Skateboards That Rock

Graphic Design of a Counterculture

By Rhyn Noll

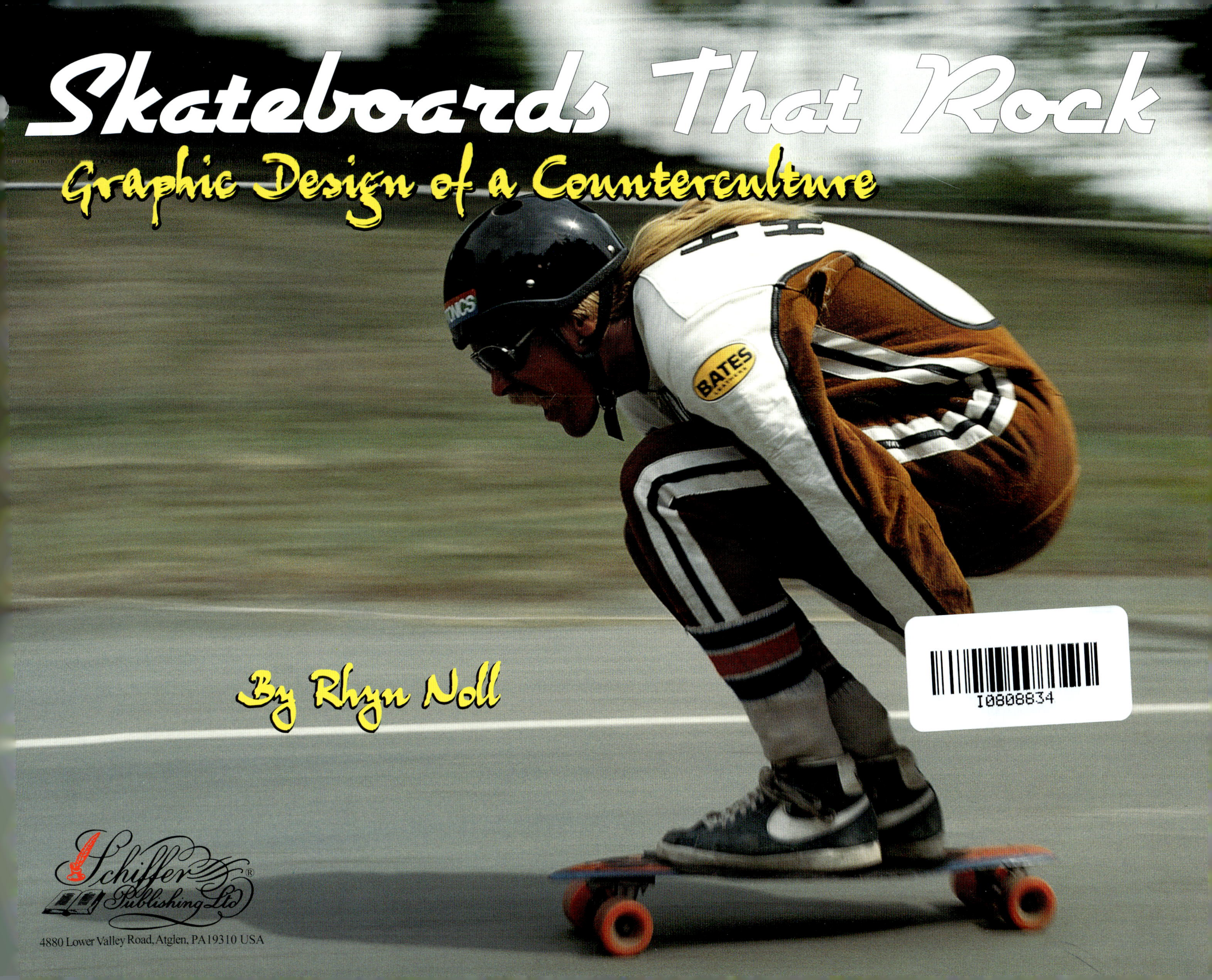

Schiffer Publishing Ltd®
4880 Lower Valley Road, Atglen, PA19310 USA

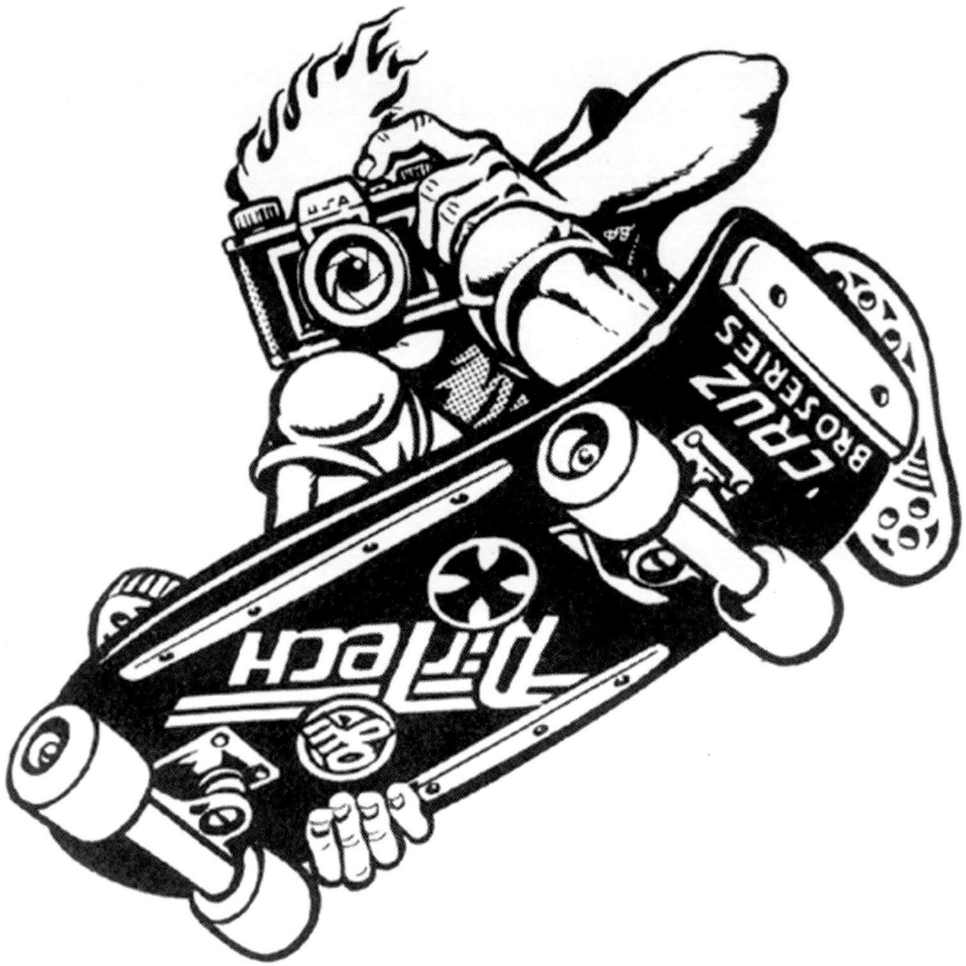

Title page: Downhill, Henry Hester. Signal Hill and Downhill was big in the 1970s; speed was hot. *Photo: James O'Mahoney.*

Inside front cover: *Photo courtesy Dale Smith.*

Library of Congress Control Number: 2002116685

Designed by Bonnie M. Hensley
Cover design by Bruce M. Waters
Type set in Airstream/Humanst521 BT

ISBN: 0-7643-1790-3
Printed in China
1 2 3 4

Published by Schiffer Publishing Ltd.
4880 Lower Valley Road
Atglen, PA 19310
Phone: (610) 593-1777; Fax: (610) 593-2002
E-mail: Schifferbk@aol.com
Please visit our web site catalog at **www.schifferbooks.com**
We are always looking for people to write books on new and related subjects. If you have an idea for a book, please contact us at the above address.

This book may be purchased from the publisher.
Include $3.95 for shipping. Please try your bookstore first.
You may write for a free catalog.

In Europe, Schiffer books are distributed by
Bushwood Books
6 Marksbury Ave. Kew Gardens
Surrey TW9 4JF England
Phone: 44 (0)20 8392-8585; Fax: 44 (0)20 8392-9876
E-mail: Bushwd@aol.com
Free postage in the UK. Europe: air mail at cost.
Please try your bookstore first.

Dedication

To the Noll family, for their support and encouragement enabling me to write this book. Thanks to Sarah, my wife; Remy Hannah and Sienna Rose, my daughters; Dane, my son; Beverly, my mom; Ira and Bettie Roberts, my grandpa and granny; Tate and Jed, my brothers; Ashlyne, my sister; Laura and Greg Noll, my dad; Jim Noll and Steve Zalabak, my uncles; Nancy Noll, my aunt; A.J. and Luke Noll and Kyler Whaley, my nephews; Grace and Ash Noll, my grandparents; the Campbell family; and Pete and Strider Zalabak.

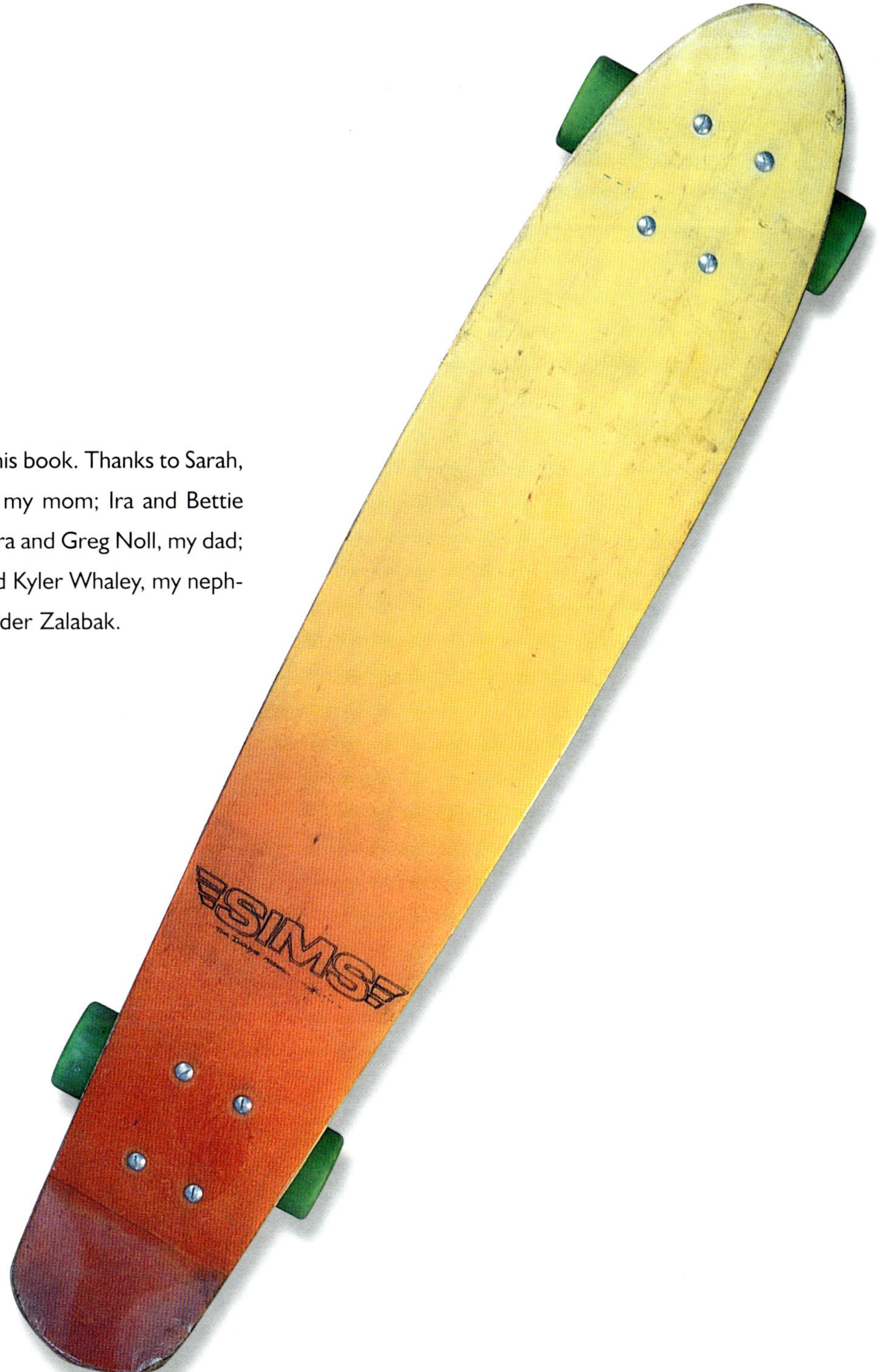

Acknowledgements

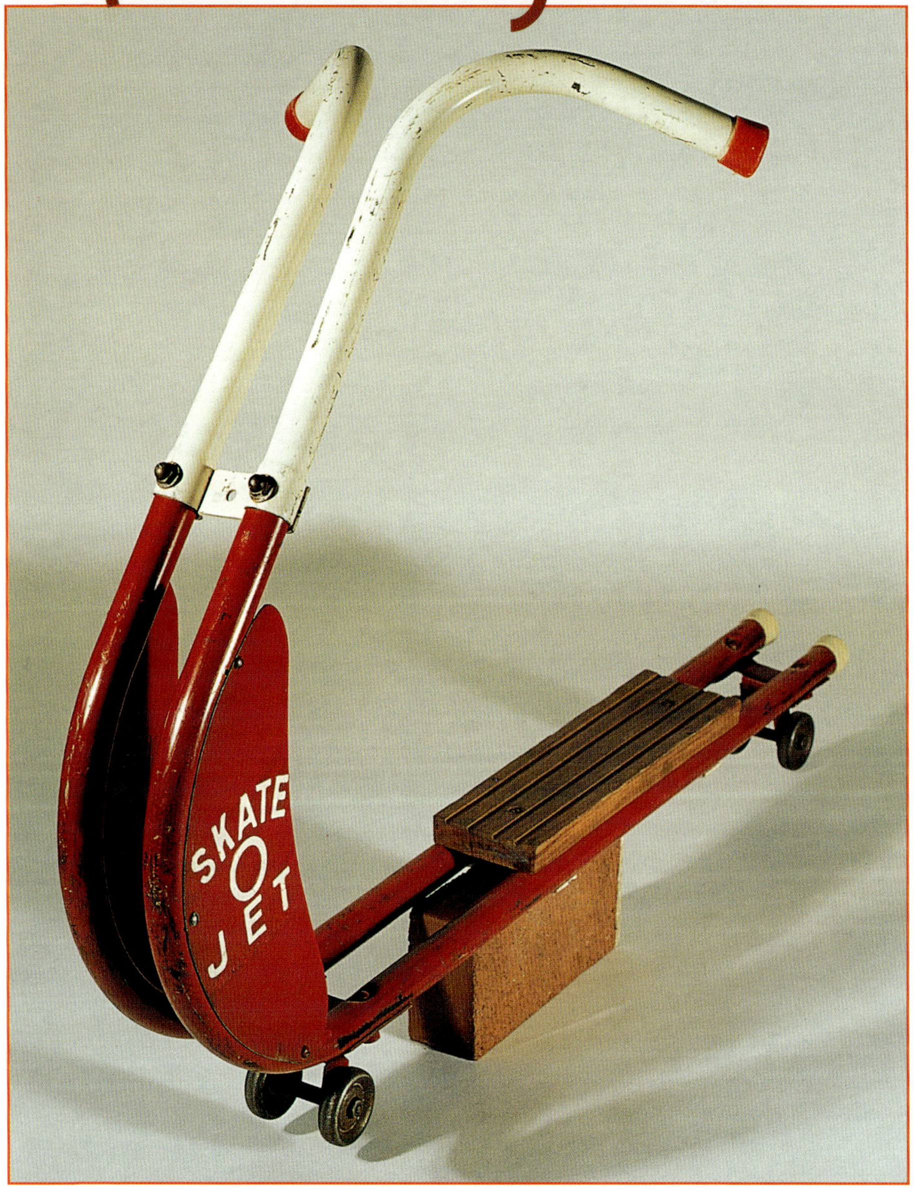

Beverly Noll

Bettie Roberts

Sarah Noll, editor

Remy Noll, associate editor

Dane Noll

Greg Noll

Jim Noll

Bills Wheels

Randal Fuller

Dale Smith

Ed Economy.

Todd Huber of Skatelab

Richard Barnick of Tsunami Surf & Sport

Roy Gonzalas

Cleave Gardner

Jean Cooper

Buddy Carr of Tracker Trucks

Liz Barbee

Leroy Granis

Atilla Azsodi

Michael Breem of Gravity

Brad Edwards

Rich Novak of NHS Skateboards

Jim Phillips

ET Surf and Skate

Just Long Boards

Streetsurfer™

Jail House™

Jim O'Mahoney.

Carrasco family

Katch Art

Natural Concepts

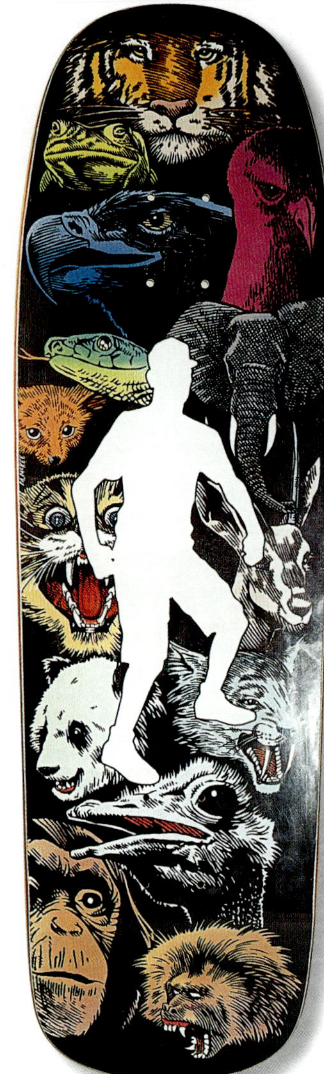

Contents

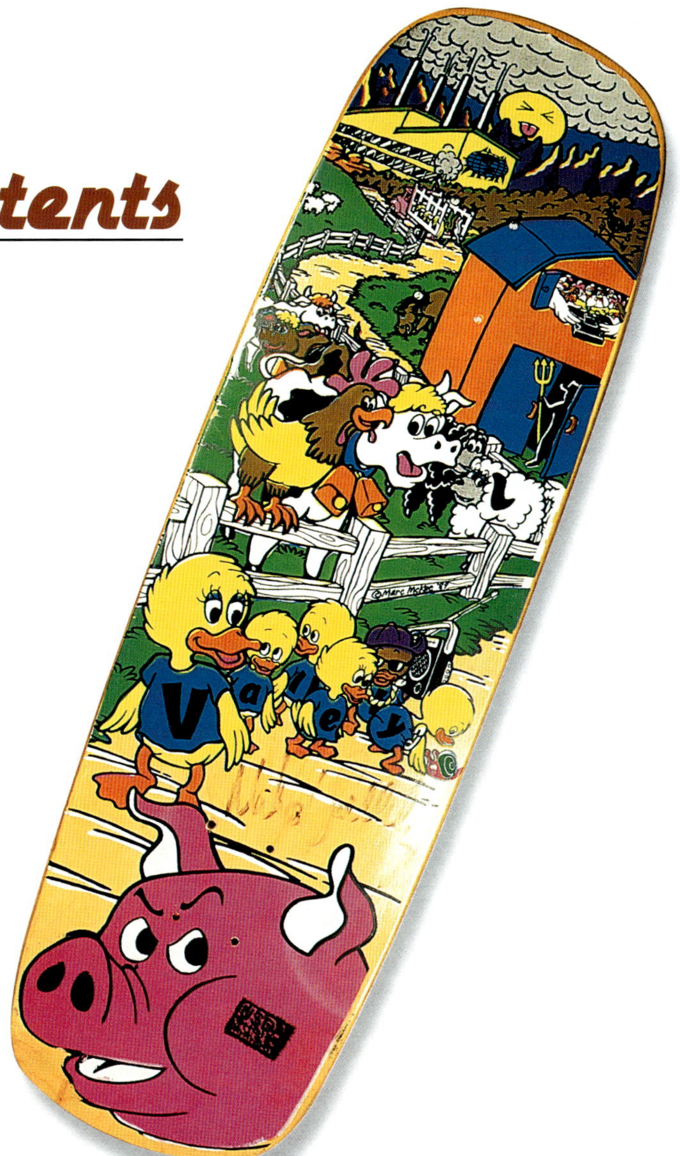

Preface

The skateboard industry is a funny place. You have some people behind the manufacturing companies who are soulful and believe in the sport. Then you have companies that just have no idea what they are doing. Some make as many boards as they can in order to make as much money as they can. That's all it's about for them. They don't care about the legacy or the riders; and let's face it, if you can't be involved in history, if you can't contribute a little bit of time towards skate history, should you be in the business? I don't think so. If there is one thing I want to do with this book, it is to enlighten you. Pay attention to the companies who care about the riders and the sport. The people who ride and the whole genre. Why should you give your hard-earned dollar to someone who doesn't care about you or your sport?

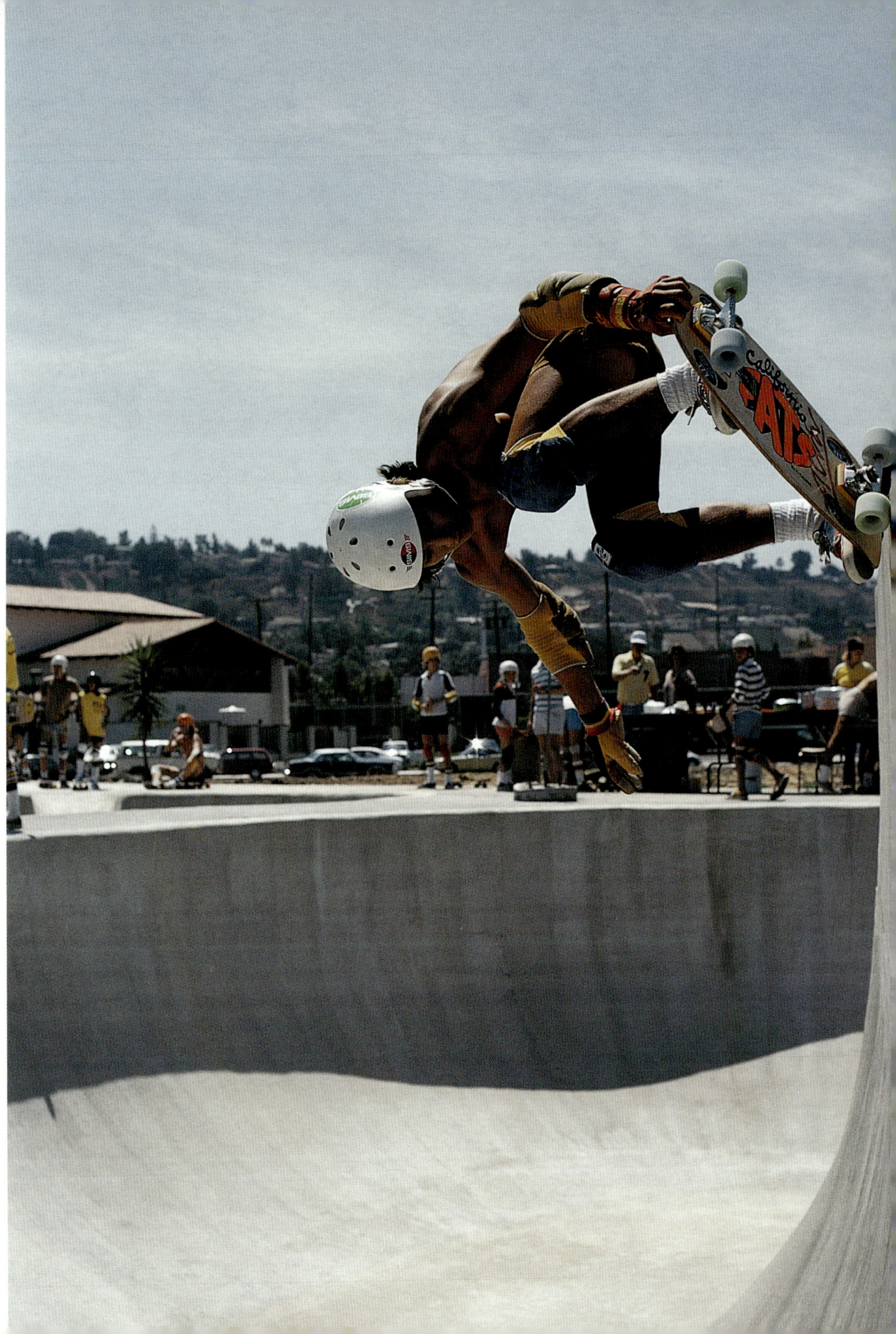

Grinding Steve's Southbay wall. *Photo James O'Mahoney.*

Introduction

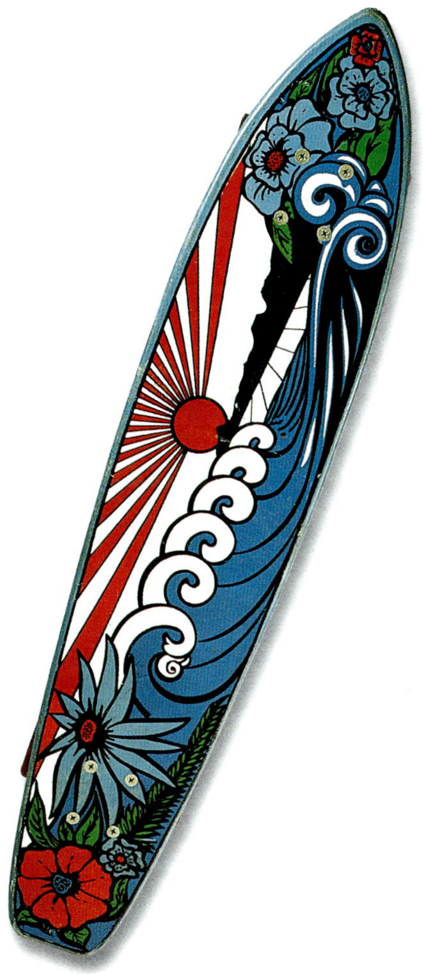

I am still waiting for boarding to go mainstream. I've been waiting since the 1970s. I wonder if, as soon as it happens, I will be disappointed and not want any part of it. That is usually how skaters are. I just hope that for one moment or hour people will wake up just long enough to see what they are missing.

Skateboarding Time Line

Skateboarding through the decades has forever been misunderstood by the masses as child's play, and you can bet that the pioneers of skateboarding never imagined the heights that the sport would reach.

Was the future of skateboarding assured in the 1960s? No, its future was uncertain. We look back on this time and know it was just the beginning of skateboarding. In the thirties, when surfing became something real, guys stood on boards and rode waves. As early as the forties, boxes were getting knocked off scooters. Did the boxes get knocked off before that? Yes, when guys like Doc Ball did it. They rode them around on one knee and pushed off with one leg. Were they standing back in those days? No, probably not, but its my belief that it happened when the Polynesian sport of surfing was introduced. The art of standing on a board became real. Board sports date all the way back to ancient Hawaiians who rode the surf on boards made of koa. Trace the lineage. If you want the holy grail of board sports, it is the surfboards of the ancient Hawaiians.

Time flies like the wind, and before you know it you're looking back on a lifetime and it becomes apparent time waits for no man or woman. Time is the essence that shows who we are. 1960s skaters are the first generations of skateboard pioneers; they are the grandfathers. 1970s skaters are the second generation, the urethane revolutionaries. The 1980s skaters are the third, and most rebellious, generation.

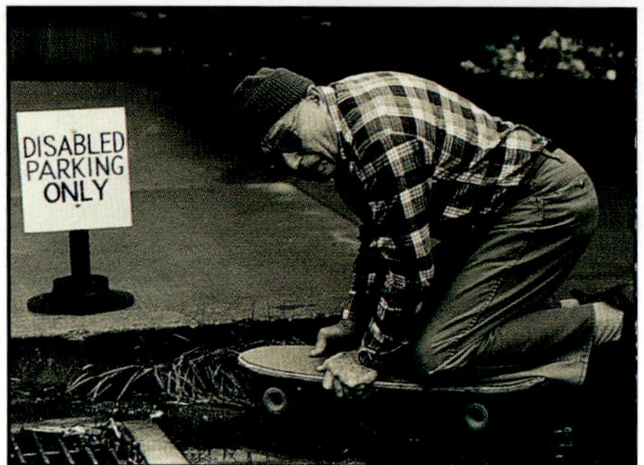

Doc Ball explains that this is how they used to do it when he was a kid. Back in the early part of the century. *Courtesy of Ball Family*.

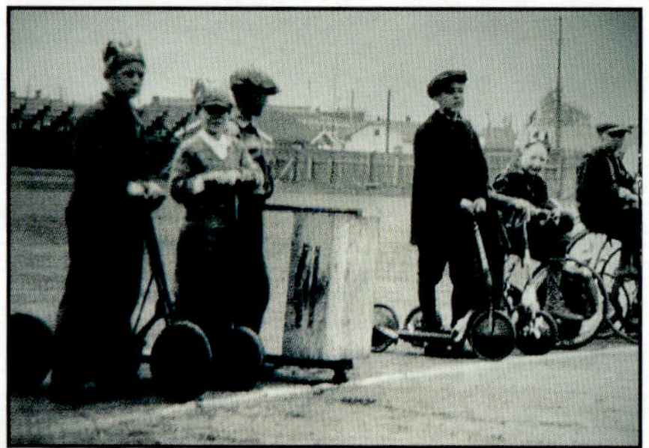

Pre-1950. Scooters were the fundamental transportation of the day. *Courtesy Dale Smith*.

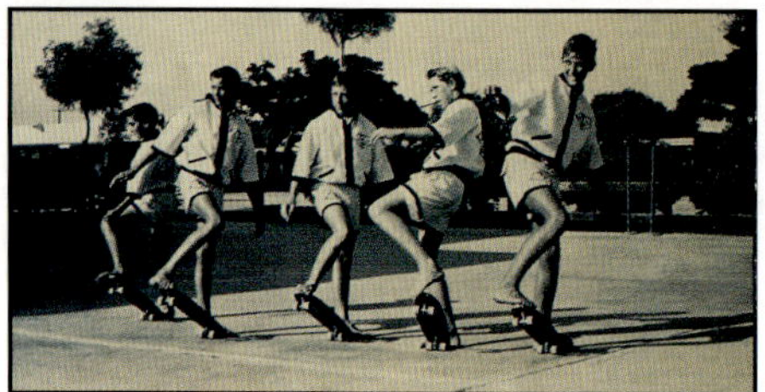

Circa 1964 High production of skateboards and team demos help propel the sport into the future. *Courtesy Classic Stoner Photos*

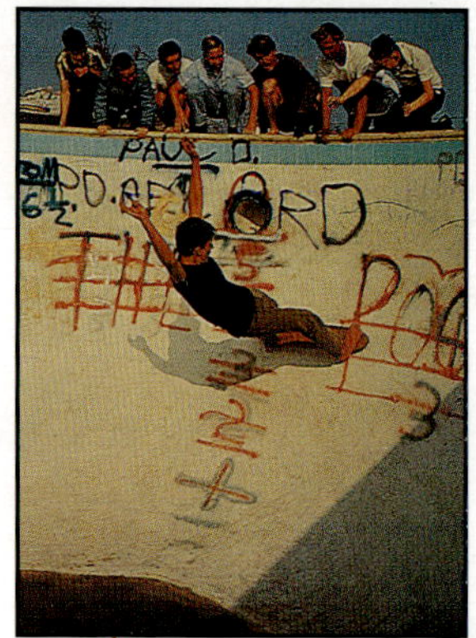

The first vert ever experienced at Fox Tail Pool. 1965. *Courtesy Classic Stoner Photographs*

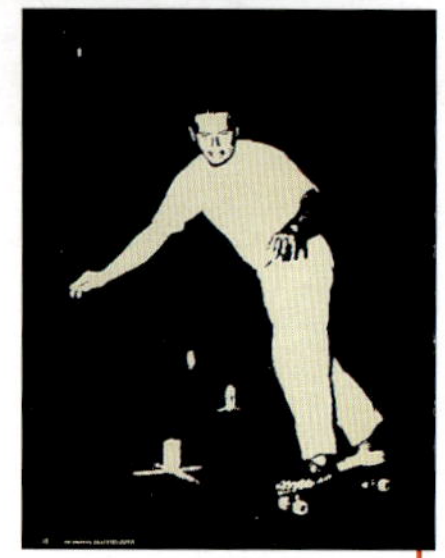

Skateboarding is all but outlawed in the later 1960s due to injuries and even deaths. Forced to go underground, skaters went out at night. *Courtesy Classic Stoner Photographs*.

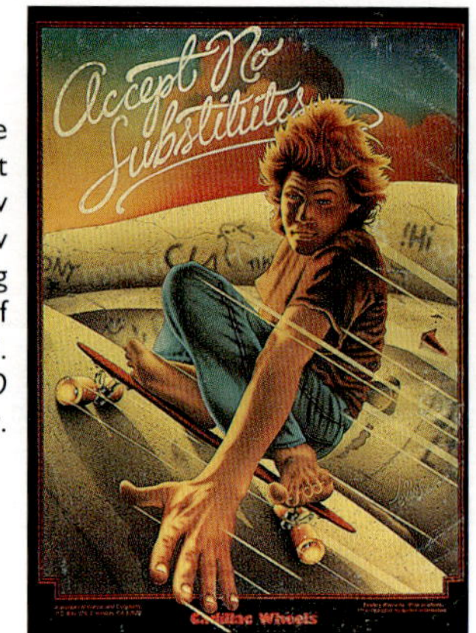

The urethane revolution brought forth many new possibilities. New surfaces were being skated with new self reliance emerged. *Courtesy of James O Mahoney*.

1900 **1920** **1960** **1965** **1970** **1975**

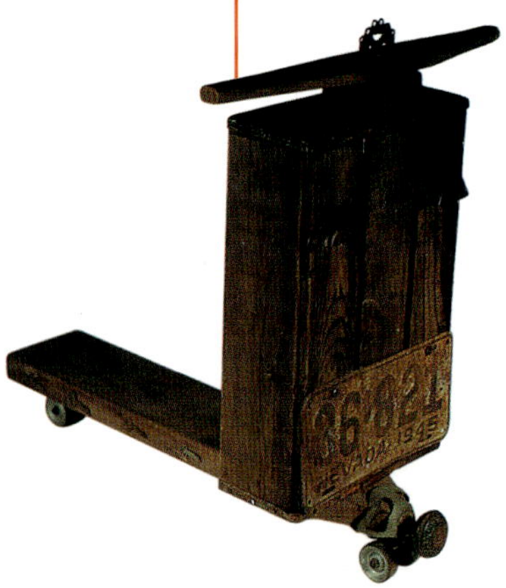

Fruit box skater. *Courtesy Dale Smith*.

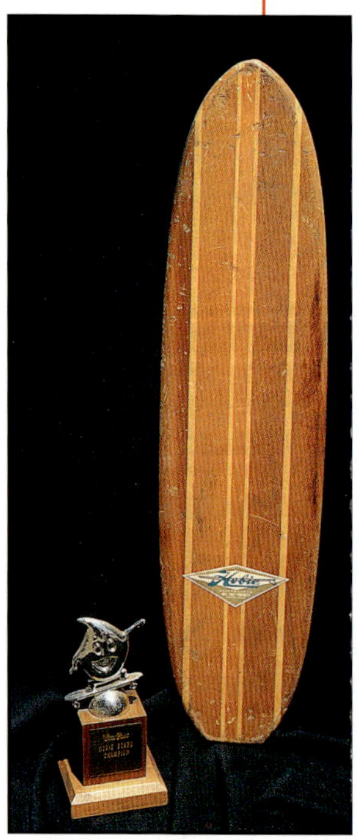

Hobie Vita Pak, laminated ash and mahogany, and the Vita Pak trophy. The quintessential board from the 1960s. *Courtesy J O'Mahoney*. $ 2500.00 for both

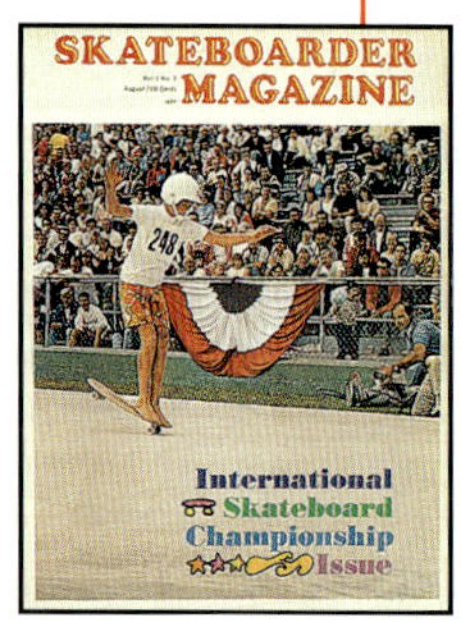

Skateboarding has its first major first competition and its featured in the magazine devoted to skateboarding. *Courtesy of Todd Huber*

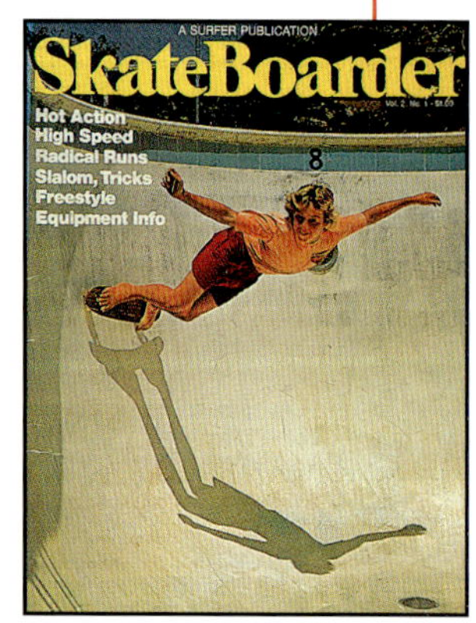

Skateboarder Magazine is on the scene and Greg Weaver's style was influencing a generation of kids, just like me. *Courtesy of Ed Economy*.

By the late 1970s, skate parks are everywhere. Vert was being conquered, Howard Hood Rock and Roll Runaway Pro Contest USSAA. *Courtesy James O'Mahoney.*

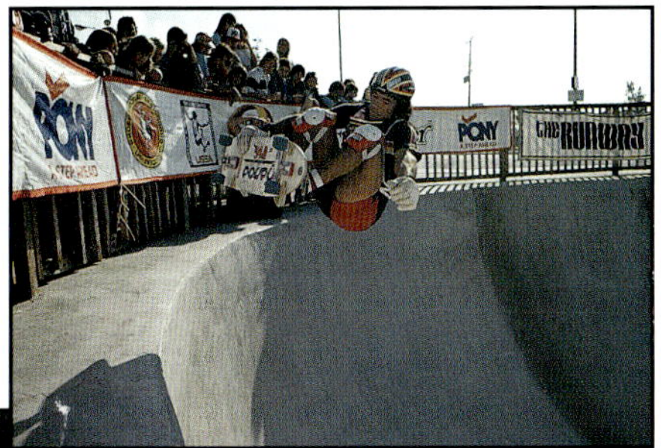

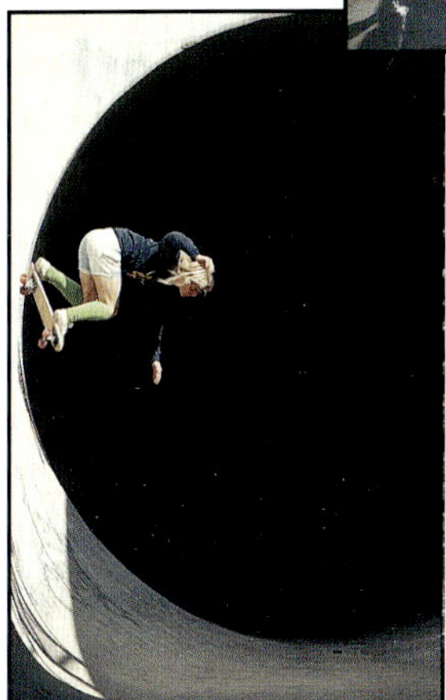

Waldo Autry amazes us all with his extension into vertical terrain. Baldy, circa 1975. *Courtesy James O'Mahoney.*

Vert and *air* were the buzzwords of the 1980s. Highflying technical routines are developed all through this era. *Courtesy of NHS.*

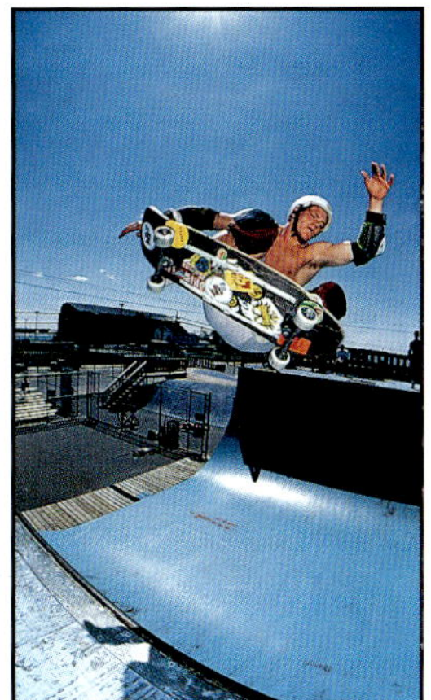

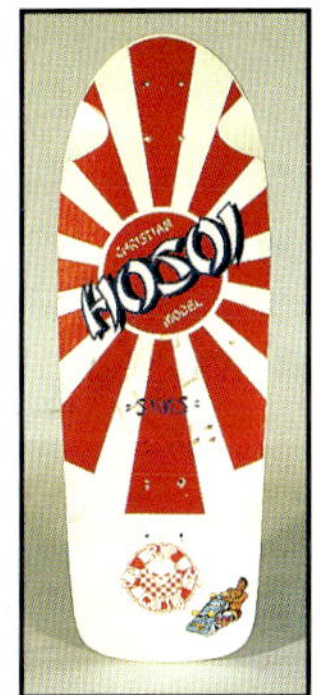

It's hard to pick the board of the 1980s, there are so many. I couldn't resist this Hasoi model because its design has been reused years later and, besides, some say Christian Hasoi was the essence of the 1980s. *Courtesy of Jim (Rip City) Photo R. Noll.* $2000-3000.

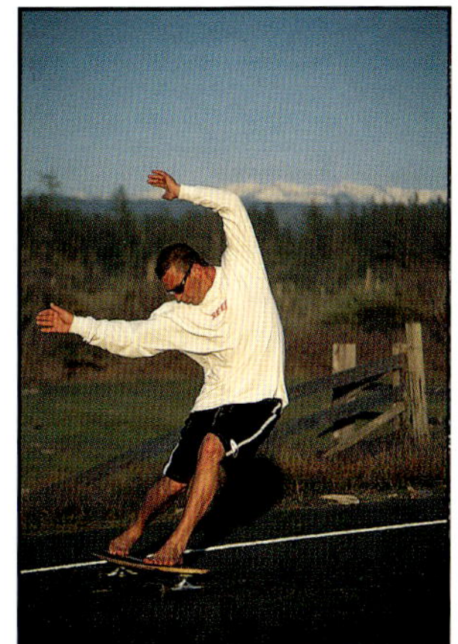

The longboard revolution arrives and sends ripples through the industry. What happens is nothing short of rebirth. *Photo S. Noll.*

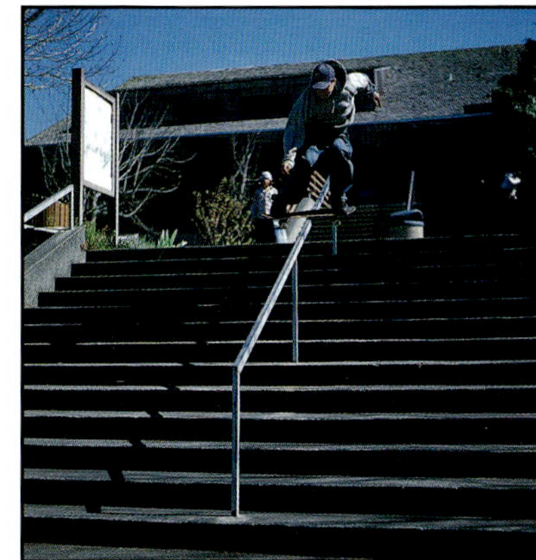

Street skating plays a major part influencing the industry. *Photo R. Noll*

1980 1985 1990 1995 2000

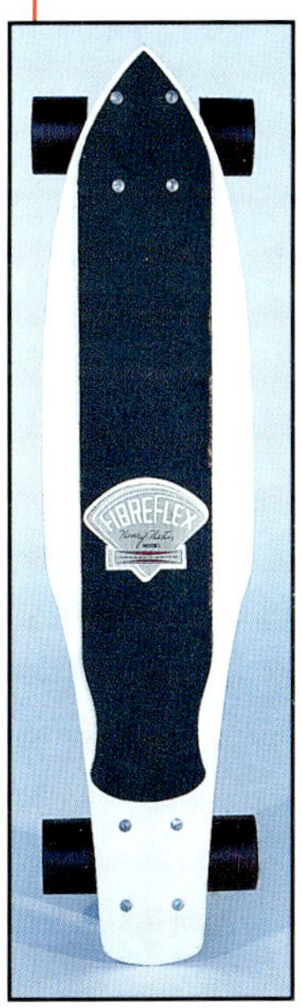

One of the quintessential boards of the 1970s Fiber Flex, Circa 1975. *Photo R. Noll. Courtesy Ed Economy.*

The 1980s ushered in a new era in design and function. Attitudes were shifting and skateboarding struggled for its identity. *Courtesy Jim Phillips.*

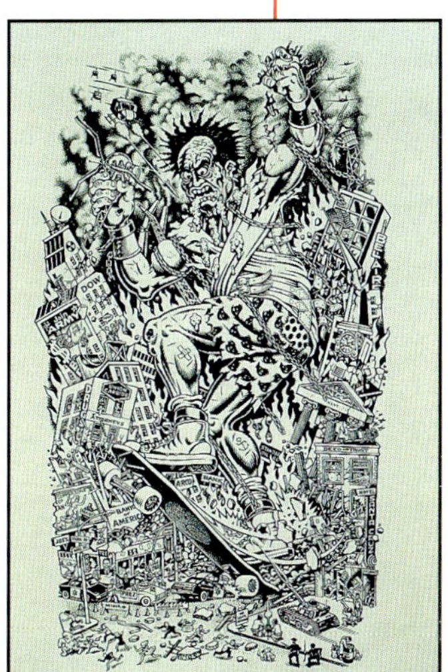

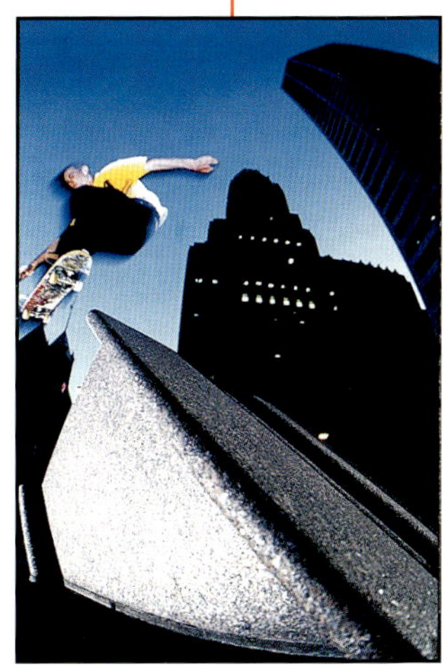

Cities and bridges were being gapped. Hugh stairs and huge airs the industry is firmly in place. *Courtesy NHS.*

By the end of the century, skate parks were springing up allover America and practically every small town got their own facility so local kids could get more, and safer, skate time.

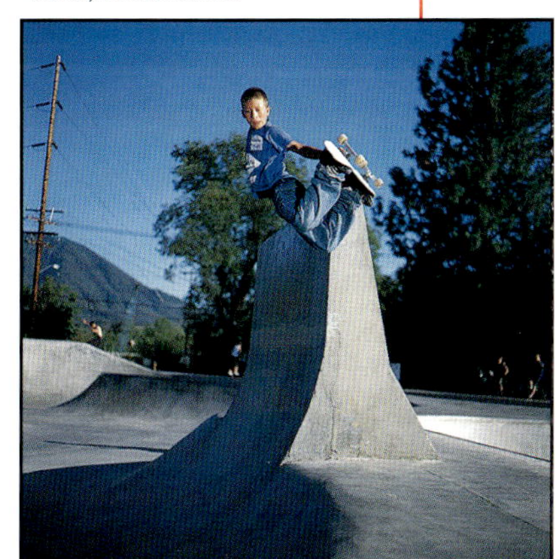

Rock Music Time Line

Boards that rock include some that relate to rock music groups, like Black Fag. So many people mistook the punk rock music for some kind of sadomasochistic worship. In reality, bands like the Dead Kennedy's (one of my personal favorites) sang, not about things that they were stoked about but things that pissed them off. Their lyrics reflect this. Now that we have the neutron bomb, its nice and quick and clean; it gets things done. They are not saying how bitchin' they think that is or lets go do it. They are saying how ludicrous this way of thinking is. Perception is always an opinion.

As far as music is concerned, what was influencing the skateboarding scene was not always the same as what was influencing the rest of America.

1960- Elvis Presley appears on *The Ed Sullivan Show* following his Army stint.

1963- Surf music rules the airwaves.

1964- The Beatles hit America, leading the British Invasion in music.

1969- Woodstock Music & Arts Festival draws half a million fans to Max Yesgar's farm in New York. The Who's rock opera "Tommy" is introduced.

1973- Led Zeppelin's tour is a record breaker. Pink Floyd releases "Dark Side of the Moon."

1976- Stevie Wonder's album *Songs In The Key Of Life* won five Grammy Awards. Frampton's *Comes Alive* is released.

1978- Van Halen releases their first album.

1980- John Lennon is murdered in front of his New York apartment.

1985- "We Are The World" is recorded by 46 U.S. artists in support of suffering people in the USA and Africa.

1992- Seattle becomes the core of Grunge Rock, with groups like Nirvana and Pearl Jam.

1995- The Rock and Roll Hall Of Fame and Museum opens in Cleveland, Ohio. Alanis Morissette's *Jagged Little Pill* is a multi-million dollar seller. Neil Young and Pearl Jam perform and record together.

2000- Hip-hop invades the airways and there is a retro revival.

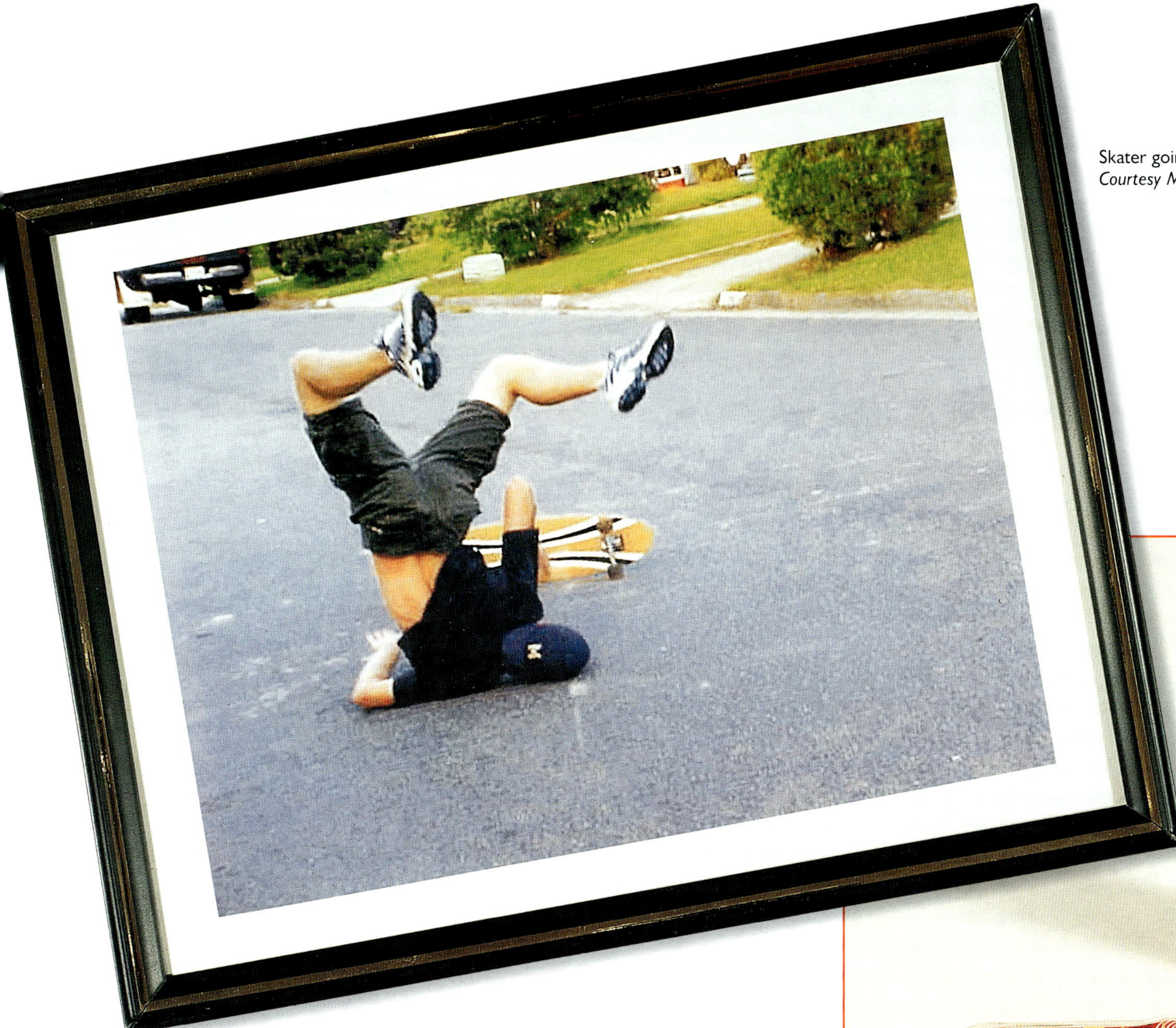

Skater going down for the count.
Courtesy Michael Bream.

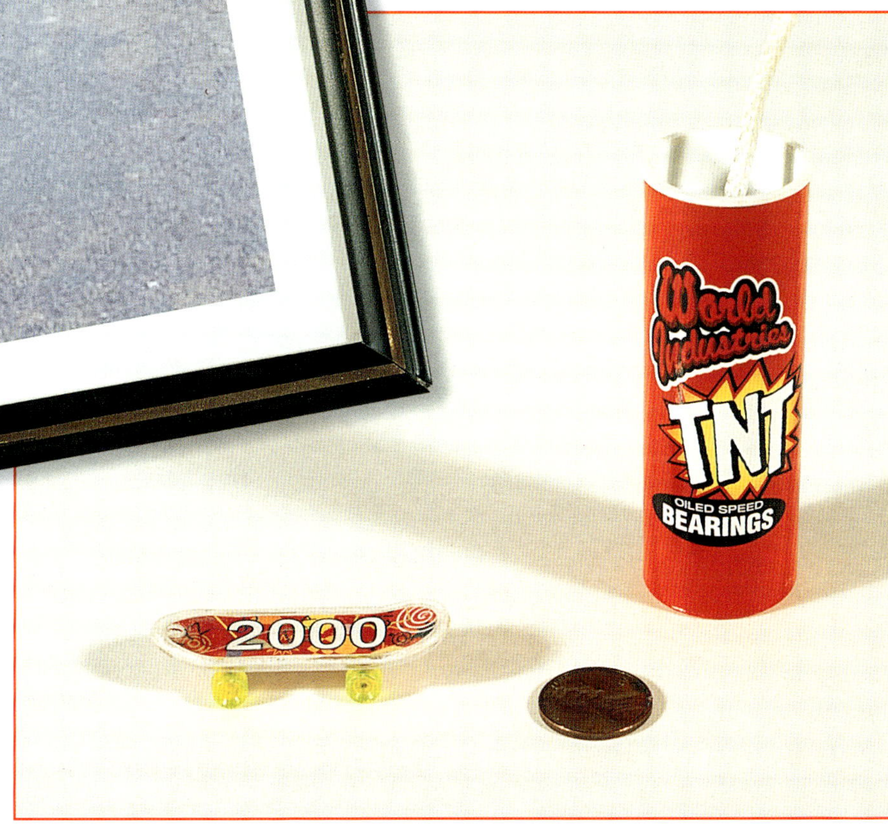

World industries bearings. $15.
The smallest skateboard replica I've ever seen. $10.

Skateboard Stickers

You have to remember that skateboarders pride themselves on being counter culture. Therefore, what we say, hear, and know today will quite possibly be rebelled against sometime in the near future.

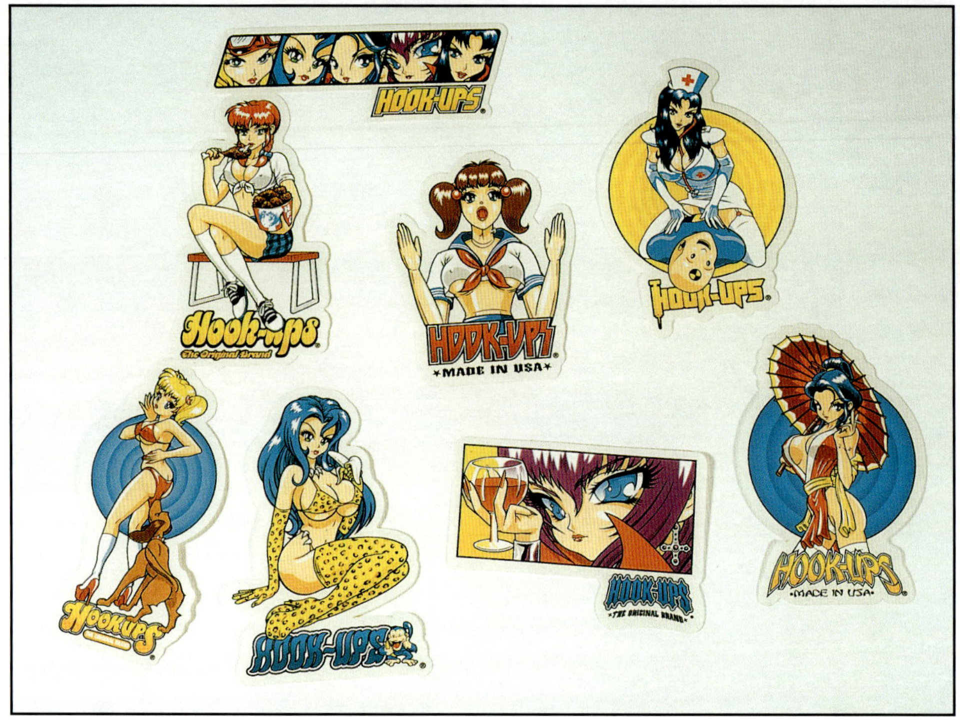

Some stickers I've collected from today's companies. $1-3.

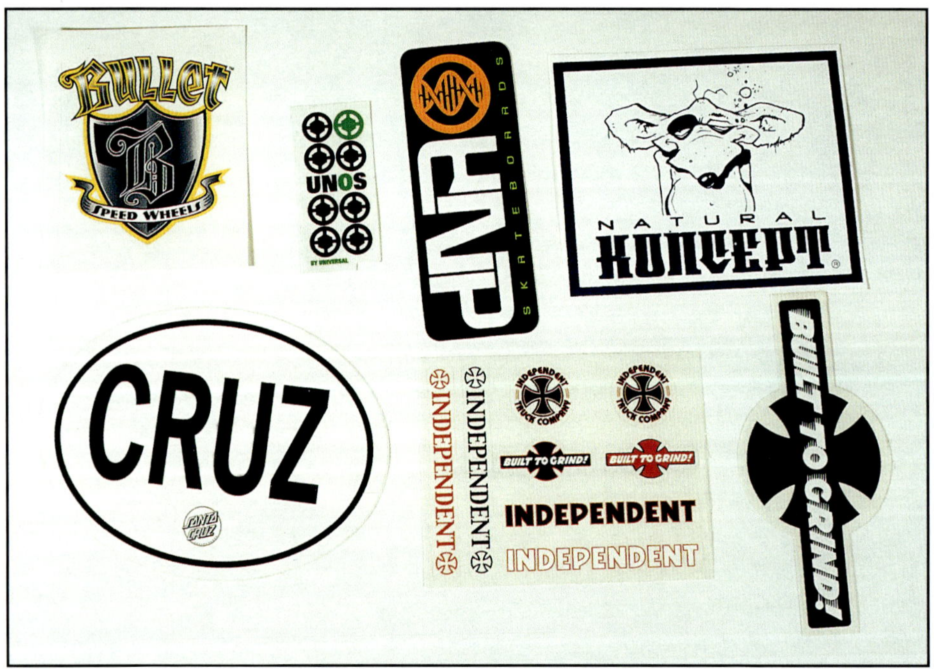

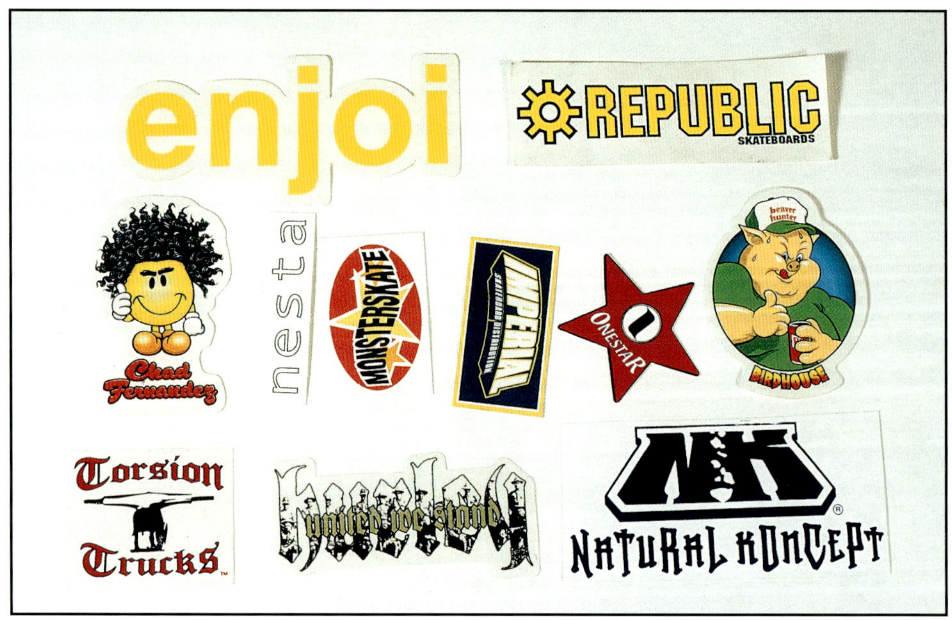

Skateboard Memorabilia

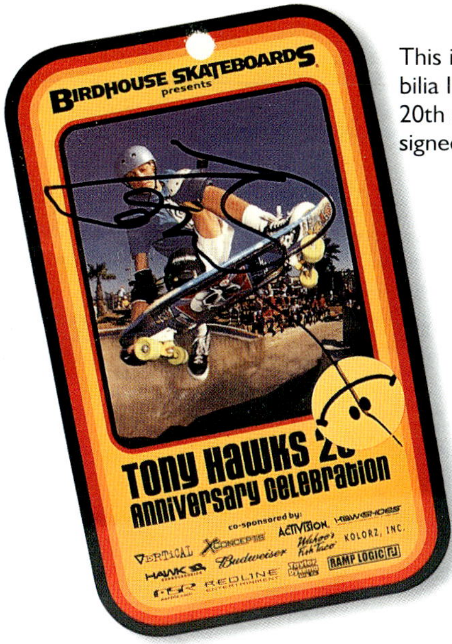

This is some modern memorabilia I picked up at Tony Hawk's 20th anniversary party. Pass signed by Tony Hawk. $20.

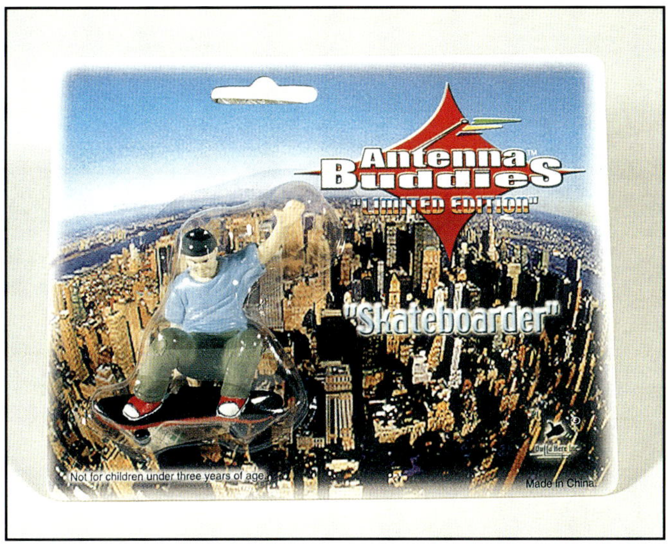

Antenna Buddies. *Courtesy Noll Surf and Skate*. $7.

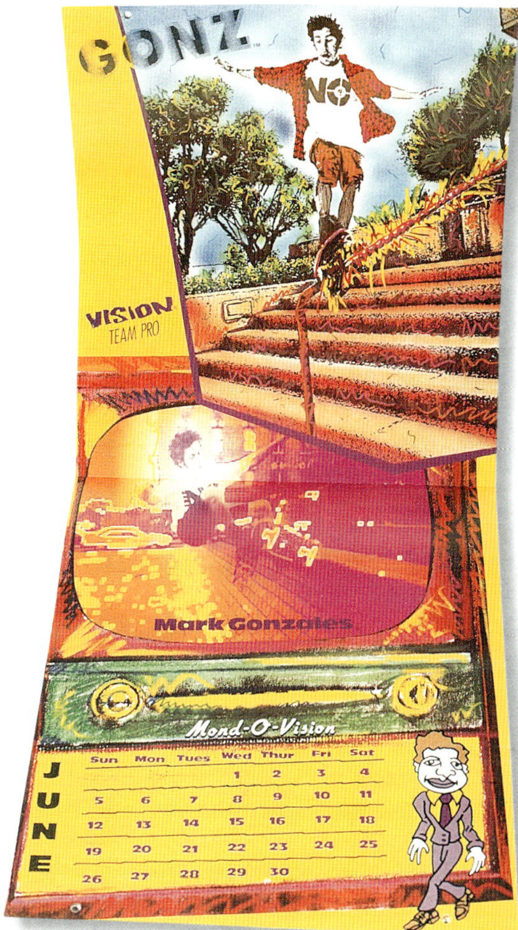

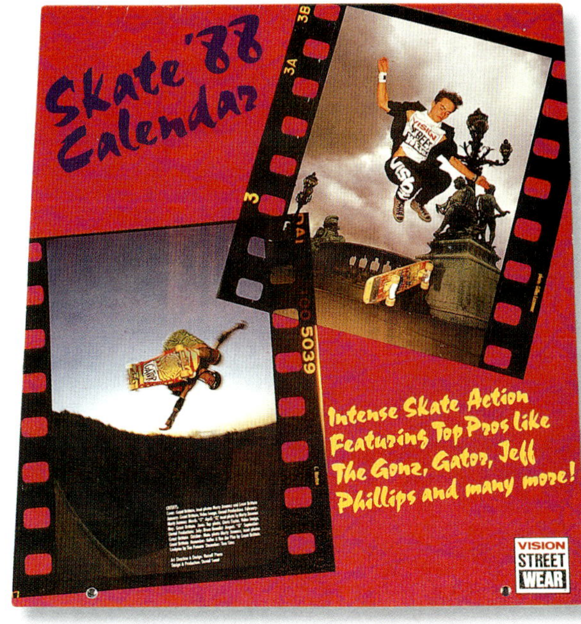

1980s Vision calendar. *Courtesy Vision*. $20.

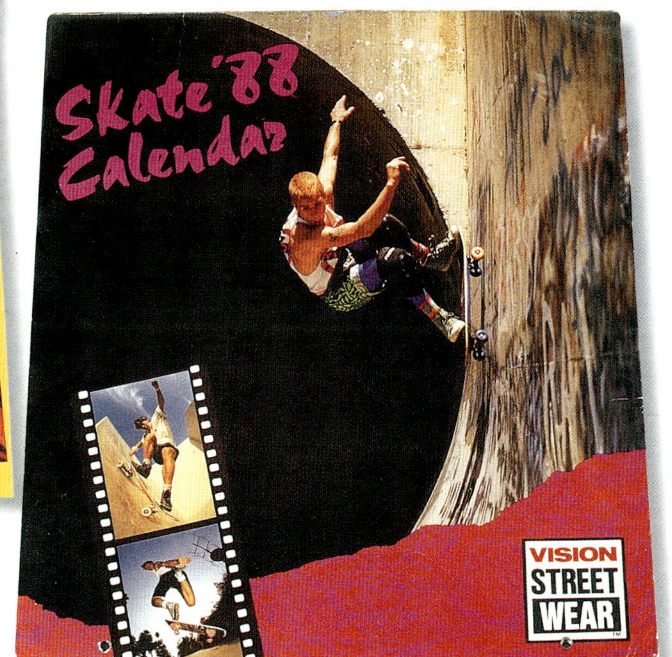

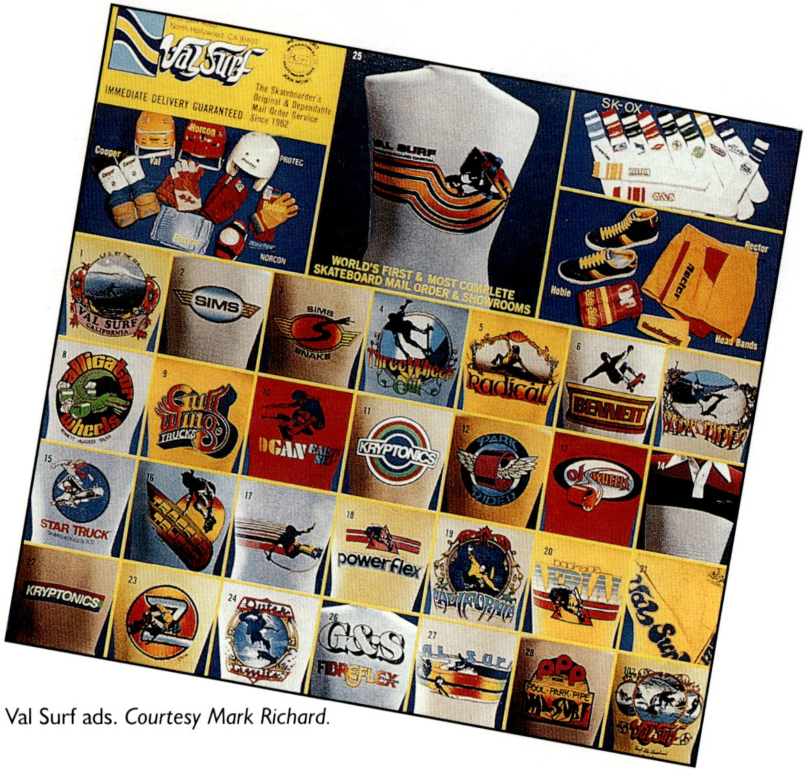

Val Surf ads. *Courtesy Mark Richard.*

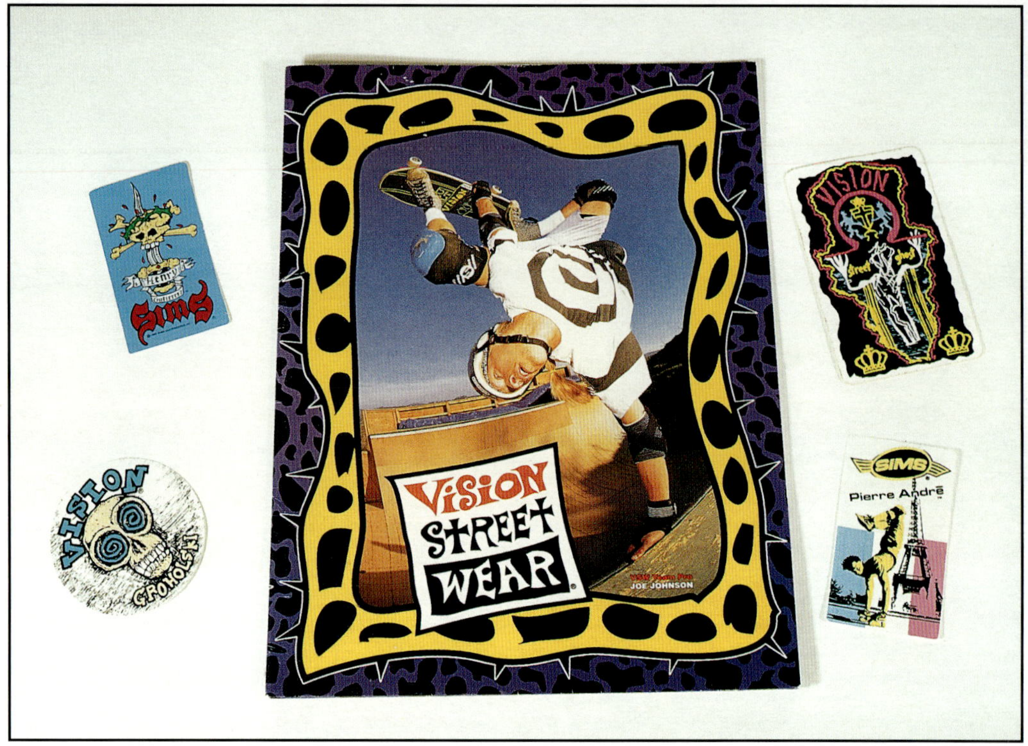

Vision stickers and folder *Courtesy Vision.* $25.

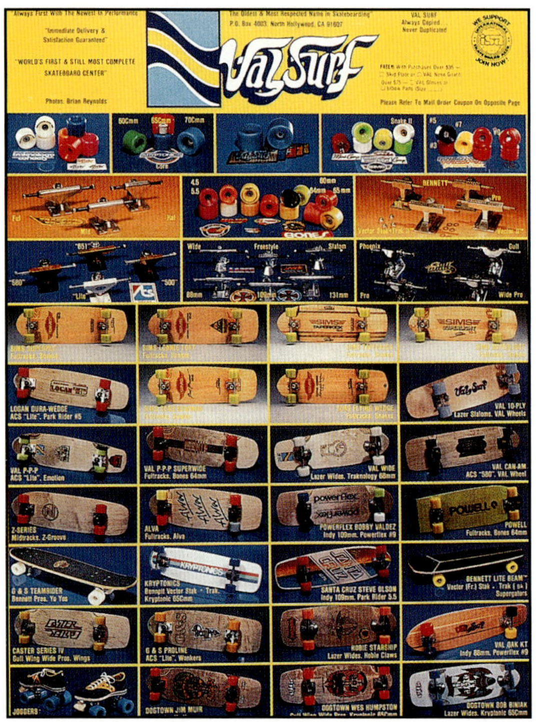

Courtesy Mark Richards.

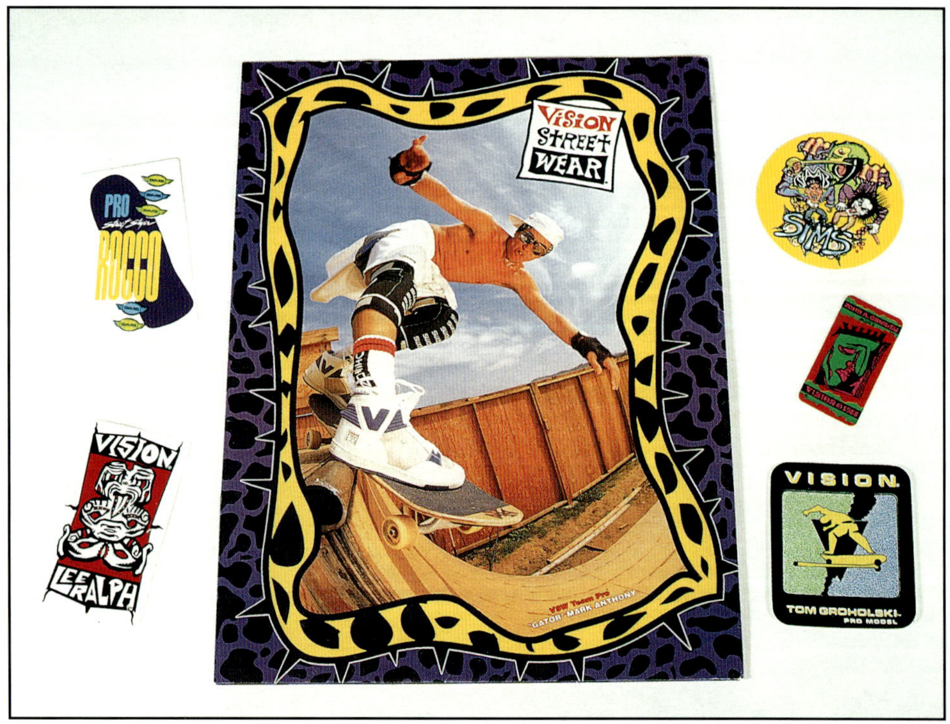

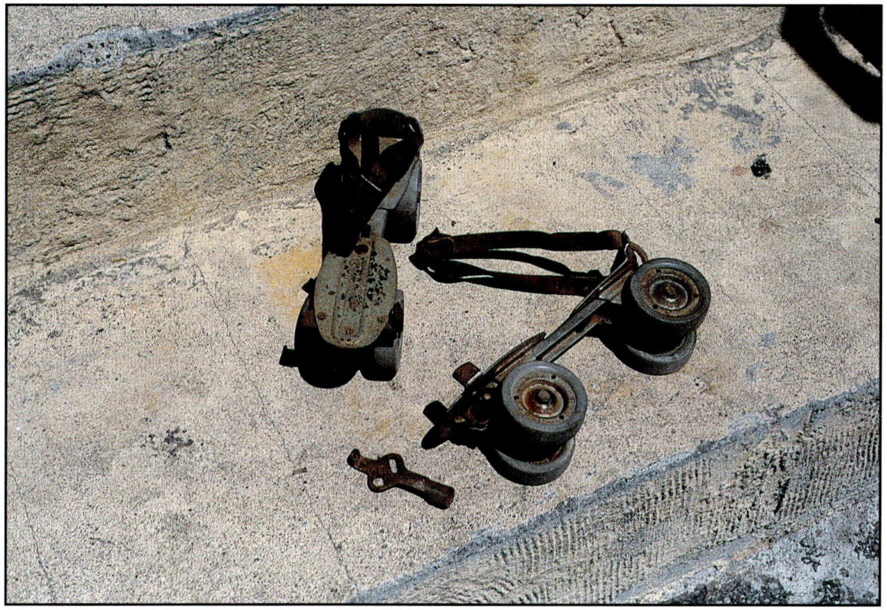

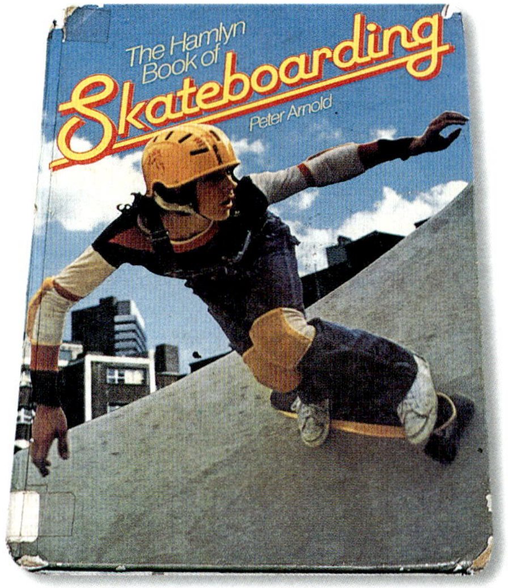

Two books: *Skateboarding* by Peter Arnold and *Skateboard Mania* by The Radlaurs. *Courtesy Jim O'Mahoney.* $20-40.

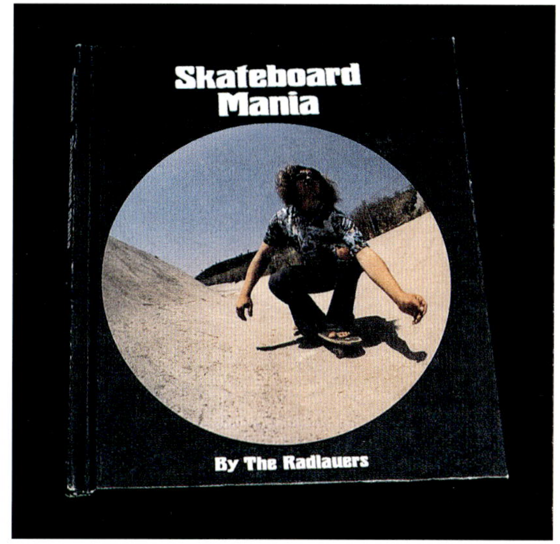

This pair of skates from the 1920s had an early clay wheel. *Courtesy Jim O'Mahoney.* $100.

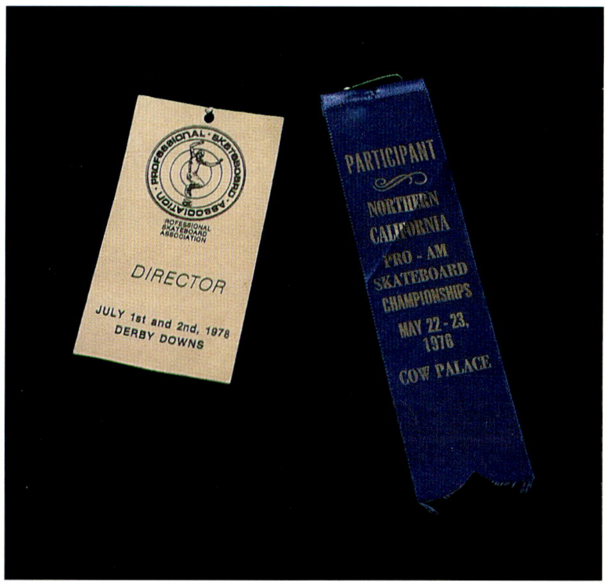

Badge of the Professional Skateboarding Association Director and a ribbon from the Pro-Am Skateboarding Championships in 1976. *Courtesy Jim O'Mahoney.* $25-40.

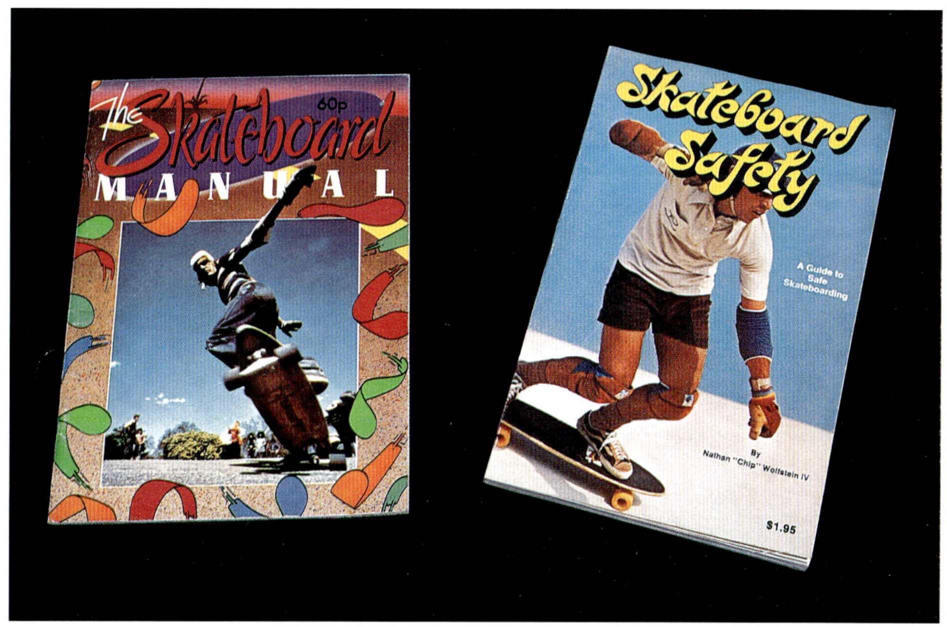

Here are a couple of paperbacks: *Skateboard Safety* and *The Skateboard Manual*. *Courtesy Jim O'Mahoney.* $15-30.

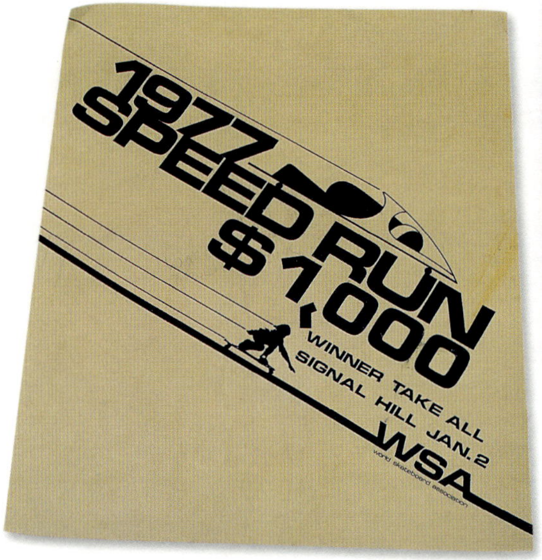
1977
SPEED RUN
$1,000
WINNER TAKE ALL
SIGNAL HILL JAN. 2
WSA
world skateboard association

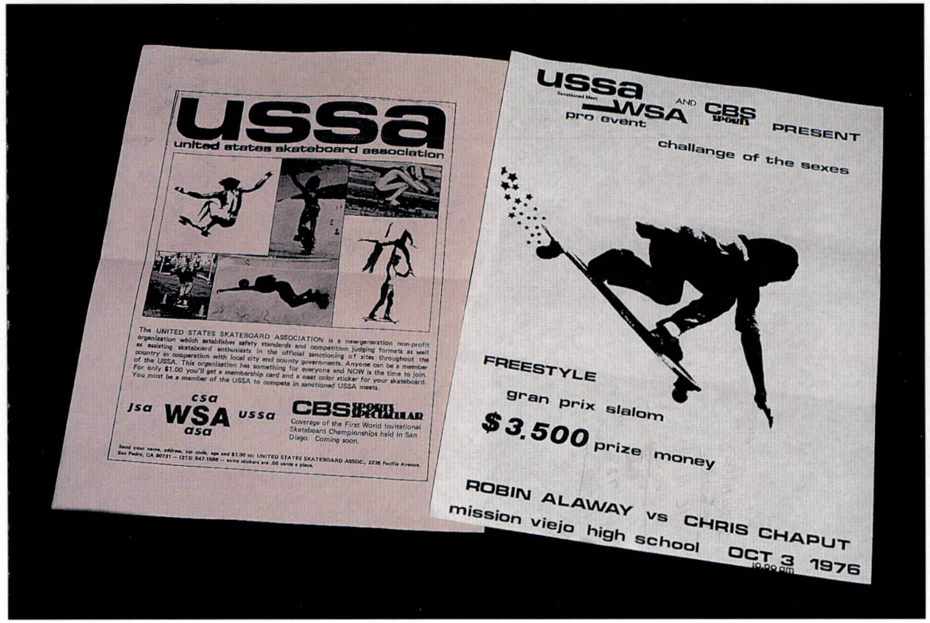
ussa
united states skateboard association
jsa
csa
WSA
asa
ussa
CBS SPORTS SPECTACULAR
ussa
WSA
AND
CBS
pro event
PRESENT
challange of the sexes
FREESTYLE
gran prix slalom
$3.500 prize money
ROBIN ALAWAY vs CHRIS CHAPUT
mission viejo high school
OCT 3 1976

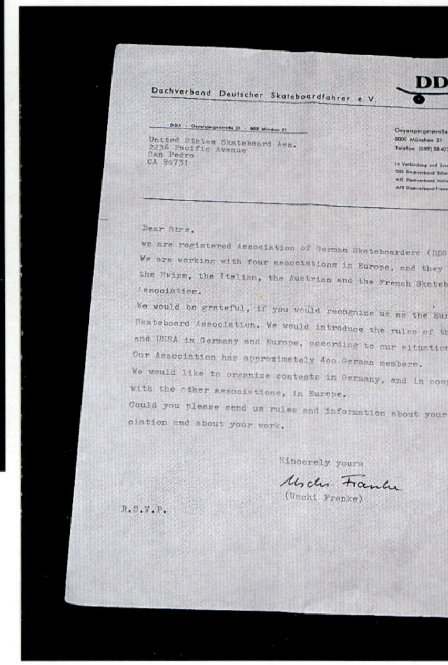
Dachverband Deutscher Skateboardfahrer e.V.
DDS
United States Skateboard Ass.
2236 Pacific Avenue
San Pedro
CA 90731
Dear Sirs,
Sincerely yours
(Uschi Franke)
R.S.V.P.

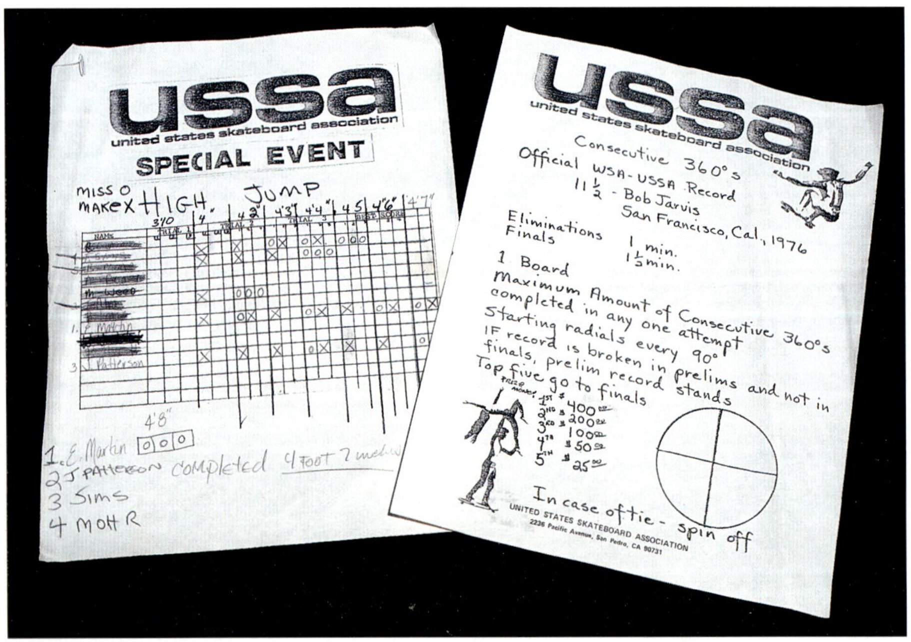
ussa
united states skateboard association
SPECIAL EVENT
HIGH JUMP
1. E. Martin
2 J Patterson
3 Sims
4 Moth R
ussa
united states skateboard association
Consecutive 360°s
Official WSA-USSA Record
11½ - Bob Jarvis
San Francisco, Cal, 1976
Eliminations 1 min.
Finals 1½ min.
1 Board
Maximum Amount of Consecutive 360°s completed in any one attempt
Starting radials every 90°
If record is broken in prelims and not in finals, prelim record stands
Top five go to finals
In case of tie - spin off
UNITED STATES SKATEBOARD ASSOCIATION
2236 Pacific Avenue, San Pedro, CA 90731

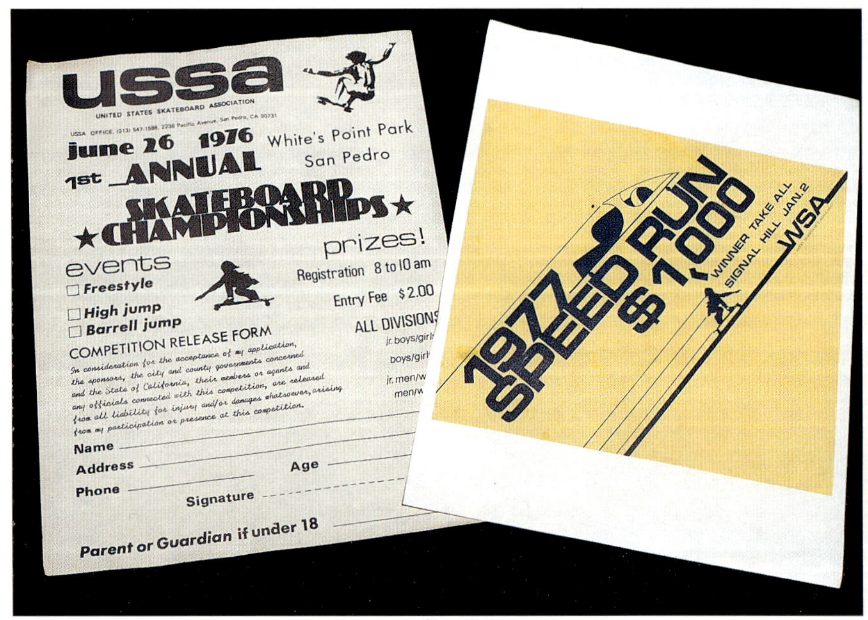
ussa
UNITED STATES SKATEBOARD ASSOCIATION
june 26 1976
White's Point Park
San Pedro
1st ANNUAL
SKATEBOARD CHAMPIONSHIPS
events
Freestyle
High jump
Barrell jump
prizes!
Registration 8 to 10 am
Entry Fee $2.00
ALL DIVISIONS
COMPETITION RELEASE FORM
Name
Address
Age
Phone
Signature
Parent or Guardian if under 18
1977
SPEED RUN
$1,000
WINNER TAKE ALL
SIGNAL HILL JAN. 2
WSA

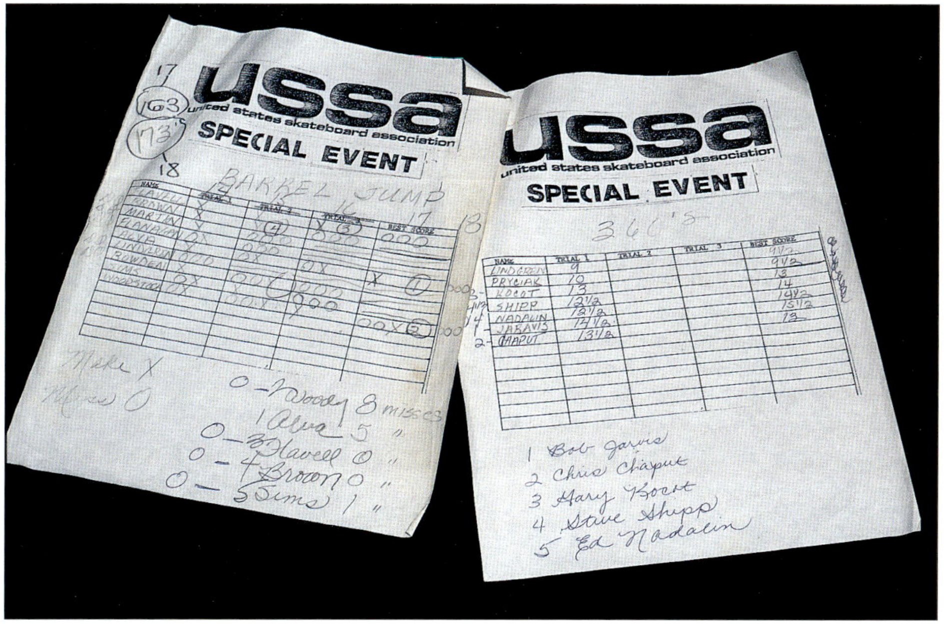

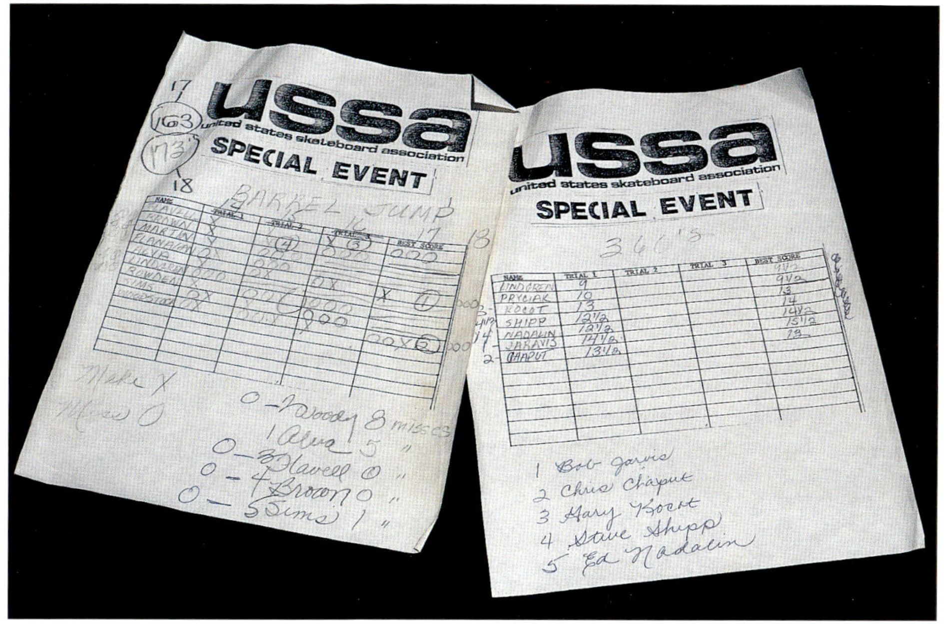

These are just a few of the event flyers and format sheets out of the hundreds that Jim O. was responsible for. *Courtesy Jim O'Mahoney.* $200-500 for collection.

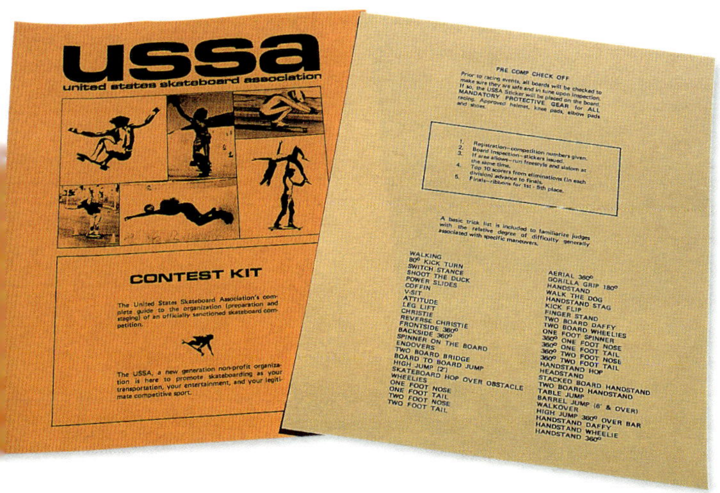

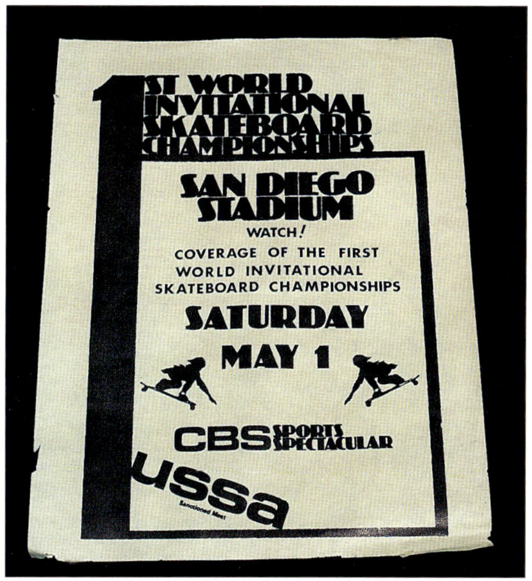

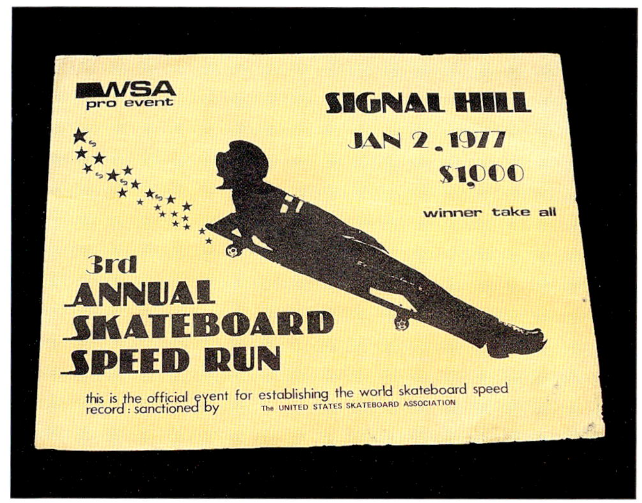

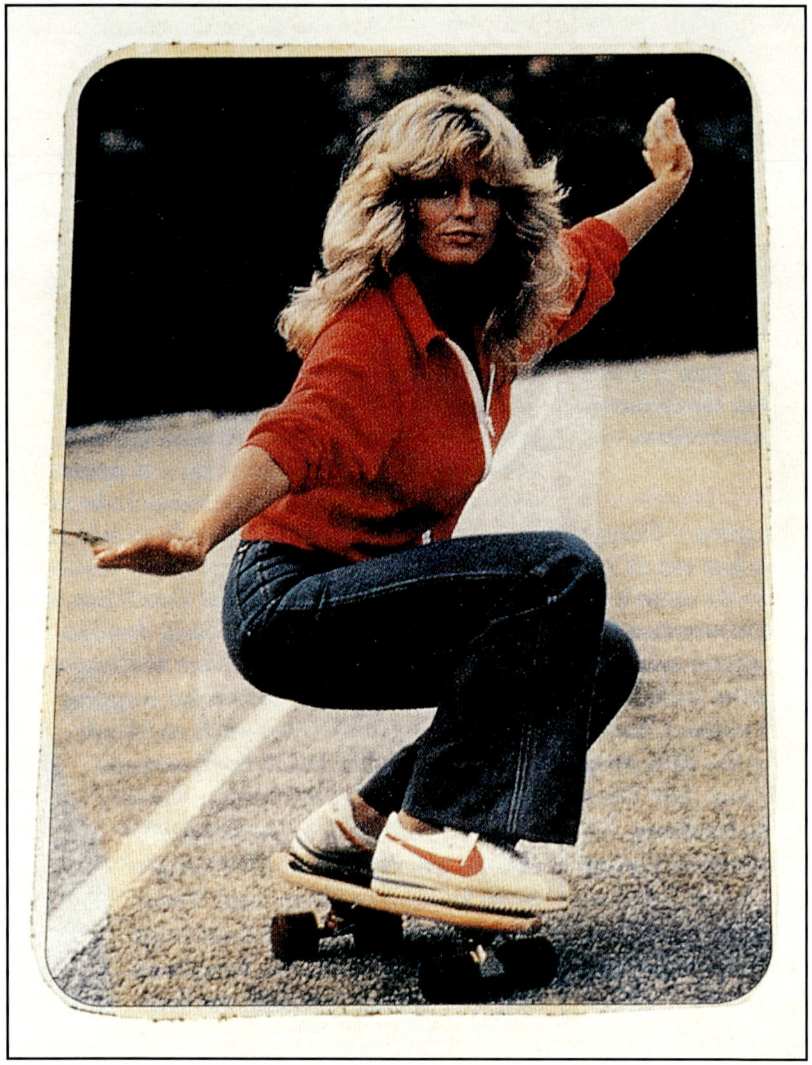

Does this shot of Farrah bring back any memories?
Courtesy Jim O'Mahoney. $25.

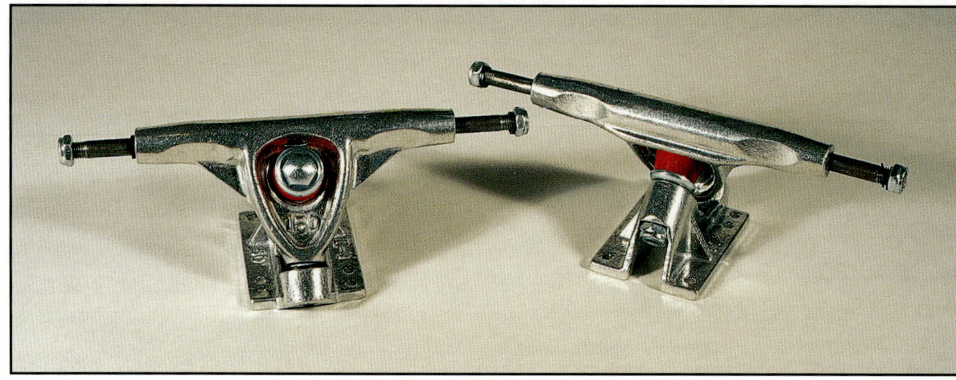

New Randal trucks, 150s. *Courtesy Randal*. $50 set.

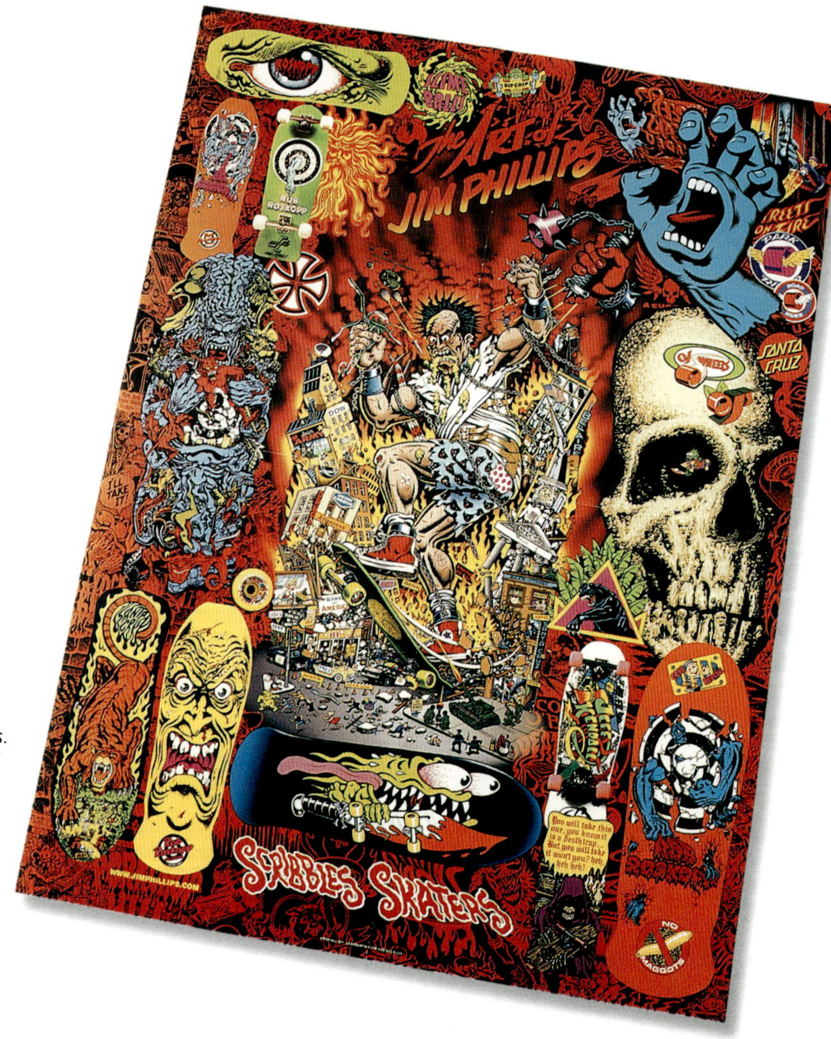

Old art revisited by Jim Phillips. *Courtesy Jim Phillips.*

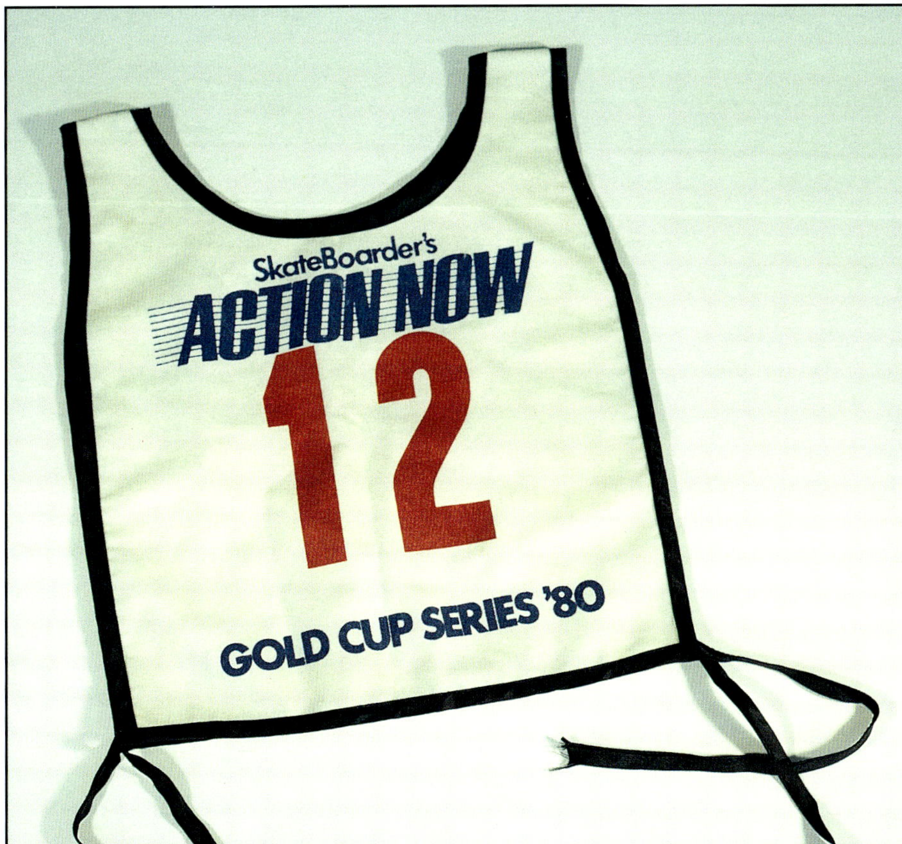

Racing vest. *Courtesy Ed Economy.* $100.

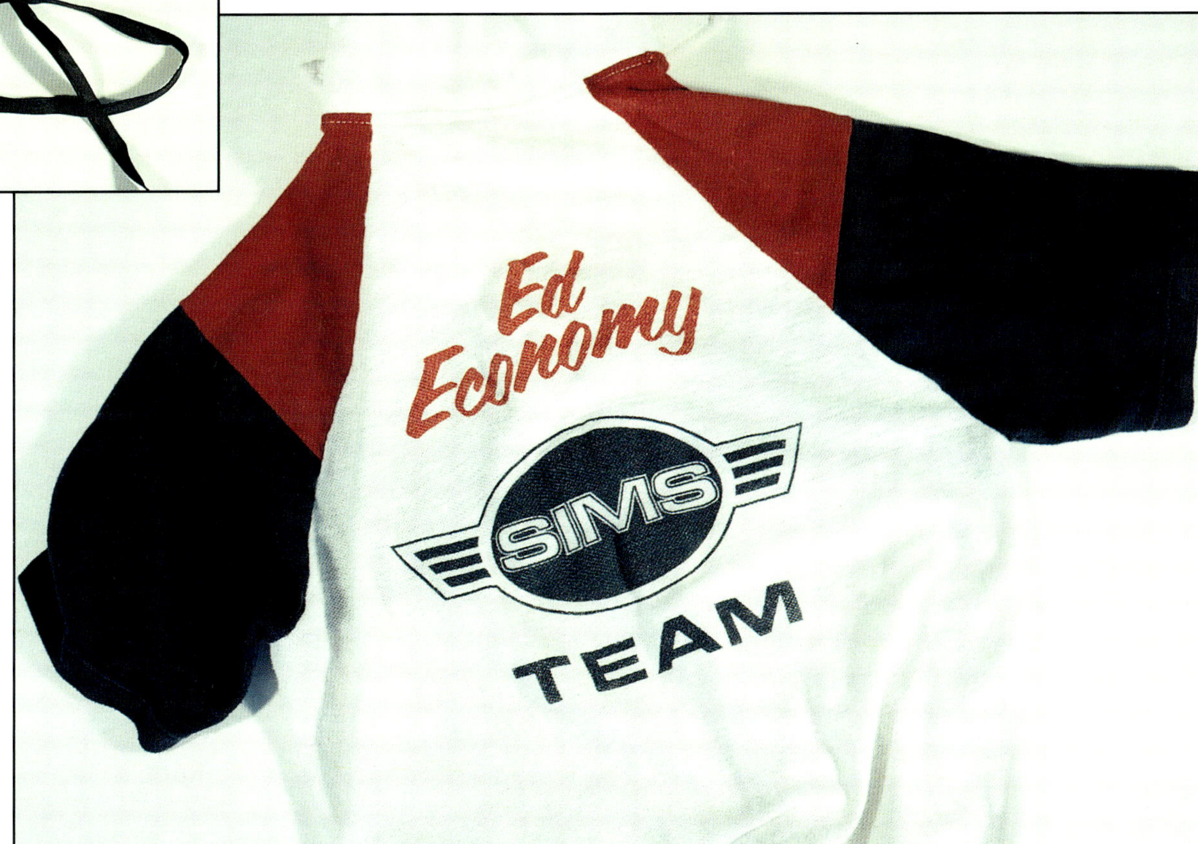

Ed Economy.'s personal team jersey. *Courtesy Ed Economy.* $500.

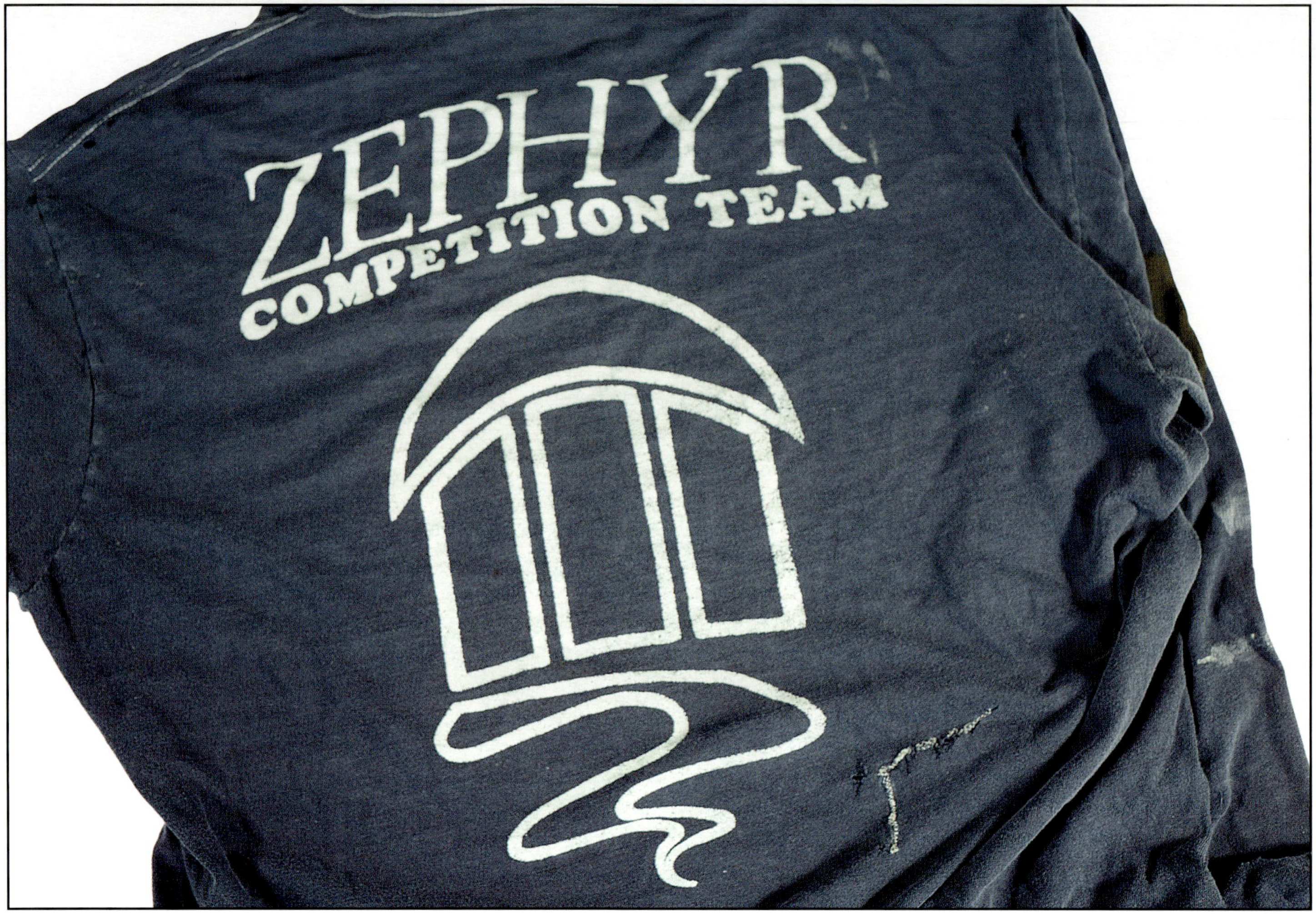

Original Zeffer t-shirt. This design is being reproduced, so watch out. *Courtesy Ed Economy.* $2000.

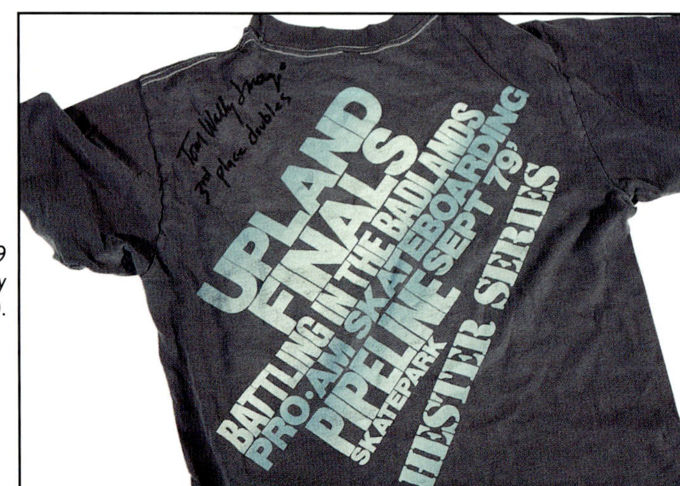

The Upland pro-am tee, 1979 signed by Tom Inouye. *Courtesy Ed Economy.* $2000.

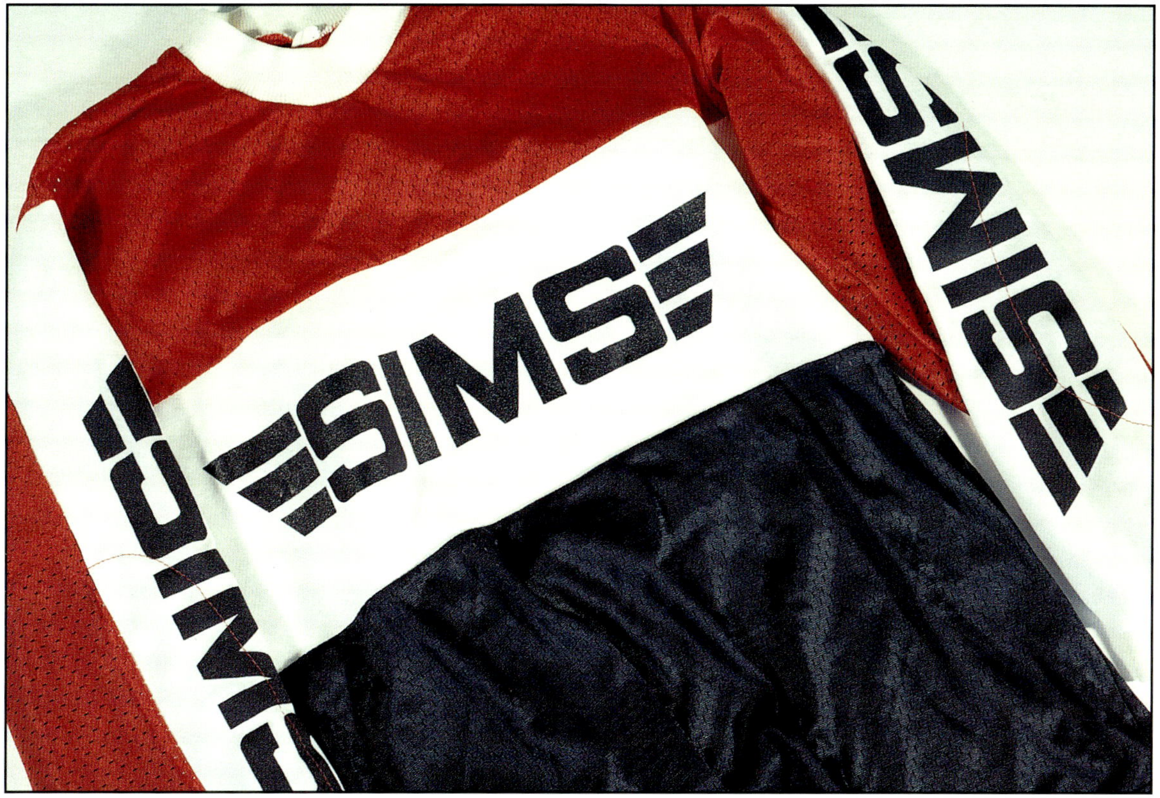

Sims team jersey. *Courtesy Ed Economy.* $300.

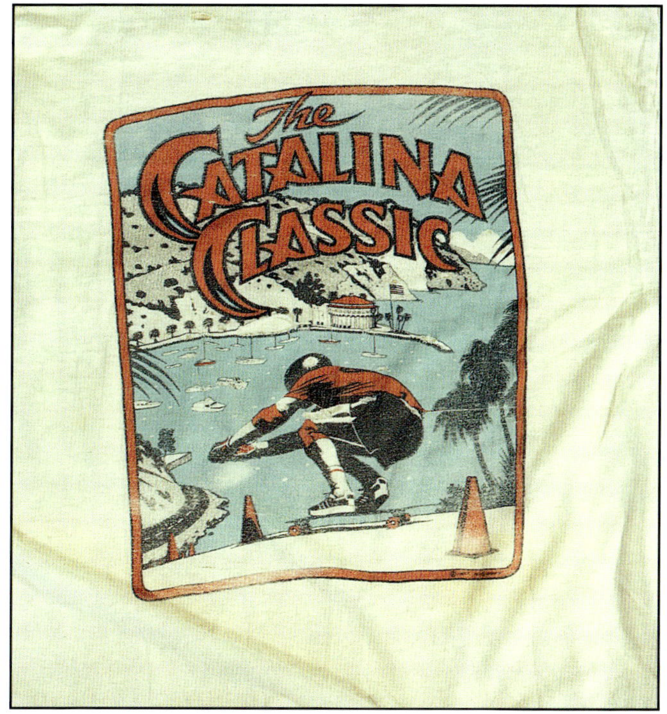

Original Catalina Classic tee. *Courtesy Ed Economy.* $200.

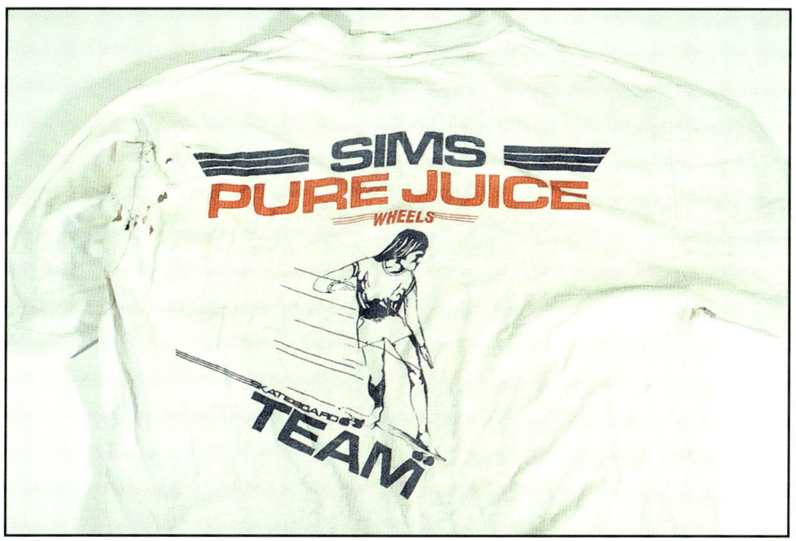

Courtesy Ed Economy.

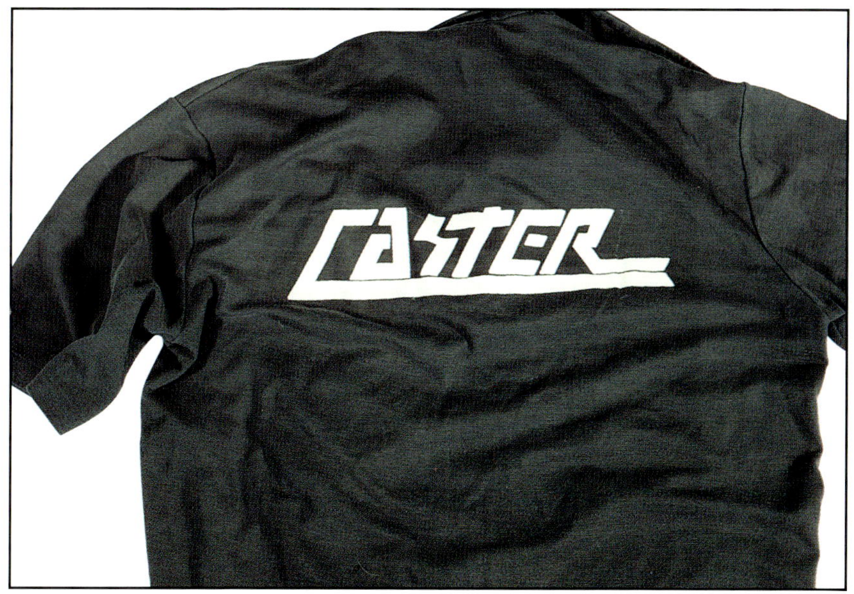

Caster tee. *Courtesy Ed Economy.* $500.

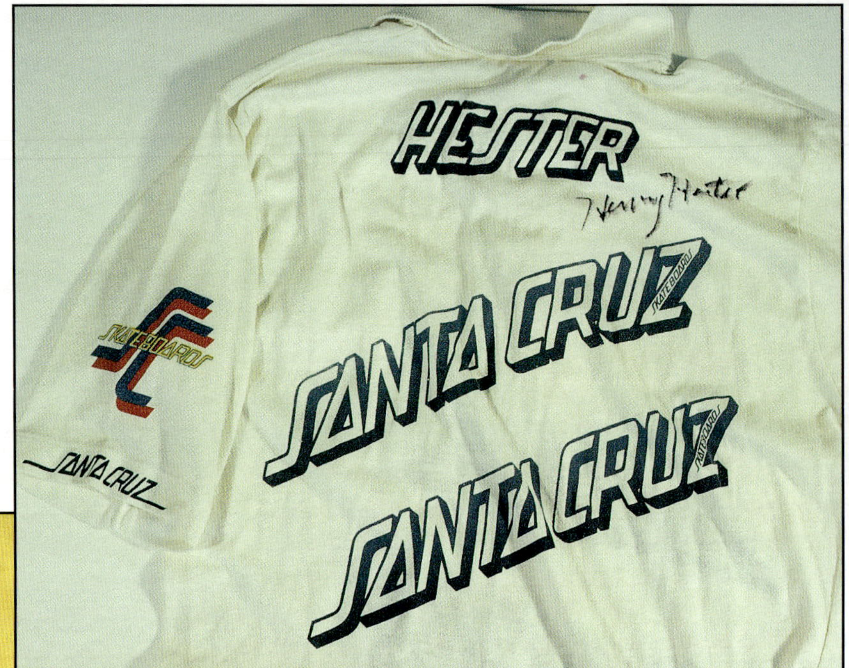

Henry Hester's Santa Cruz team jersey singed by Henry. *Photo R. Noll. Courtesy Ed Economy.* $1000.

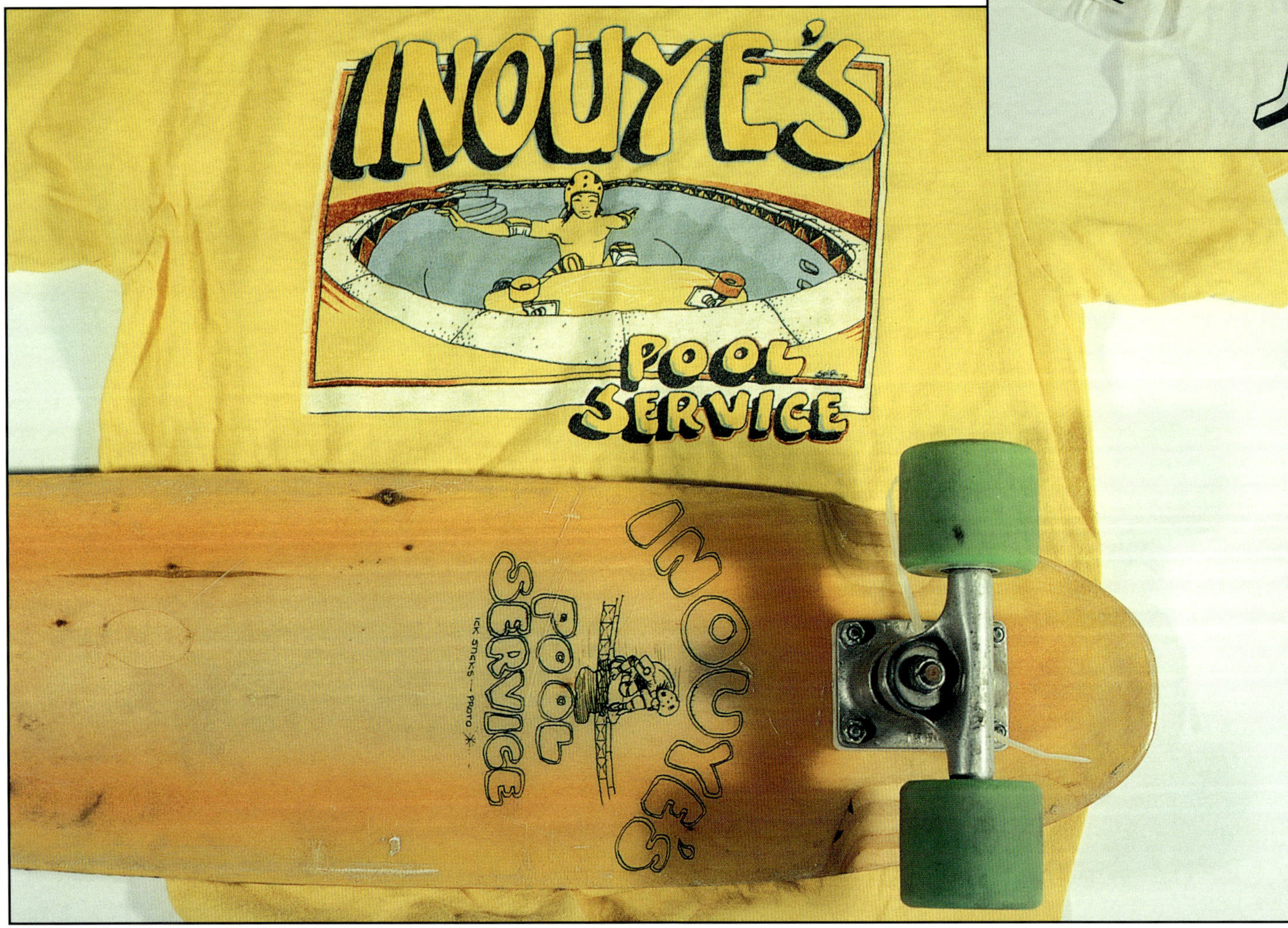

Inouye's Pool Service tee and skateboard. *Courtesy Ed Economy.* $2000.

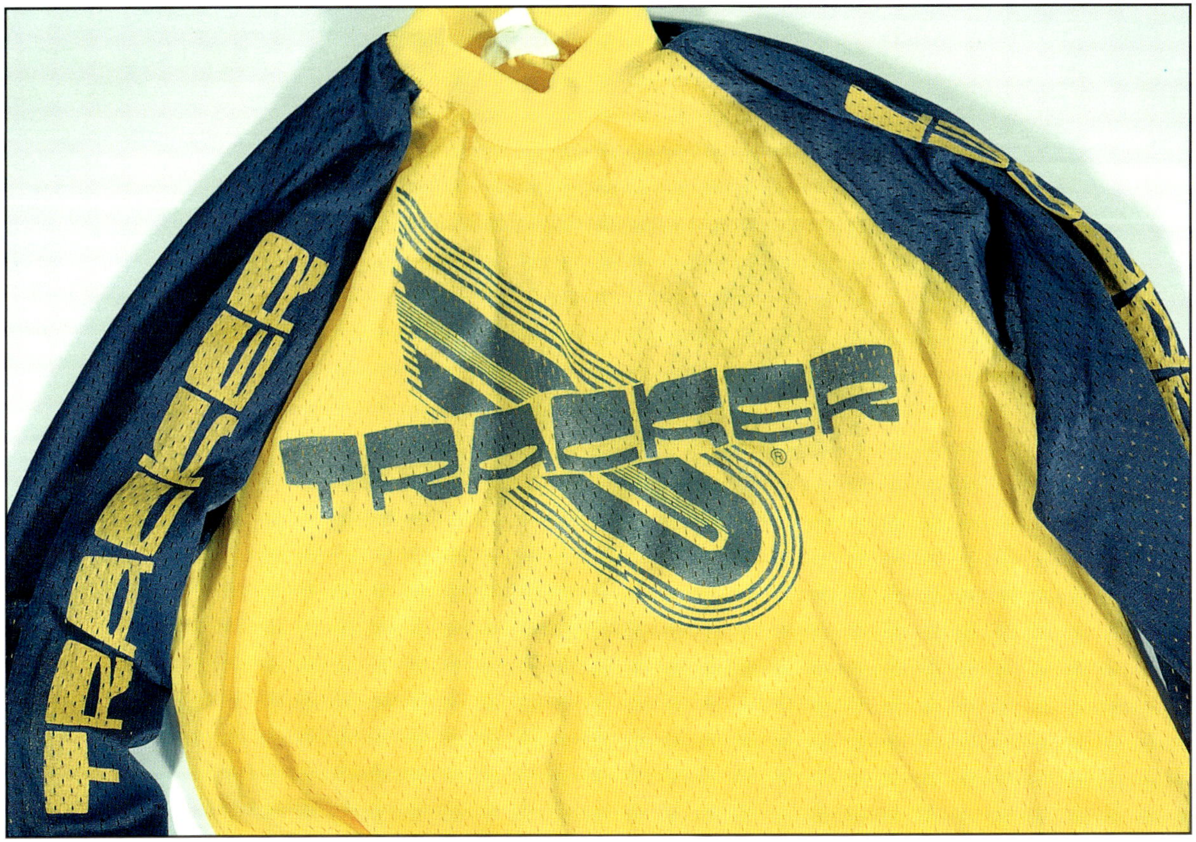

An original Tracker team jersey.
Courtesy Ed Economy. $300.

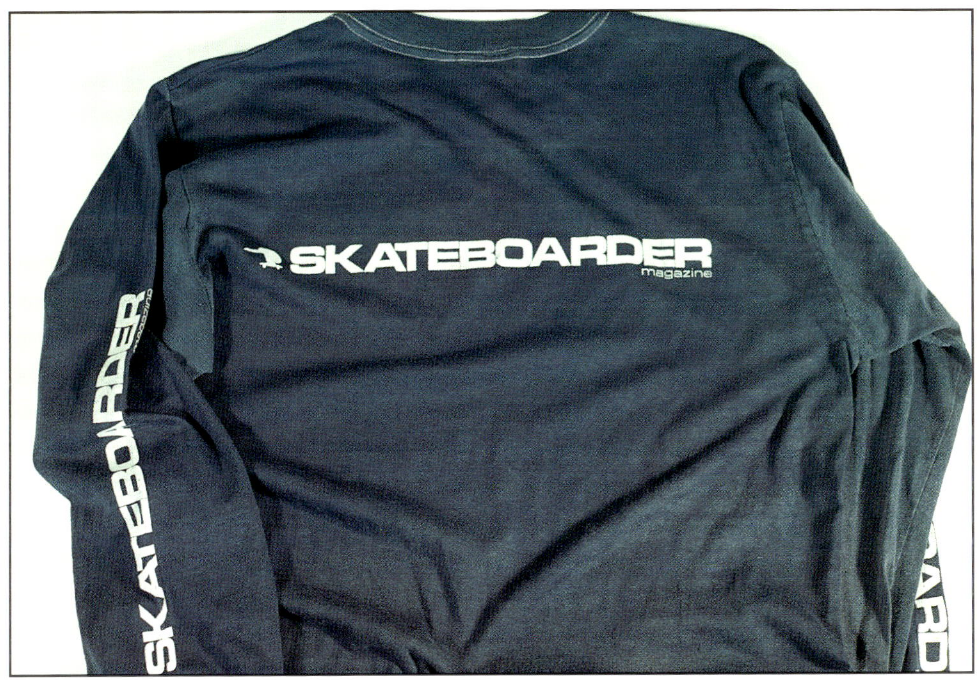

Skateboarder magazine tee.
Courtesy Ed Economy. $100.

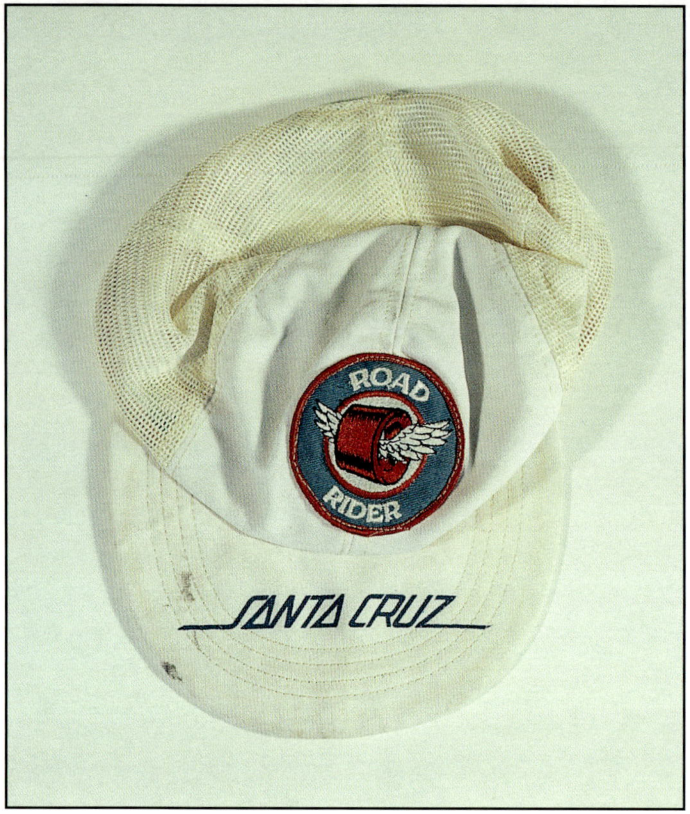

Road rider hat by Santa Cruz. *Courtesy Ed Economy.* $45.

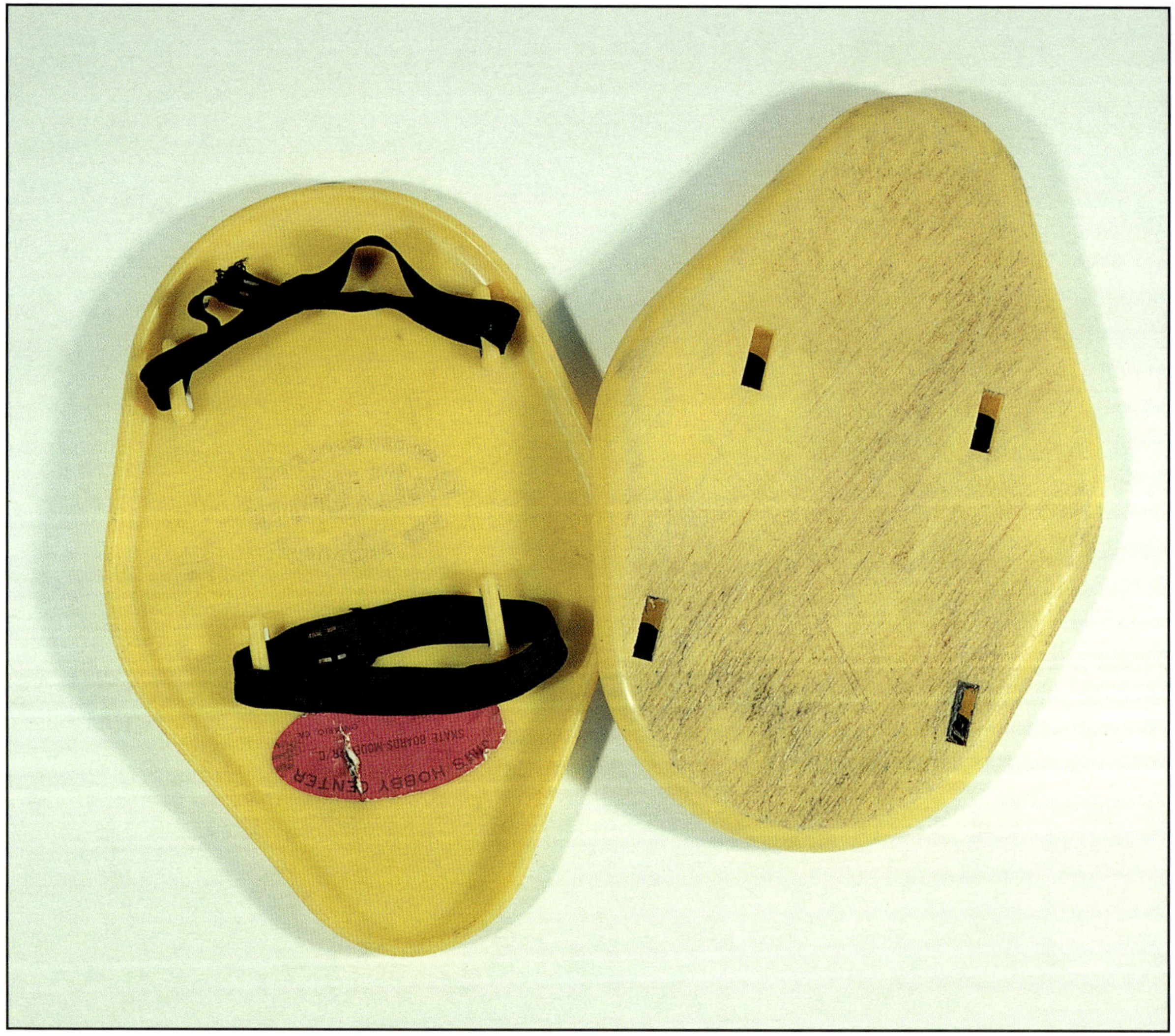

These are plastic hand grind pads. *Courtesy Ed Economy.* $50.

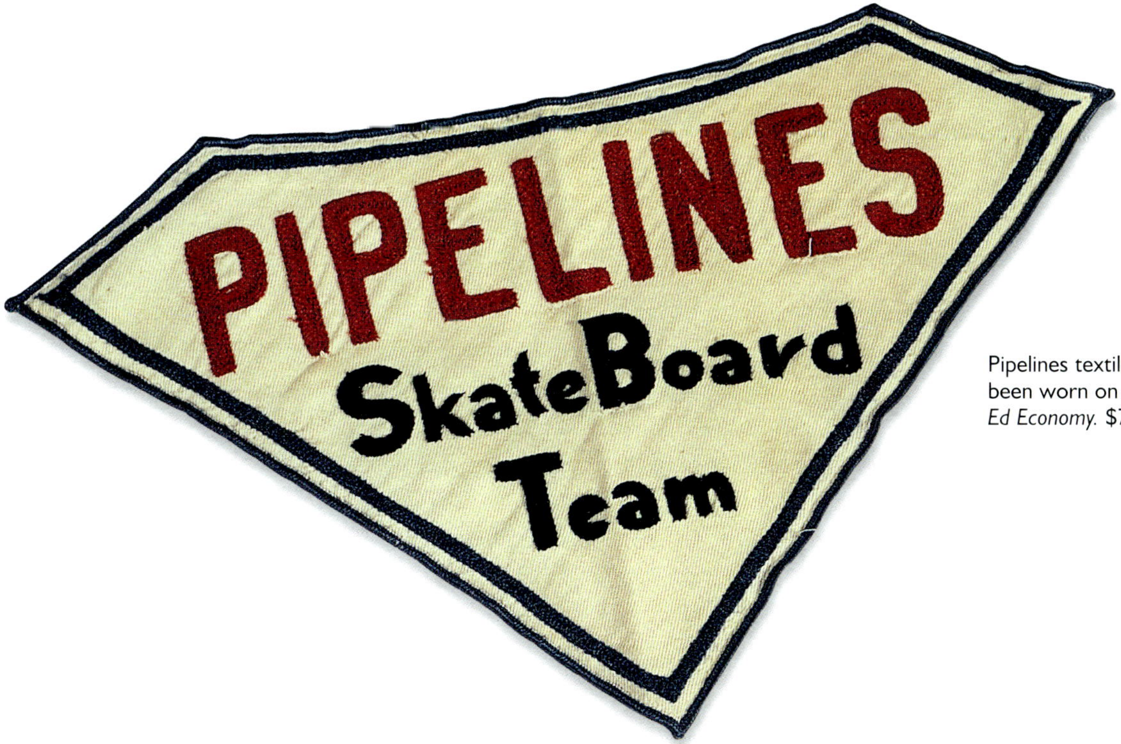

Pipelines textile team patch would have been worn on the back of a jacket. *Courtesy Ed Economy.* $700.

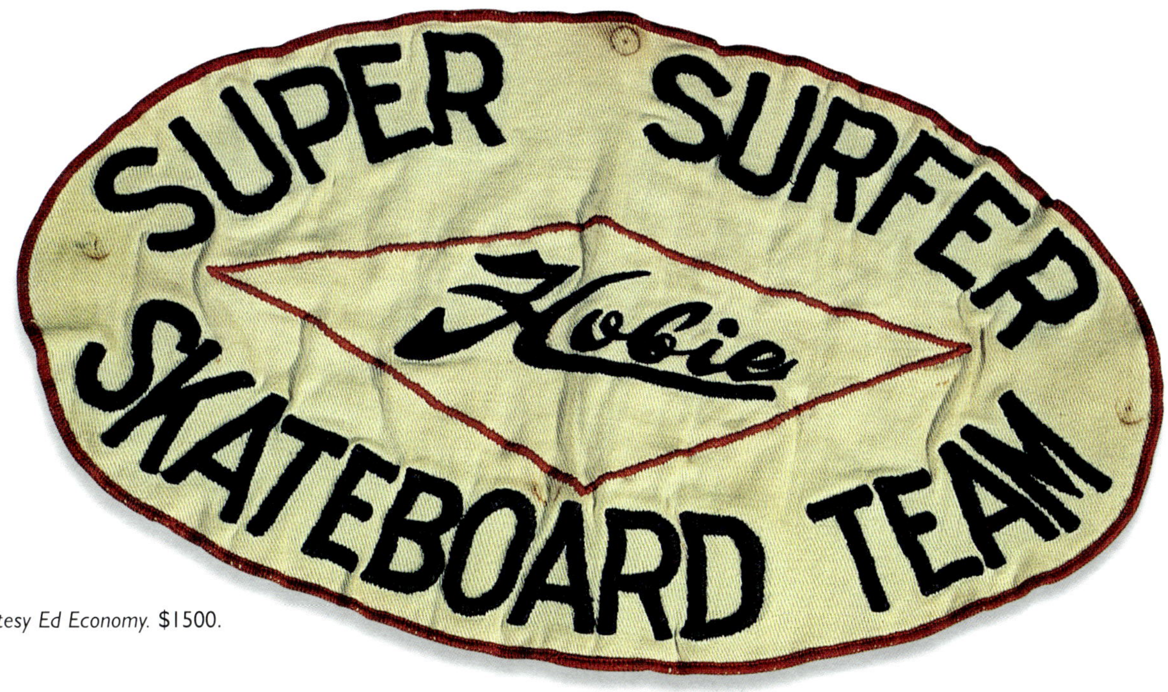

Super Surfer skateboard patch. *Courtesy Ed Economy.* $1500.

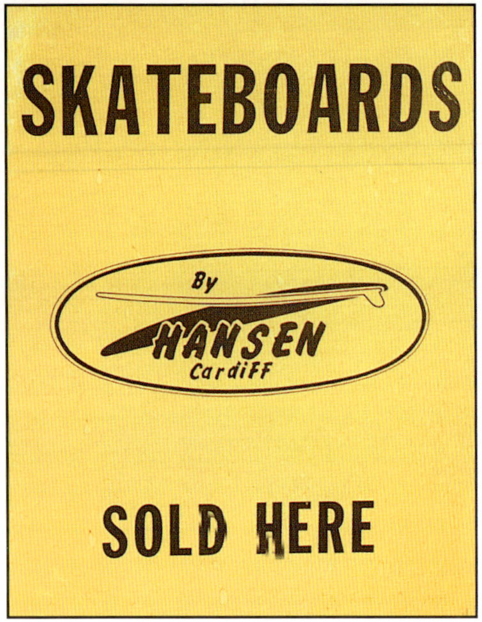

A rare window sign for Hanson skateboards. *Courtesy Todd Huber.* $50-70.

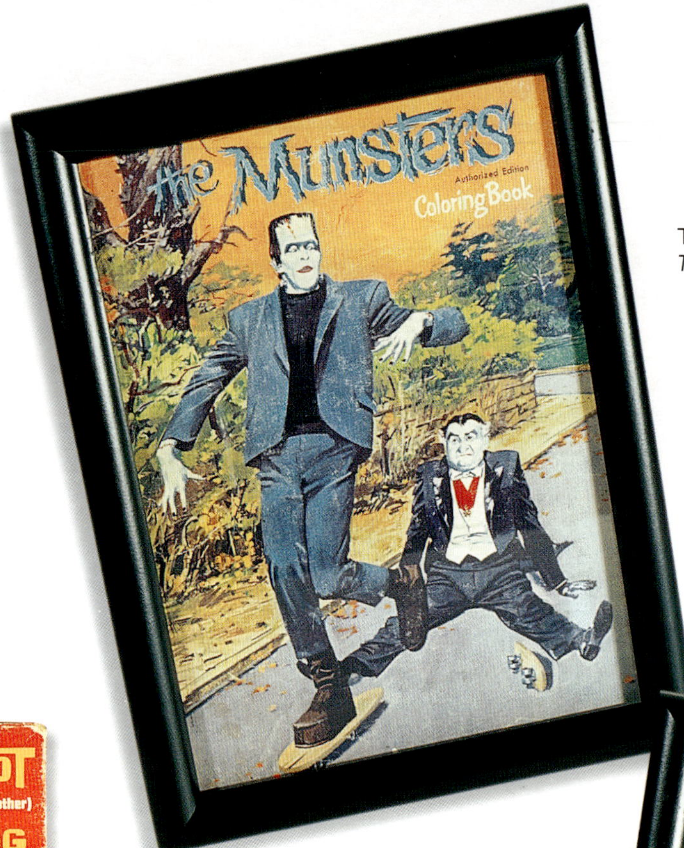

The Munsters' rare coloring book. *Courtesy Todd Huber.* $25.

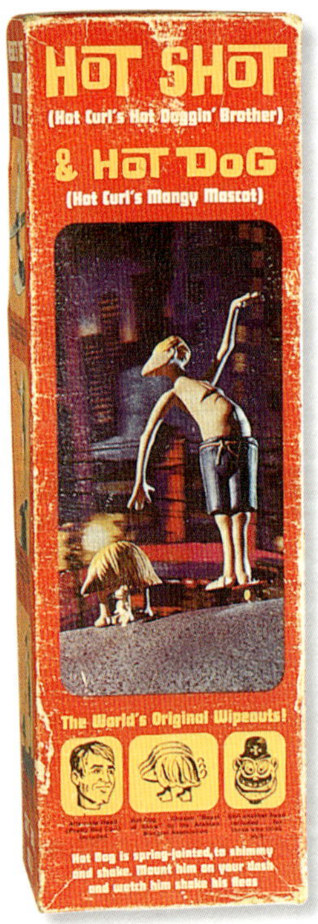

Hot Shot and Hot Dog.

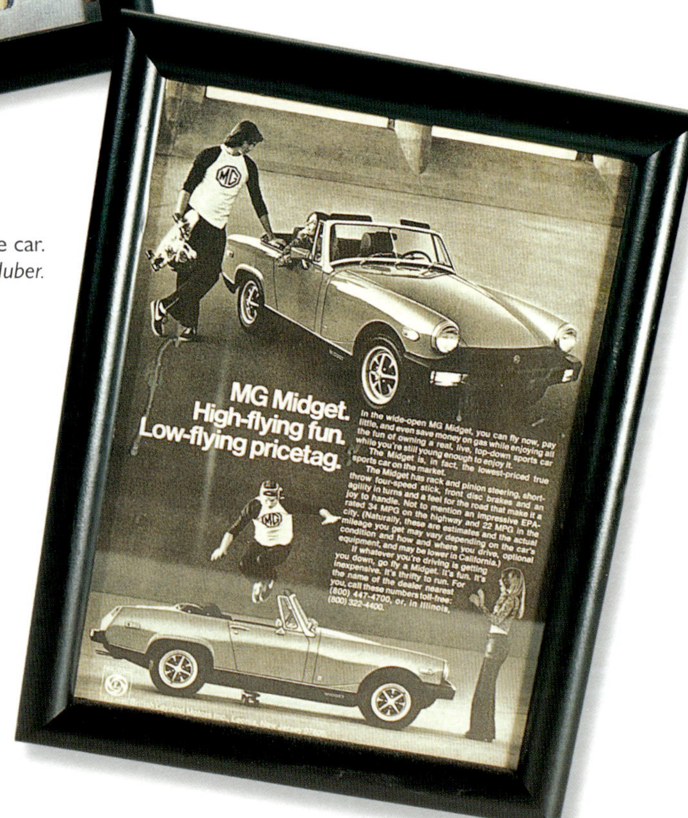

M.G. car ad with midget jumping the car. *Courtesy Todd Huber.*

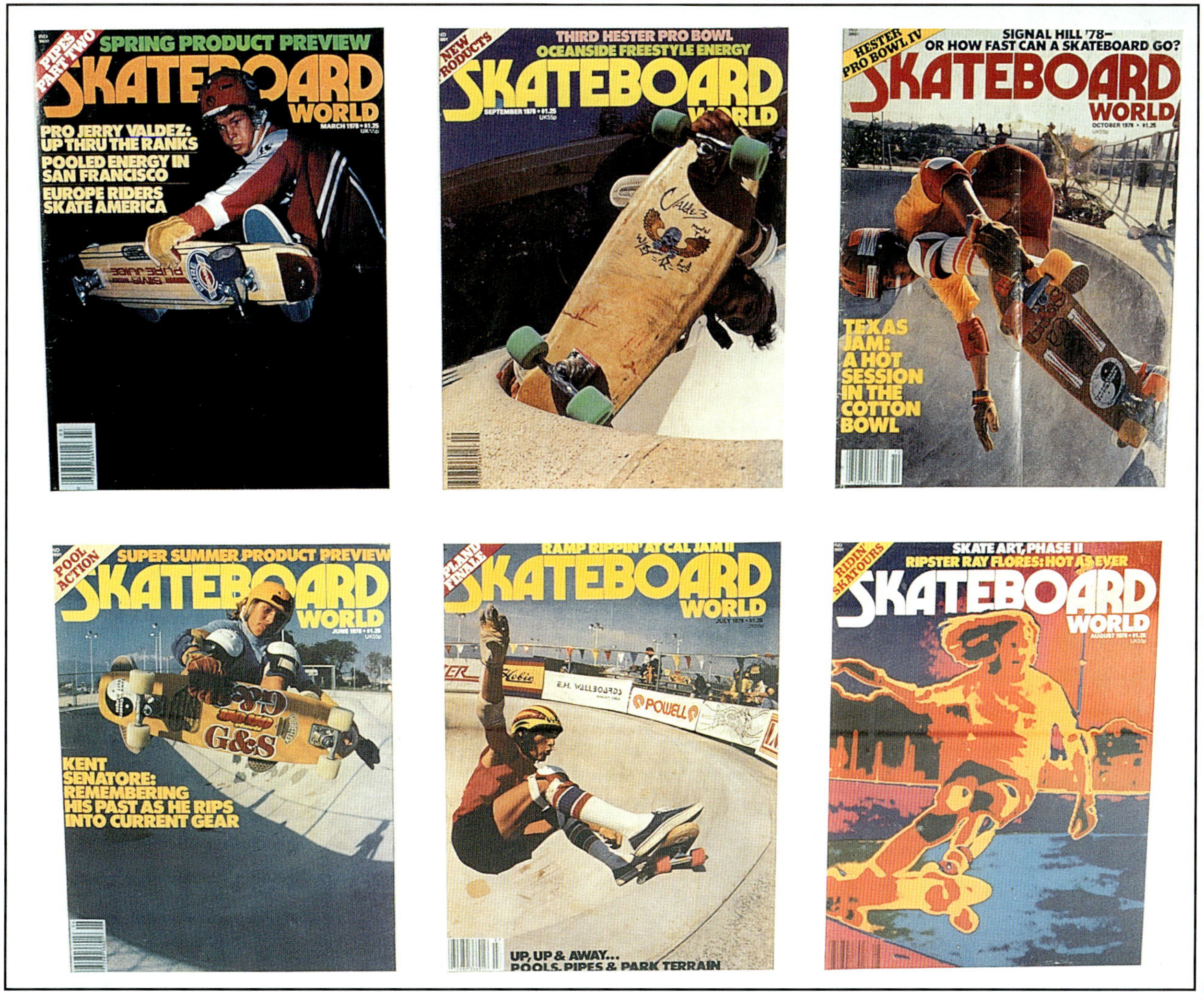

Skateboard World cover shots from the late '70s for collectors. *Courtesy Todd Huber.* $75-100.

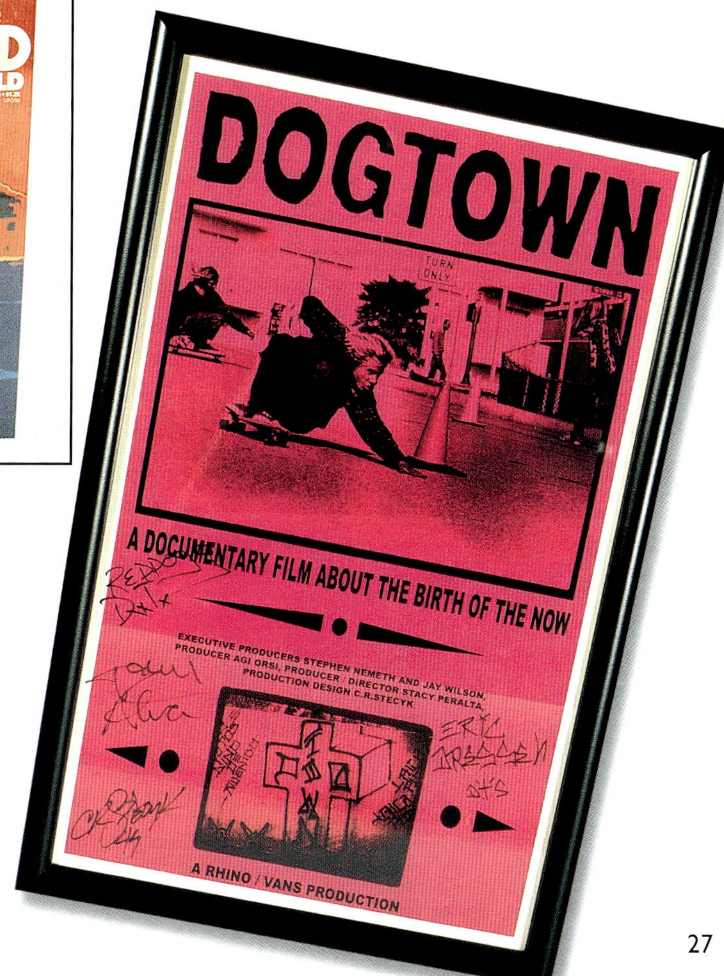

Dogtown movie poster signed by Dogtowners. *Courtesy Todd Huber.* $30-40.

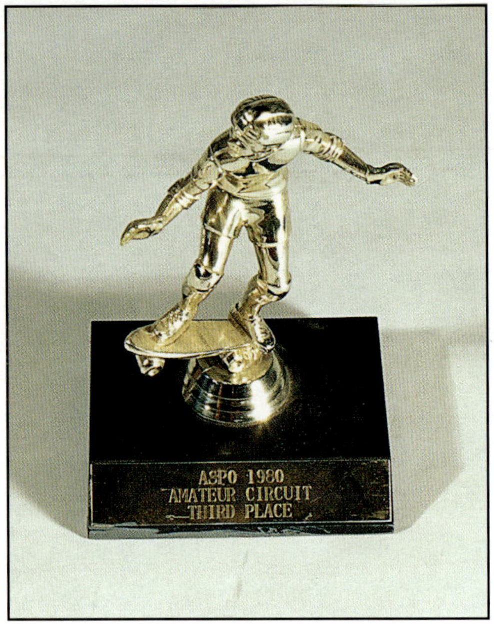

A couple of skateboarding awards. *Courtesy Todd Huber.* $20 each

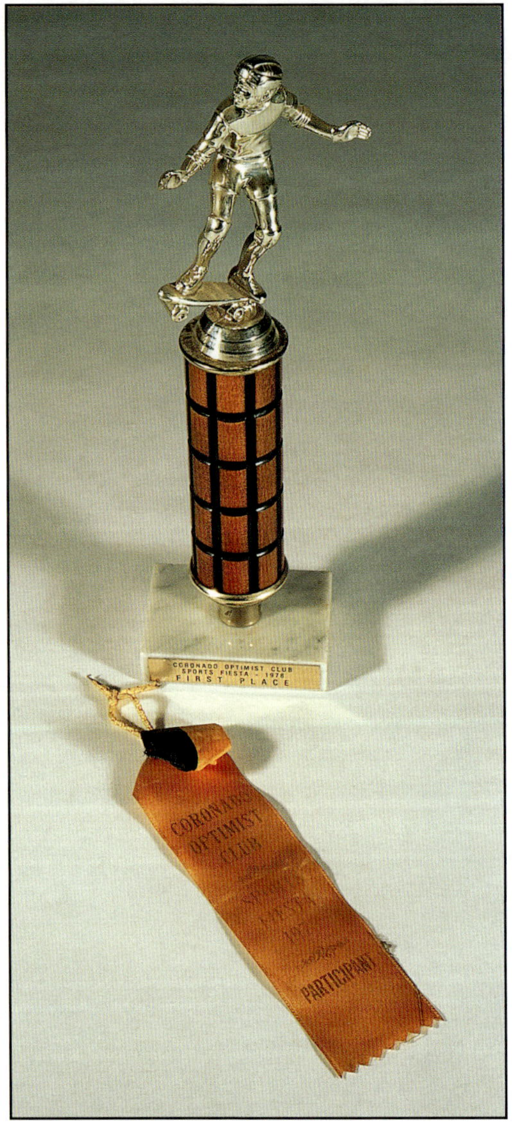

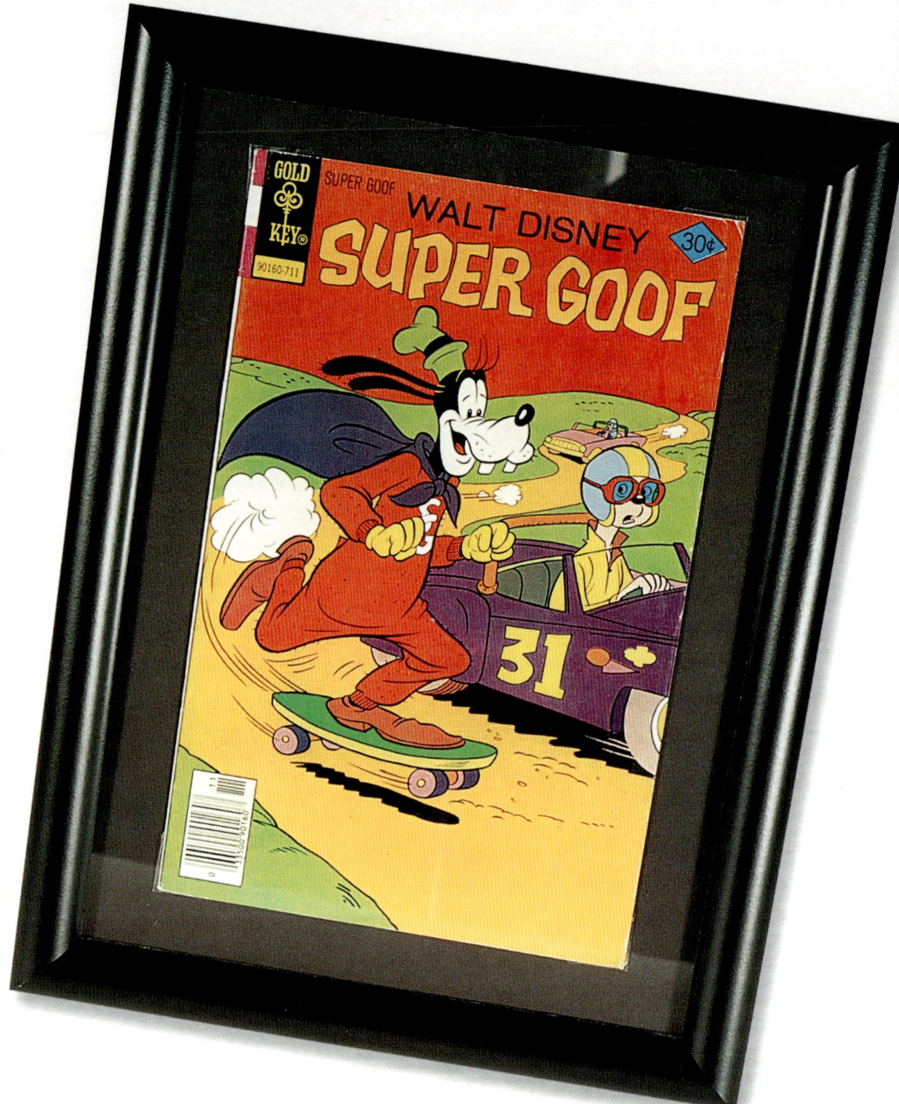

Walt Disney's Super Goof skateboard comic. *Courtesy Todd Huber.* $10-20.

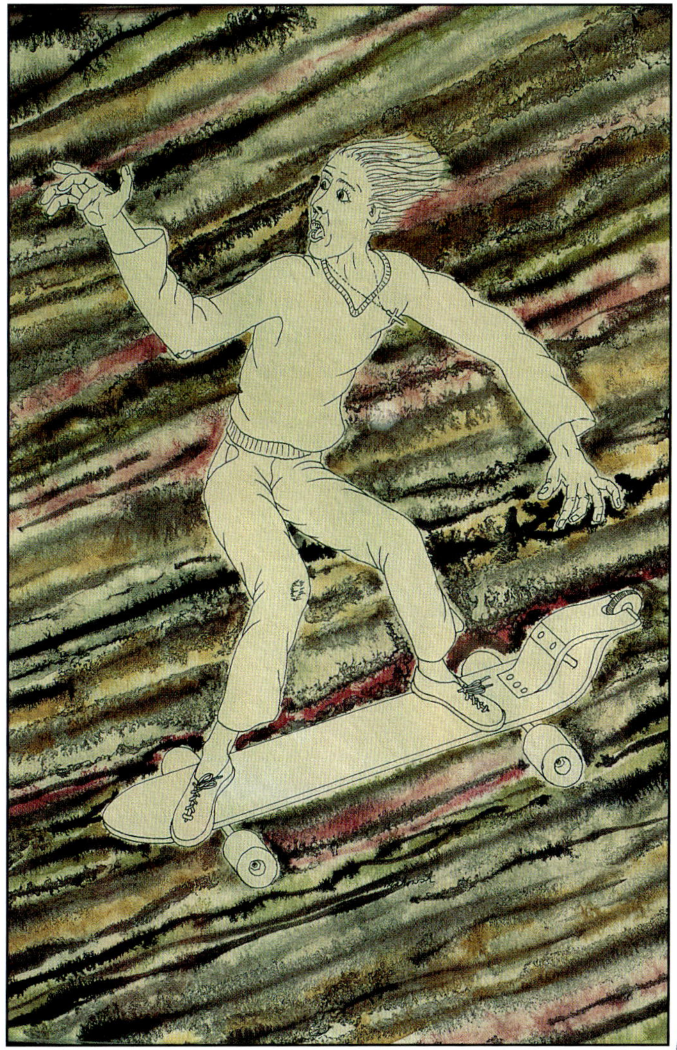

Skate art; check the wheelie bar. *Courtesy Todd Huber.* $50.

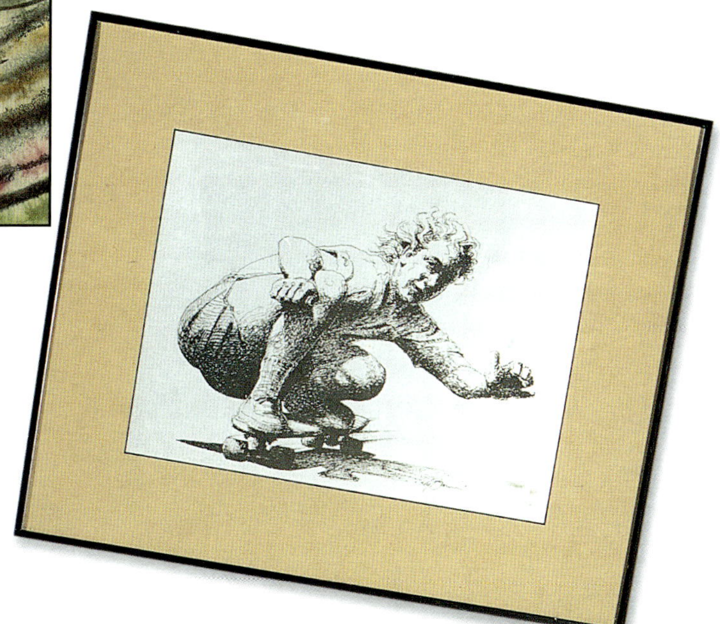

Skate art by Roy Brown. *Courtesy Todd Huber.*

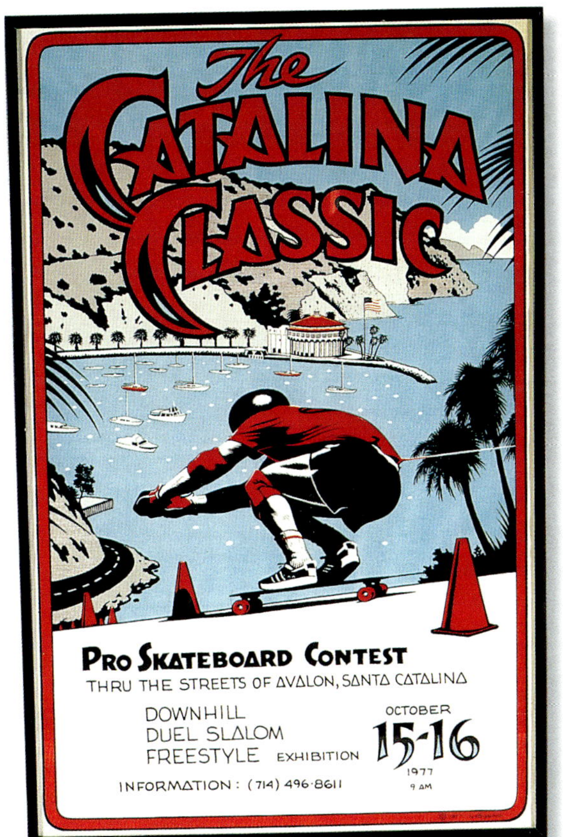

The Catalina Classic event poster. *Courtesy Todd Huber.* $40-50.

The Skatelab, in Simi Valley, California, is set up as a museum; behold the treasures. *Courtesy Todd Huber.*

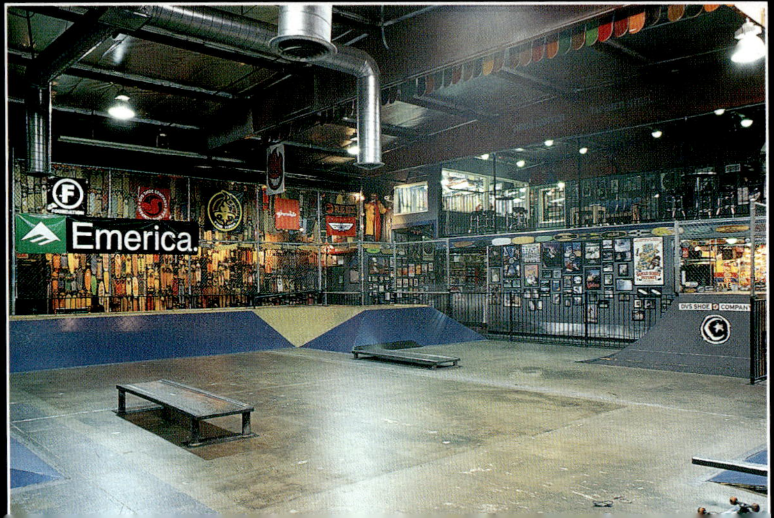

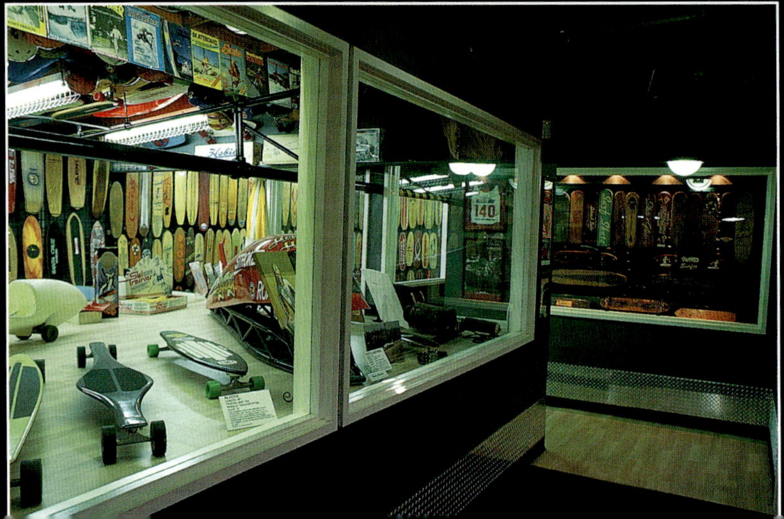

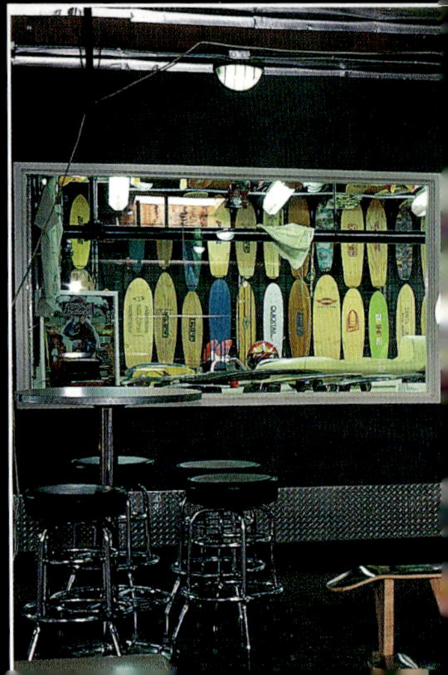

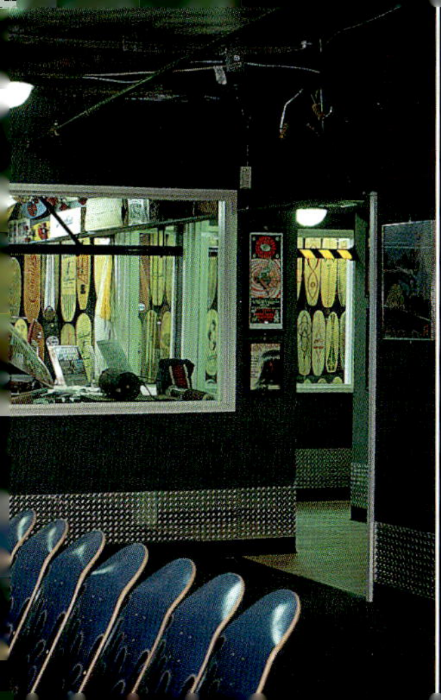

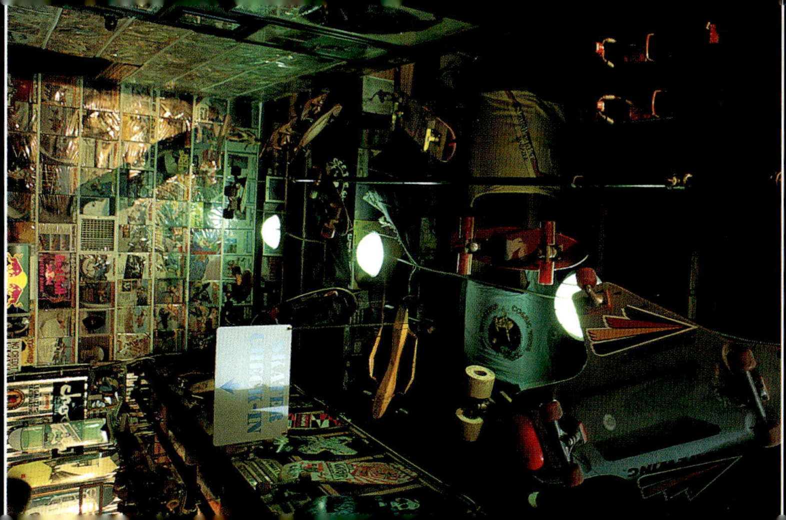
SKATER CHECK-IN

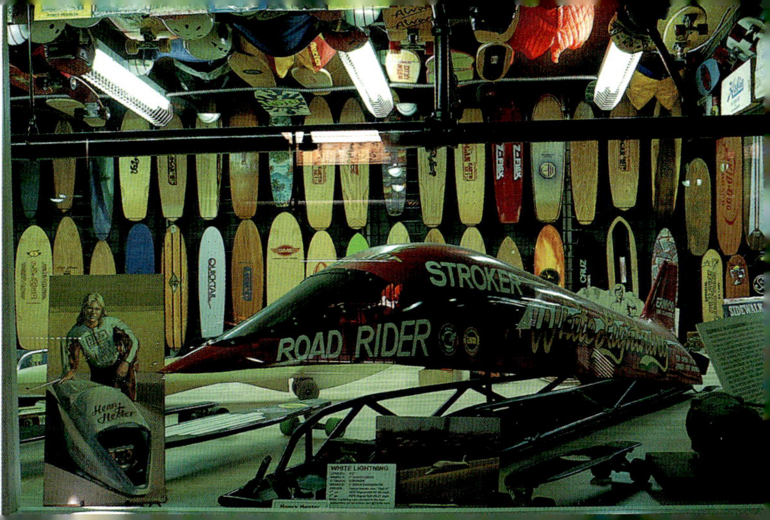
STROKER
ROAD RIDER
WHITE LIGHTNING

Gaze at the collectibles that are now locked away but preserved for all to see. The Skatelab collection is so significant that you can no longer find similar items. *Courtesy Todd Huber.*

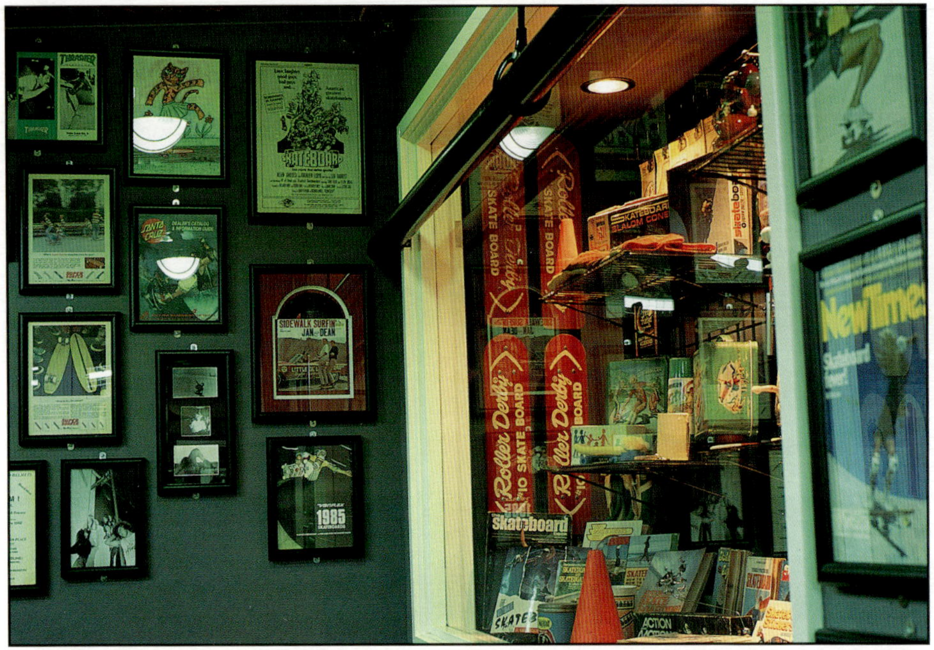

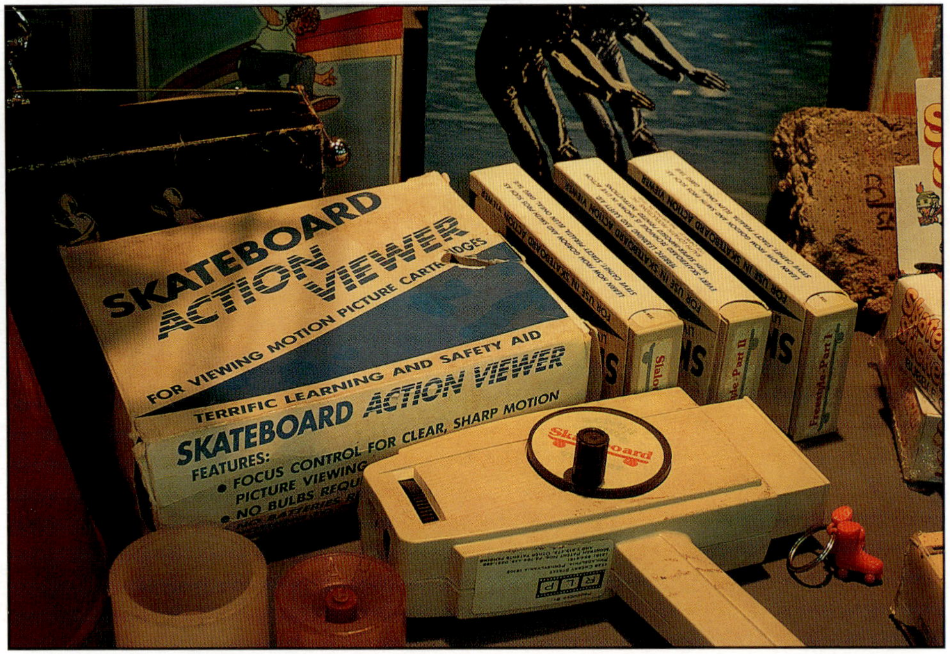

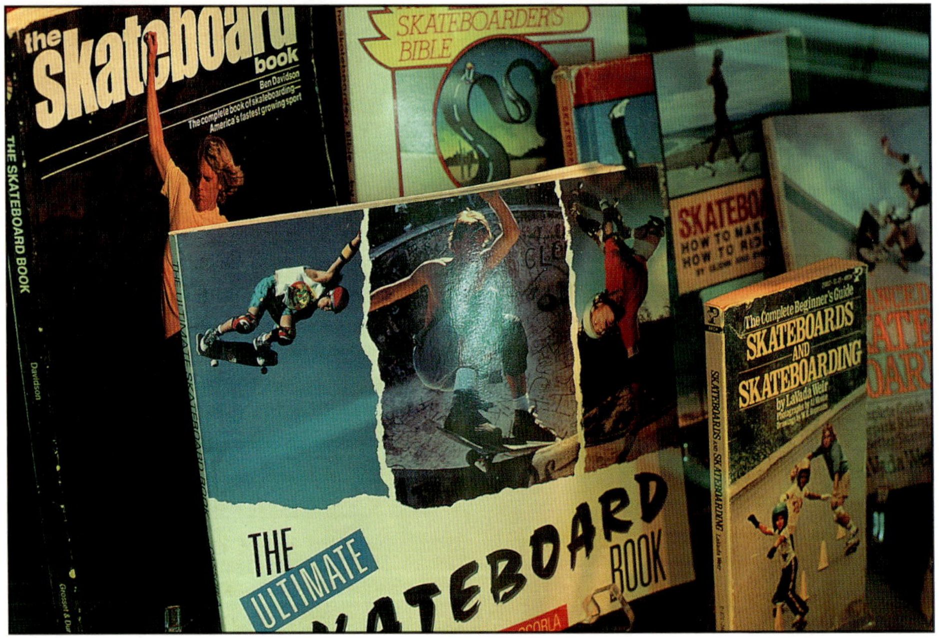

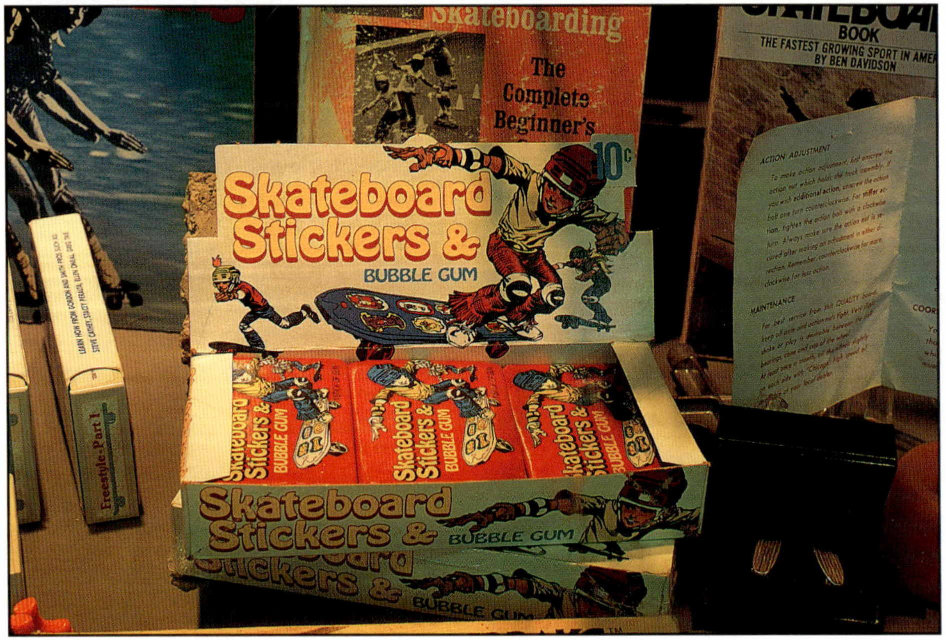

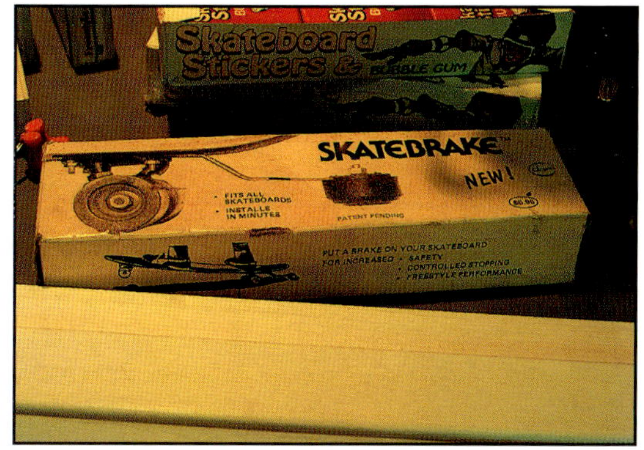
Skateboard Stickers & Bubble Gum
SKATEBRAKE
NEW!
FITS ALL SKATEBOARDS
INSTALLS IN MINUTES
PUT A BRAKE ON YOUR SKATEBOARD

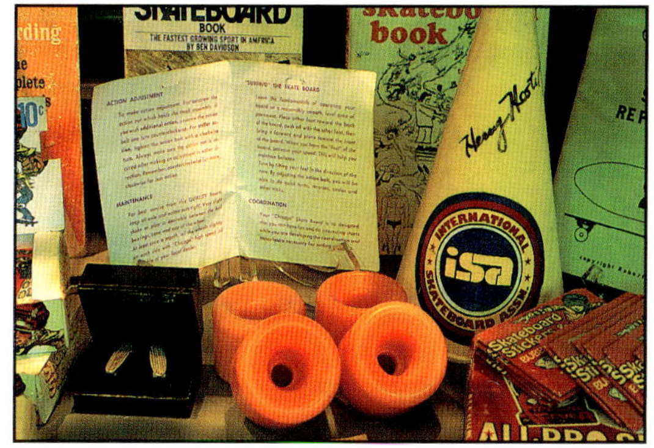
SKATEBOARD BOOK
THE FASTEST GROWING SPORT IN AMERICA
BY BEN DAVIDSON
book
INTERNATIONAL
isa
SKATEBOARD ASSN.

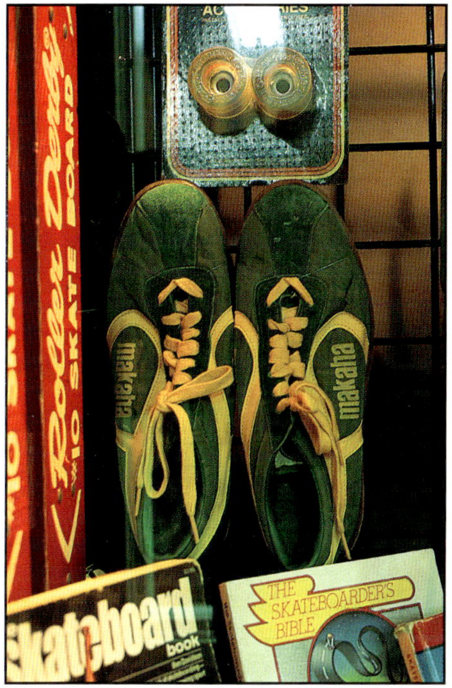
Roller Derby
#10 SKATE BOARD
makaha
makaha
skateboard
book
THE SKATEBOARDER'S BIBLE

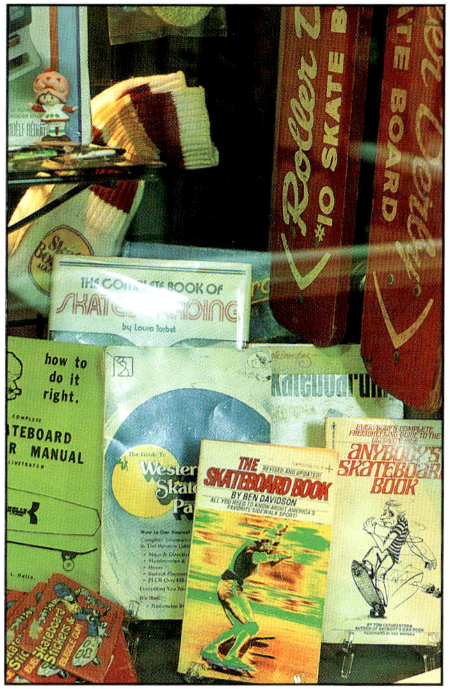
Roller Derby
#10 SKATE BOARD
THE COMPLETE BOOK OF SKATEBOARDING
by Laura Torbet
how to do it right.
THE SKATEBOARD BOOK
REVISED AND UPDATED
BY BEN DAVIDSON
ALL YOU NEED TO KNOW ABOUT AMERICA'S FAVORITE SIDEWALK SPORT!
ANYBODY'S SKATEBOARD BOOK

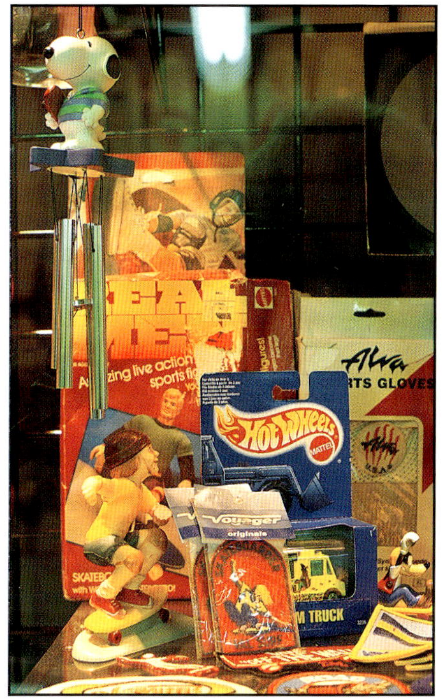
Hot Wheels
MATTEL
Voyager
originals
Alva
TRUCK

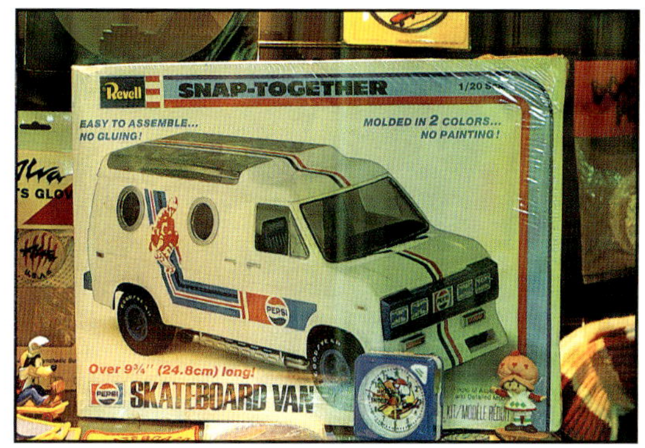
Revell
SNAP-TOGETHER
EASY TO ASSEMBLE...
NO GLUING!
MOLDED IN 2 COLORS...
NO PAINTING!
Over 9¾" (24.8cm) long!
PEPSI
SKATEBOARD VAN

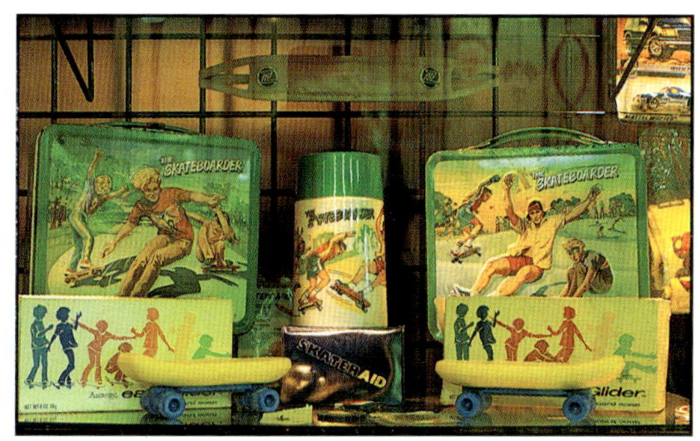
THE SKATEBOARDER
THE SKATEBOARDER
SKATERAID

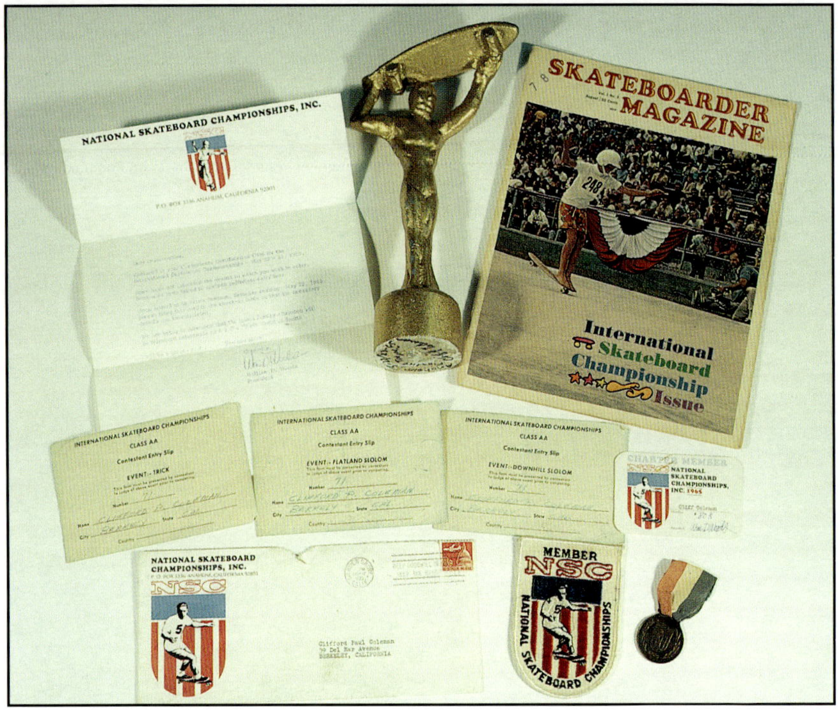

Skateboarder Magazine trophy, official documents, and medal. As usual, *Ed Economy.* wins the grand prize for vision. *Courtesy Ed Economy.* $5000-7000.

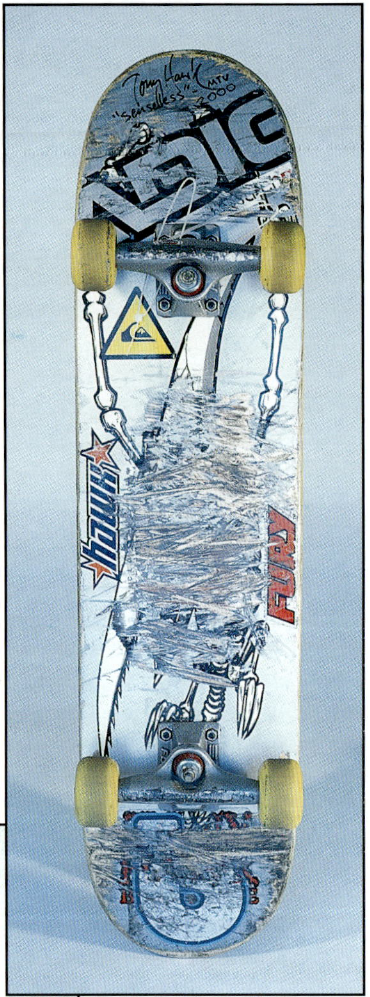

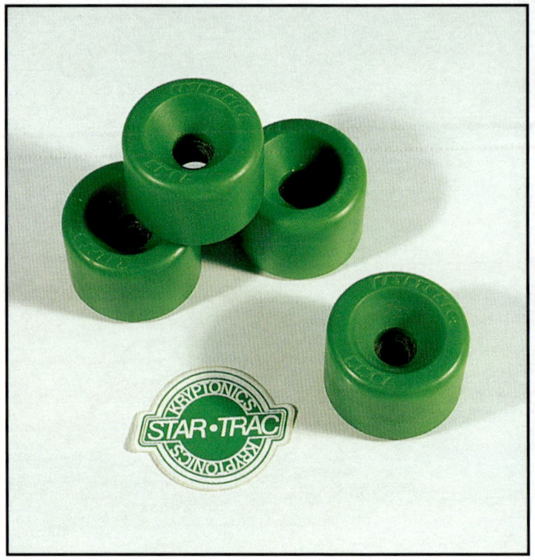

Set of Star-Trac Kryptonics wheels and sticker. *Courtesy Ed Economy.* $75-80.

Tony Hawk's singed photo and skateboard from the event in New York in 2000. *Courtesy Ed Economy.* $1000-1500 for both.

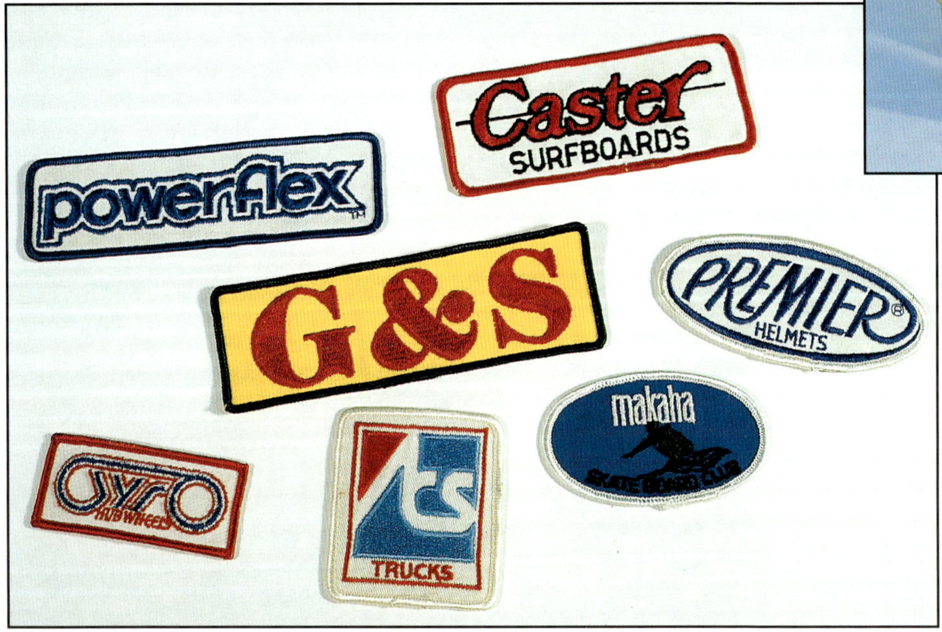

Sporting patches. *Courtesy Ed Economy.* $30 each.

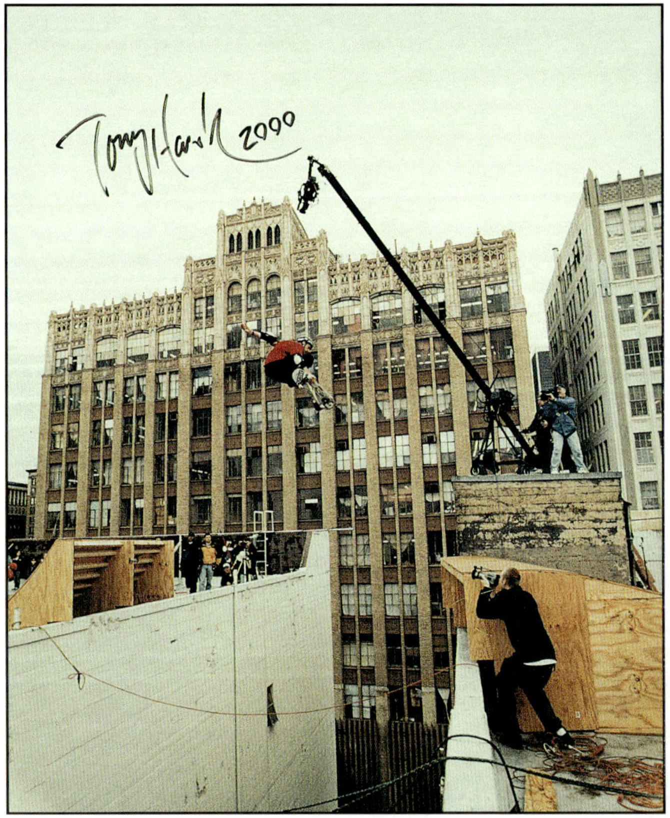

Tony Hawk jumped these buildings in New York with no nets. If he didn't make it, he would have gone straight to the ground. *Courtesy Ed Economy.*

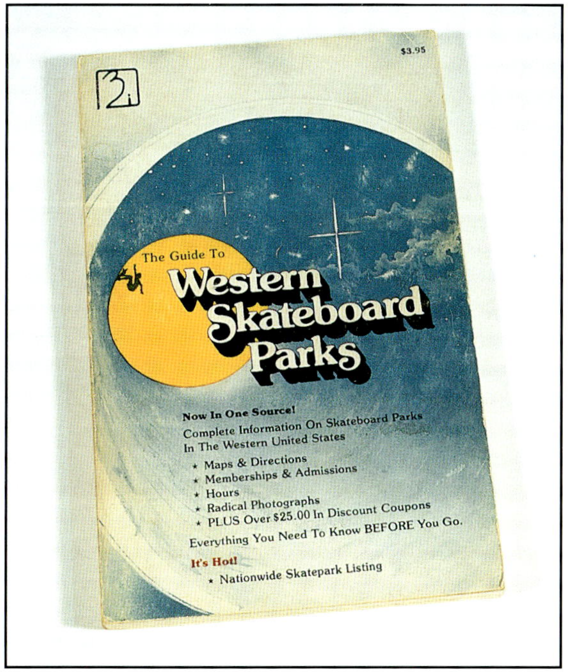

The Guide To Western Skateboard Parks. *Courtesy Ed Economy.* $20.

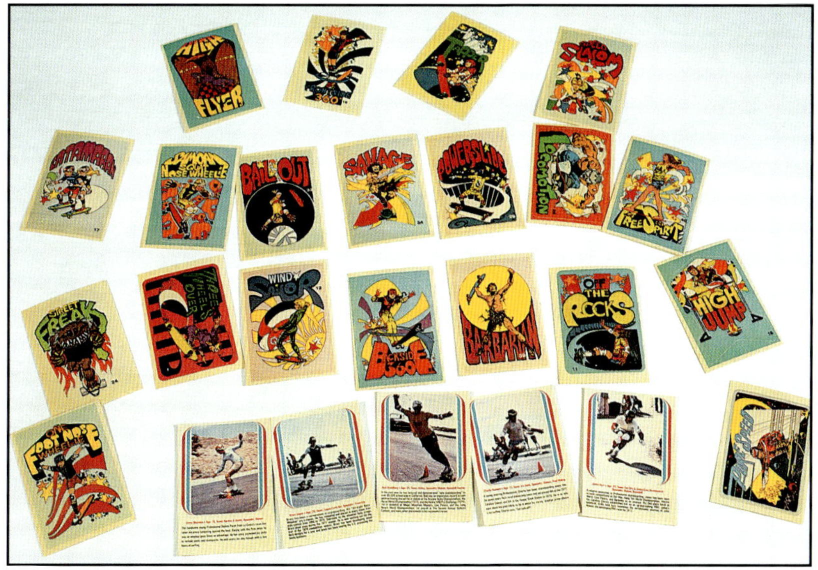

Bubblegum skateboarding trading cards from the 1970s. *Courtesy Ed Economy.* $10 each.

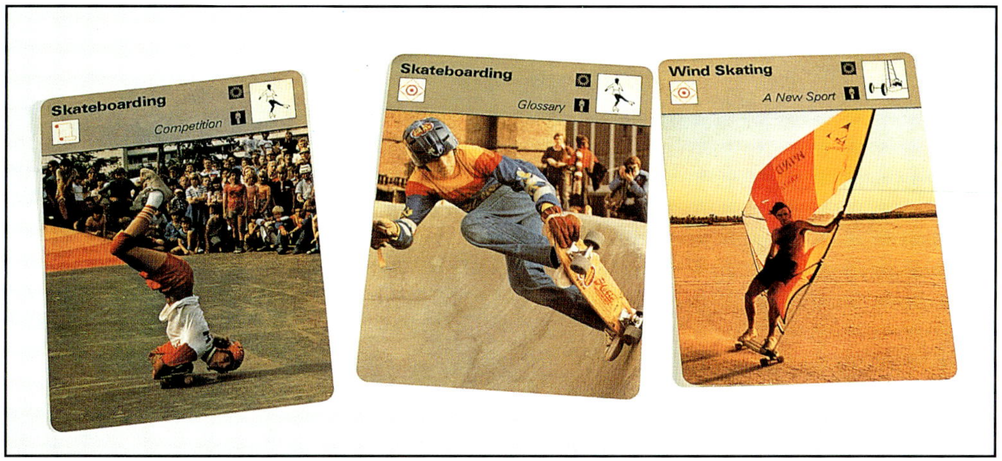

Classic skateboarding trading cards. *Courtesy Ed Economy.* $10.

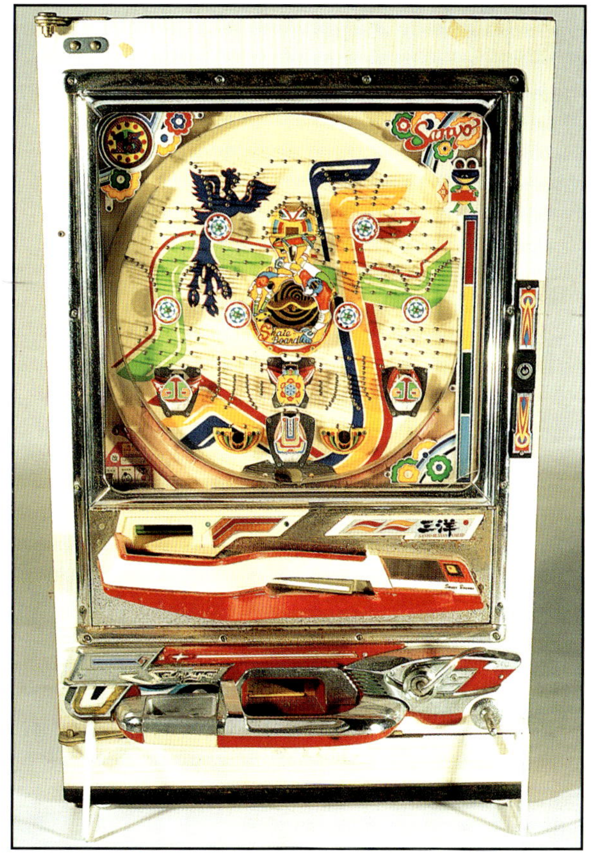

Skateboard ballgame by Sanyo. It is a Japanese gambling machine called a pachinko game. *Courtesy Todd Huber.* $500.

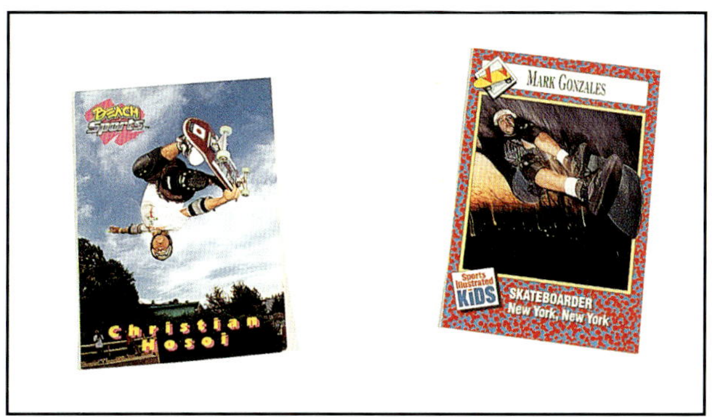

Skateboarding trading cards from the 1980s. *Courtesy Todd Huber.*

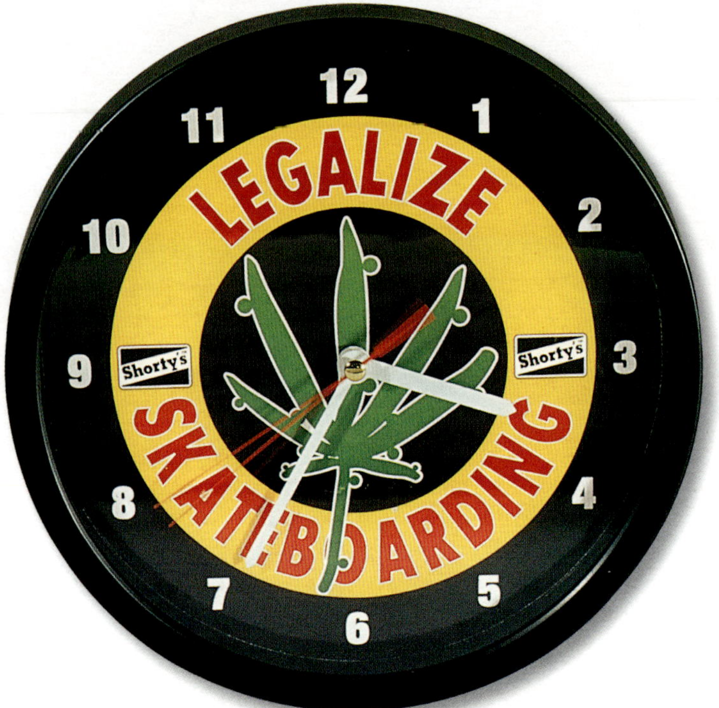

Time to Legalize it. *Courtesy Todd Huber.* $10.

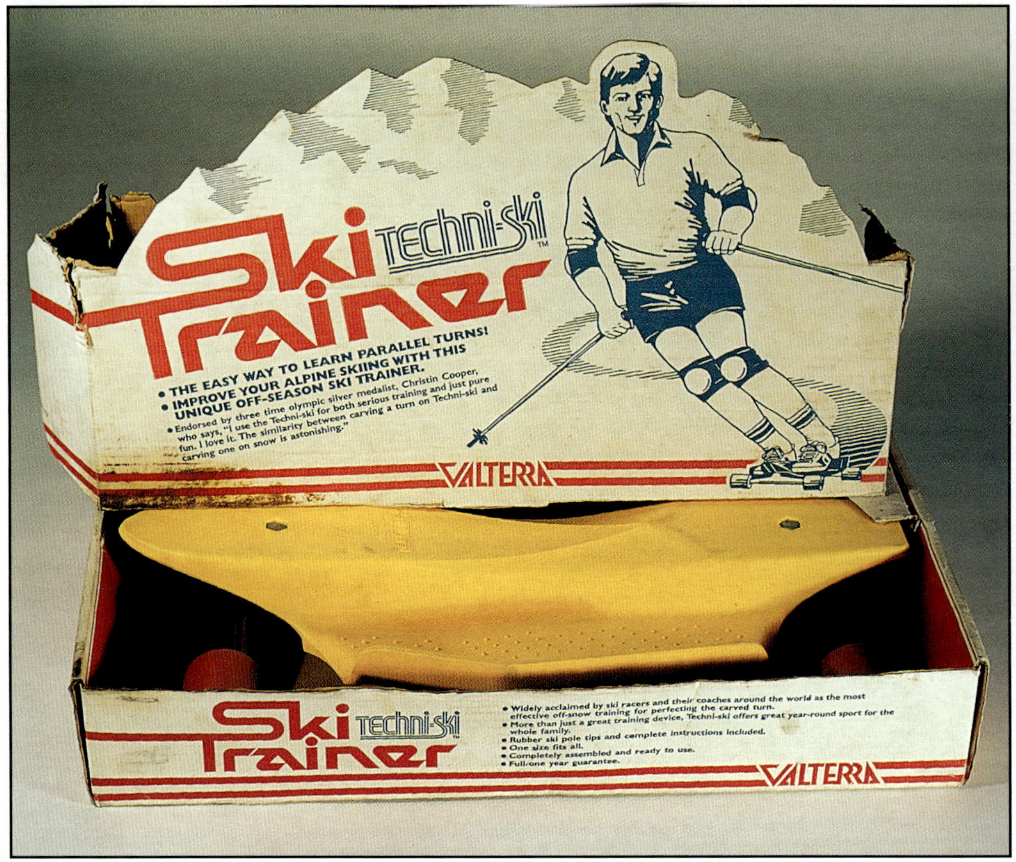

Ski Trainer, still in the box. *Courtesy Todd Huber.* $75-90.

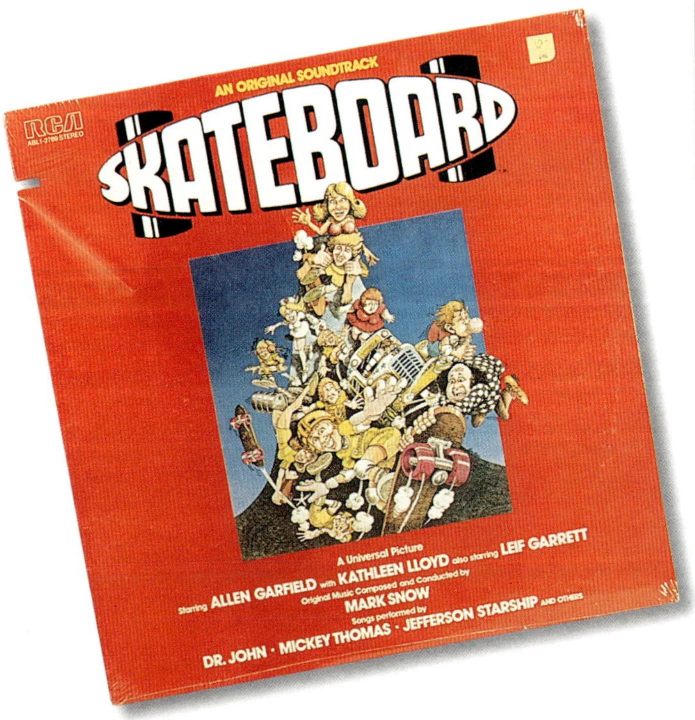

The original soundtrack to the movie *Skateboard. Courtesy Todd Huber.* $20.

1960s Skateboards

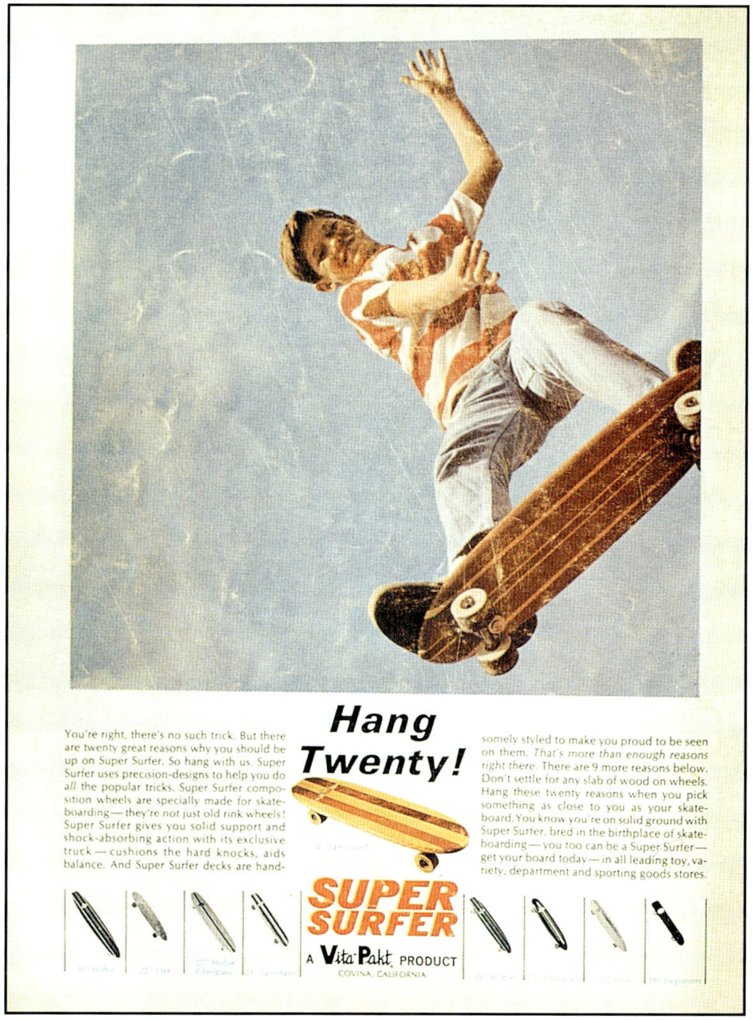

Super Surfer ad, 1960.

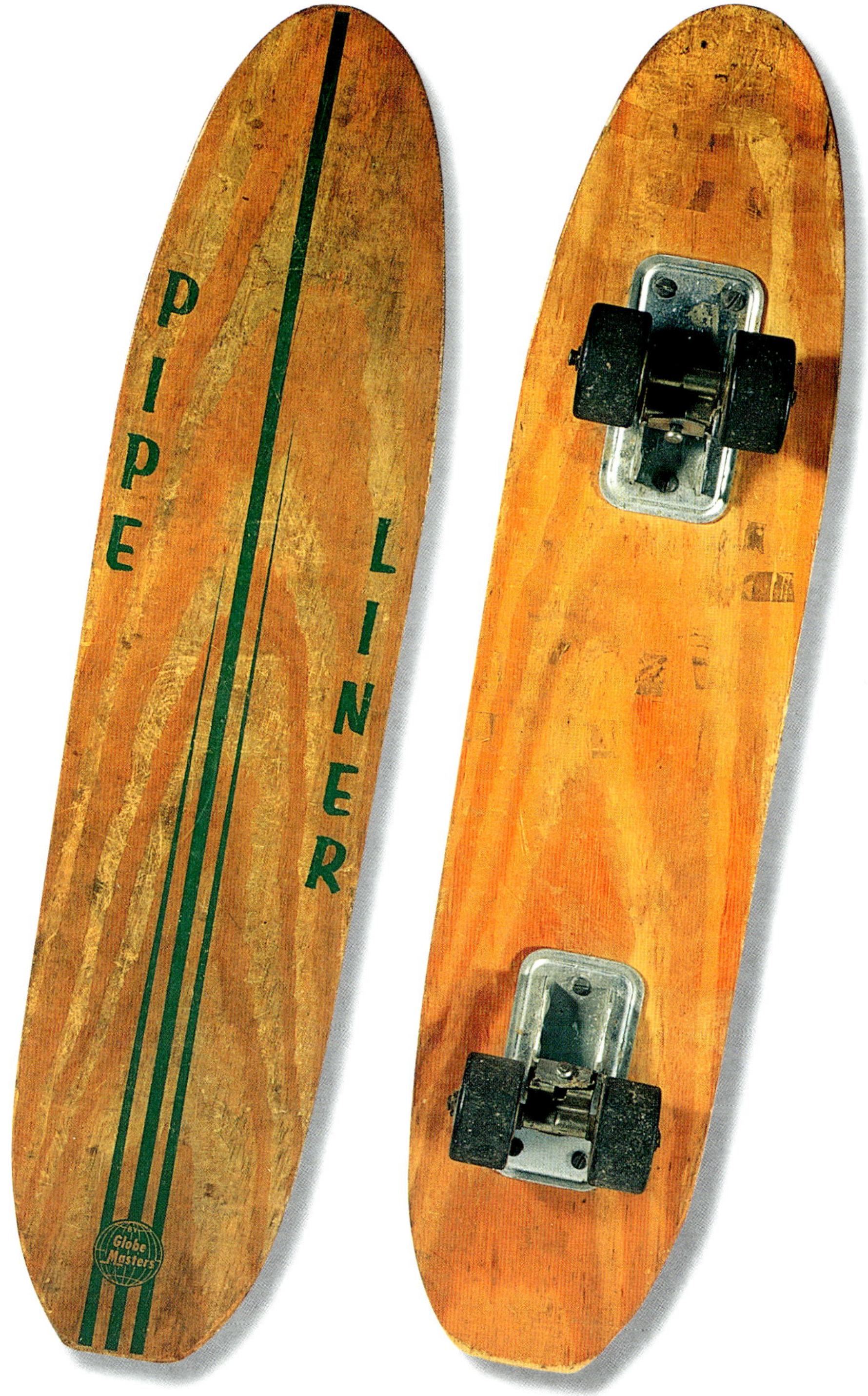

The Pipe Liner from Globe Masters with early plastic wheels. *Courtesy Todd Huber.* $200.

The Nash Keep On Boarding, mahogany. *Courtesy Todd Huber.* $75.

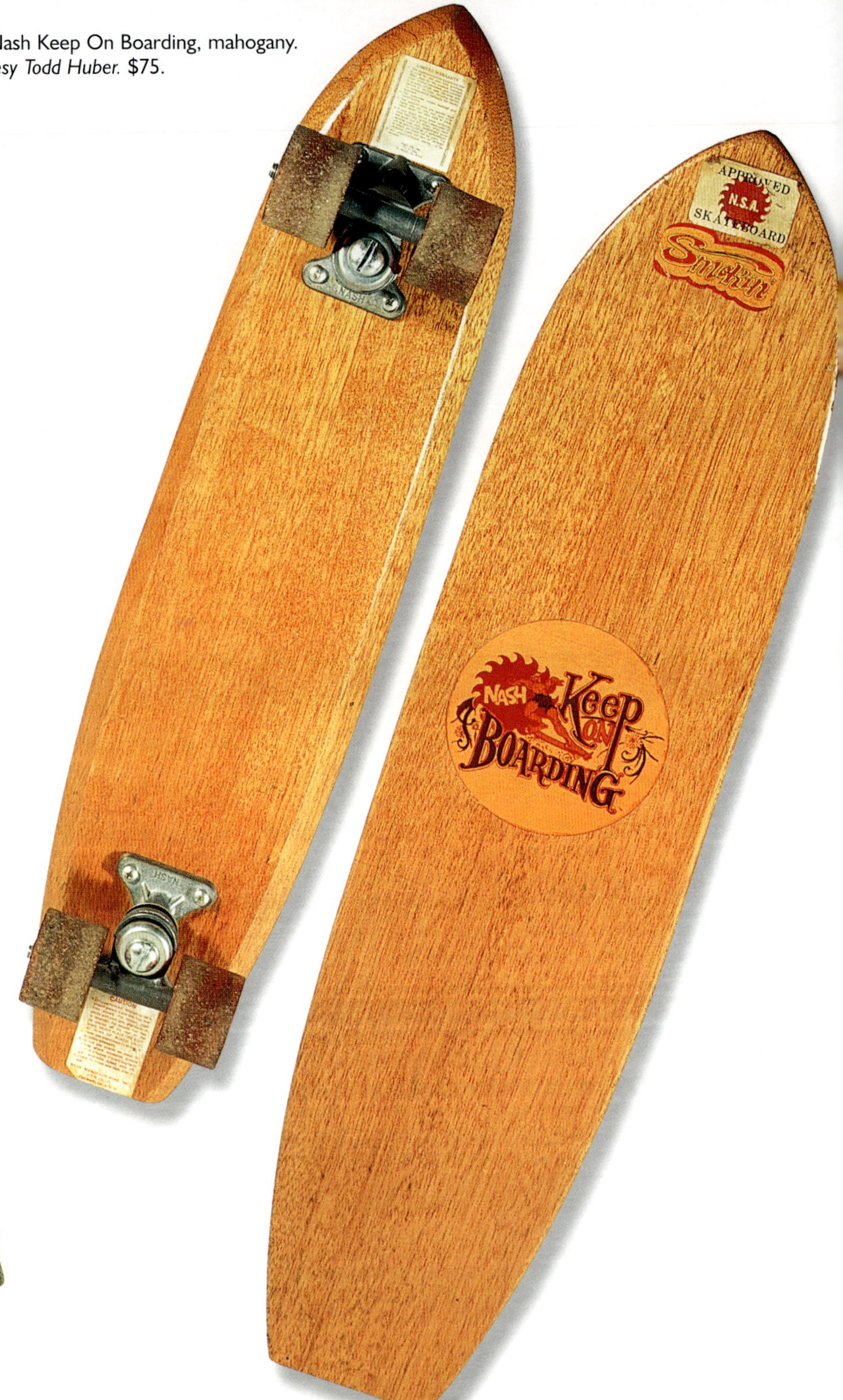

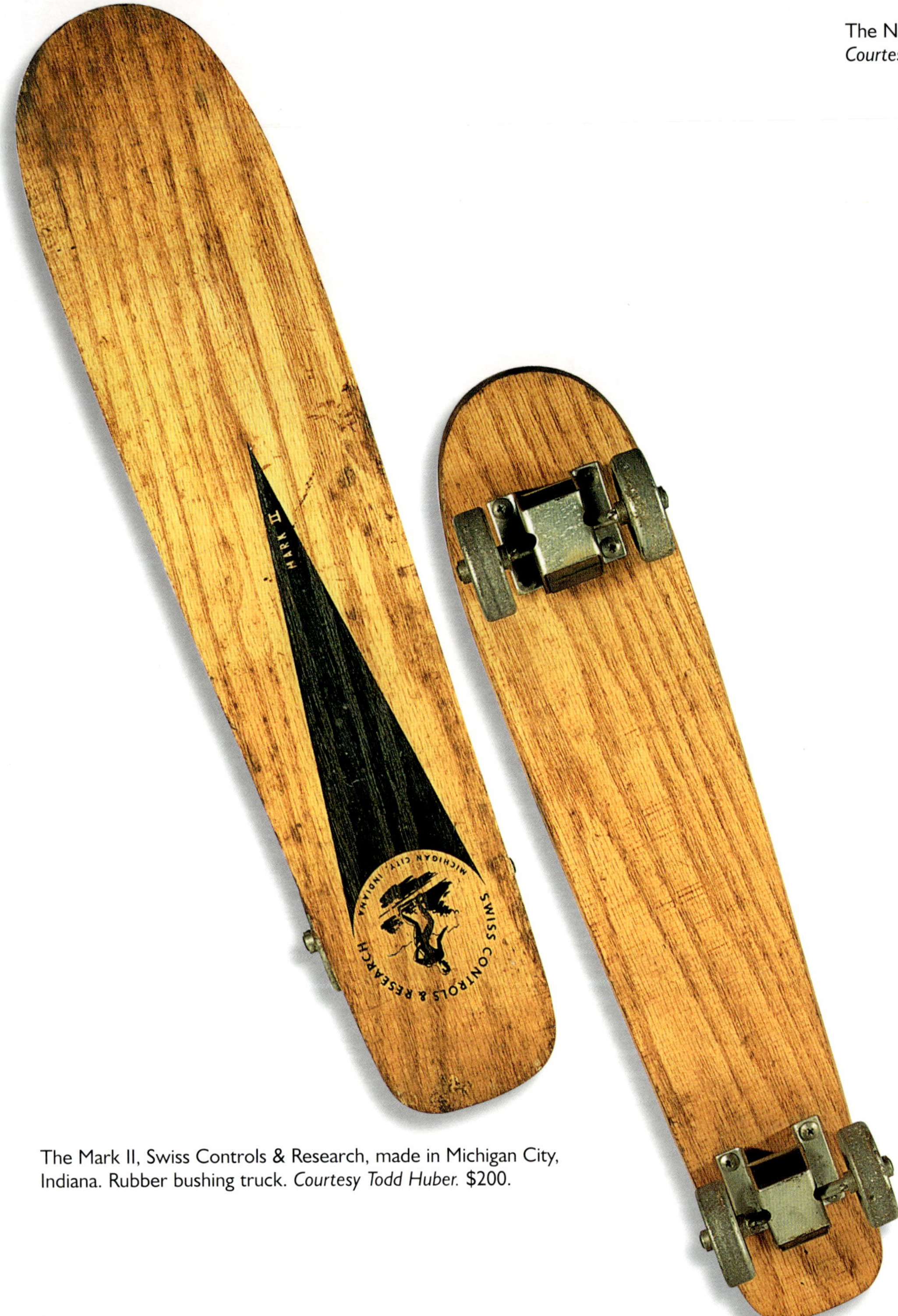

The Mark II, Swiss Controls & Research, made in Michigan City, Indiana. Rubber bushing truck. *Courtesy Todd Huber.* $200.

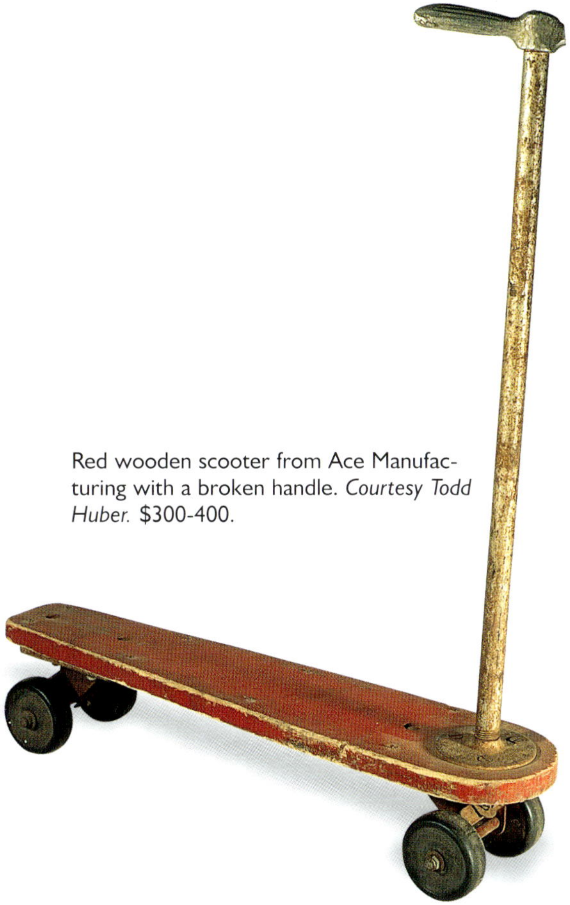

Red wooden scooter from Ace Manufacturing with a broken handle. *Courtesy Todd Huber.* $300-400.

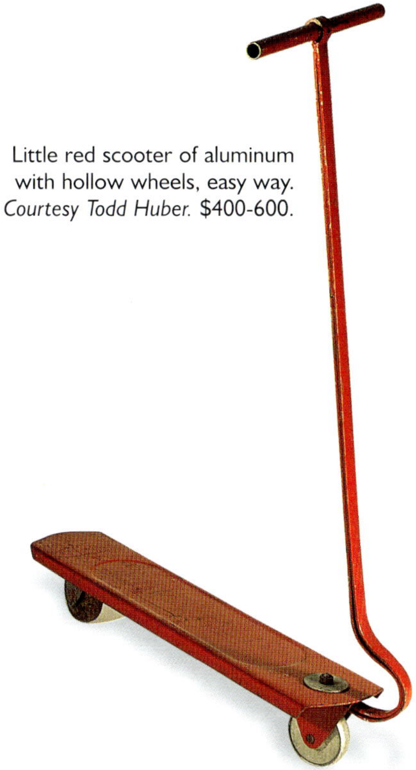

Little red scooter of aluminum with hollow wheels, easy way. *Courtesy Todd Huber.* $400-600.

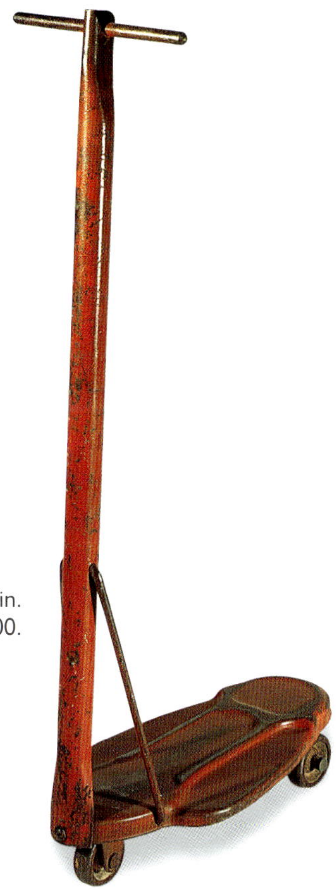

Red scooter of unknown origin. *Courtesy Todd Huber.* $300-400.

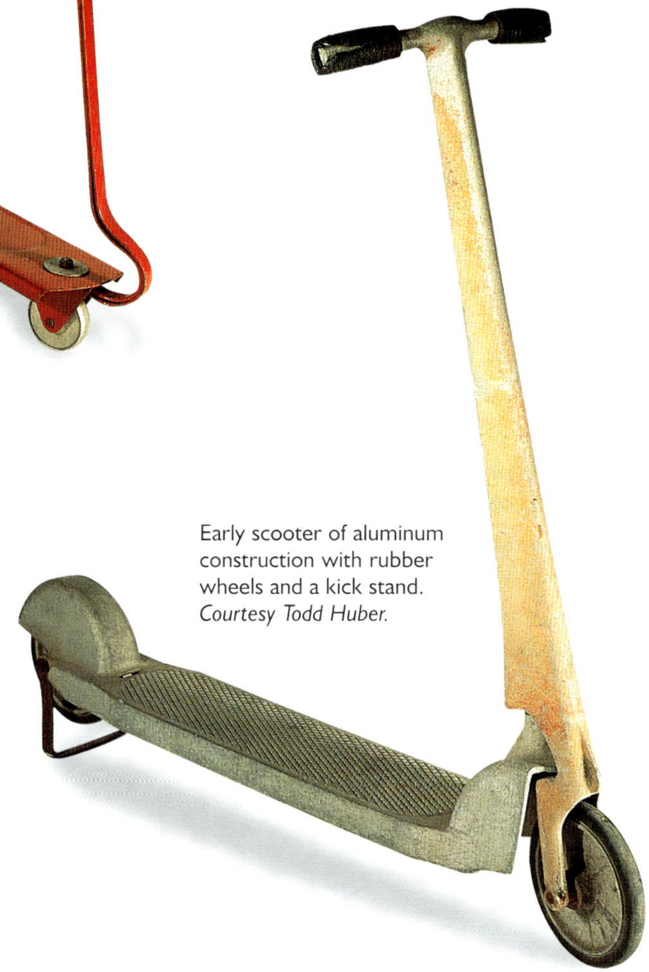

Early scooter of aluminum construction with rubber wheels and a kick stand. *Courtesy Todd Huber.*

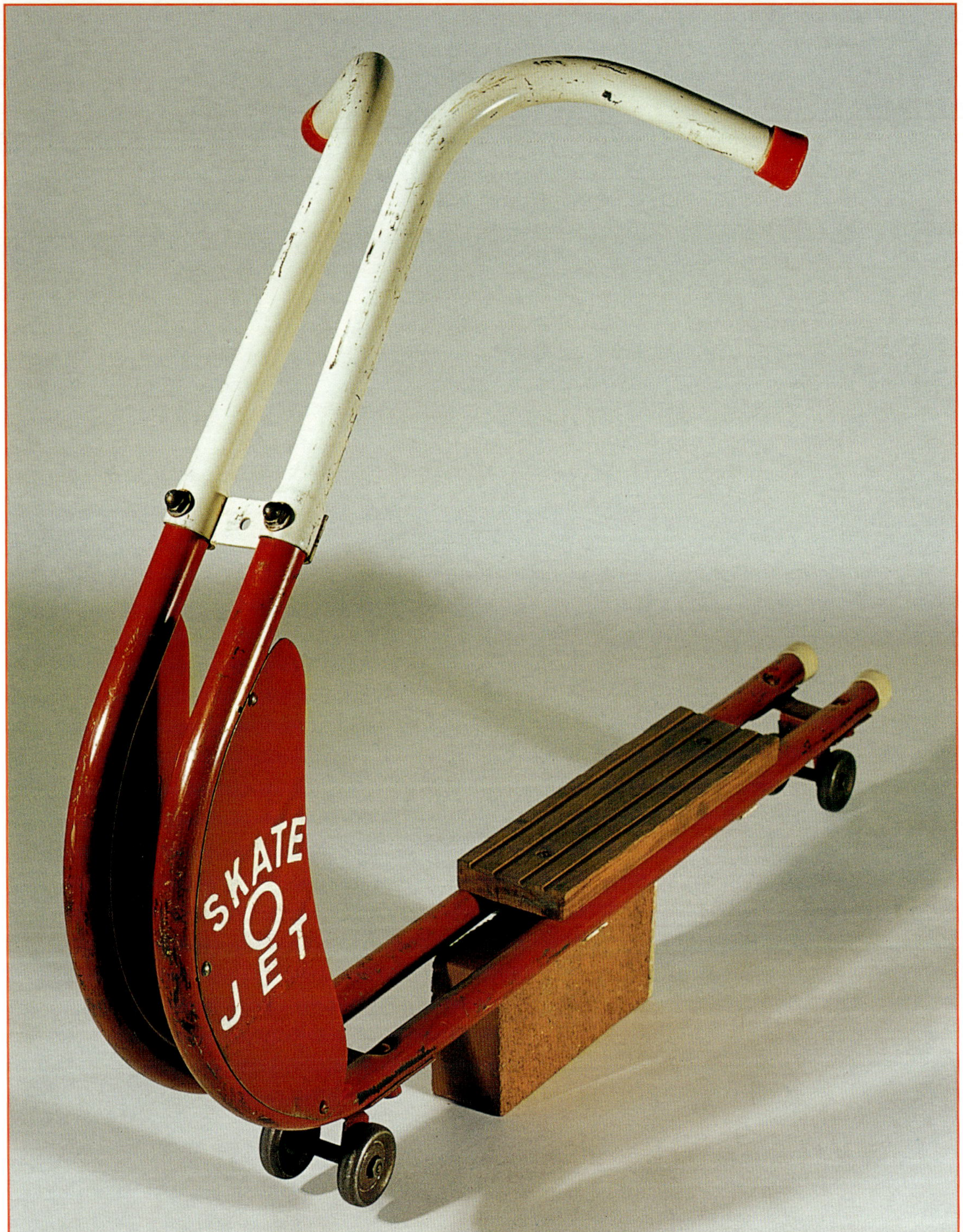

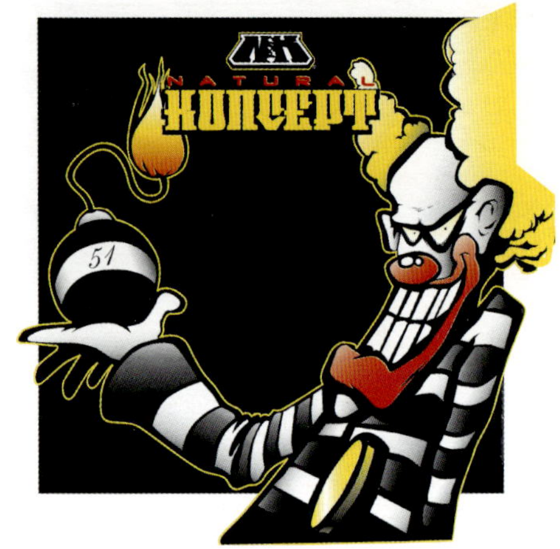

Clown, Katch Art. *Courtesy Natural Concepts.*

The skate jet. *Courtesy Todd Huber.* $400-500.

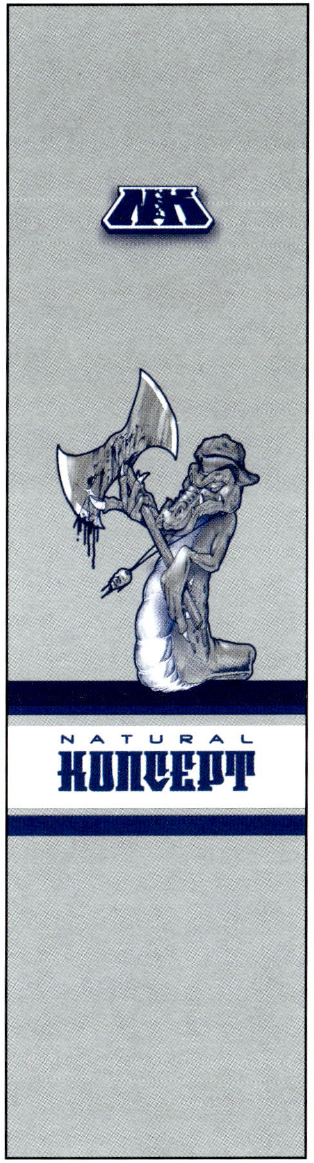

Alligator, Katch Art. *Courtesy Natural Concepts.*

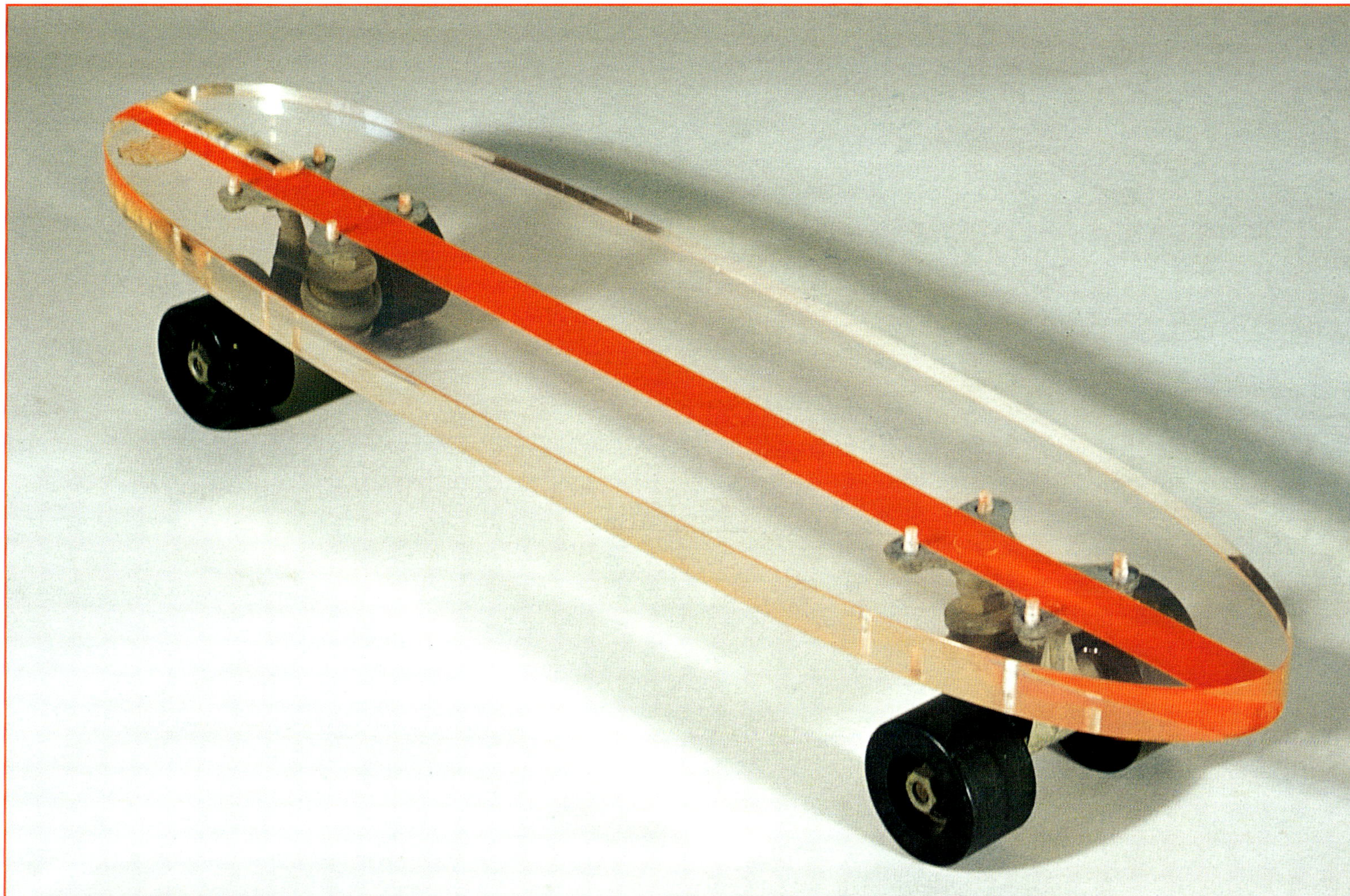

Plexiglas skateboard. *Courtesy Todd Huber.* $200.

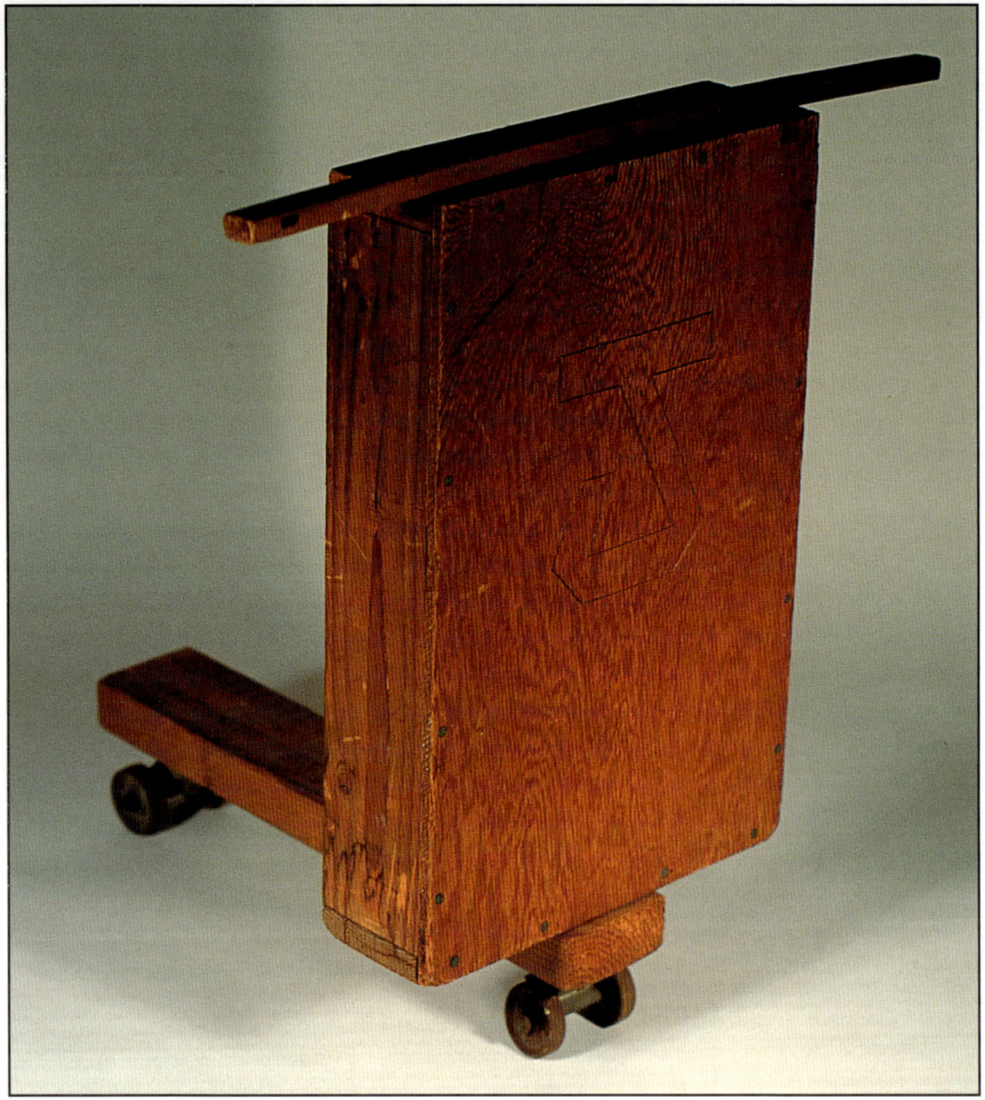

Cool old scooter. *Courtesy Dale Smith.* $200.

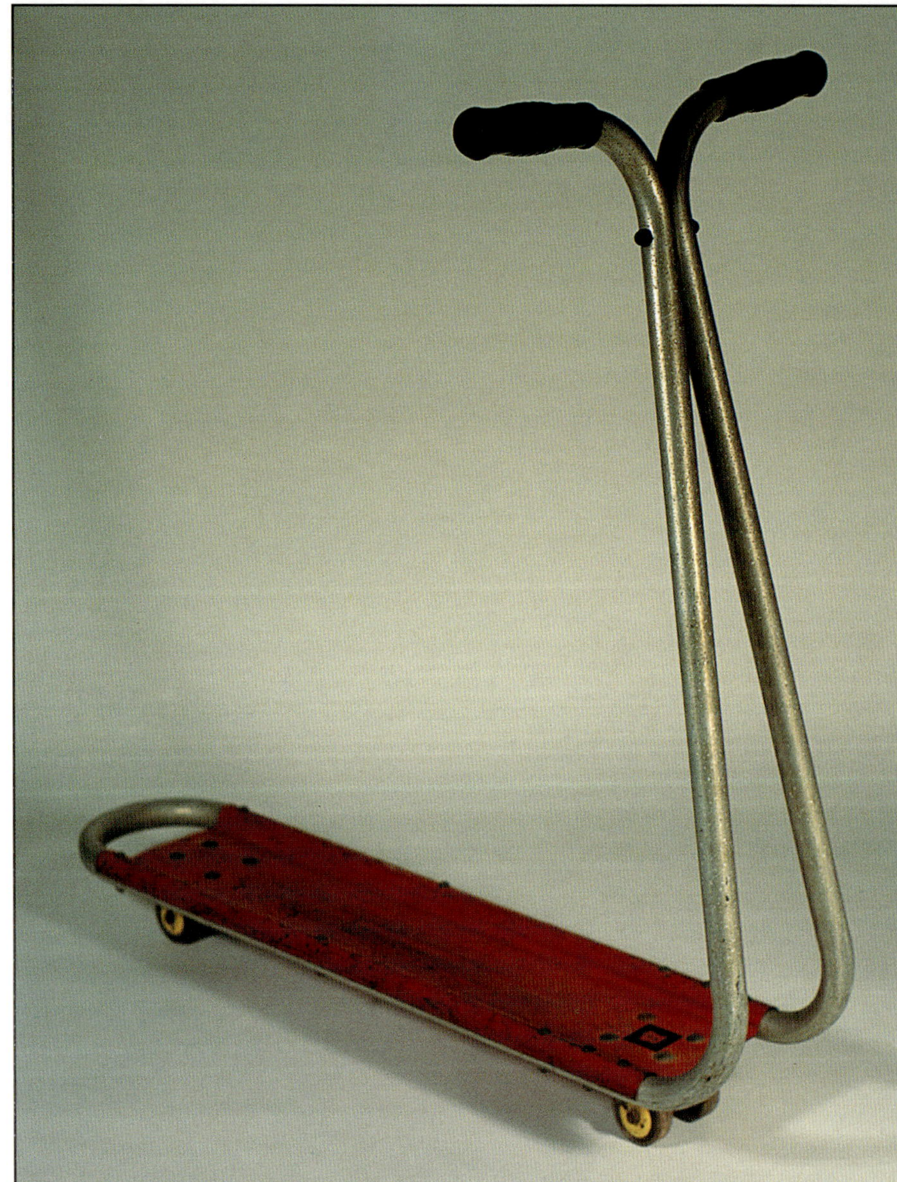

Aluminum scooter with plastic handle grips. *Courtesy Dale Smith.* $400-600.

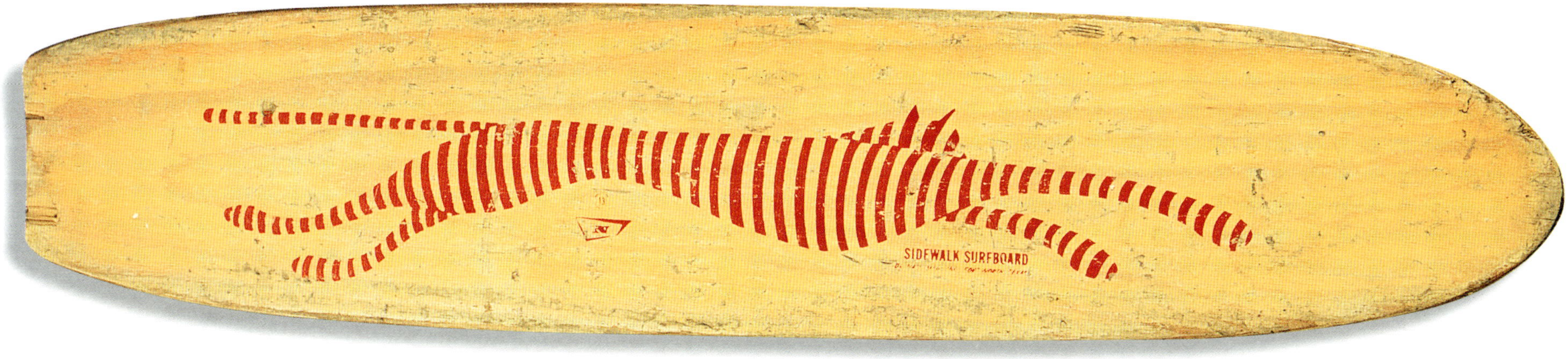

The Nash Cat. *Courtesy Todd Huber.* $150-200.

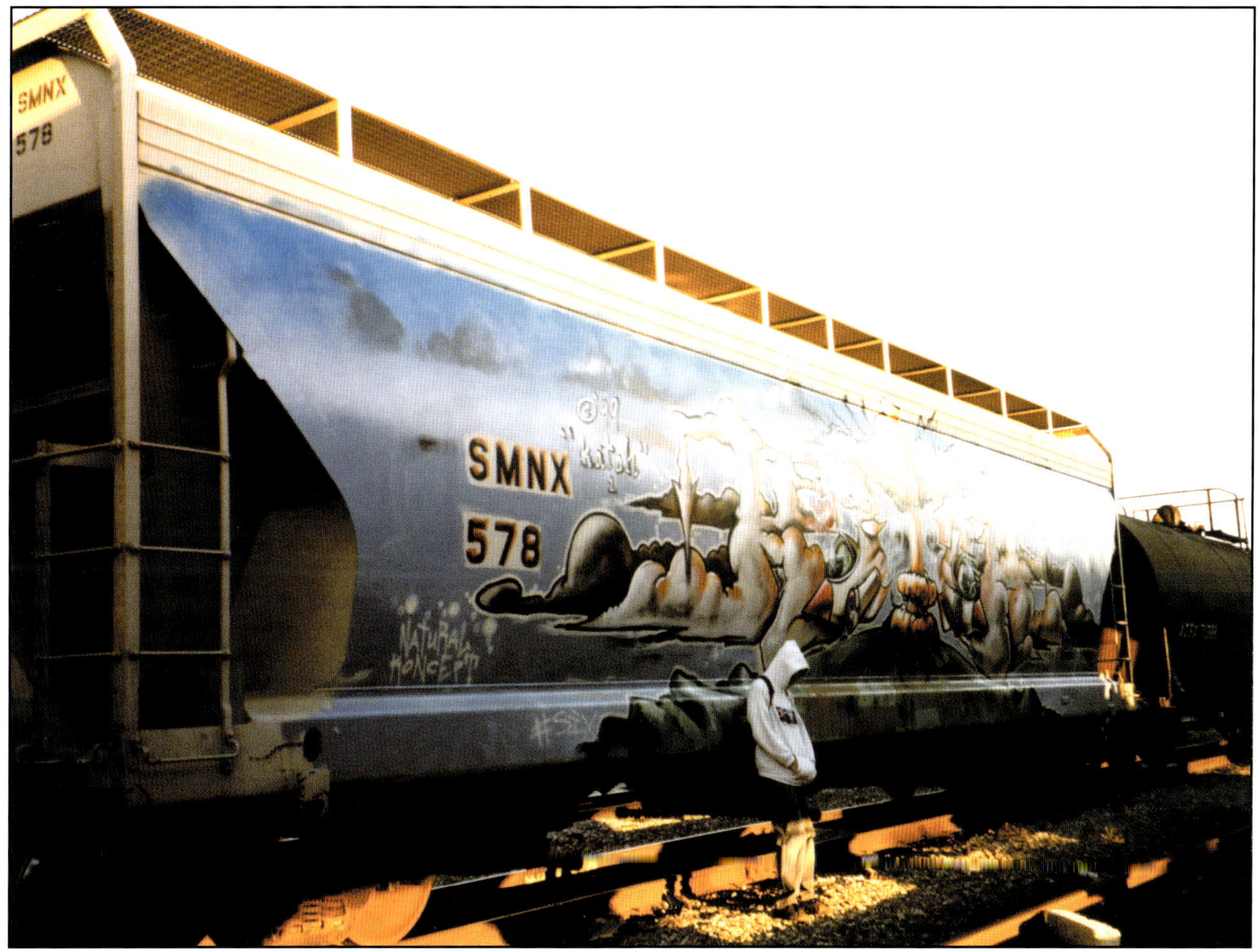

Katch at the Railway. *Courtesy Natural Concepts.*

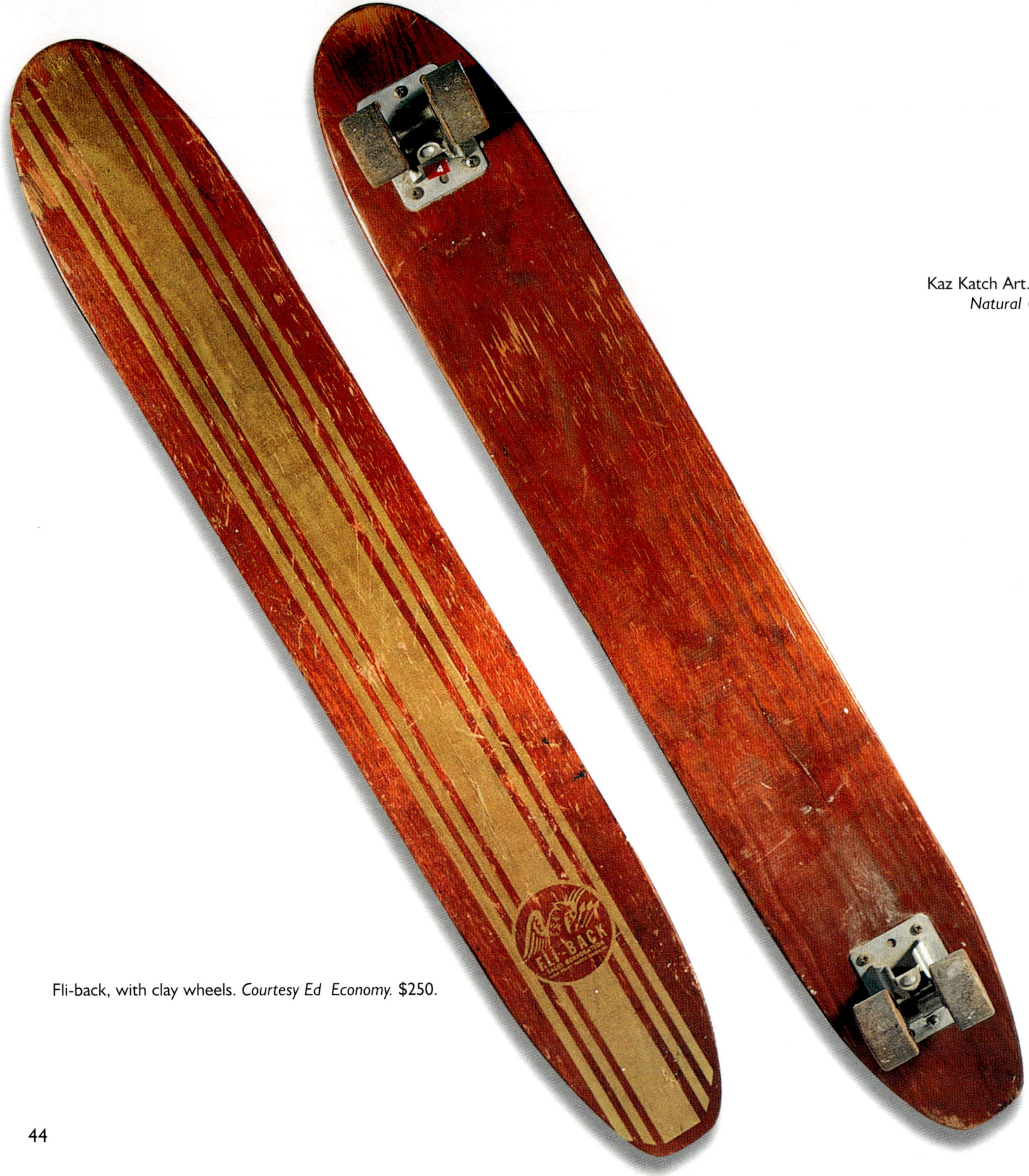

Fli-back, with clay wheels. *Courtesy Ed Economy.* $250.

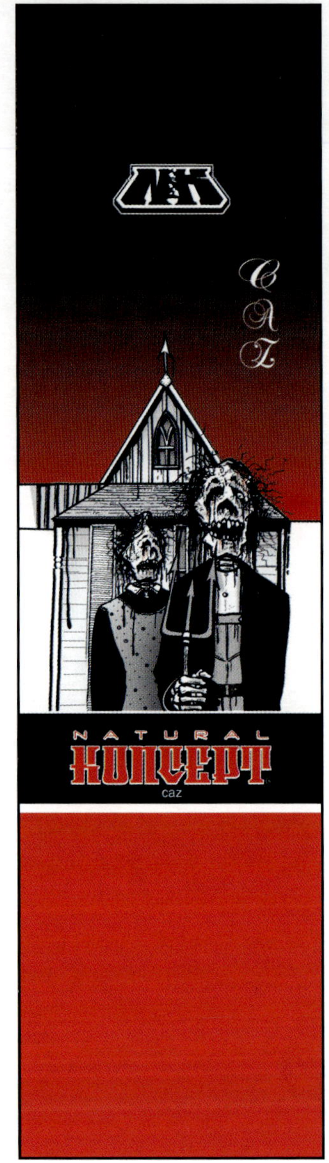

Kaz Katch Art. *Courtesy Natural Concepts.*

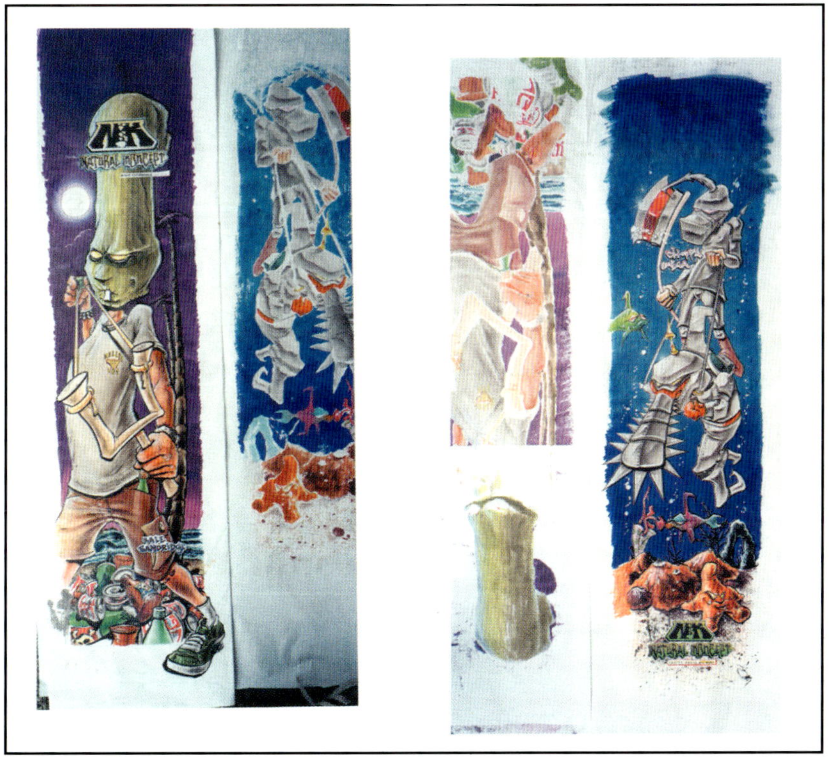

Kale, Katch Art. *Courtesy Natural Concepts.*

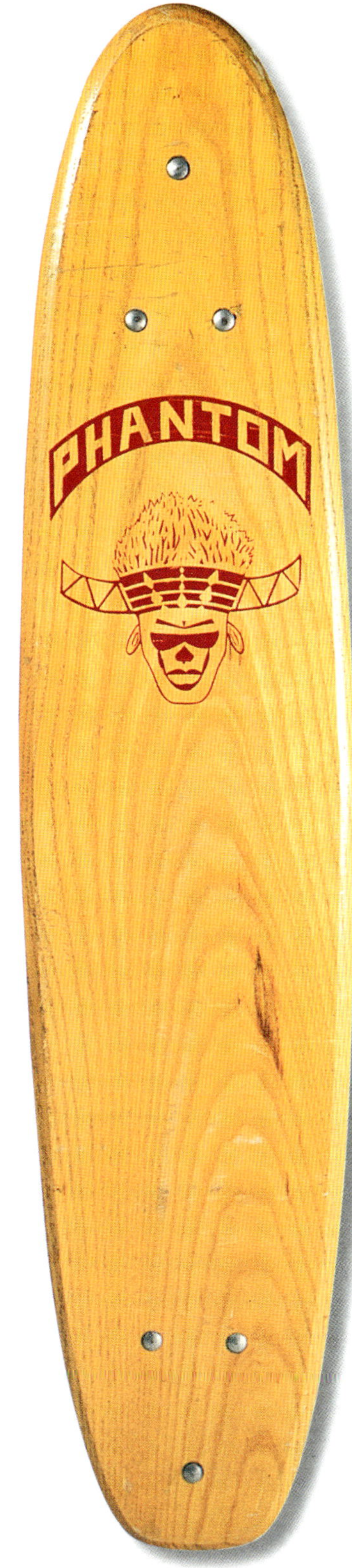

The Phantom, solid ash. *Courtesy Ed Economy.* $250.

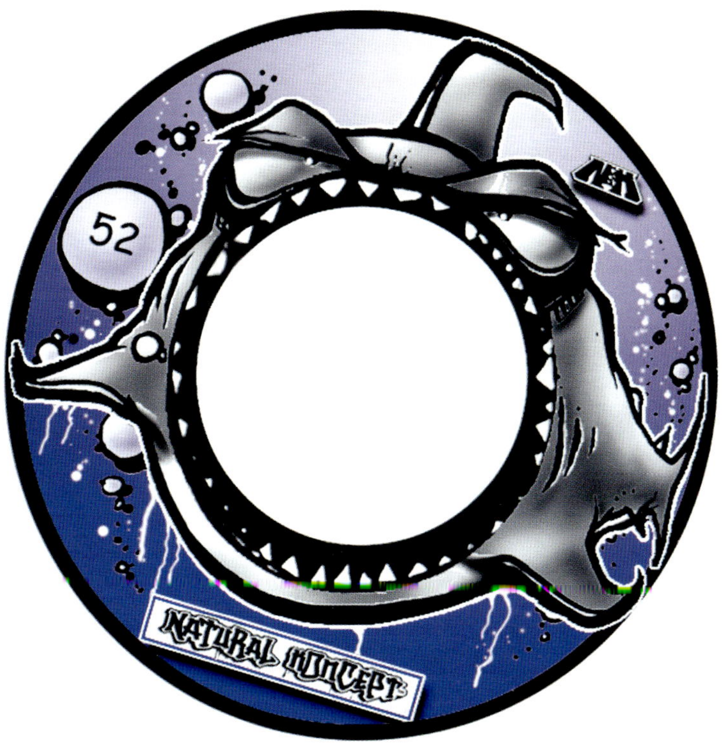

Fish Food, Katch Art. *Courtesy Natural Concepts.*

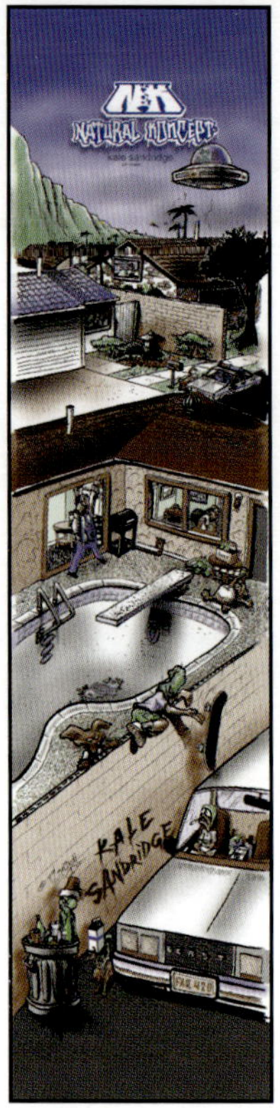

Kale, Katch Art. *Courtesy Natural Concepts.*

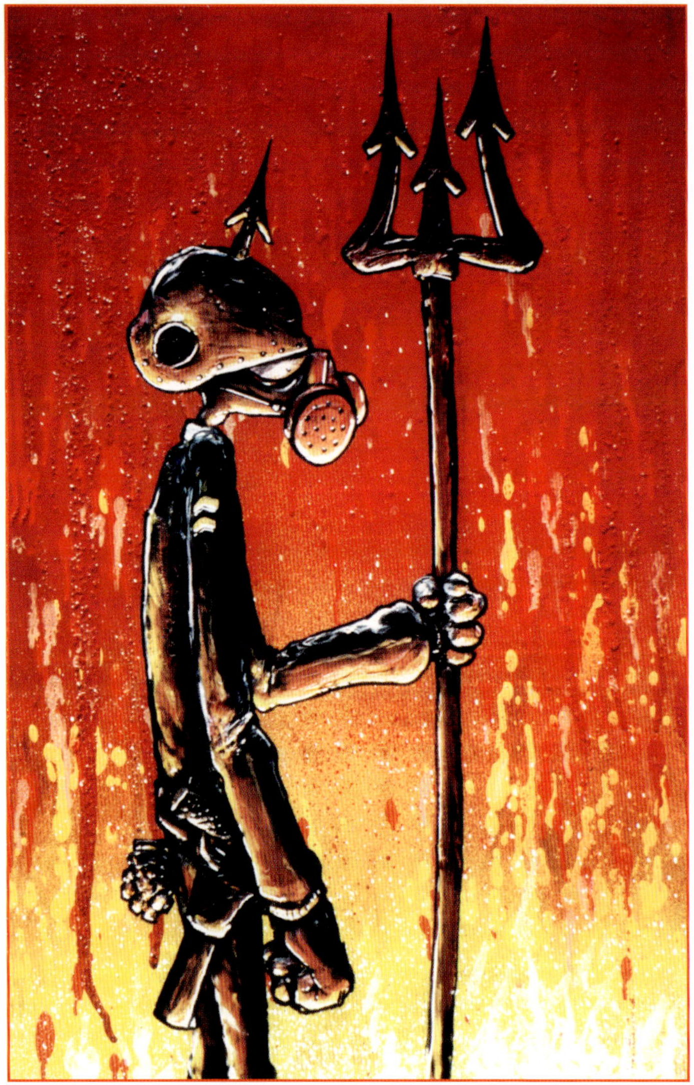

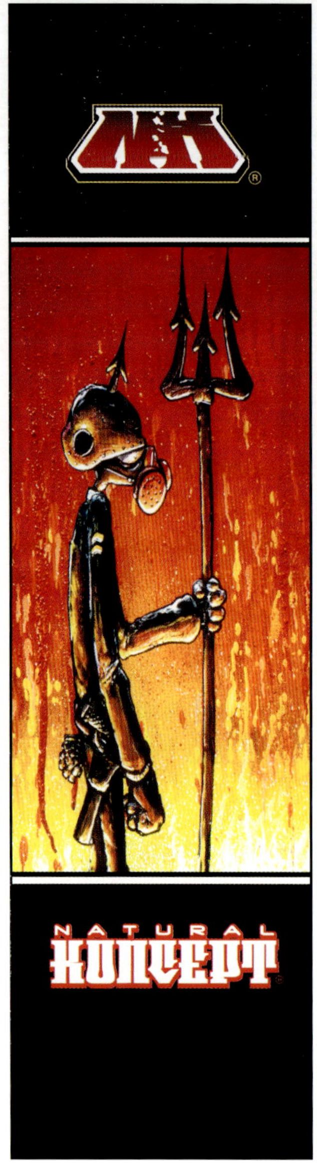

Guardian, Katch Art. *Courtesy Natural Concepts.*

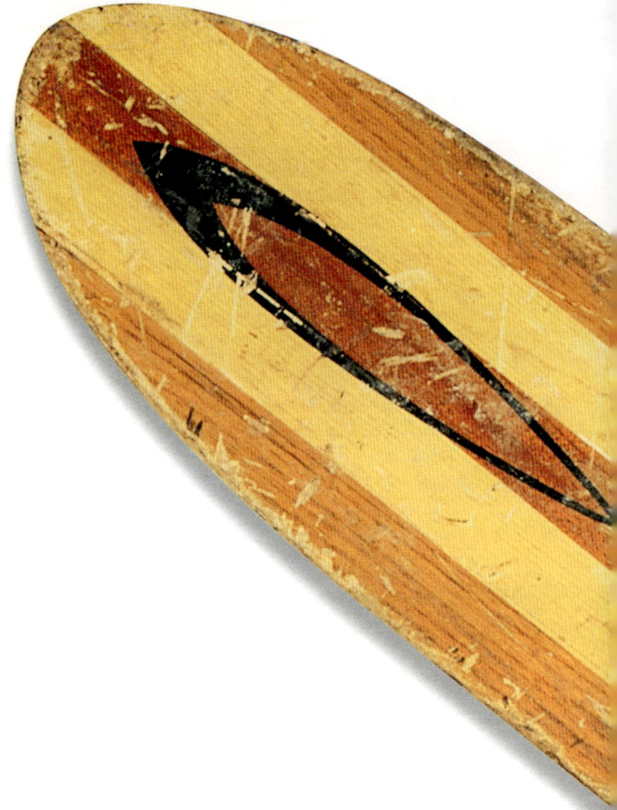

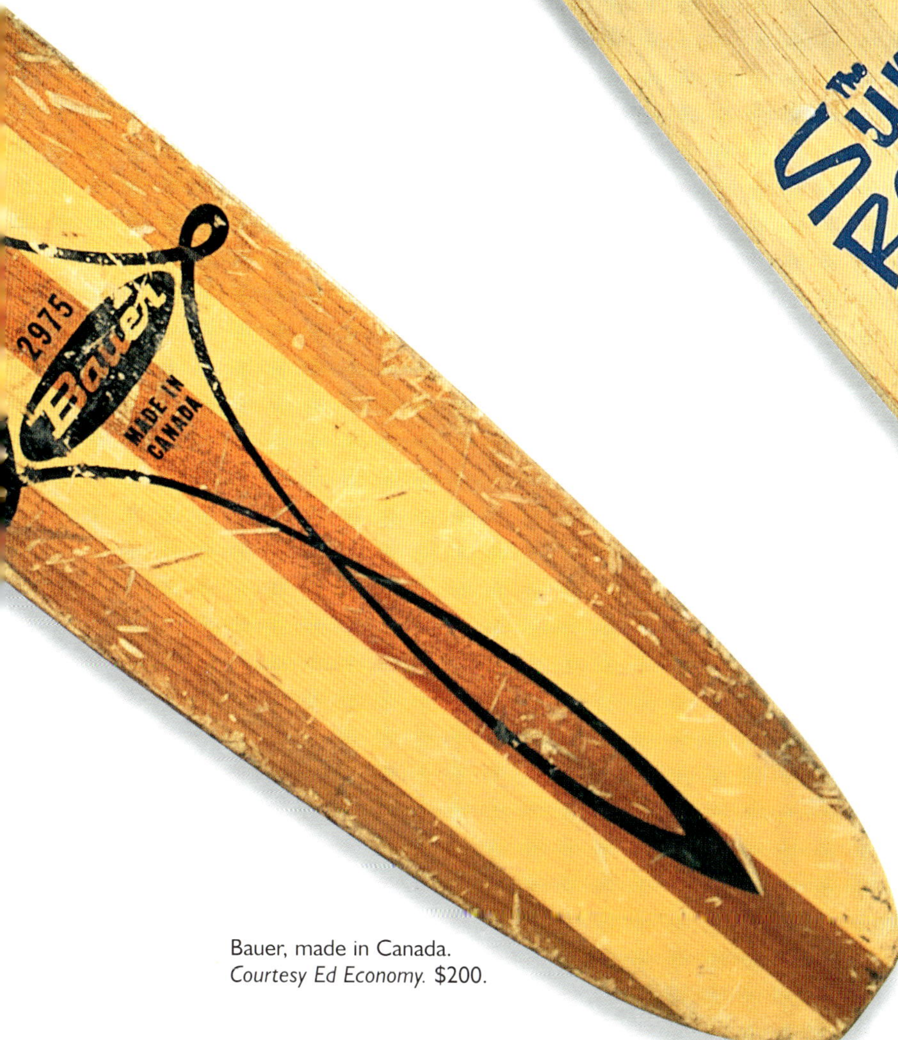

Bauer, made in Canada.
Courtesy Ed Economy. $200.

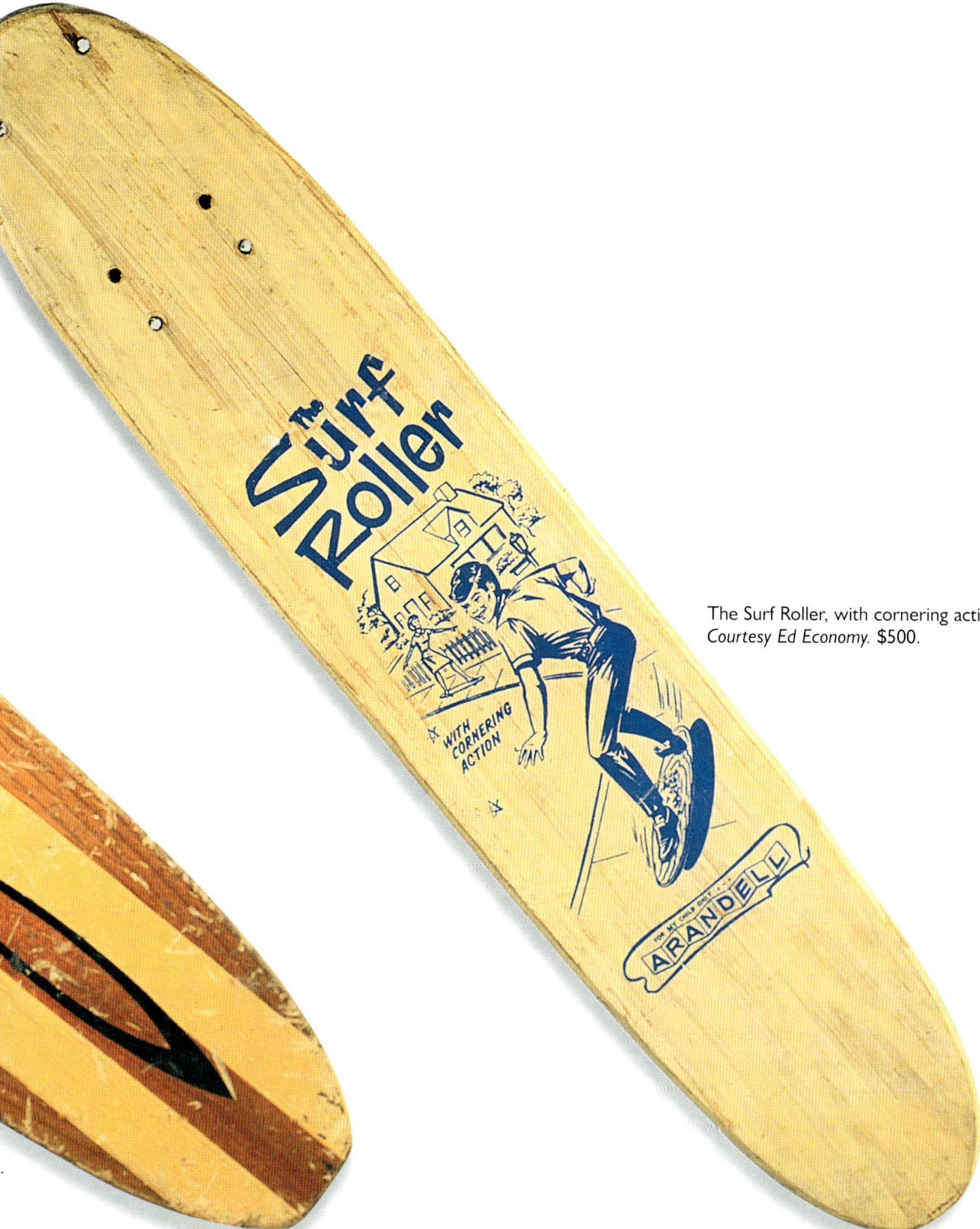

The Surf Roller, with cornering action.
Courtesy Ed Economy. $500.

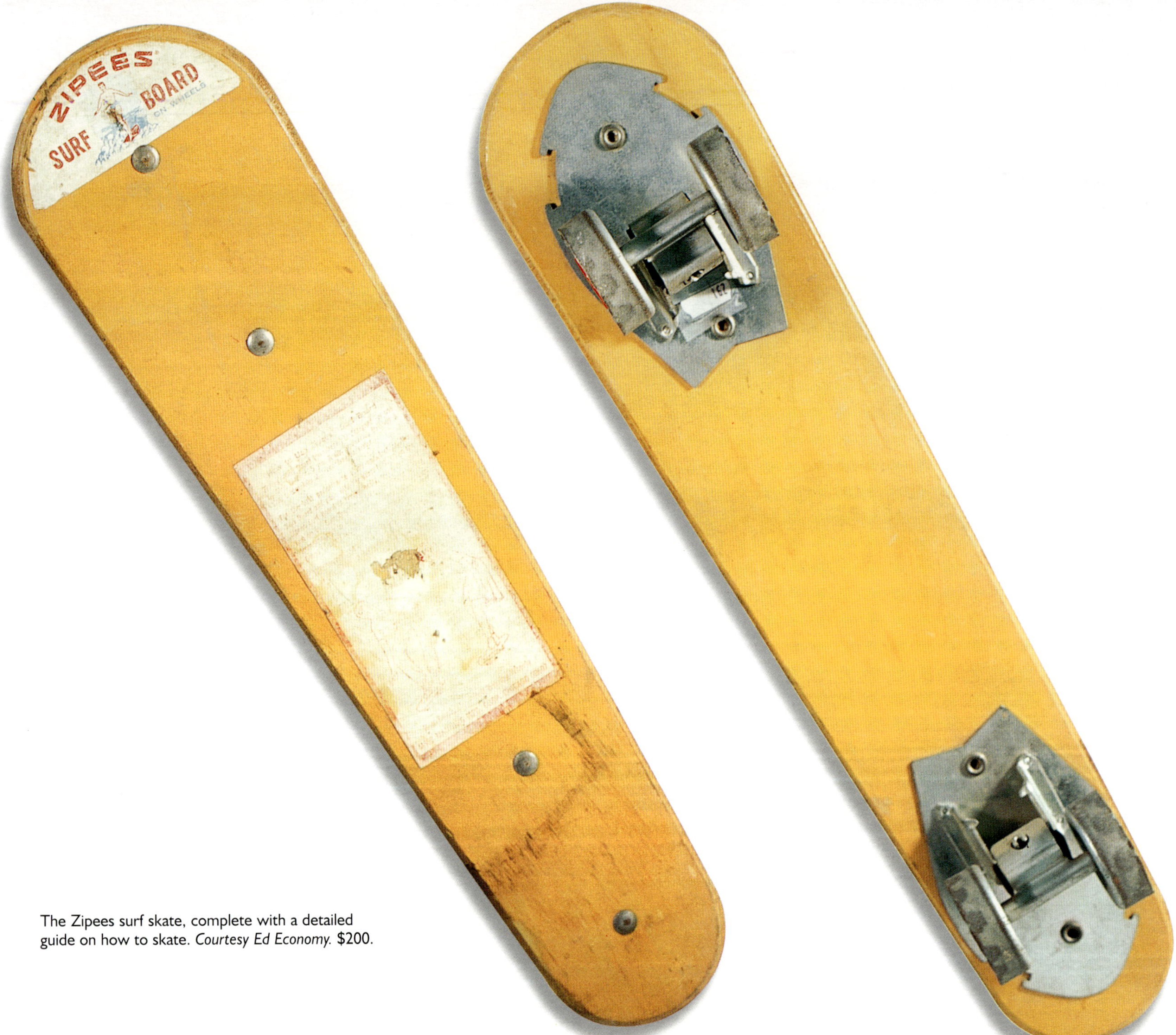

The Zipees surf skate, complete with a detailed guide on how to skate. *Courtesy Ed Economy.* $200.

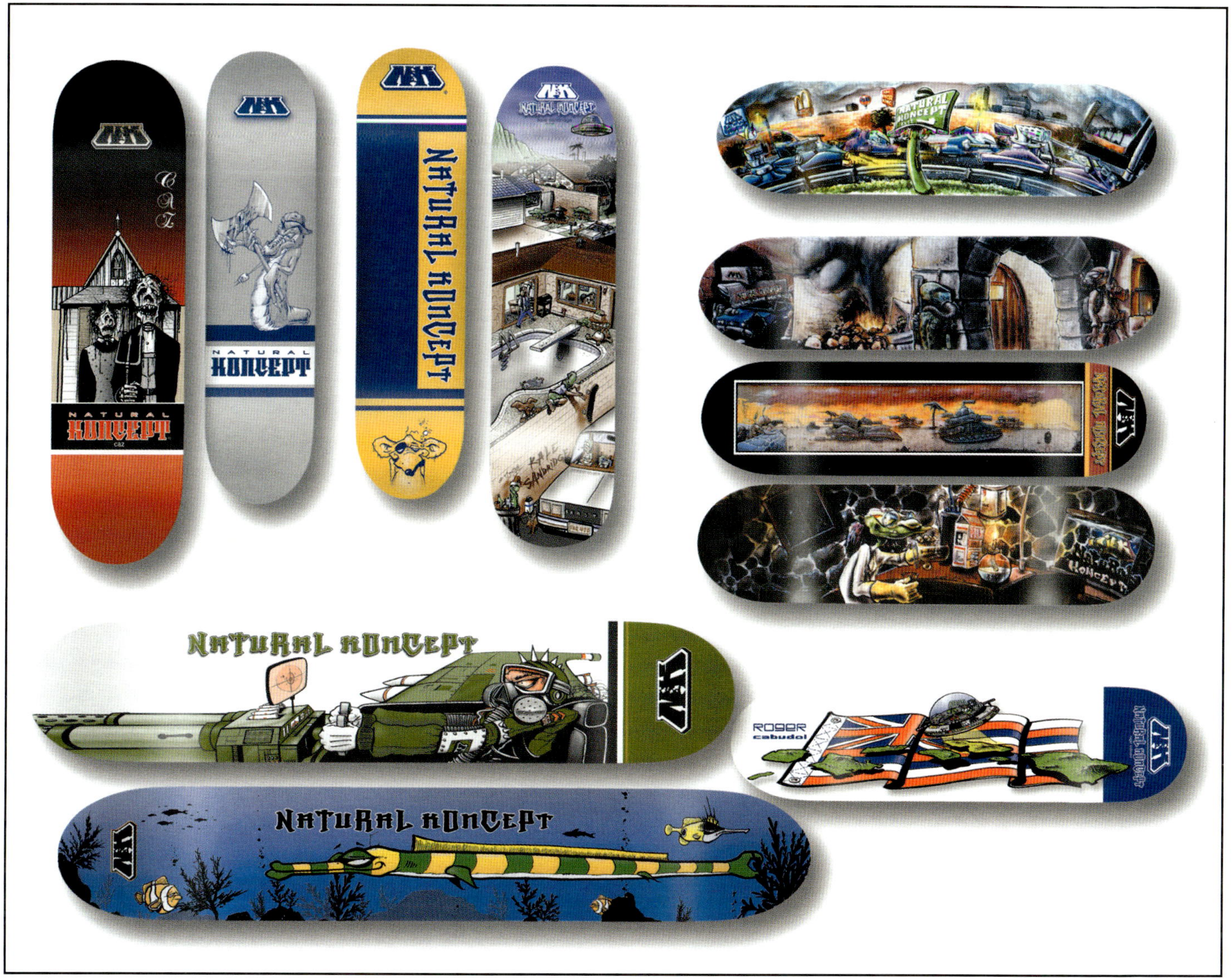

Katch Art Skateboards. *Courtesy Natural Concepts.*

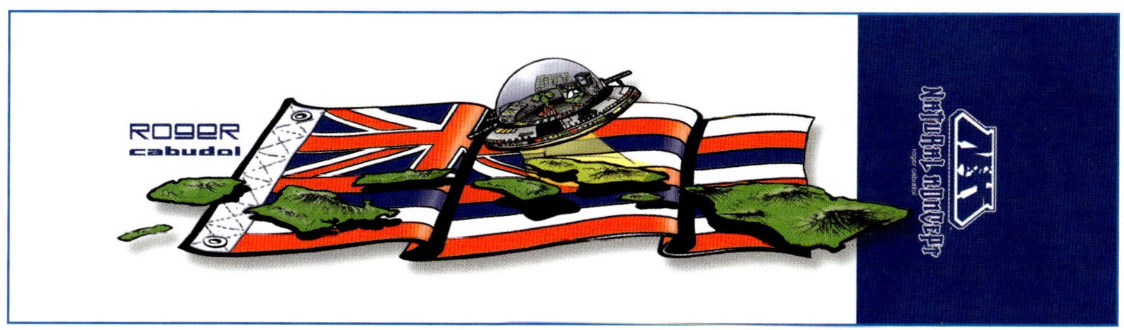

Ruger, Katch Art. *Courtesy Natural Concepts.*

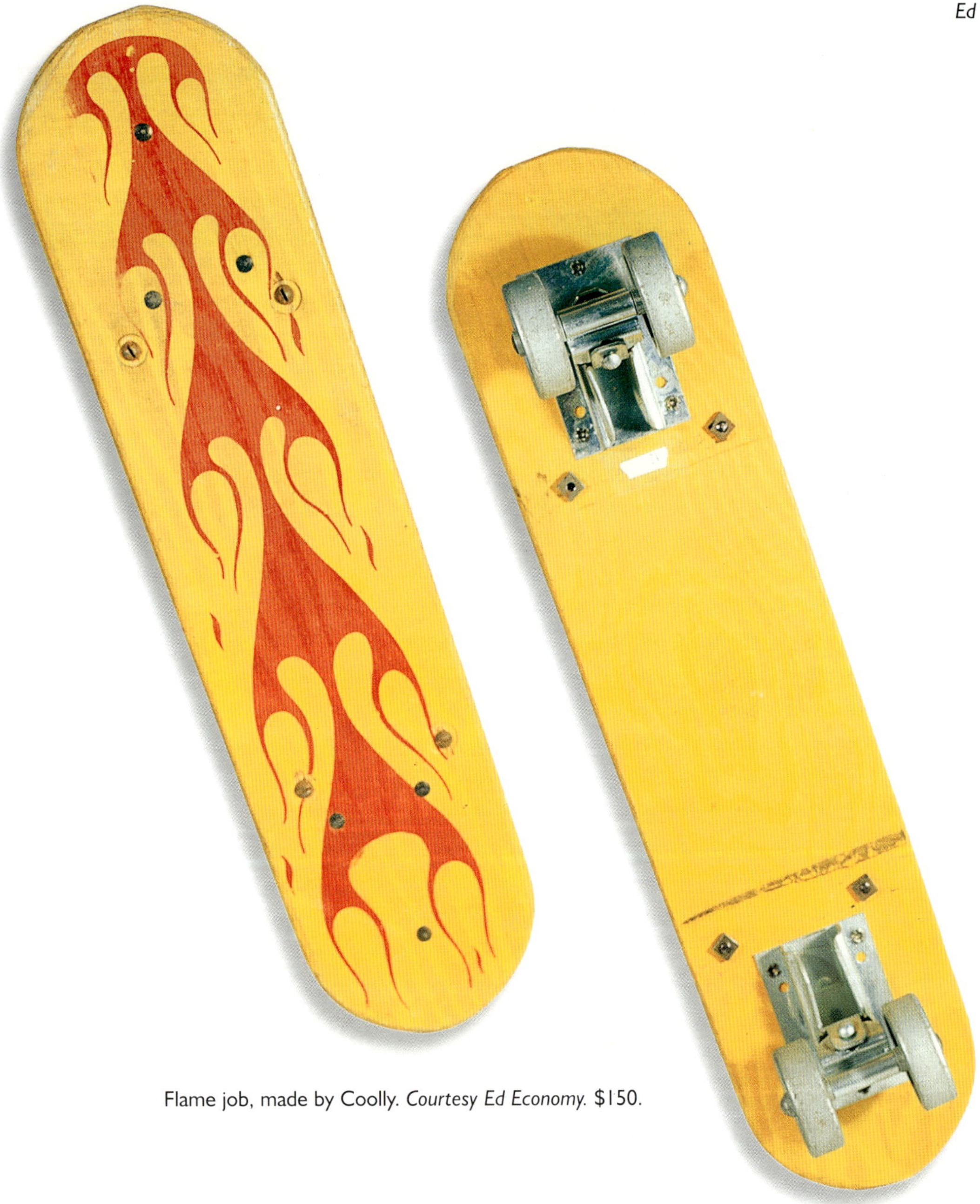

Flame job, made by Coolly. *Courtesy Ed Economy.* $150.

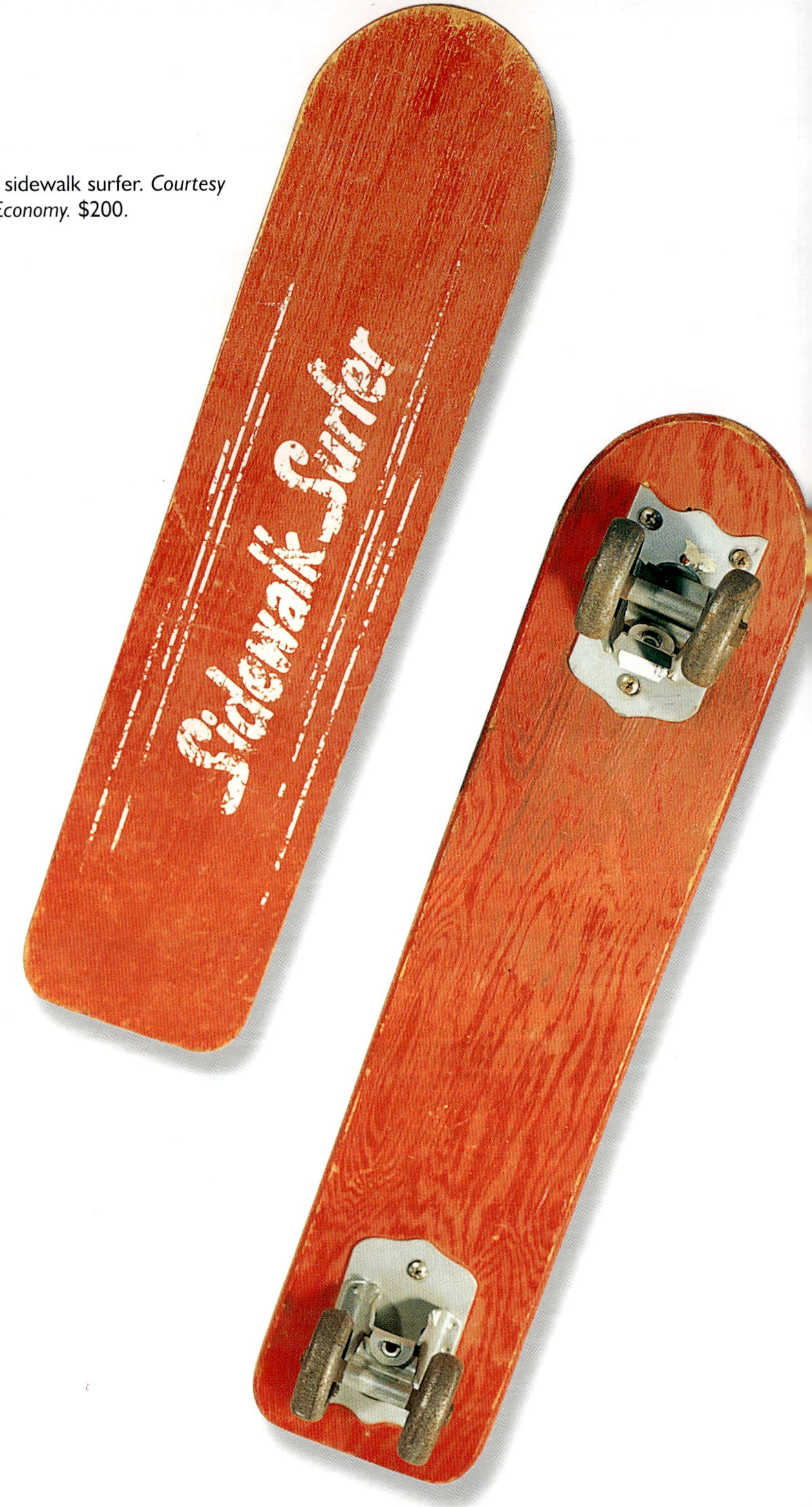

Red sidewalk surfer. *Courtesy Ed Economy.* $200.

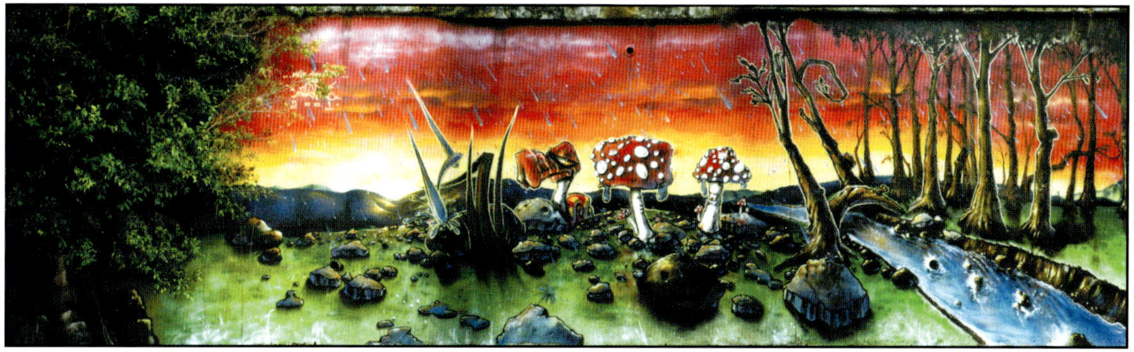

Big Shroom, Katch Art. *Courtesy Natural Concepts.*

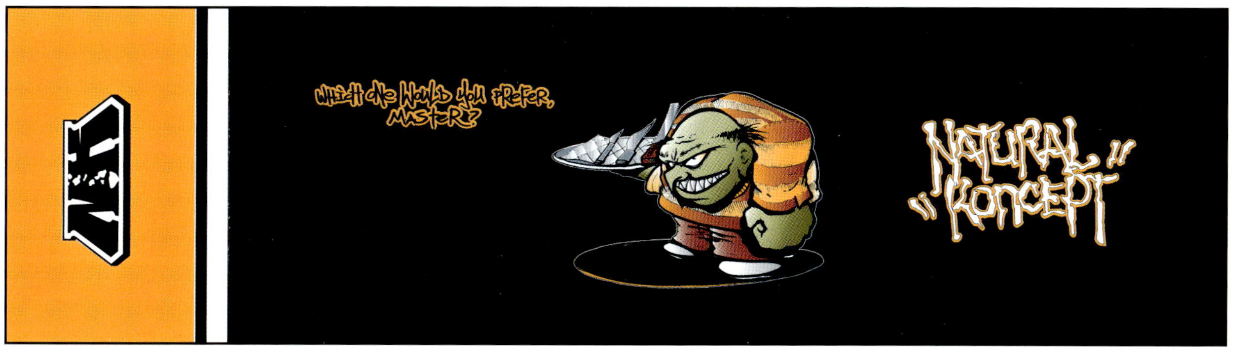

Assistant, Katch Art. *Courtesy Natural Concepts.*

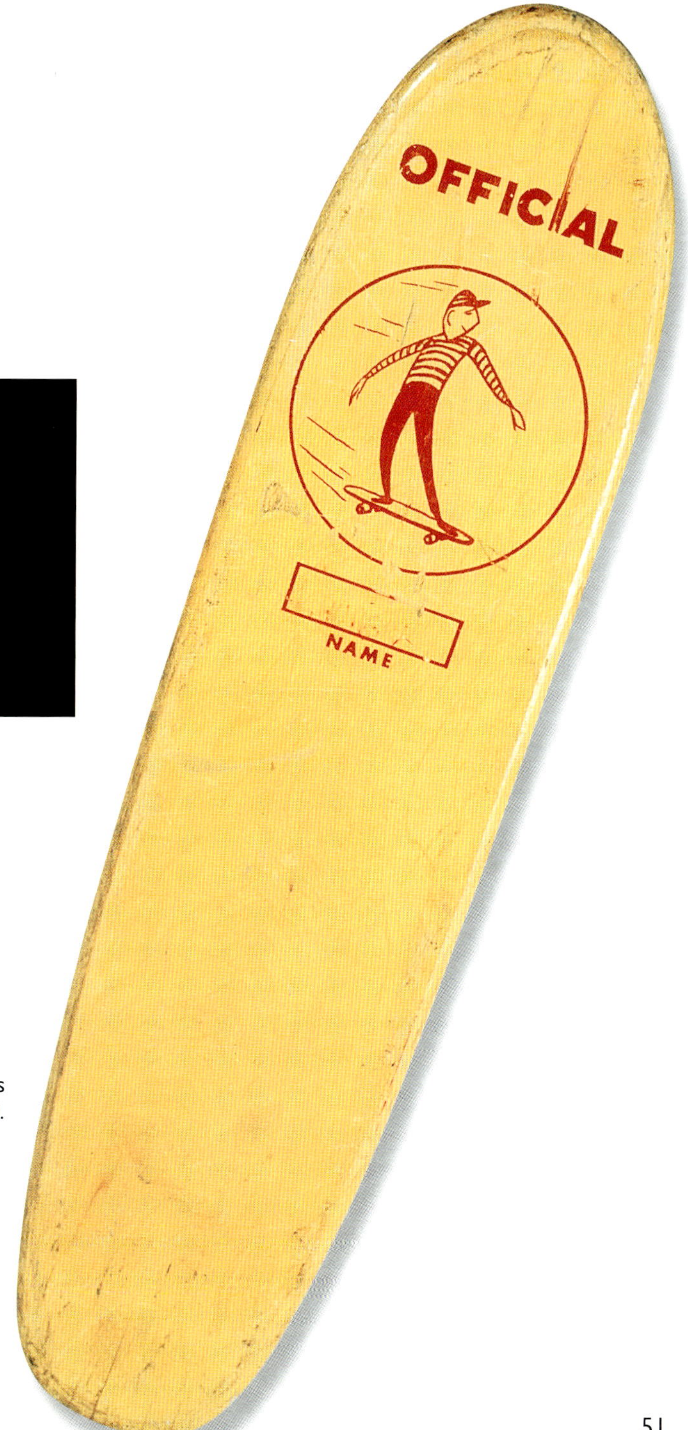

The Official with a place for the skater's name. *Courtesy Ed Economy.* $250.

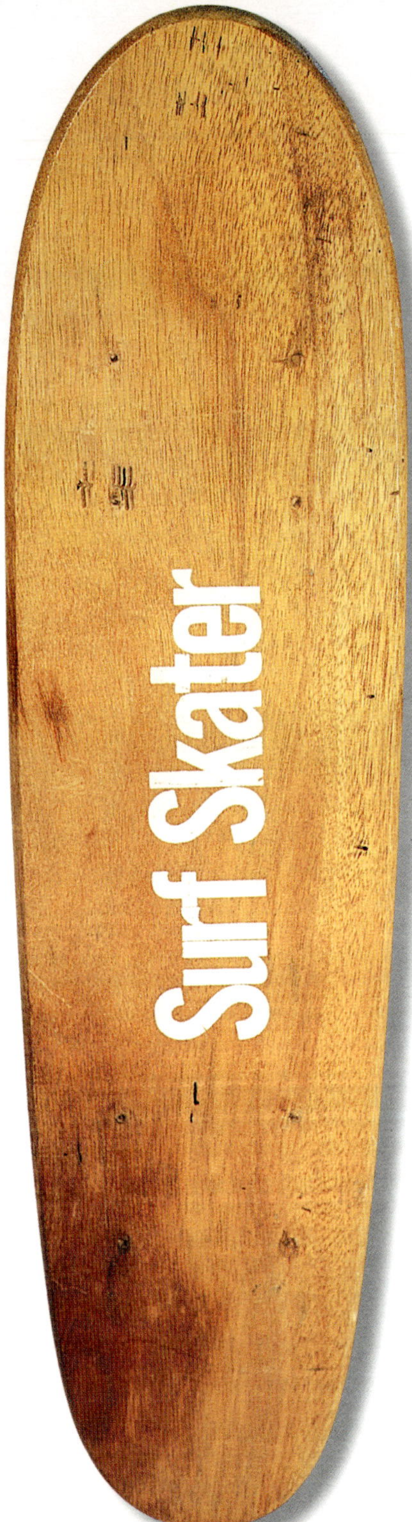

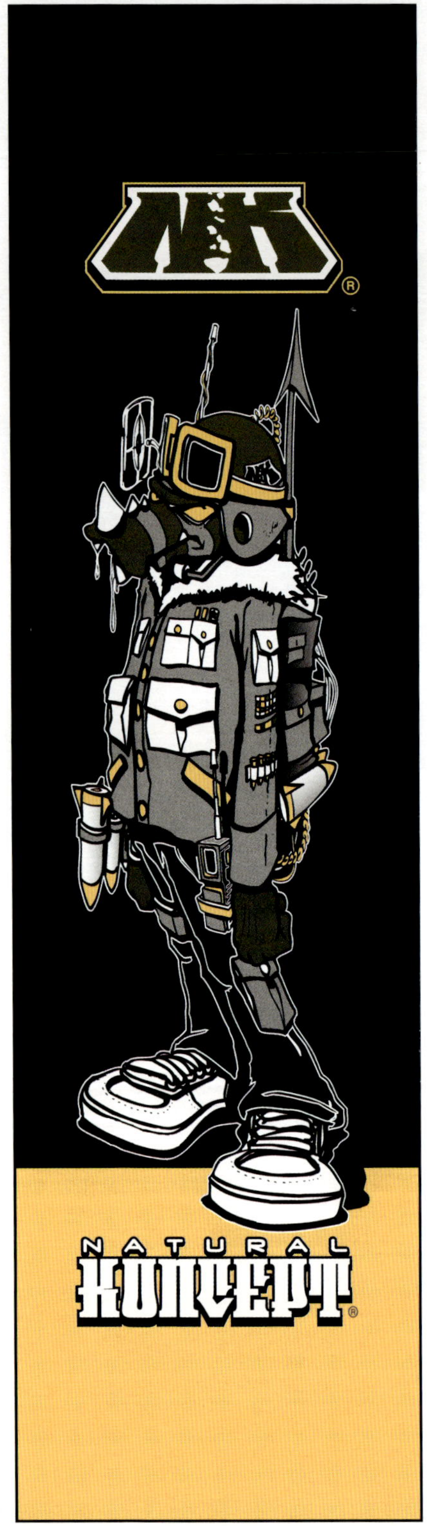

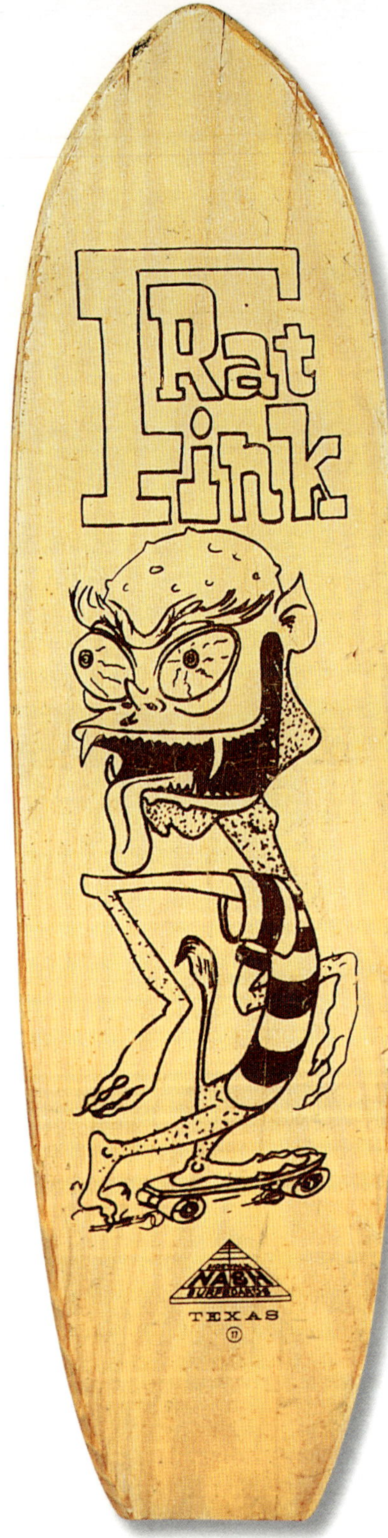

Left to right:
The Surf Skater in solid mahogany. *Courtesy Ed Economy.* $150.

Lizard Bomber, Katch Art. *Courtesy Natural Concepts.*

The Rat Fink by Nash. *Courtesy Ed Economy.* $200.

Red Makaha. *Courtesy Ed Economy.* $300.

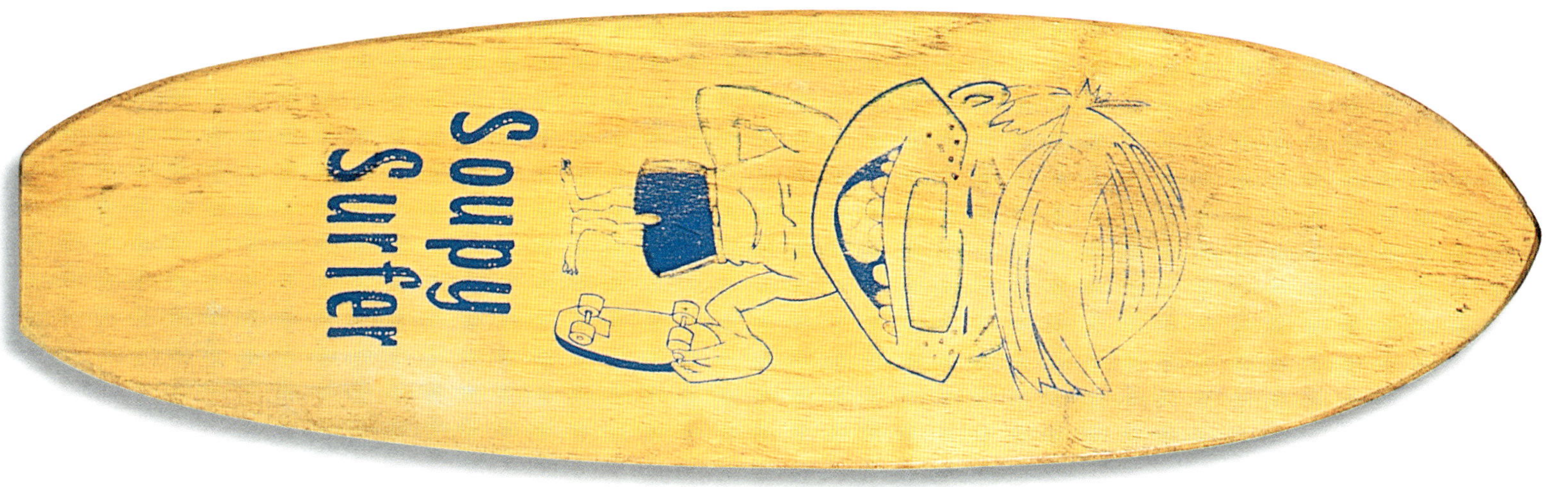

The Soupy Surfer in solid ash. *Courtesy Ed Economy.* $250-300.

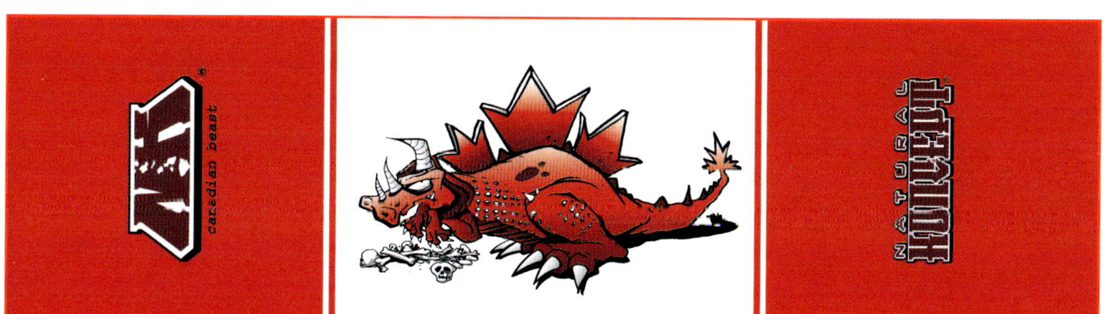

Beast, Katch Art. *Courtesy Natural Concepts.*

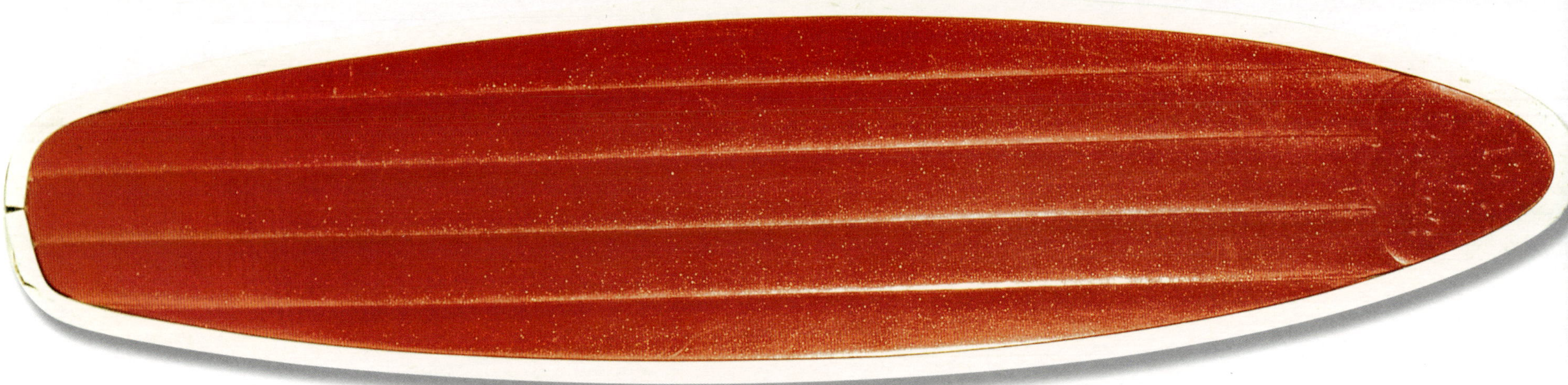

Red Tuck and Roll. *Courtesy Ed Economy.* $400.

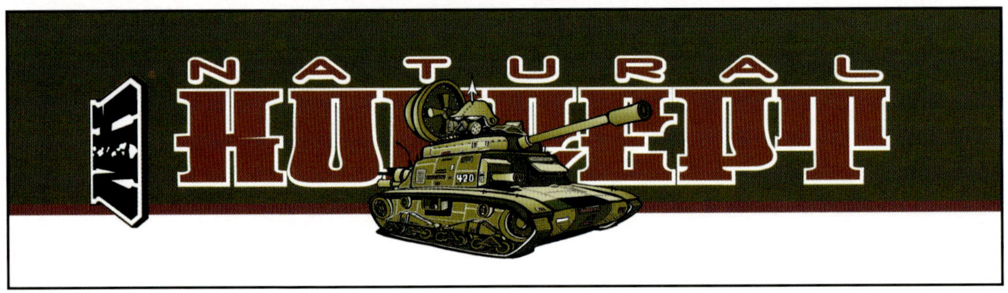

Tank, Katch Art. *Courtesy Natural Concepts.*

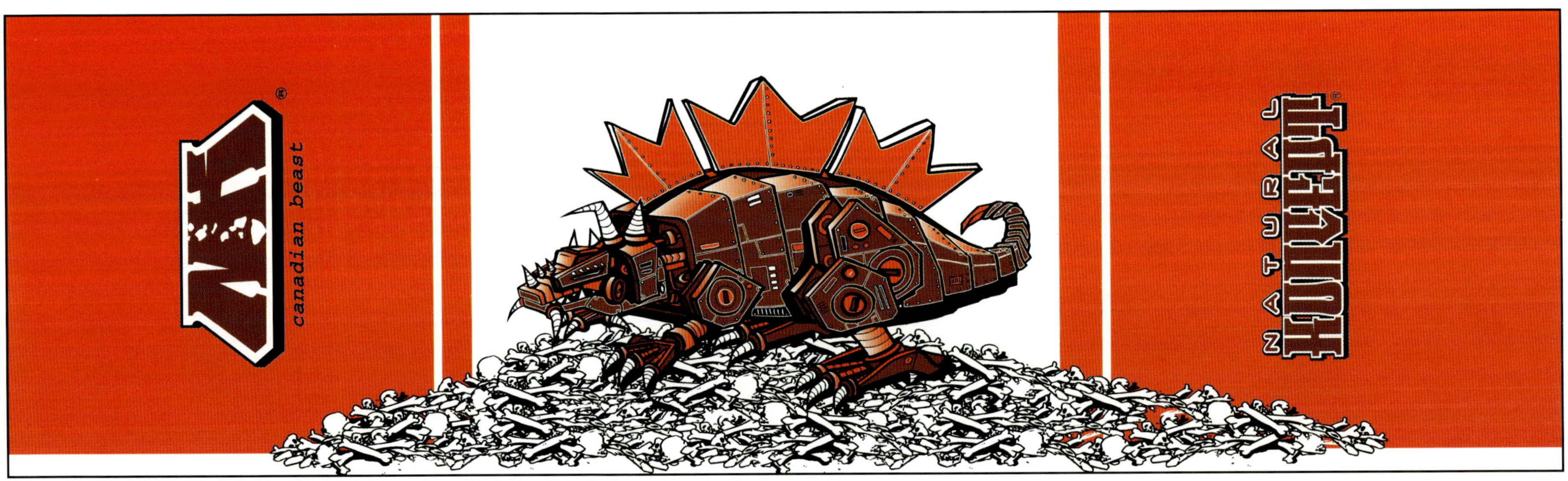

Katch Art. *Courtesy Natural Concepts.*

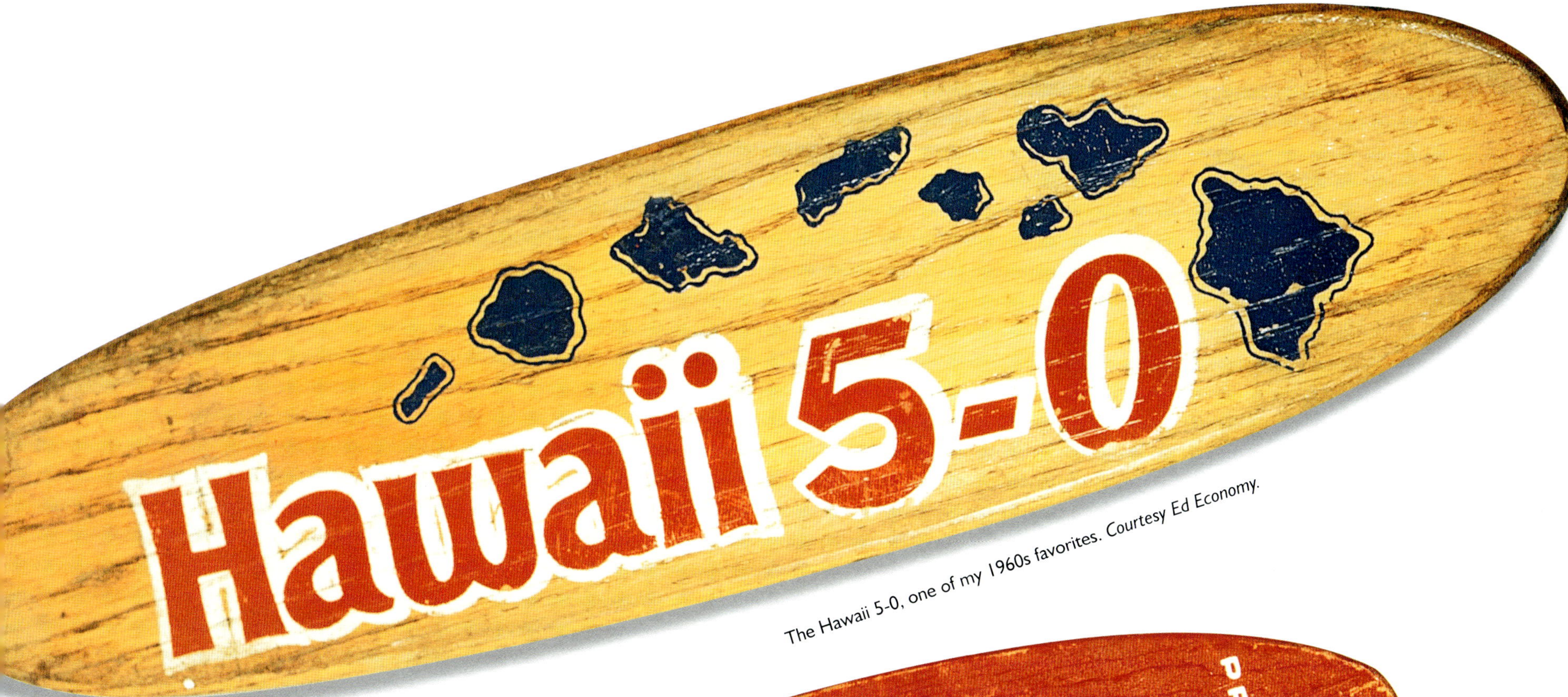

The Hawaii 5-0, one of my 1960s favorites. Courtesy Ed Economy.

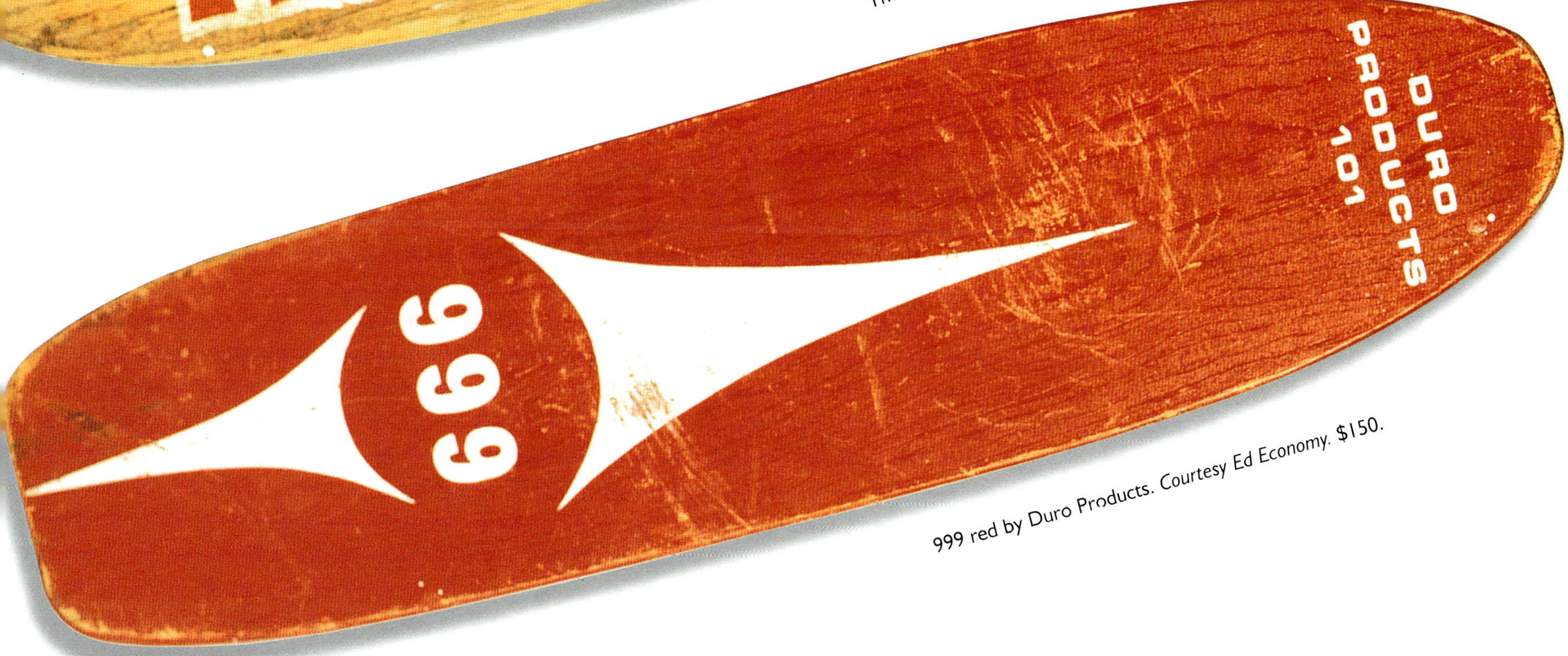

999 red by Duro Products. Courtesy Ed Economy. $150.

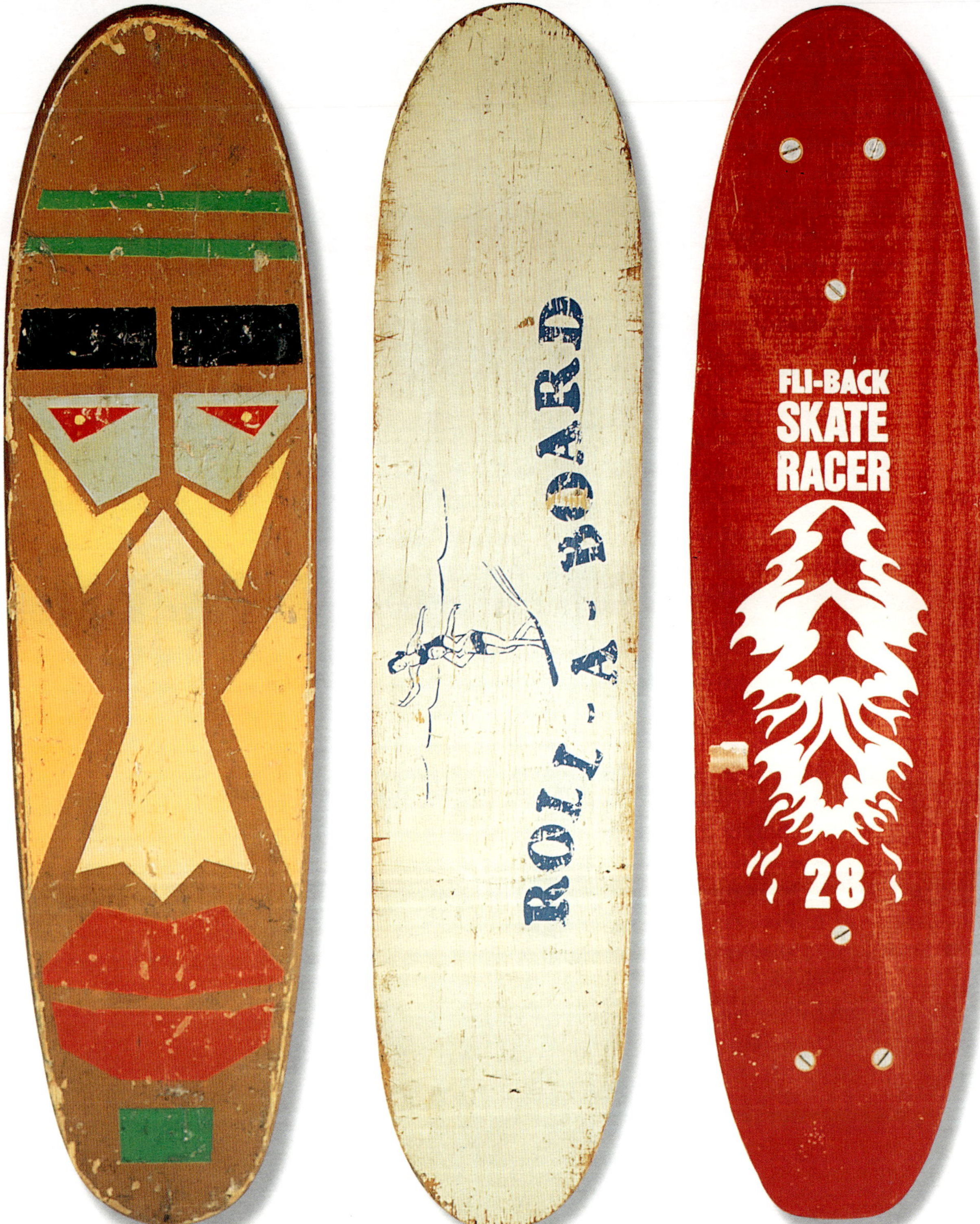

Left to right:
Tiki board. *Courtesy Ed Economy.* $200.

Roll-a-Board from Britain. *Courtesy Ed Economy.* $250.

Fli-Back Skate Racer #28, red. *Courtesy Ed Economy.* $150-200.

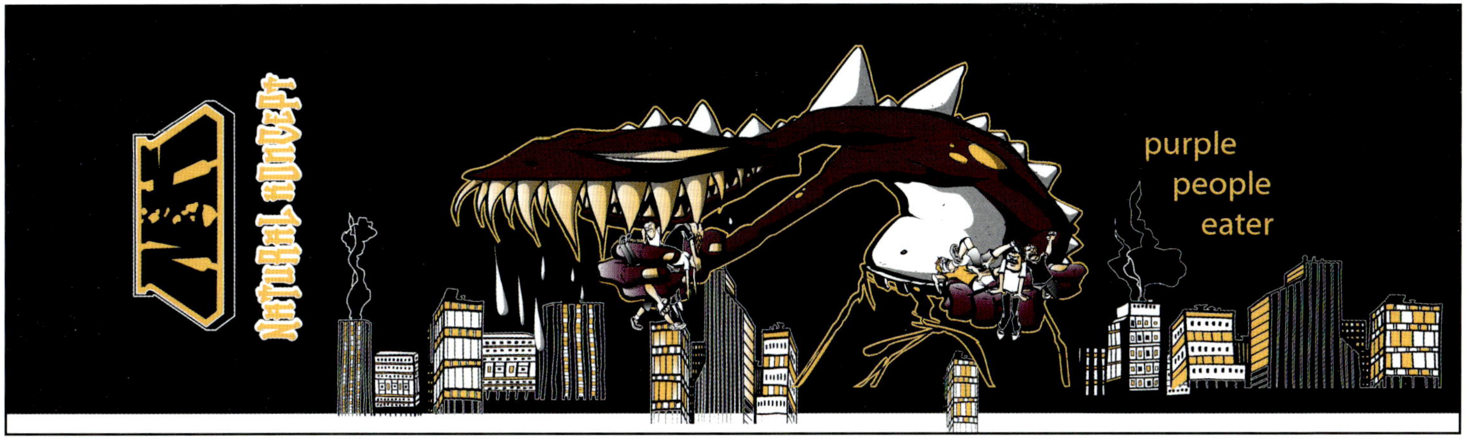

Purple people eater, Katch art. *Courtesy Natural Concepts.*

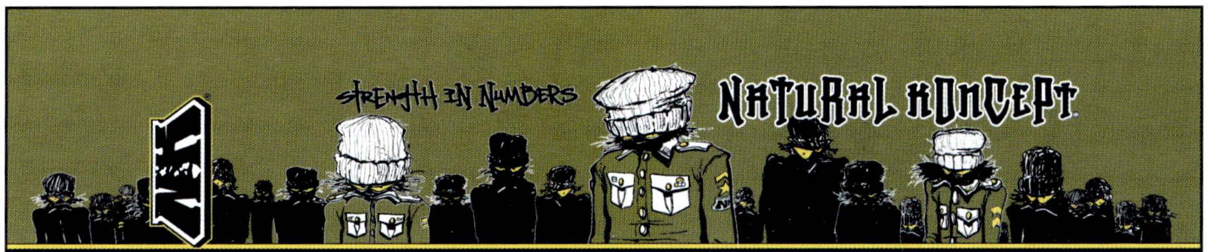

Katch art. *Courtesy Natural Concepts.*

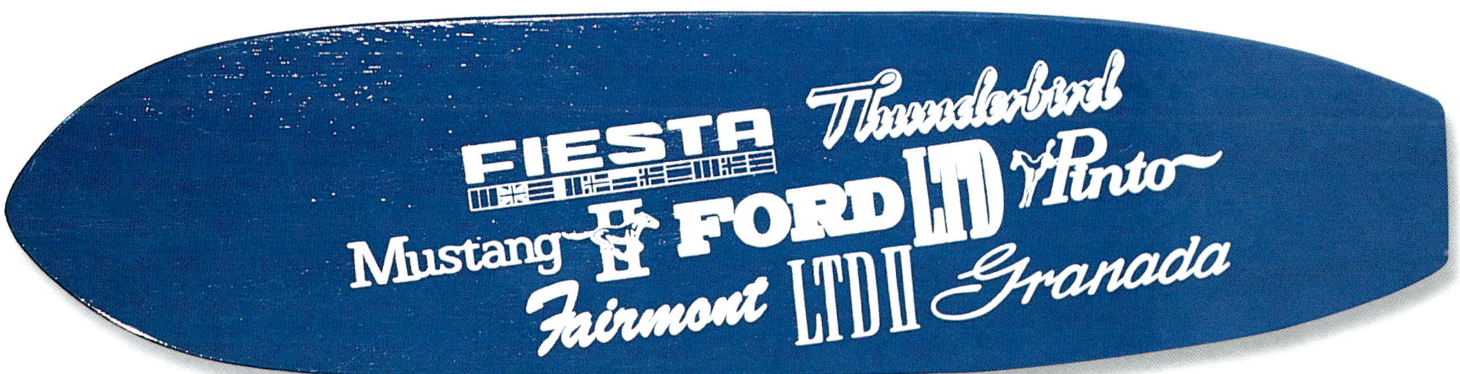

Looks like some car dealers got together and decorated a Nash. *Courtesy Ed Economy.* $150.

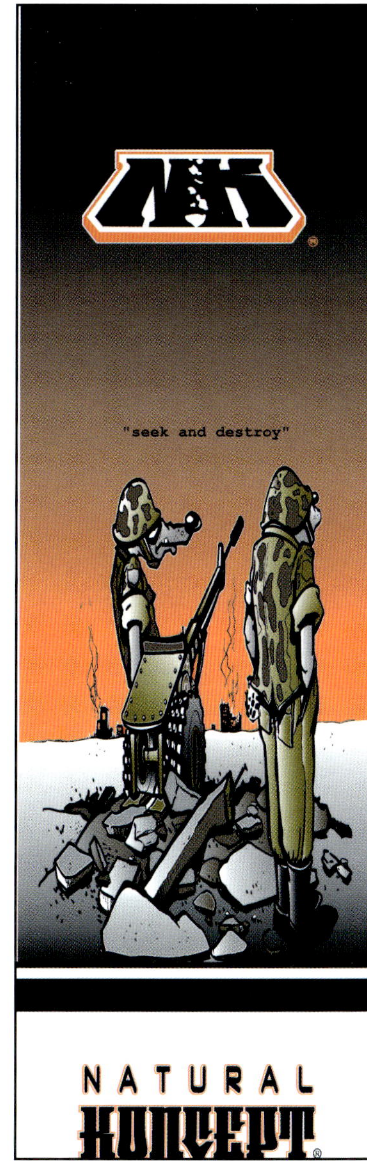

Seek and Destroy, Katch Art. *Courtesy Natural Concepts.*

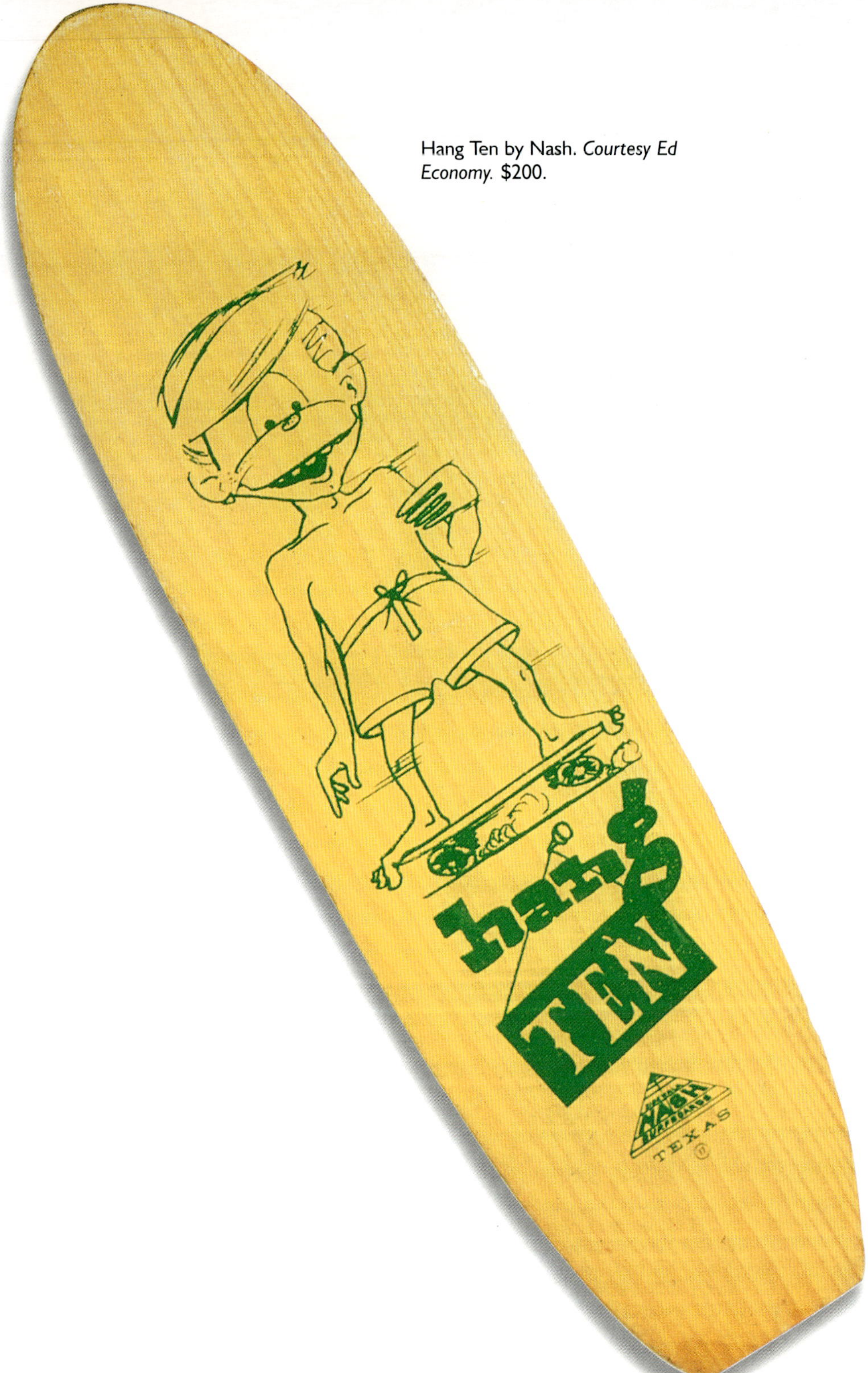

Hang Ten by Nash. *Courtesy Ed Economy.* $200.

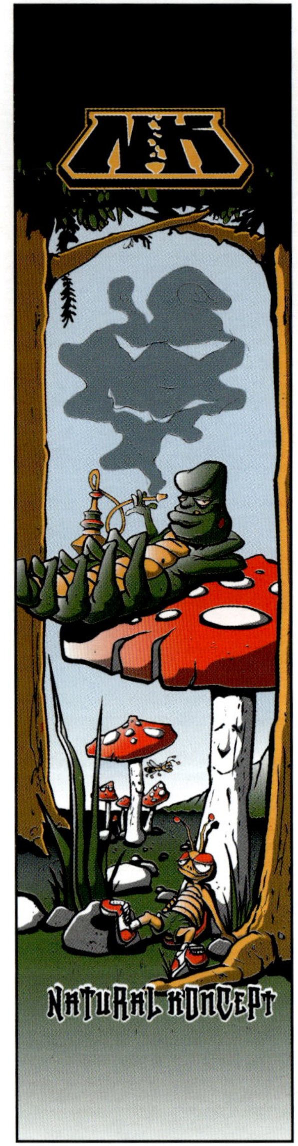

Shroom, Katch art. *Courtesy Natural Concepts.*

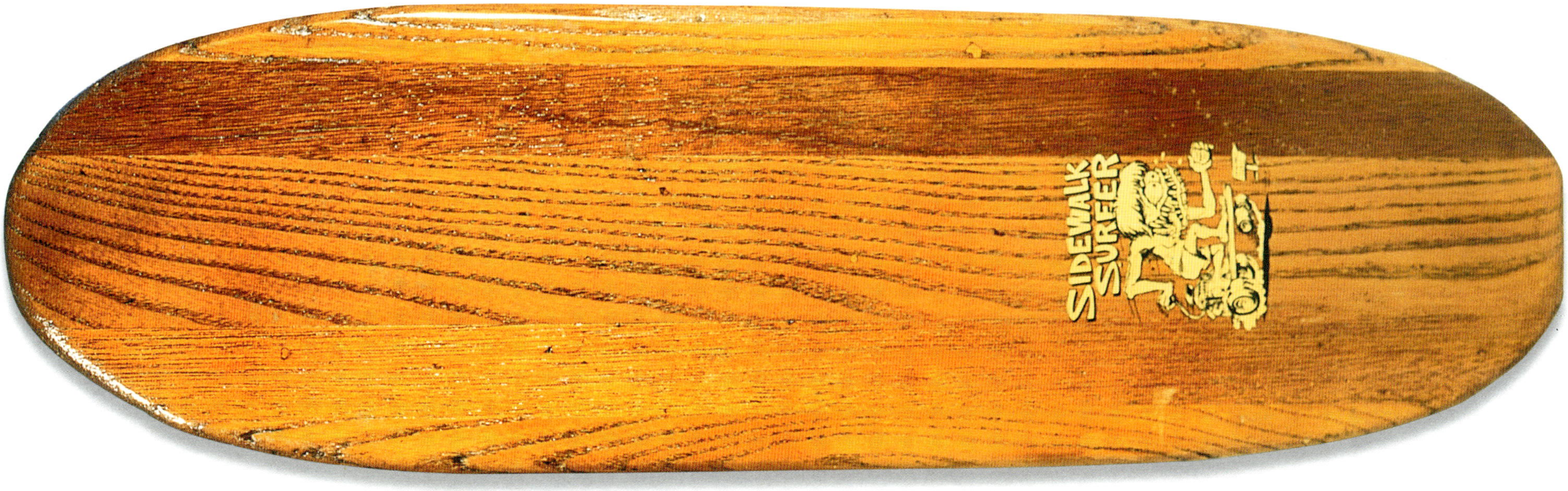

The Sidewalk Surfer with hot, red graphics. *Courtesy Ed Economy.* $100.

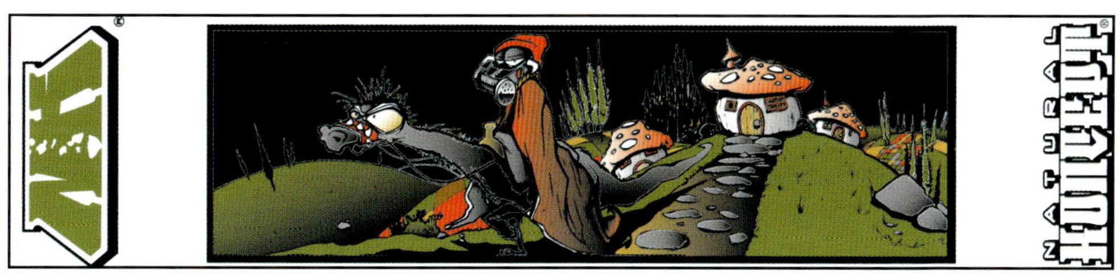

Shroom Land, Katch Art. *Courtesy Natural Concepts.*

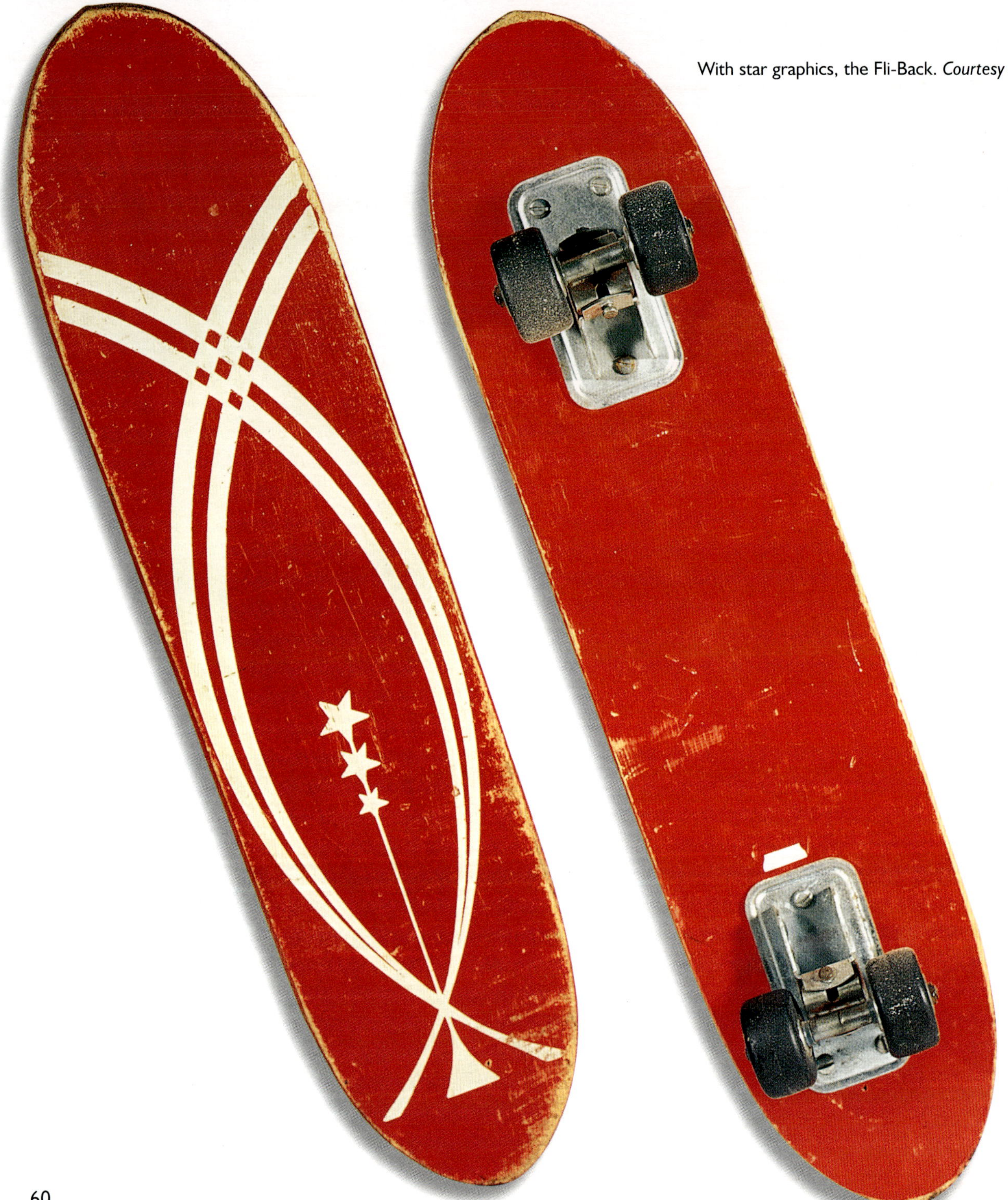

With star graphics, the Fli-Back. *Courtesy Ed Economy.*

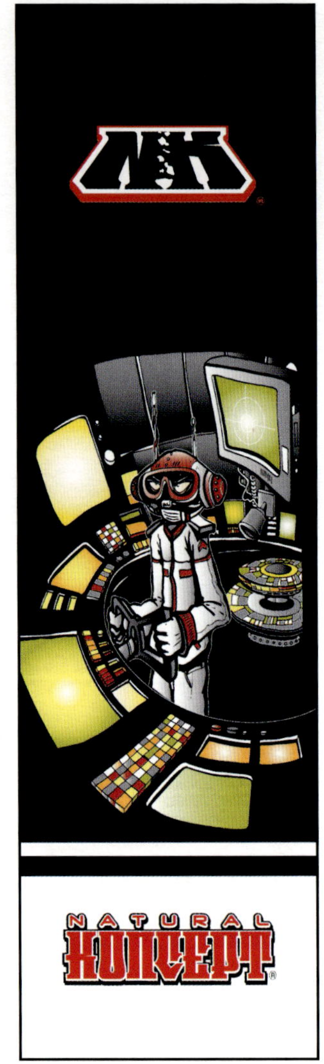

Space Pilot, Katch art.
Courtesy Natural Concepts.

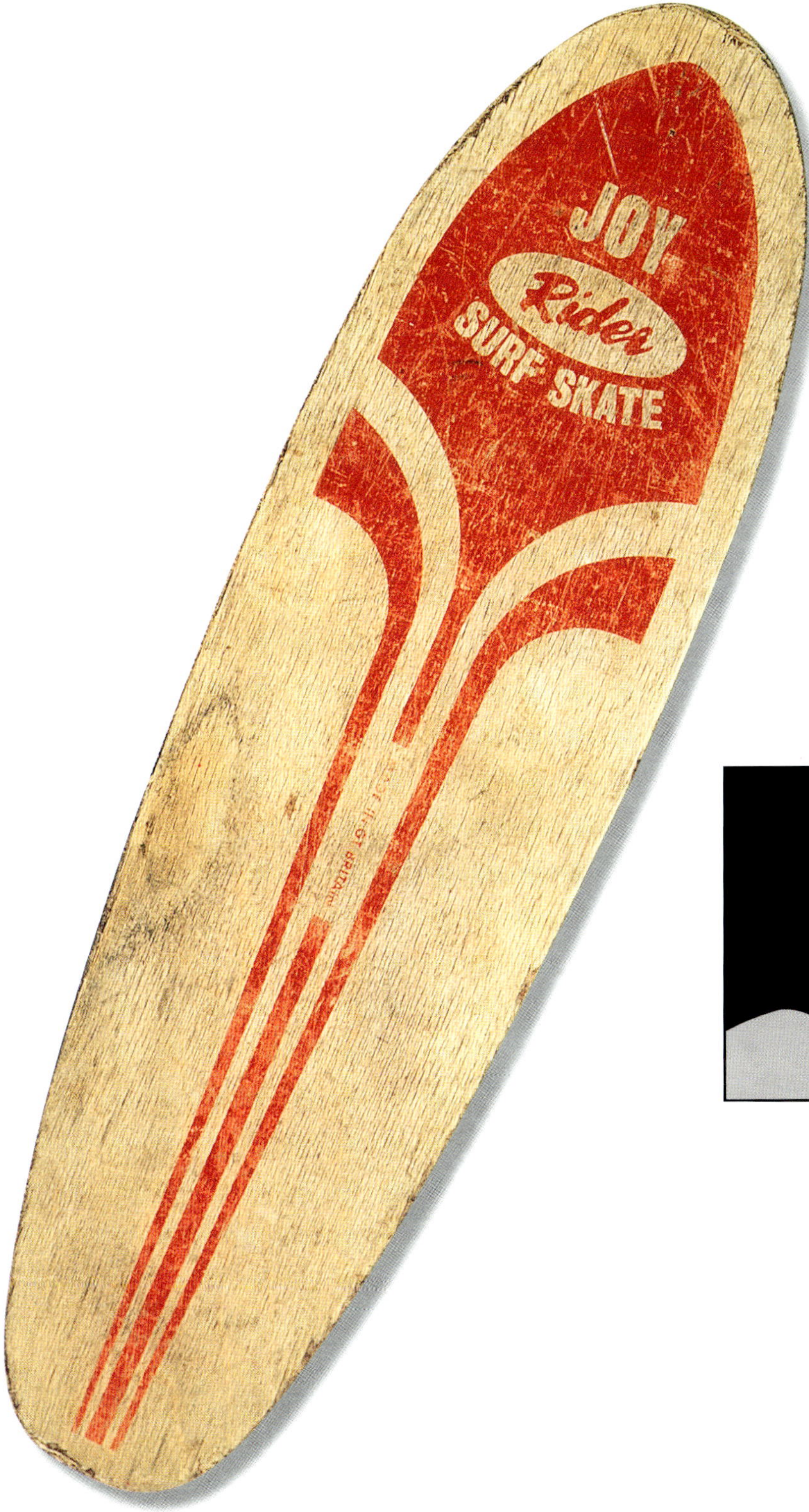

Joy Rider Surf Skate. *Courtesy Ed Economy.* $75.

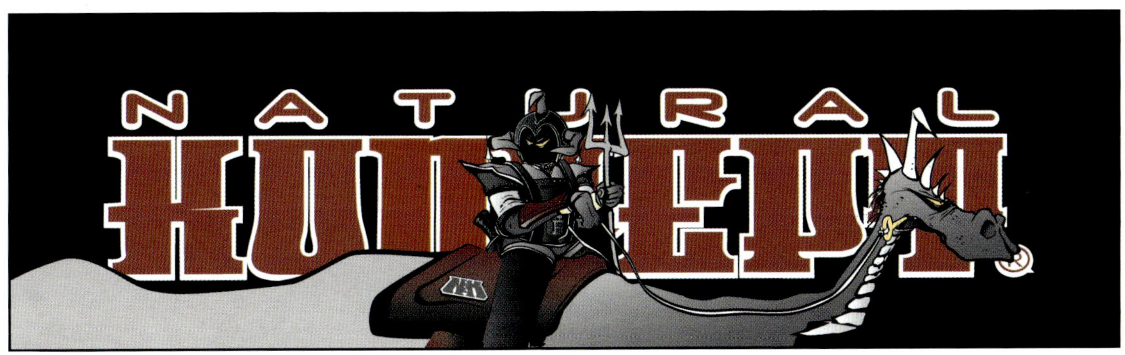

Night Marauder, Katch art. *Courtesy Natural Concepts.*

I spoke to a guy from the *Chicago Tribune* about collectible skateboards from the sixties, because he did a piece on it. He told me that through his travels he met a guy who made skateboards of the '60s called Big Wheeler. His name was Adolph Kefer and he lived back east somewhere. The Tribune guy was telling Adolf how much these boards were worth now. Adolf laughed and said he used to use them for firewood.

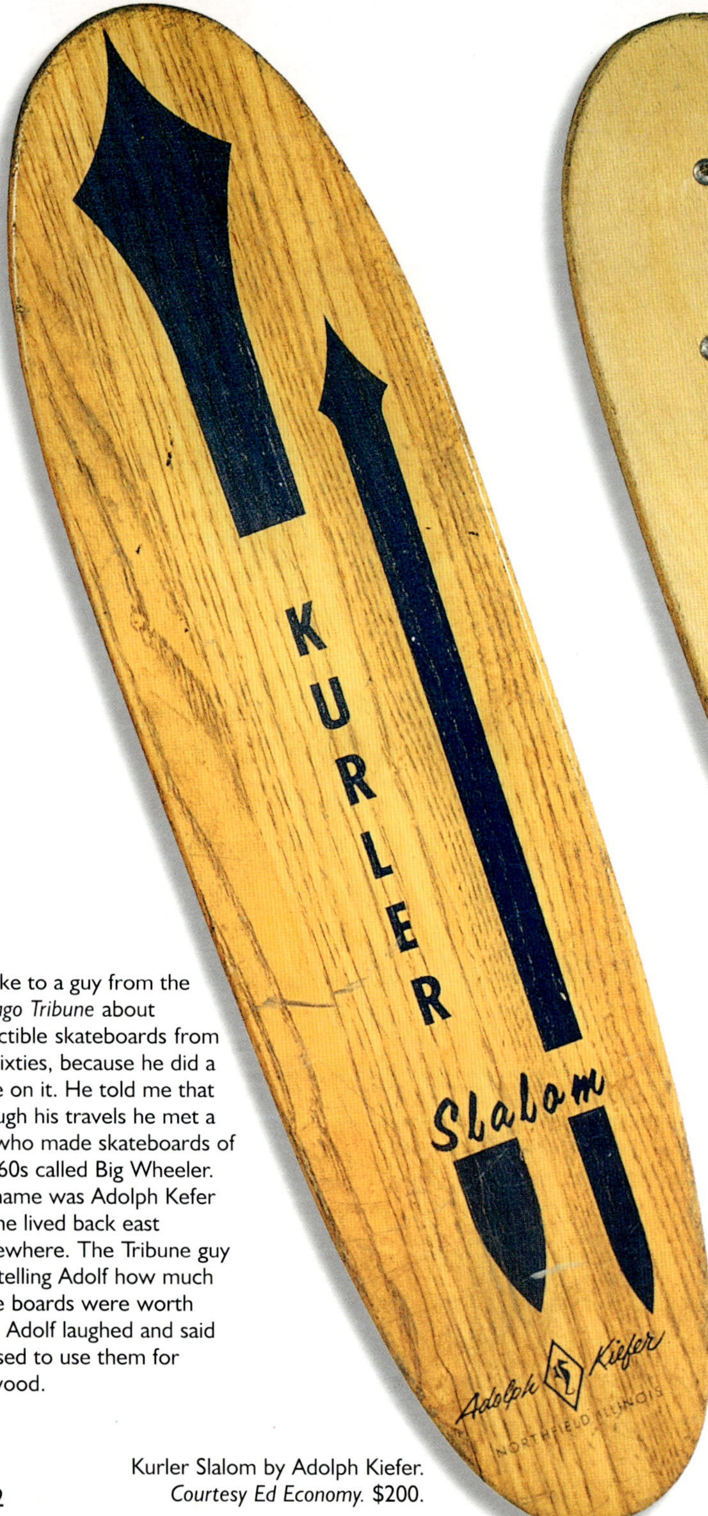

Kurler Slalom by Adolph Kiefer. *Courtesy Ed Economy.* $200.

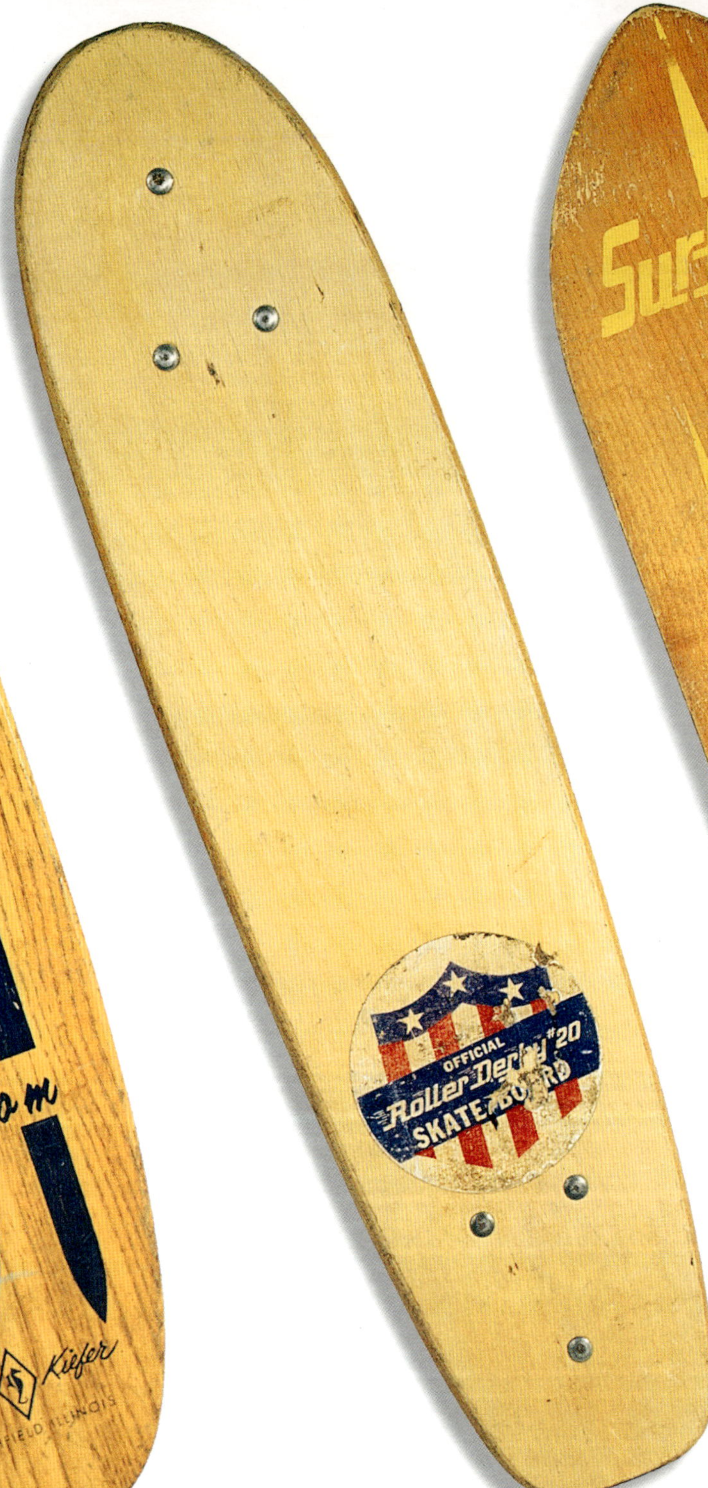

Roller Derby, a 20-incher. *Courtesy Ed Economy.* $100.

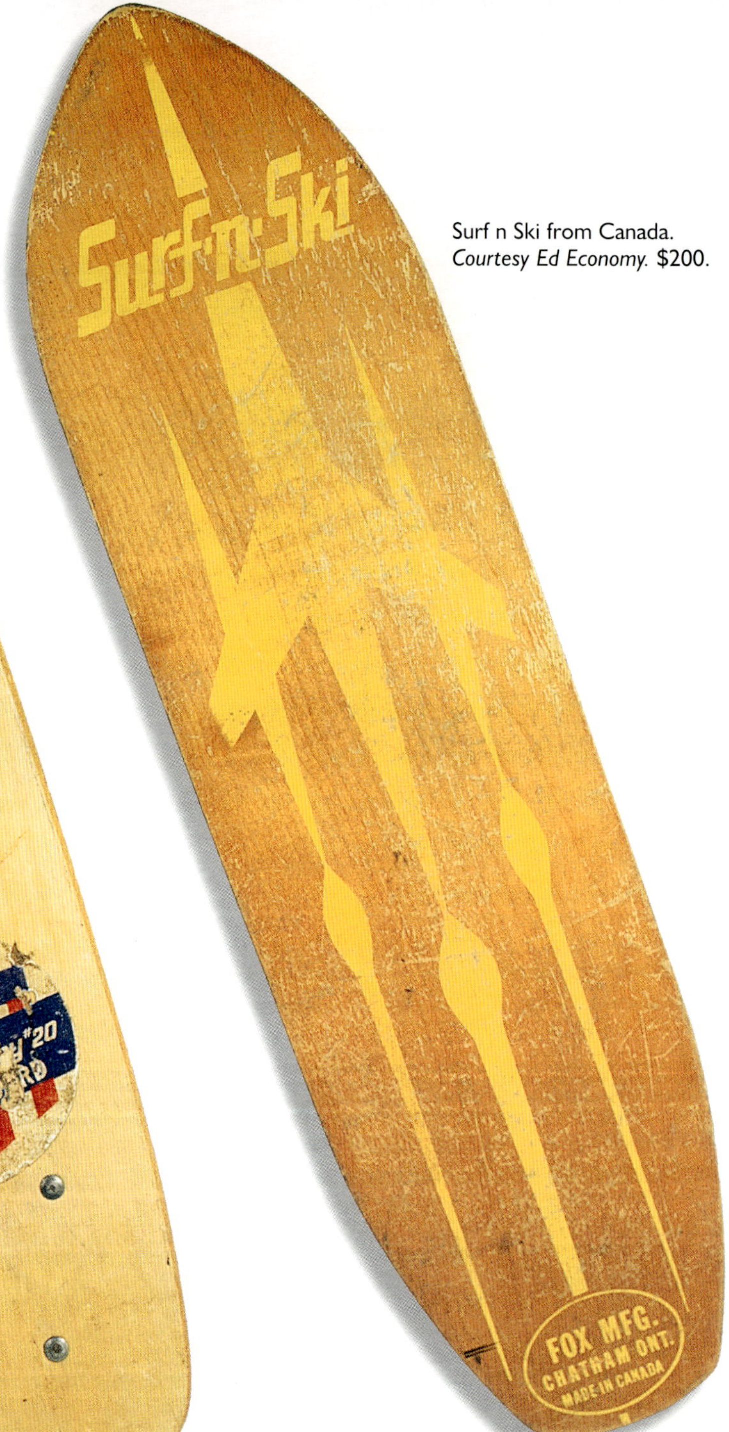

Surf n Ski from Canada. *Courtesy Ed Economy.* $200.

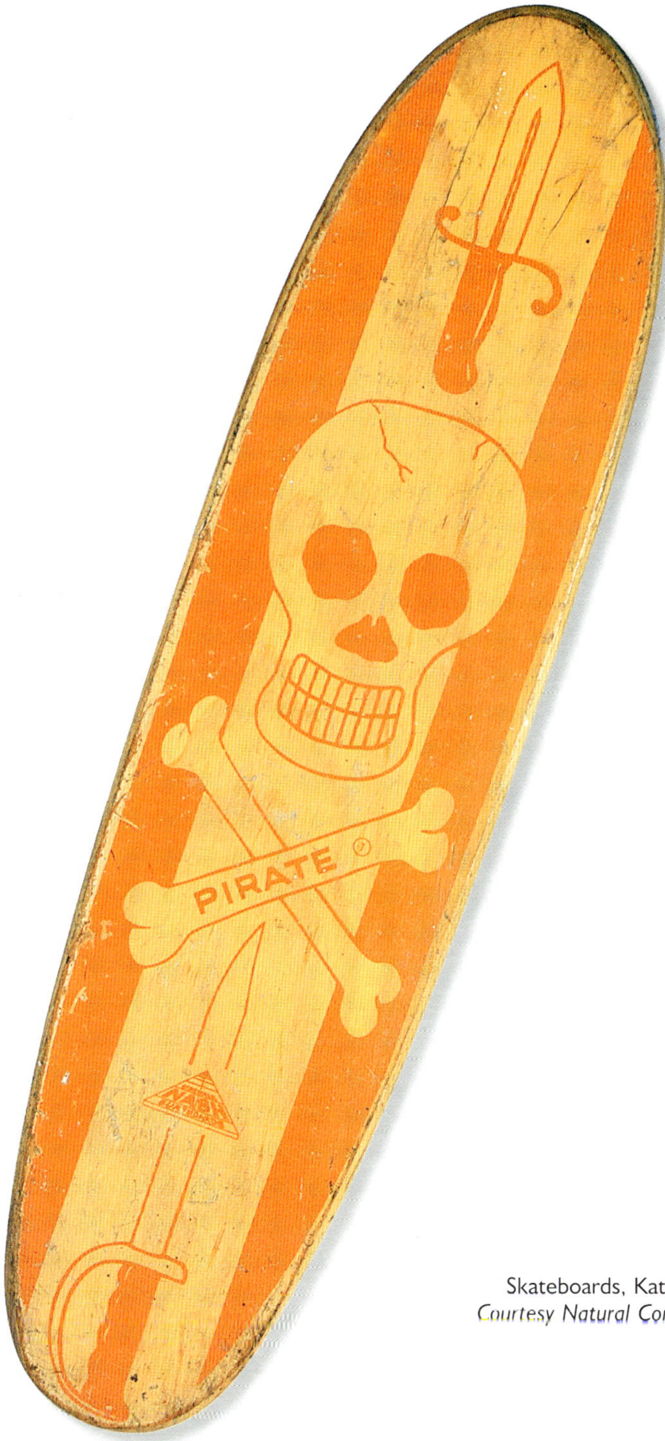

The Pirate, complete with daggers. *Courtesy Ed Economy.* $500.

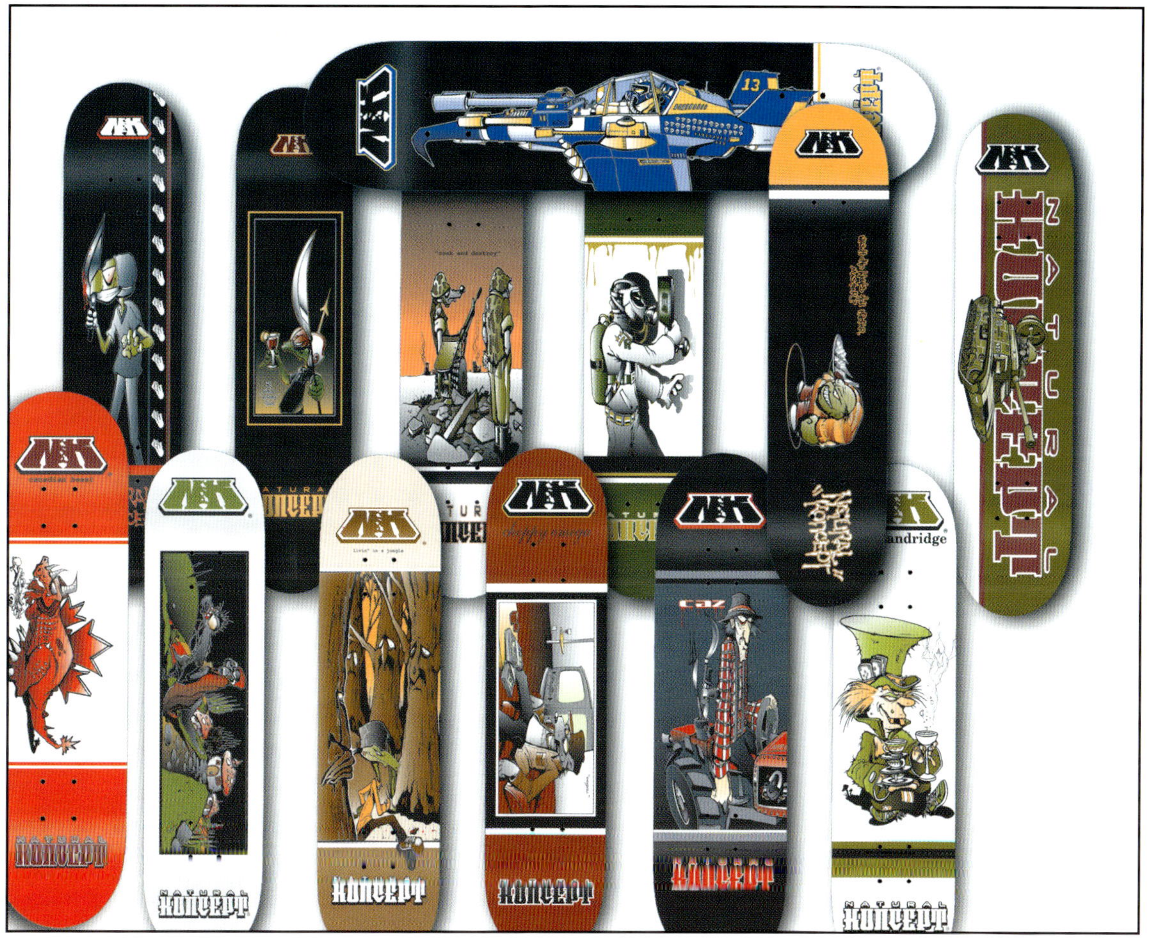

Skateboards, Katch art. *Courtesy Natural Concepts.*

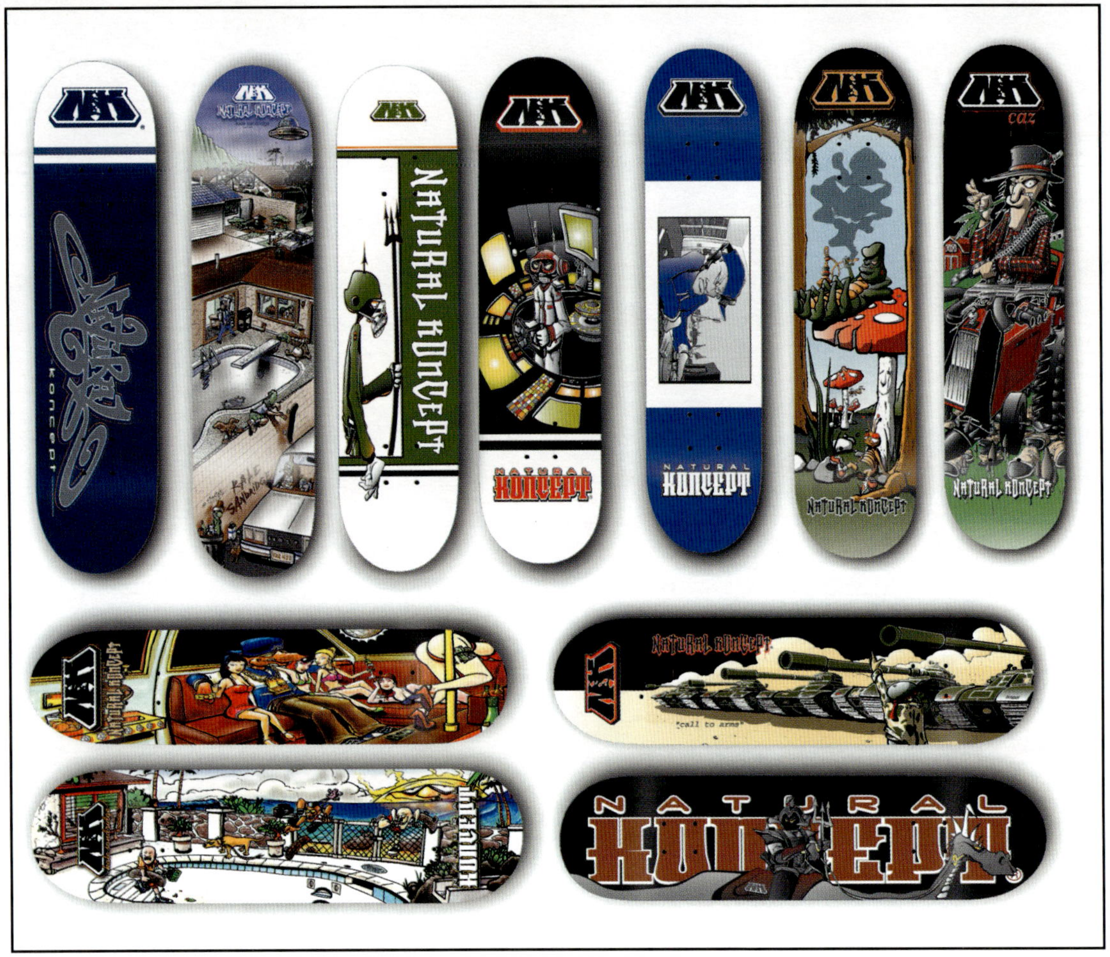

Skateboards, Katch art. *Courtesy Natural Concepts.*

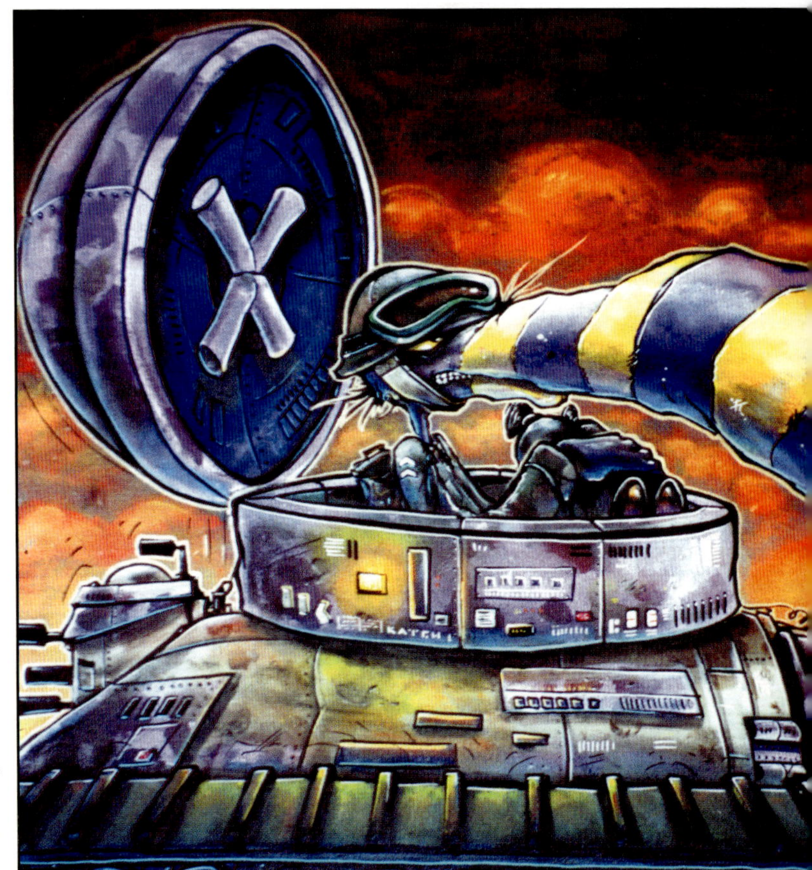

Tank Bug, Katch Art. *Courtesy Natural Concepts.*

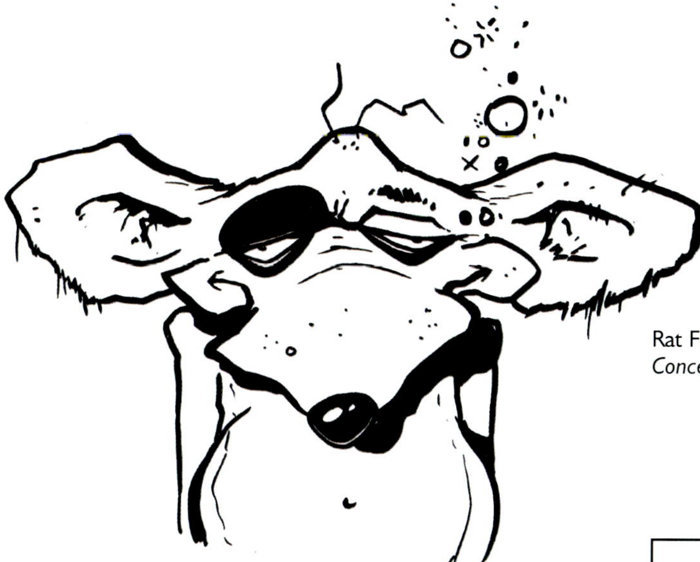

Rat Fink, Katch art. *Courtesy Natural Concepts.*

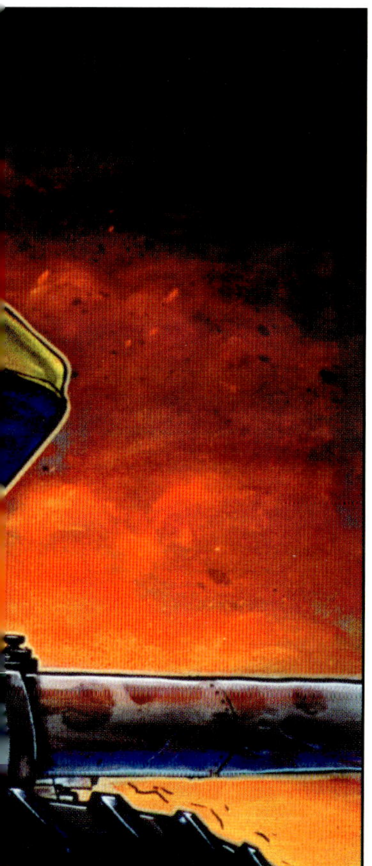

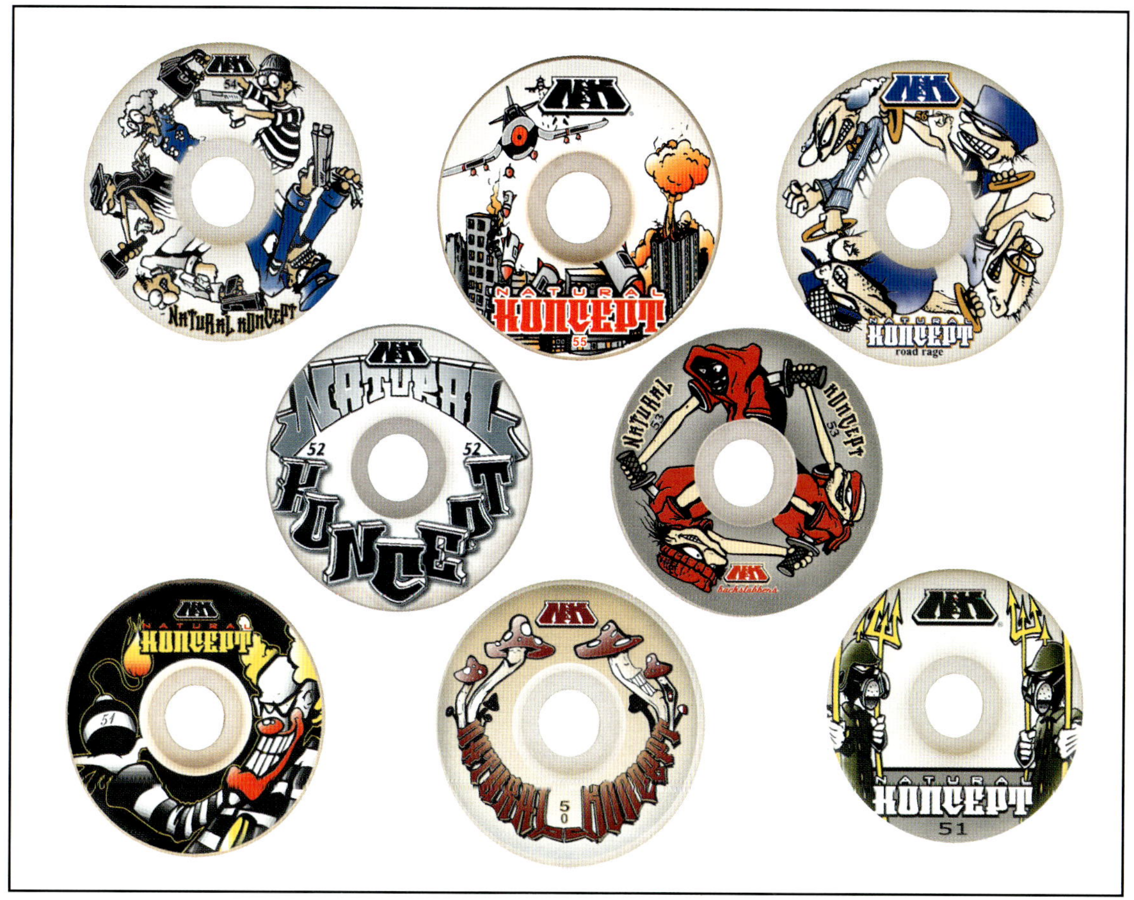

New School Wheels, Katch art. *Courtesy Natural Concepts.*

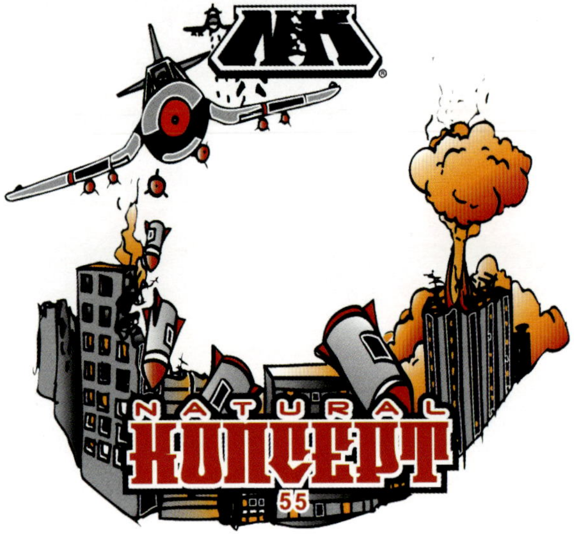

Bombers, Katch art. *Courtesy Natural Concepts.*

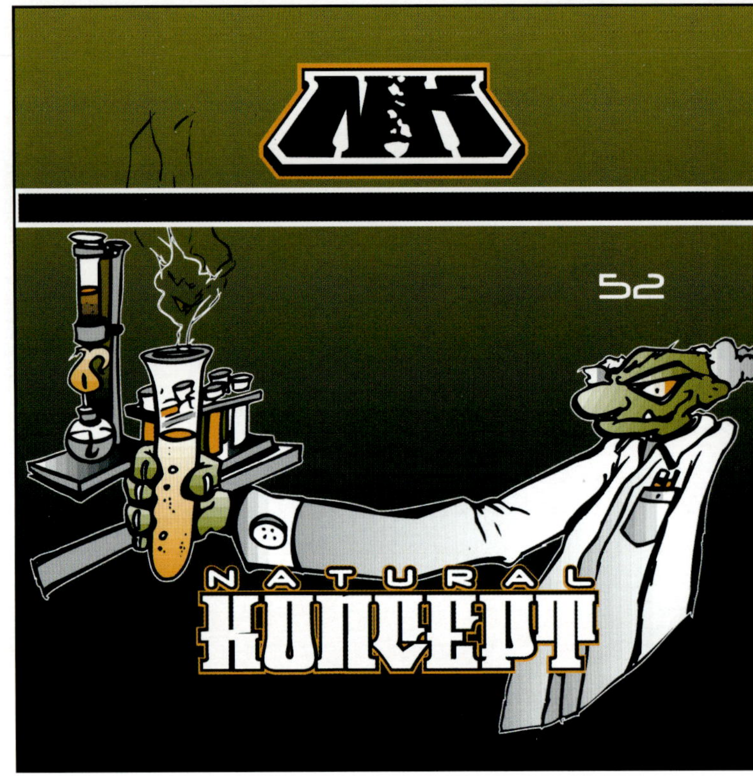

Science, Katch art. *Courtesy Natural Concepts.*

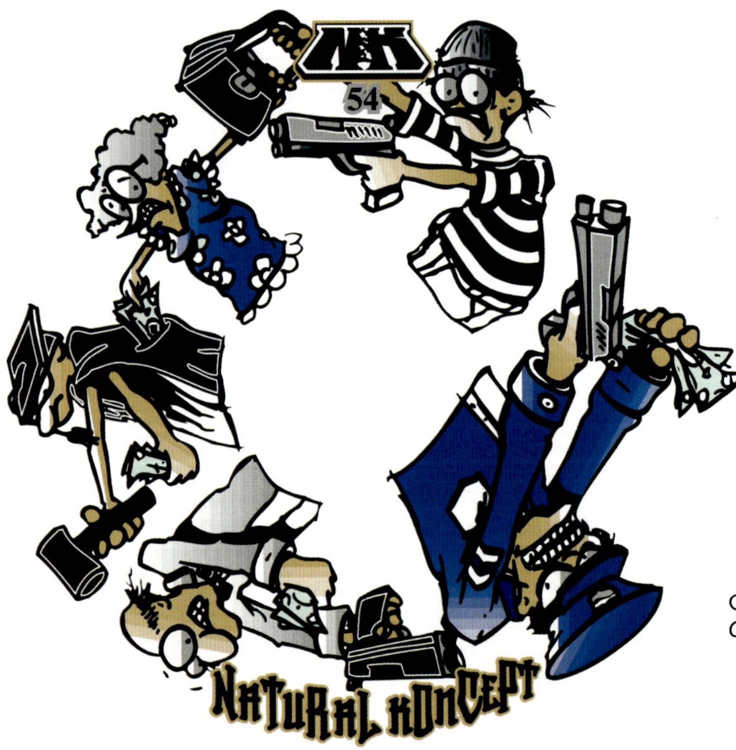

Circle of life, Katch art. *Courtesy Natural Concepts.*

1970s Skateboards

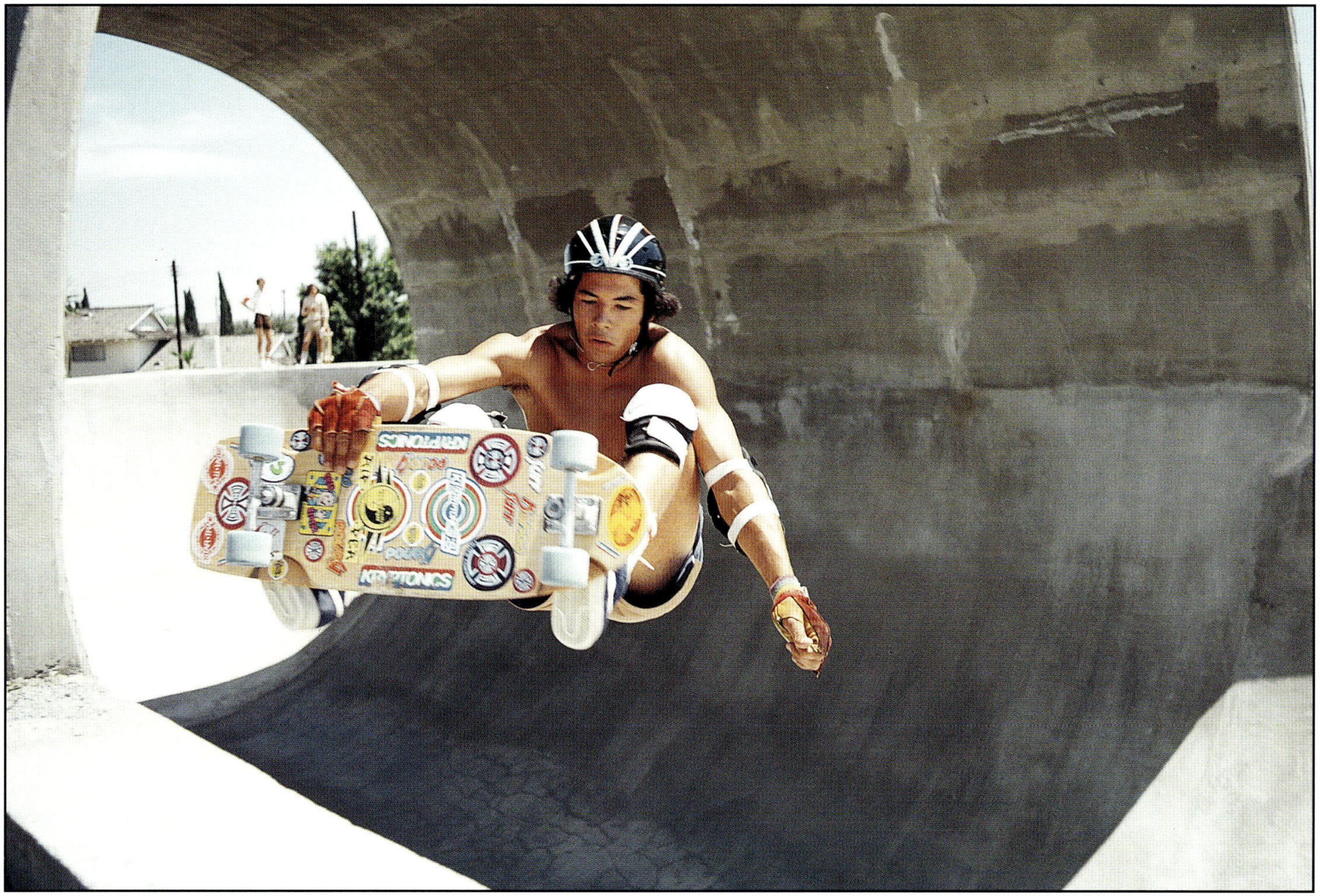

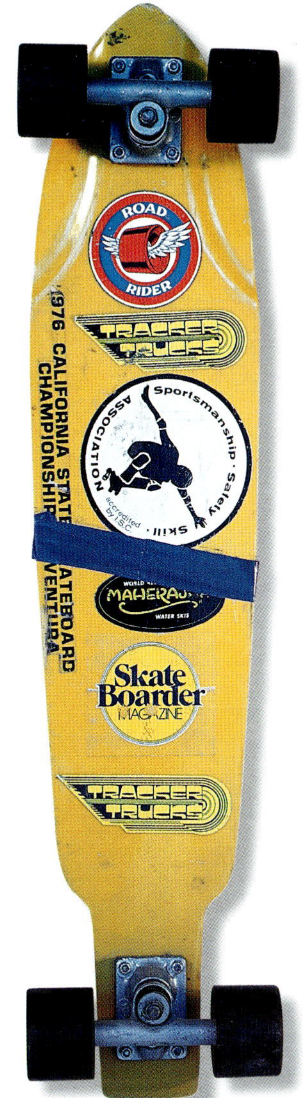

First generation yellow, Turner Road Rider with tracker trucks. *Courtesy Ed Economy.* $1500-2000.

Howard Hood shows off sticker collection. Steves Southbay Pipe. *Photo James O'Mahoney.*

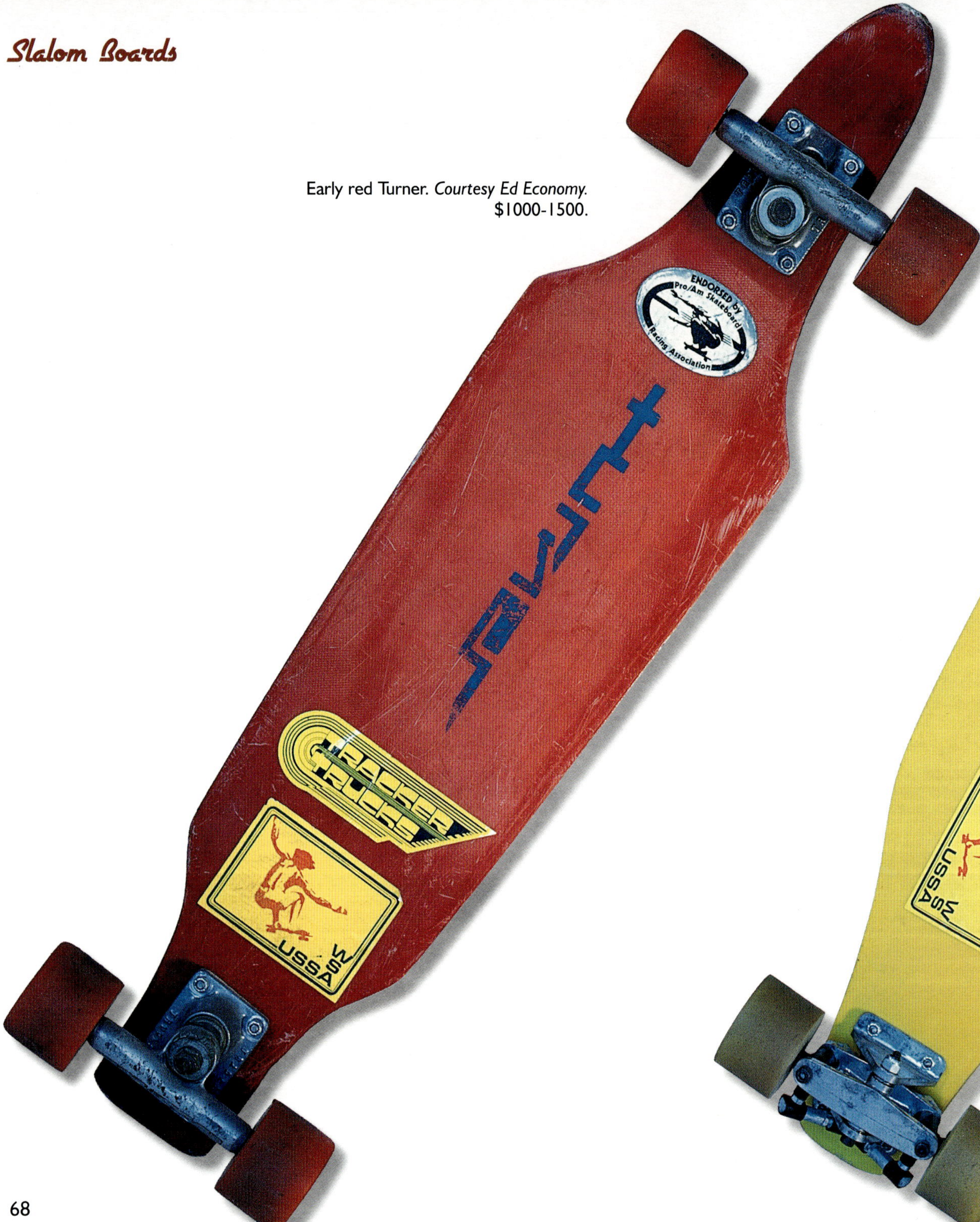

Early red Turner. *Courtesy Ed Economy.*
$1000-1500.

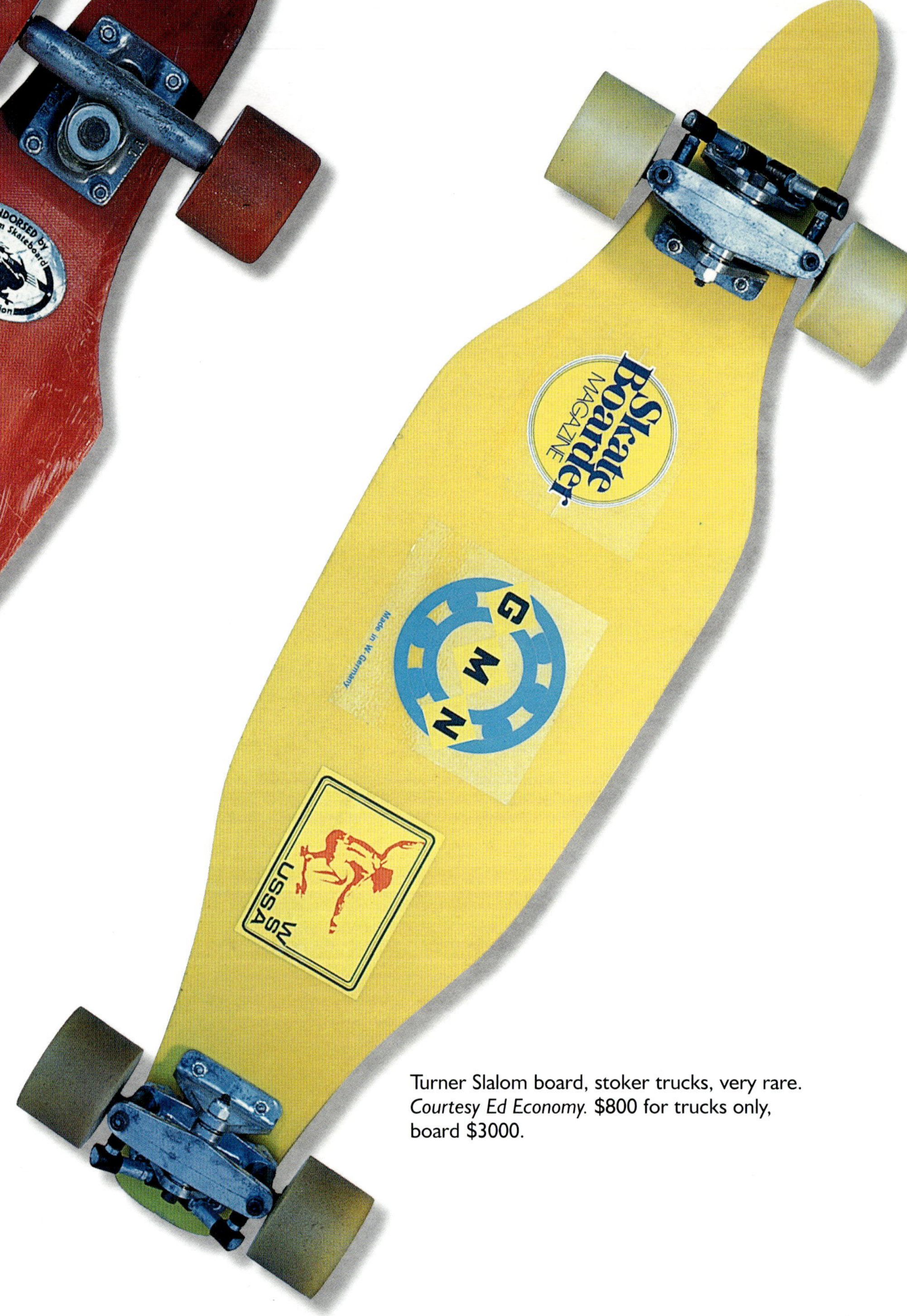

Turner Slalom board, stoker trucks, very rare. *Courtesy Ed Economy.* $800 for trucks only, board $3000.

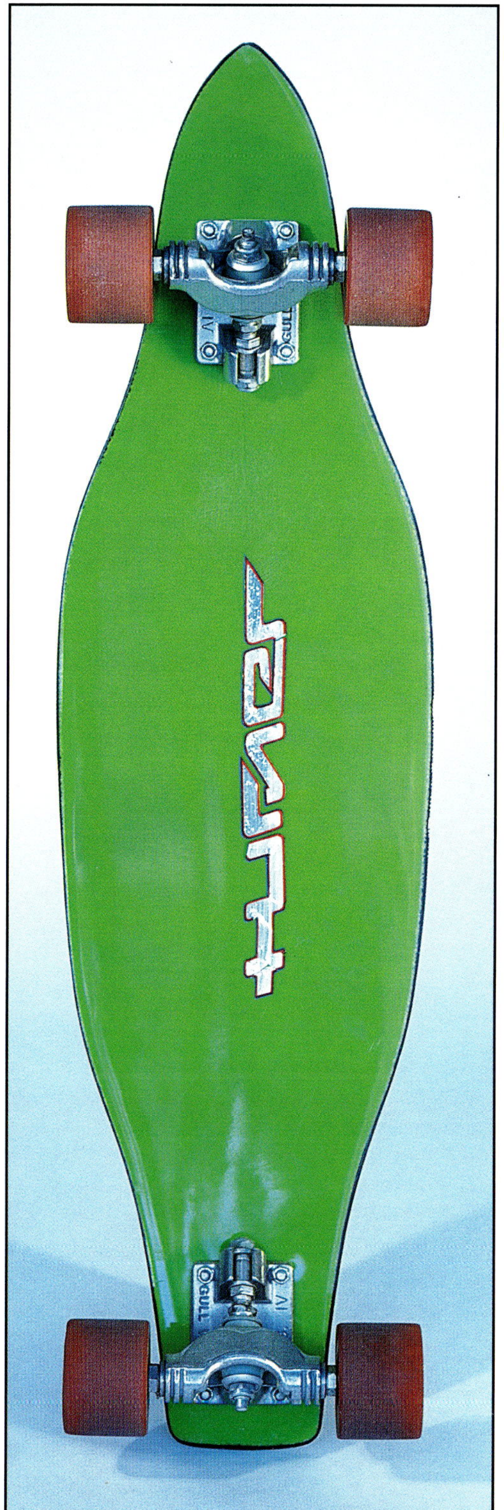

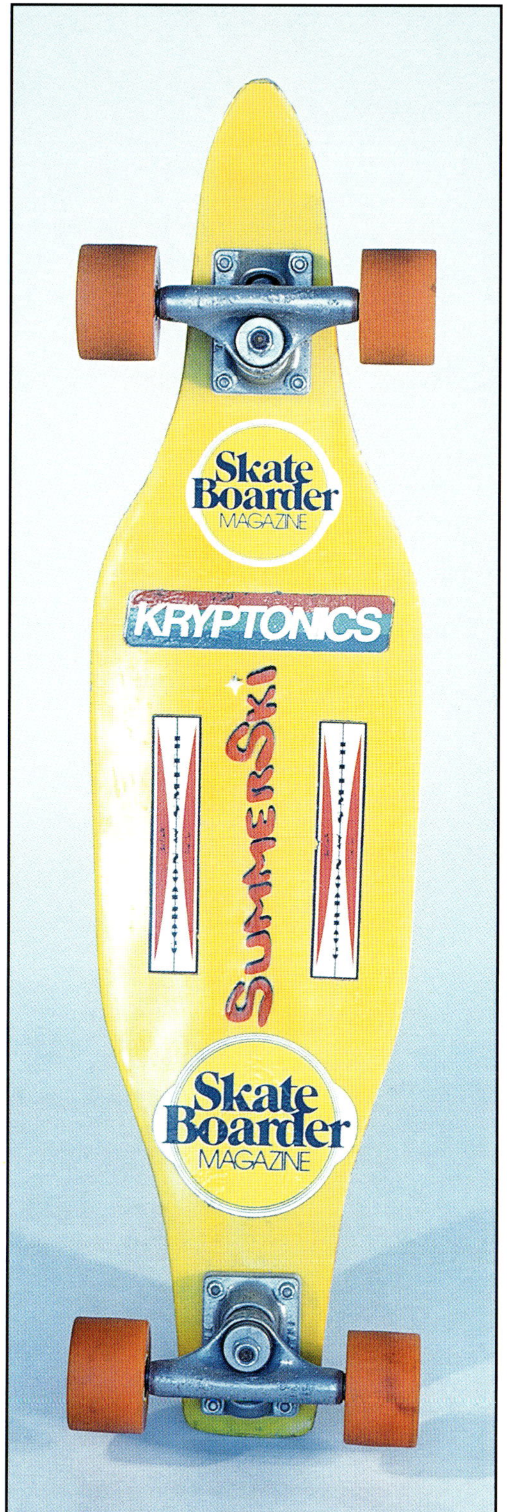

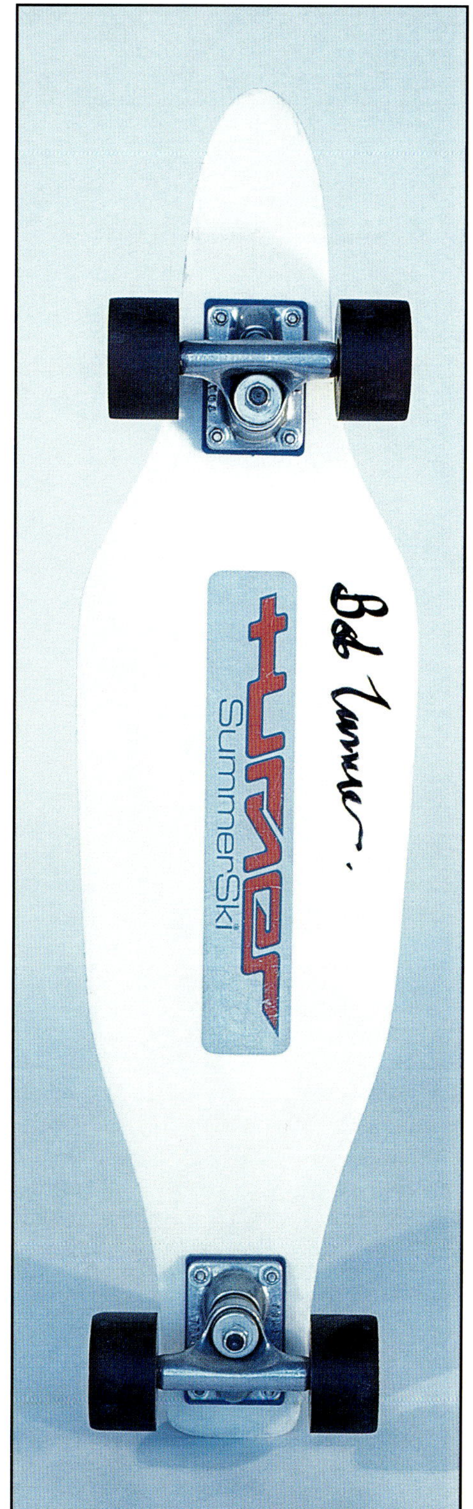

Left to right:
Black and green Turner, later model Parkrider, gull wing, split axle trucks. *Courtesy Ed Economy.* $300 a set, board $800.

Yellow Turner Kryptonics and tracker trucks. *Courtesy Ed Economy.* $1000-1500.

Henry Hester's personal board singed by Bob Turner, never been ridden. *Courtesy Ed Economy.* $2000.

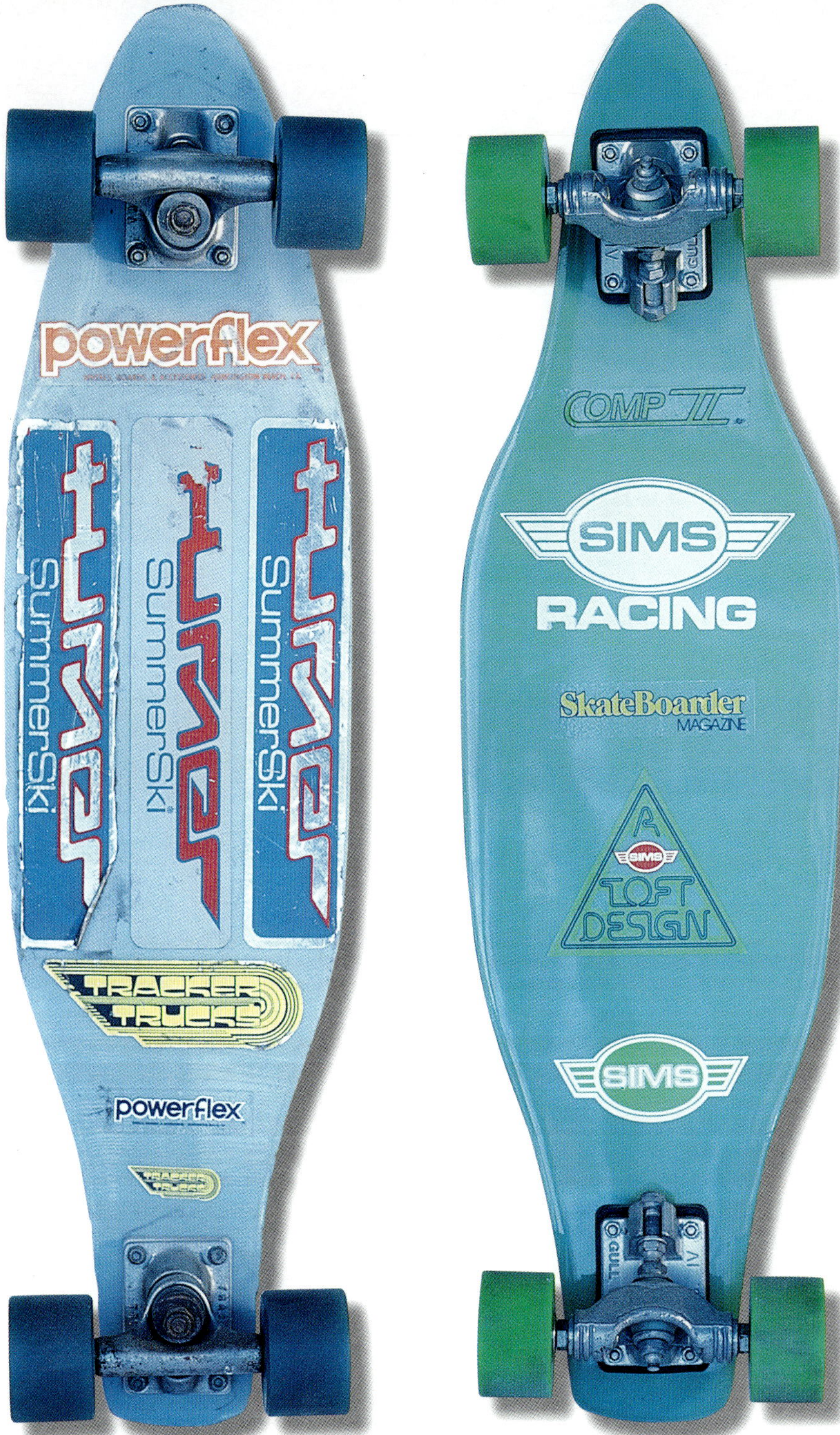

Left: Blue Turner. *Courtesy Ed Economy.* $1000.

Right: Green Turner gull wing, trucks rare, team board. *Courtesy Ed Economy.* $2500.

John Huston makes his first world speed mark, Signal Hill. *Photo James O'Mahoney.*

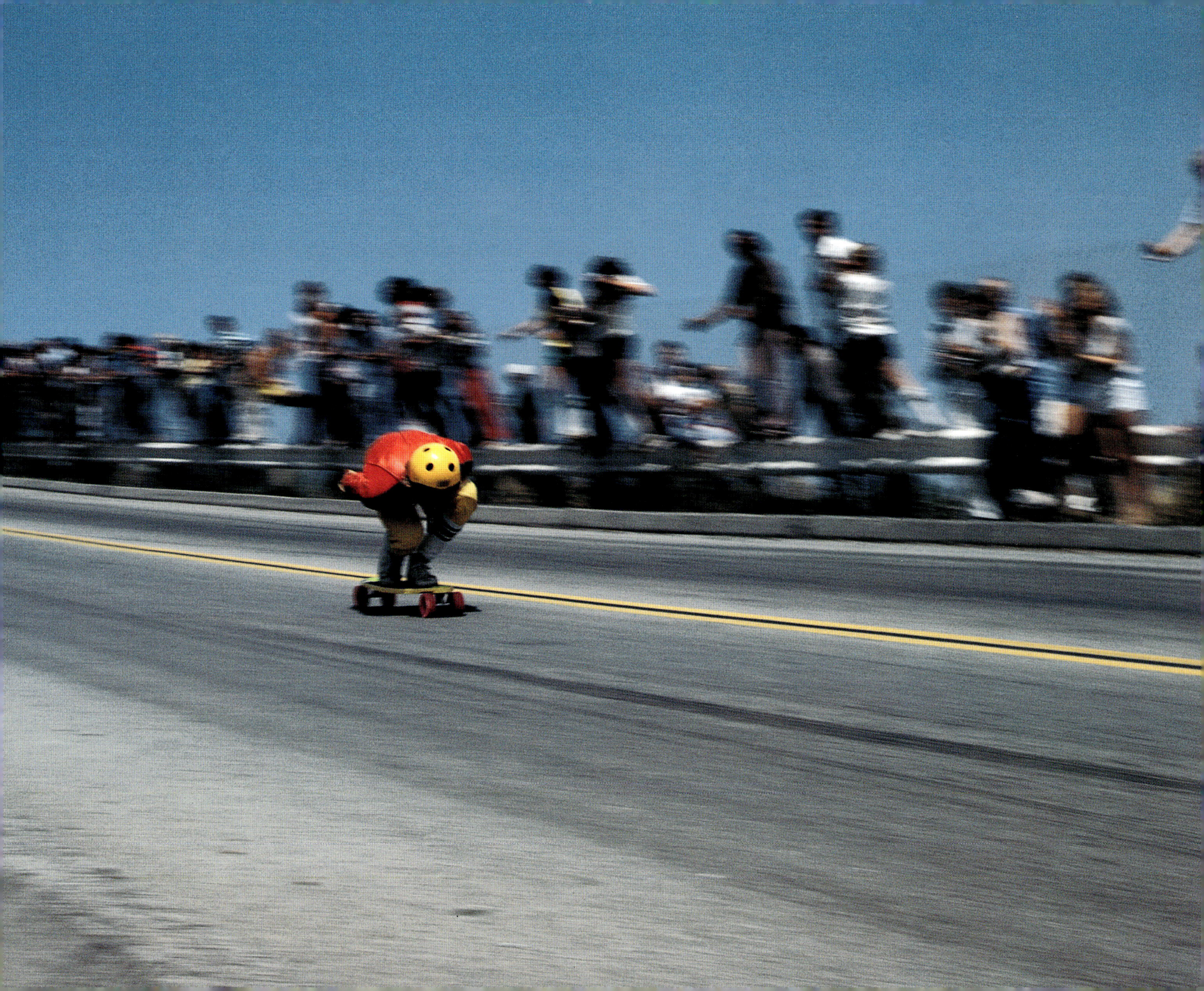

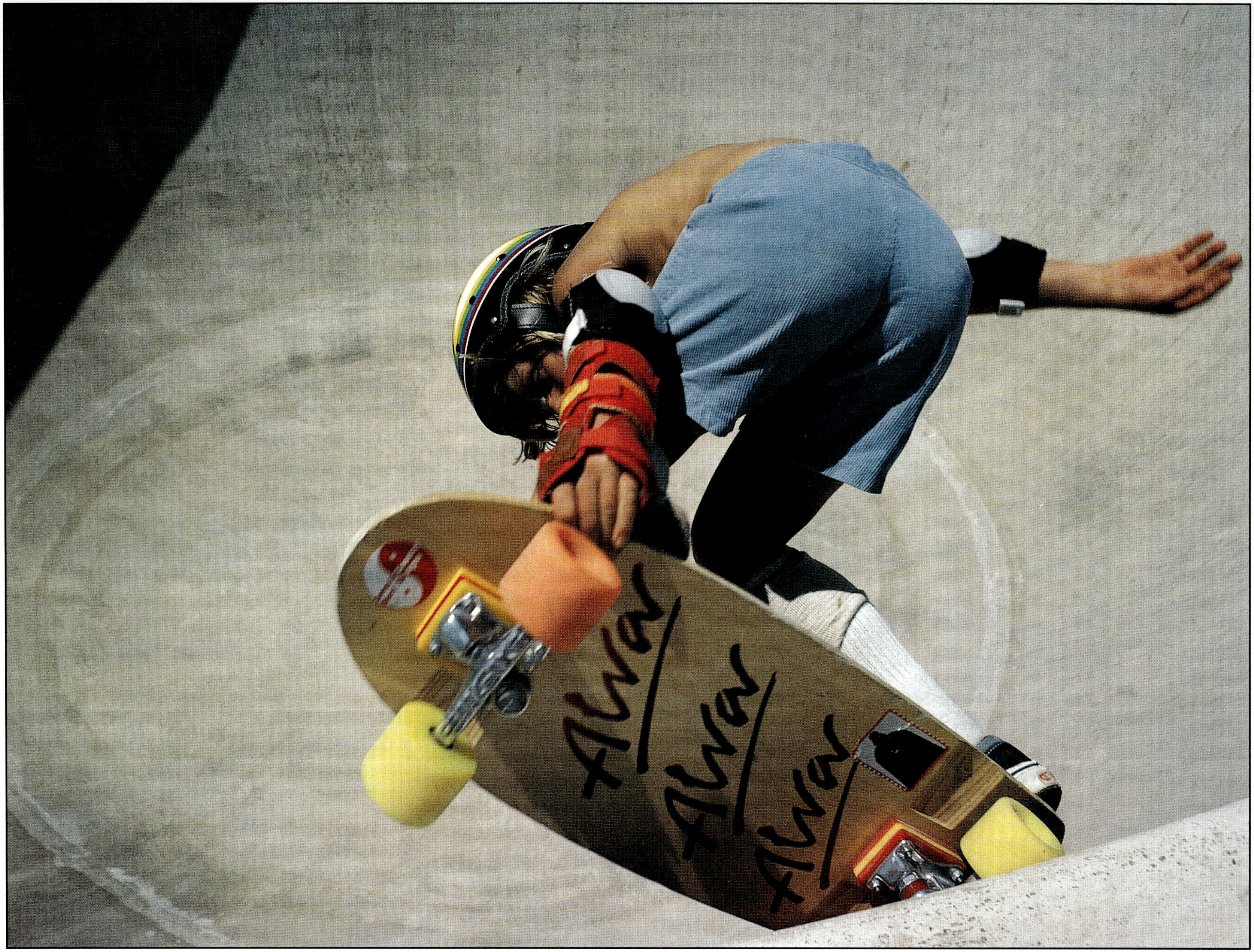

Indy grab in the bowl, early Alva board. *Photo James O'Mahoney.*

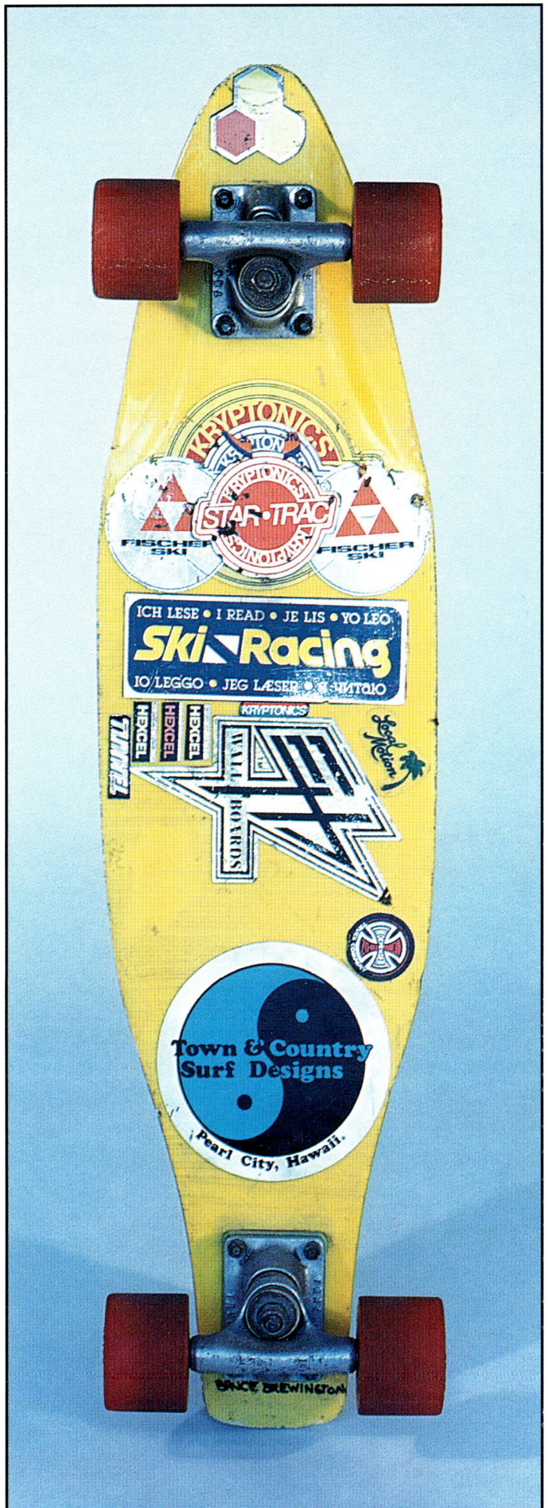

Yellow Turner, Bruce Brewington's personal racer, Kryptos trackers. *Courtesy Ed Economy.*

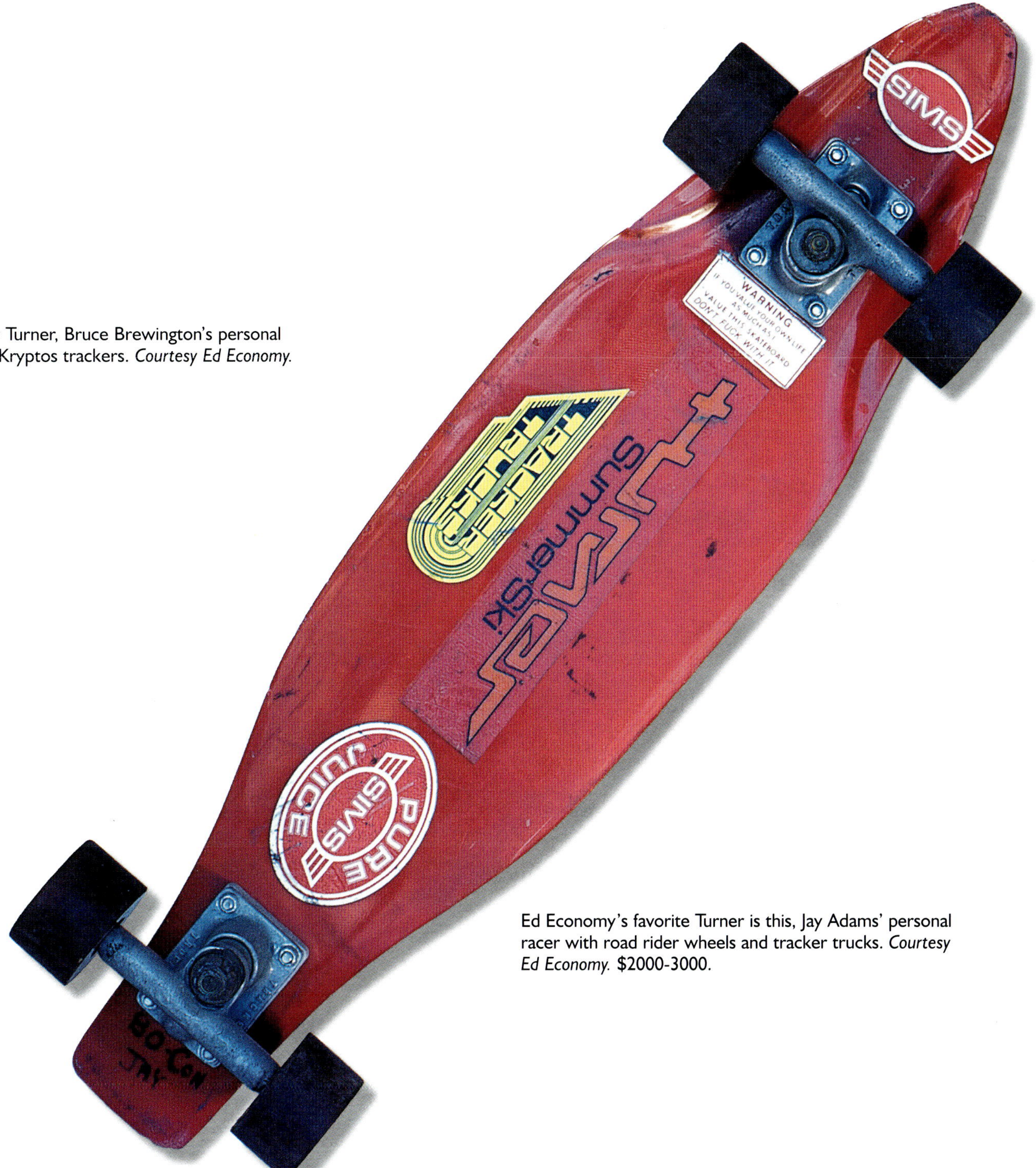

Ed Economy's favorite Turner is this, Jay Adams' personal racer with road rider wheels and tracker trucks. *Courtesy Ed Economy.* $2000-3000.

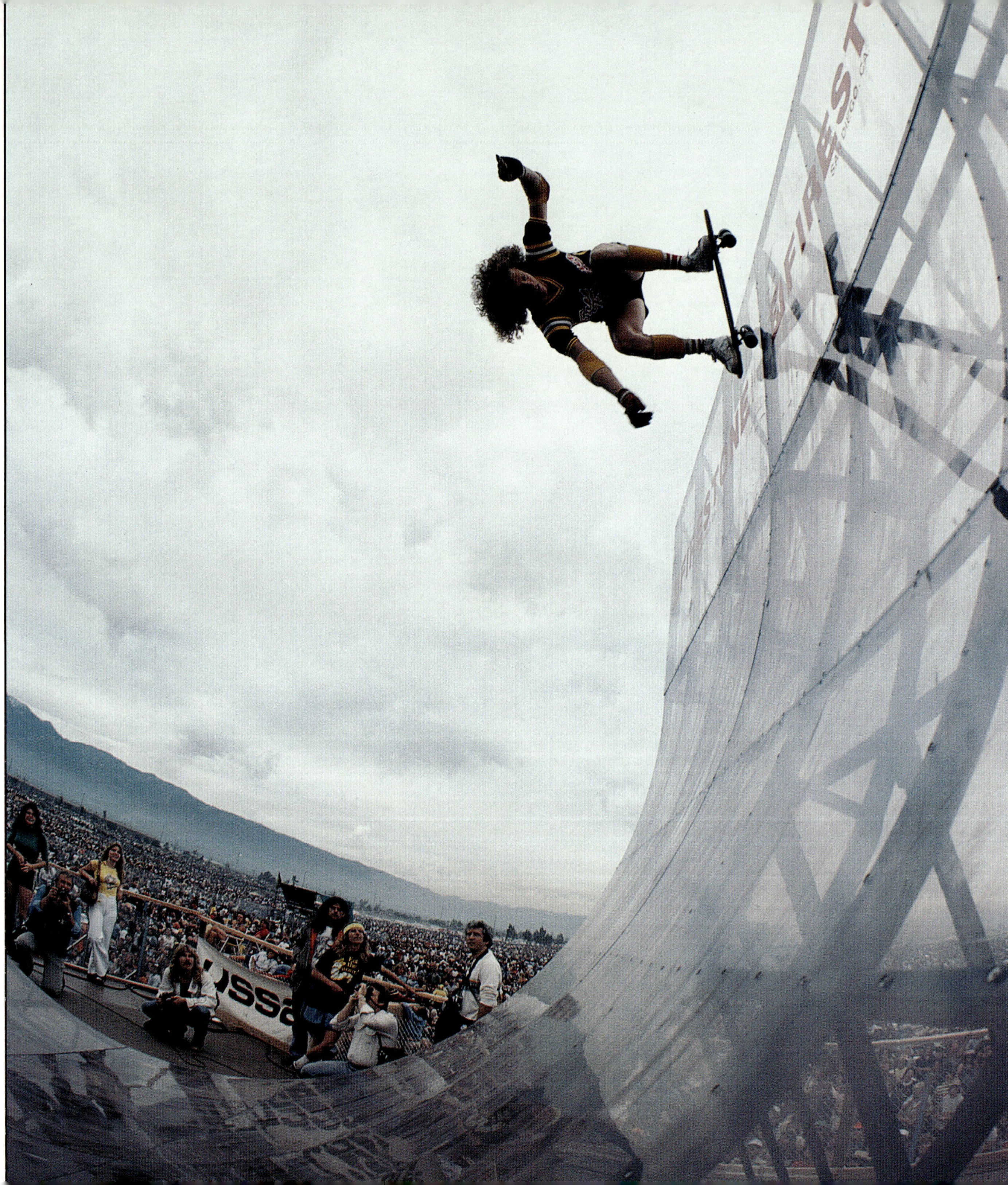

Fly Ty Page, Cal Jam, 400,000 passengers. *Photo James O'Mahoney.*

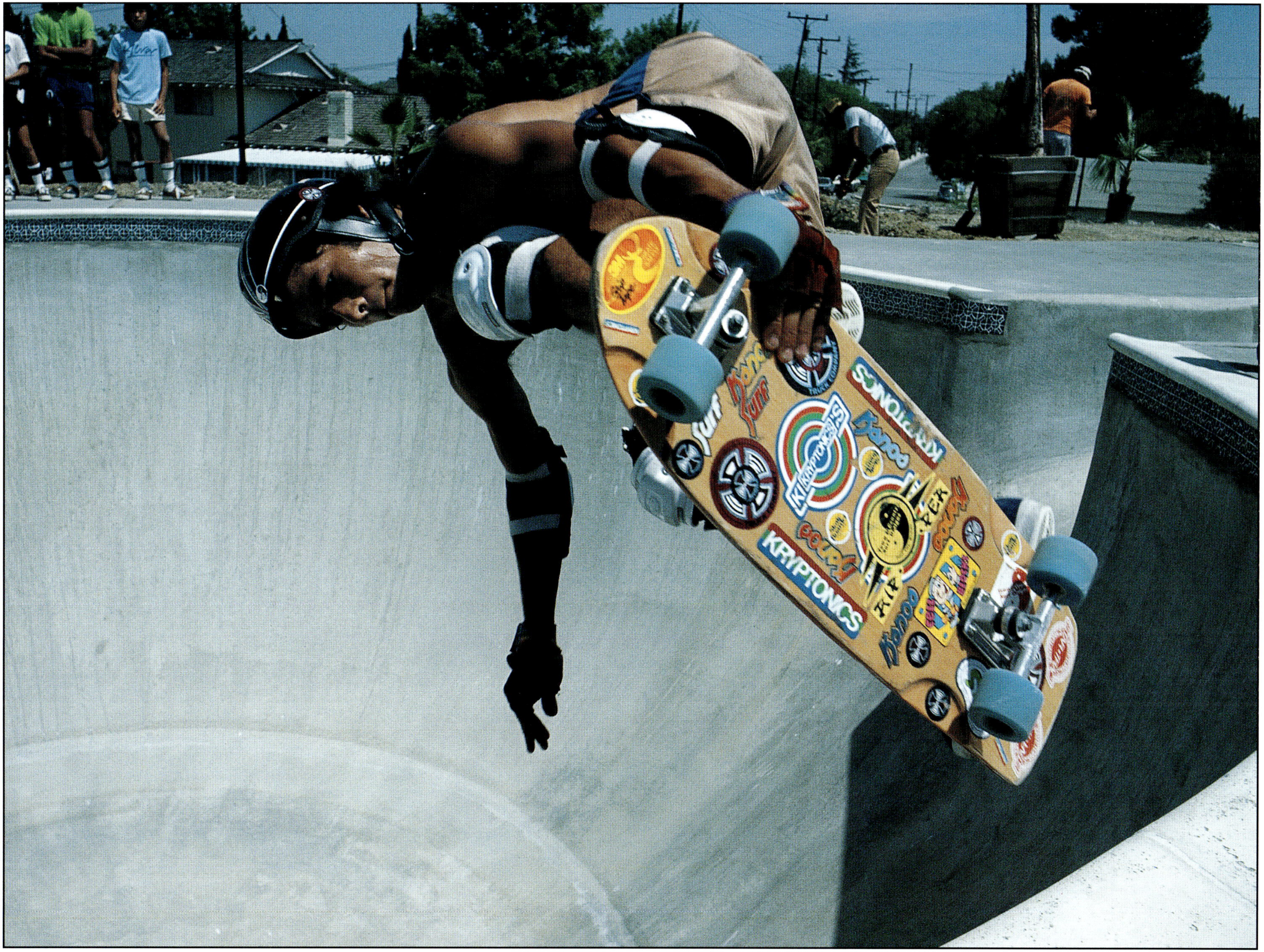

Howard Hood, Steves Southbay pool. *Photo James O'Mahoney.*

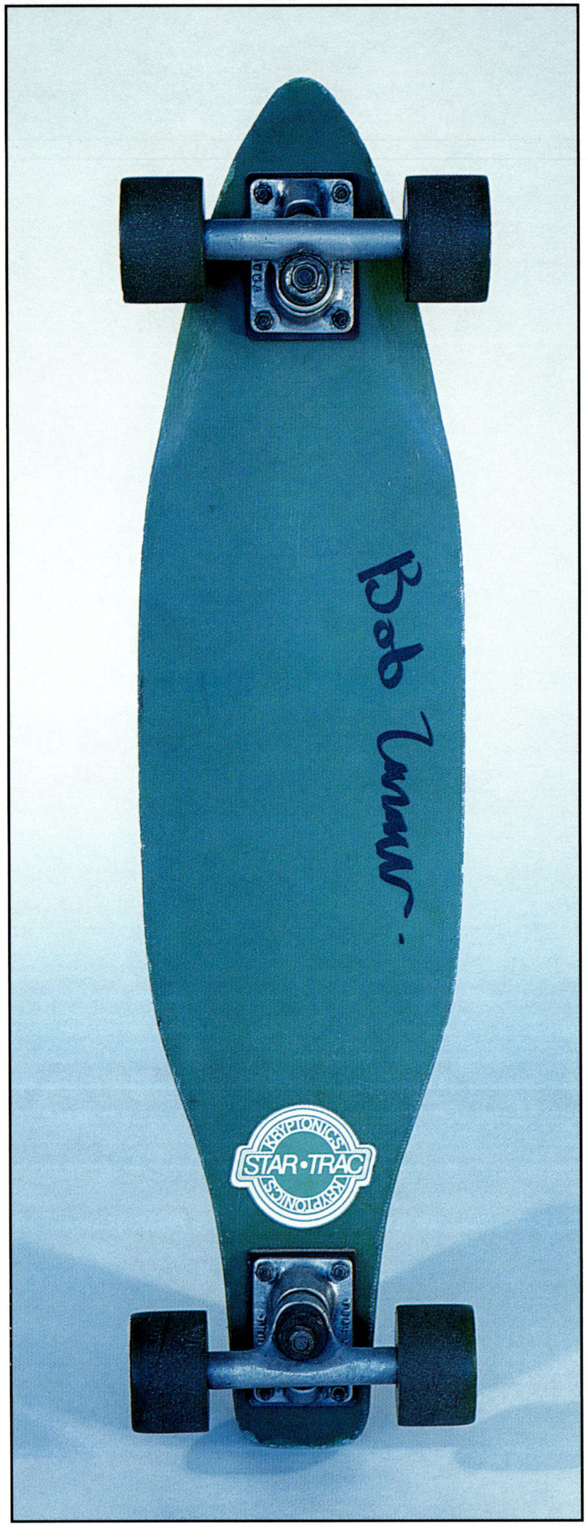
KRYPTONICS
STAR•TRAC
KRYPTONICS

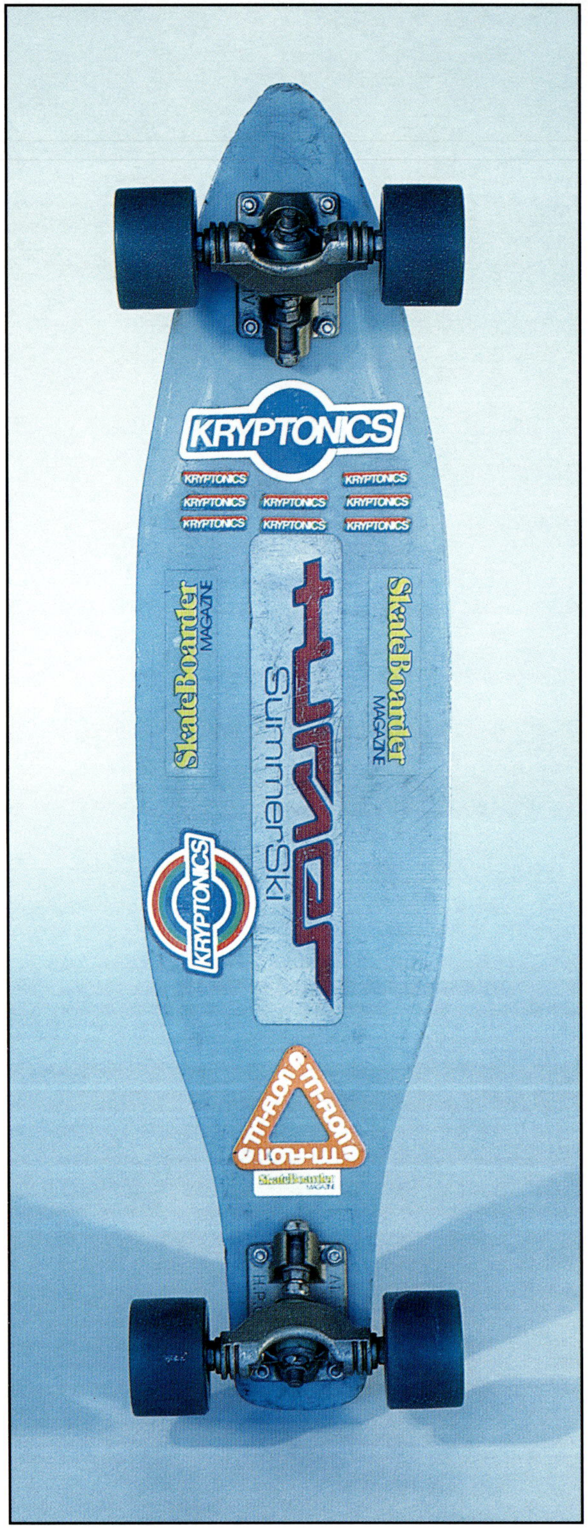
KRYPTONICS
SkateBoarder MAGAZINE
turner
SummerSki
SkateBoarder MAGAZINE
KRYPTONICS
TRI-FLON

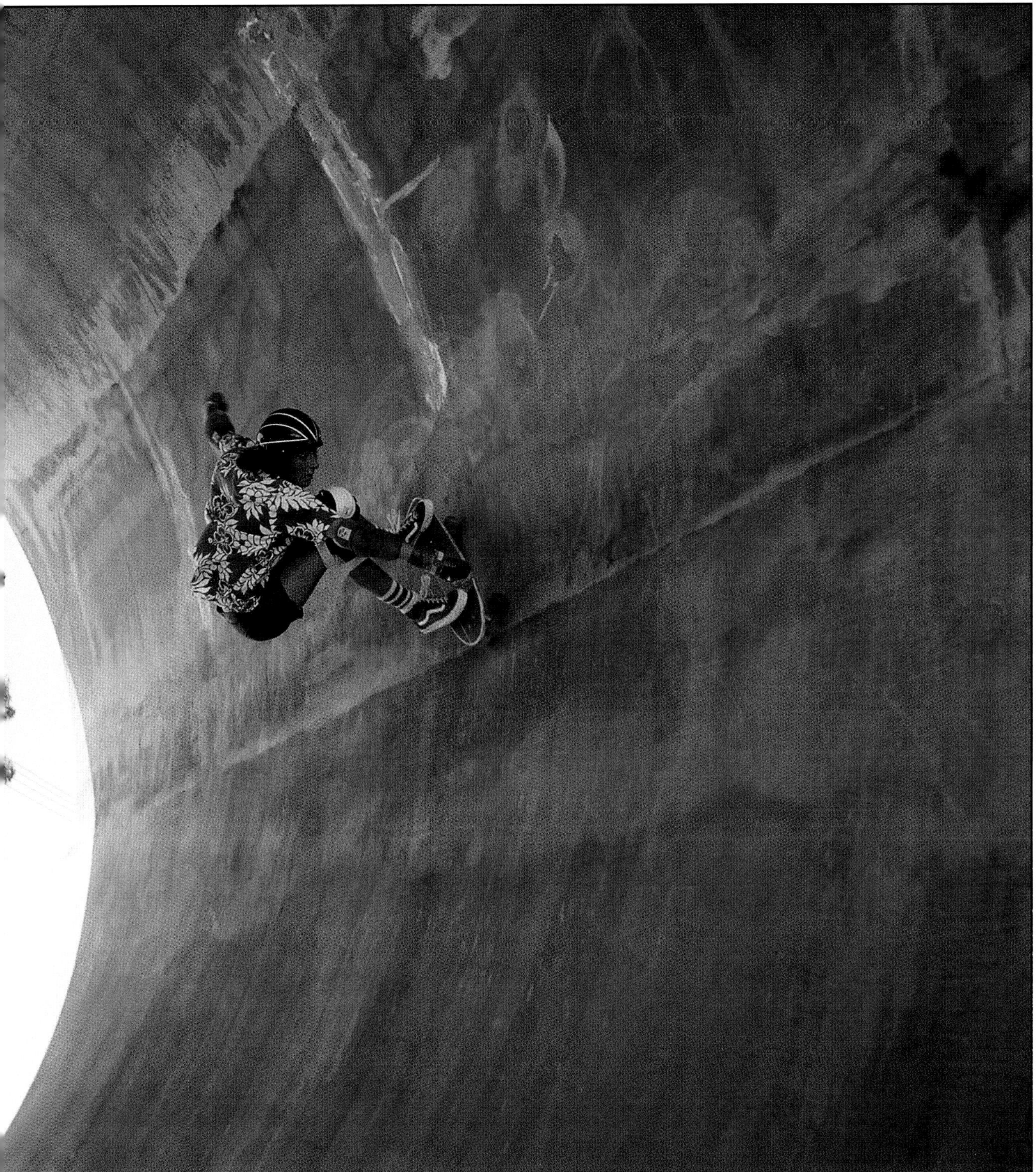

Opposite page
Left: Green Turner with matching green Kryptos wheels, singed by Bob Turner. *Courtesy Ed Economy.* $2000.

Right: Blue Turner, Binkie Concland's personal racer. *Courtesy Ed Economy.* $1500-1800.

Right: Pipe Hanging, Steves pipe contest. *Photo James O'Mahoney.*

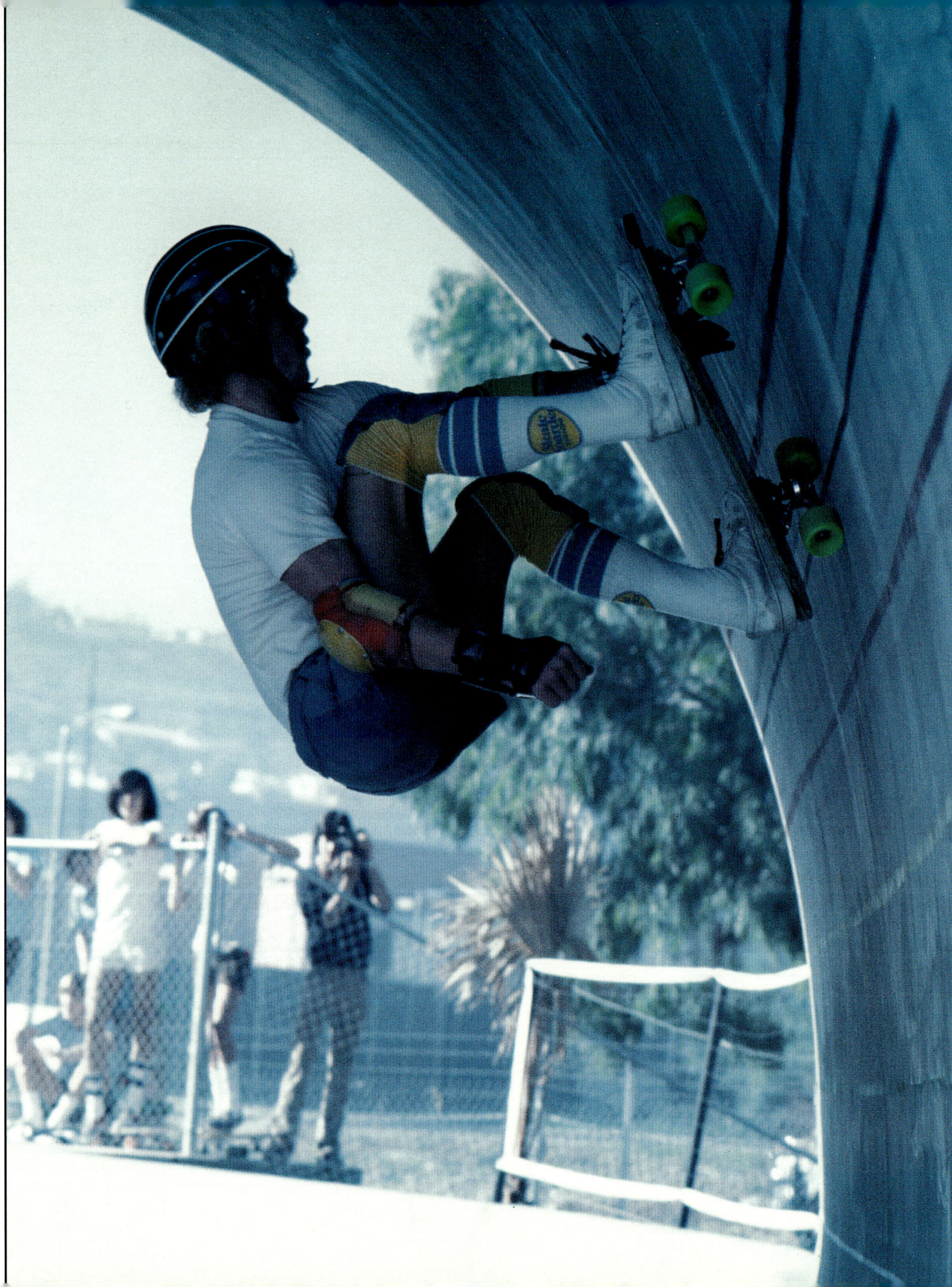

George Orton past vert, pipe contest
Steves Southbay.

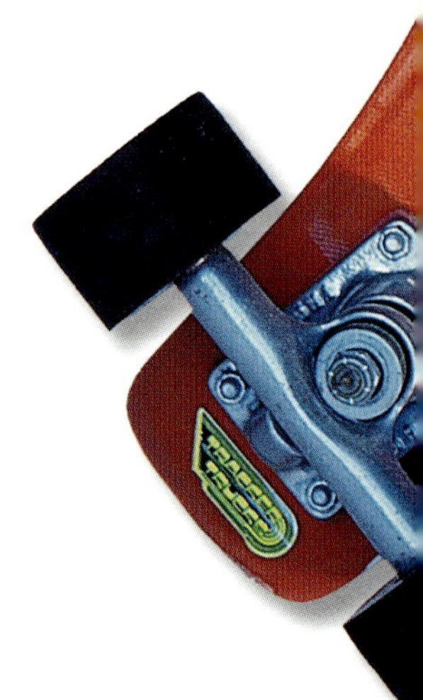

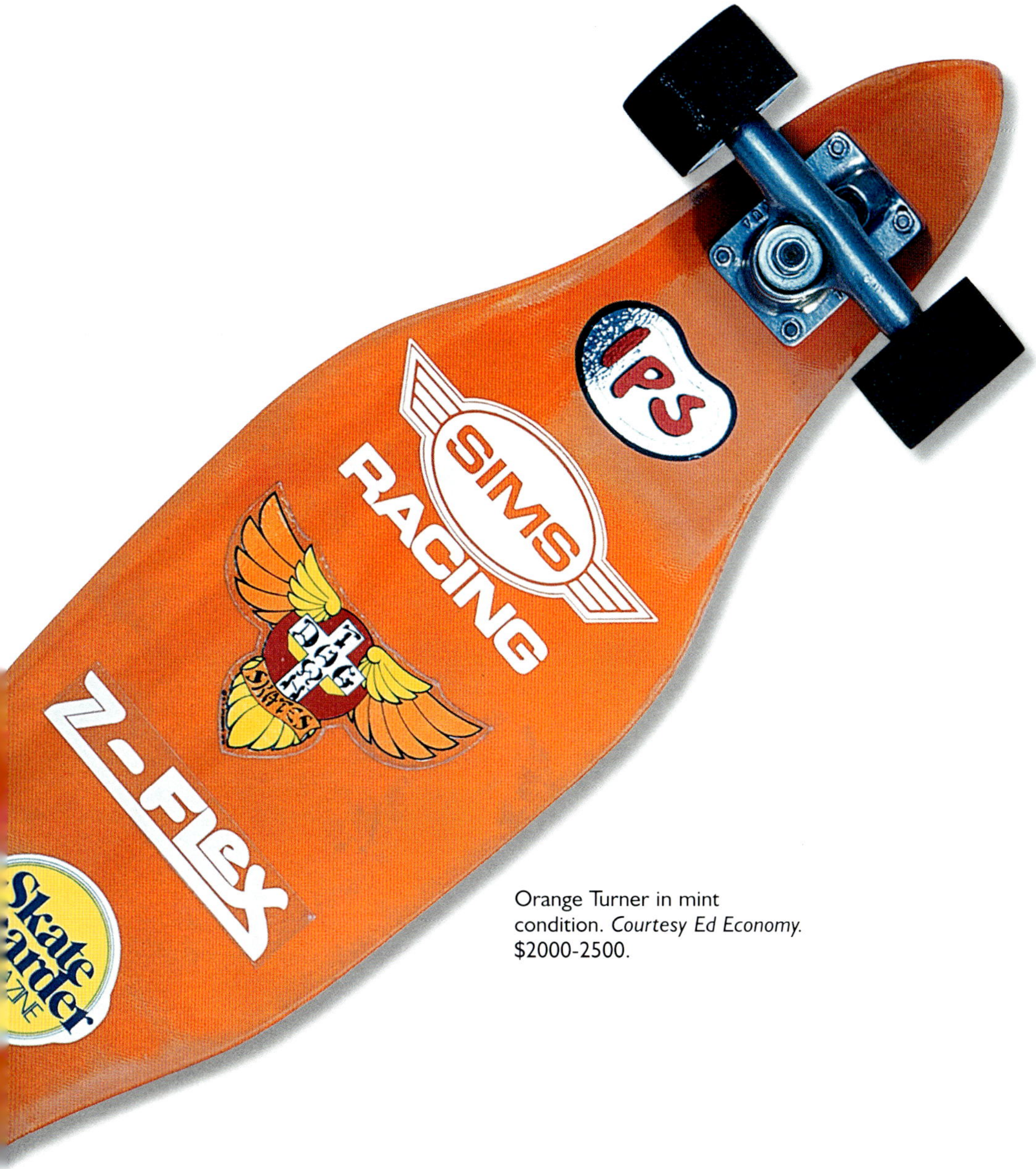

Orange Turner in mint condition. *Courtesy Ed Economy.* $2000-2500.

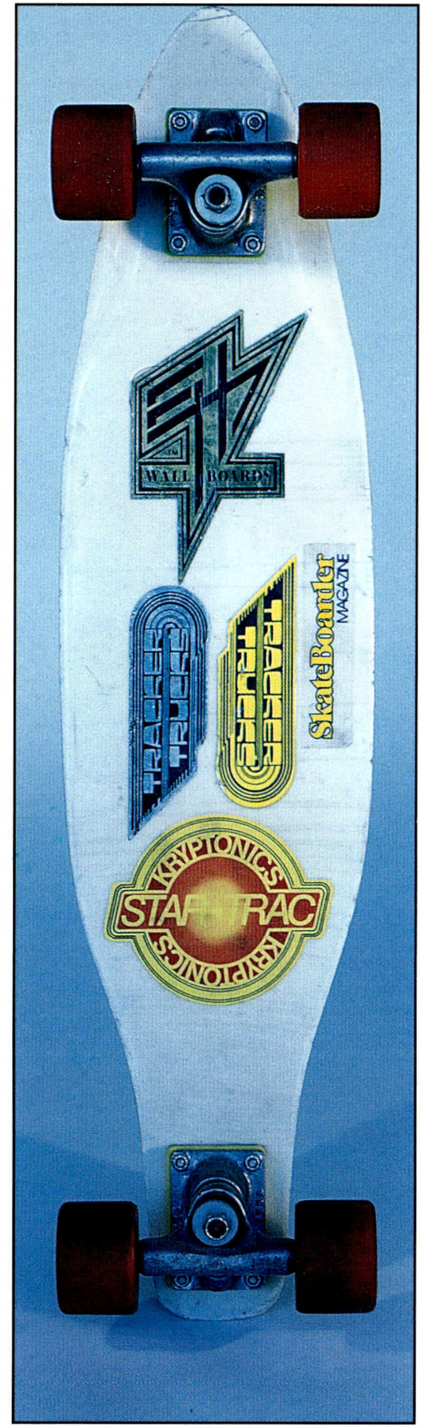

White Turner with tracker trucks. *Courtesy Ed Economy.* $1000-1500.

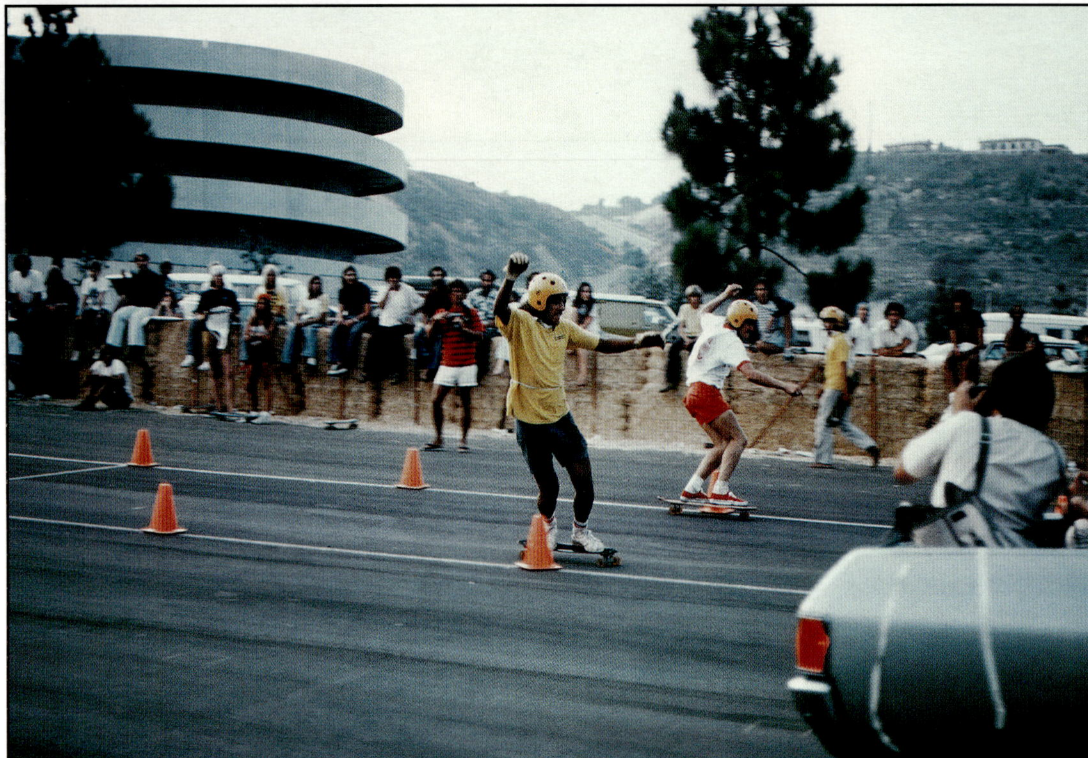

Nayo Jaime filming Chris Yandell in the slalom run for CBS in first world invitational contest. Jack Murphy. *Photo James O'Mahoney*

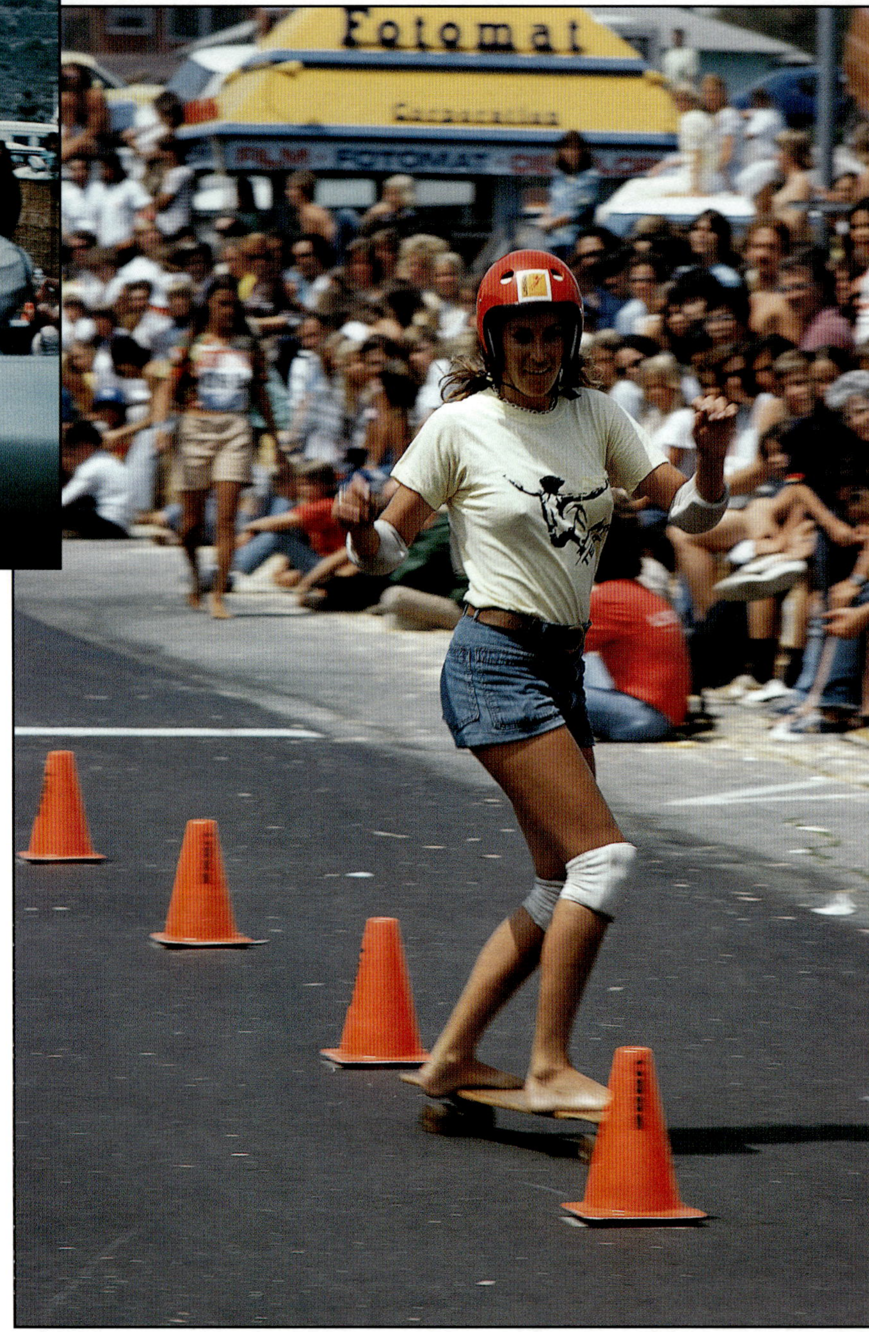

Jennifer Johnson Skateboard Mag Team Rider, Slalom Steves contest. *Photo James O'Mahoney.*

Black Turner. *Courtesy Ed Economy.* $1500-2000.

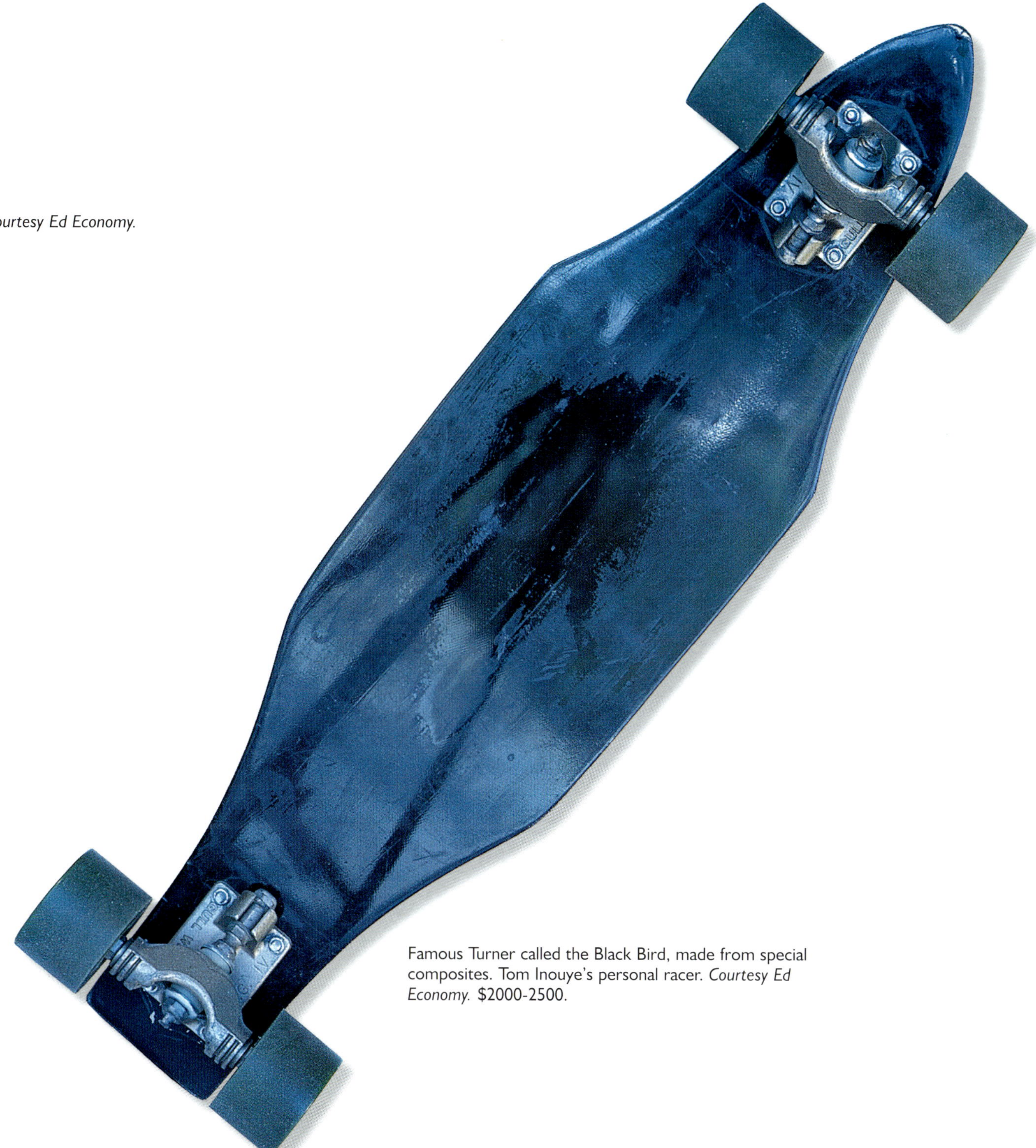

Famous Turner called the Black Bird, made from special composites. Tom Inouye's personal racer. *Courtesy Ed Economy.* $2000-2500.

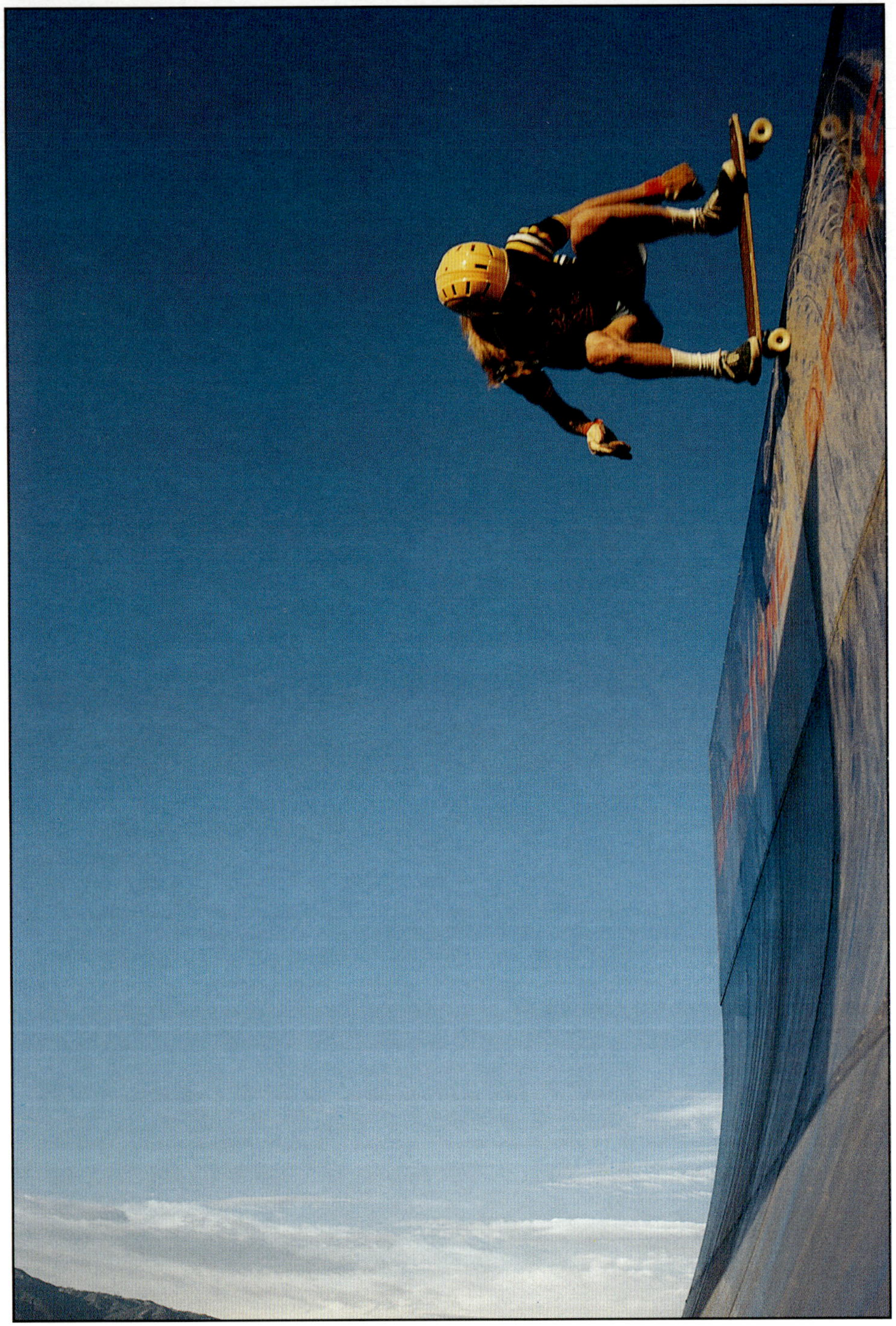

Curt Lindgrin Cal Jam Sky Touch. *Photo James O'Mahoney.*

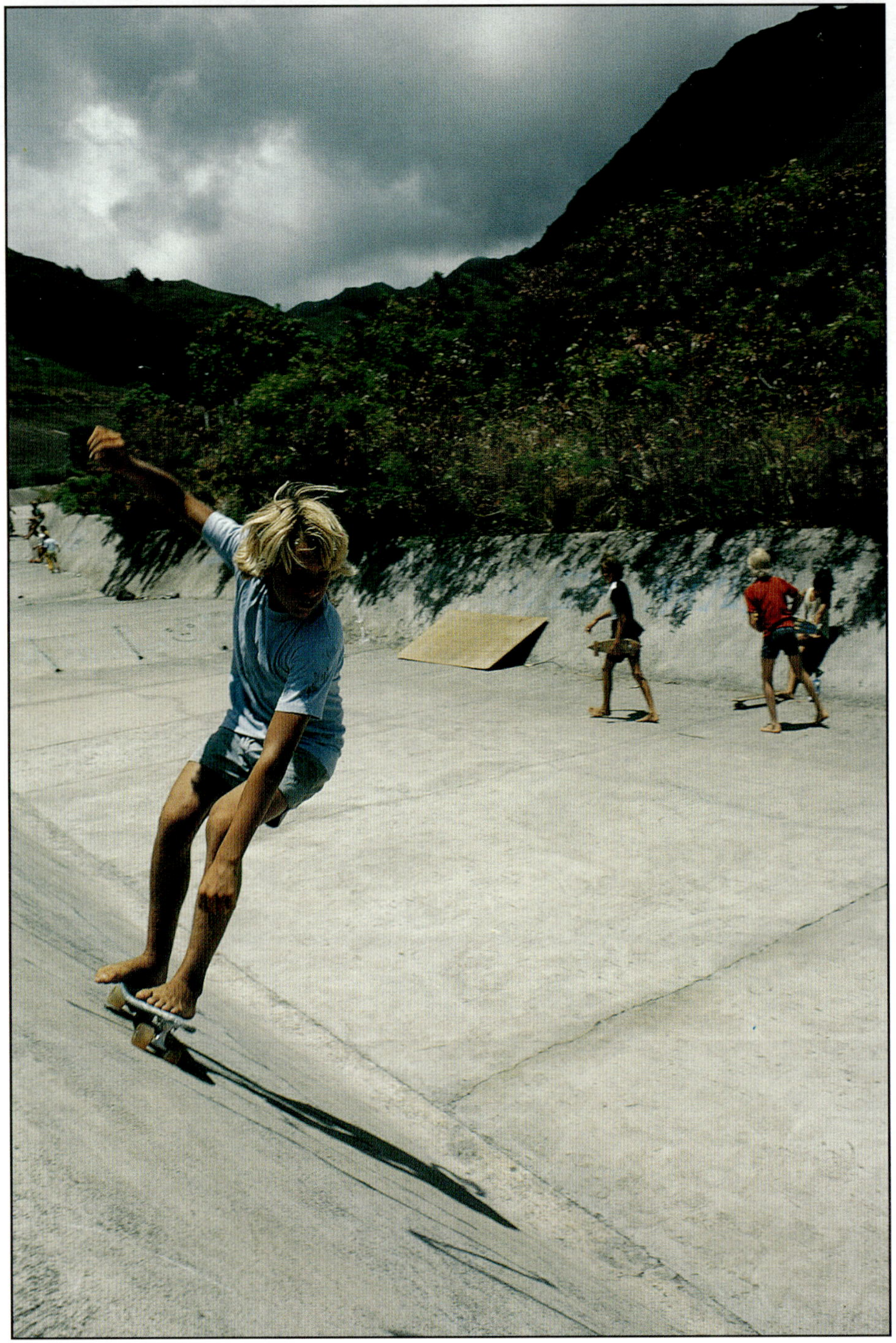

Young Jay Adams takes the drop. *Photo James O'Mahoney.*

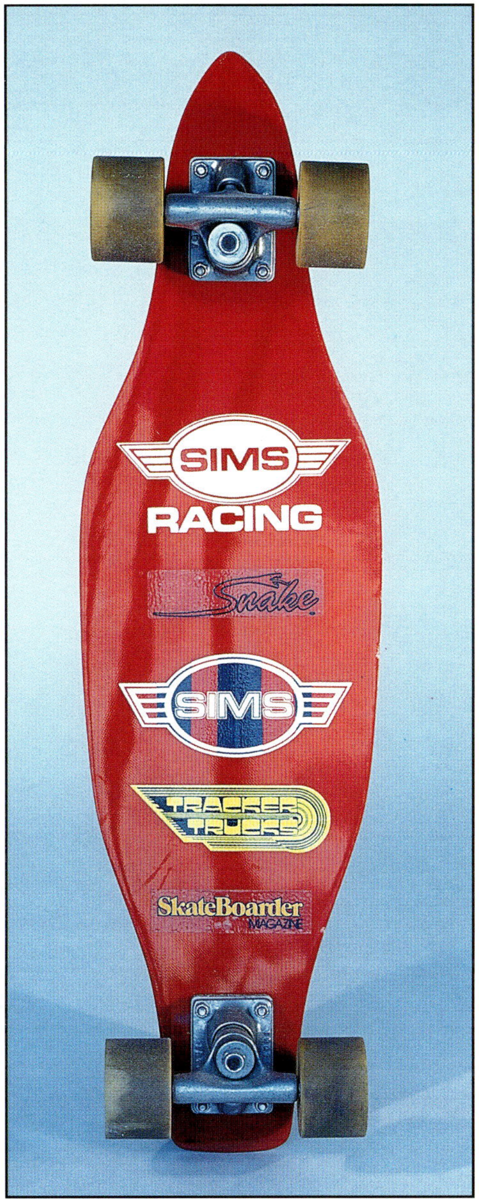

Red Turner with panther wheels and tracker trucks. *Courtesy Ed Economy.* $1500-2000.

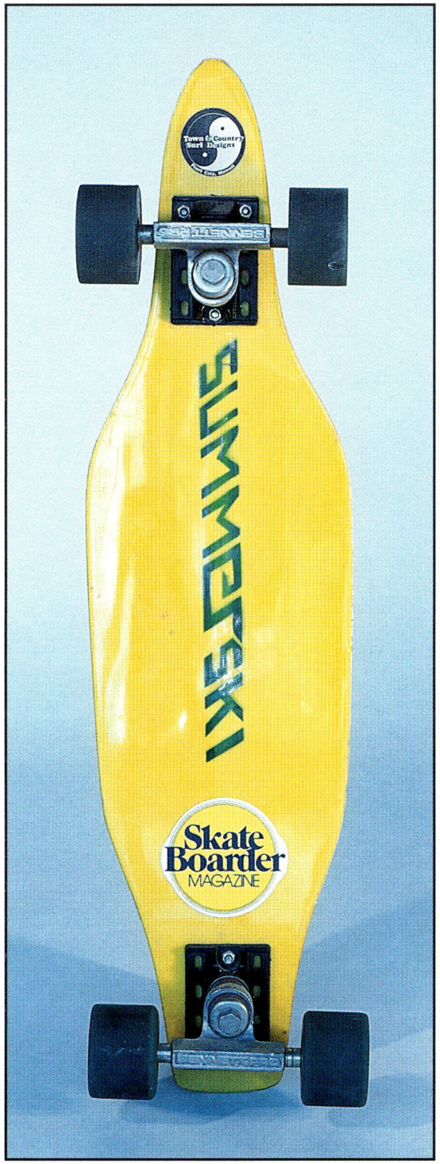

Yellow Turner with the Summerski logo, Benit trucks. Note the snow connection. *Courtesy Ed Economy.*

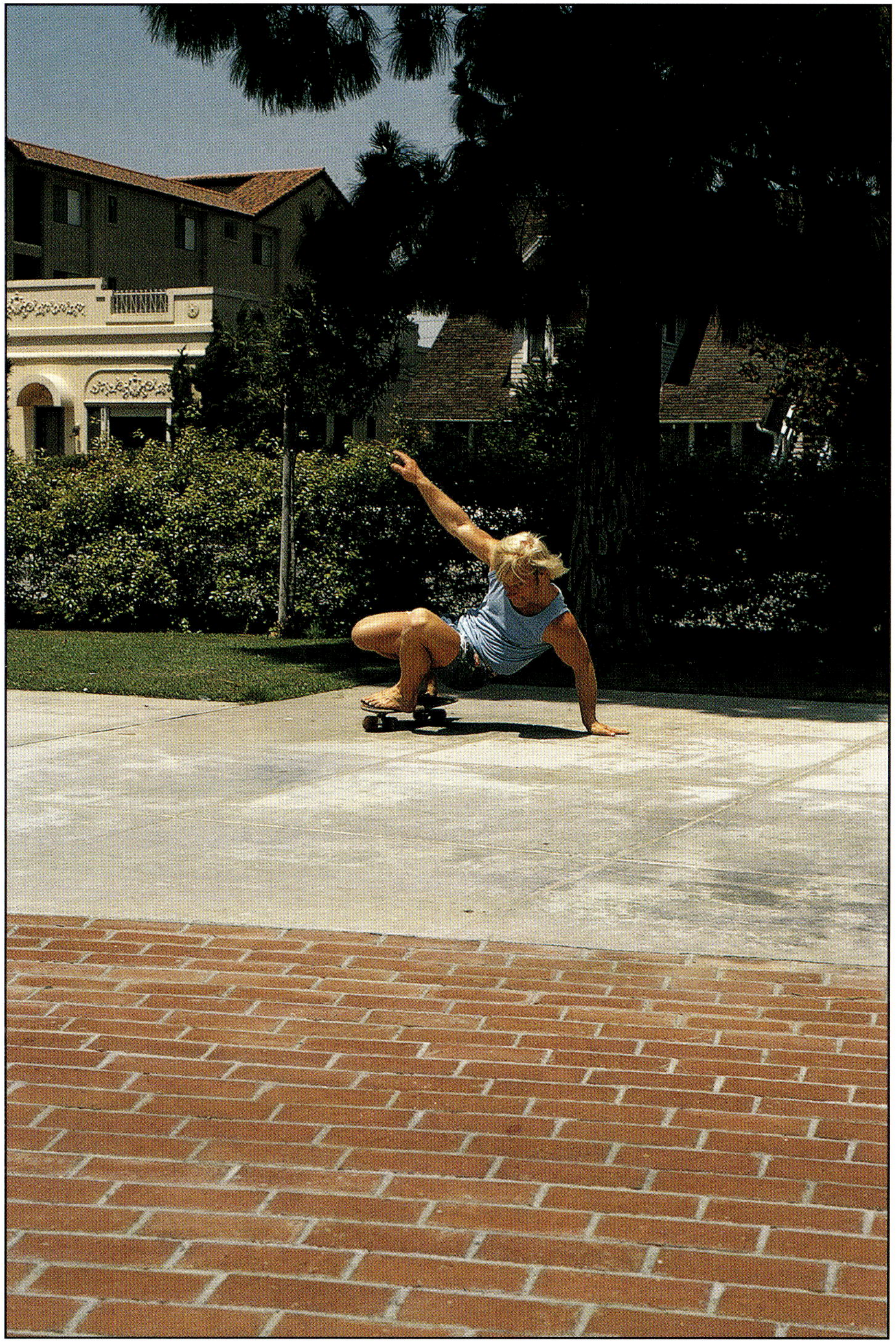

Russ Howell. *Courtesy of Leroy Grannis.*

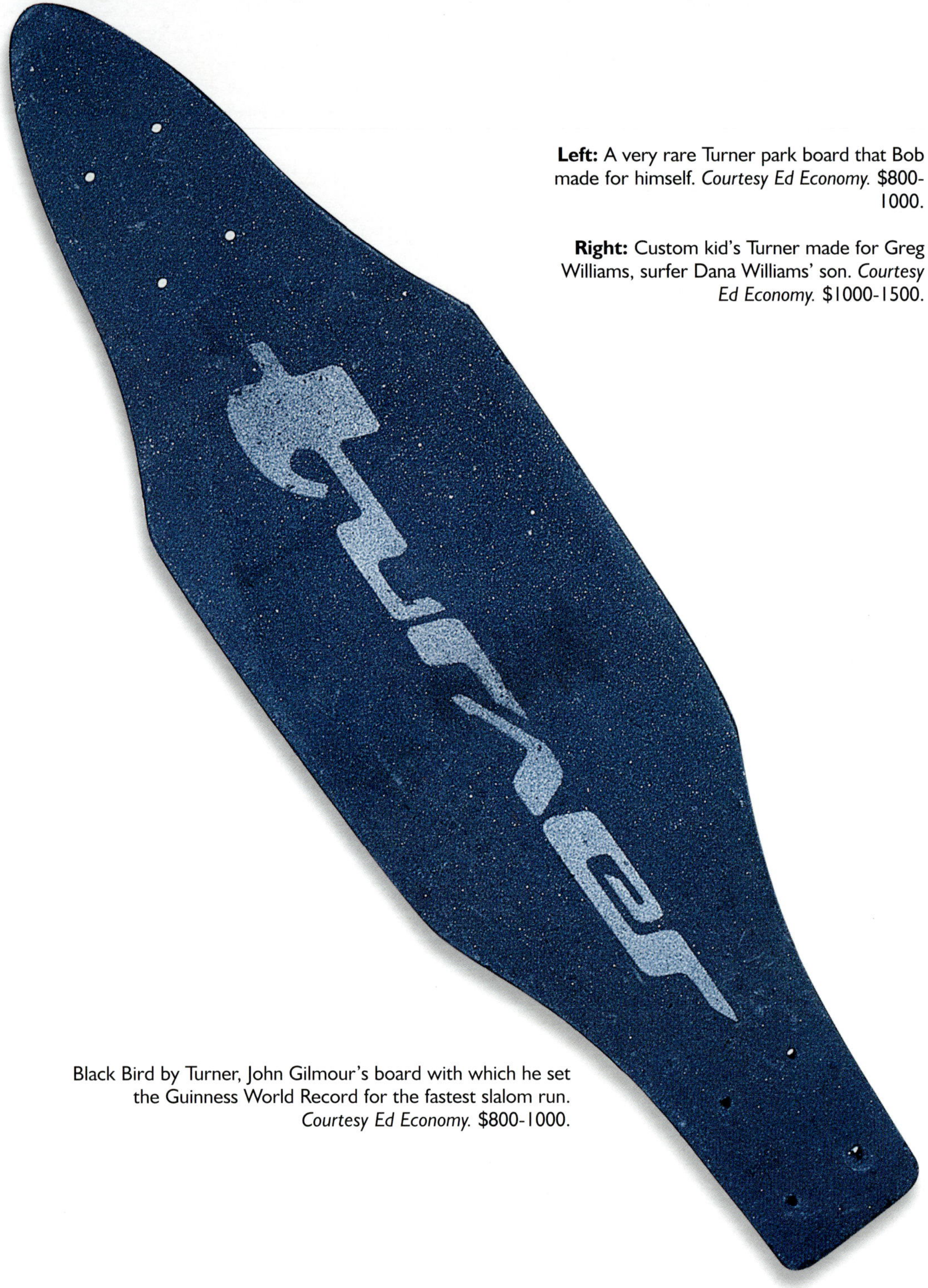

Black Bird by Turner, John Gilmour's board with which he set the Guinness World Record for the fastest slalom run. *Courtesy Ed Economy.* $800-1000.

Left: A very rare Turner park board that Bob made for himself. *Courtesy Ed Economy.* $800-1000.

Right: Custom kid's Turner made for Greg Williams, surfer Dana Williams' son. *Courtesy Ed Economy.* $1000-1500.

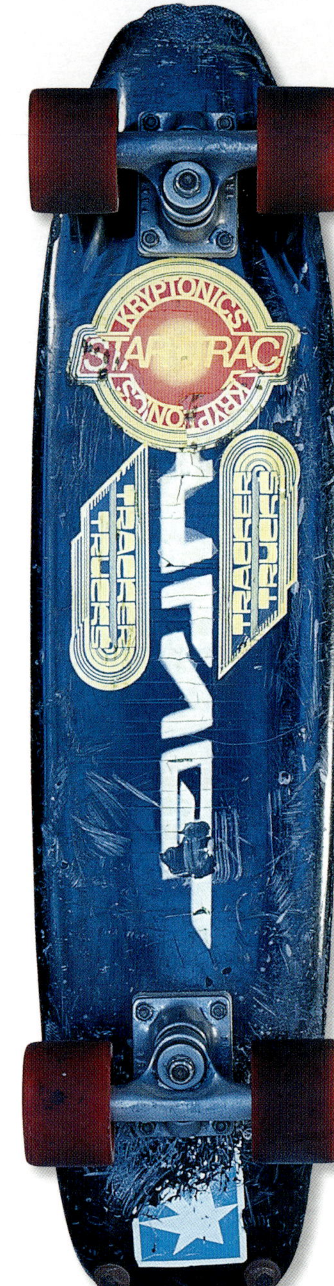

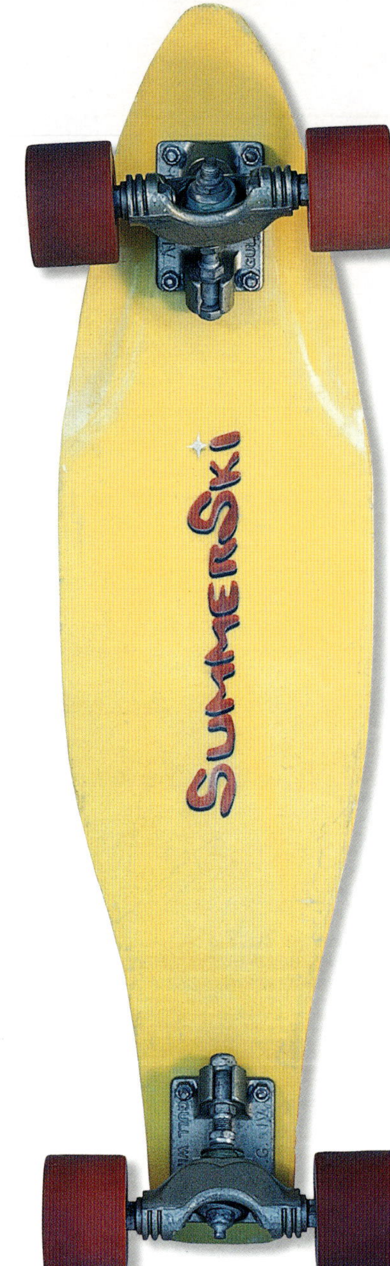

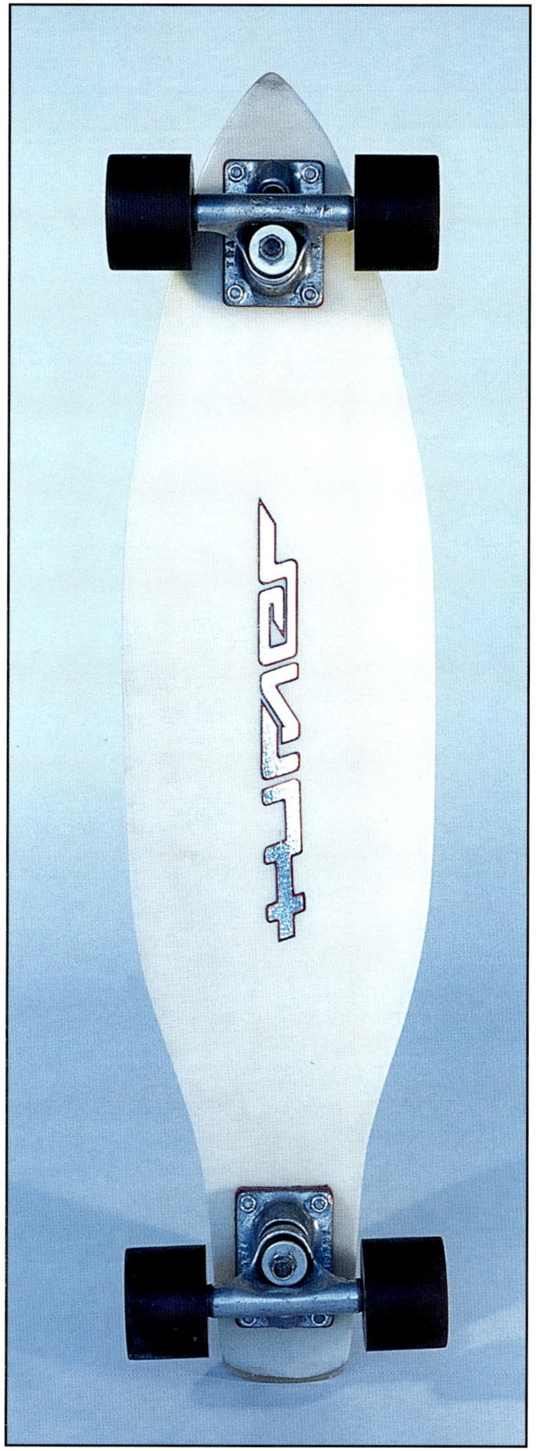

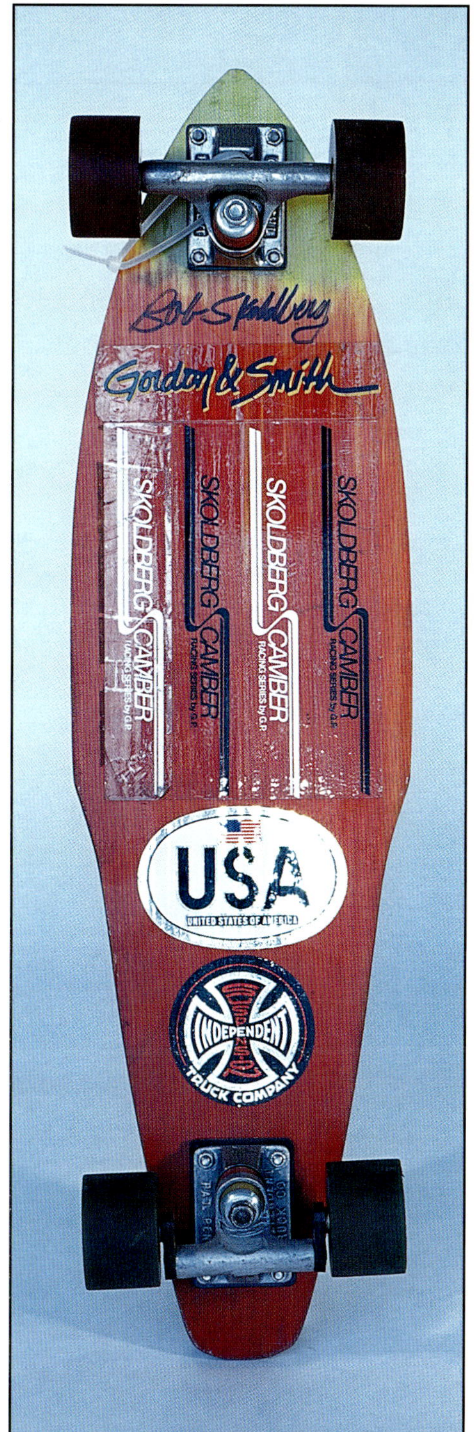

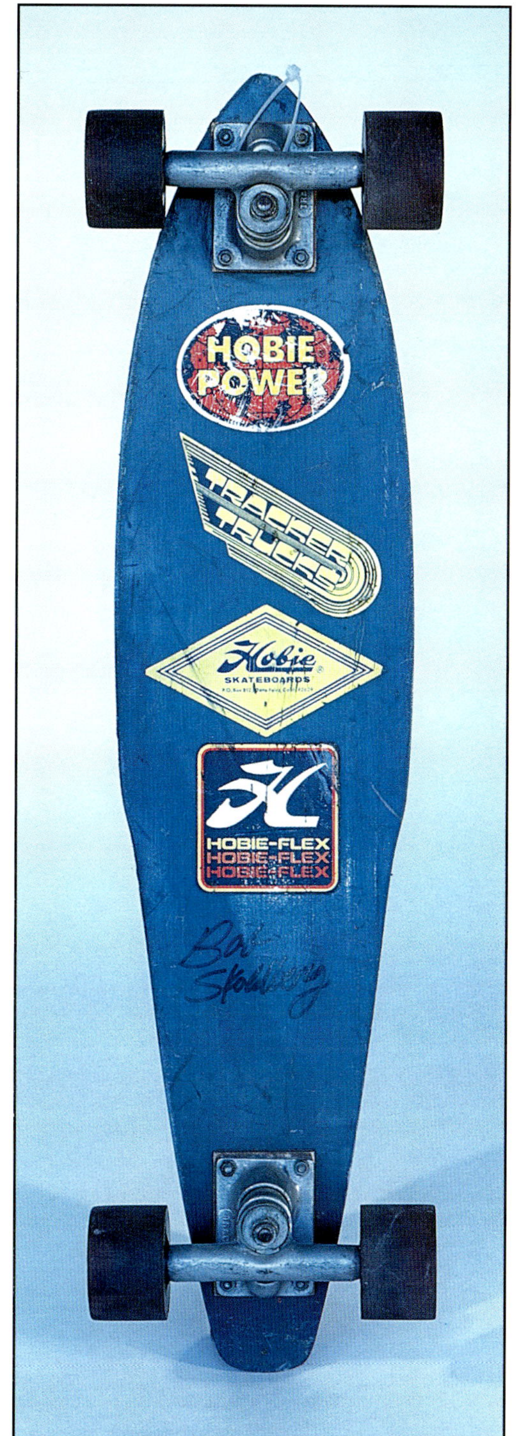

Left to right: White Turner, Adam Terimame's personal racer. *Courtesy Ed Economy.* $1000-1500.

Gordon and Smith board, Bob Scolberg's personal board with which he won the World Championships in Canada. The back truck is a rare independent, only eight sets were made. *Courtesy Ed Economy.* The truck alone is worth $700.The board and trucks together are $1000-1500.

Hobie board, Bob Scolberg model, singed by Bob. *Courtesy Ed Economy.* $1500-2000.

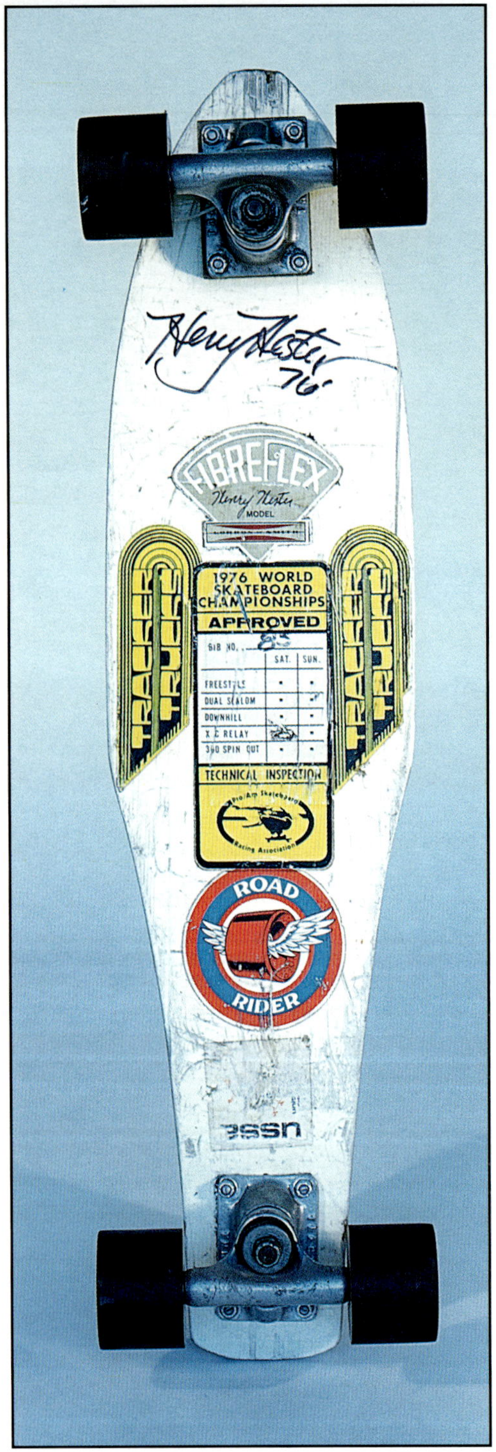

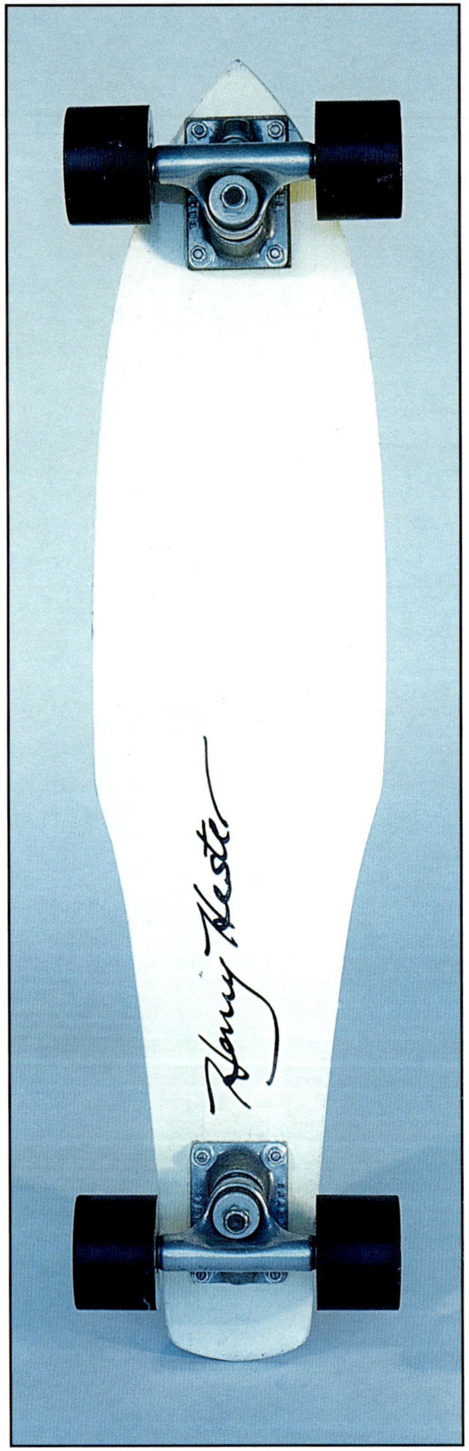

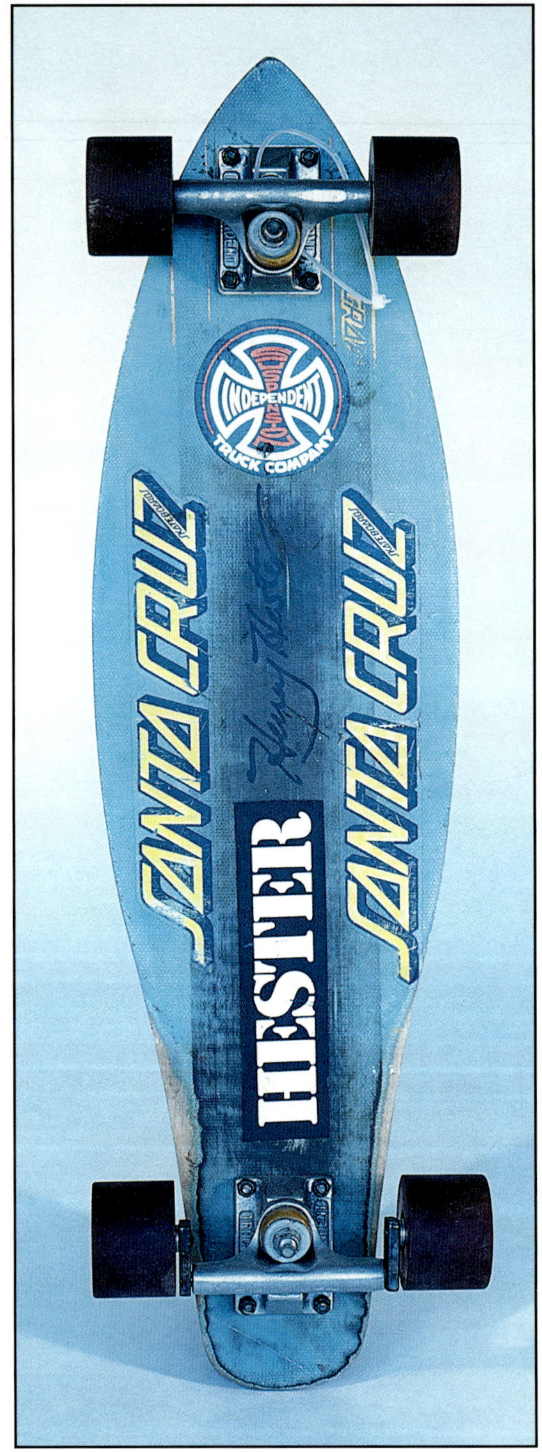

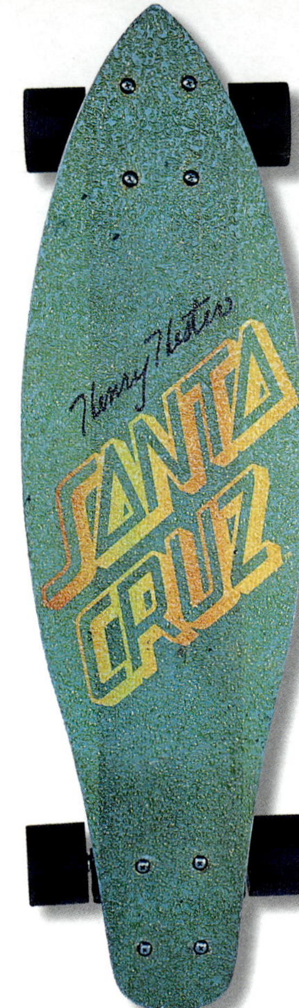

Left & above: Blue Santa Cruz slalom Henry Hester's racer from the 1980s graphite.$1500-2000. *Courtesy Ed Economy.*

Far left: The rarest of all Fiber Flexes ever made, and the one with which Henry Hester won the 1976 Carlsbad World Championships. Singed by Henry. *Courtesy Ed Economy.* $3000-5000.

Center: Henry Hester is considered to be the best racer from the 1970s. This Gordon and Smith is the prototype board for the Hester Fiber Flex model. *Courtesy Ed Economy.* $1000-1500.

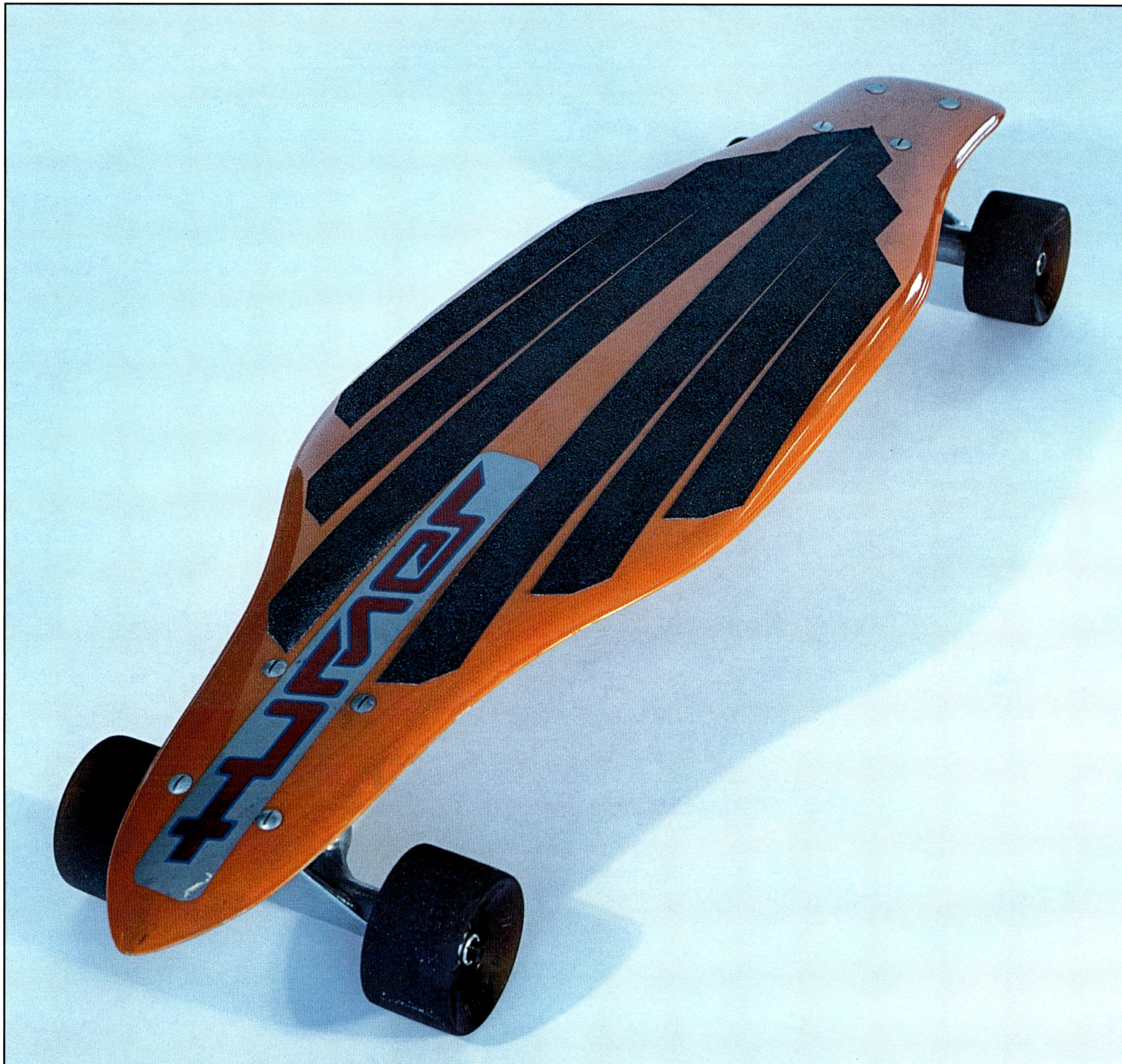

Bob Turner would make a skateboard according to your weight, so that it would have just the right flex. Therefore, every Turner is a custom board . *Courtesy Ed Economy.* $800-1000.

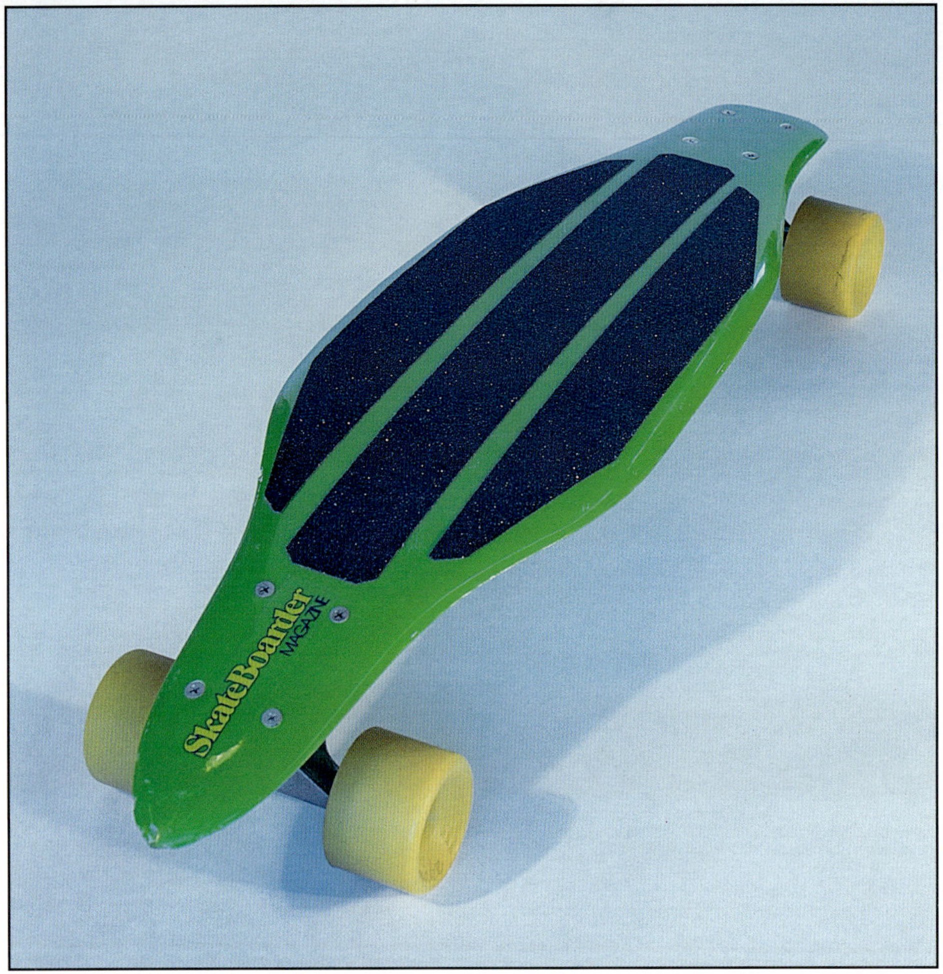

Ed Economy. thinks that racing boards are extremely collectible because almost every one was ridden by a famous team rider. Green Turner. *Courtesy Ed Economy.* $800-1000.

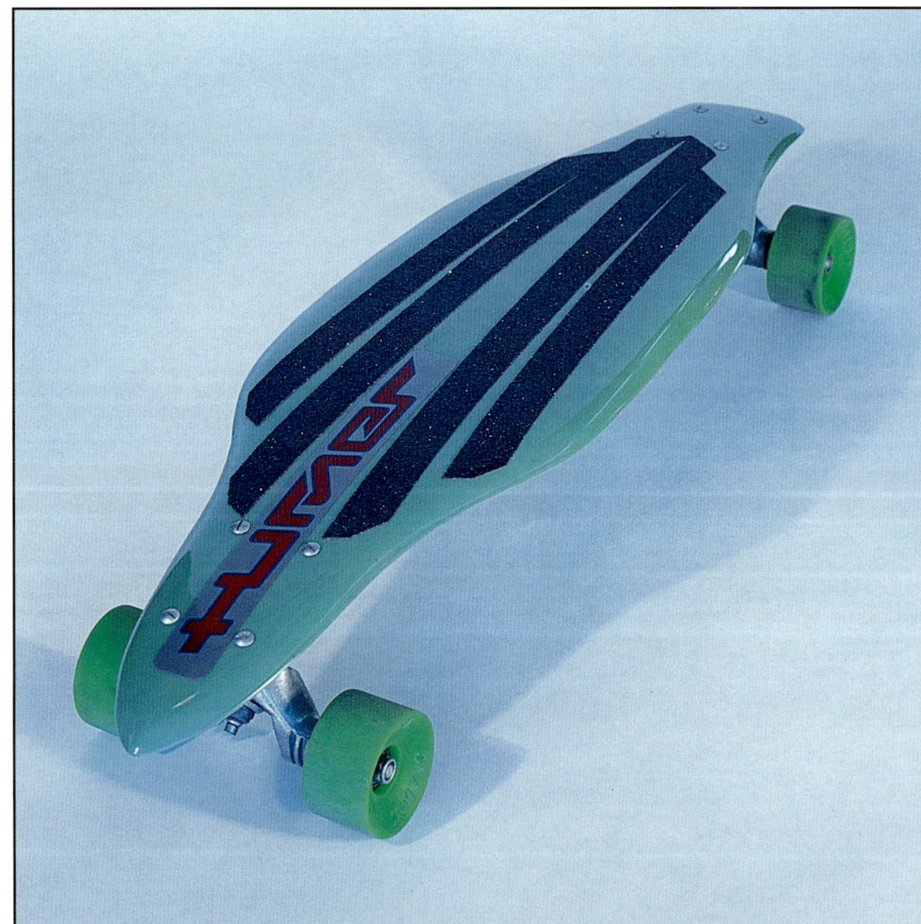

Another fine Turner. *Courtesy Ed Economy.*

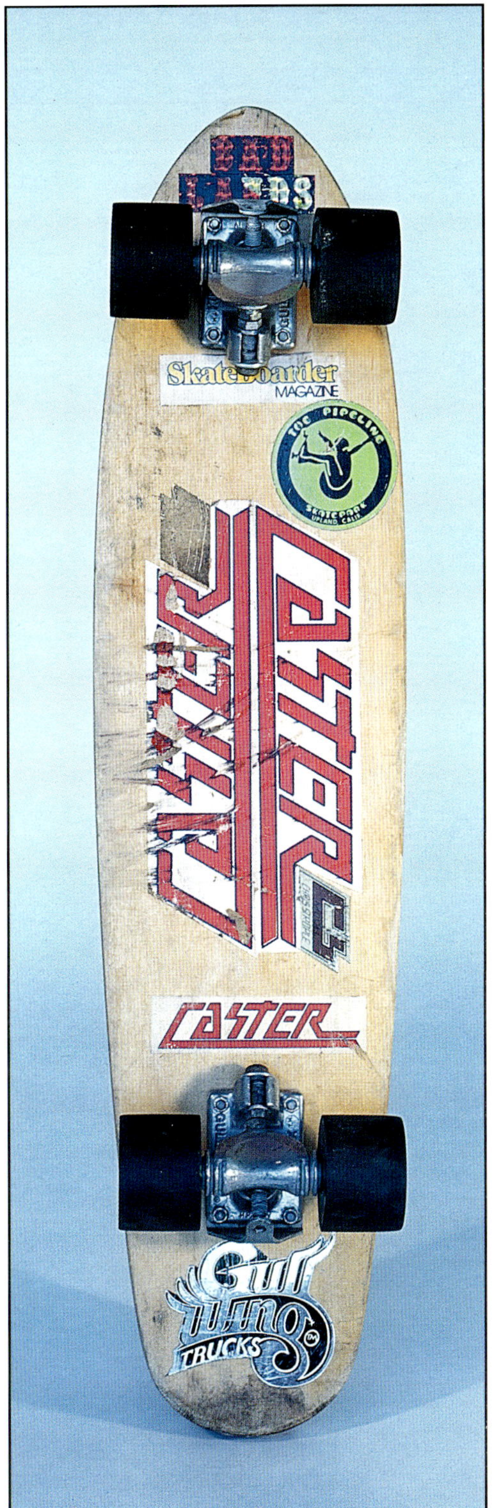

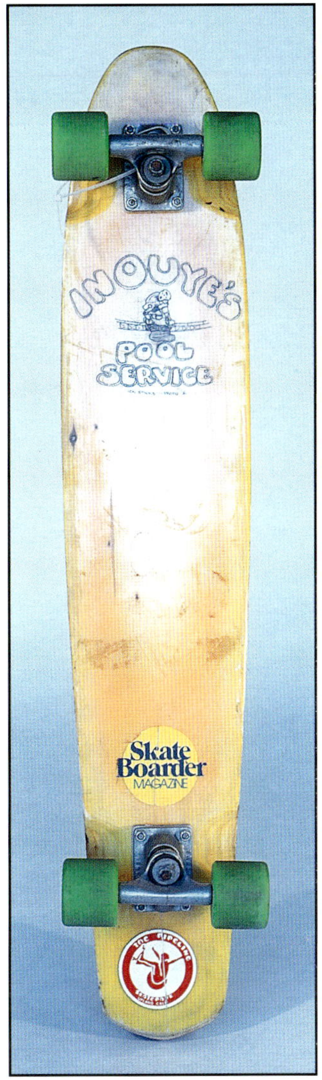

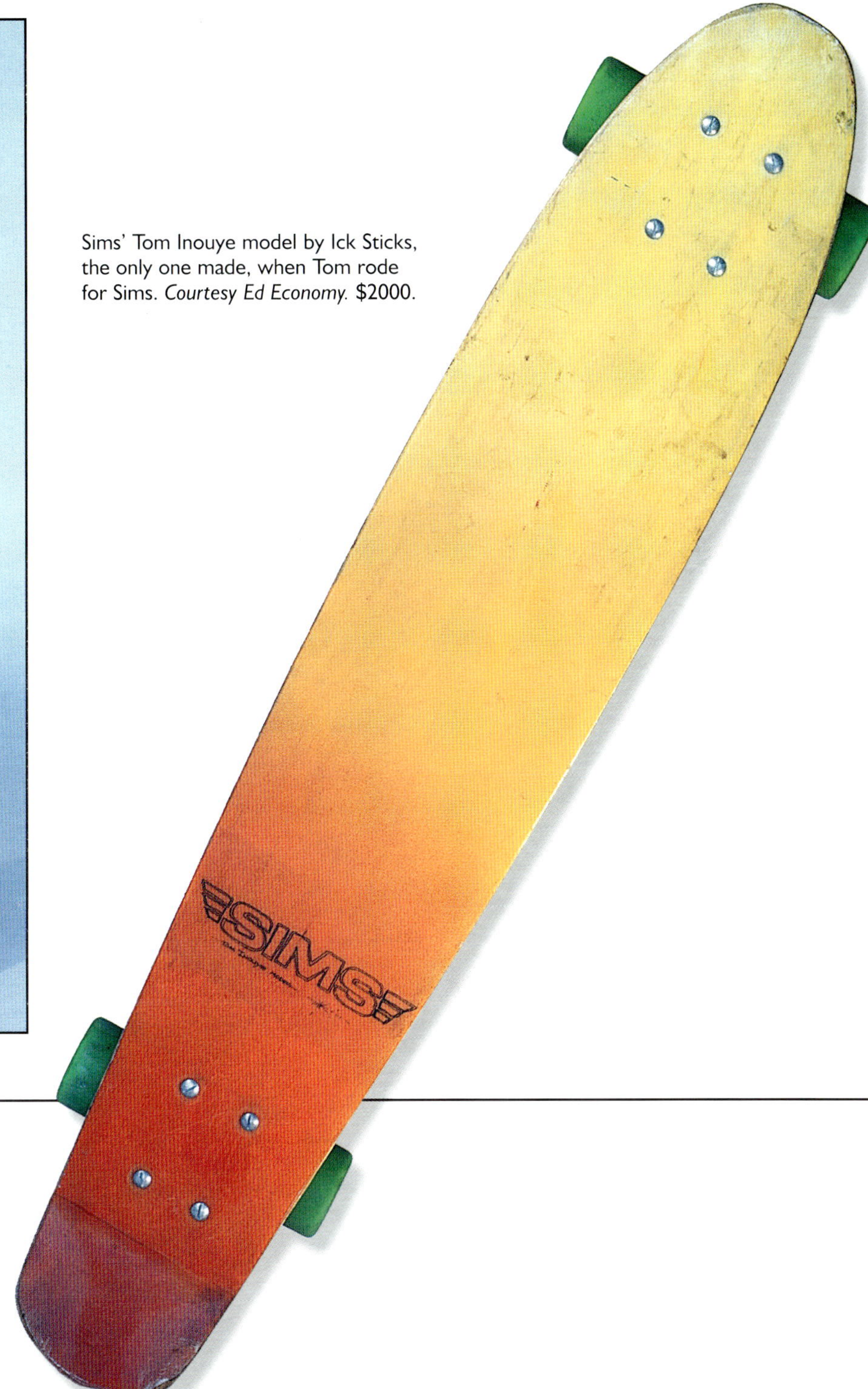

Sims' Tom Inouye model by Ick Sticks, the only one made, when Tom rode for Sims. *Courtesy Ed Economy.* $2000.

Early Chris Strople model by Caster, the famous Upland Park board. *Courtesy Ed Economy.* $1000-1500.

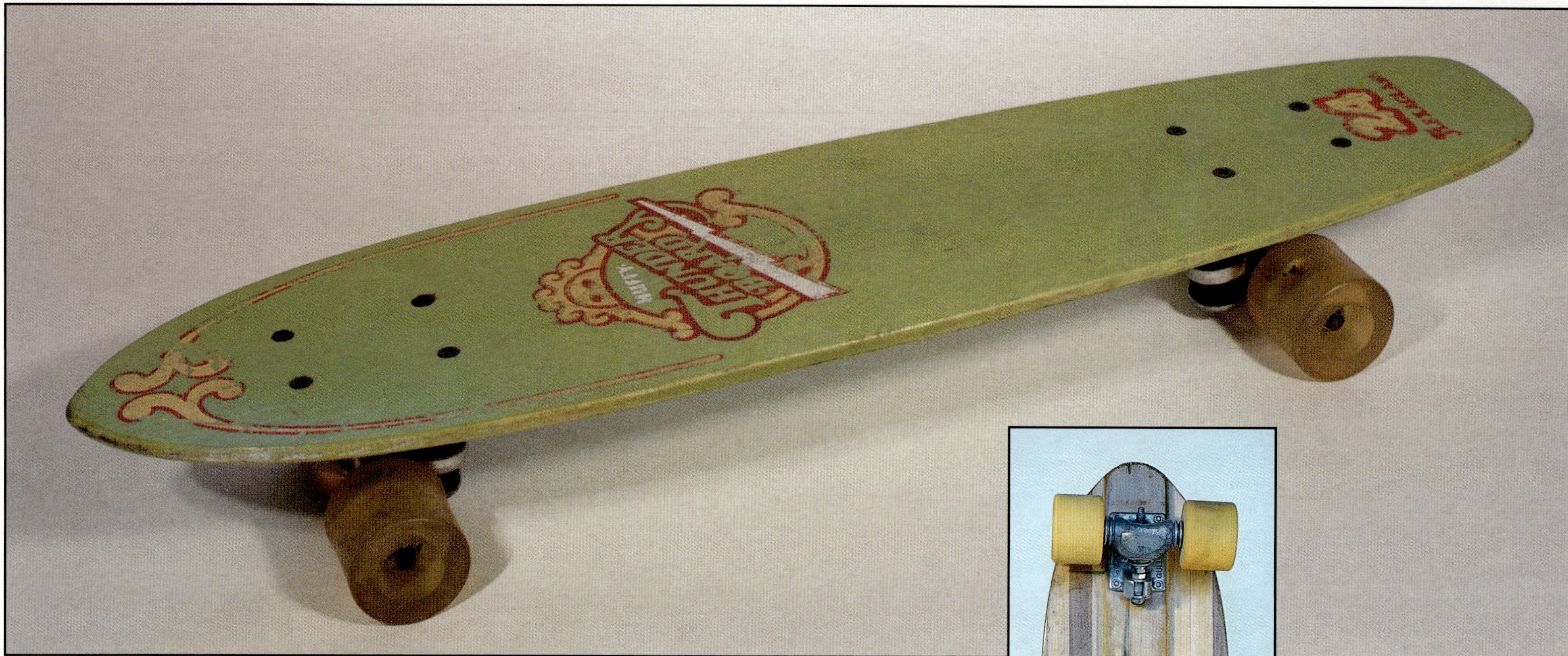

Huffy Thunder Board of fiberglass. *Courtesy Ricky Young Family.* $150-200.

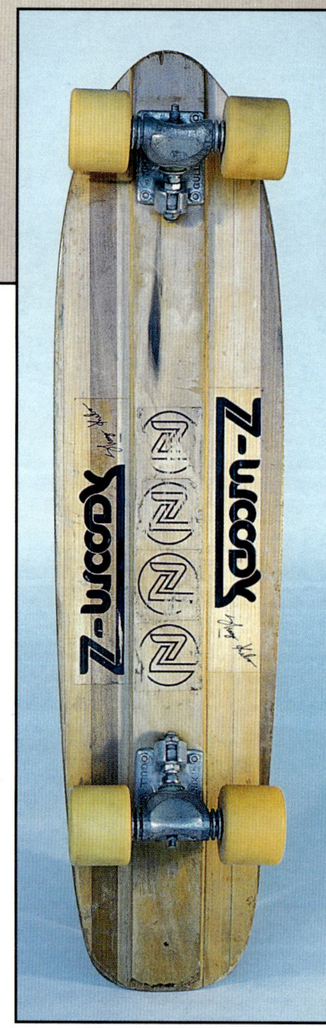

Z-woody board, singed by Shogo Kubo, with gullwings, trucks, and Sims wheels. *Courtesy Ed Economy.* $500-800.

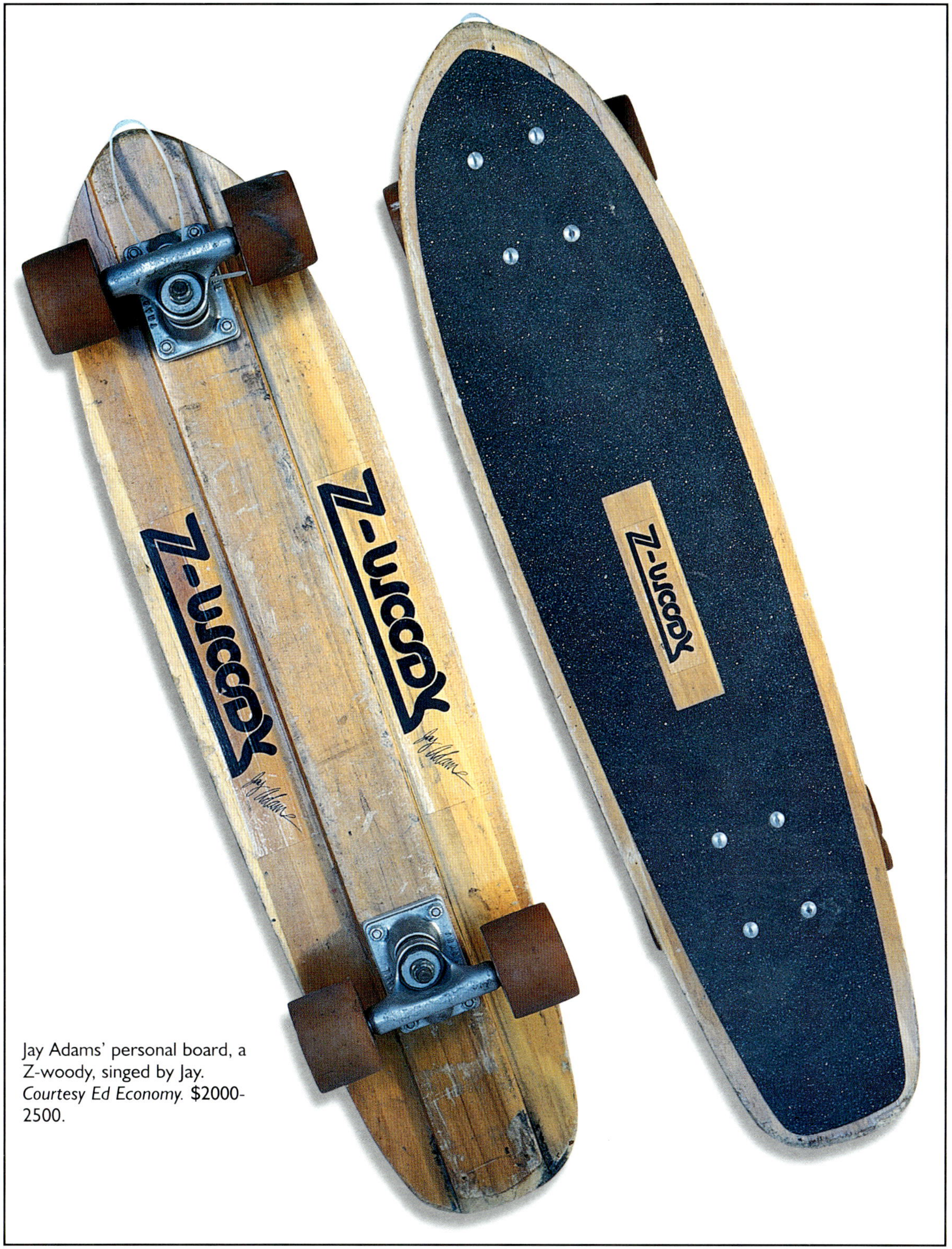

Jay Adams' personal board, a Z-woody, singed by Jay. *Courtesy Ed Economy.* $2000-2500.

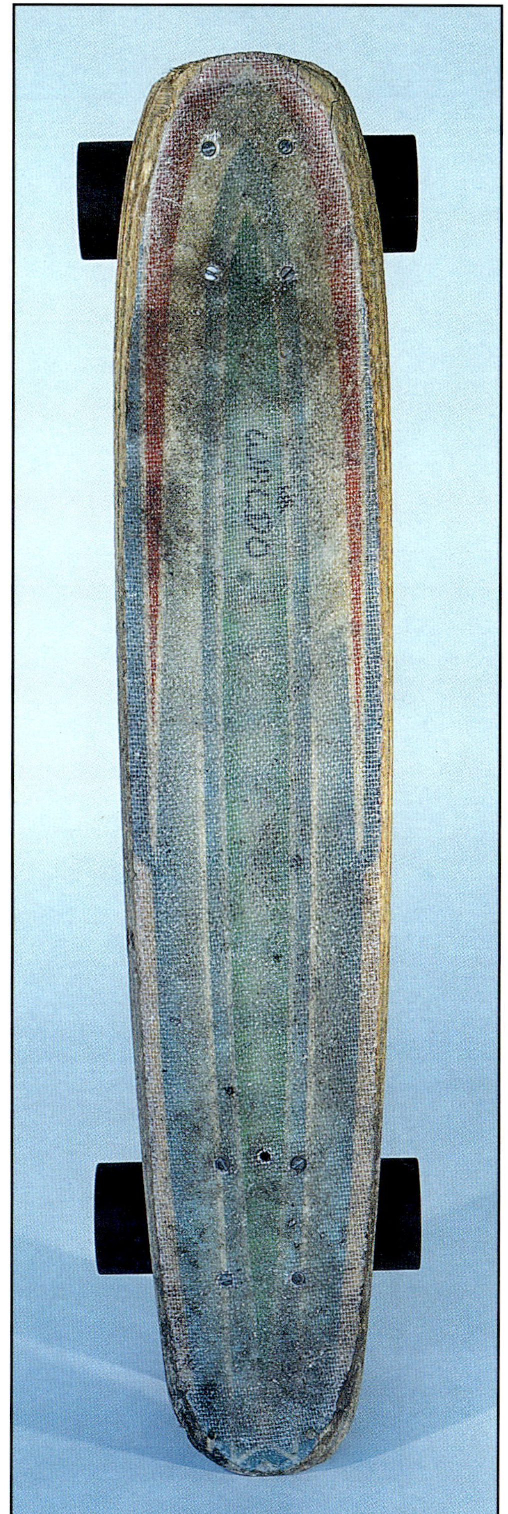

Waldo Autrey's personal board, custom made. *Courtesy Ed Economy.* $1000-1500.

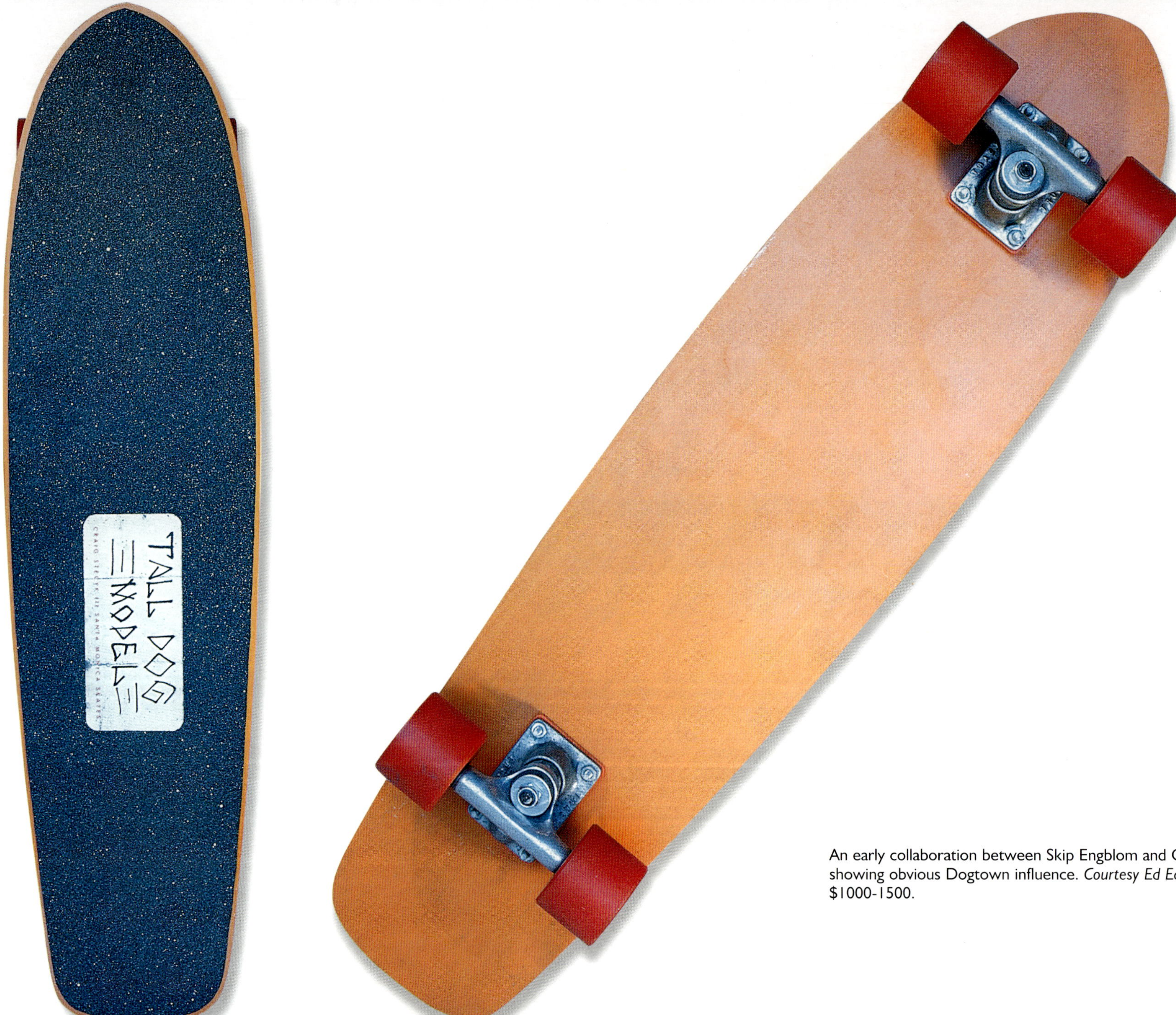

An early collaboration between Skip Engblom and Craig Stecyk, showing obvious Dogtown influence. *Courtesy Ed Economy.* $1000-1500.

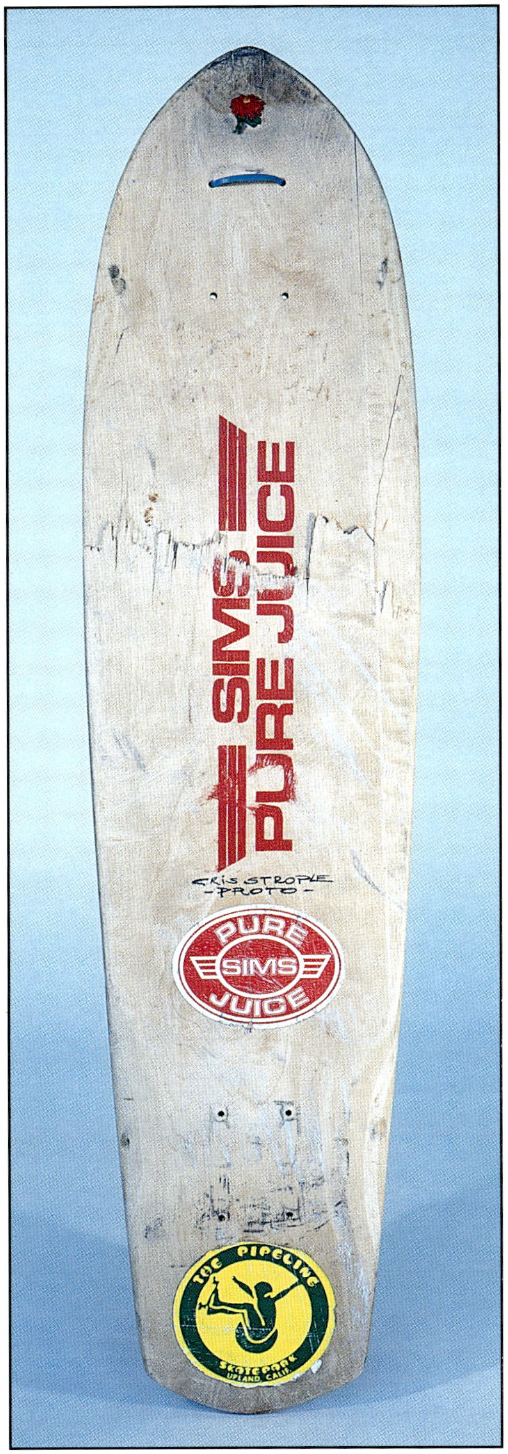

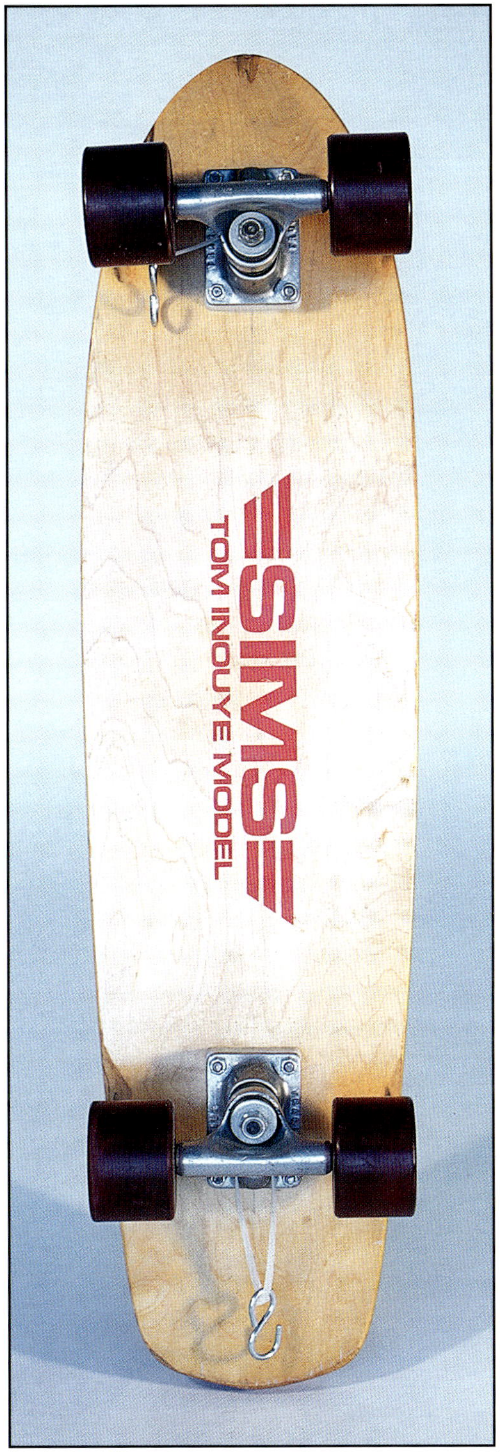

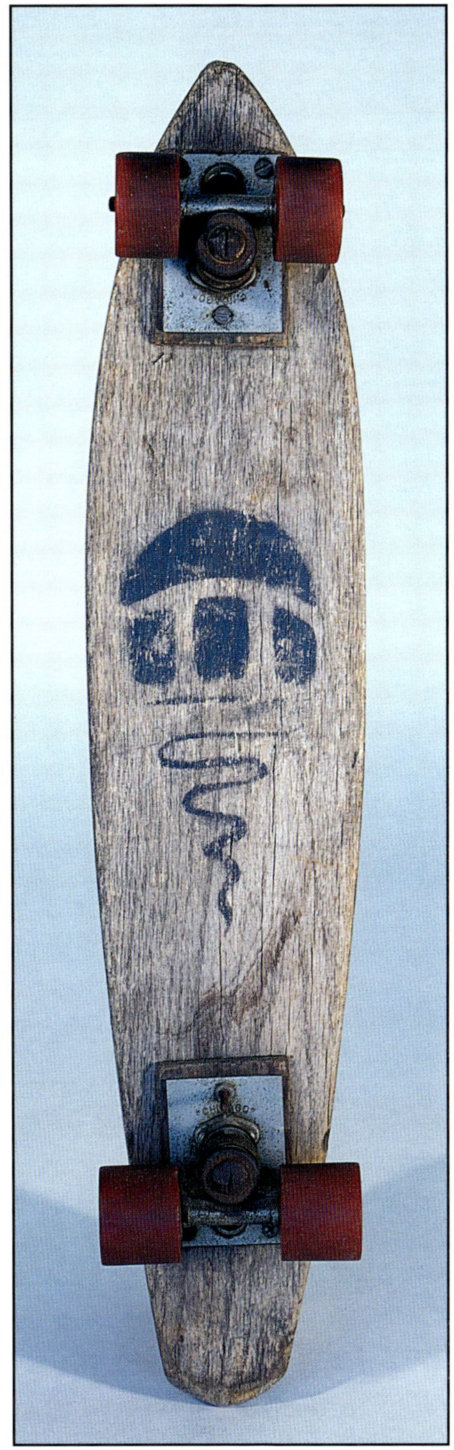

Left to right:

The only Chris Strople board Sims ever made, the prototype was broken by Chris. *Courtesy Ed Economy.* $800-1000.

Sims' Tom Inouye model prototype, only two made. *Courtesy Ed Economy.* $2000-2500.

Dogtown / Z-boys, it all started here. Zeffer surfboards air brush, Jay Adams. *Courtesy Ed Economy.* $2500-3000.

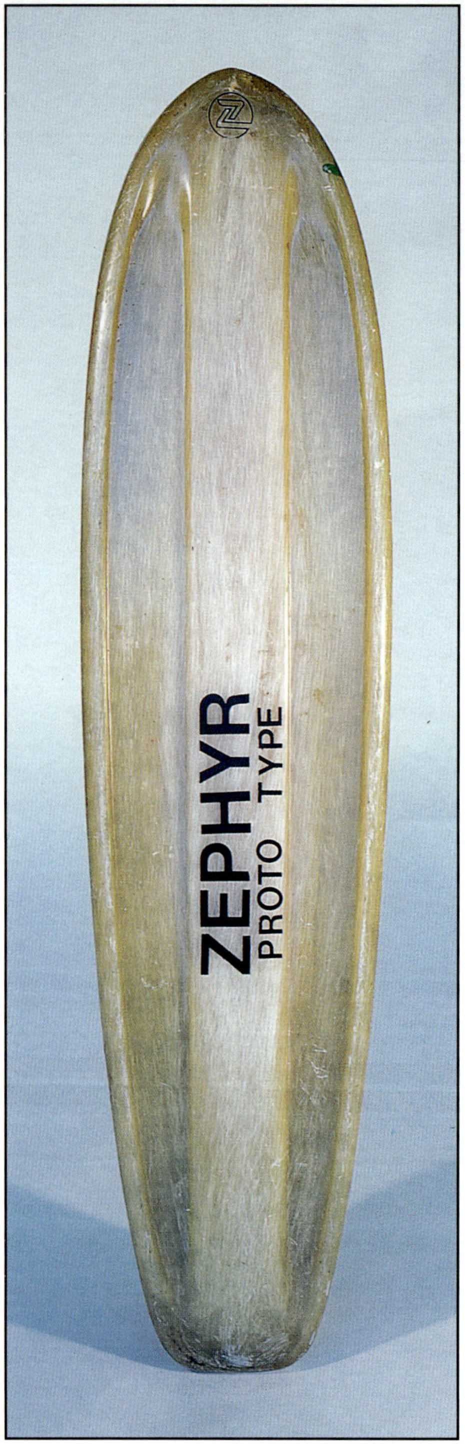

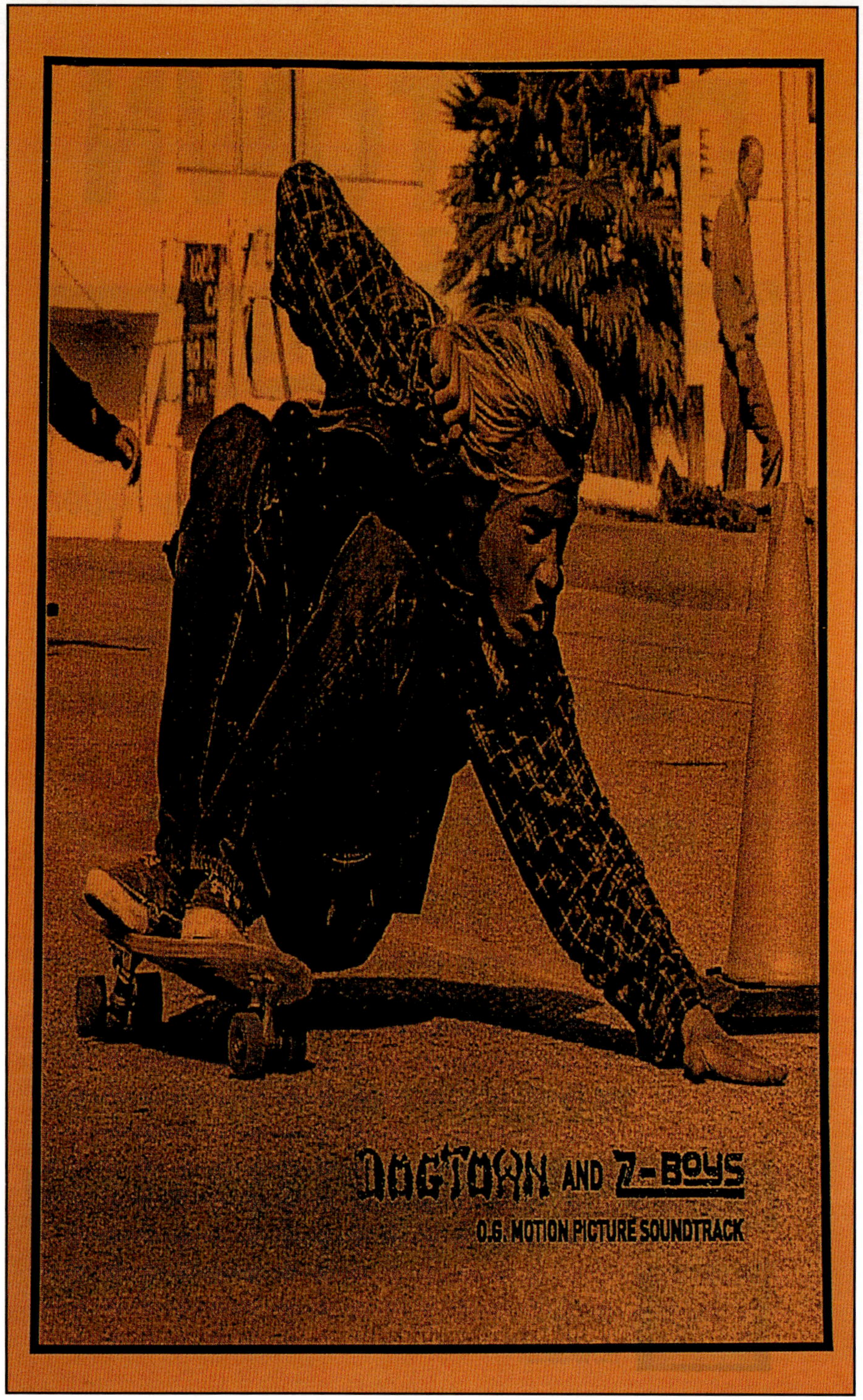

Left: Zeffer mold that made a lot of the boards you are about to see. *Courtesy Ed Economy.* $2500.

Right: Dogtown / Z-boys movie flyer from Van's premiere. *Courtesy Ed Economy.* $5.

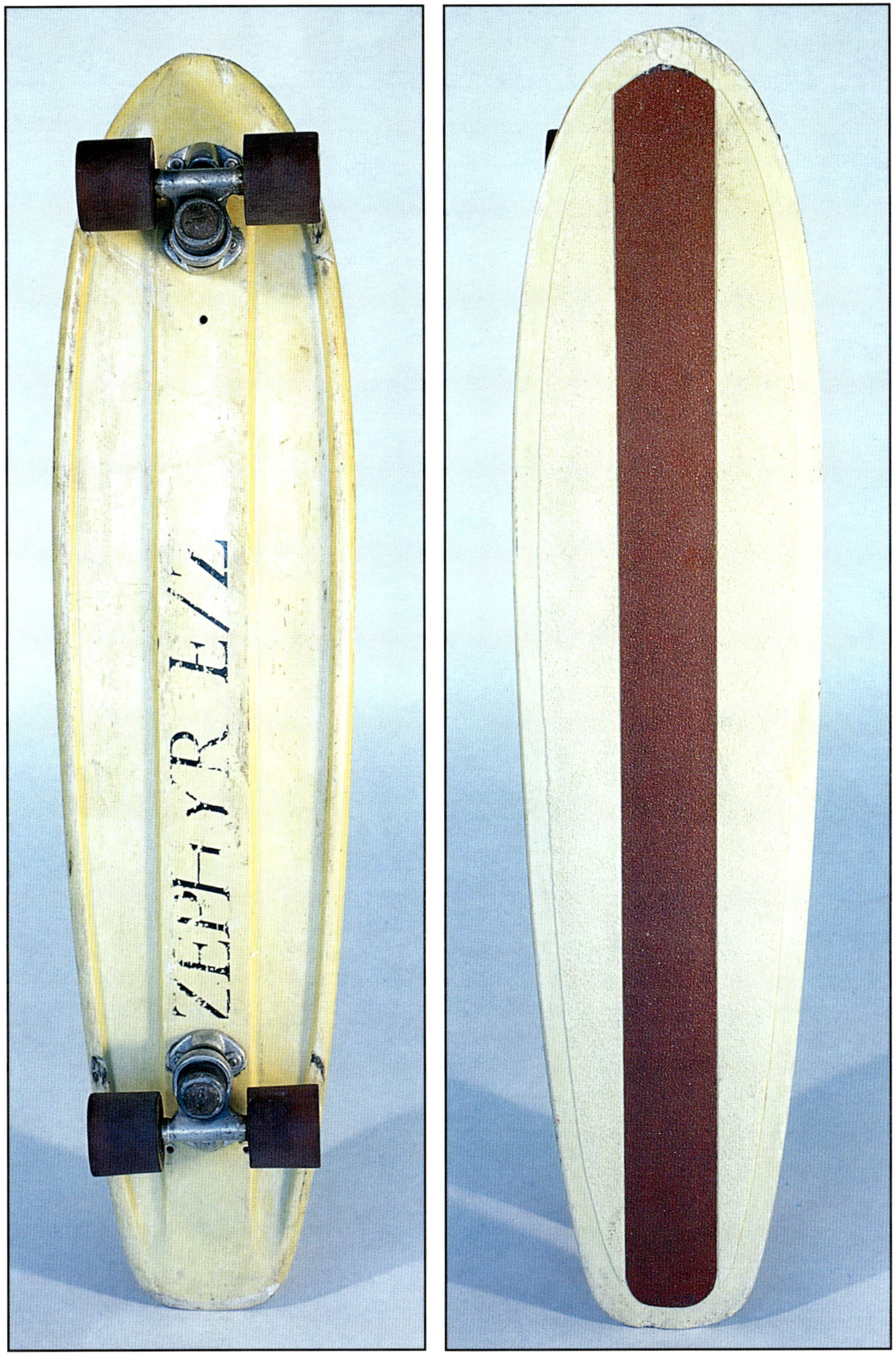

Transitional board from Zeffer surf to Z-Flex and Z-boys. Jay Adams' personal board. *Courtesy Ed Economy.* $4000.

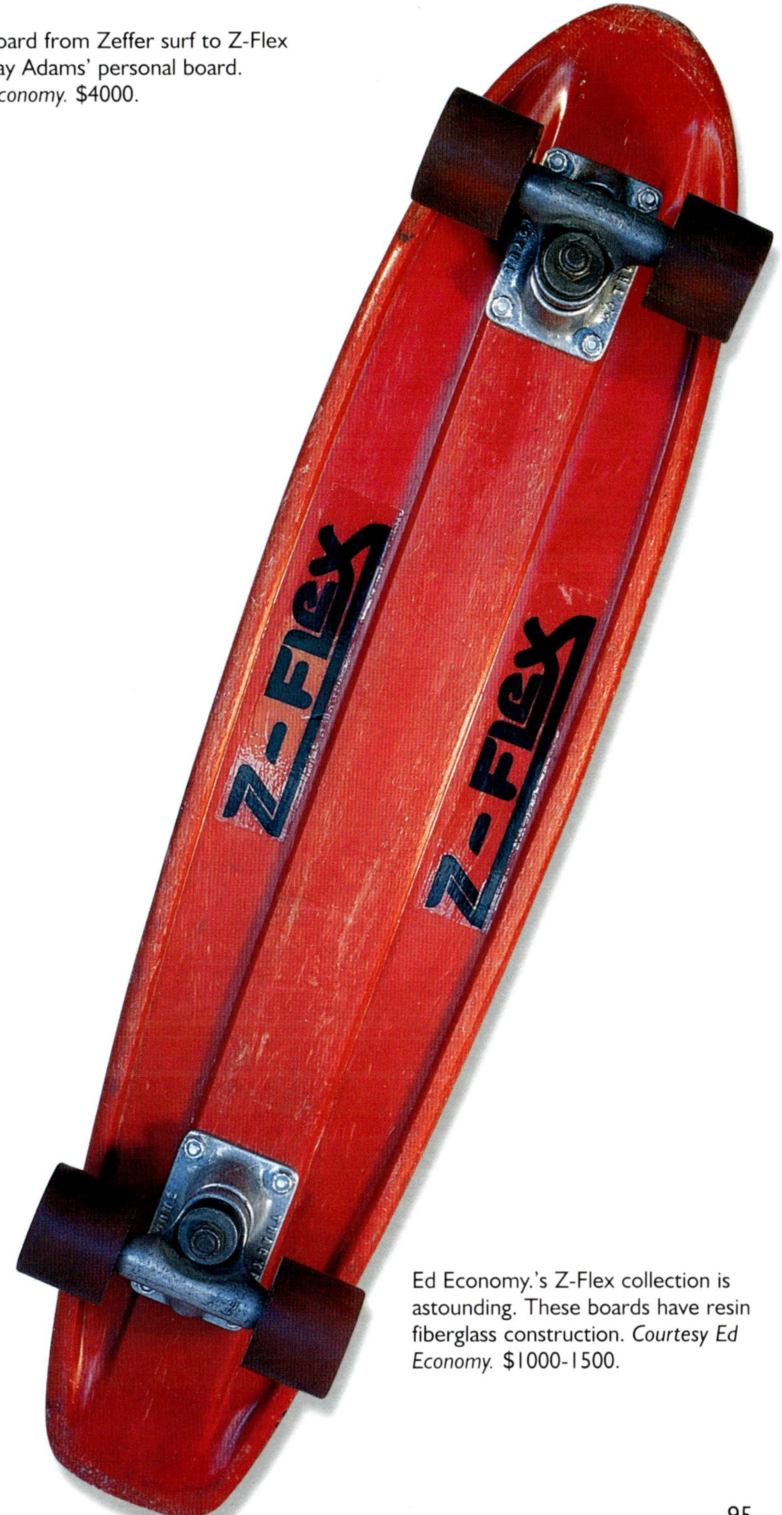

Ed Economy.'s Z-Flex collection is astounding. These boards have resin fiberglass construction. *Courtesy Ed Economy.* $1000-1500.

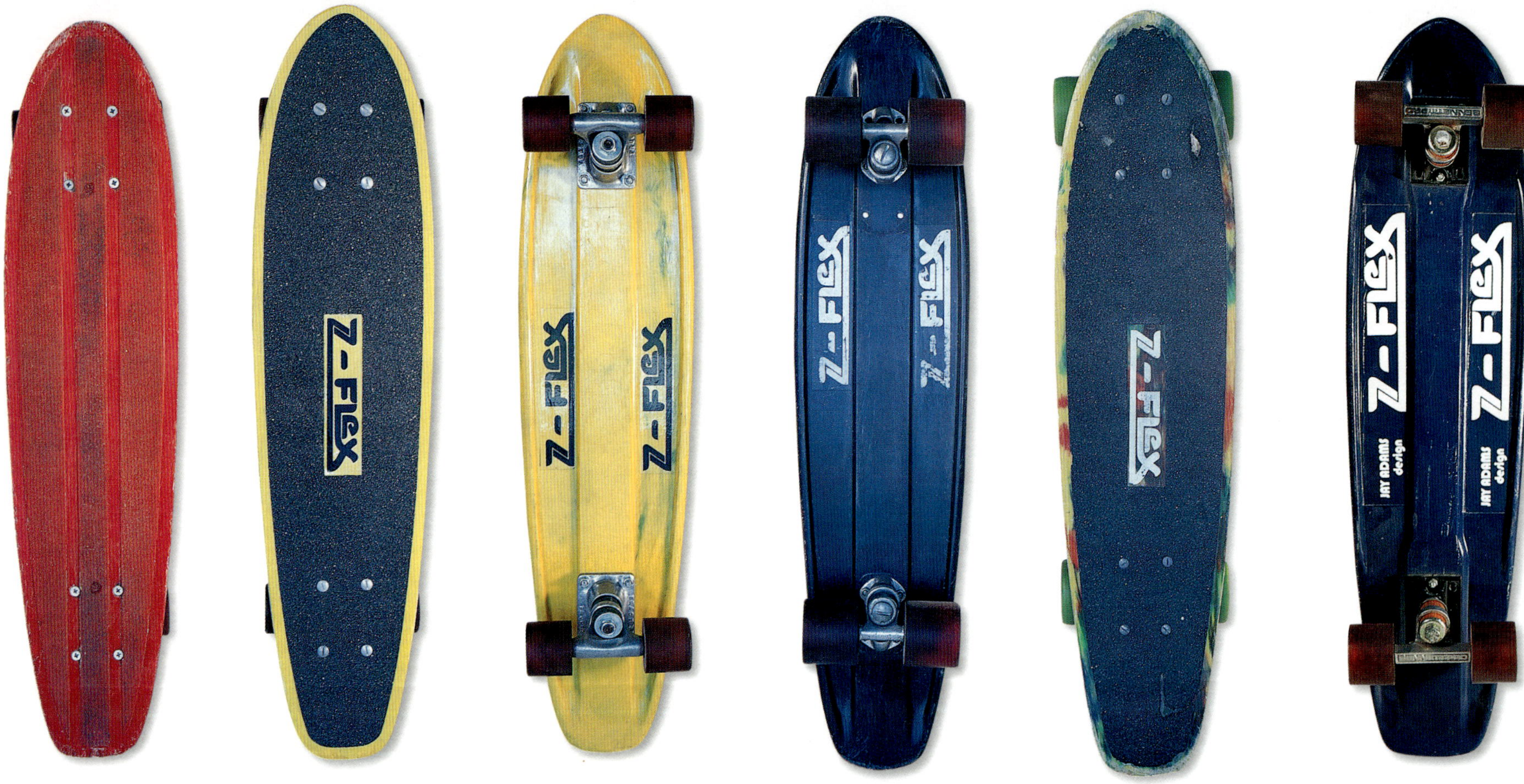

All the generations of Z-Flex are here. Originally, these boards sold for $29.95. *Courtesy Ed Economy.* Now anywhere from $800-2000.

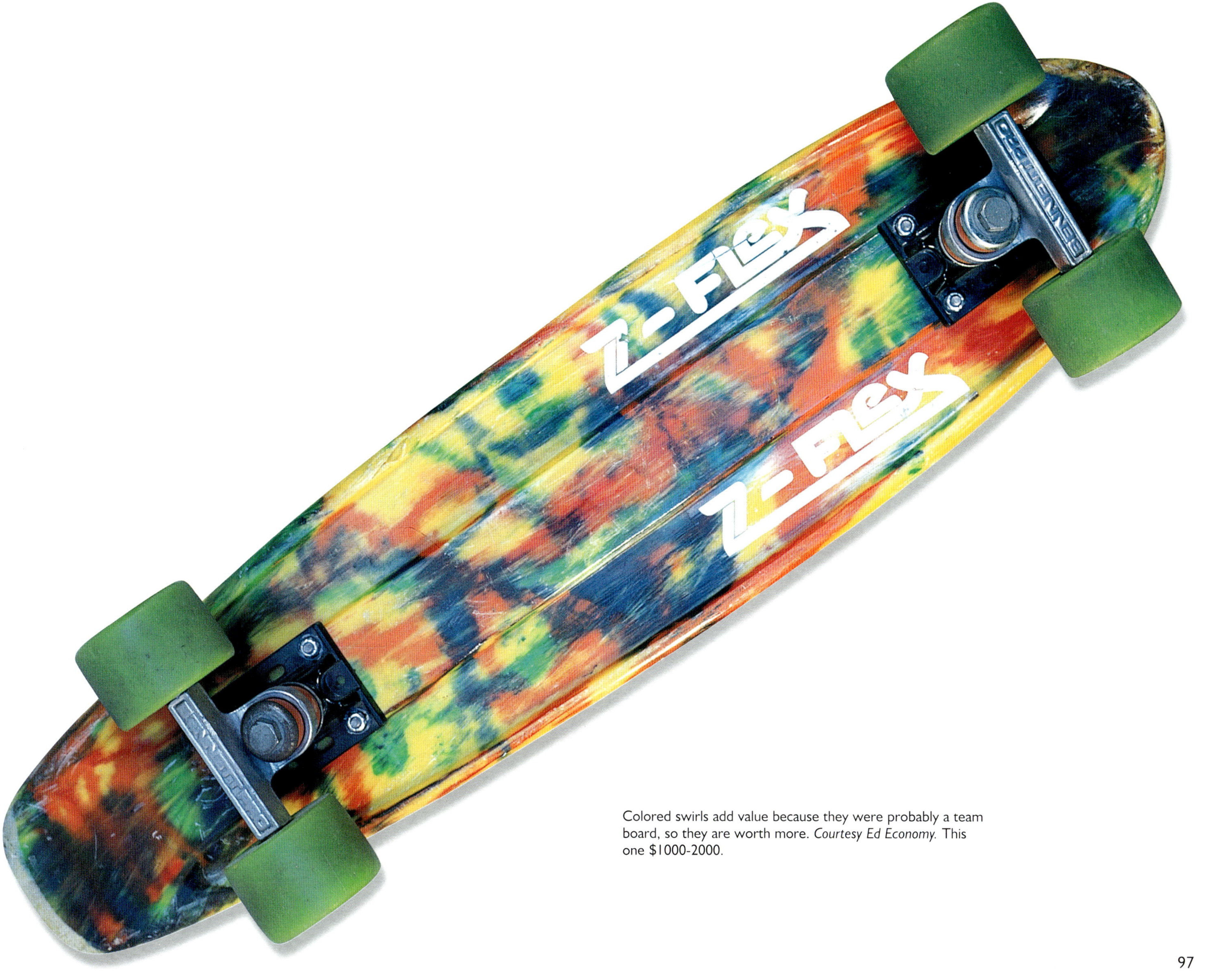

Colored swirls add value because they were probably a team board, so they are worth more. *Courtesy Ed Economy.* This one $1000-2000.

Courtesy Ed Economy. $1000-1500 each

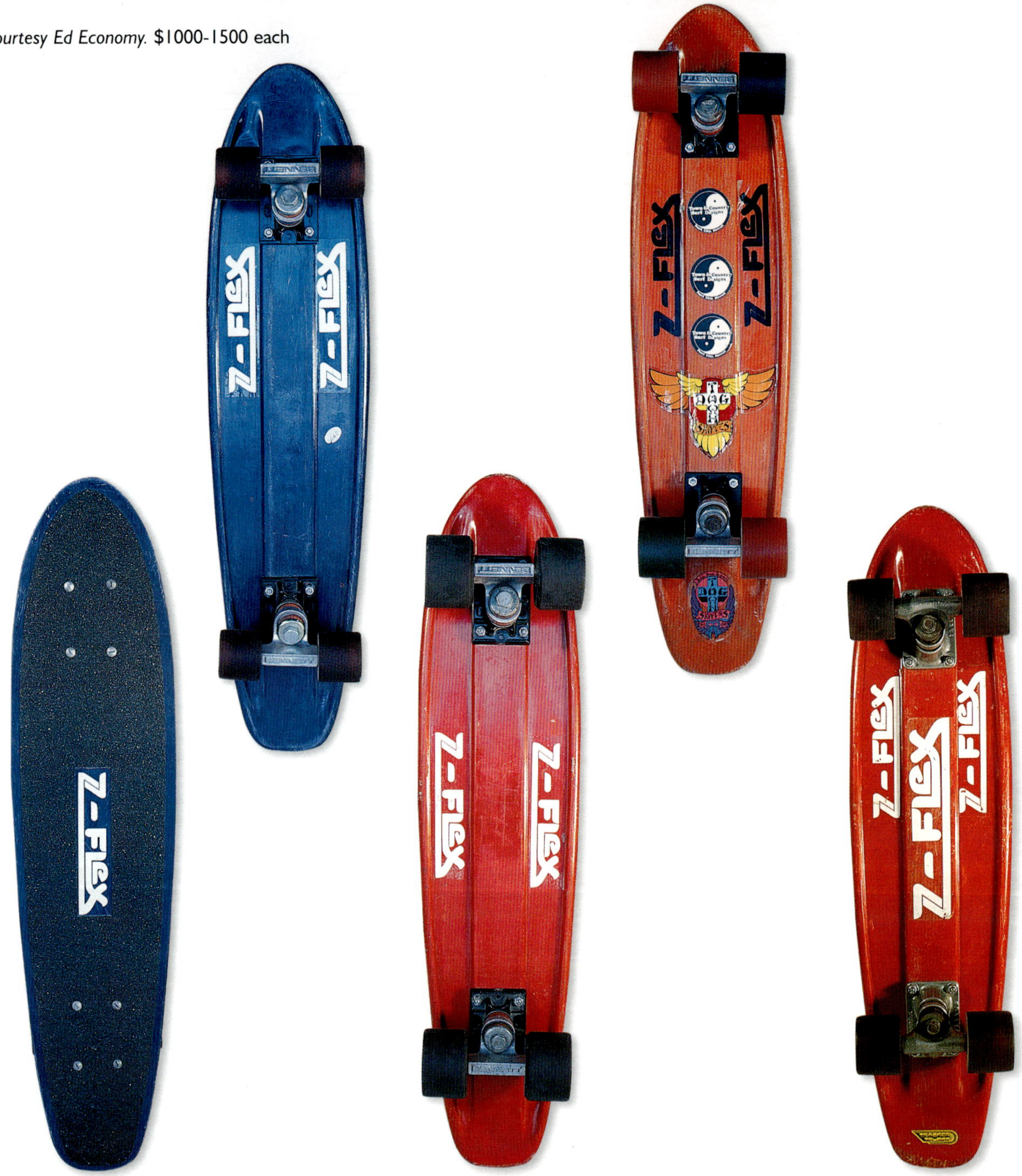

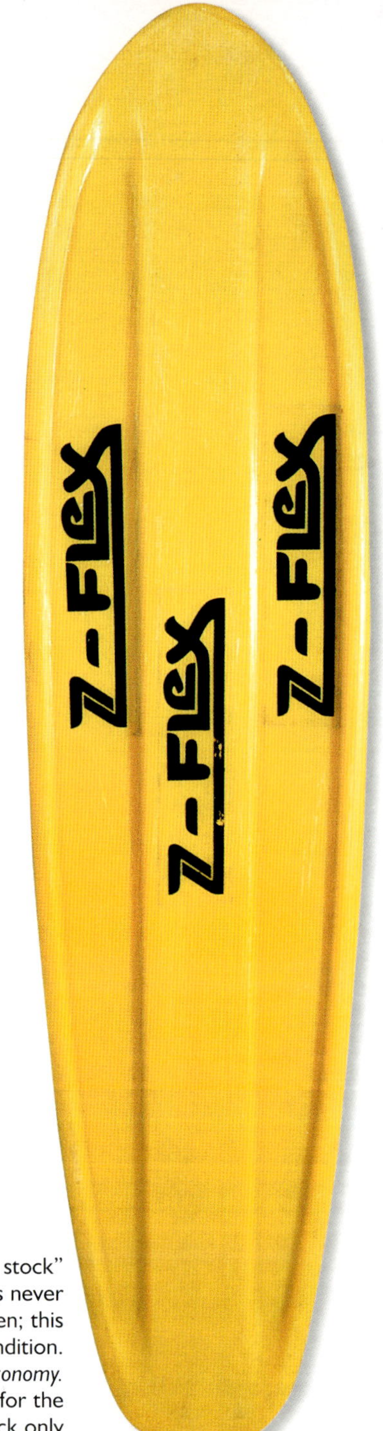

"New old stock" means that it's never been ridden; this one's mint condition. *Courtesy Ed Economy.* $500-800 for the deck only

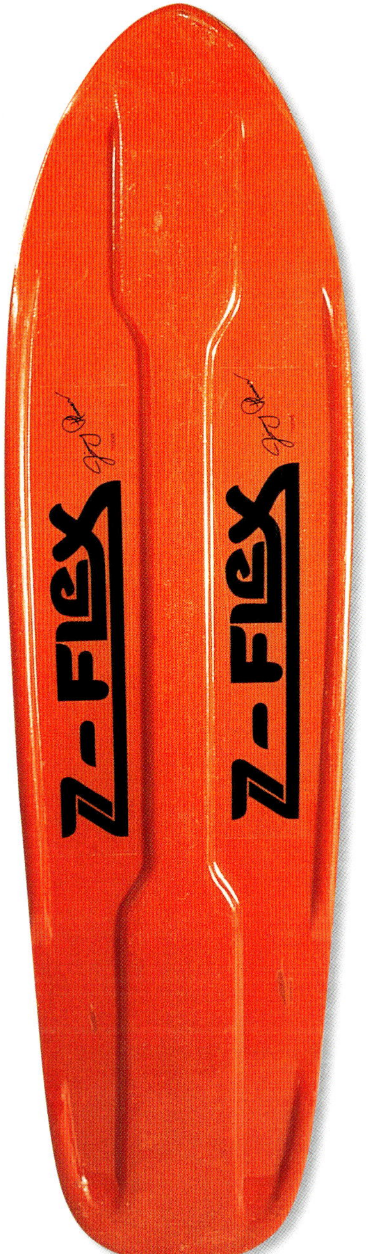

"New old stock" deck only. *Courtesy Ed Economy.* $500-800 for the deck only

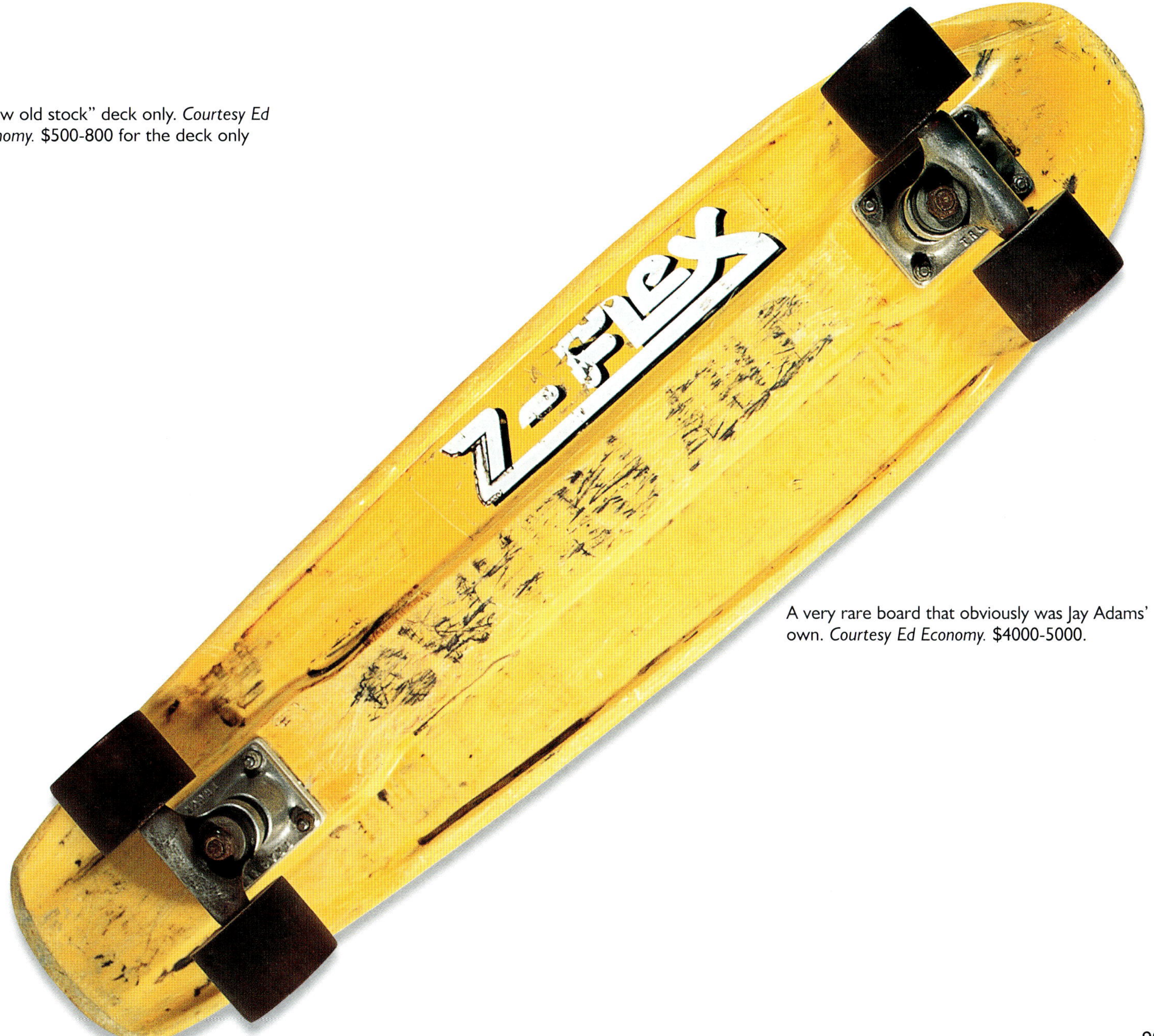

A very rare board that obviously was Jay Adams' own. *Courtesy Ed Economy.* $4000-5000.

A transparent Jay Adams model. *Courtesy Ed Economy.* $2000-2500.

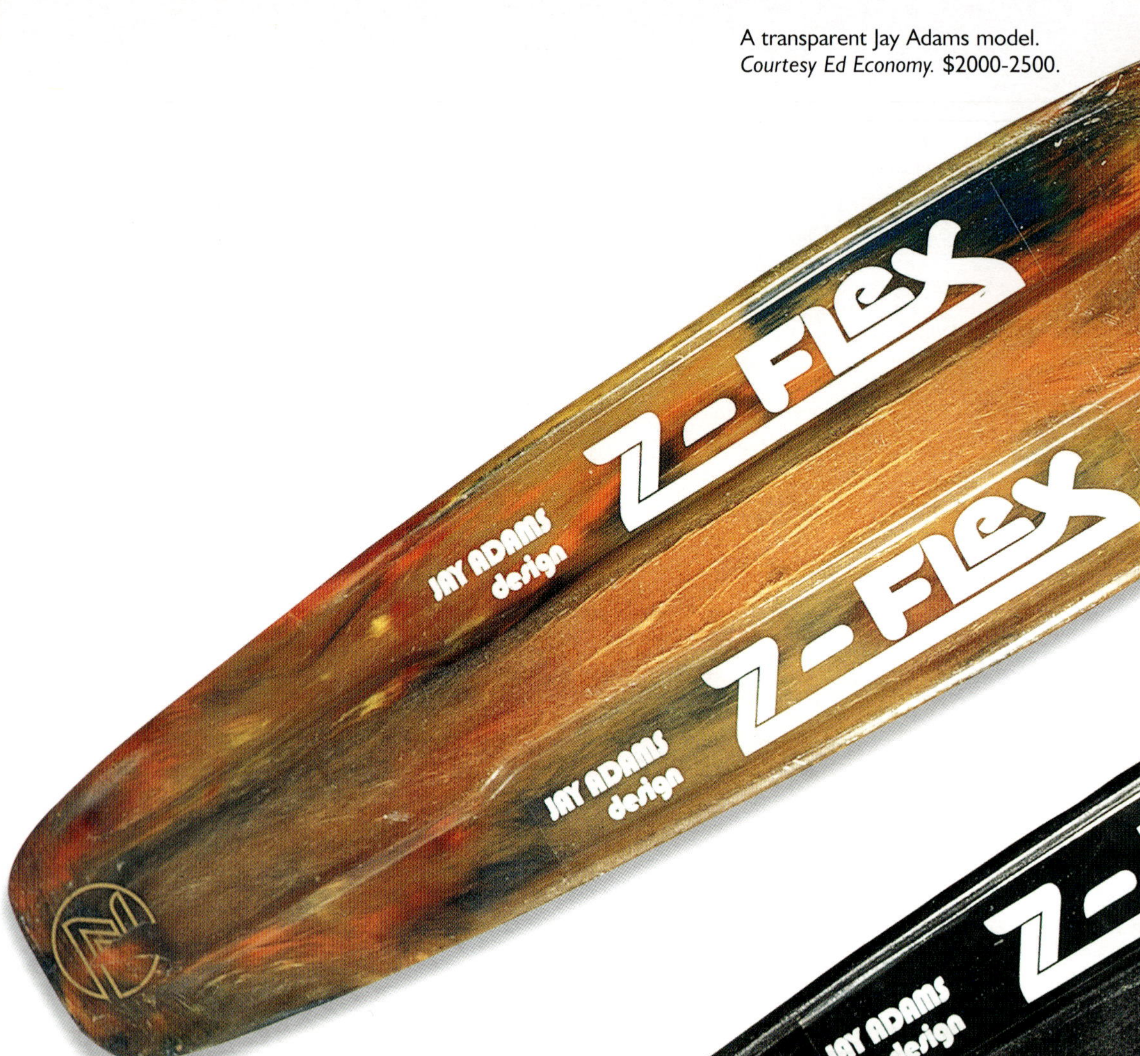

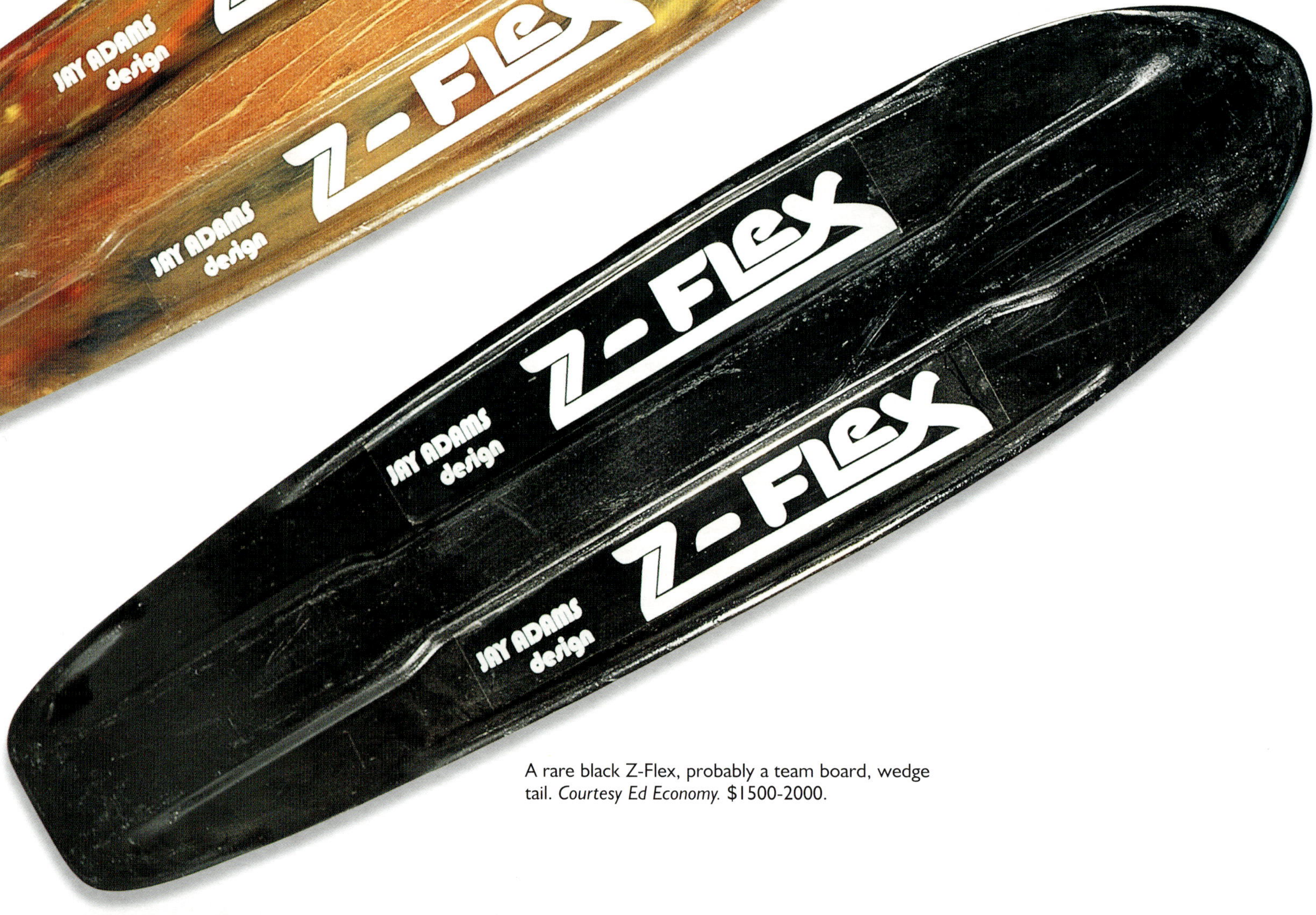

A rare black Z-Flex, probably a team board, wedge tail. *Courtesy Ed Economy.* $1500-2000.

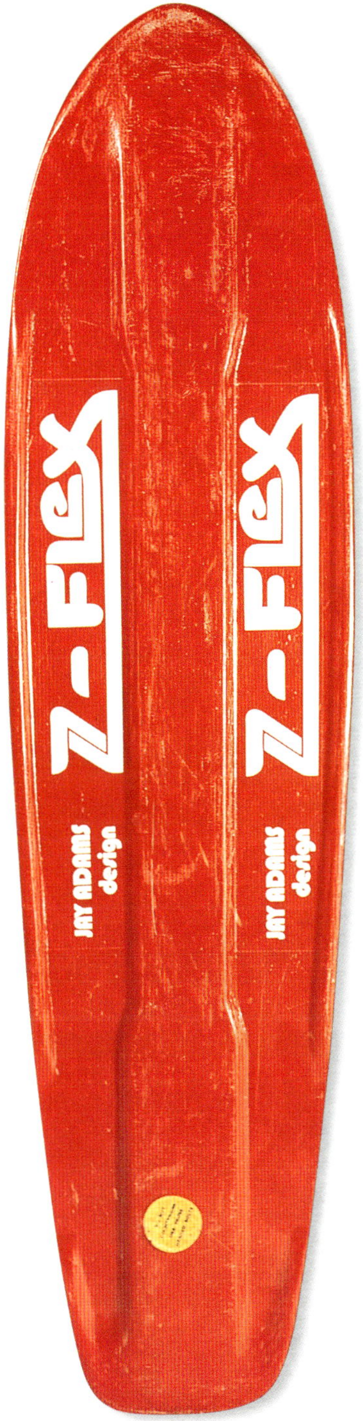

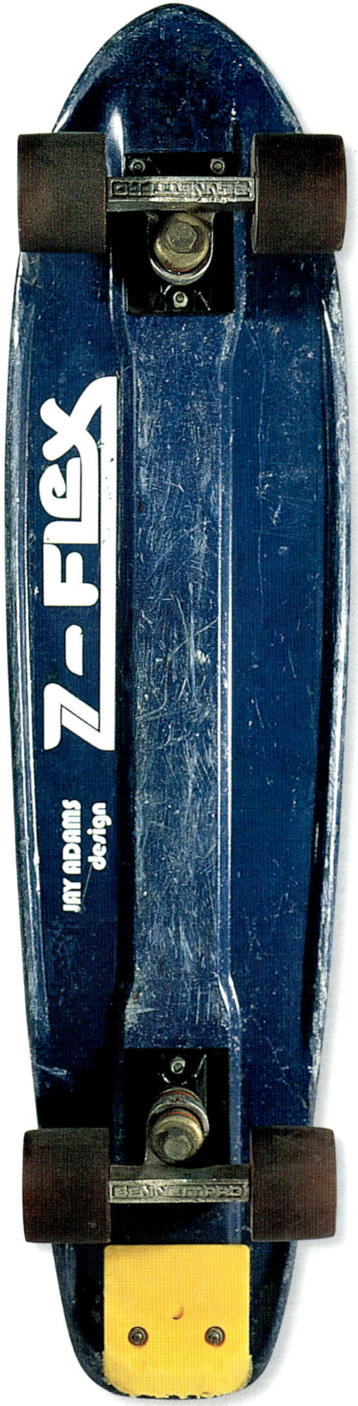

Left: Z-Flex. *Courtesy Ed Economy.* $500-800.

Right: Jay Adams model. *Courtesy Ed Economy.* $1000-1500.

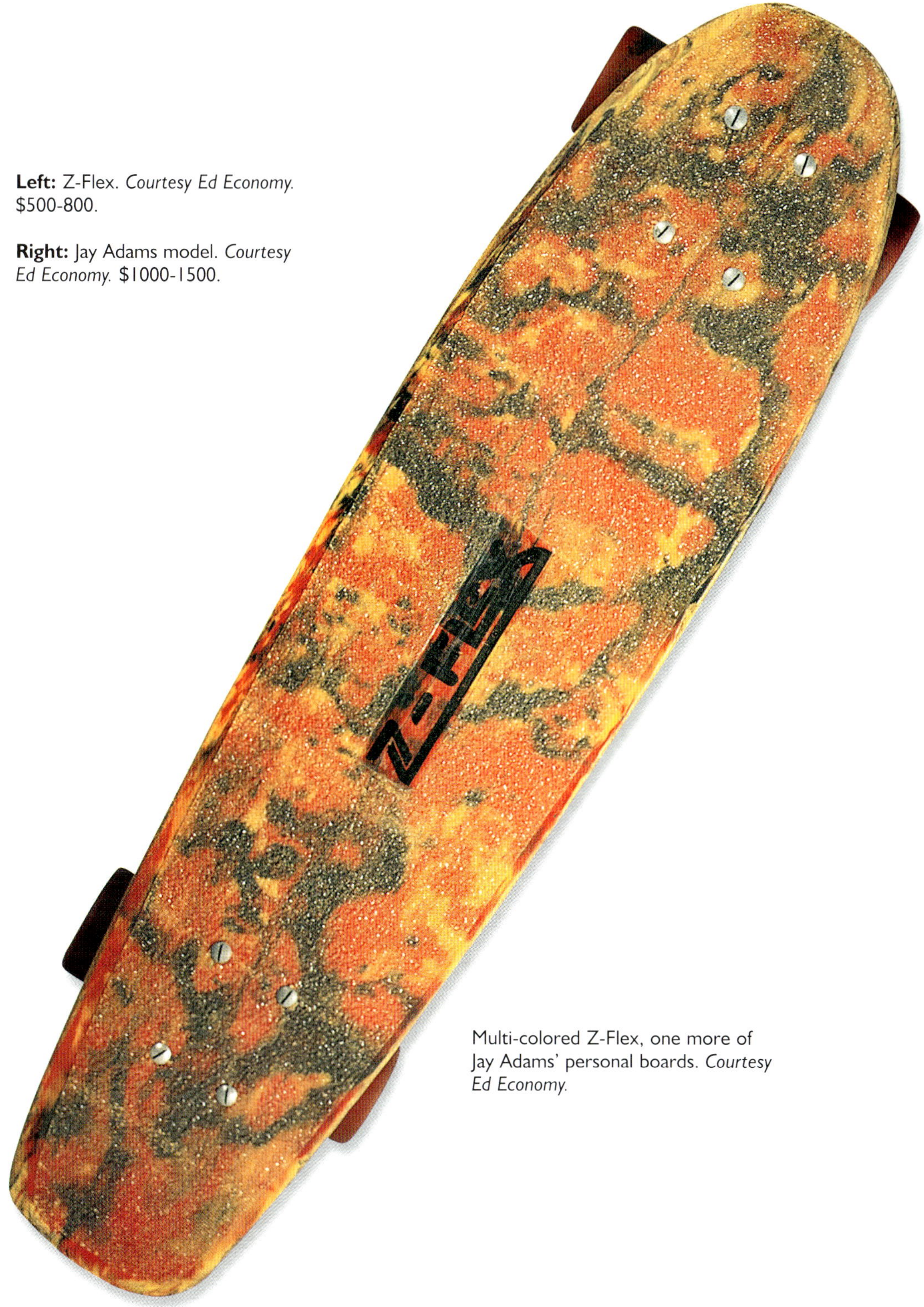

Multi-colored Z-Flex, one more of Jay Adams' personal boards. *Courtesy Ed Economy.*

Courtesy Ed Economy. $800-1500 each

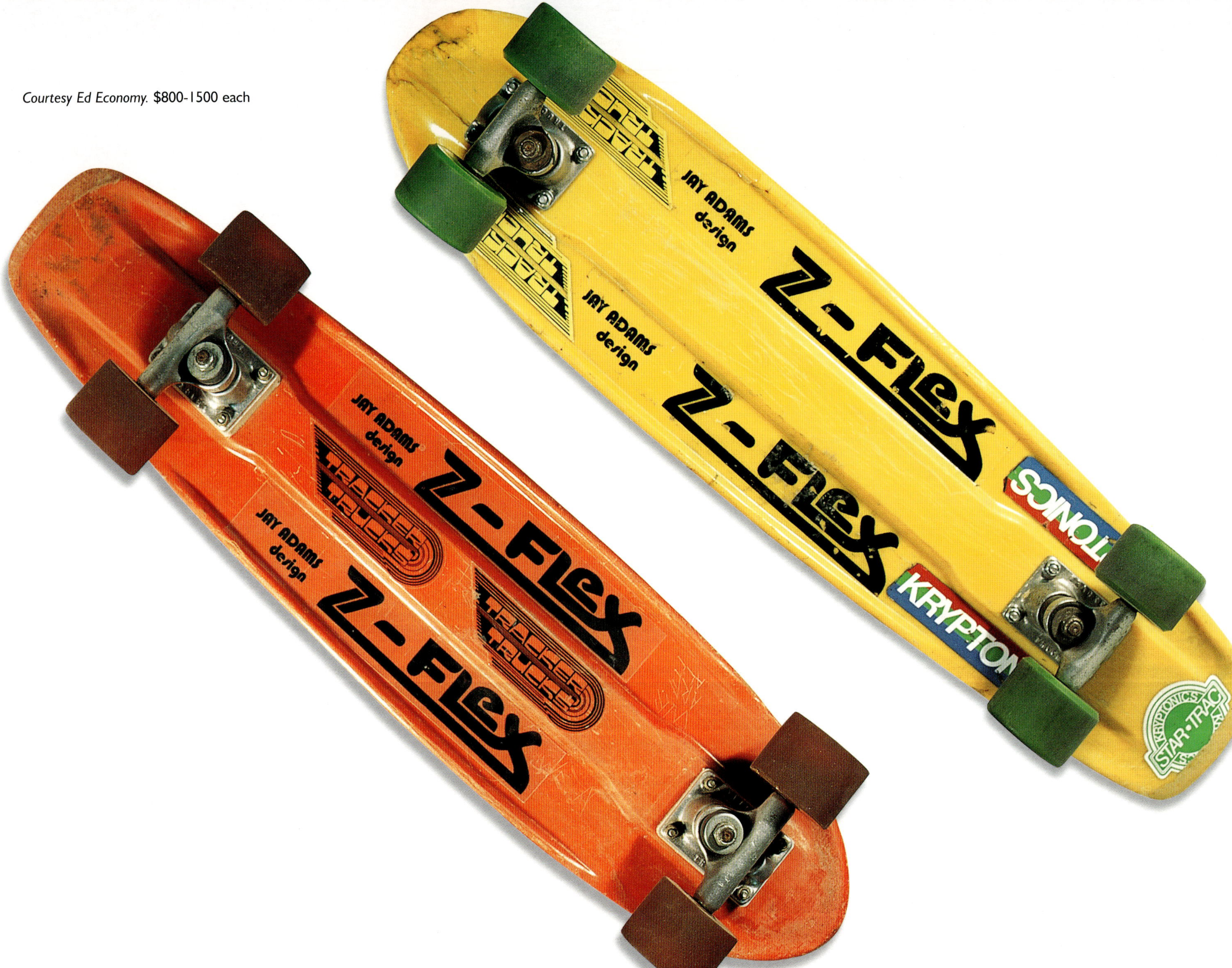

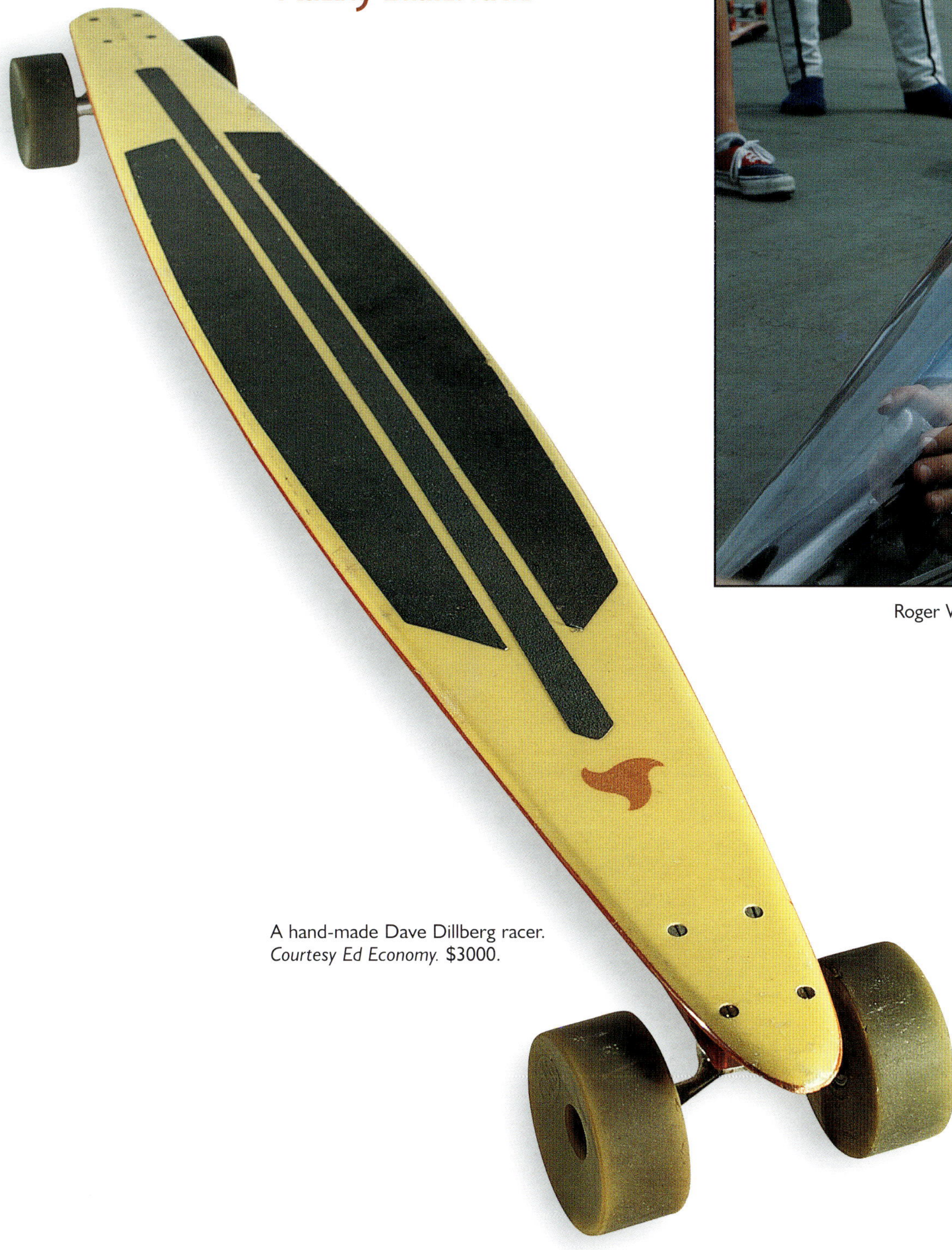

A hand-made Dave Dillberg racer.
Courtesy Ed Economy. $3000.

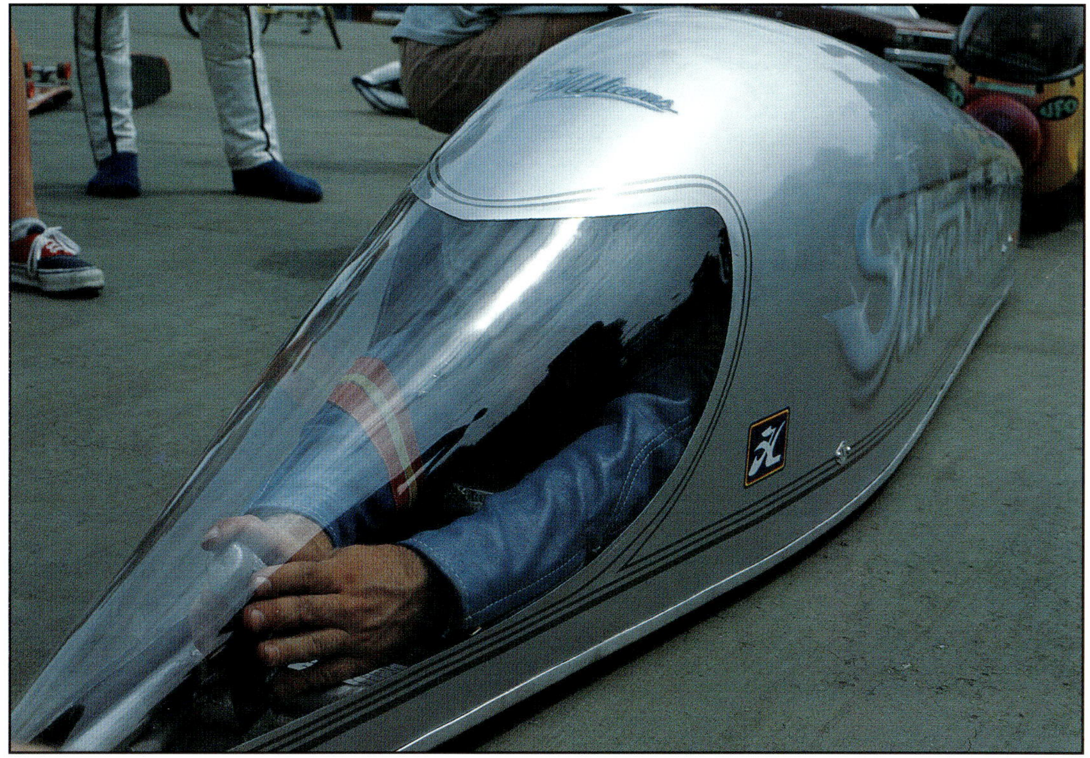

Roger Williams, Hobie Silverstreak, Signal Hill. *Photo James O'Mahoney.*

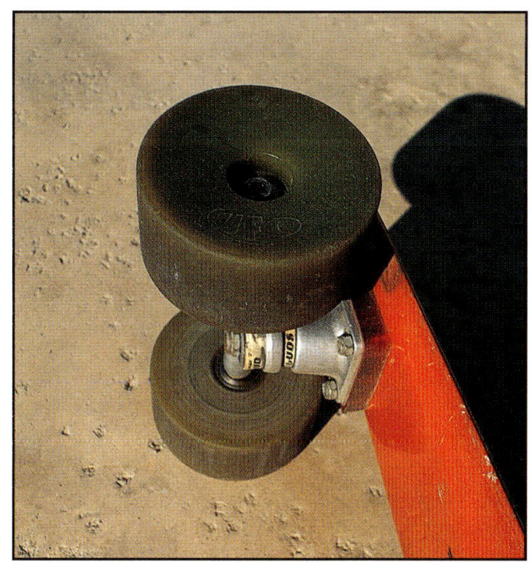

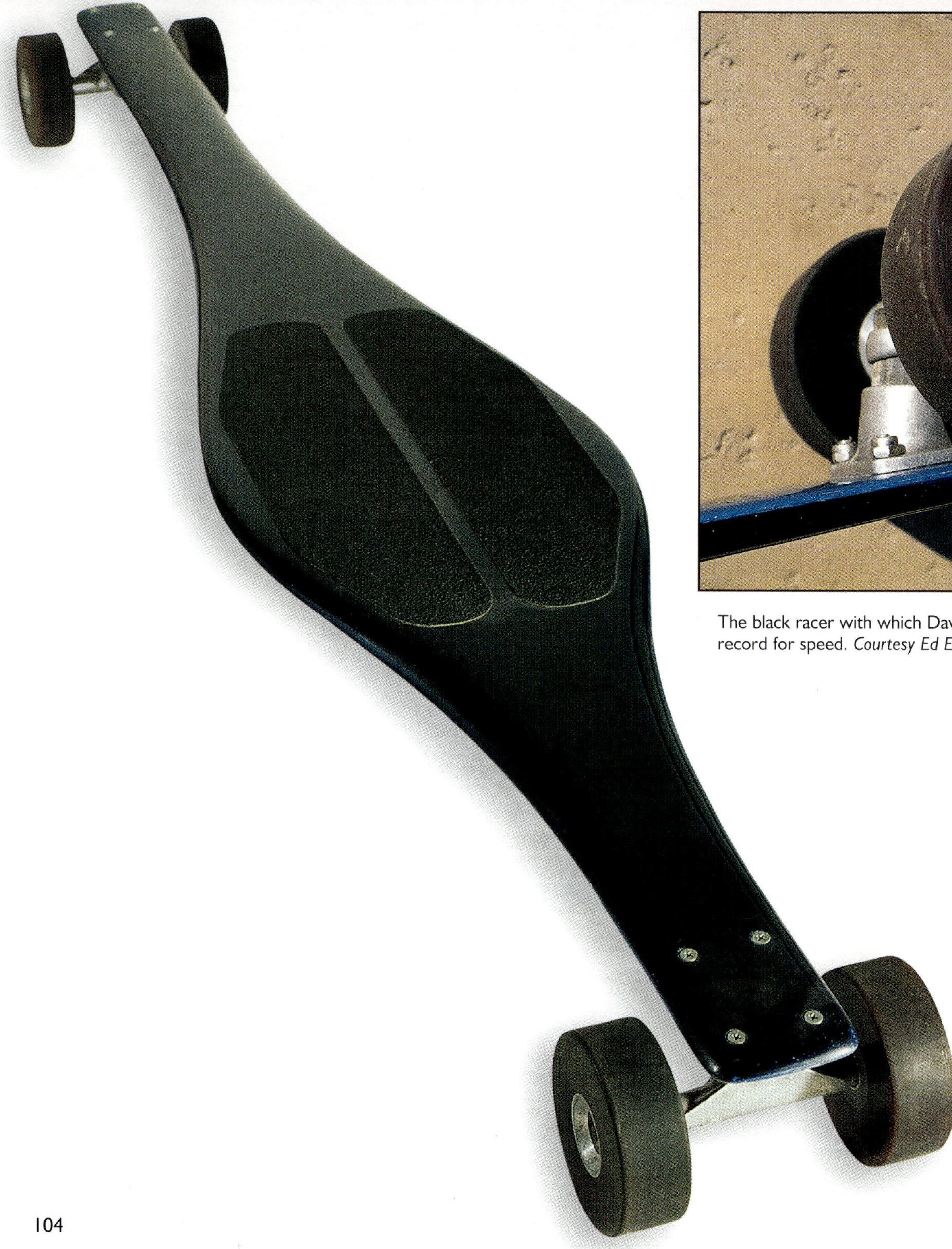

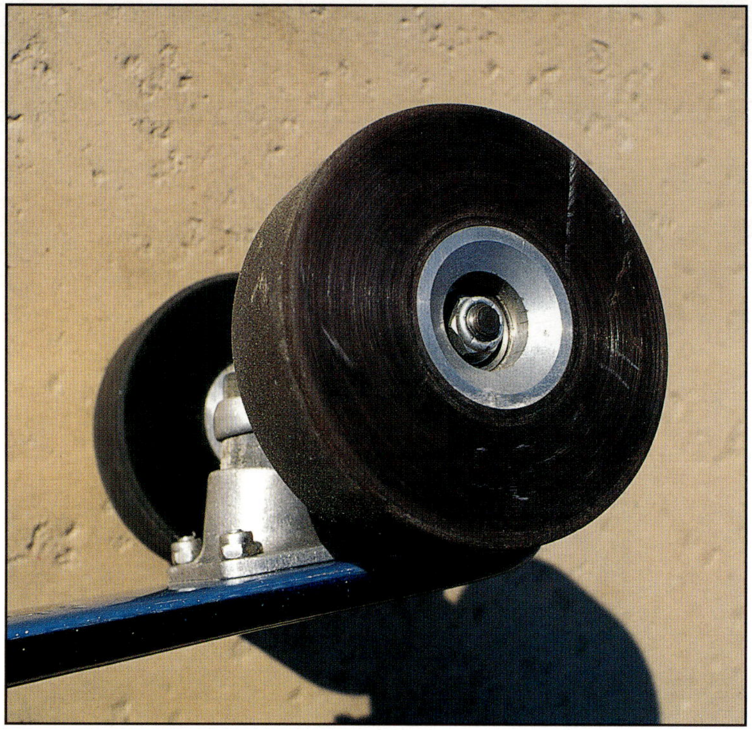

The black racer with which Dave Dillberg set the world record for speed. *Courtesy Ed Economy.* $5000.

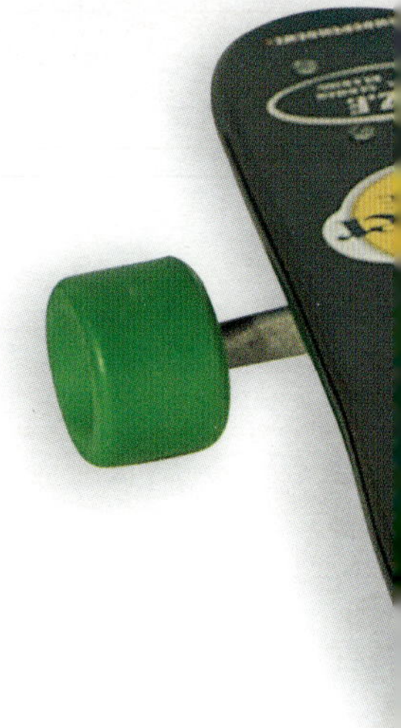

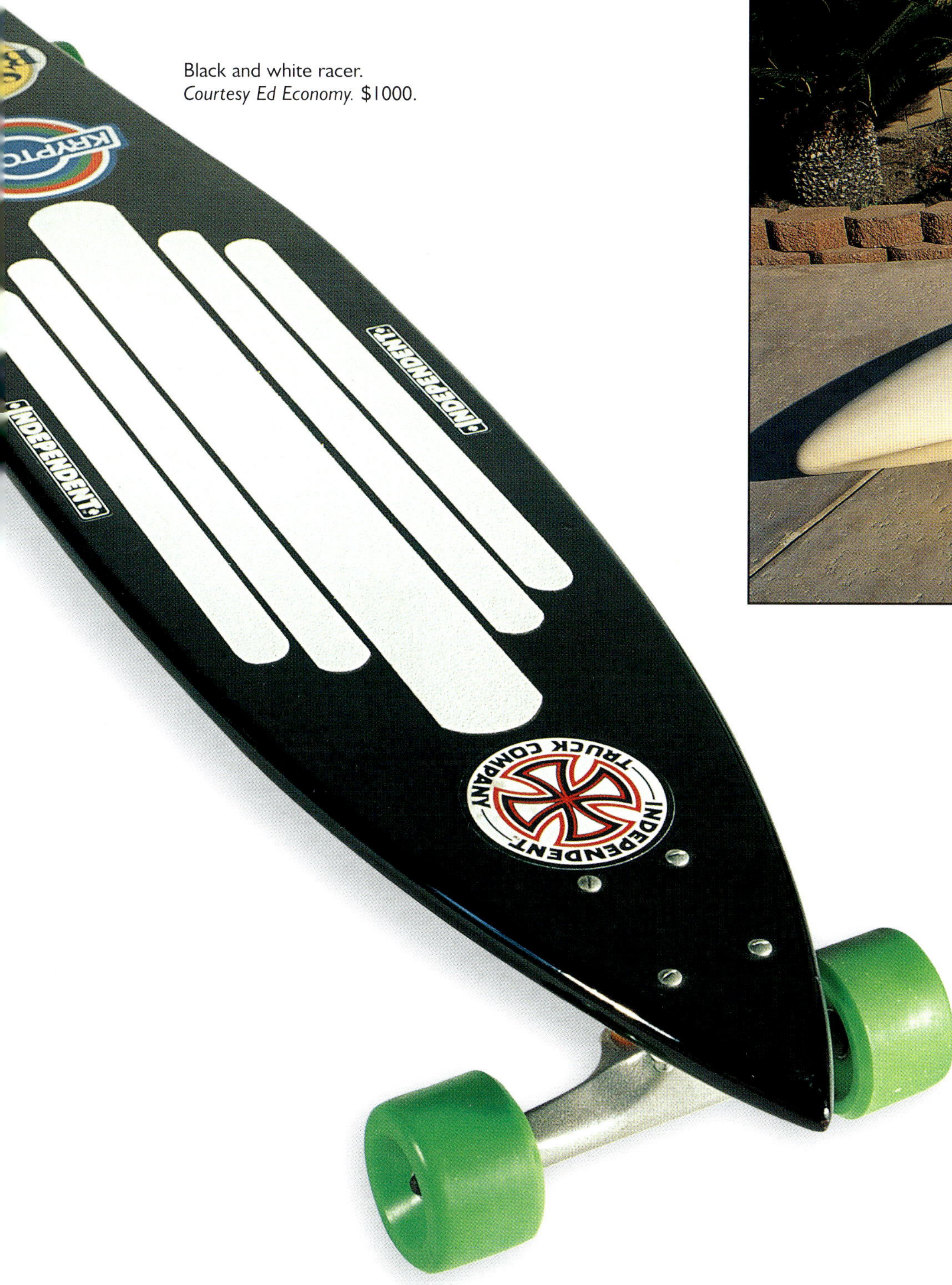

Black and white racer.
Courtesy Ed Economy. $1000.

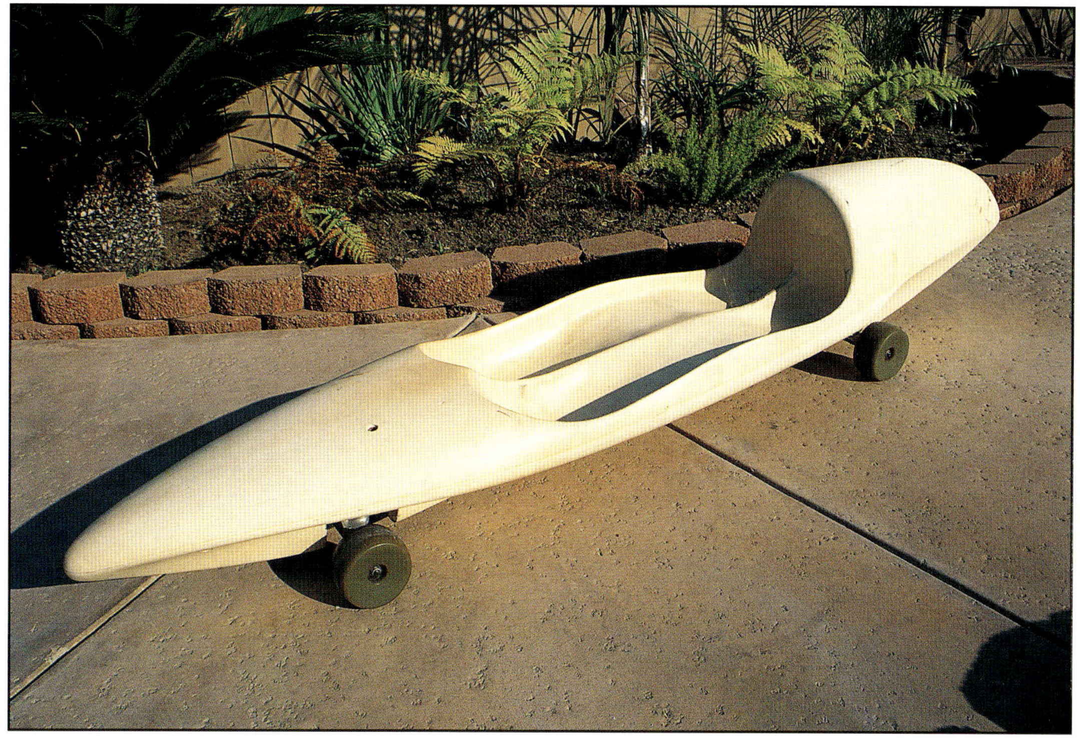

Tommy Ryan's knee skate car. This racer was weighted down for sustained momentum. *Courtesy Ed Economy.* $3000-4000.

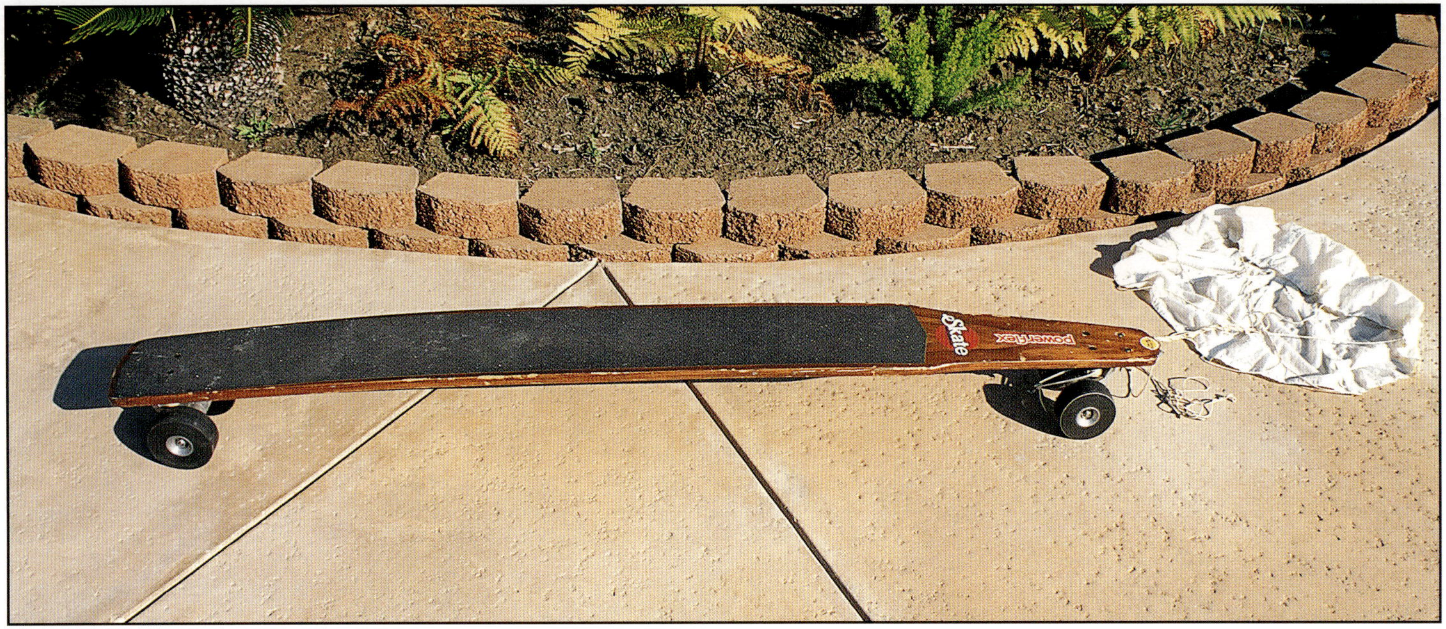

Don Boma's downhill racer equipped with a parachute and floating axle. *Courtesy Ed Economy.* $3000-4000.

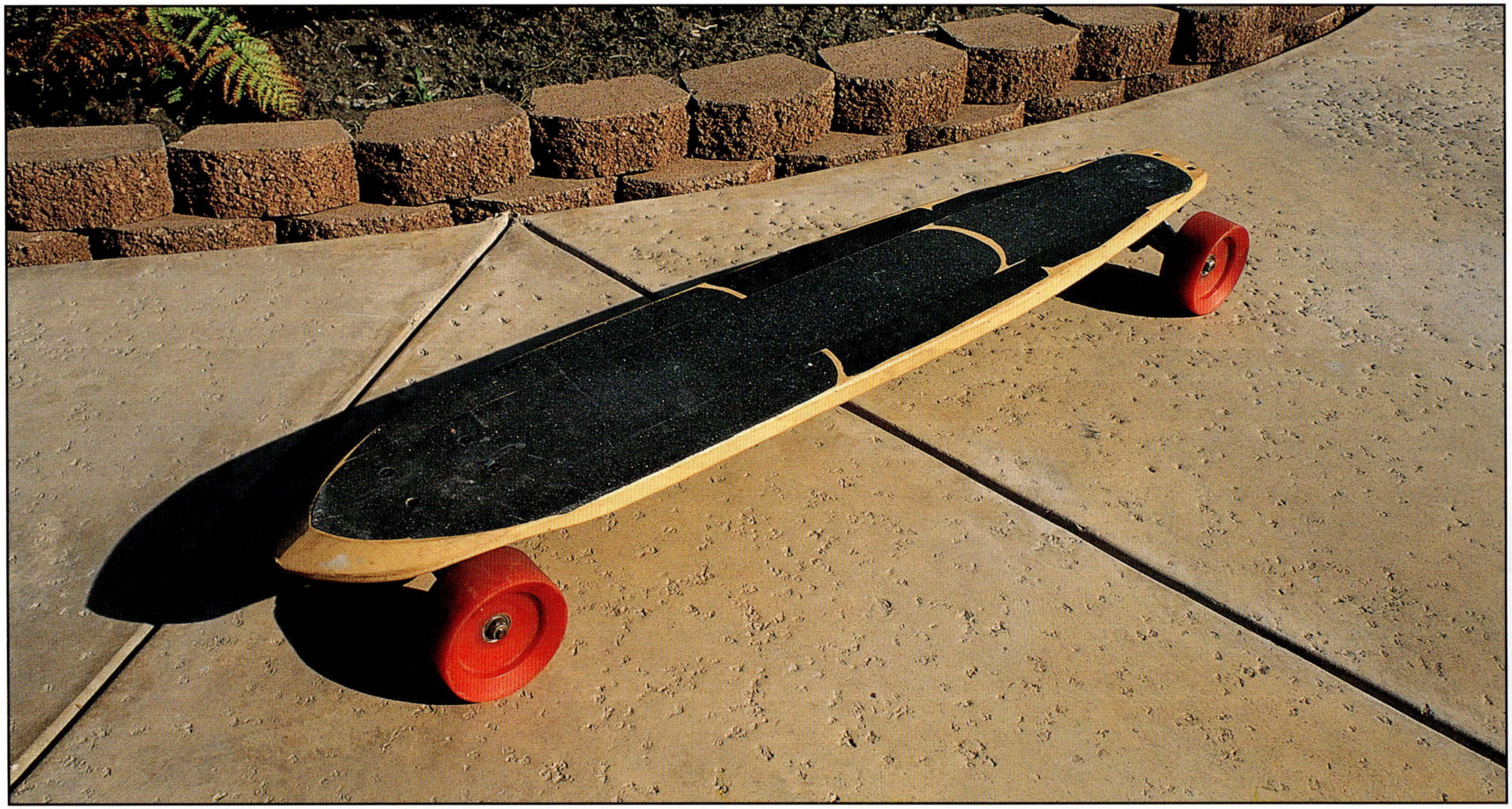

Beveled nose with black grip that was Cliff Coleman's personal board. He rode at Signal Hill with a speed of 51.05 mph. *Courtesy Ed Economy.* $4000.

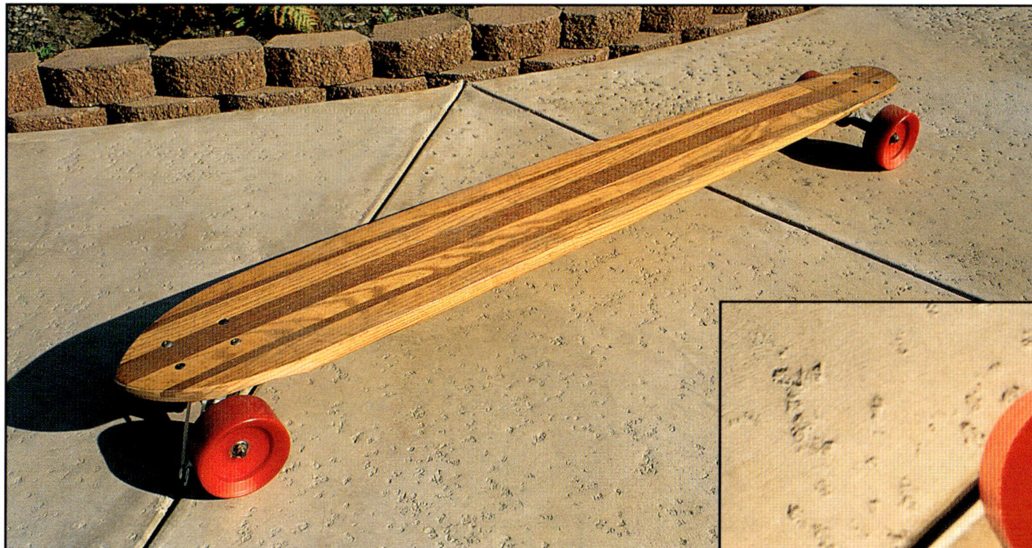

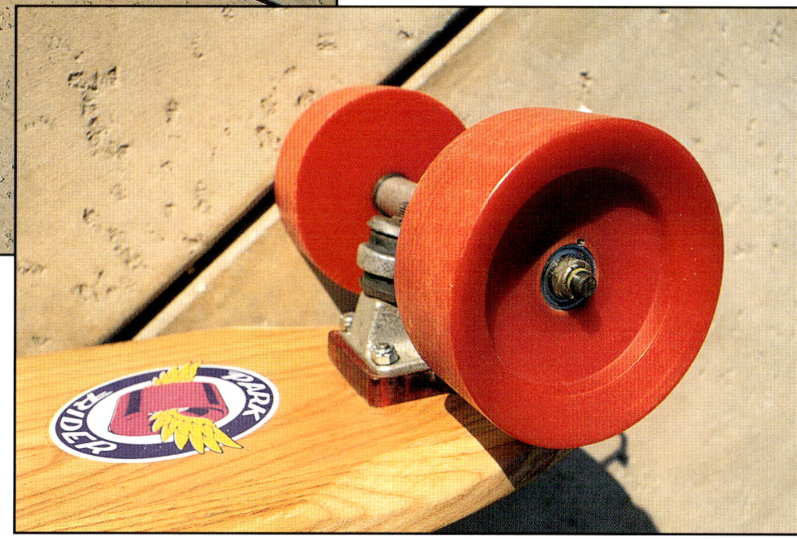

Laminated Racer *Courtesy Ed Economy.* $2000.

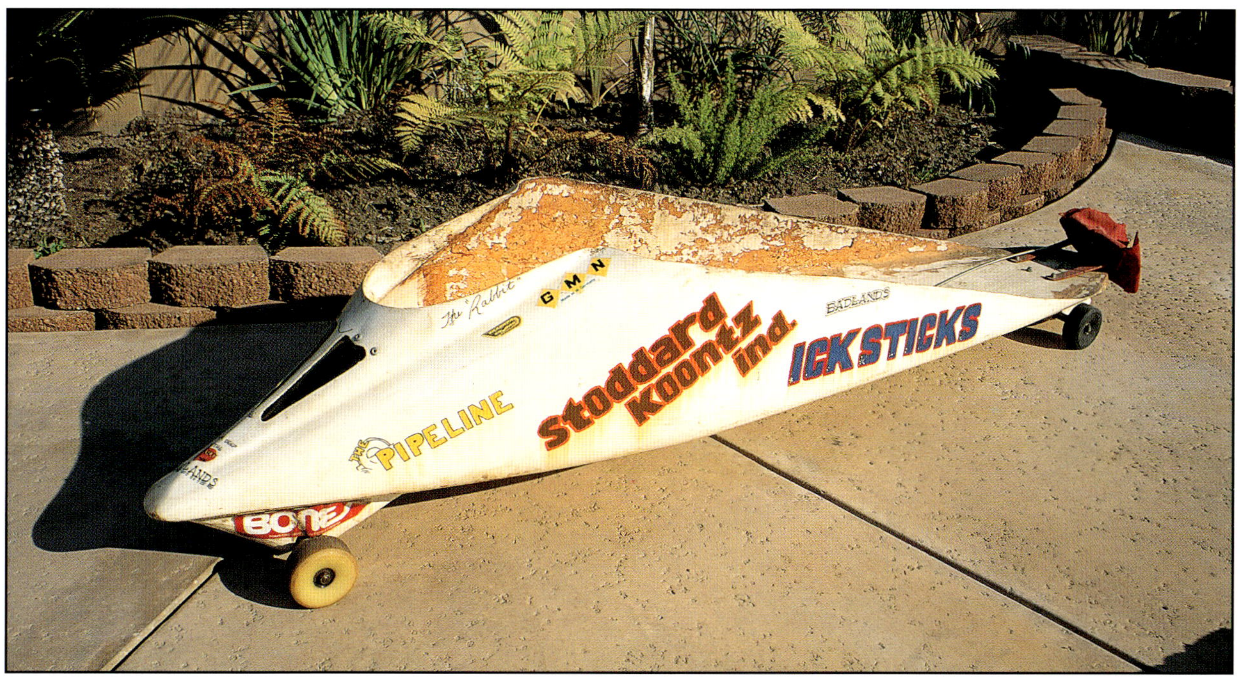

Baddlens skate car made by Rick Howell. Harvey Hawks rode it in the prone position. *Courtesy Ed Economy.* $5000-6000.

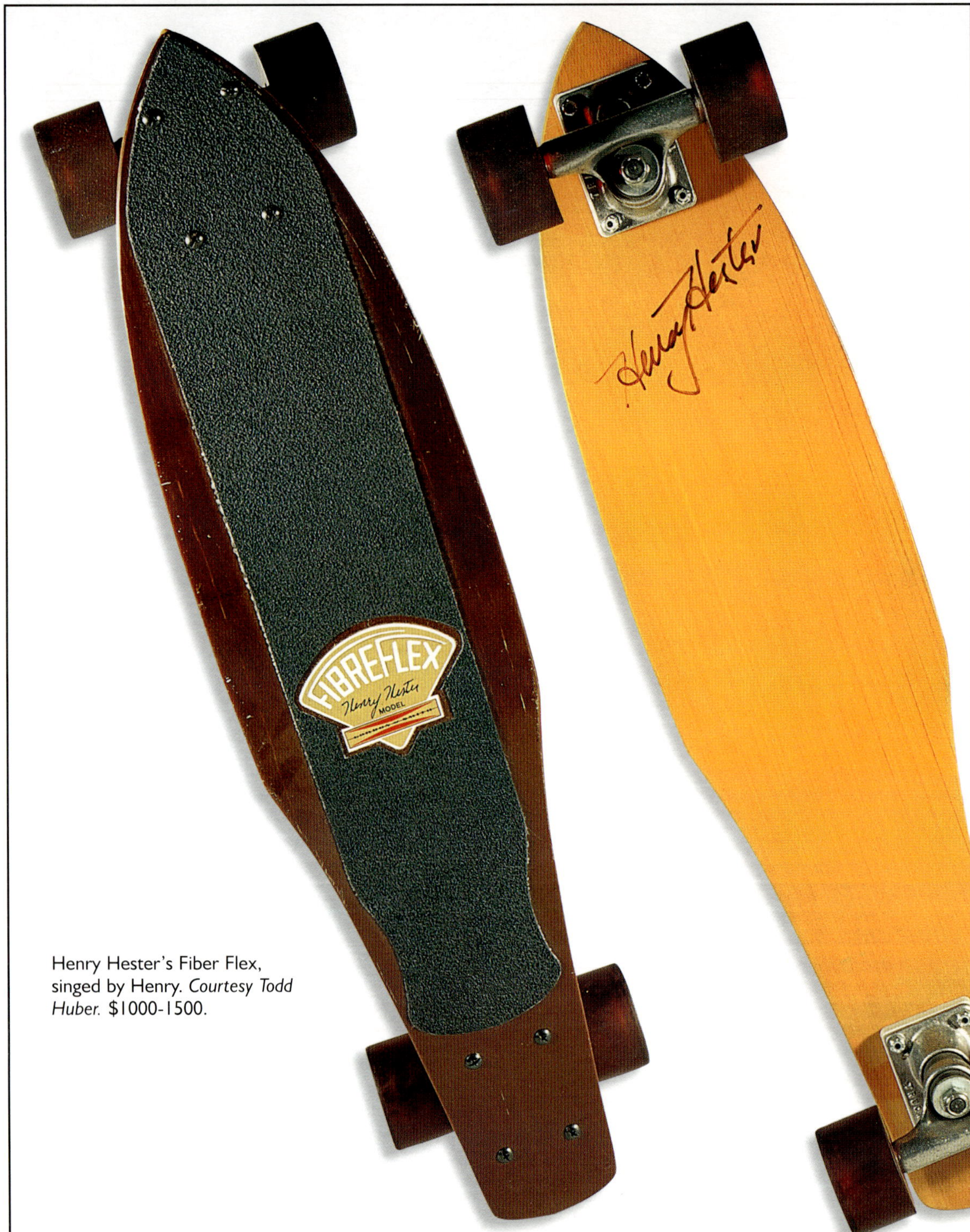

Henry Hester's Fiber Flex, singed by Henry. *Courtesy Todd Huber.* $1000-1500.

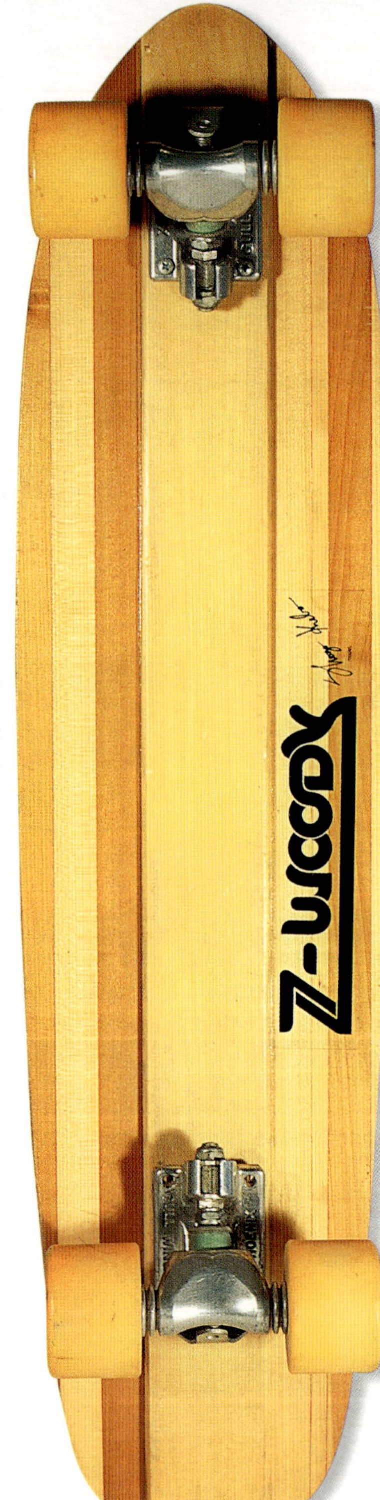

Z-woody laminated with a kicktail. *Photo R. Noll. Courtesy Jim at Rip City.* $6000.

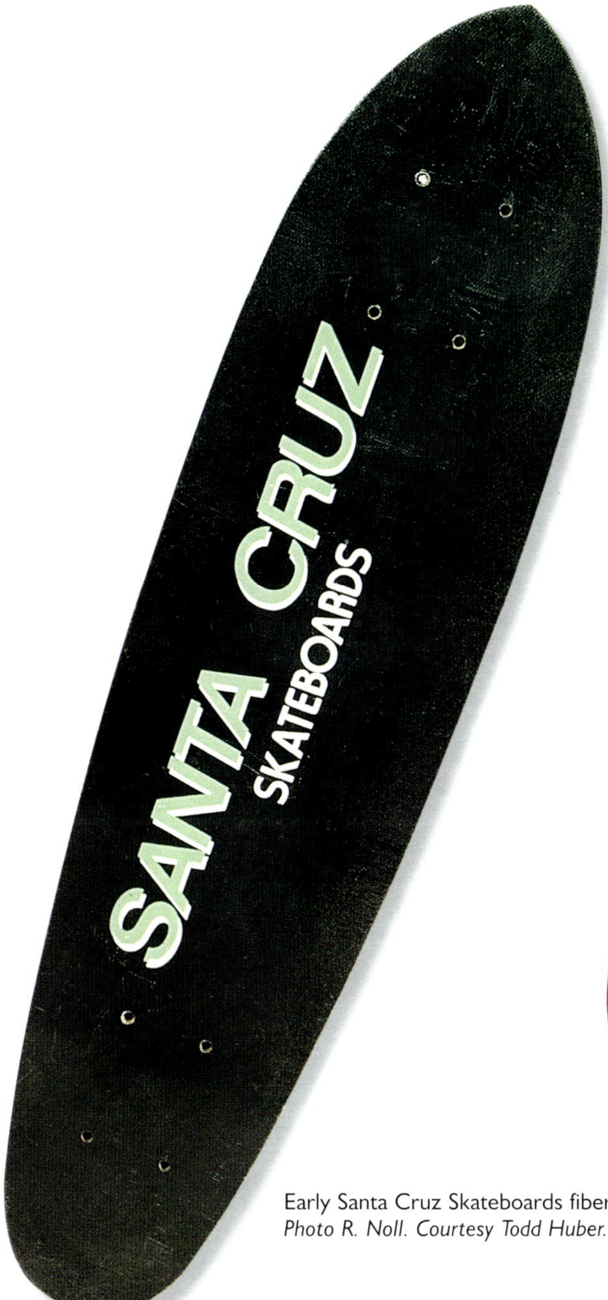

Early Santa Cruz Skateboards fiberglass deck. *Photo R. Noll. Courtesy Todd Huber.* $100.

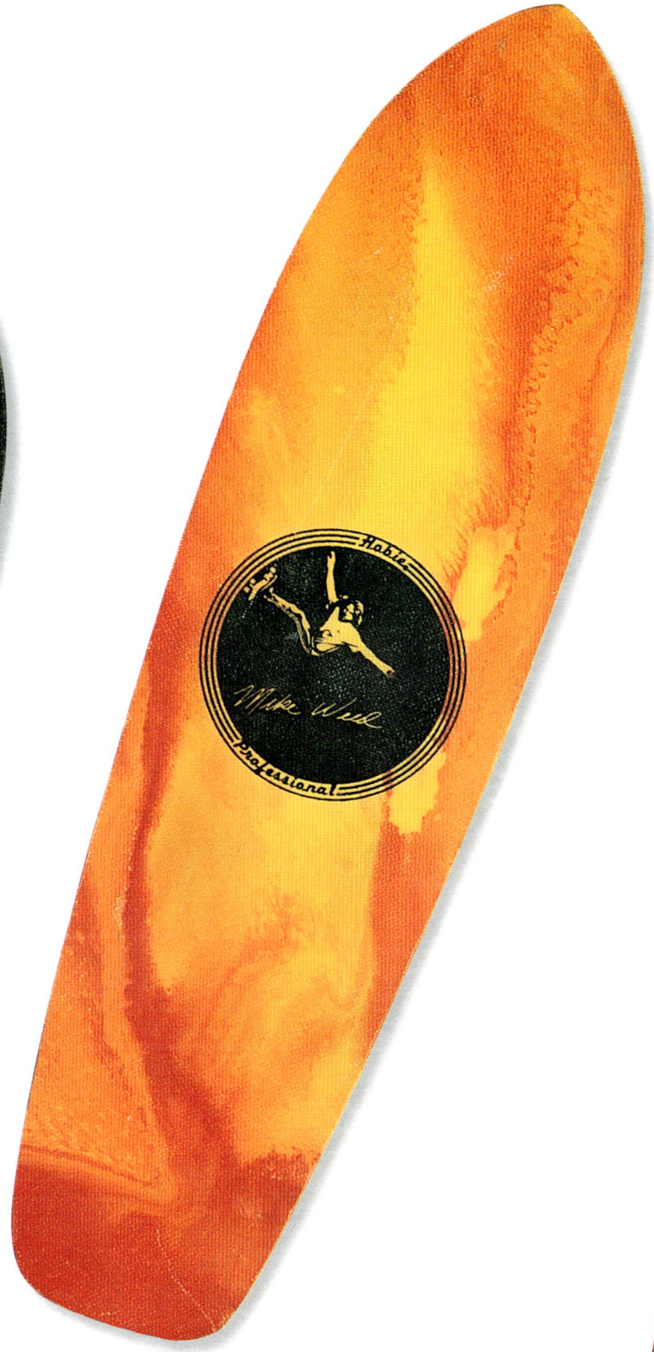

Mike Weed model. *Photo R. Noll. Courtesy Todd Huber.* $200.

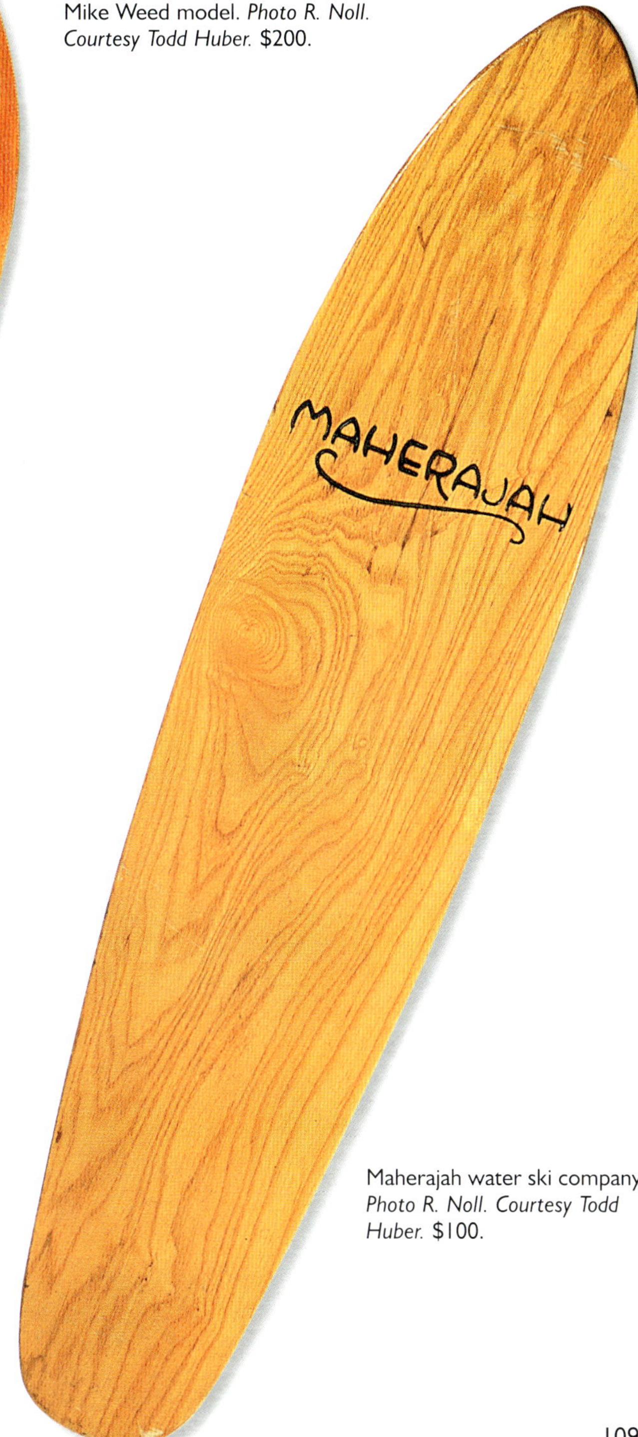

Maherajah water ski company. *Photo R. Noll. Courtesy Todd Huber.* $100.

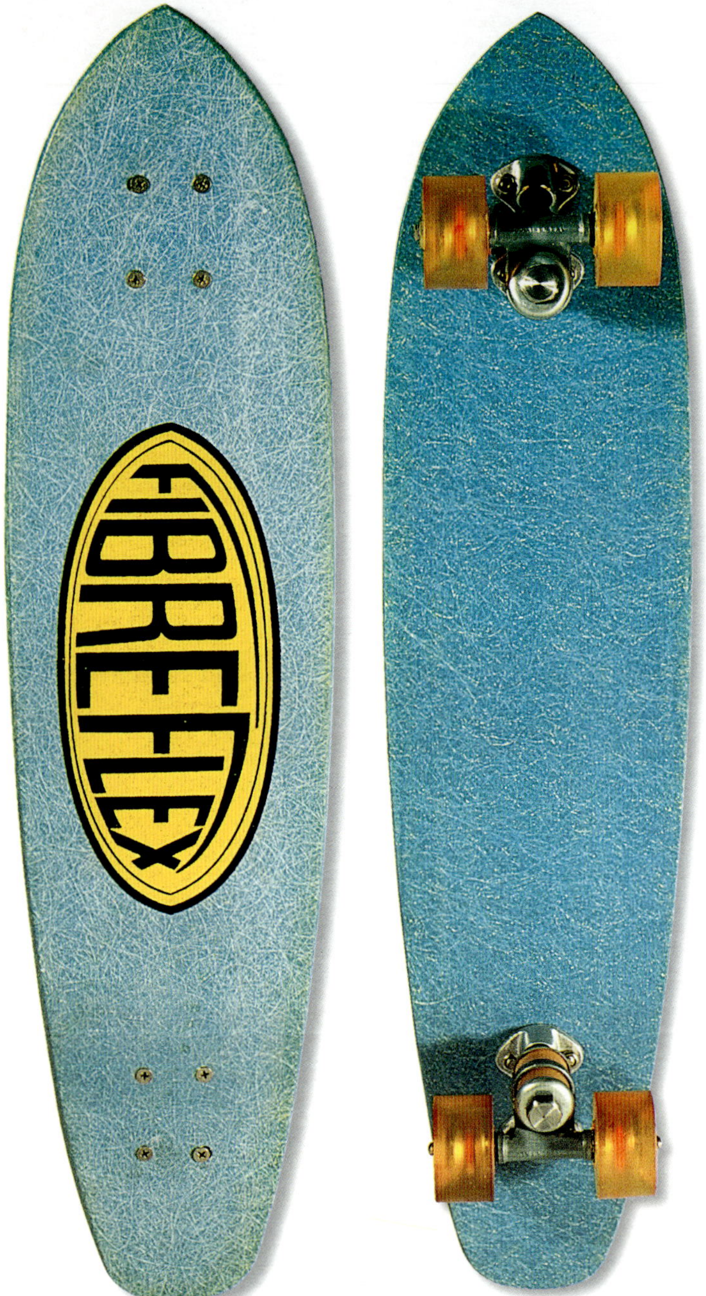

Bogus "FibreFlex." *Photo R. Noll. Courtesy Todd Huber.* $100.

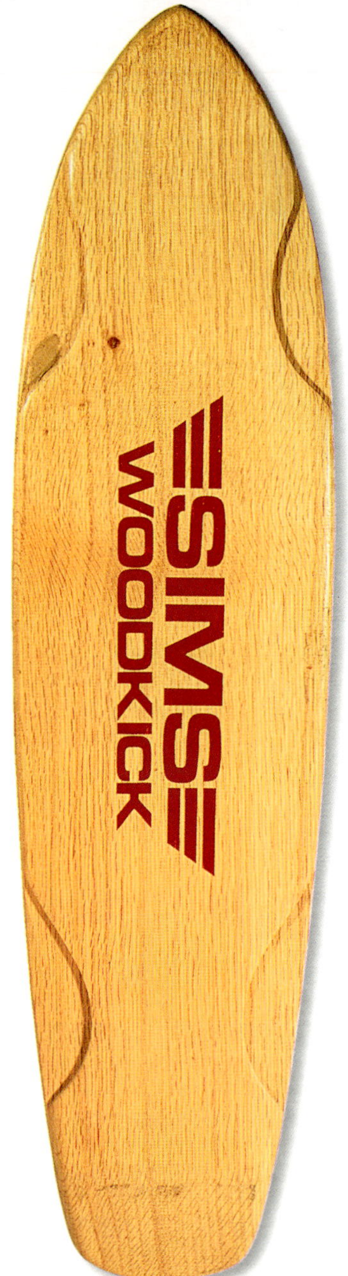

Sims wood kick. *Photo R. Noll. Courtesy Todd Huber.* $200-250.

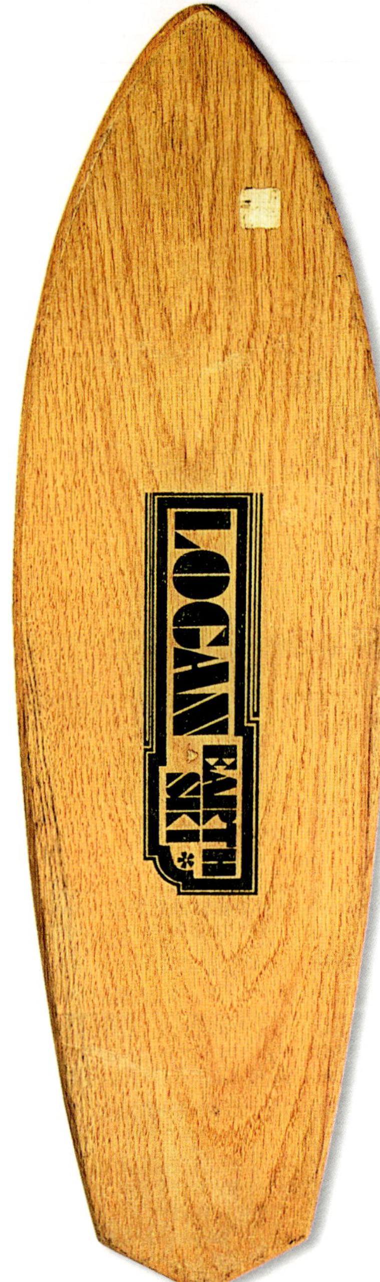

Logan Earth Ski. *Photo R. Noll. Courtesy Todd Huber.* $150.

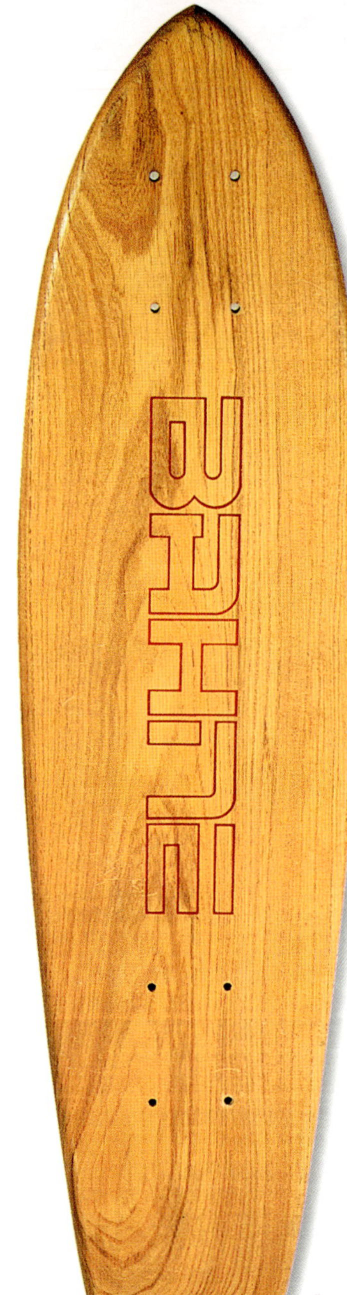

Bahne solid ash. *Photo R. Noll. Courtesy Todd Huber.* $150.

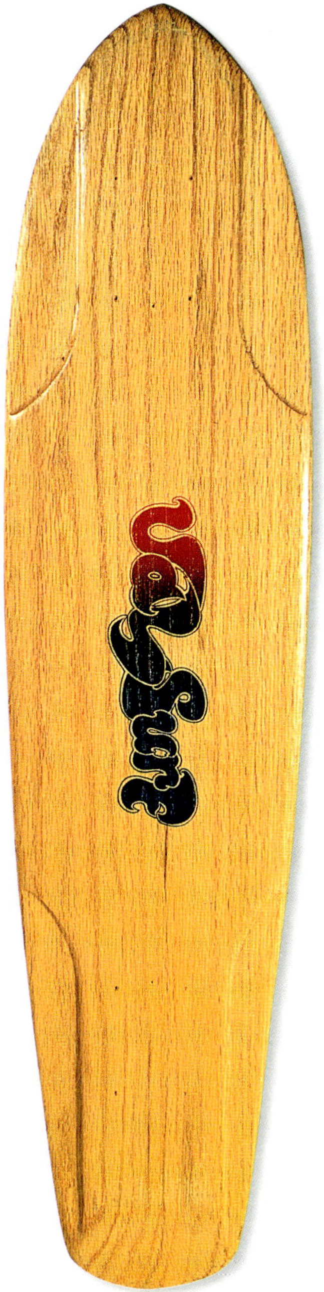

Oak Val Surf kick tail. *Photo R. Noll. Courtesy Todd Huber.* $100-150.

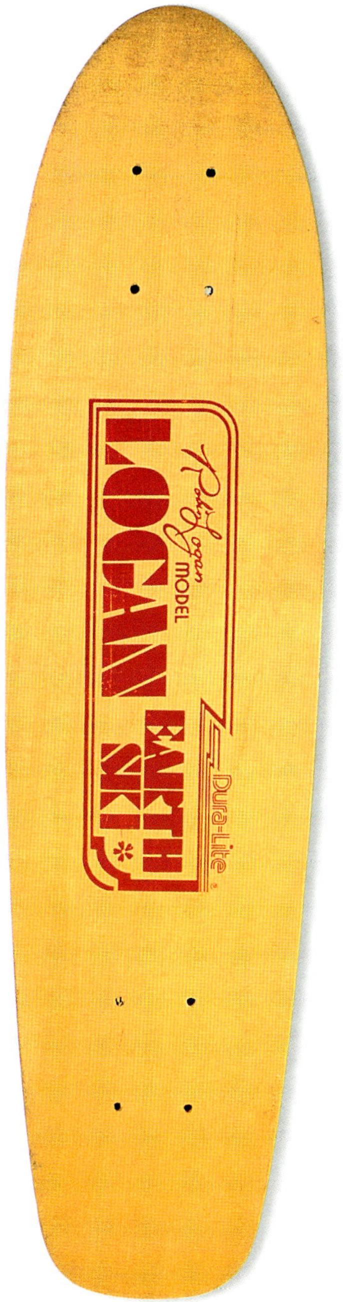

The Robin Logan model, Logan Earth Ski, Dura Light, kick tail. *Photo R. Noll. Courtesy Todd Huber.* $200.

Bahne fiberglass, common style. *Photo R. Nolla. Courtesy Todd Huber.* $75-100.

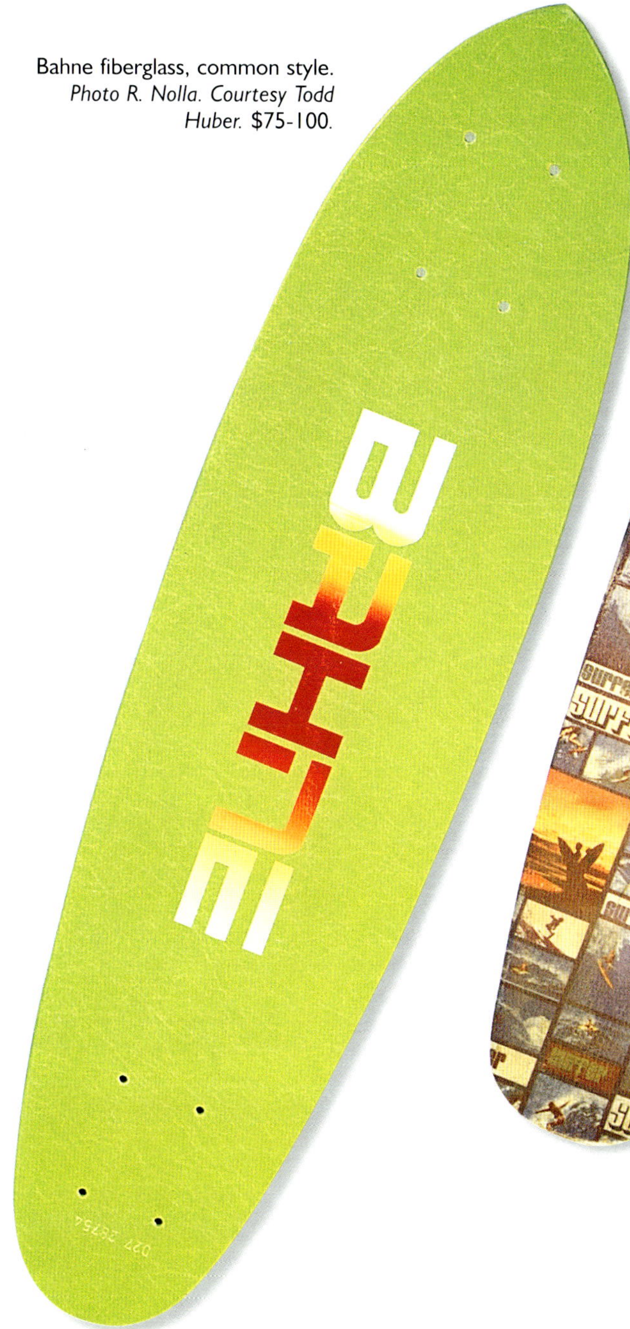

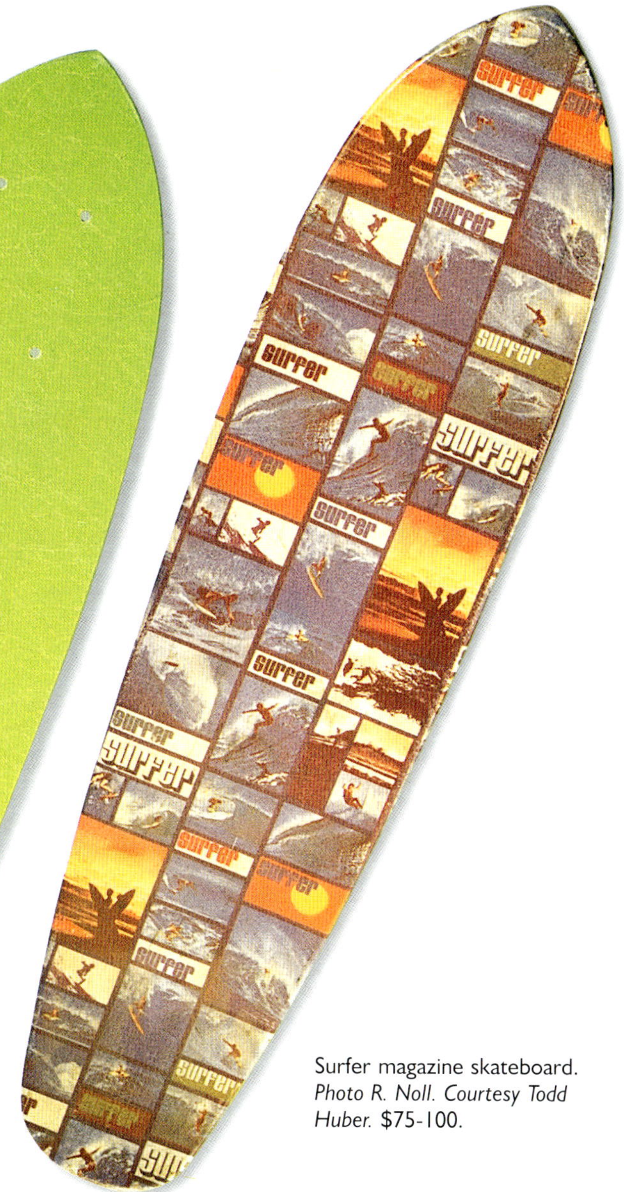

Surfer magazine skateboard. *Photo R. Noll. Courtesy Todd Huber.* $75-100.

The Bob Mohr Bullet by Bahne. *Photo R. Noll. Courtesy Todd Huber.* $300.

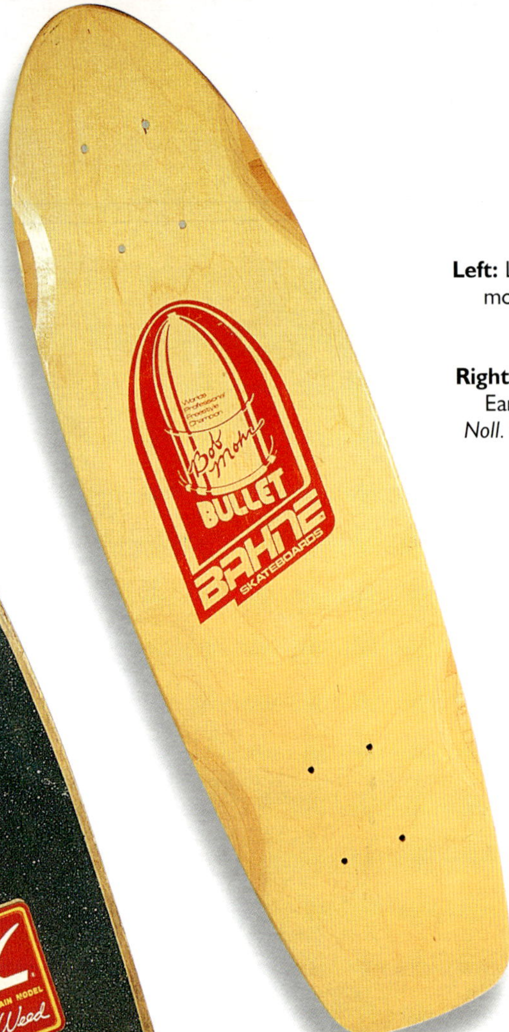

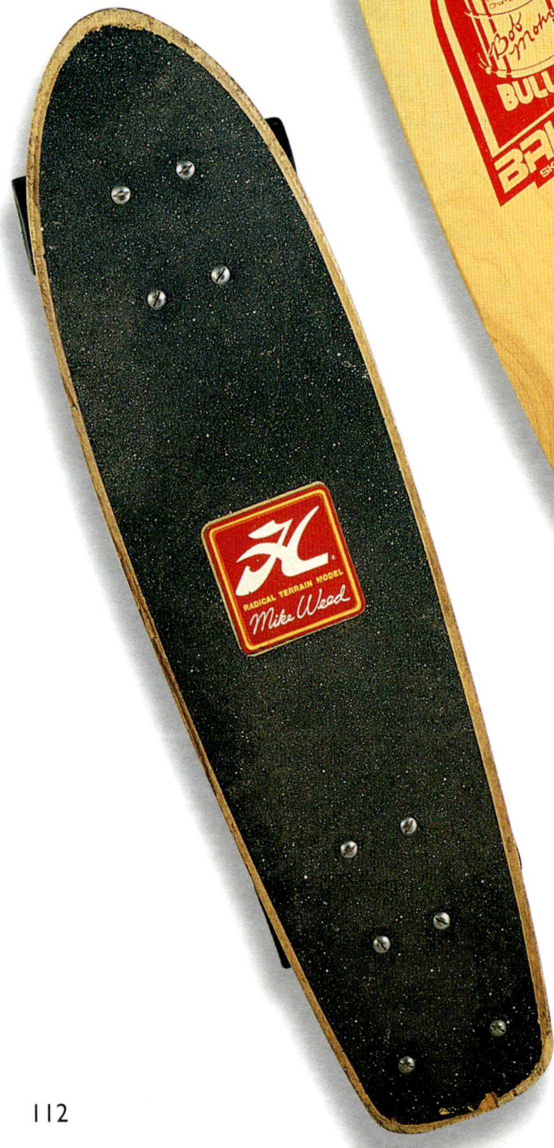

The Hobie, Mike Weed rough terrain model. *Photo R. Noll. Courtesy Todd Huber.* $200-300.

Left: Logan Earth Ski, Bob Biniak model. *Photo R. Noll. Courtesy Todd Huber.* $250.

Right: Brad Logan model, Logan Earth Ski, wedge tail. *Photo R. Noll. Courtesy Todd Huber.* $250.

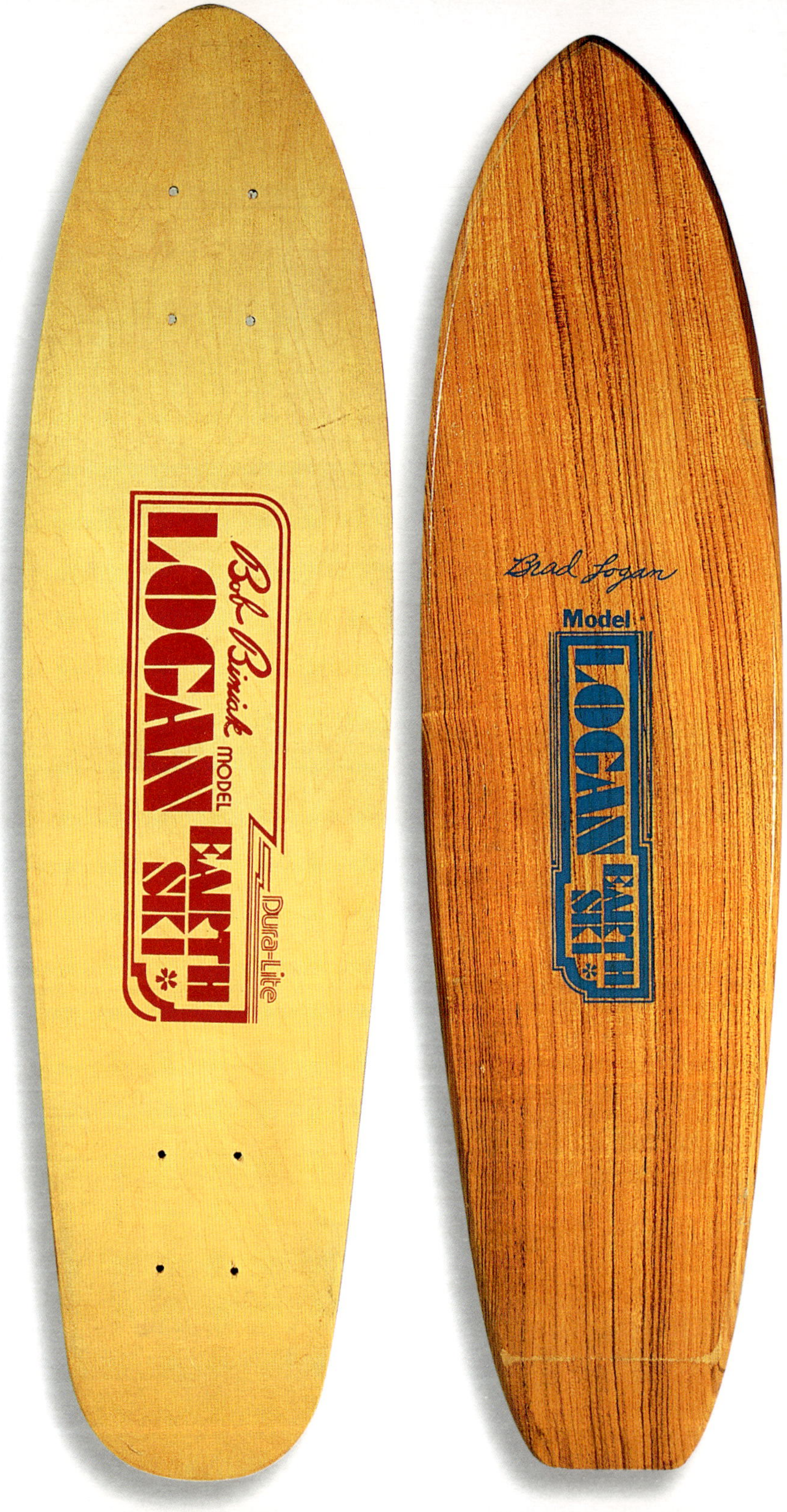

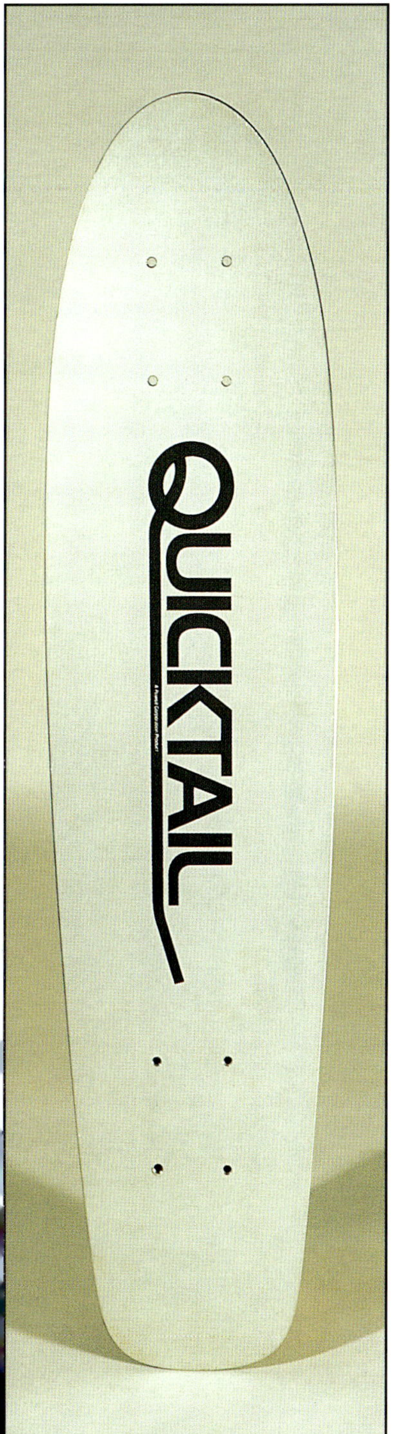

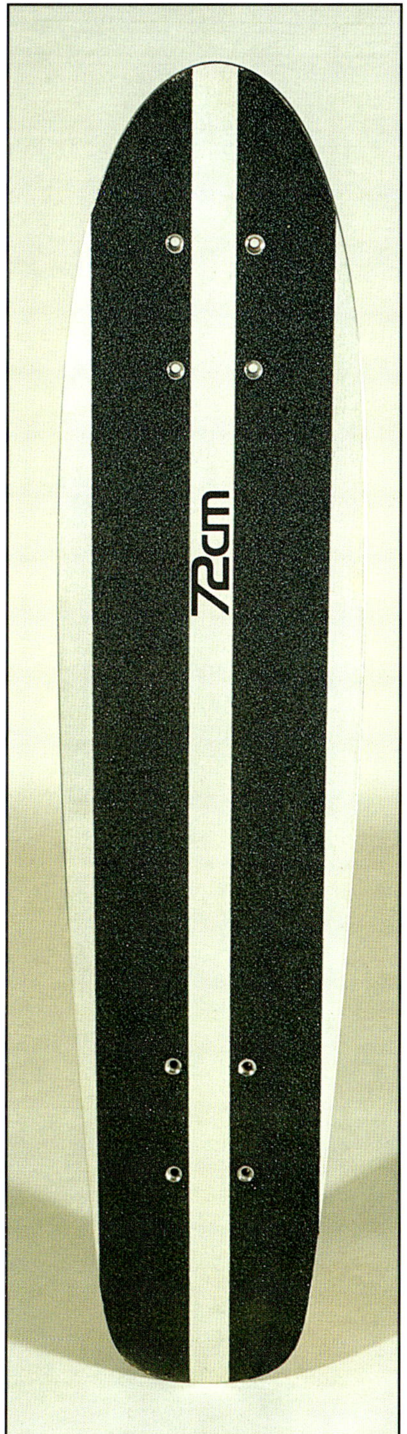

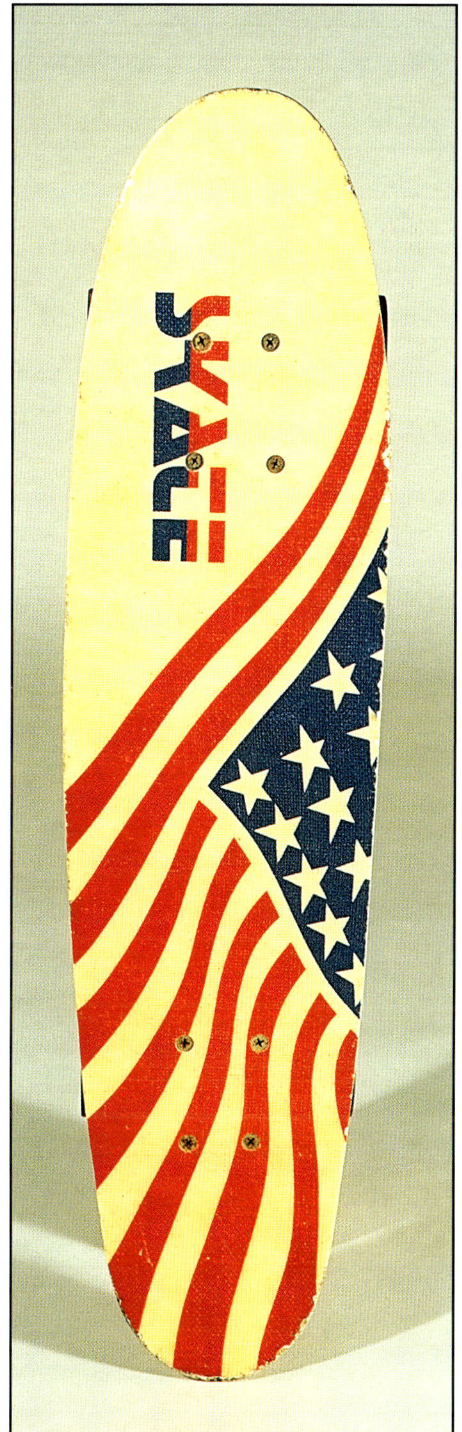

Left to right:
Powell Quicktail. *Photo R. Noll. Courtesy Todd Huber.* $250.

Photo R. Noll. Courtesy Todd Huber.

Simply the American skate. *Photo R. Noll. Courtesy Todd Huber.* $100.

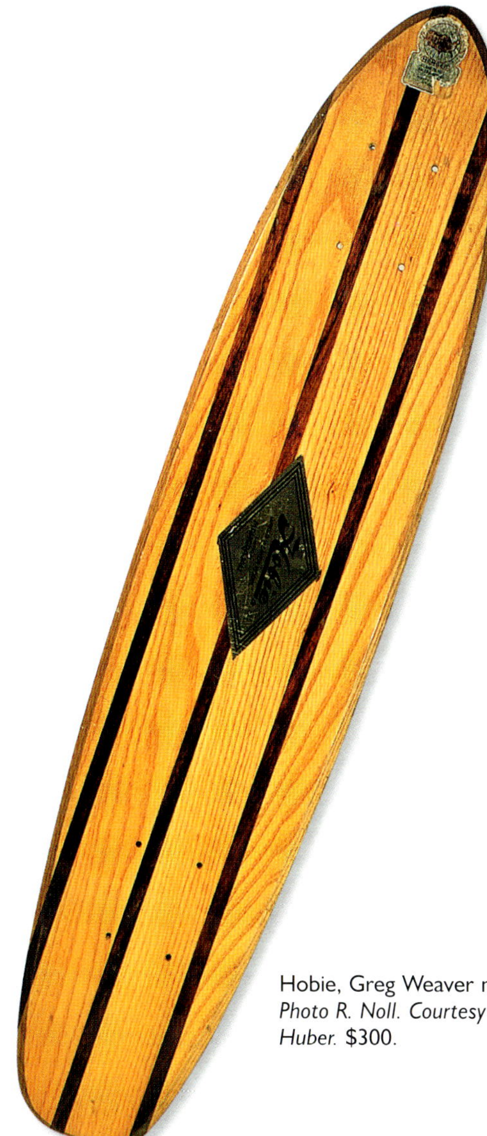

Hobie, Greg Weaver model. *Photo R. Noll. Courtesy Todd Huber.* $300.

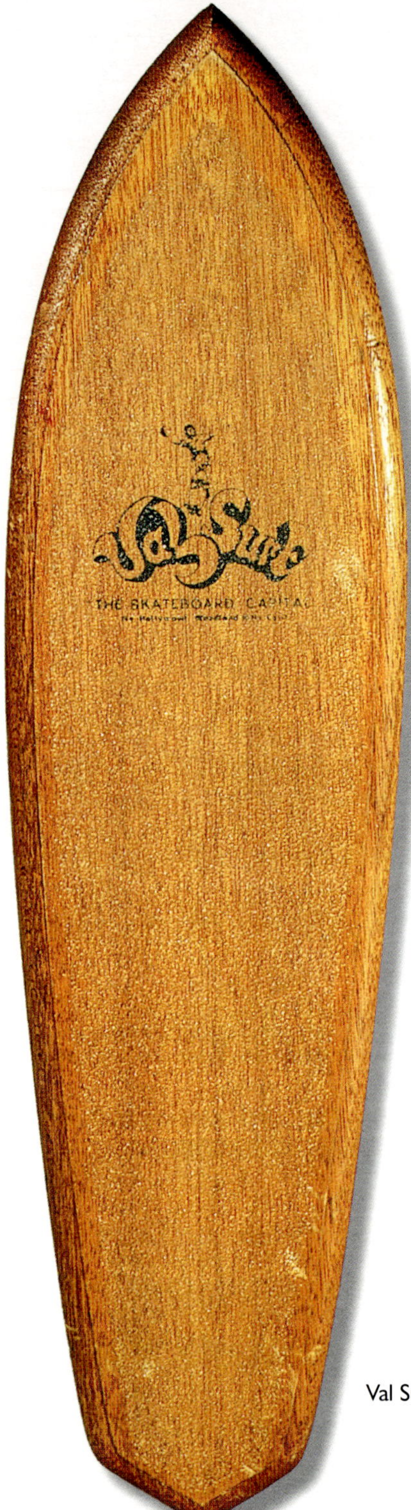

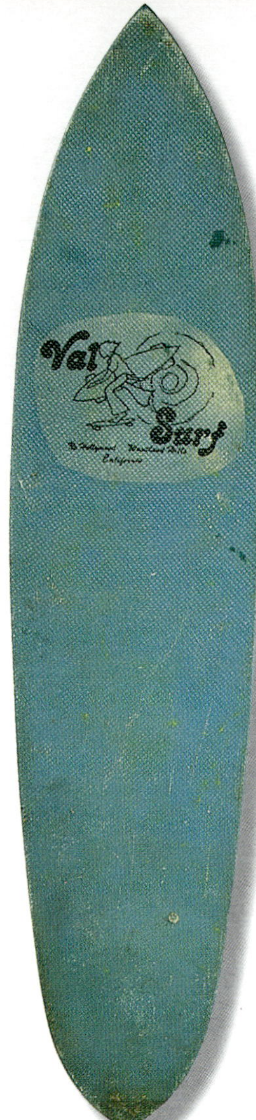

Val Surf. *Photo R. Noll. Courtesy Todd Huber.* $50.

Val Surf. *Photo R. Noll. Courtesy Todd Huber.* $75.

Hobie fiber-flex, mint condition deck only. *Photo R. Noll. Courtesy Todd Huber.* $75.

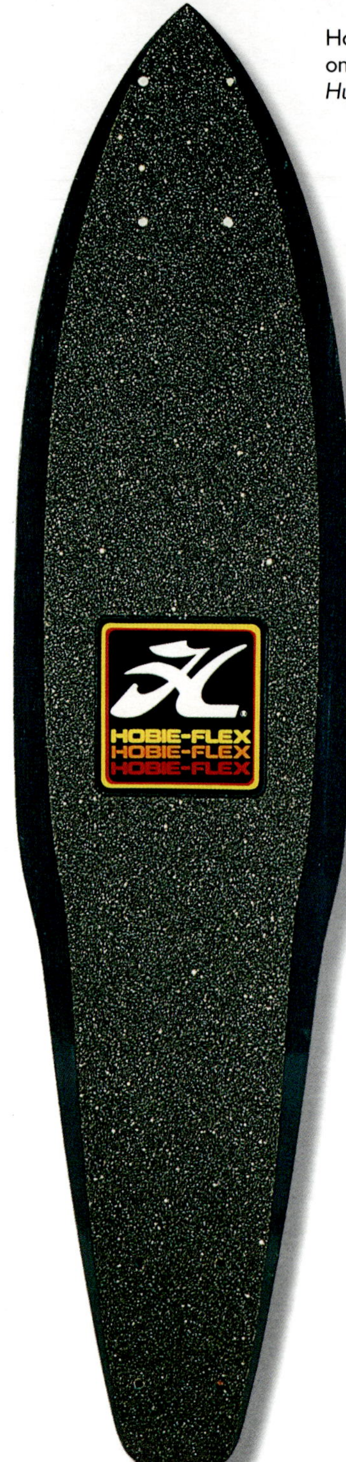

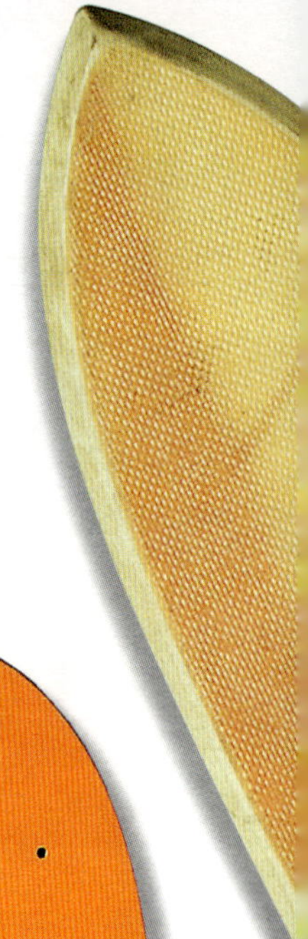

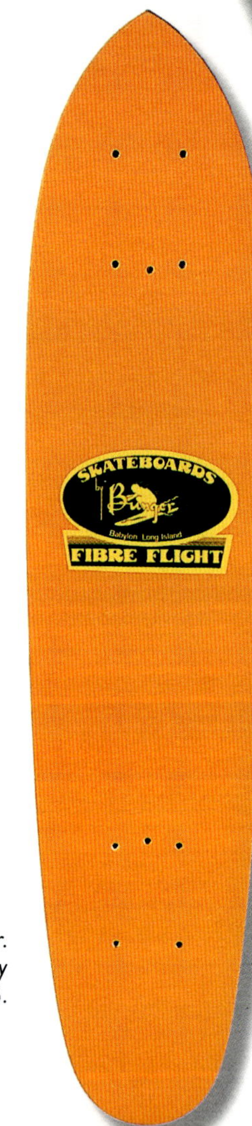

Fibre Flight by Bunger. *Photo R. Noll. Courtesy Todd Huber.* $75.

One of my favorites because this is what I rode in the 1970s. E T Surfboards, fiberglass. *Photo R. Noll. Courtesy Todd Huber.* $75.

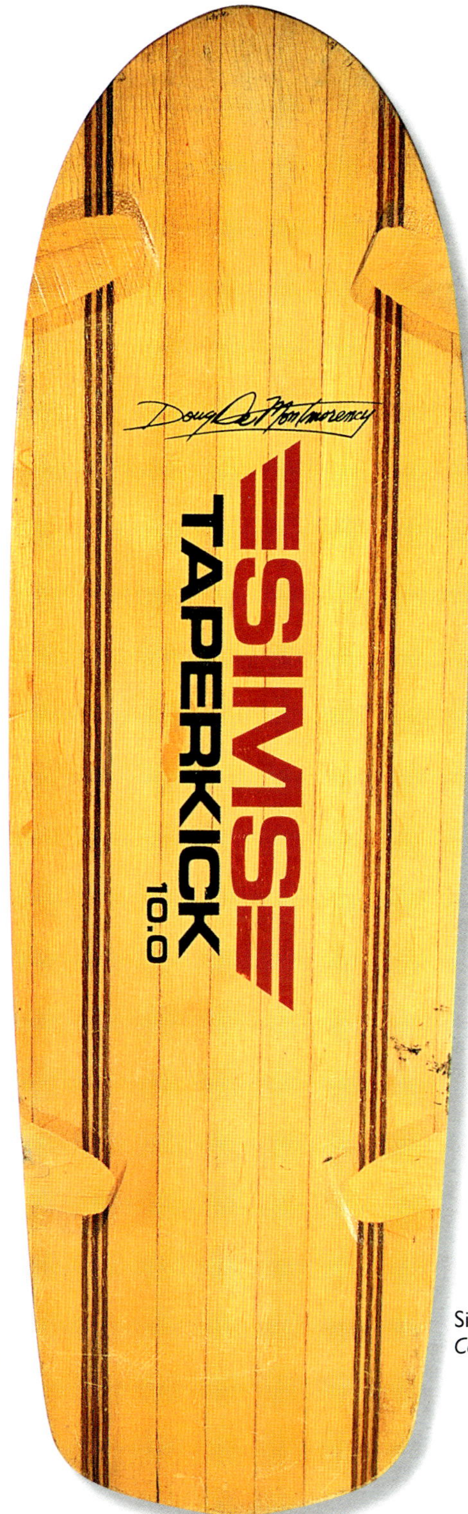

Sims Taperkick. *Photo R. Noll. Courtesy Todd Huber.* $300.

Surfer magazine skateboard with a glitch nose that wasn't printed. *Photo R. Noll. Courtesy Todd Huber.* $80.

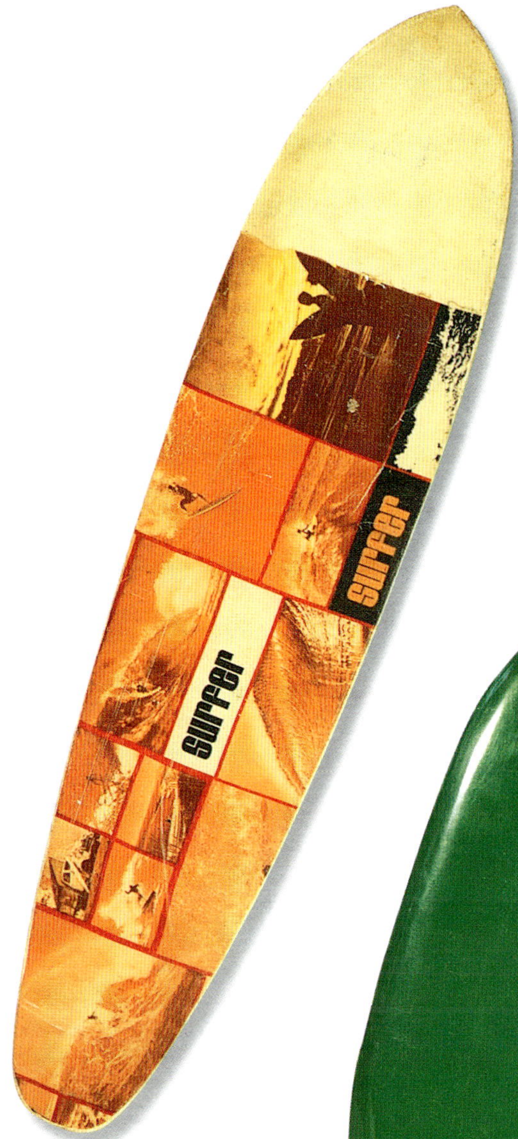

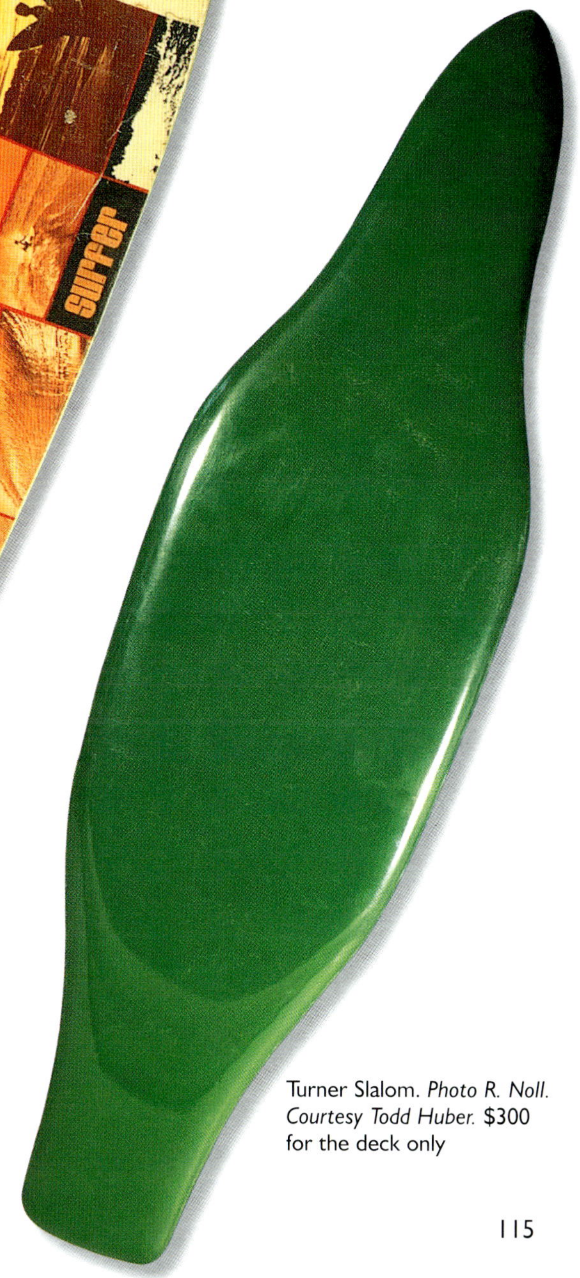

Turner Slalom. *Photo R. Noll. Courtesy Todd Huber.* $300 for the deck only

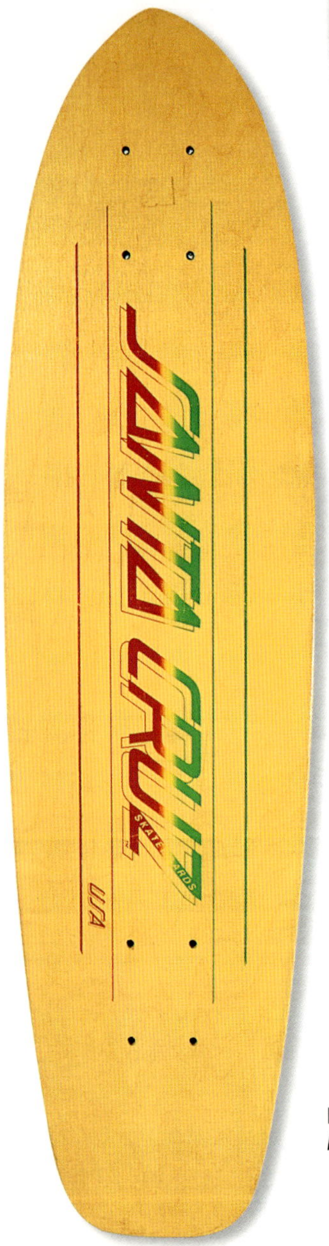

Early Santa Cruz deck. *Photo R. Noll. Courtesy Todd Huber.* $150.

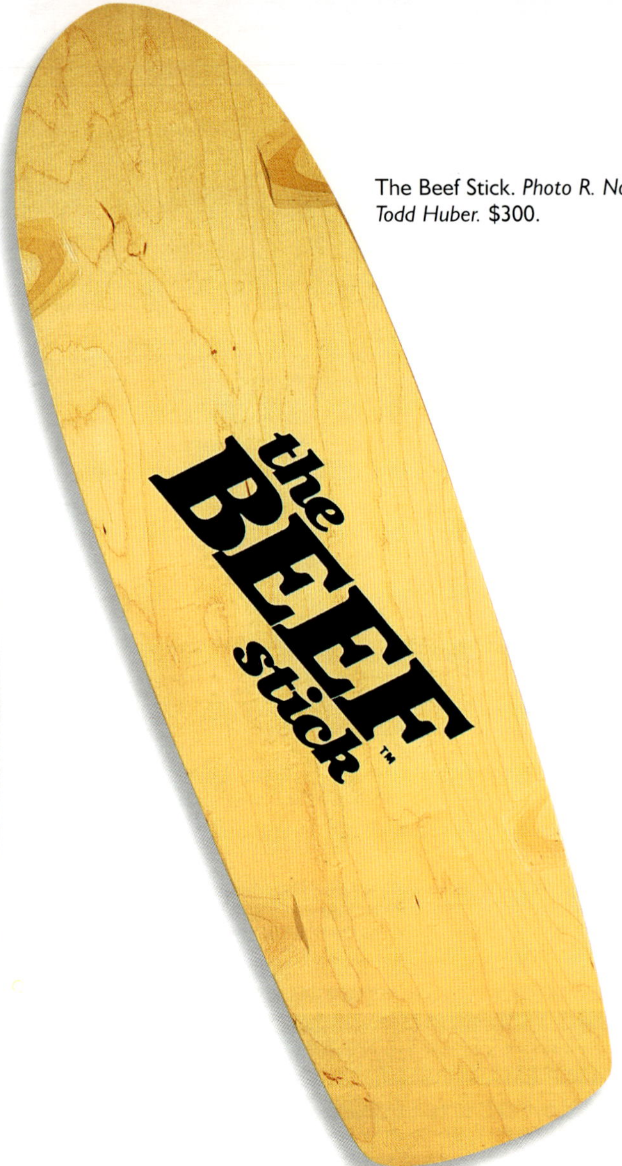

The Beef Stick. *Photo R. Noll. Courtesy Todd Huber.* $300.

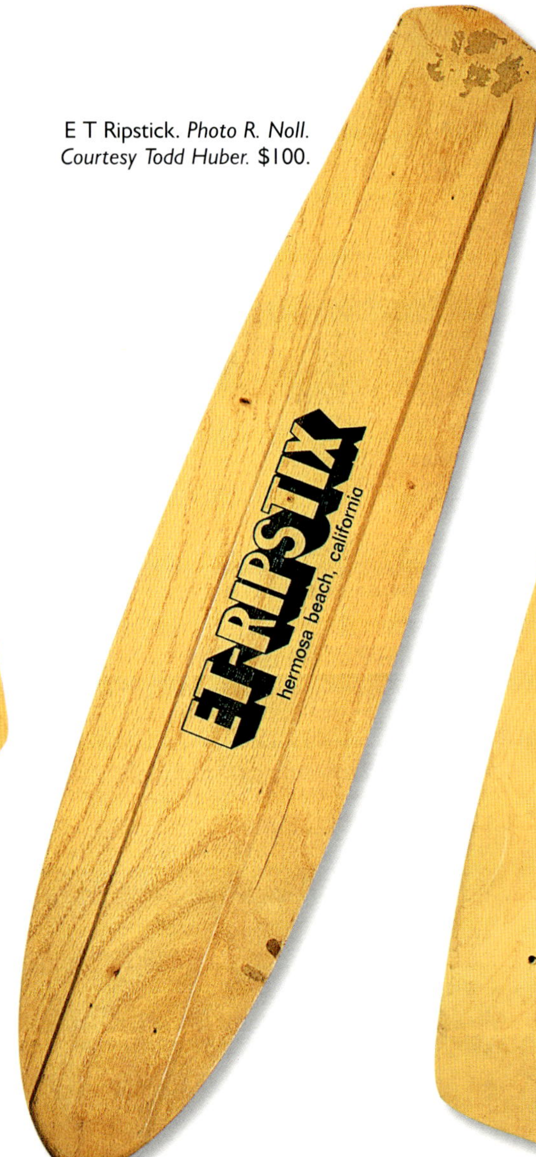

E T Ripstick. *Photo R. Noll. Courtesy Todd Huber.* $100.

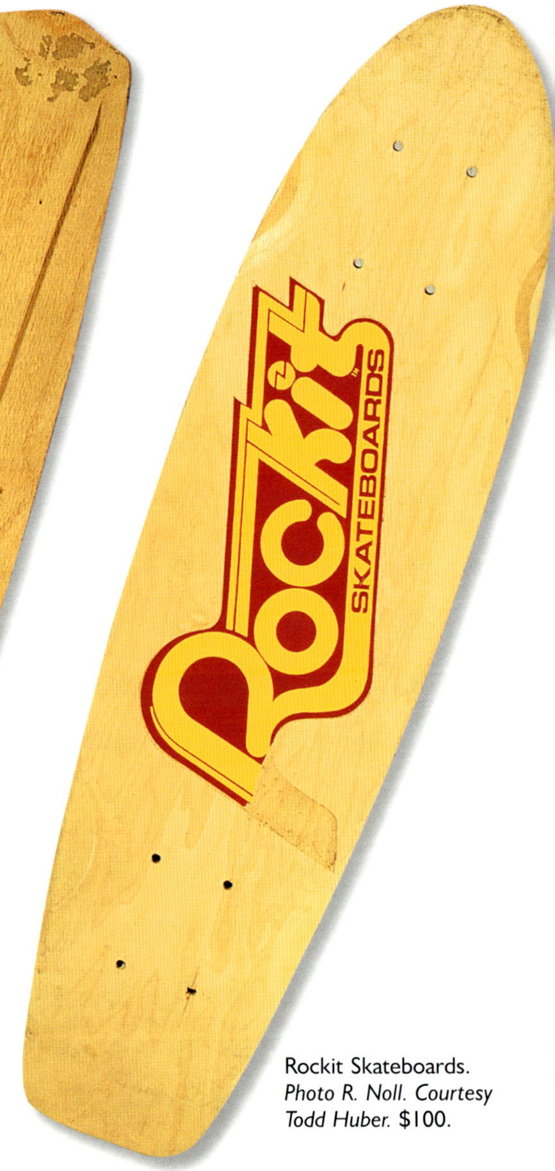

Rockit Skateboards. *Photo R. Noll. Courtesy Todd Huber.* $100.

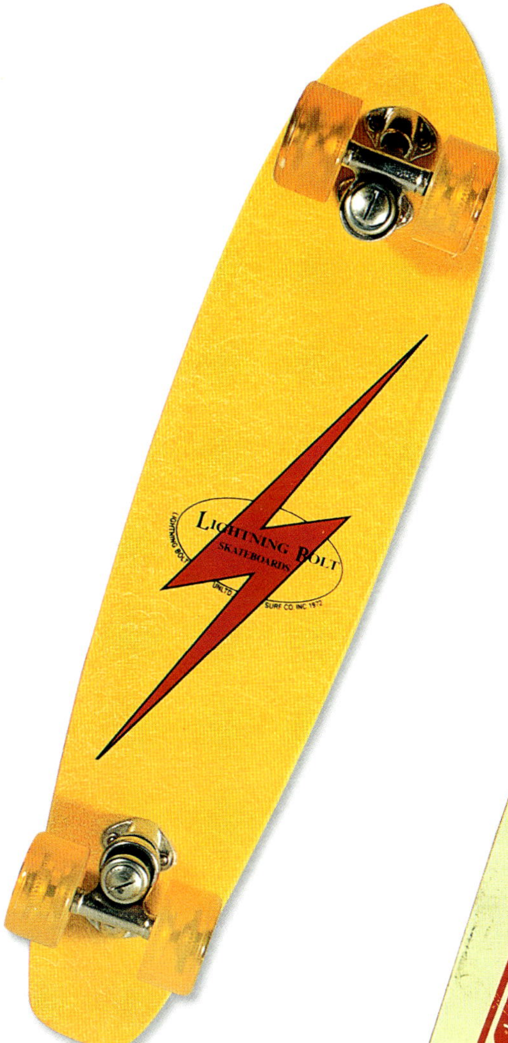

Lightning Bolt skateboard. *Photo R. Noll. Courtesy Todd Huber.* $150.

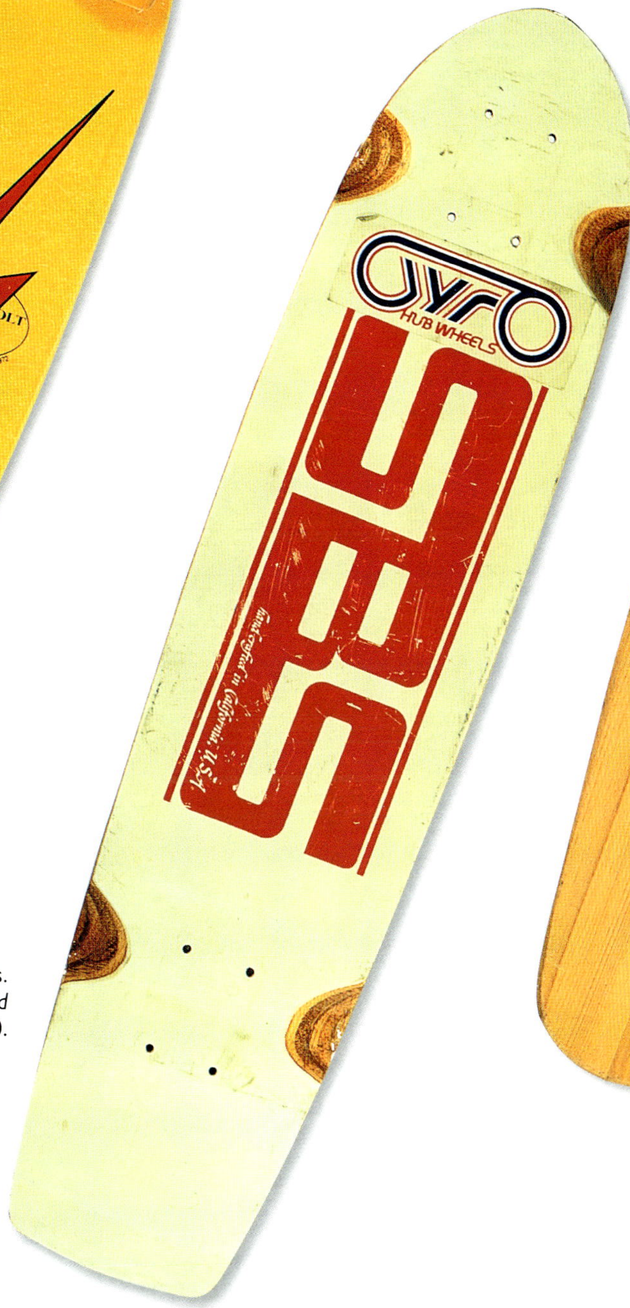

Santa Barbara Skateboards. *Photo R. Noll. Courtesy Todd Huber.* $150-200.

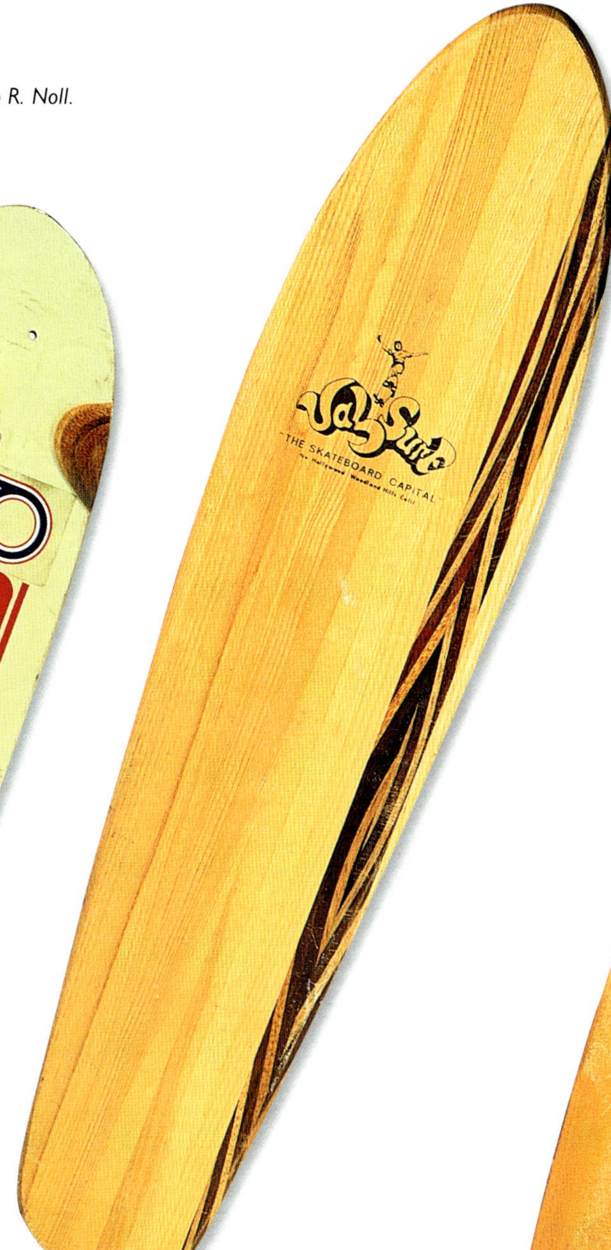

Val Surf board with inlay. *Photo R. Noll. Courtesy Todd Huber.* $300.

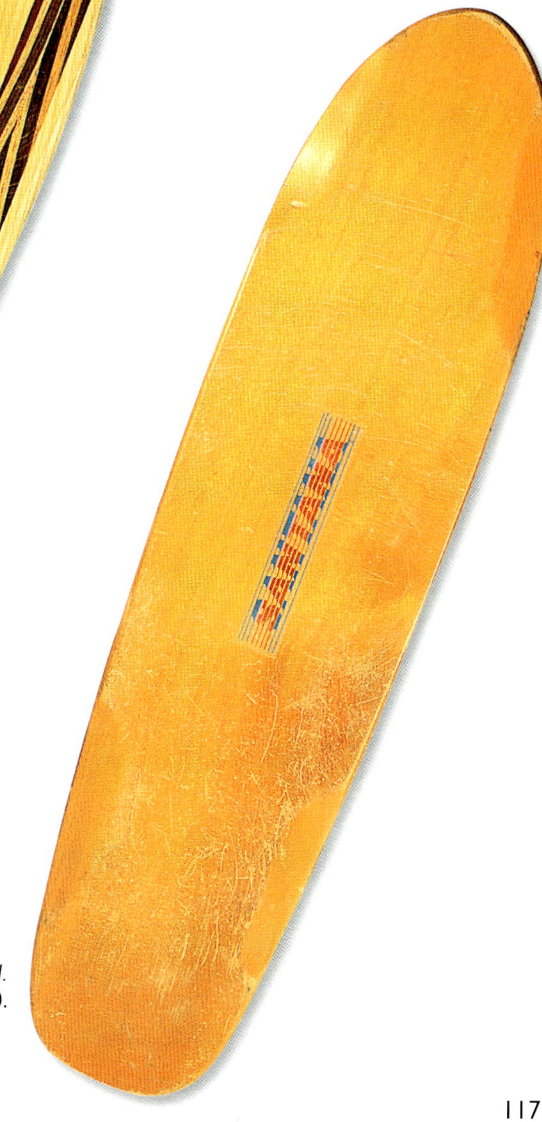

The Santana. *Photo R. Noll. Courtesy Todd Huber.* $150.

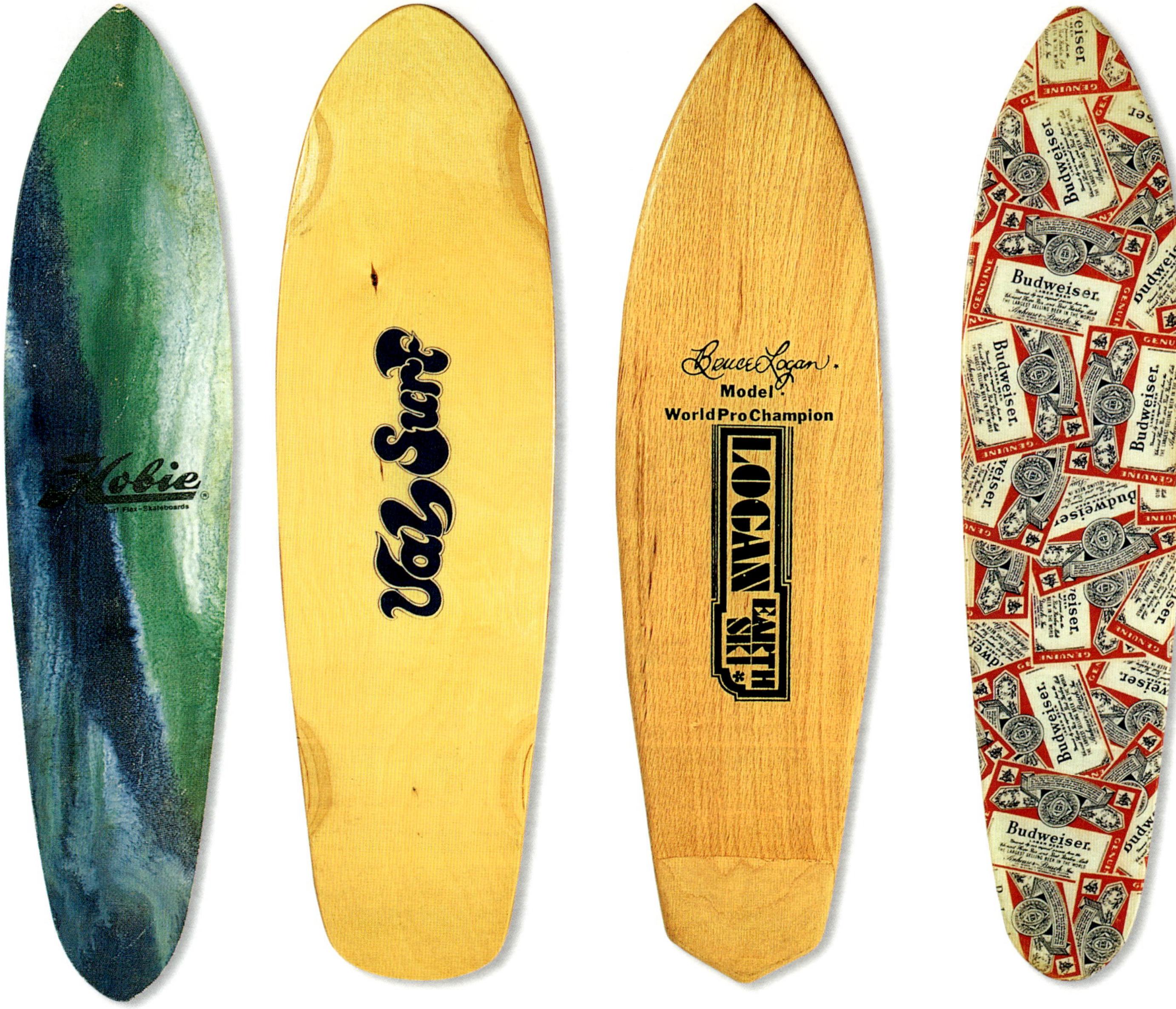

Left to right:
Hobie fiberglass board. *Photo R. Noll. Courtesy Todd Huber.* $150.

Val Surf kicktail. *Photo R. Noll. Courtesy Todd Huber.* $100.

The Bruce Logan model, Logan Earth Ski. *Photo R. Noll. Courtesy Todd Huber.* $100.

The Bud board. *Photo R. Noll. Courtesy Todd Huber.* $75.

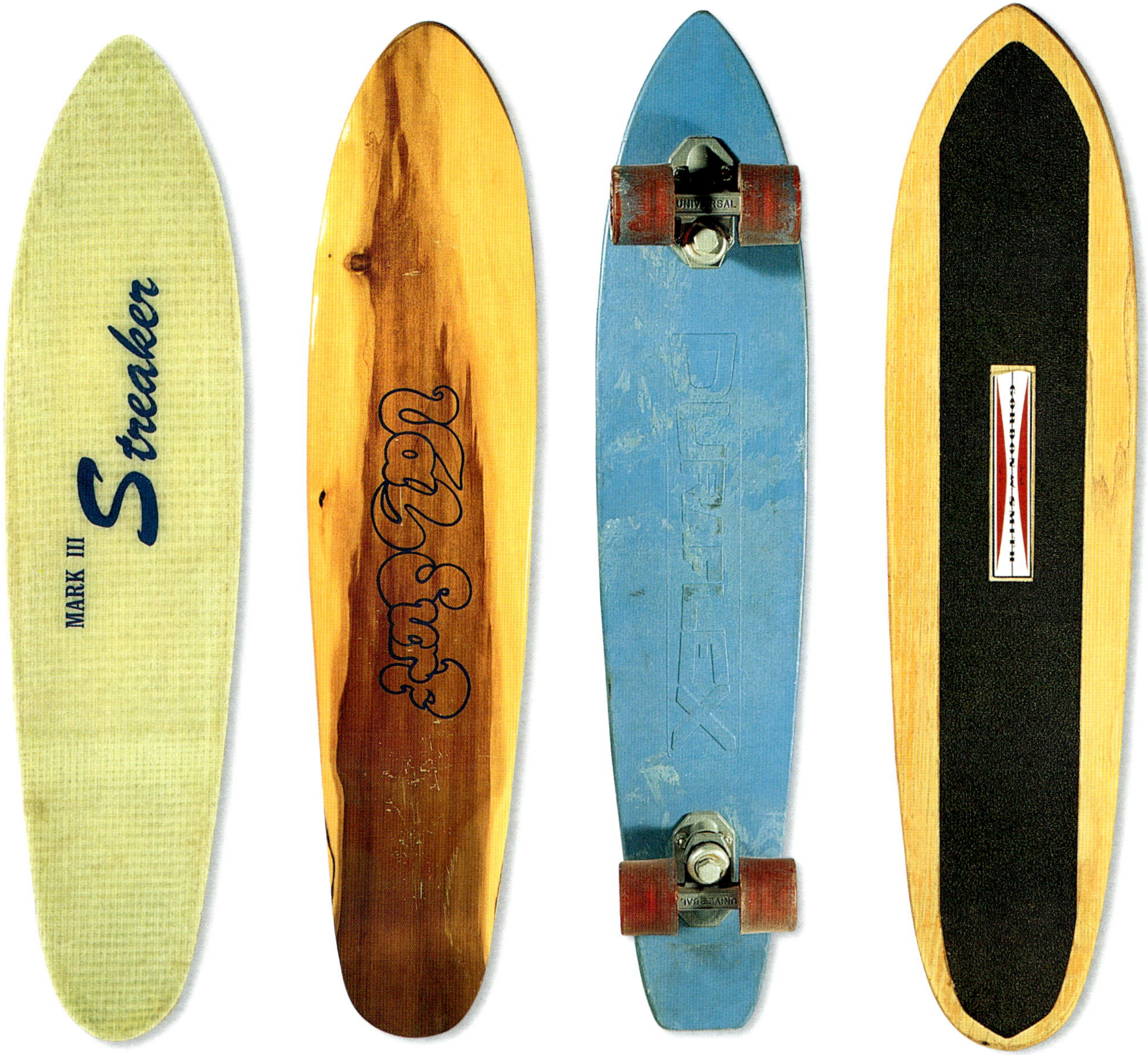

Left to right:
The Mark III Streaker. Remember, the 1970s was the "streaking" decade. *Photo R. Noll. Courtesy Todd Huber.* $150.

Val Surf kicktail. *Photo R. Noll. Courtesy Todd Huber.* $75.

Duraflex. *Photo R. Noll. Courtesy Todd Huber.* $75.

Gordon and Smith kicktail. *Photo R. Noll. Courtesy Todd Huber.* $100-150.

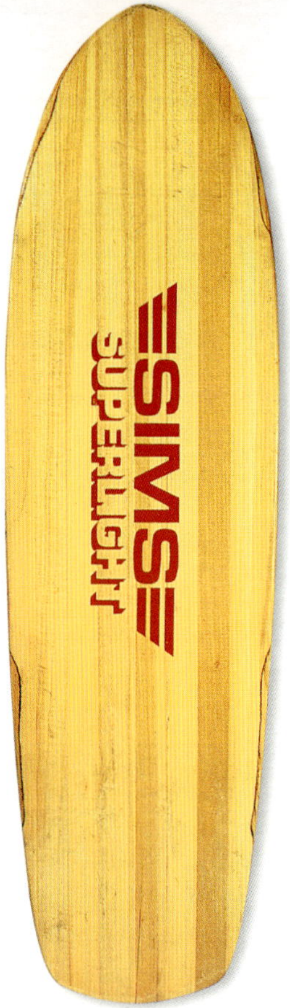

Sims Superlight kicktail. *Photo R. Noll. Courtesy Todd Huber.* $300.

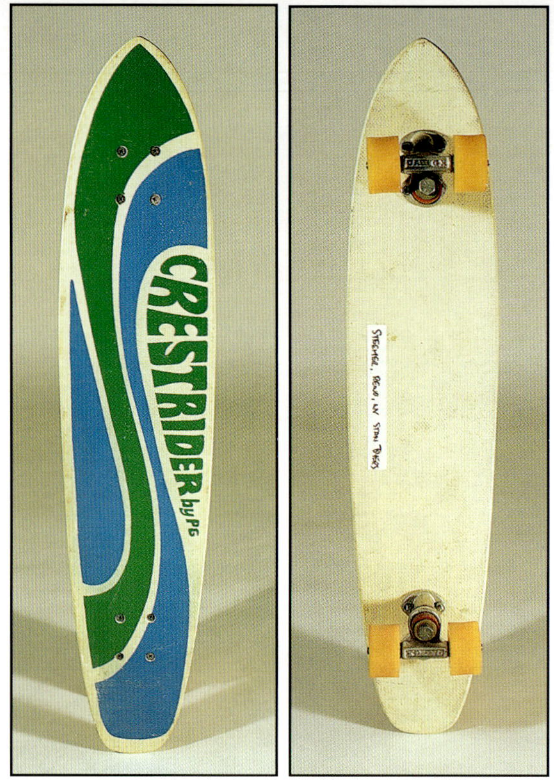

The Crestrider by PG. *Photo R. Noll. Courtesy Todd Huber.* $75.

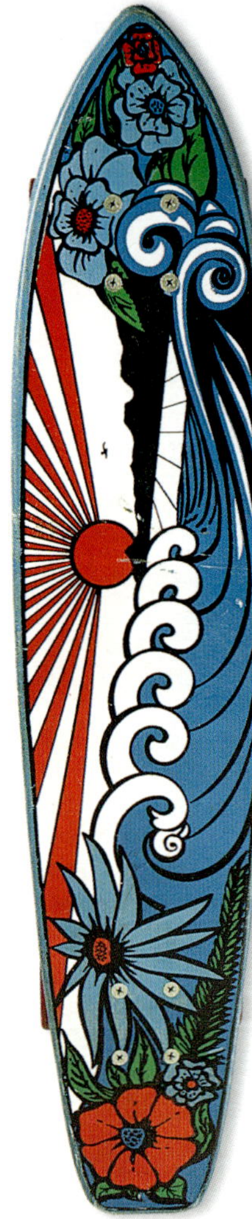

Unknown 1970s board. *Photo R. Noll. Courtesy Todd Huber.* $100.

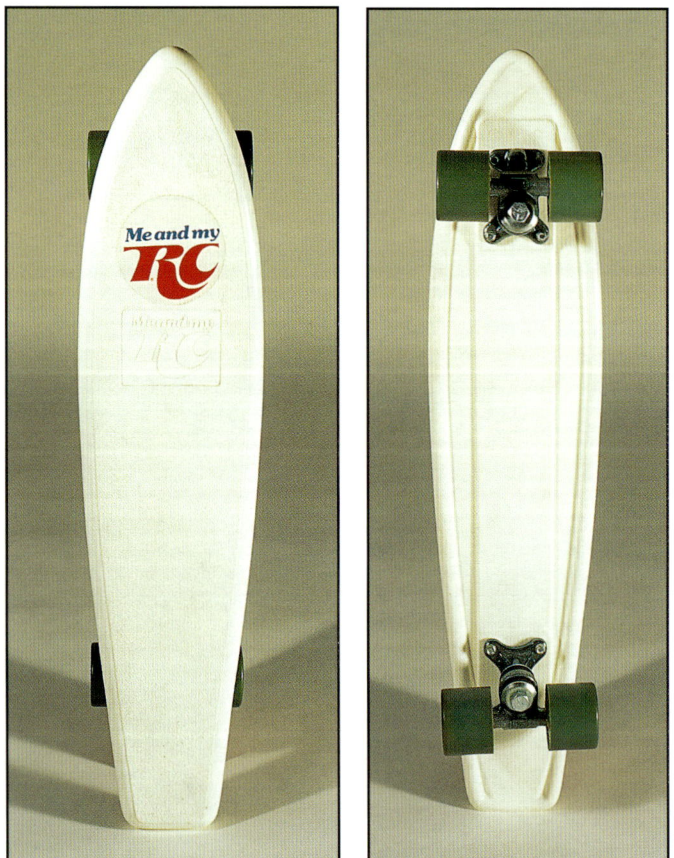

R C Cola board. *Photo R. Noll. Courtesy Todd Huber.* $50.

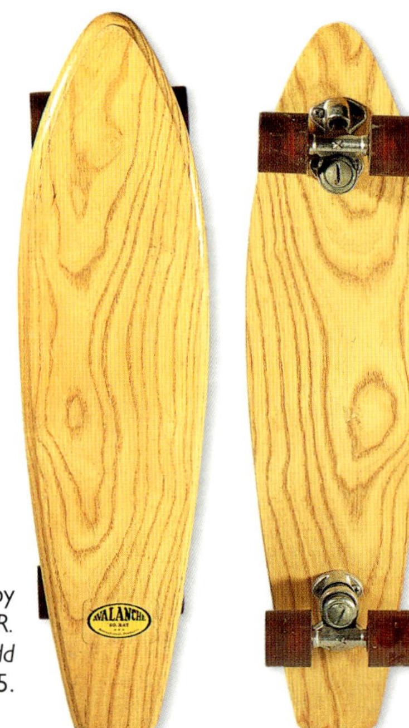

The Avalanche by South Bay. *Photo R. Noll. Courtesy Todd Huber.* $75.

1980s Skateboards

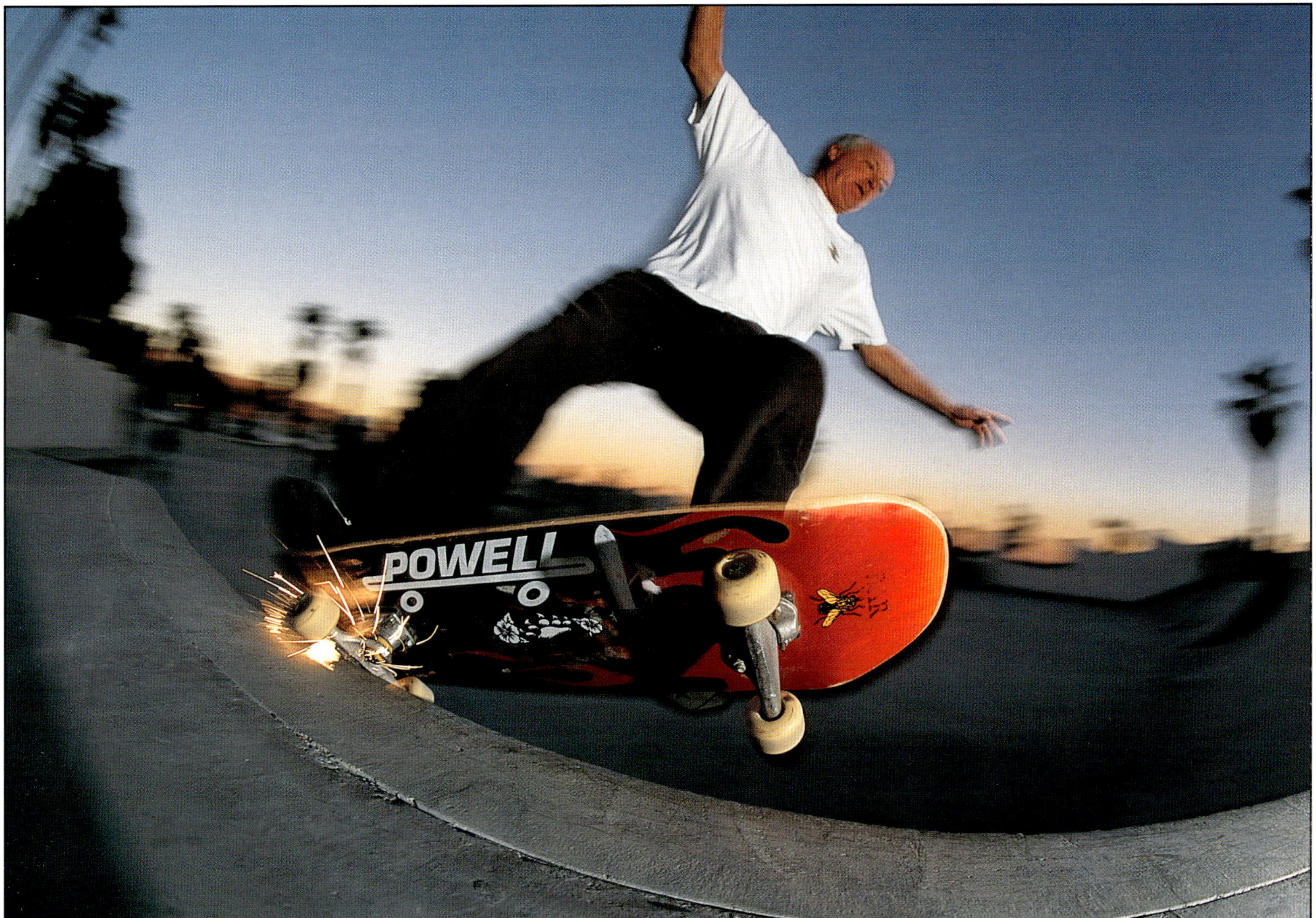

Jim O'Mahoney with his curbburner. *Photo Scott Starr. Courtesy James O'Mahoney.*

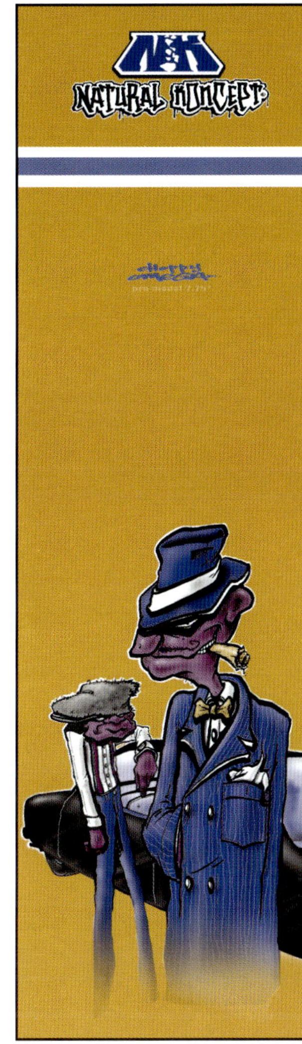

Choppy Thug, Katch Art. *Courtesy Natural Concepts.*

When I remember the 1980s, I think of Mohawk haircuts, punk bands, neon, and rebellion. These times were some of the best of my life. It has been said that Christian Hasoi was the essence of the '80s, and the buzzwords of the day were "big air" and "wild hair." New attitudes prevailed and the '80s held much change for the skateboarding world. Skaters rejected old traditions and tried to create new ones. Hence, the term "new school."

The 1980s rocked in more ways than one. Besides all the insane music that was produced, some punk rock bands even had skateboards made with their logos. I suppose a lot of folks were glad the '80s are over, but I kind of miss them. In fact, I still listen to a lot of '80s music.

The unsettled '80s has finally found its place and settled into history where it belongs. It is a piece of the great puzzle that brings us to today.

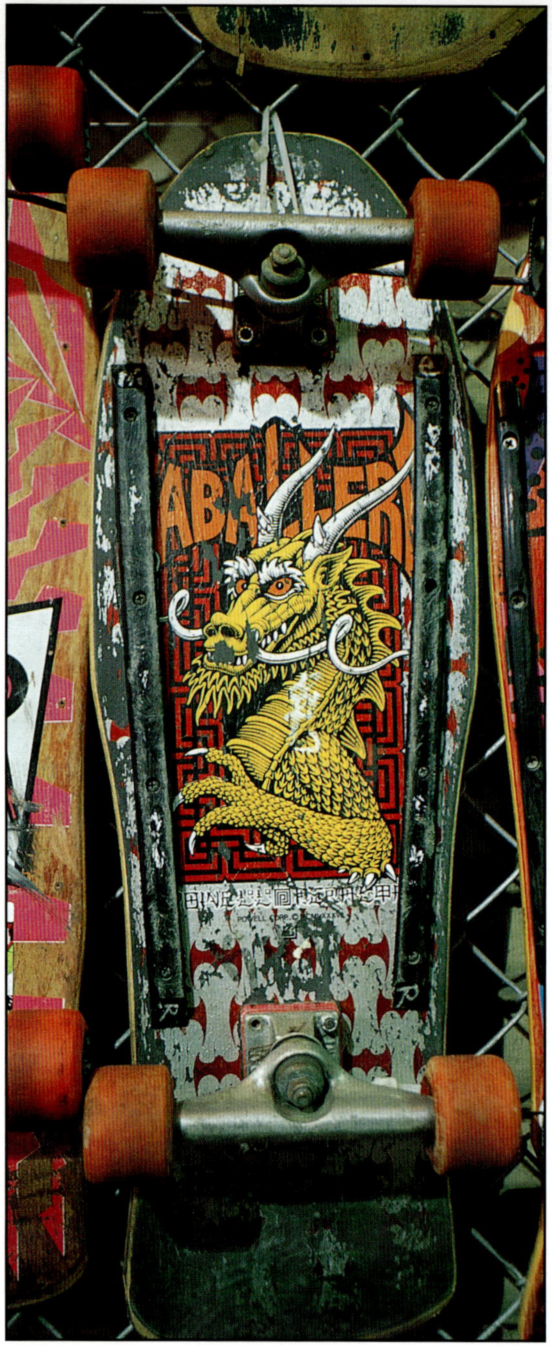

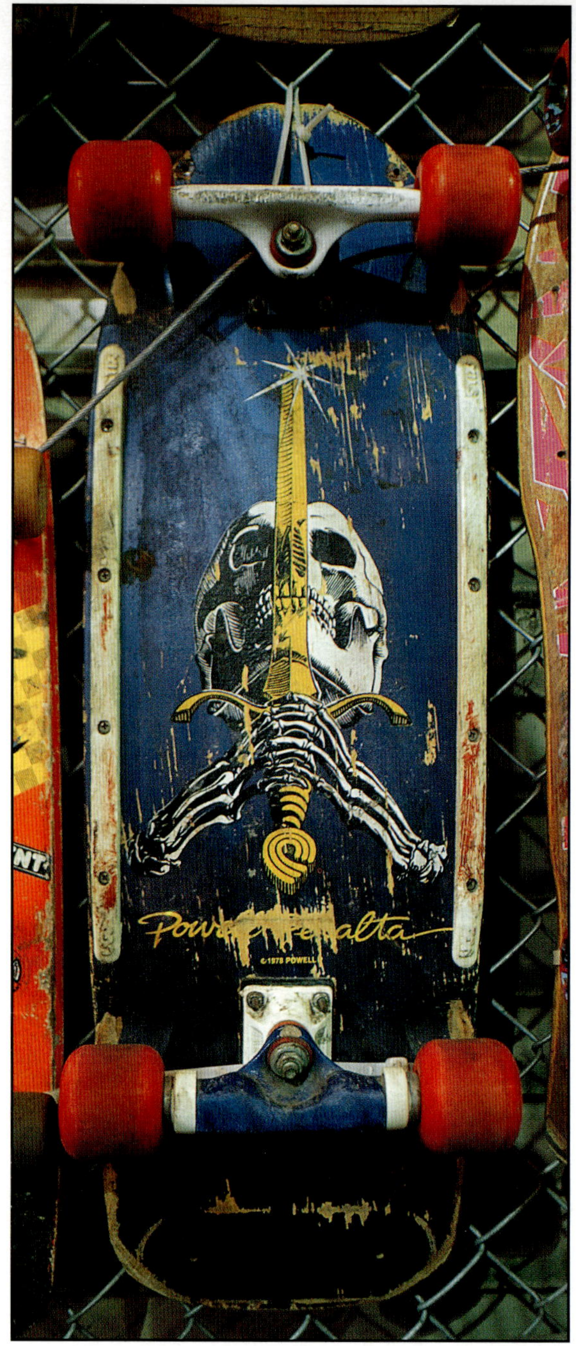

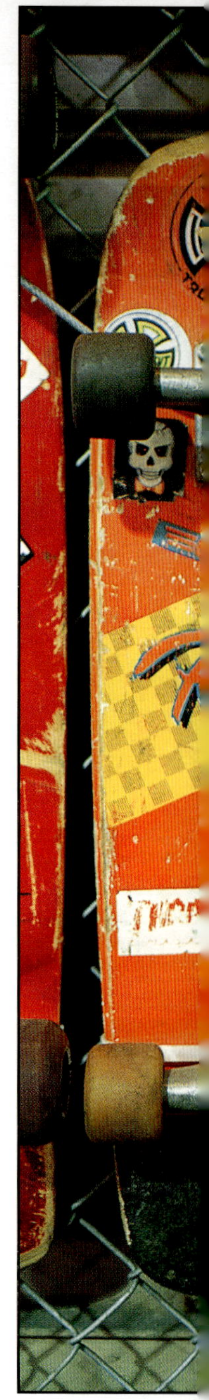

Together, these 1980s boards create an array of color and design. *Photos R. Noll. Courtesy Todd Huber.*
Caballero model. $200-300.
Powell Peralta. $500-600.
Roco freestyle. $300-400.
Powell Peralta, Rodney Mullen model. $300-400.
Alva, Eddie Reatrgui model. $200-300.
Vision, Gator model. $200-400.

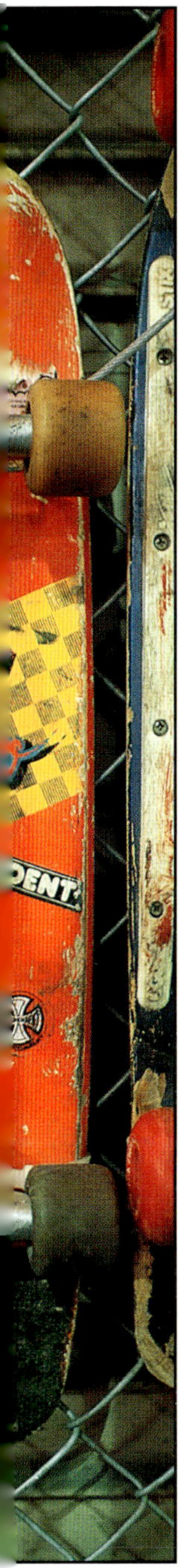

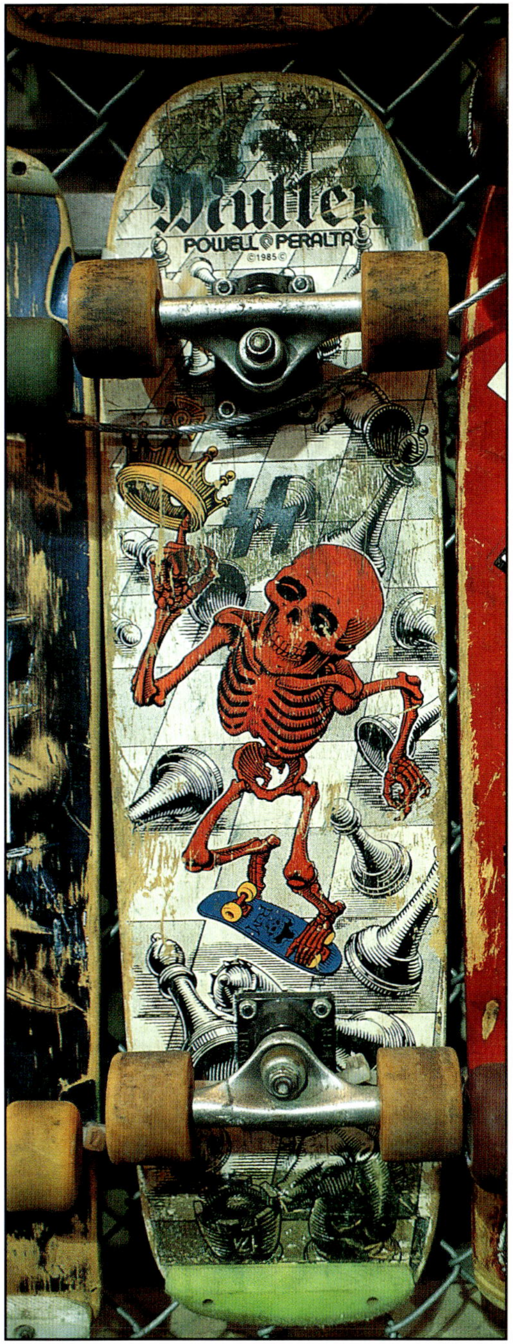
Mullen
POWELL PERALTA
©1985©

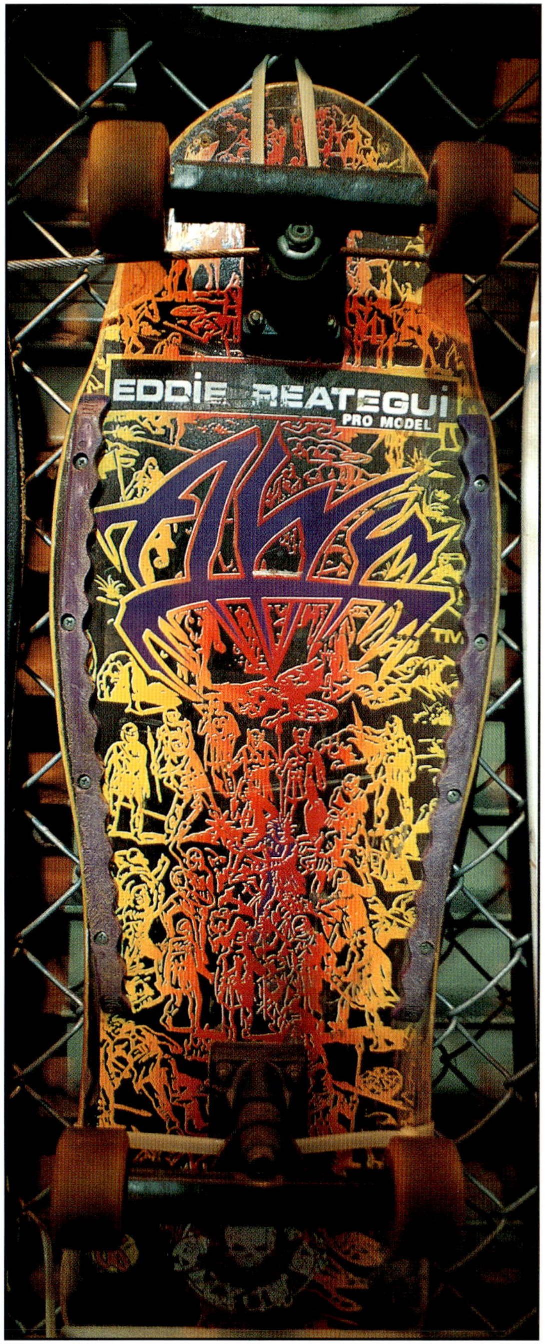
EDDIE REATEGUI
PRO MODEL

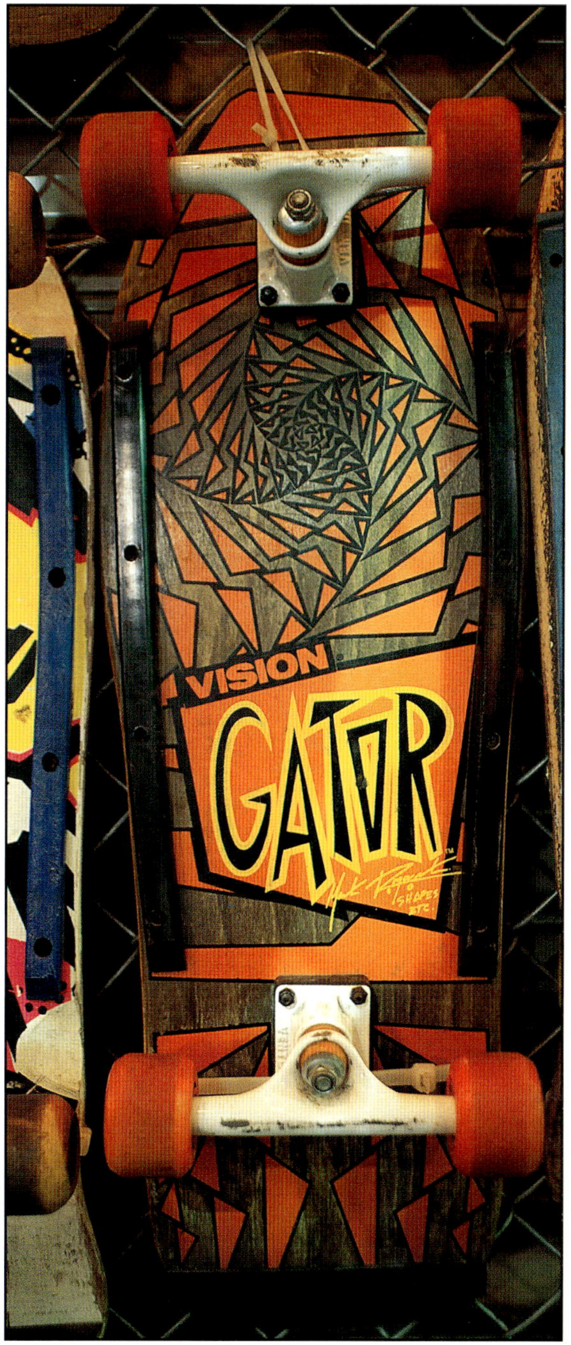
VISION
GATOR

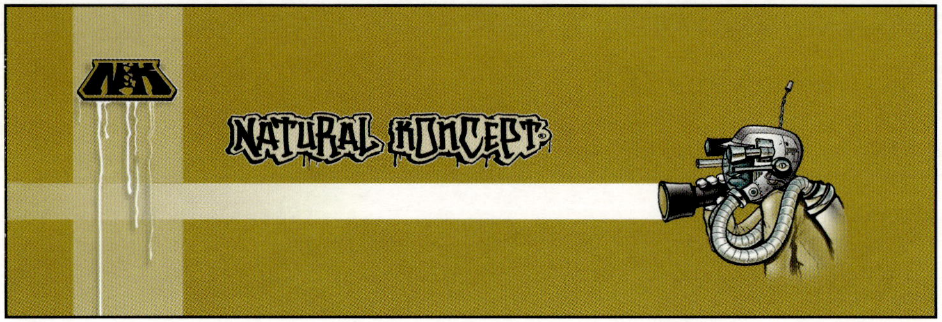

Future Police, Katch art. *Courtesy Natural Concepts*.

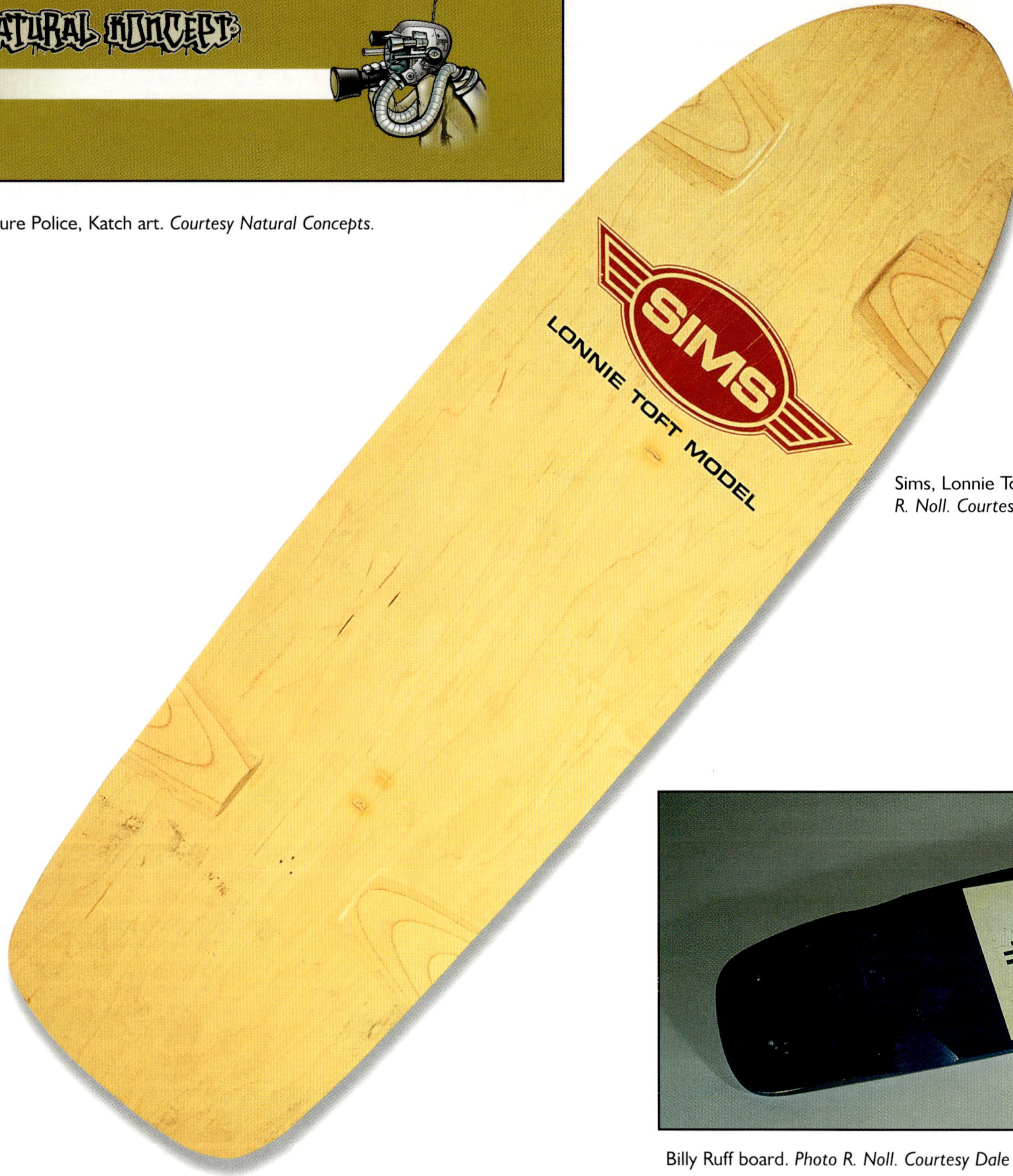

Sims, Lonnie Toft model kicktail. *Photo R. Noll. Courtesy Todd Huber.* $300-400.

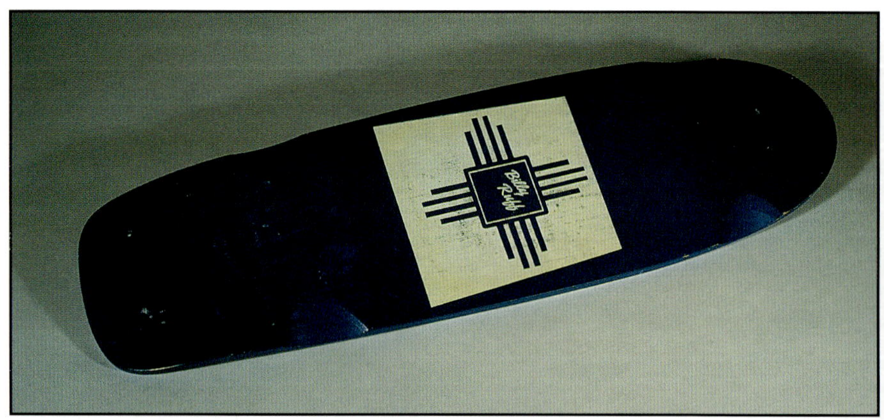

Billy Ruff board. *Photo R. Noll. Courtesy Dale Smith.* $100-200.

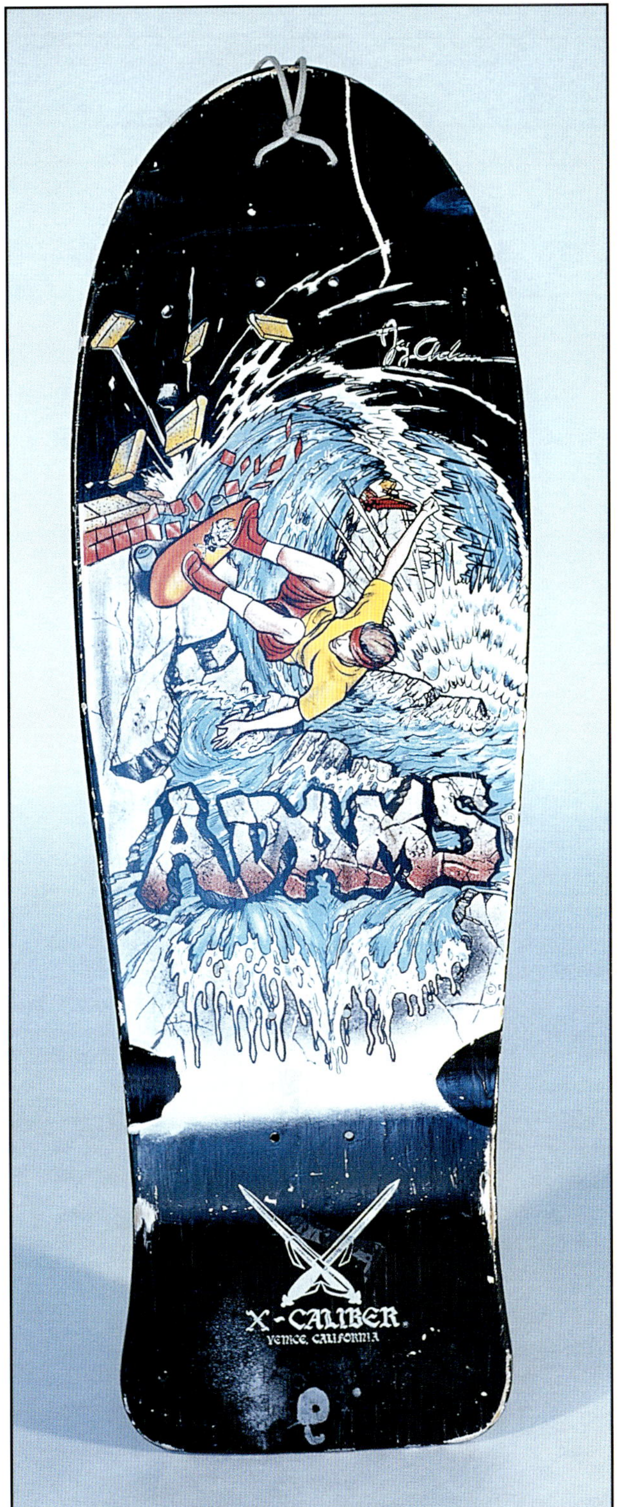

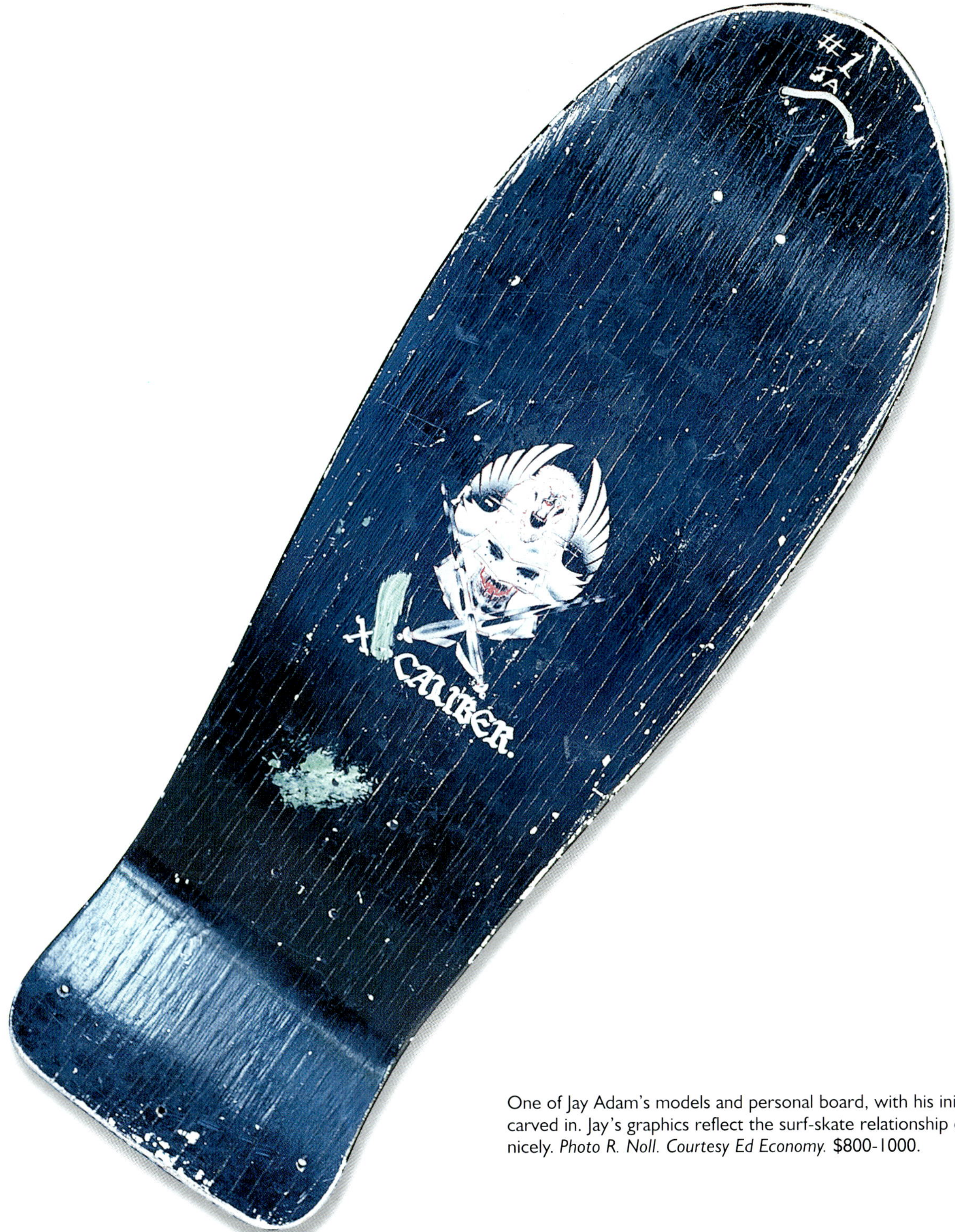

One of Jay Adam's models and personal board, with his initials carved in. Jay's graphics reflect the surf-skate relationship quite nicely. *Photo R. Noll. Courtesy Ed Economy.* $800-1000.

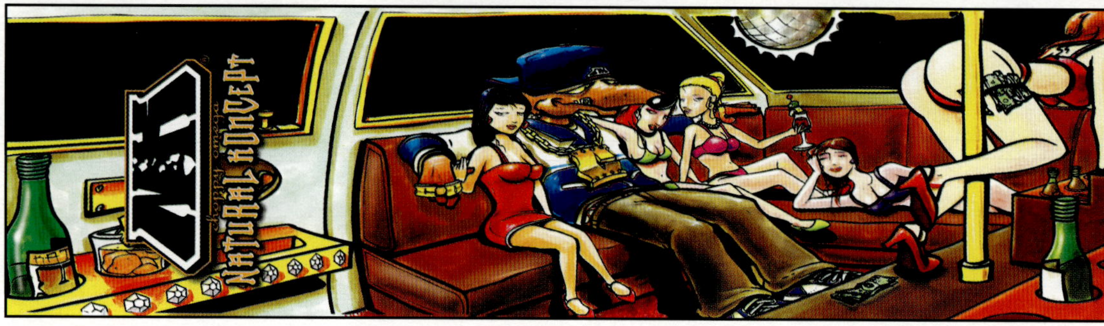

Choppy, Katch art. *Courtesy Natural Concepts.*

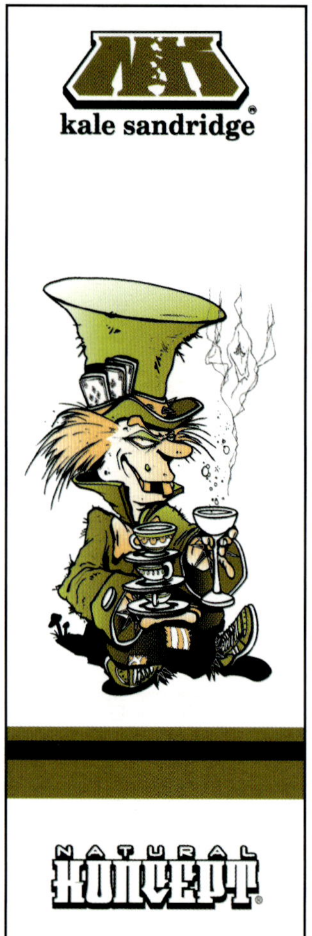

Kale, Katch Art. *Courtesy Natural Concepts.*

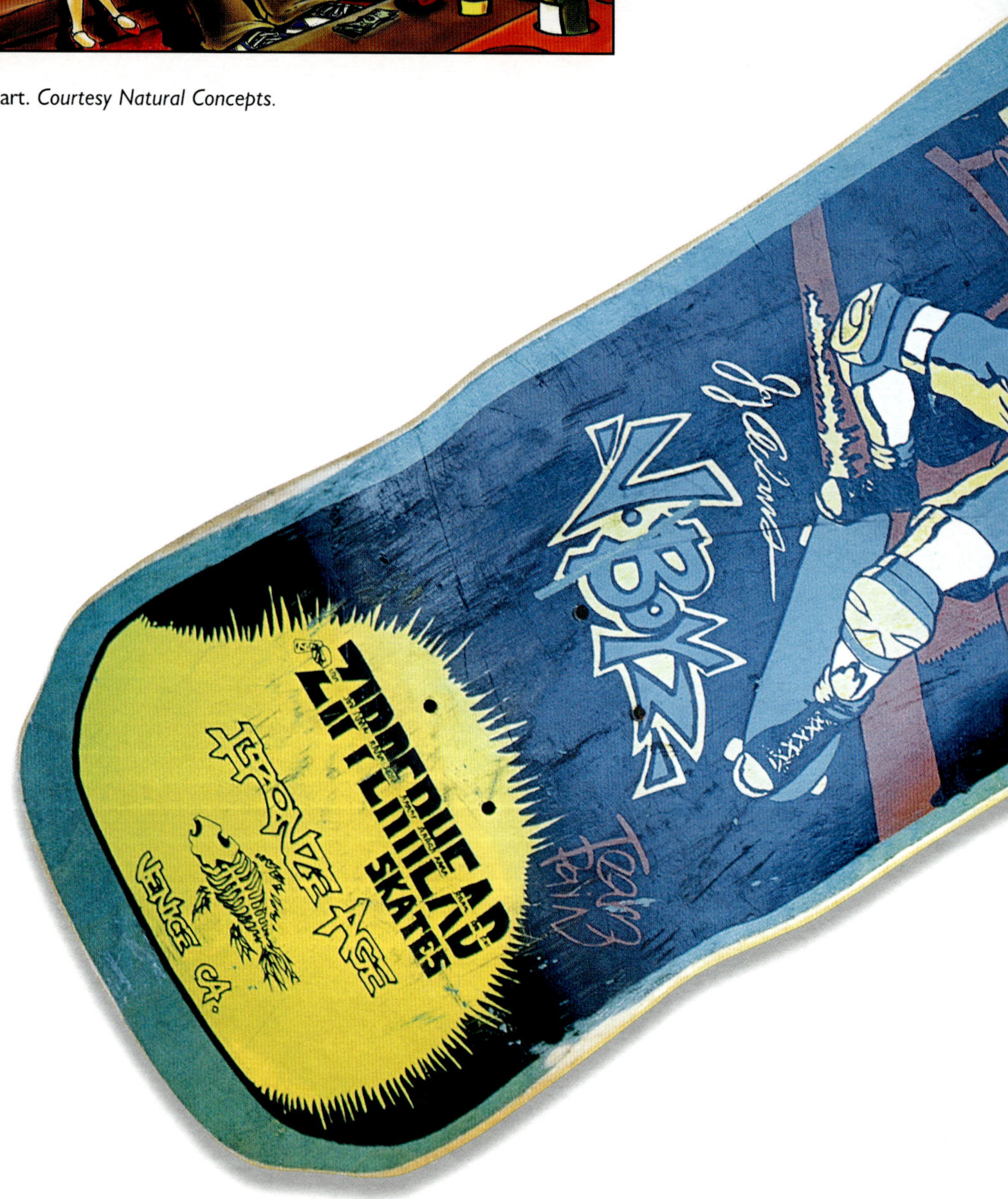

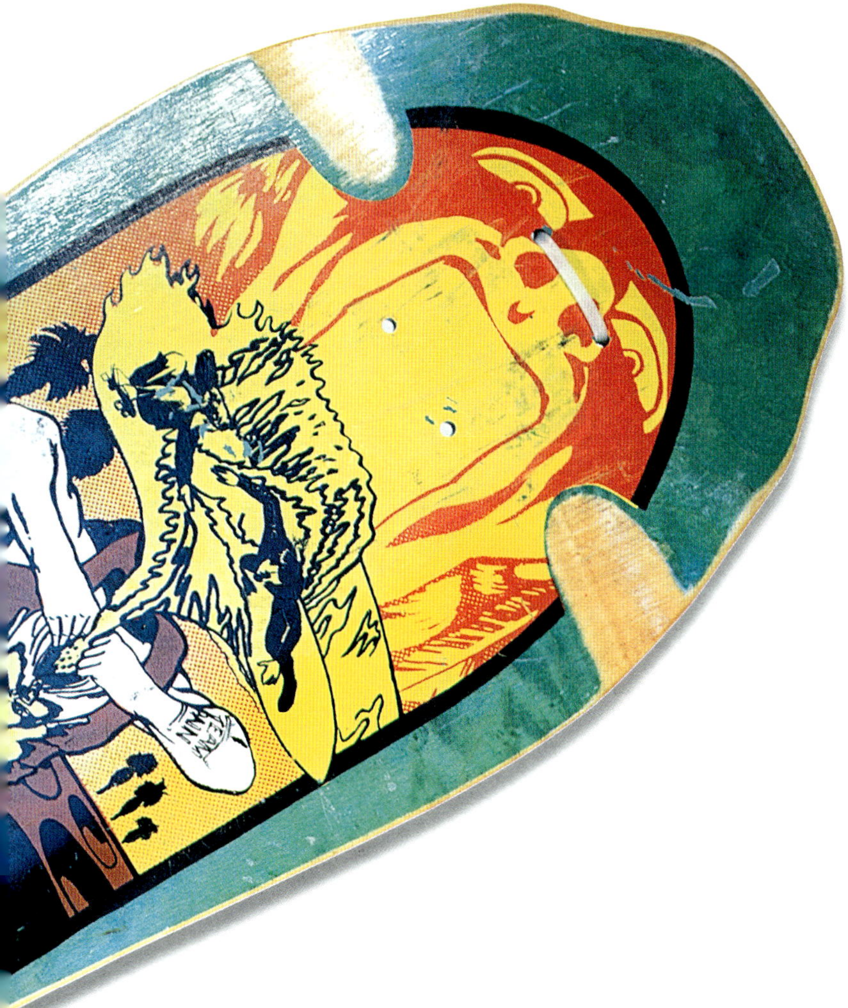

Jay Adams' Zipperhead skate shows Jay surfing and skating. "V-boyz" is for Venice boys, I'm guessing. *Photo R. Noll. Courtesy Ed Economy.* $500-800.

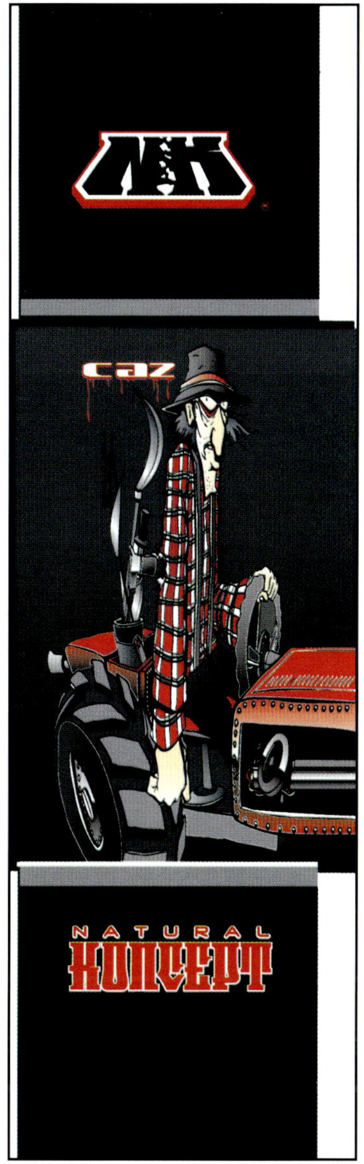

Kaz, Katch art. *Courtesy Natural Concepts.*

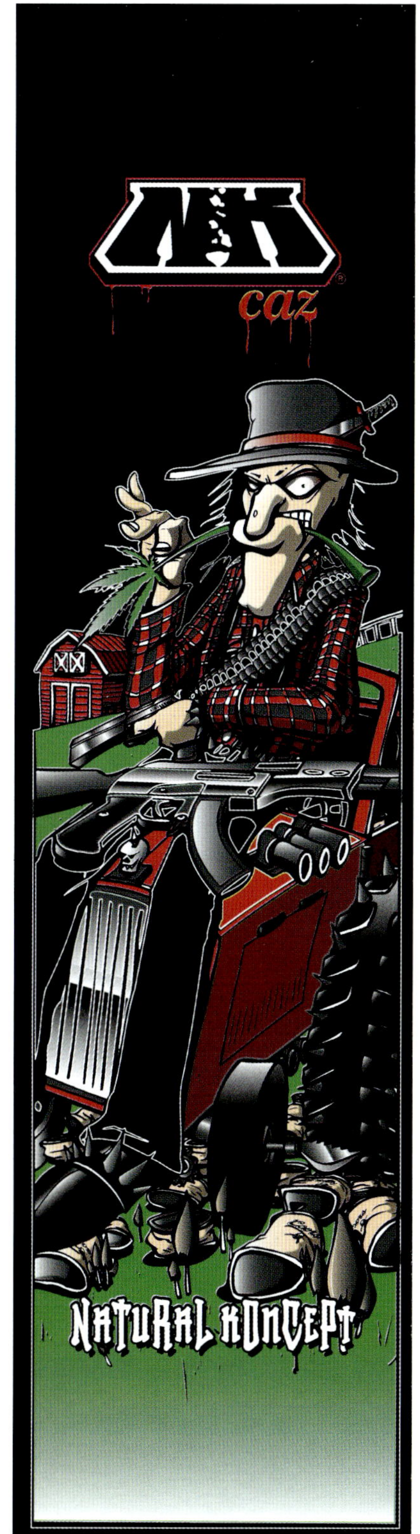

Kaz Farm, Katch Art. *Courtesy Natural Concepts.*

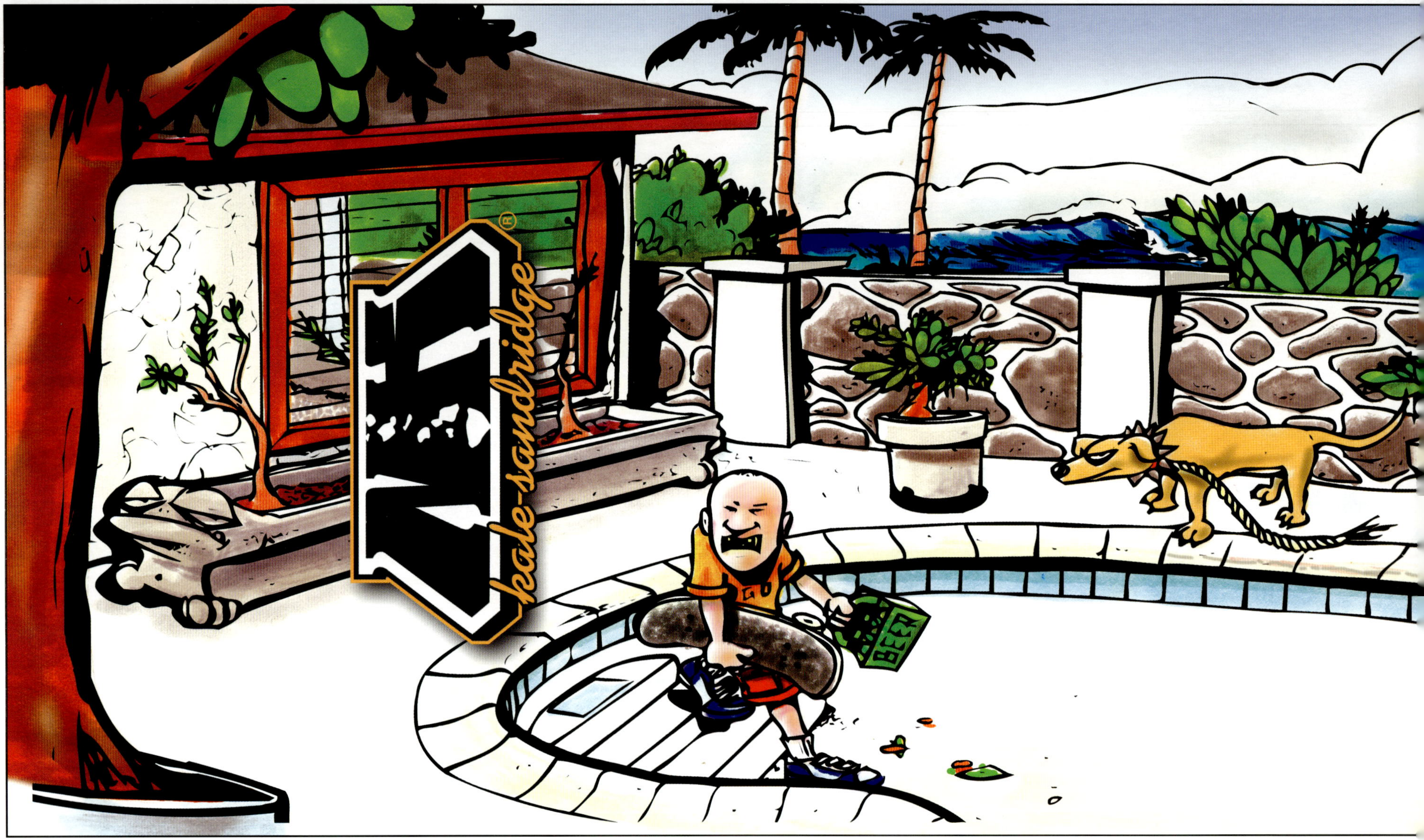

Kale, Katch Art. *Courtesy Natural Concepts.*

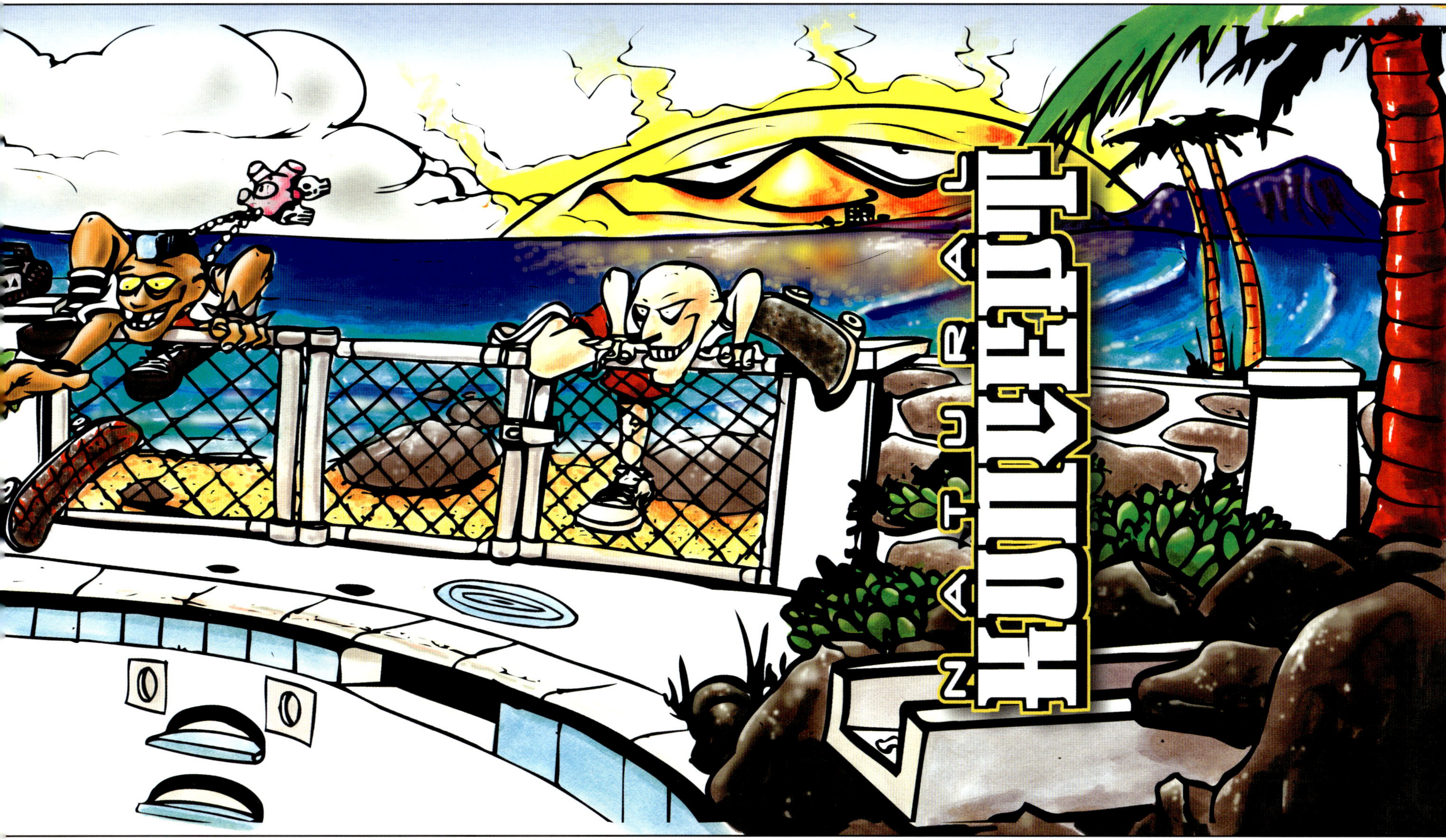

Call to Arms, Katch art. *Courtesy Natural Concepts.*

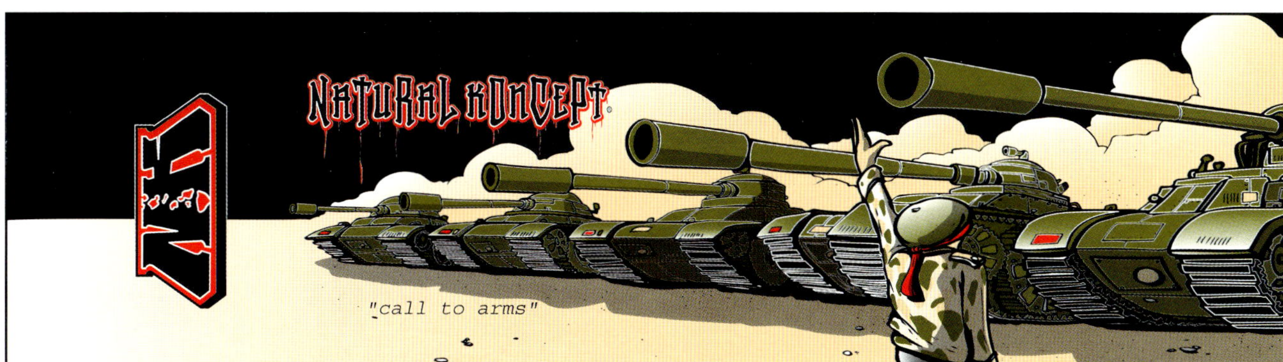

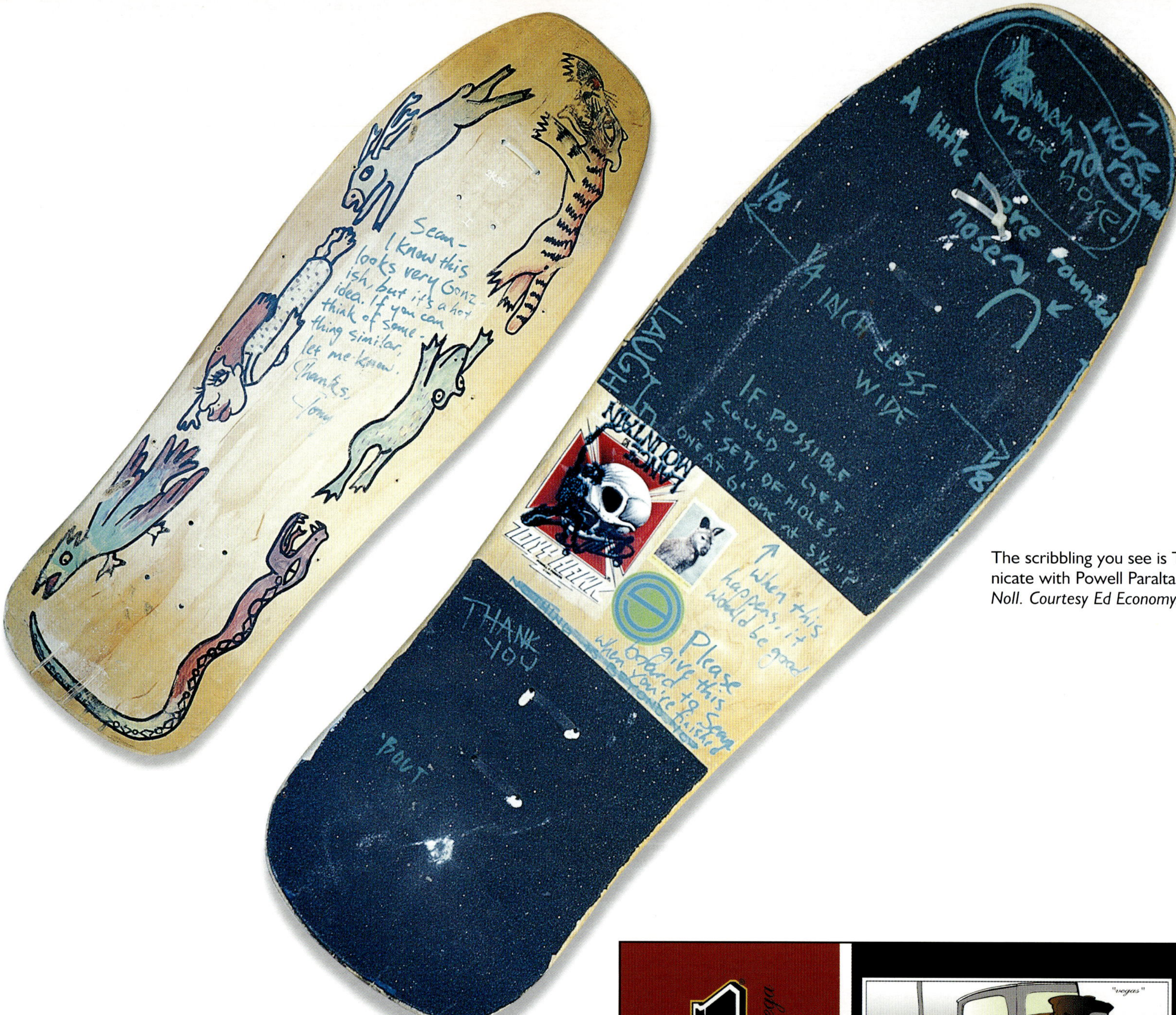

The scribbling you see is Tony Hawk trying to communicate with Powell Paralta, his manufacturer. *Photo R. Noll. Courtesy Ed Economy.* $2000-5000.

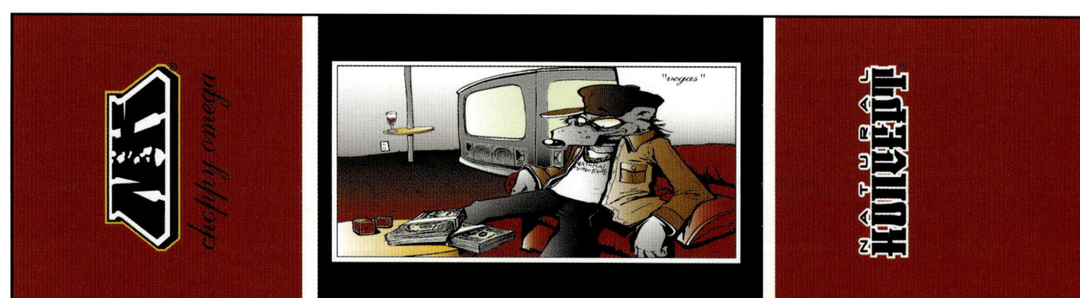

Chop, Katch art. *Courtesy Natural Concepts.*

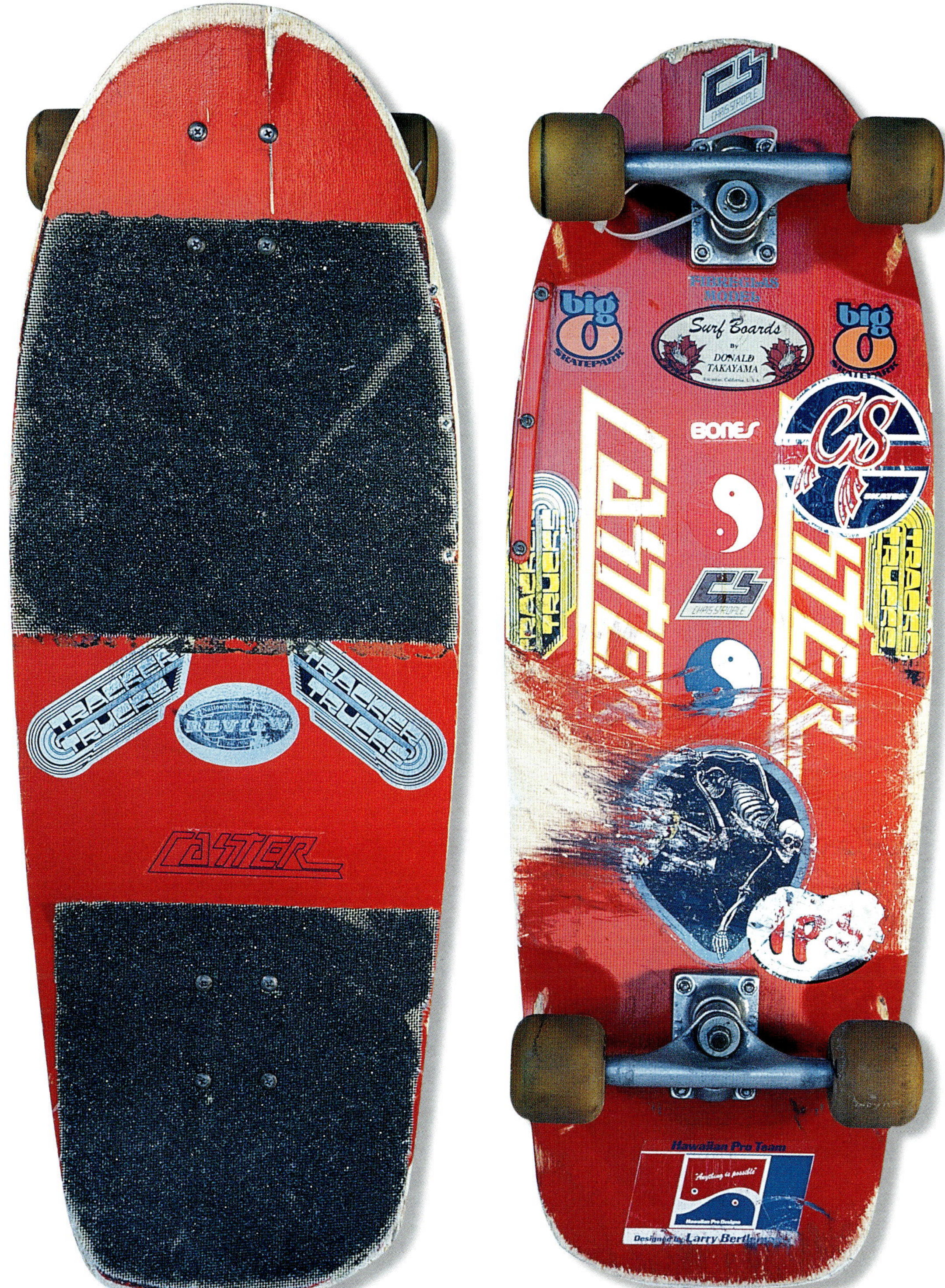

Chris Strople's personal board, the rarest of Casters, including drywall screen for grip. *Photo R. Noll. Courtesy Ed Economy.* $1500-2000.

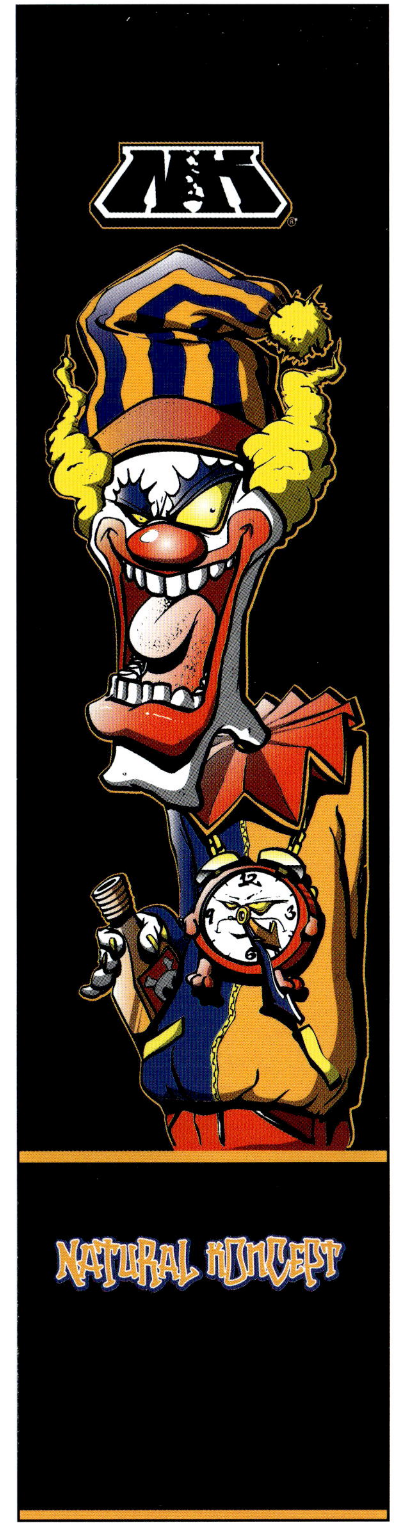

Clown, Katch art. *Courtesy Natural Concepts.*

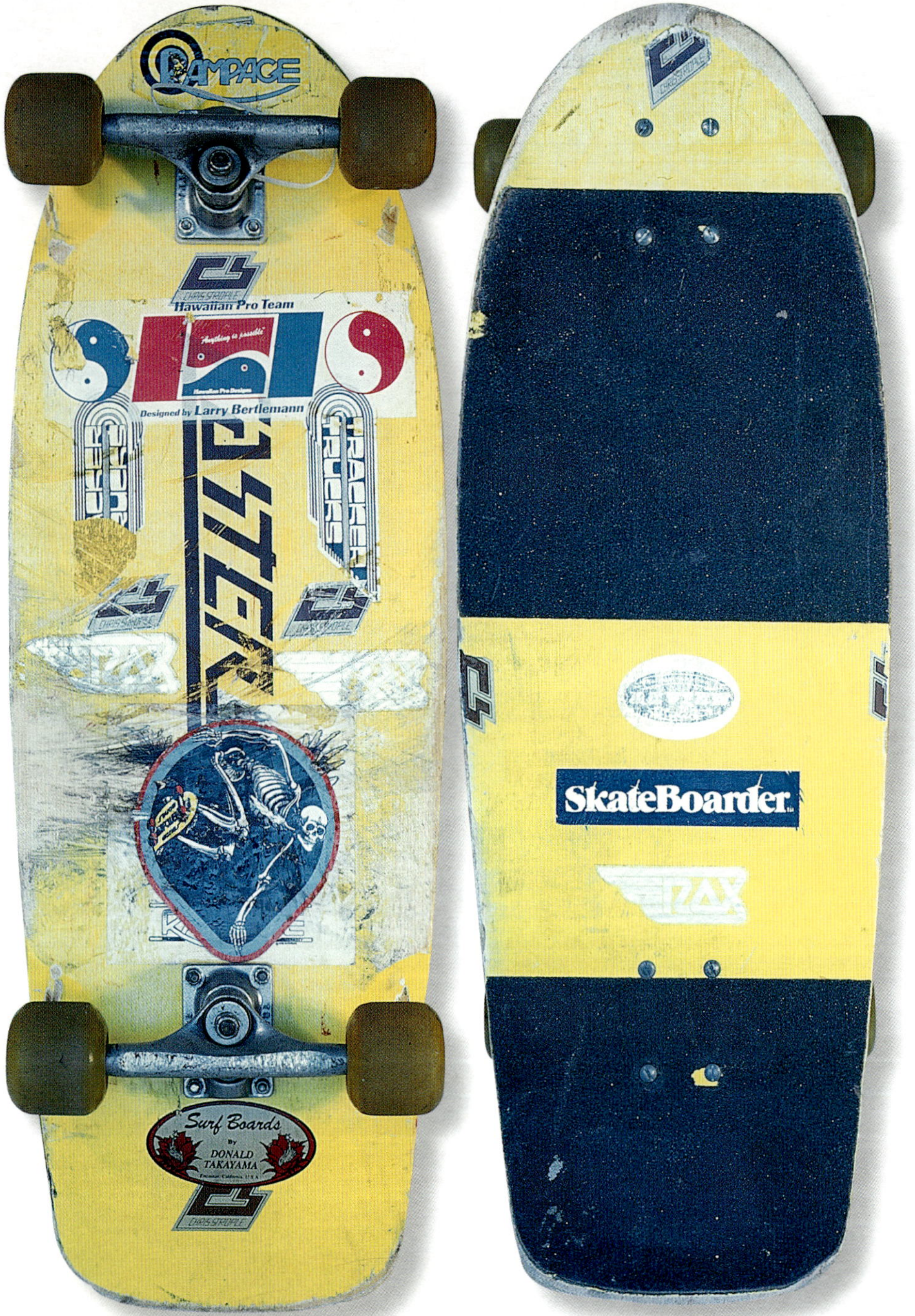

The Caster that Chris Strople rode when he toured Australia. *Photo R. Noll. Courtesy Ed Economy.* $1500-2000.

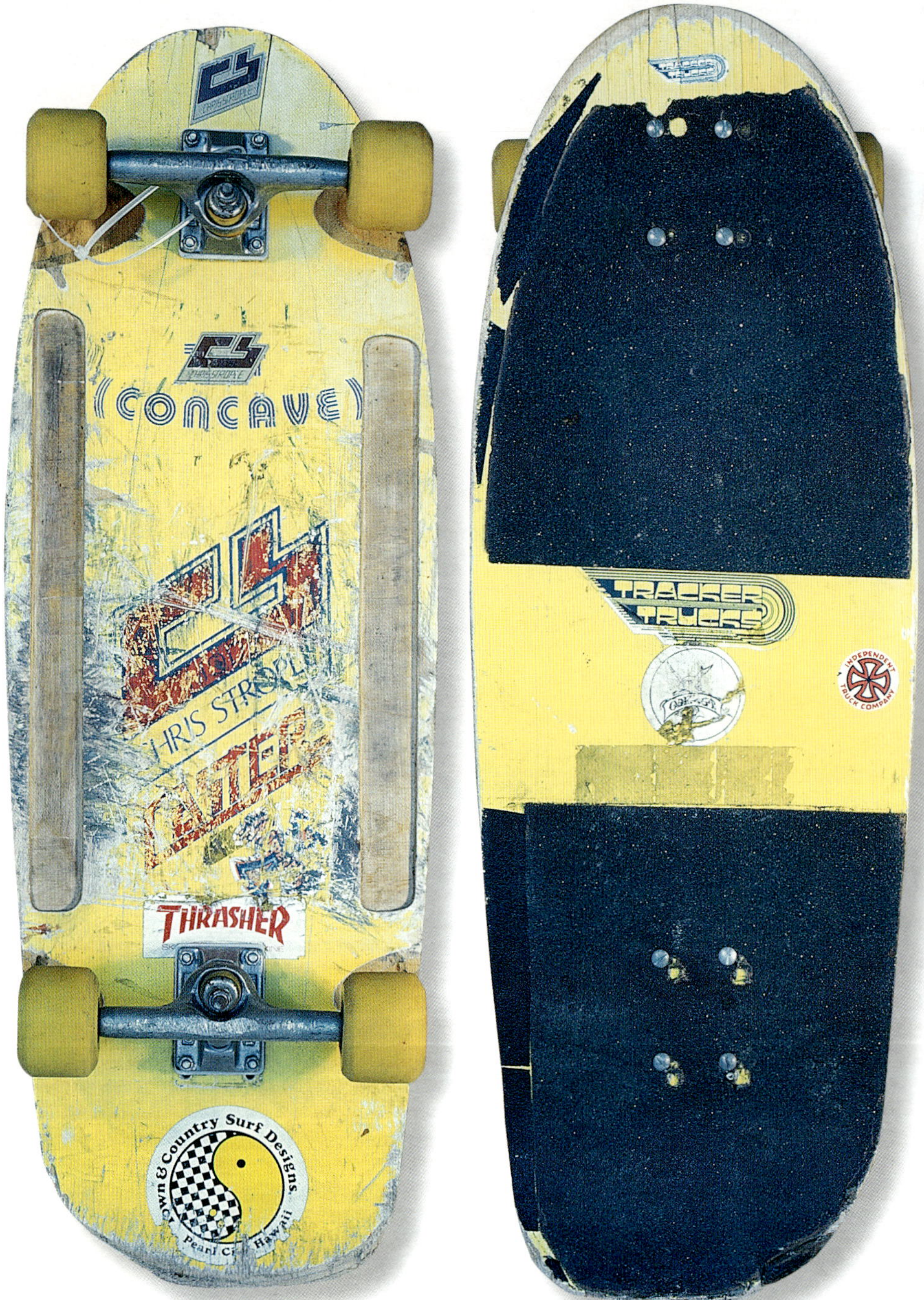

Chris Strople model that was Toms Inouye's personal board. *Photo R. Noll. Courtesy Ed Economy.* $1000-2000.

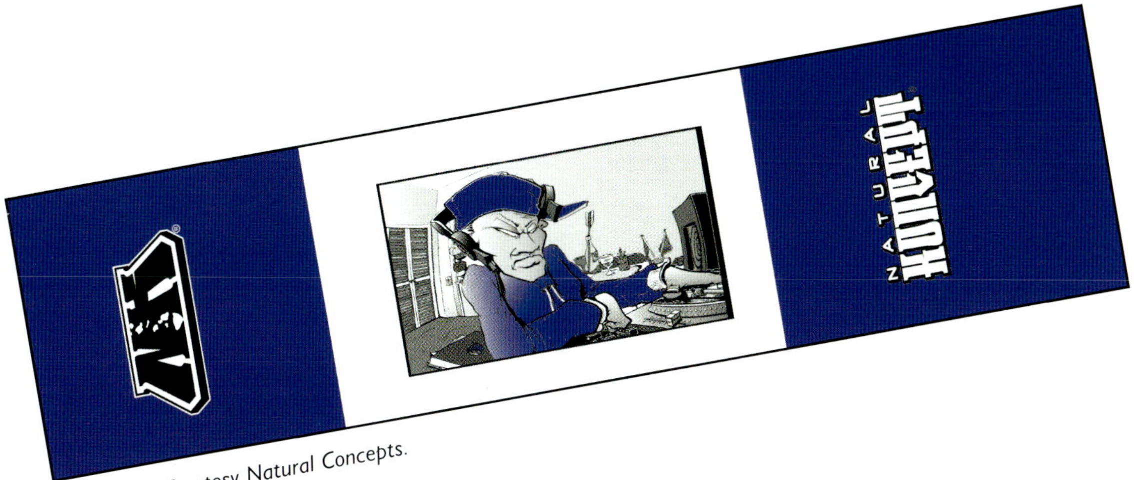

Katch art. *Courtesy Natural Concepts.*

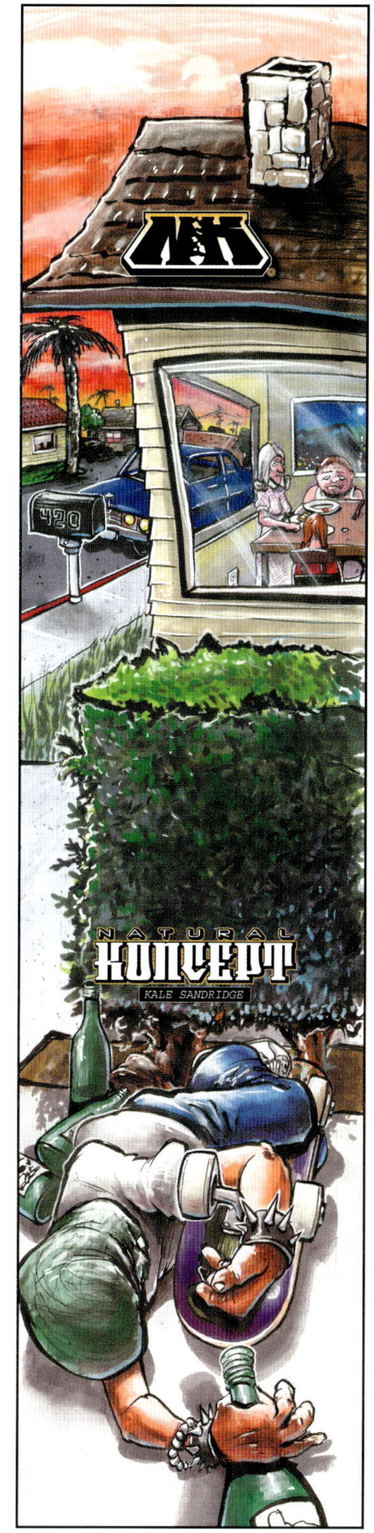

Kale, Katch art. *Courtesy Natural Concepts.*

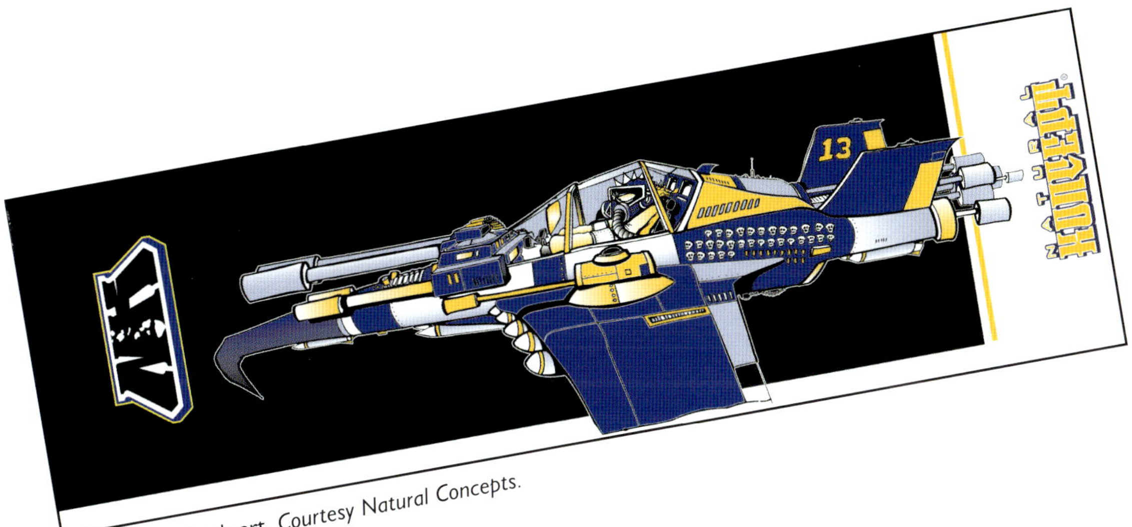

Hey Head, Katch art. *Courtesy Natural Concepts.*

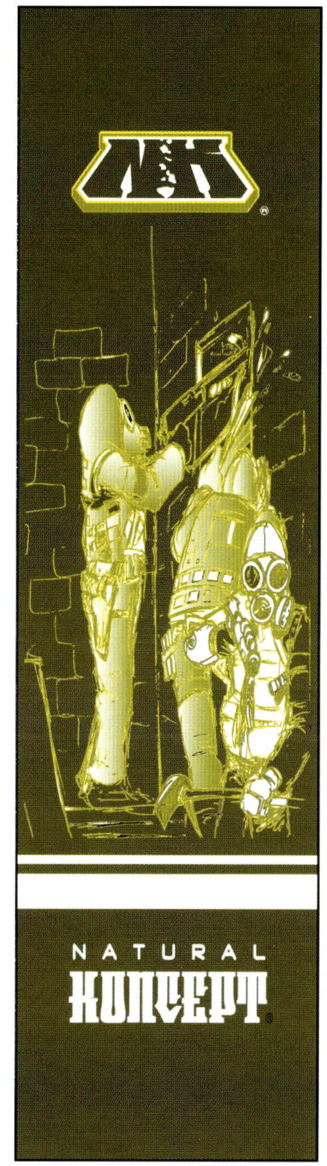

Infiltrate, Katch art. *Courtesy Natural Concepts.*

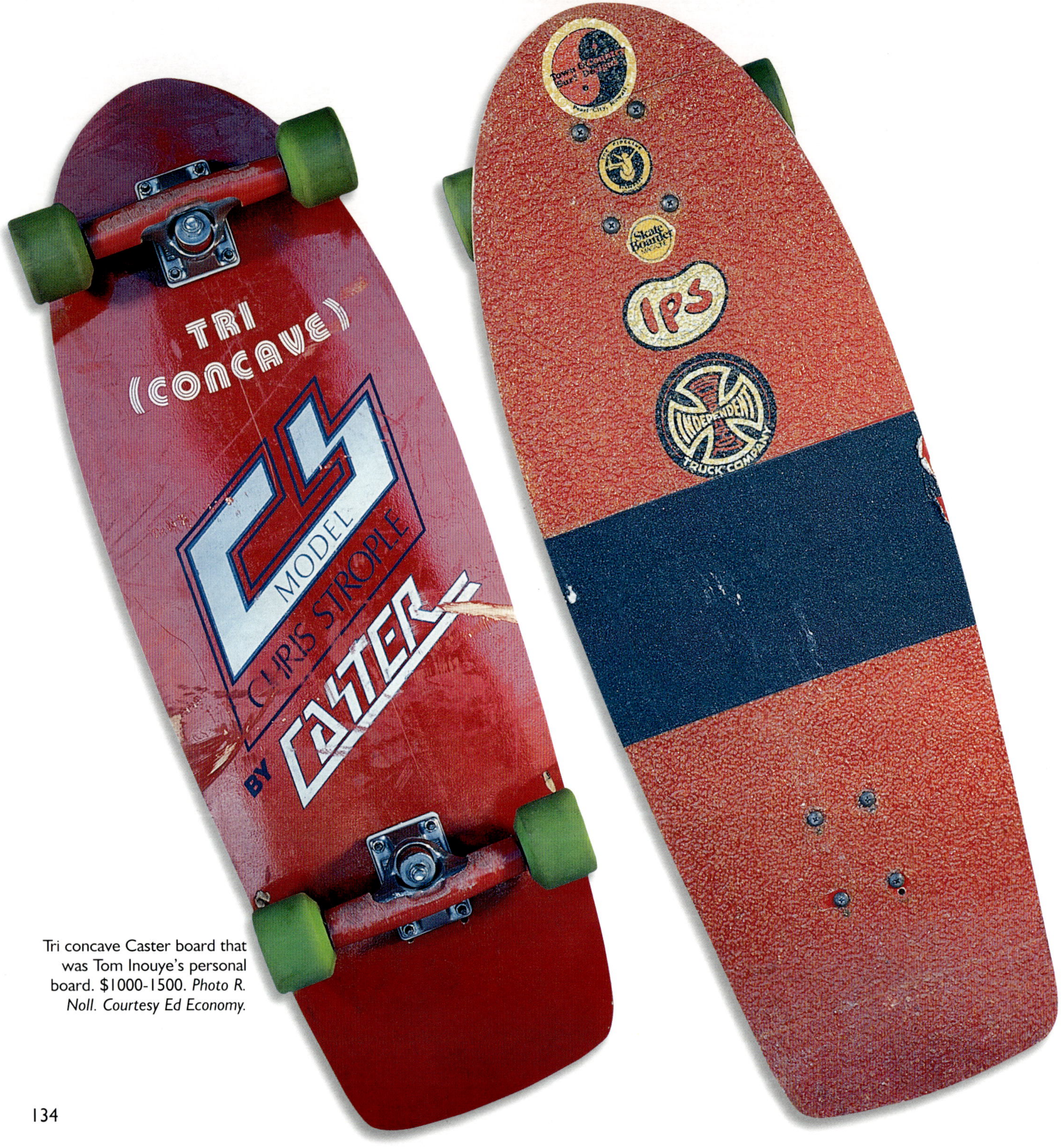

Tri concave Caster board that was Tom Inouye's personal board. $1000-1500. *Photo R. Noll. Courtesy Ed Economy.*

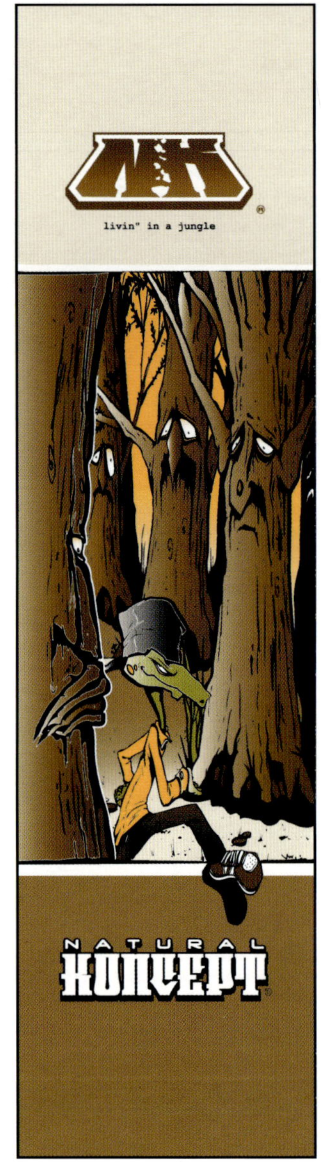

Livin in the jungle, Katch art. *Courtesy Natural Concepts.*

Caster's Tom Inouye model, one of Tom Inouye's personal boards. $1000-1500. *Photo R. Noll. Courtesy Ed Economy.*

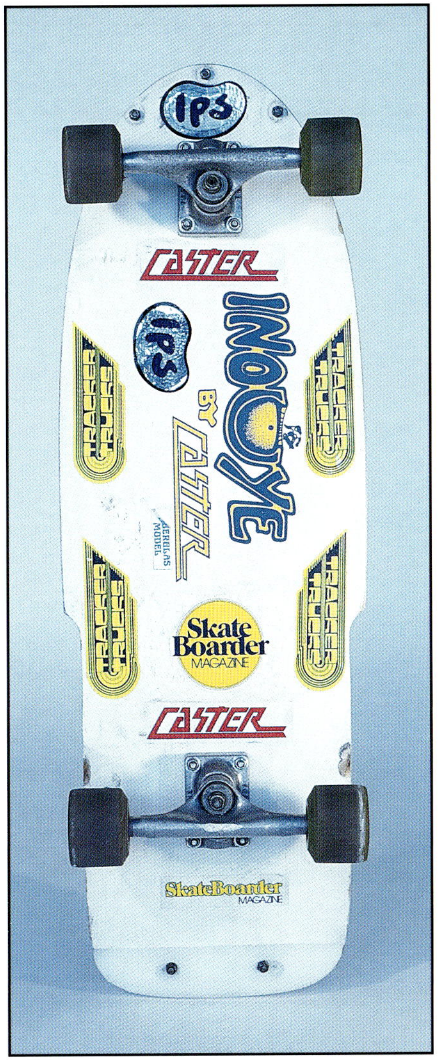

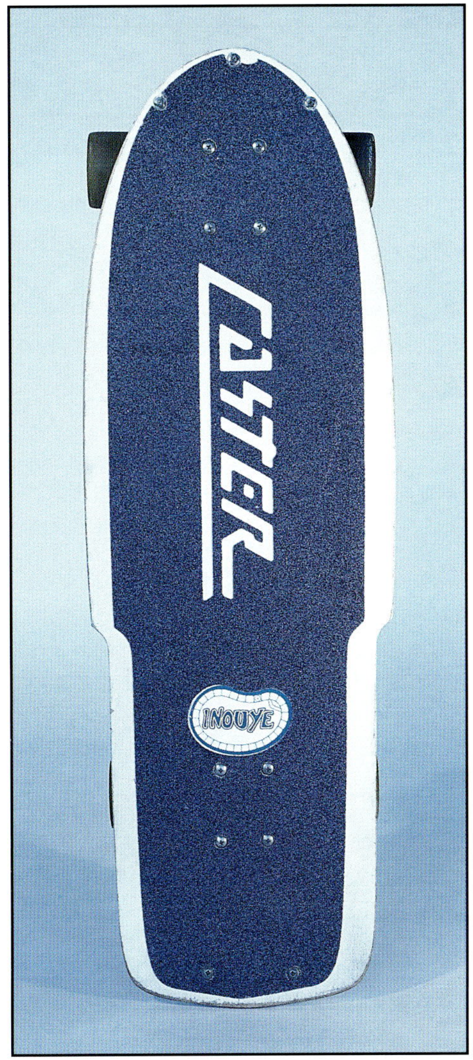

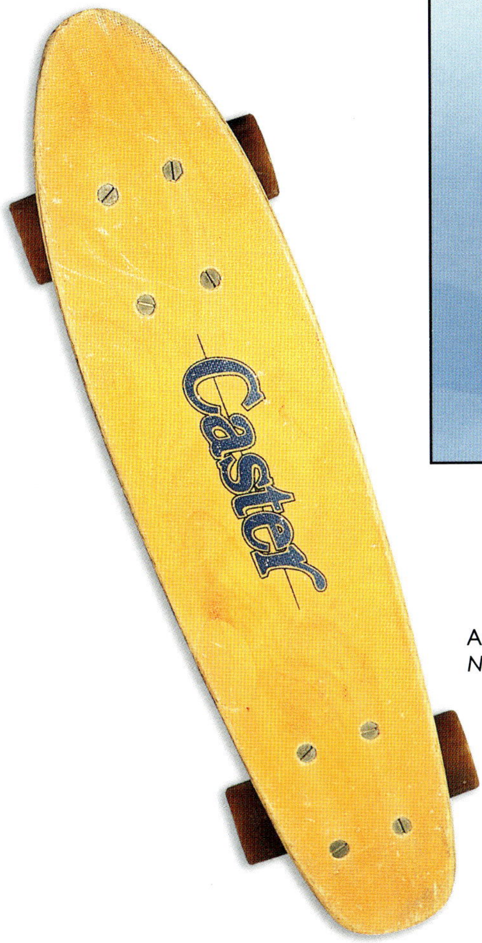

An early Caster board. *Photo R. Noll. Courtesy Ed Economy.* $400.

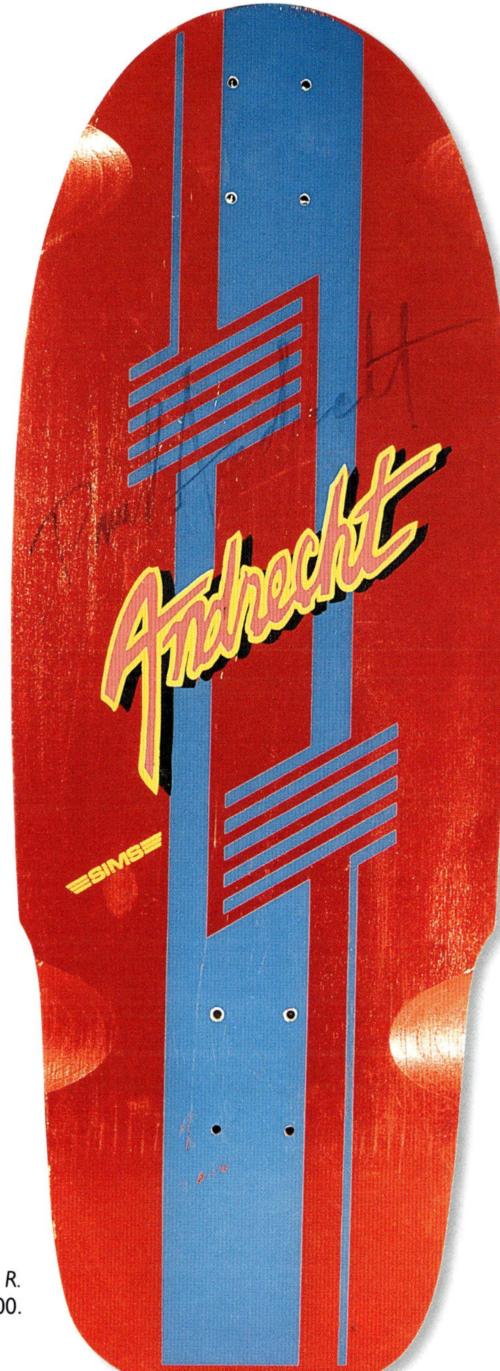

Sims Andrecht, signed by Dave. *Photo R. Noll. Courtesy Jim at Rip City.* $2000-2500.

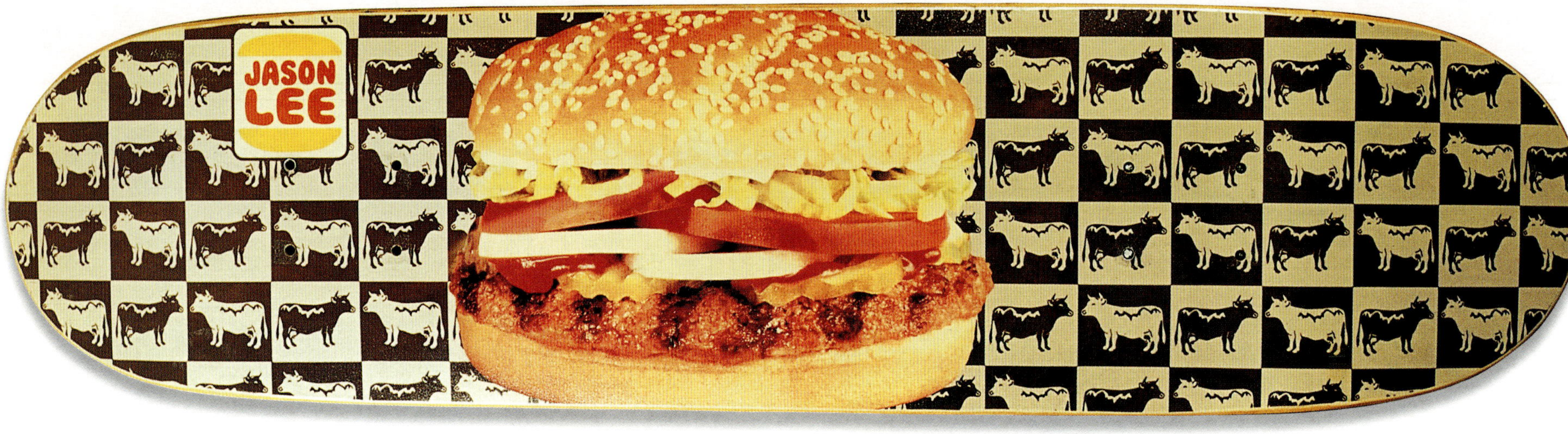

Mike Valely slick bottom. *Photo R. Noll. Courtesy Jim at Rip City.* $1500-2000.

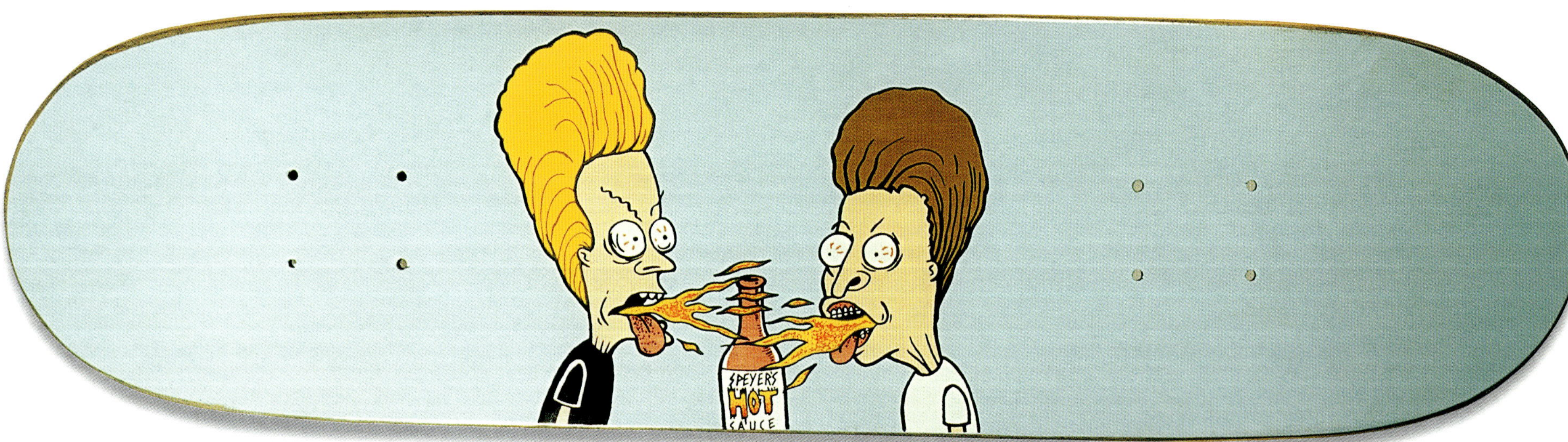

MTV's Beeves and Butthead on this board. *Photo R. Noll. Courtesy Jim at Rip City.* $800.

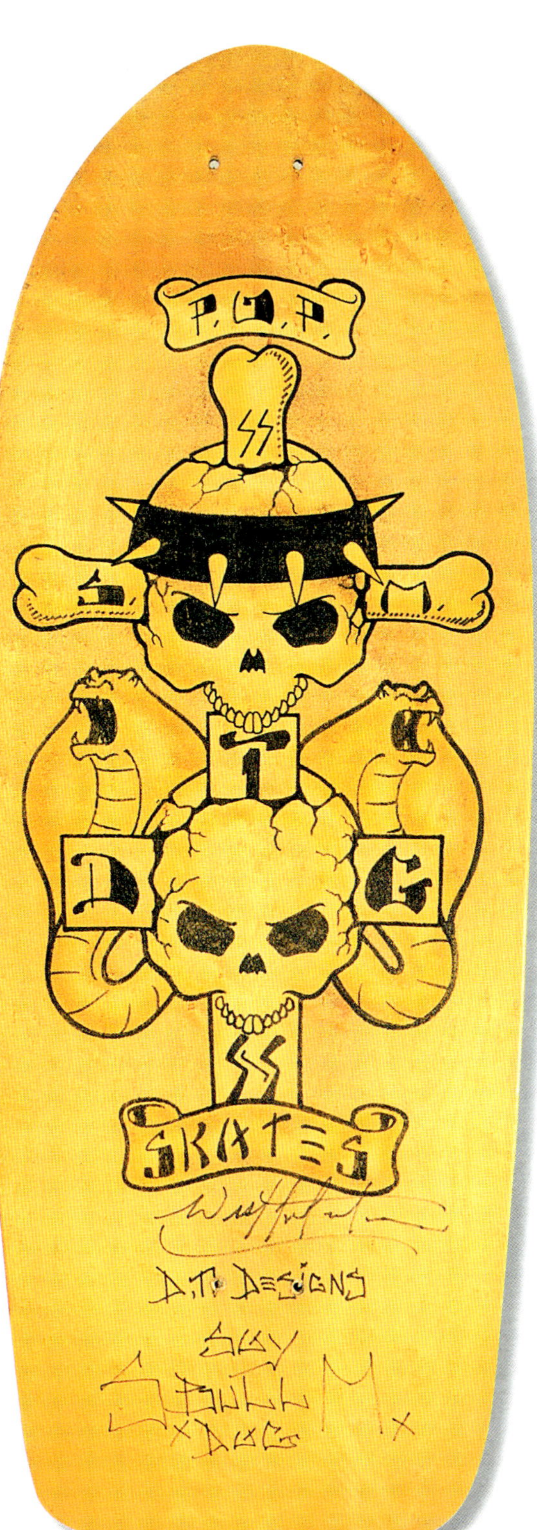

Called a kitchen table board, Wess would hand draw boards like this with Sharpie markers at home on his kitchen table. "P.O.P" stands for Pacific Ocean Park. *Photo R. Noll. Courtesy Jim at Rip City.*

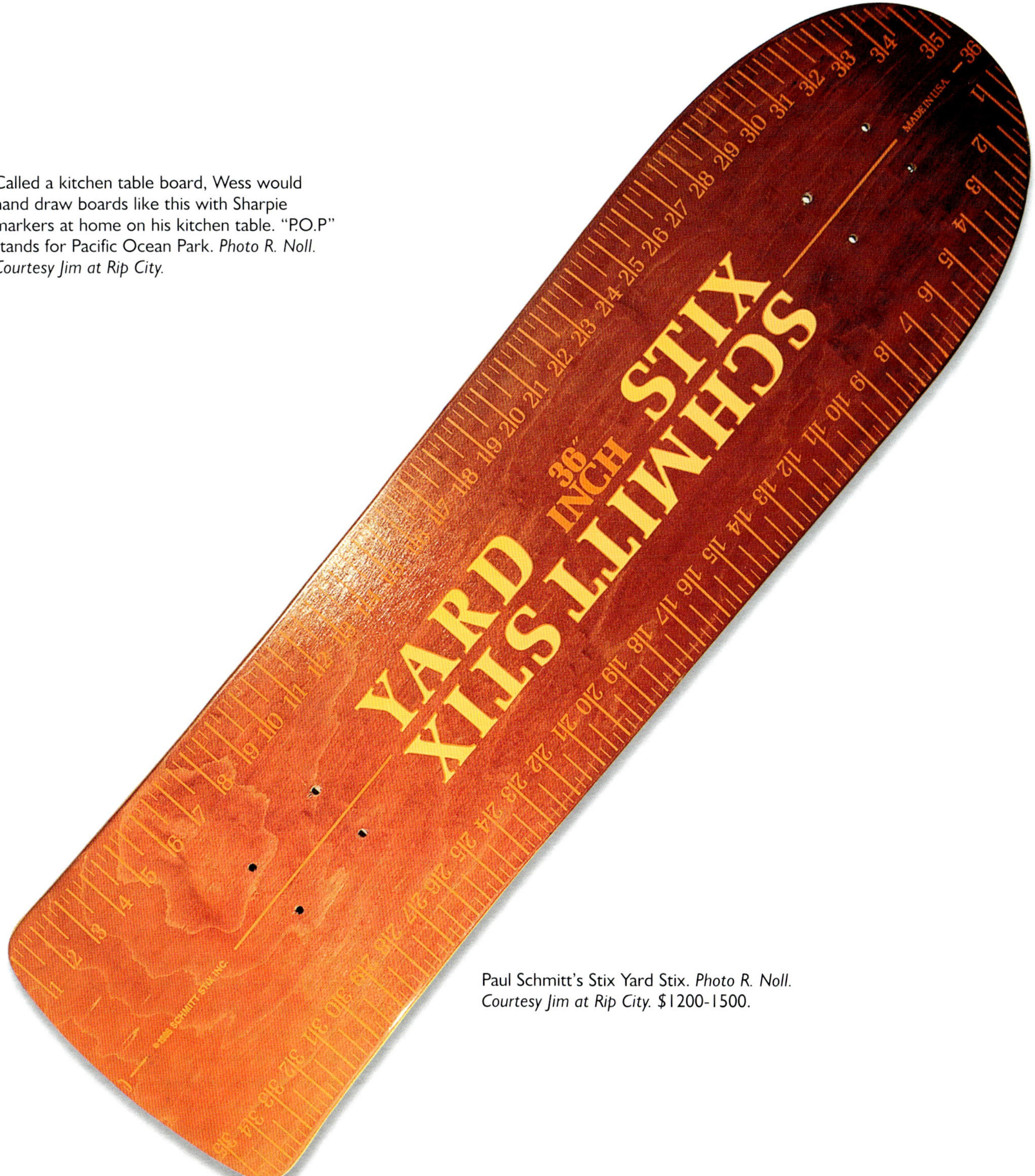

Paul Schmitt's Stix Yard Stix. *Photo R. Noll. Courtesy Jim at Rip City.* $1200-1500.

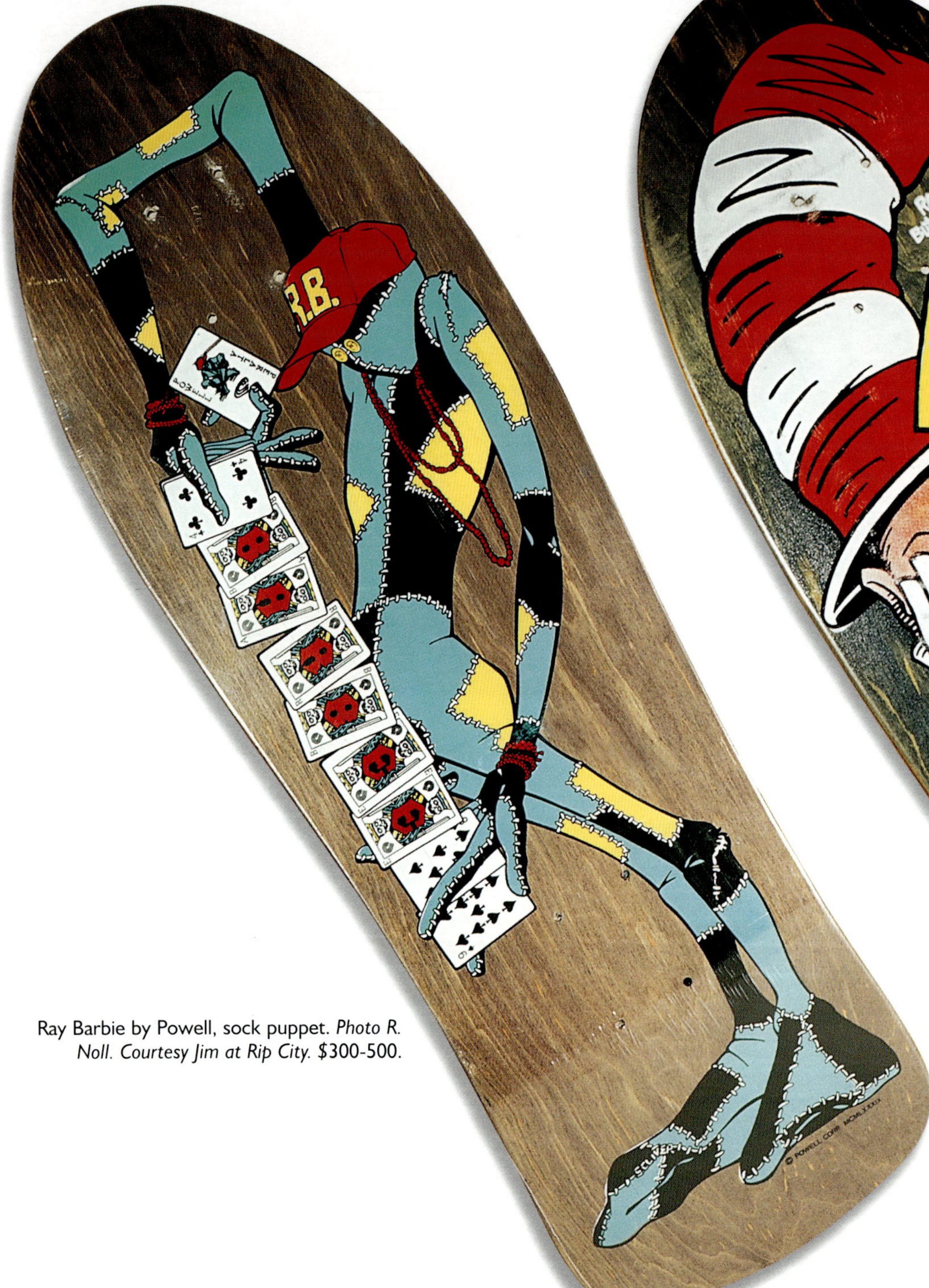

Ray Barbie by Powell, sock puppet. *Photo R. Noll. Courtesy Jim at Rip City.* $300-500.

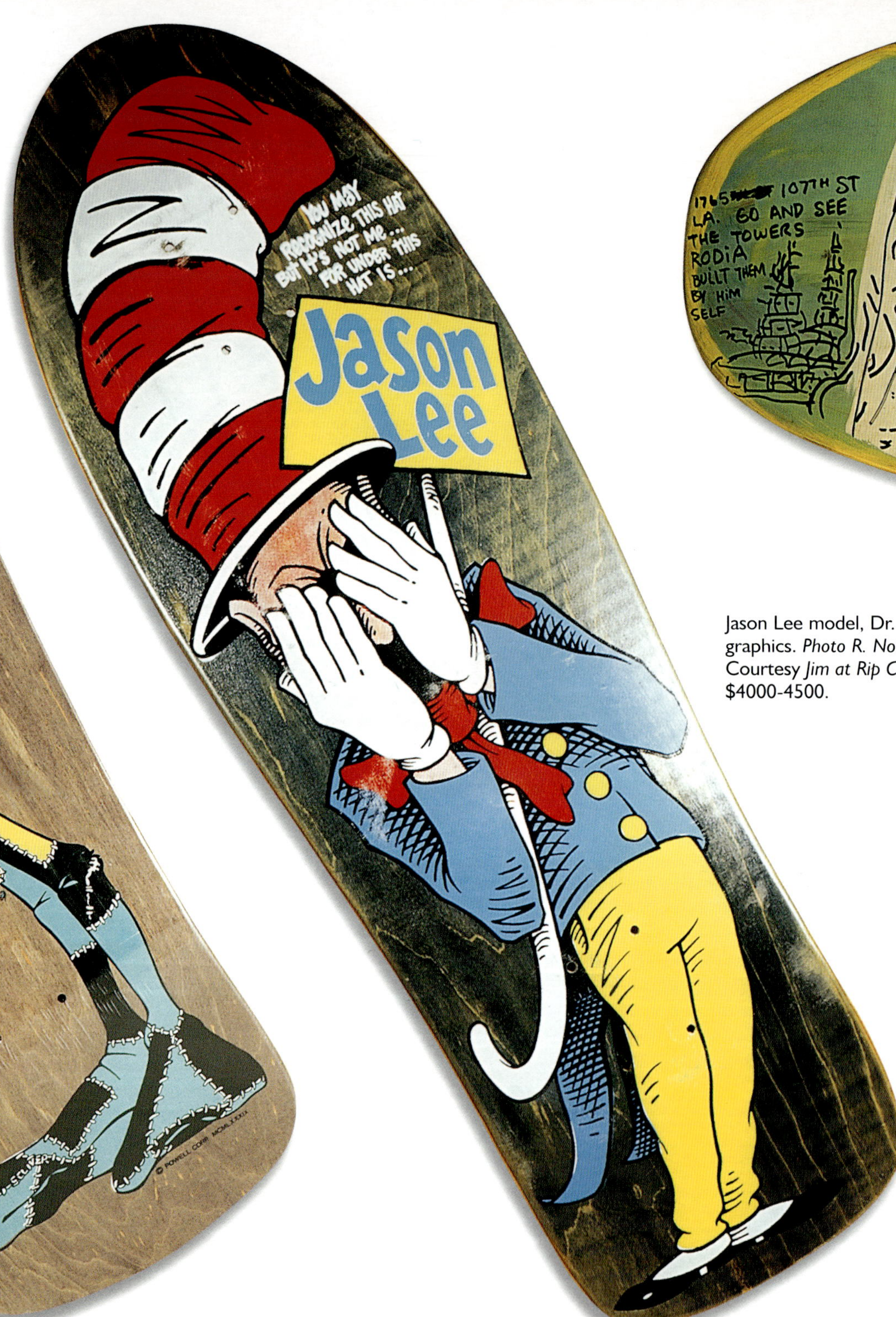

Jason Lee model, Dr. Suess graphics. *Photo R. Noll.* Courtesy *Jim at Rip City.* $4000-4500.

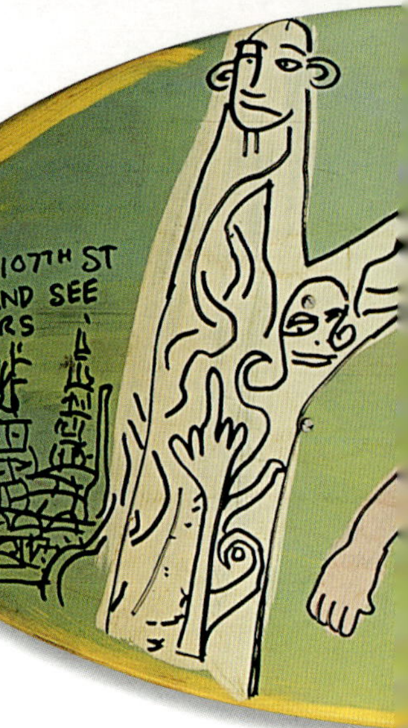

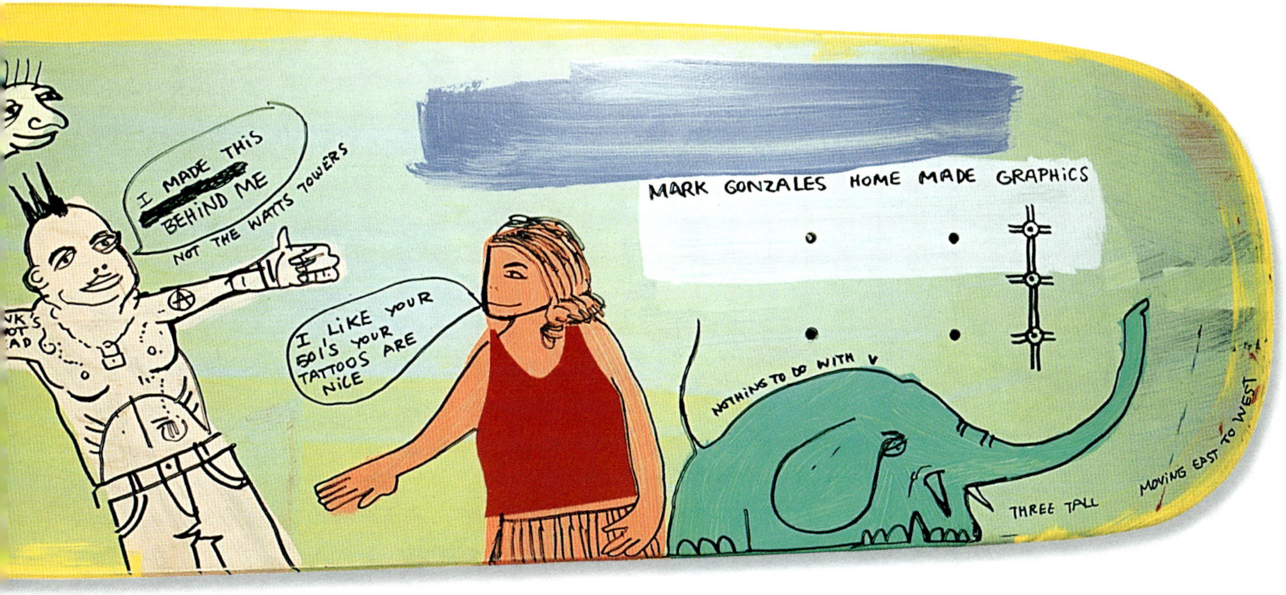

Guy Moriano model with hand drawn graphics by Mark Gonzales. *Photo R. Noll. Courtesy Jim at Rip City.* $7000-8000.

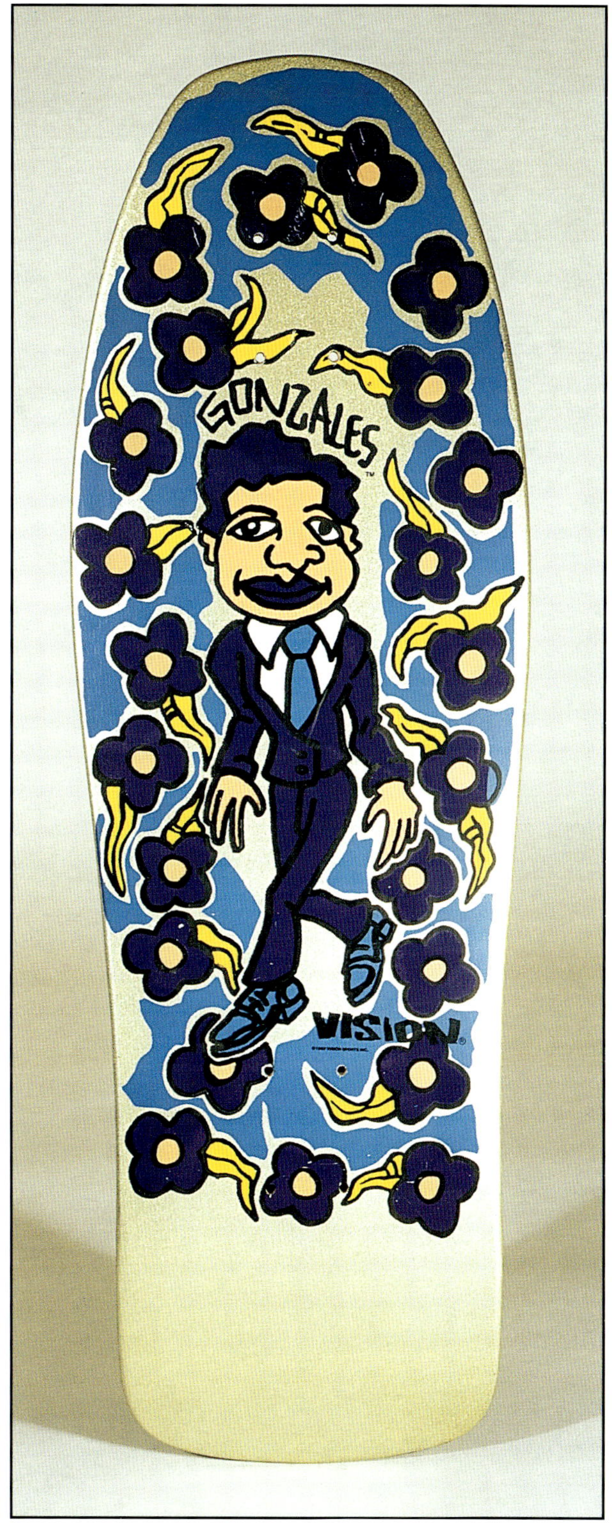

Mark Gonzales model by Vision, with purple rain influence. *Photo R. Noll. Courtesy Jim at Rip City.* $2500.

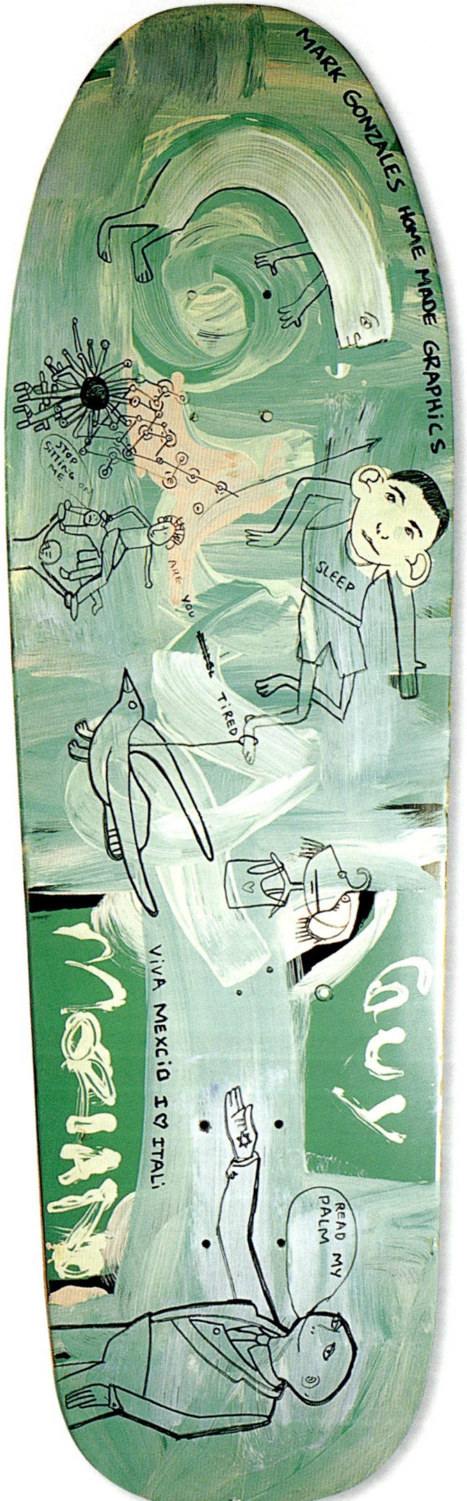

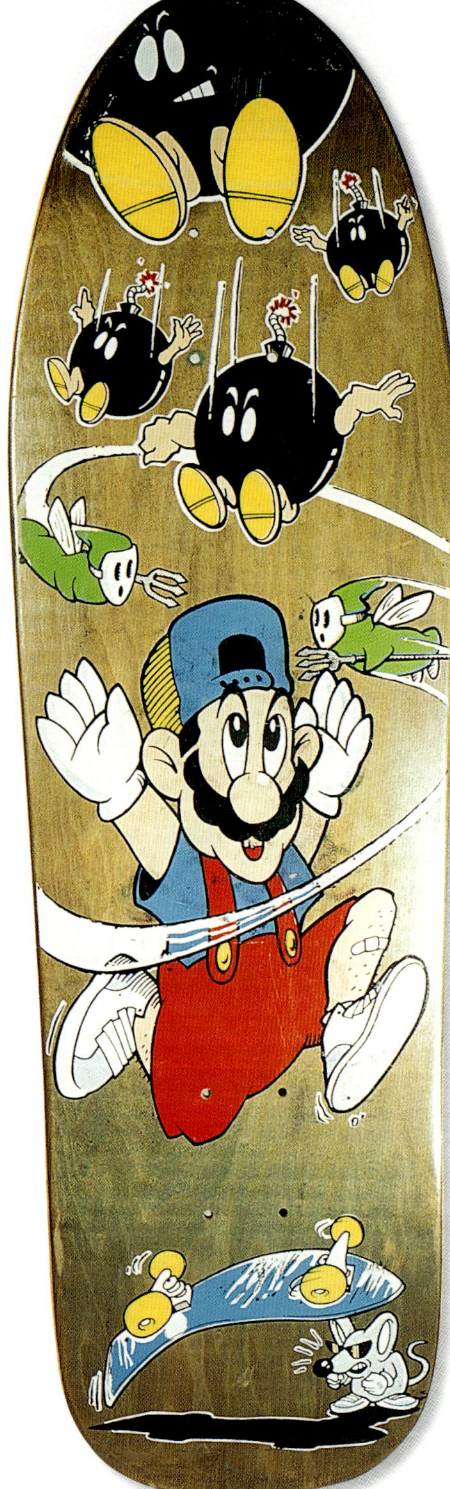

Another Guy Moriano board with hand drawn graphics by Mark Gonzales. *Photo R. Noll. Courtesy Jim at Rip City.* $7000-8000.

Guy Mariano board by World Industries. *Photo R. Noll. Courtesy Jim at Rip City.* $2500.

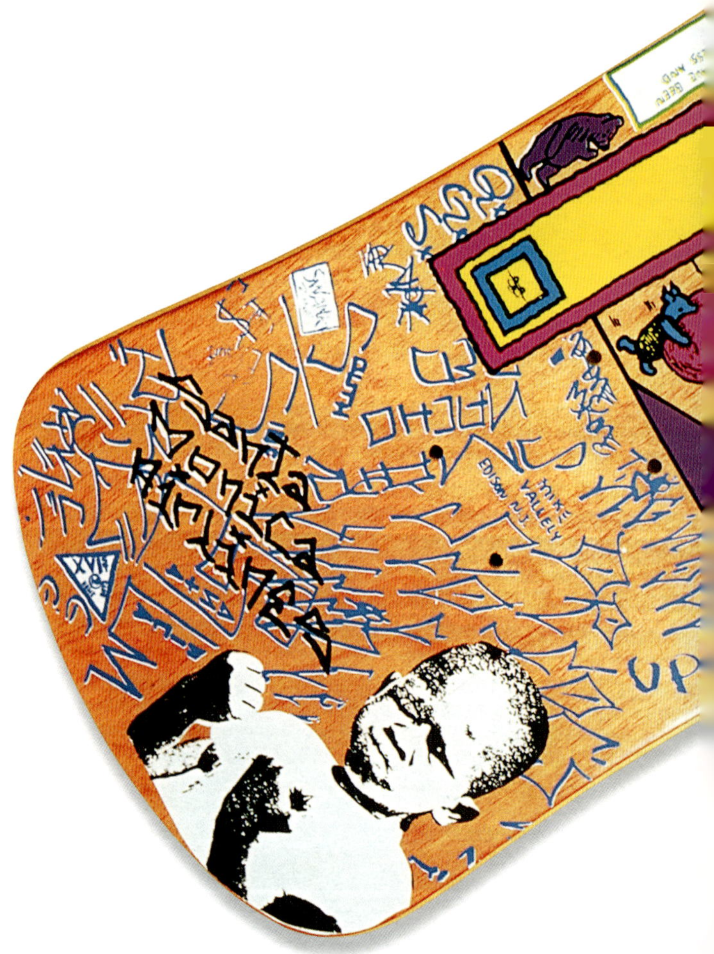

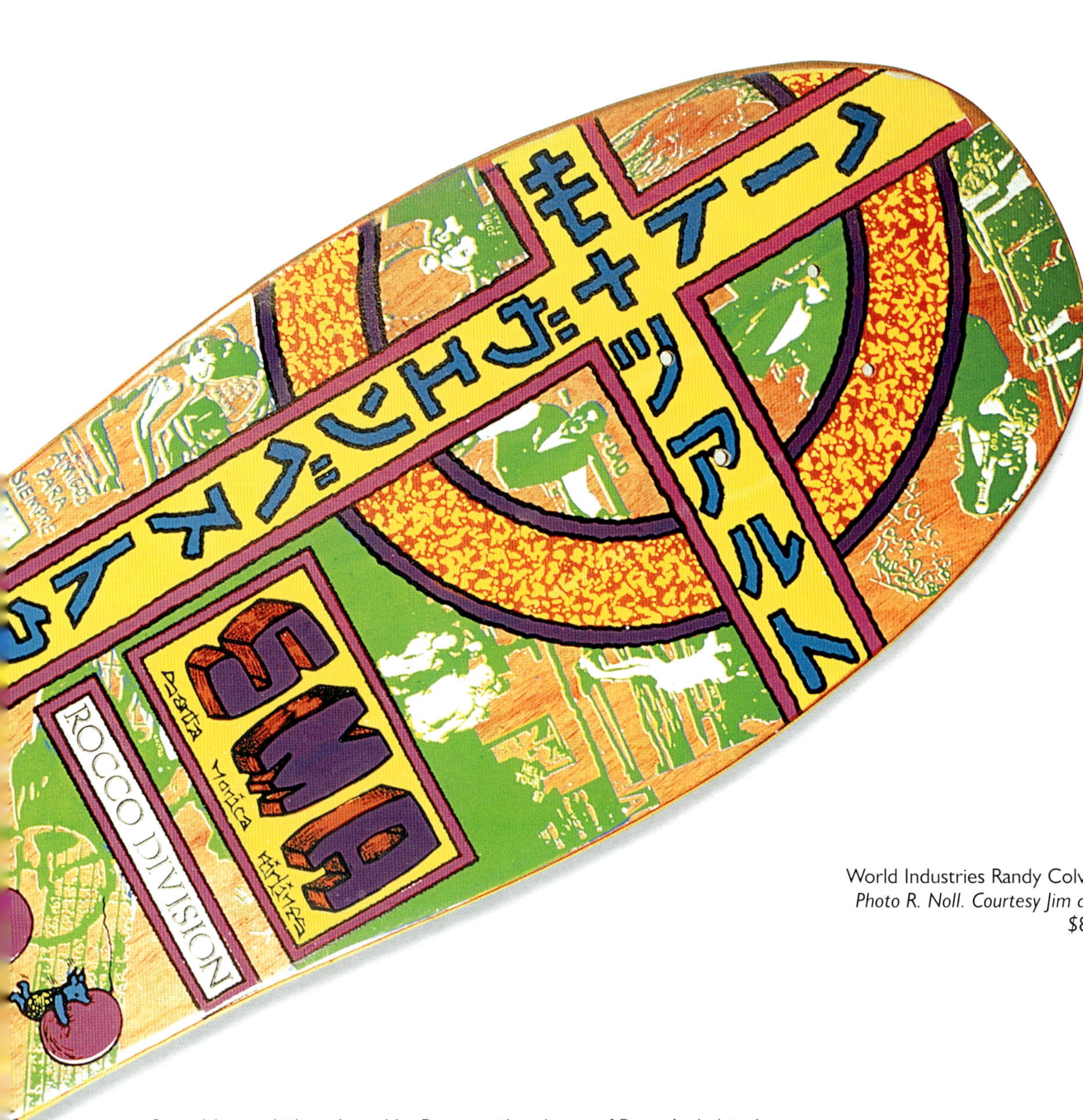

Santa Monica Airlines board by Rocco with a design of Rocco's dad in the graphics. *Photo R. Noll. Courtesy Jim at Rip City.* $1500-2000.

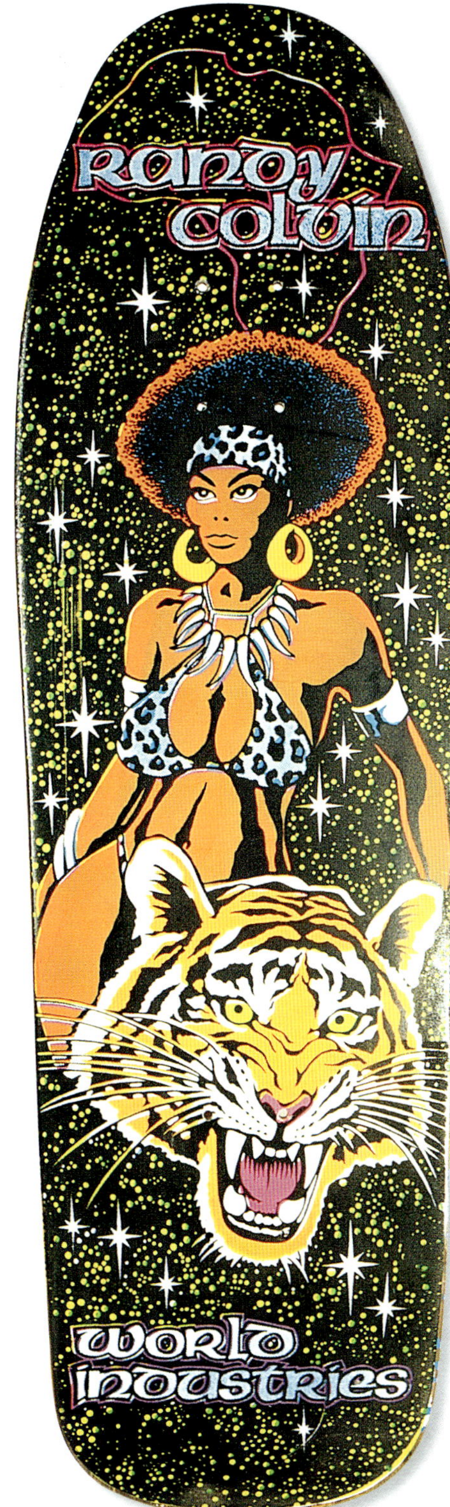

World Industries Randy Colvin model. *Photo R. Noll. Courtesy Jim at Rip City.* $800-1200.

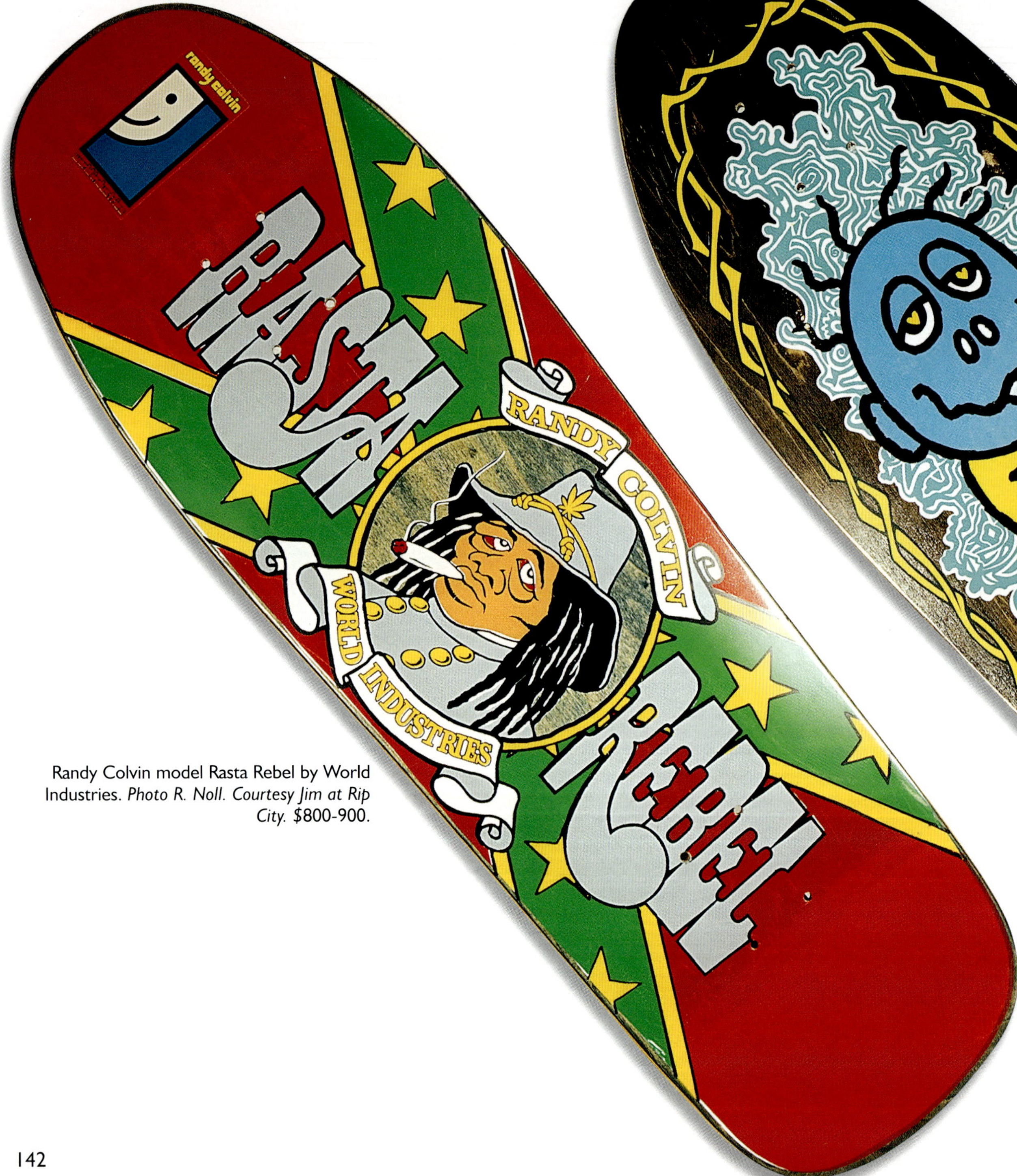

Randy Colvin model Rasta Rebel by World Industries. *Photo R. Noll. Courtesy Jim at Rip City.* $800-900.

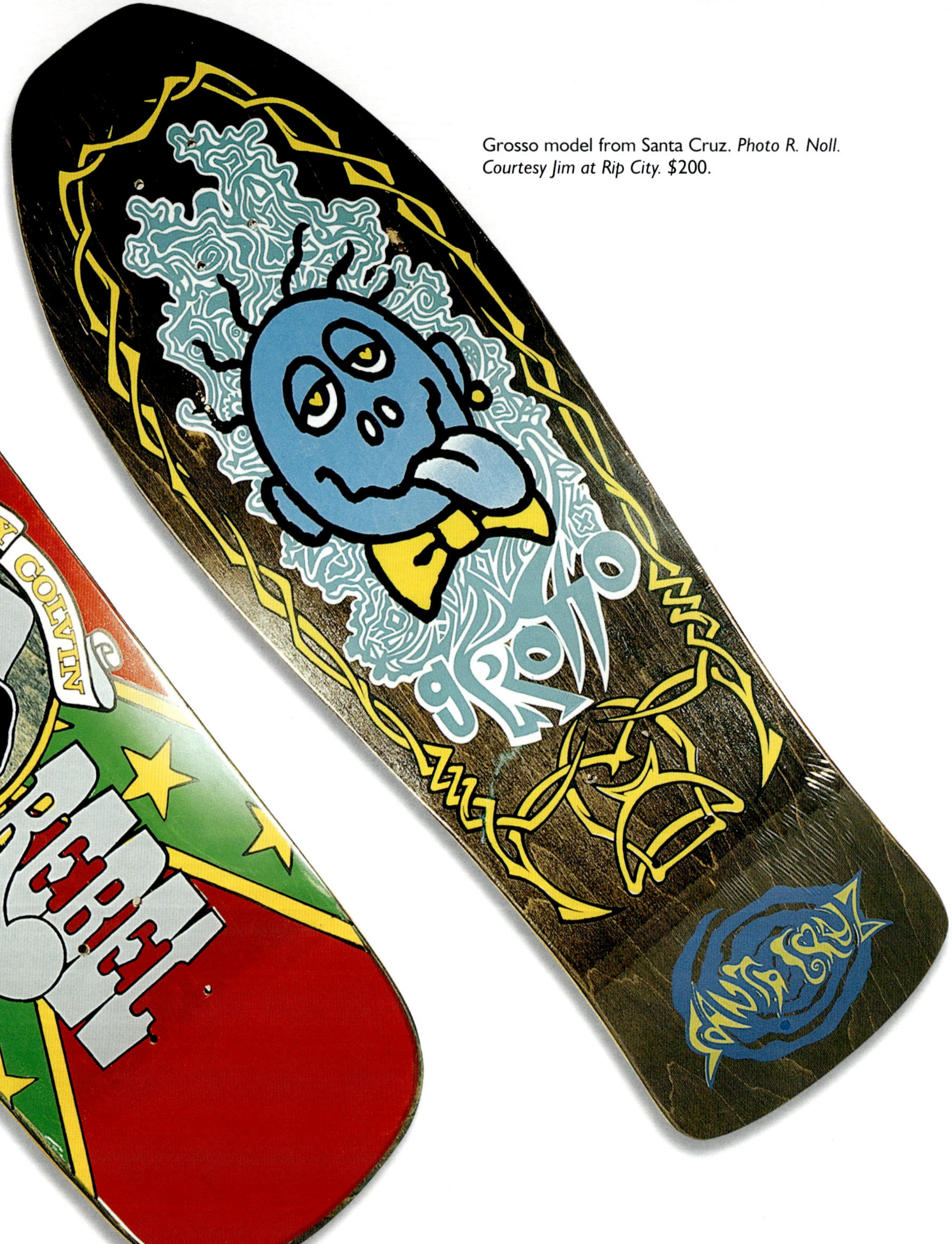

Grosso model from Santa Cruz. *Photo R. Noll. Courtesy Jim at Rip City.* $200.

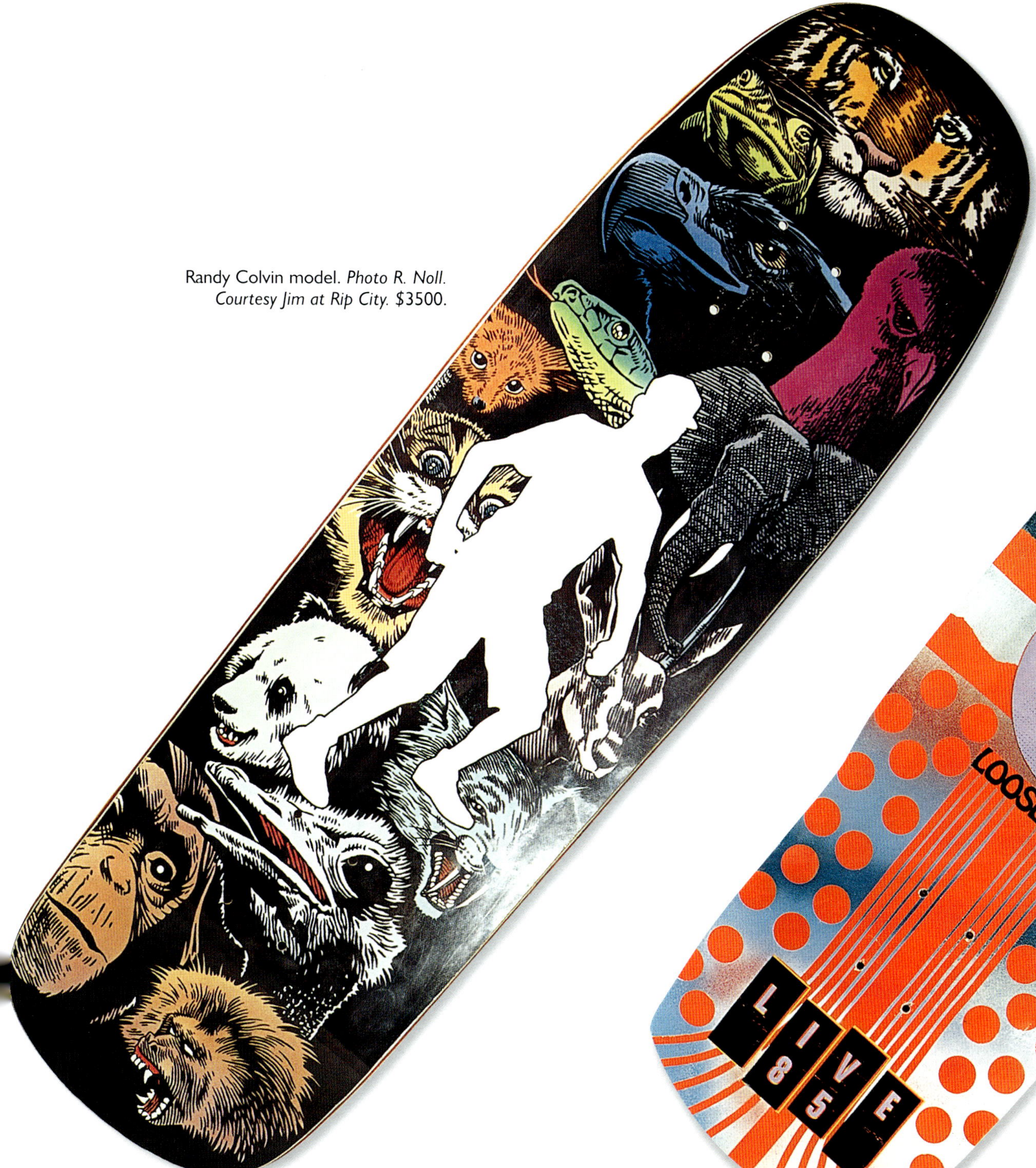

Randy Colvin model. *Photo R. Noll. Courtesy Jim at Rip City.* $3500.

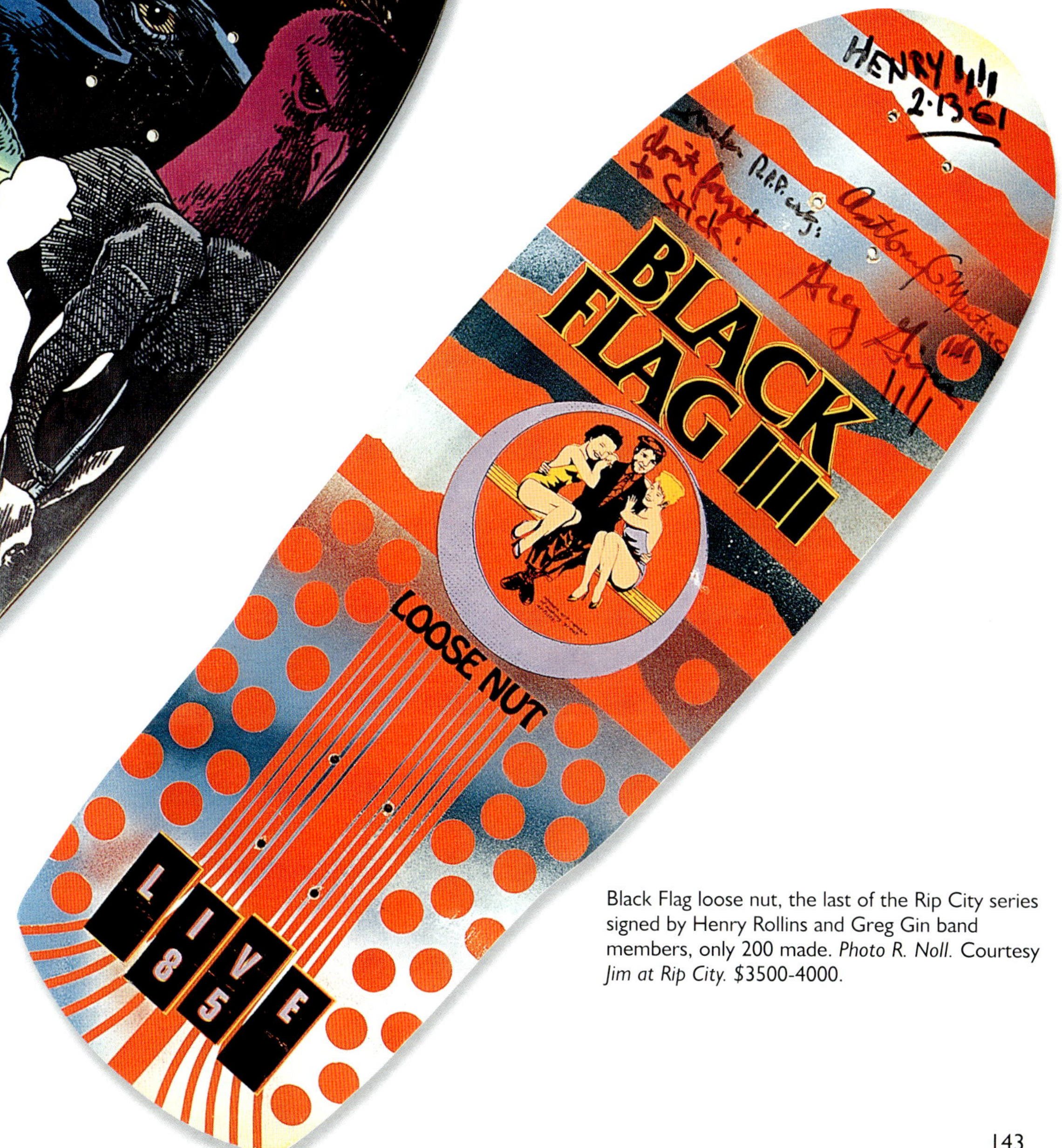

Black Flag loose nut, the last of the Rip City series signed by Henry Rollins and Greg Gin band members, only 200 made. *Photo R. Noll.* Courtesy *Jim at Rip City.* $3500-4000.

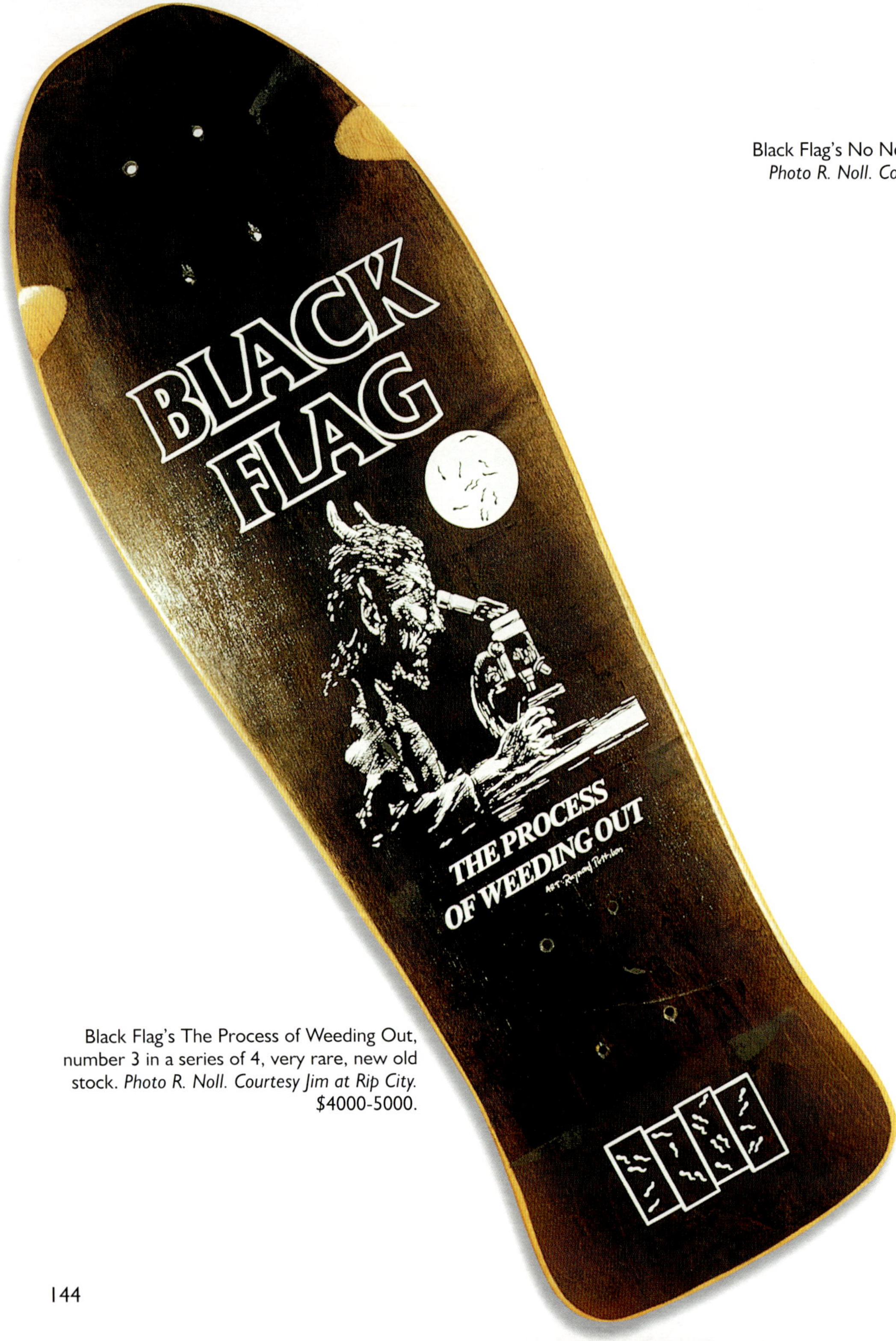

Black Flag's The Process of Weeding Out, number 3 in a series of 4, very rare, new old stock. *Photo R. Noll. Courtesy Jim at Rip City.* $4000-5000.

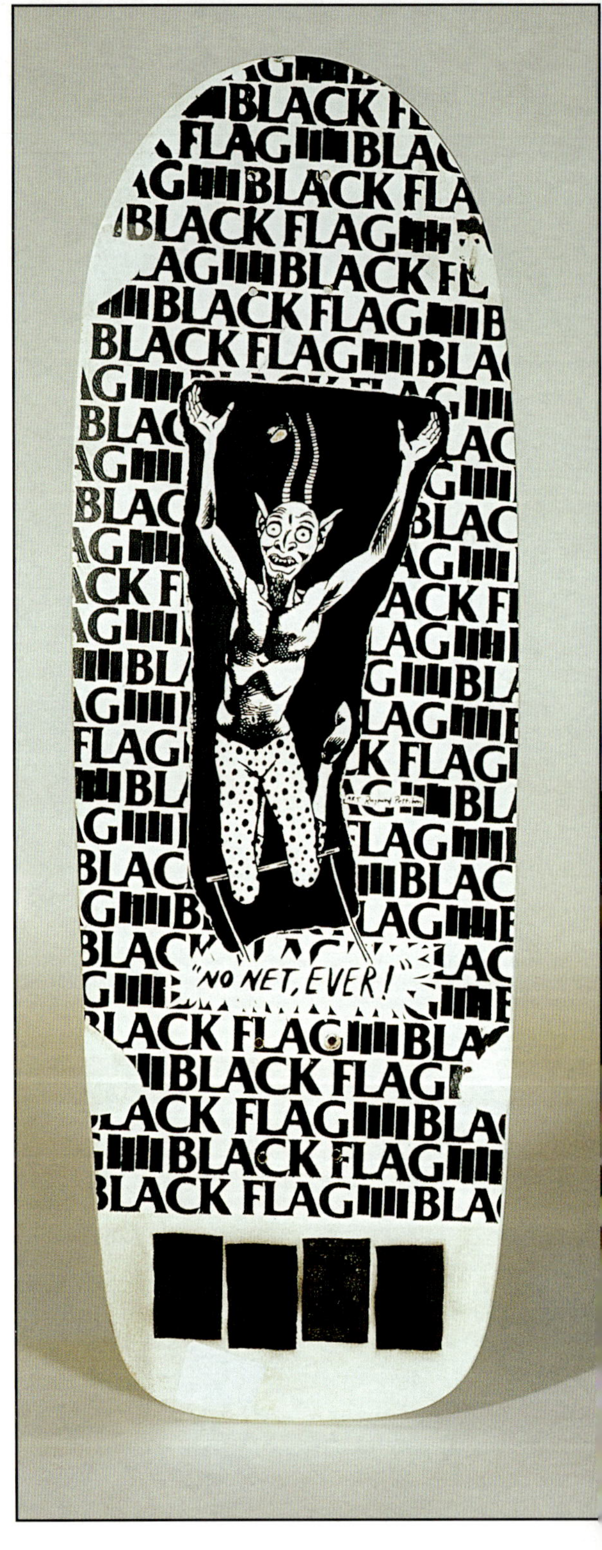

Black Flag's No Net Ever, first in a series, rare. *Photo R. Noll. Courtesy Jim at Rip City.* $5000.

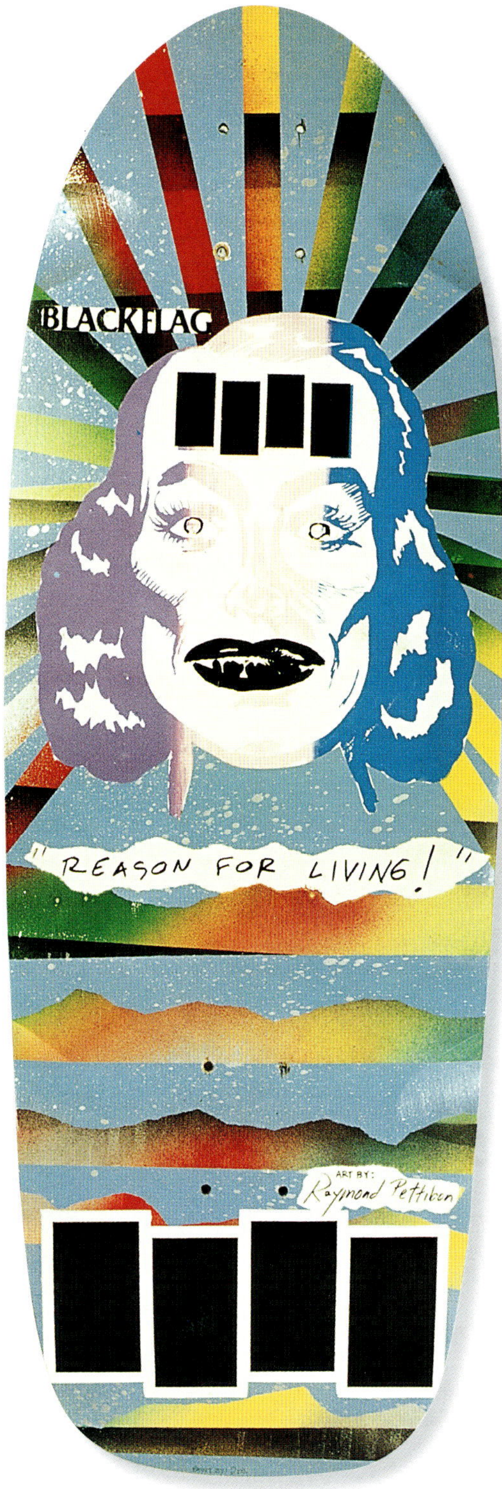

Black Flag's Reason For Living, a Joan Crawford graphic. *Photo R. Noll. Courtesy Jim at Rip City.* $2500.

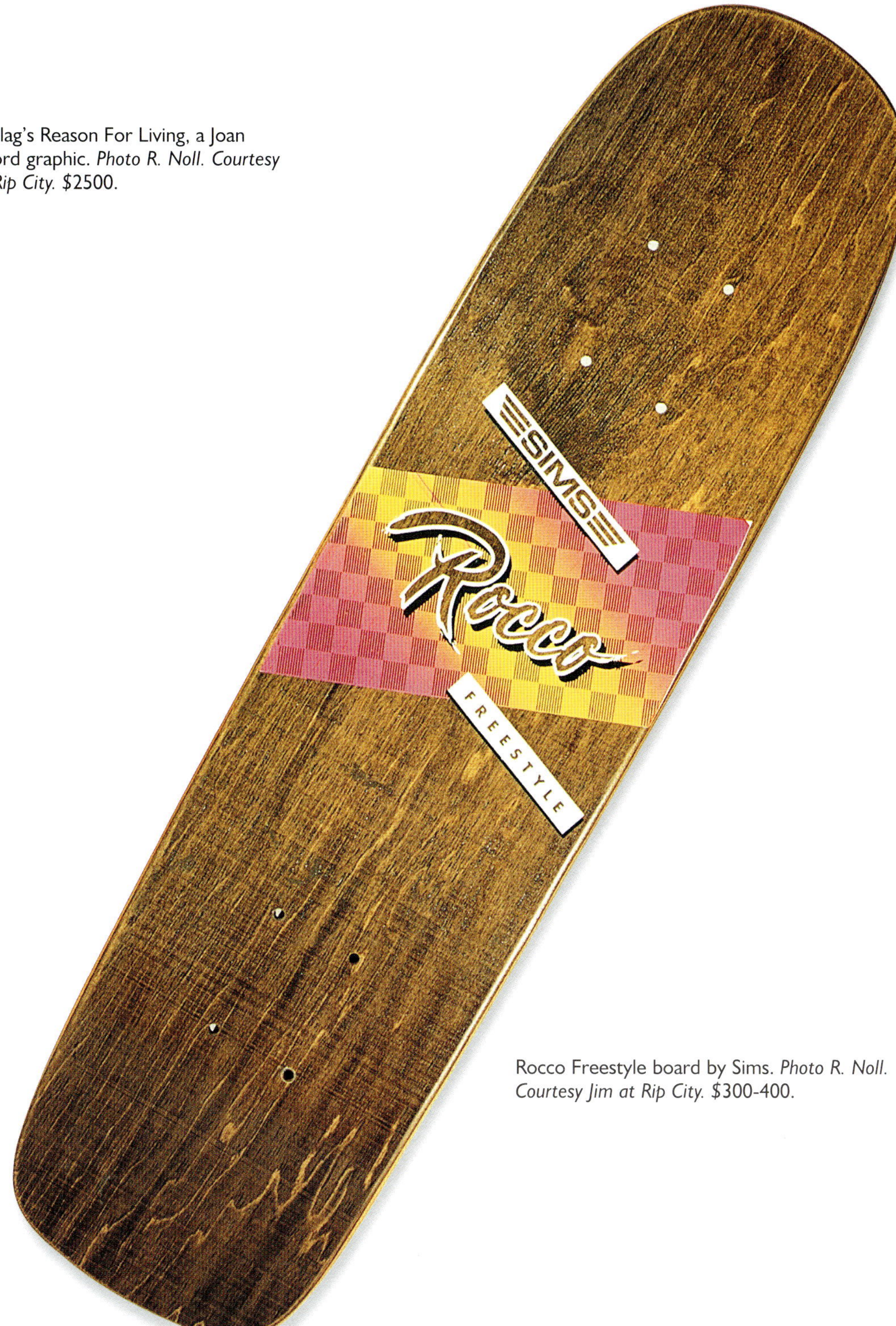

Rocco Freestyle board by Sims. *Photo R. Noll. Courtesy Jim at Rip City.* $300-400.

Natas by Santa Monica Airlines, signed by Natas. *Photo R. Noll. Courtesy Jim at Rip City.* $2500-3000.

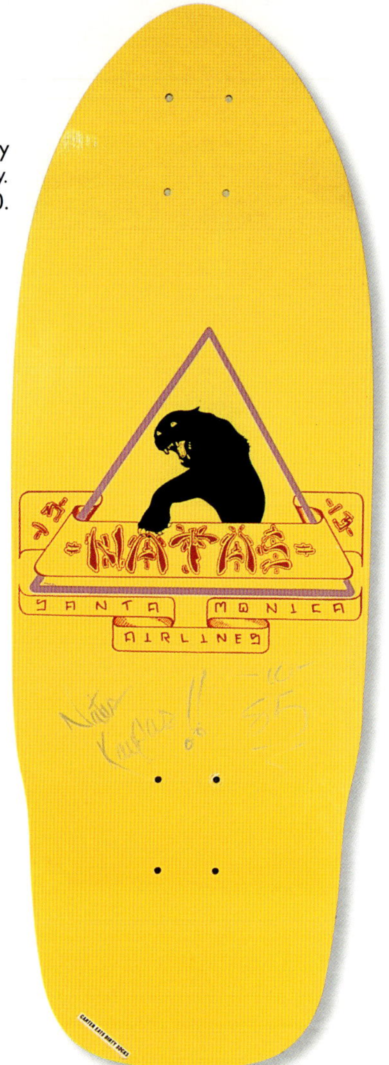

Mullen Freestyle by Powell Paralta. *Photo R. Noll. Courtesy Jim at Rip City.* $300-400.

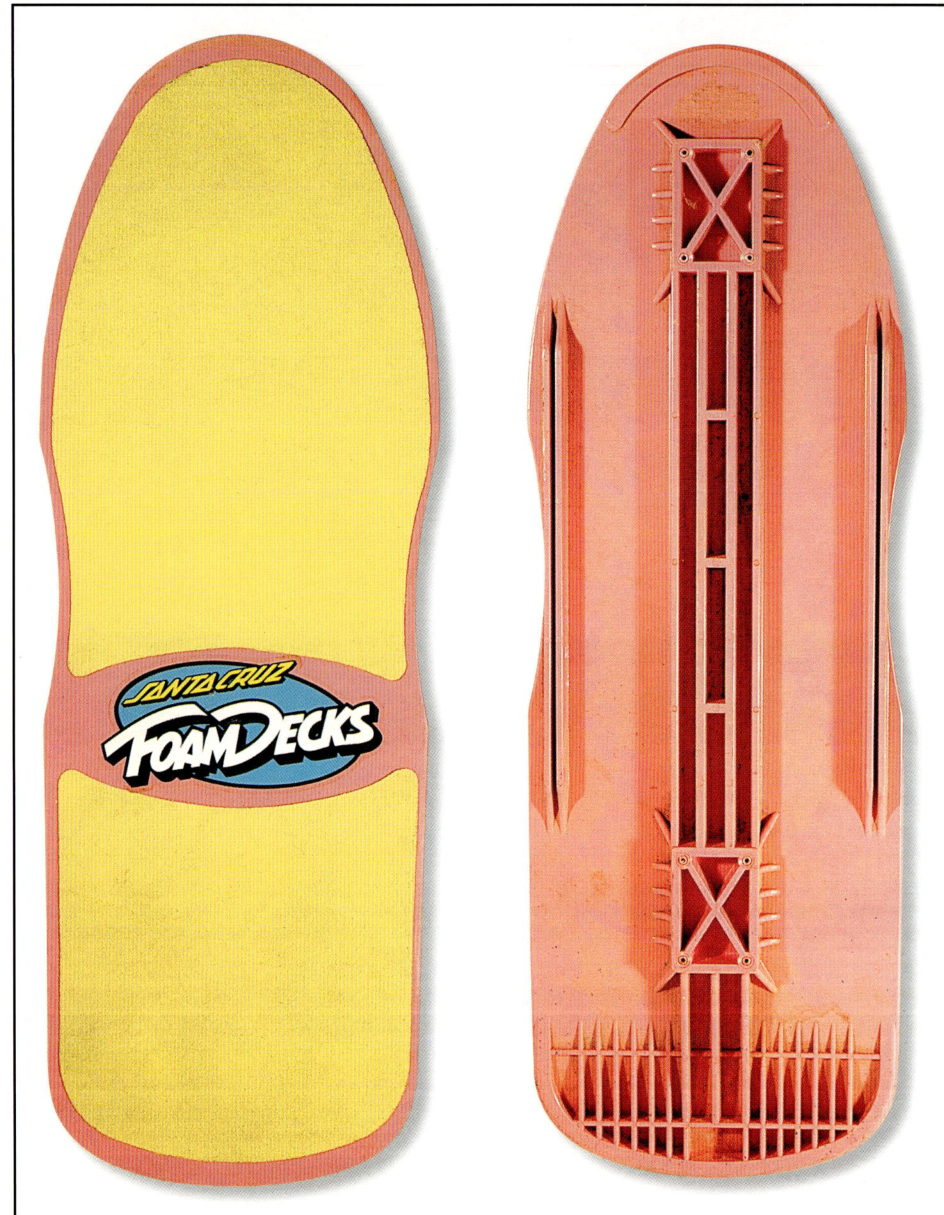

A Santa Cruz foam deck from the 1980s, but I'll bet they'd rather forget about this pink plastic model. *Photo R. Noll. Courtesy Todd Huber.* $150-200.

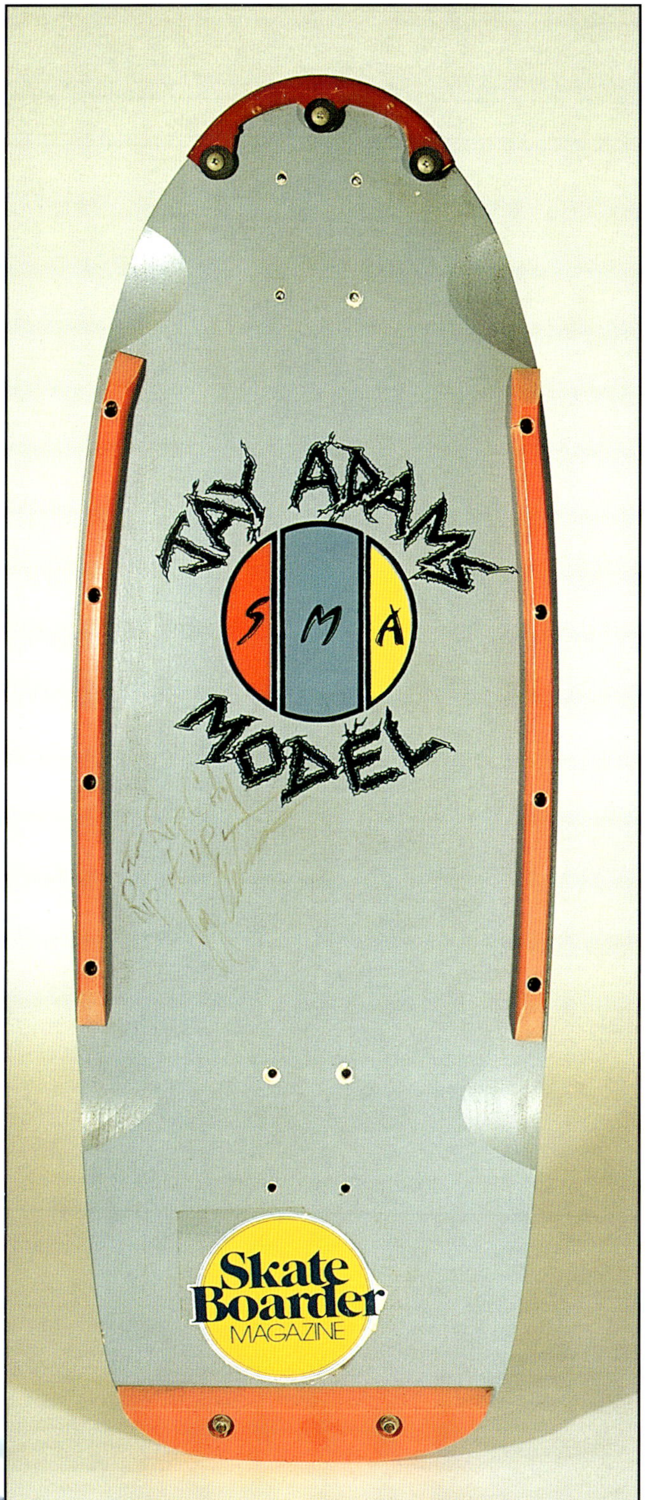

Jay Adams model by Santa Monica Airlines equipped with nose bone, tail, bone and rib bone. *Photo R. Noll. Courtesy Jim at Rip City.* $2500-3000.

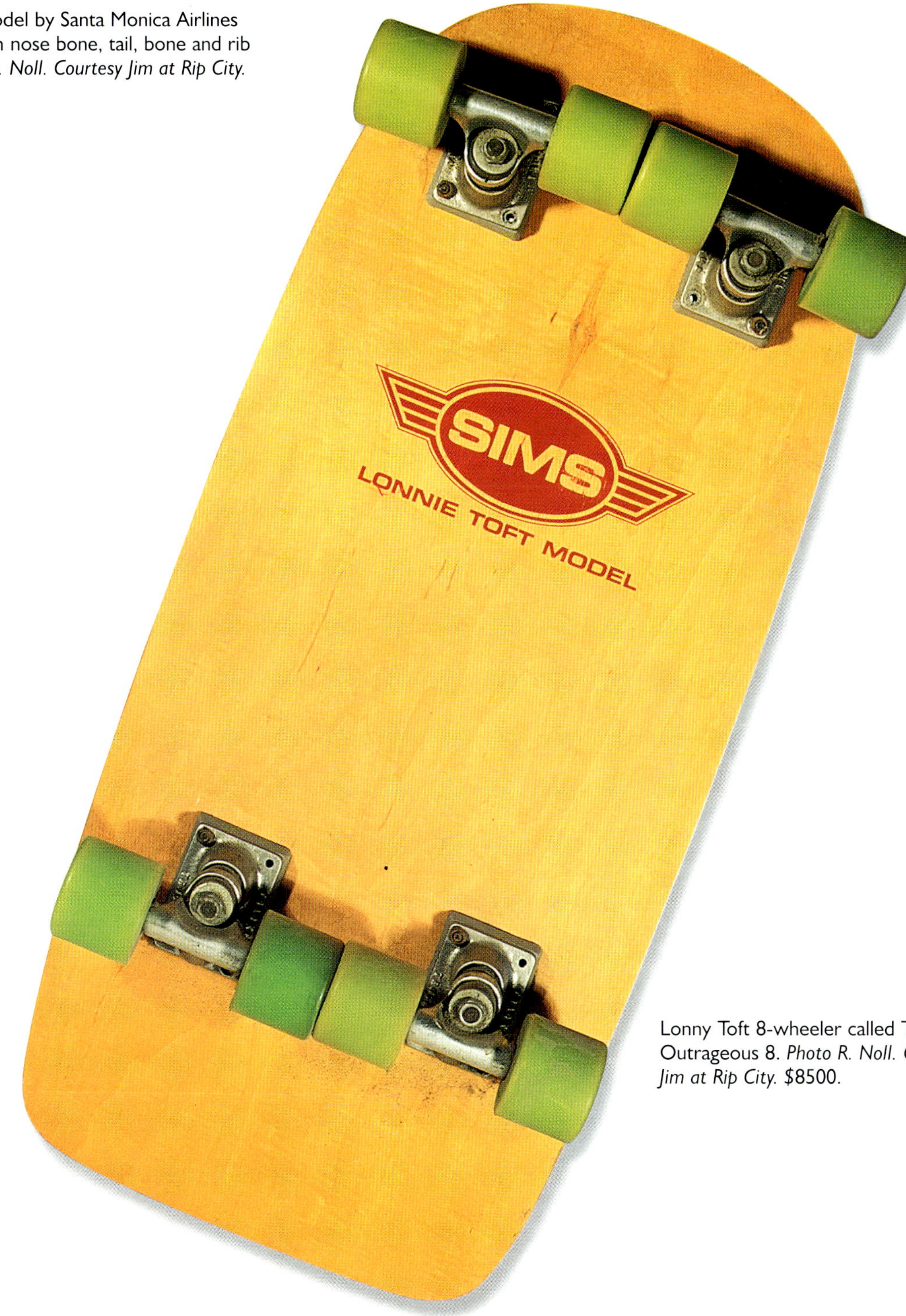

Lonny Toft 8-wheeler called The Outrageous 8. *Photo R. Noll. Courtesy Jim at Rip City.* $8500.

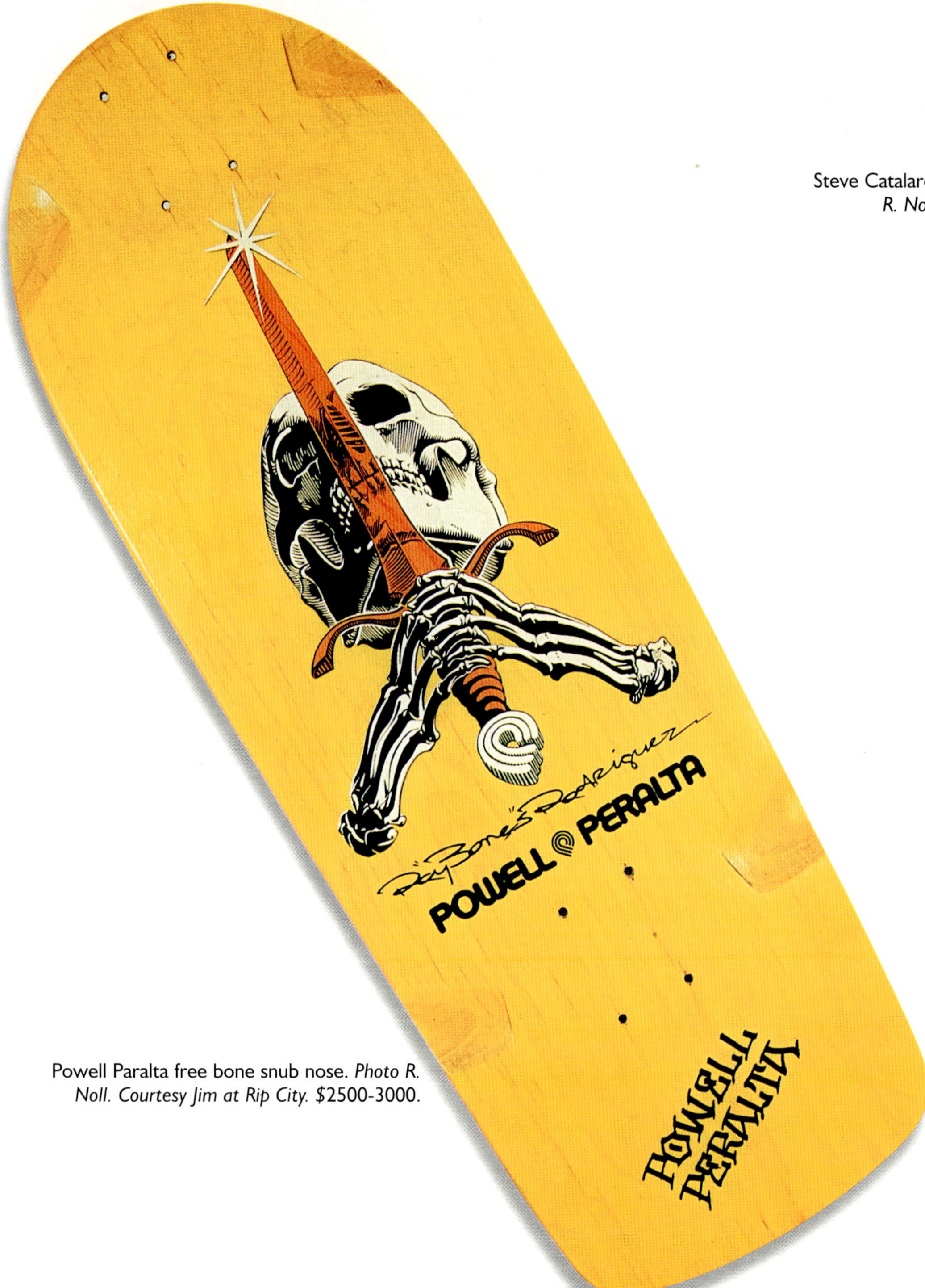

Powell Paralta free bone snub nose. *Photo R. Noll. Courtesy Jim at Rip City.* $2500-3000.

Steve Catalaro, Vision Pro, 1981. *Photo R. Noll. Courtesy Jim at Rip City.*

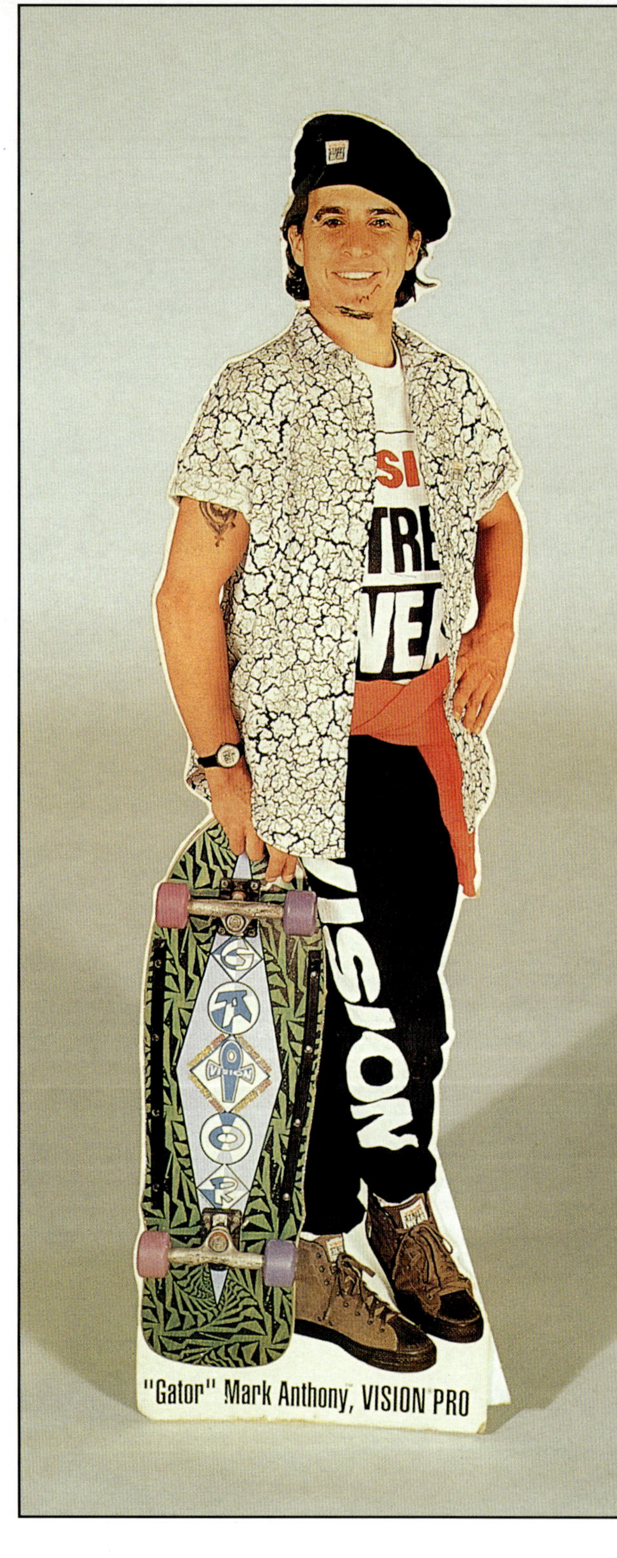

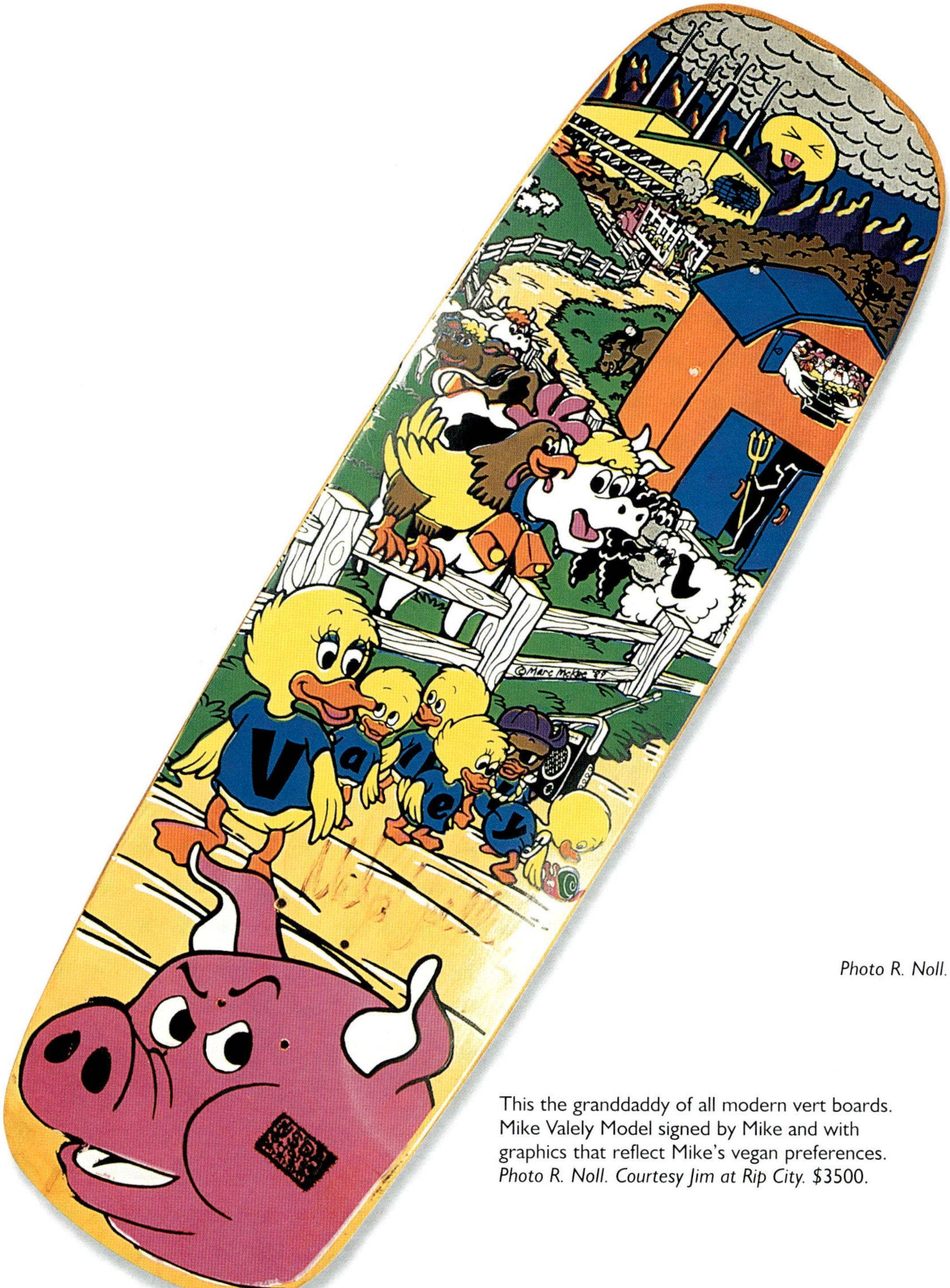

This the granddaddy of all modern vert boards. Mike Valely Model signed by Mike and with graphics that reflect Mike's vegan preferences. *Photo R. Noll. Courtesy Jim at Rip City.* $3500.

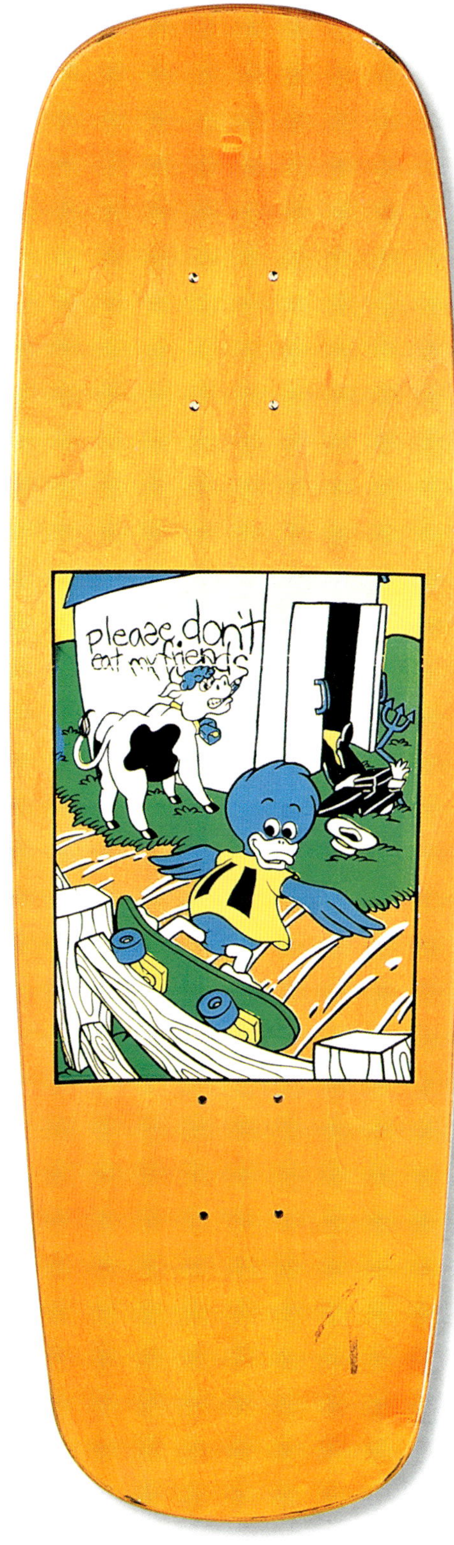

Photo R. Noll. Courtesy Jim at Rip City.

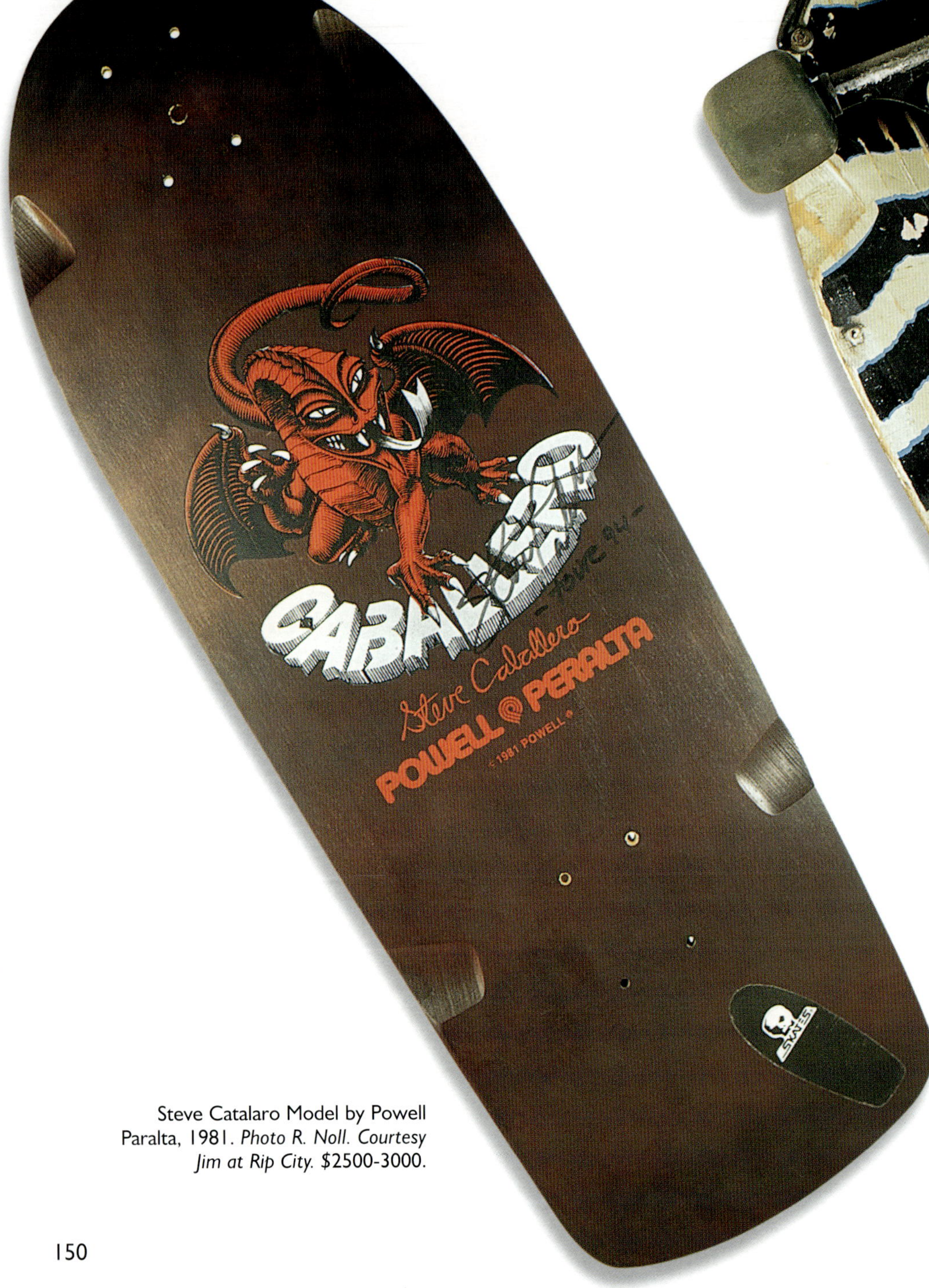

Steve Catalaro Model by Powell Paralta, 1981. *Photo R. Noll. Courtesy Jim at Rip City.* $2500-3000.

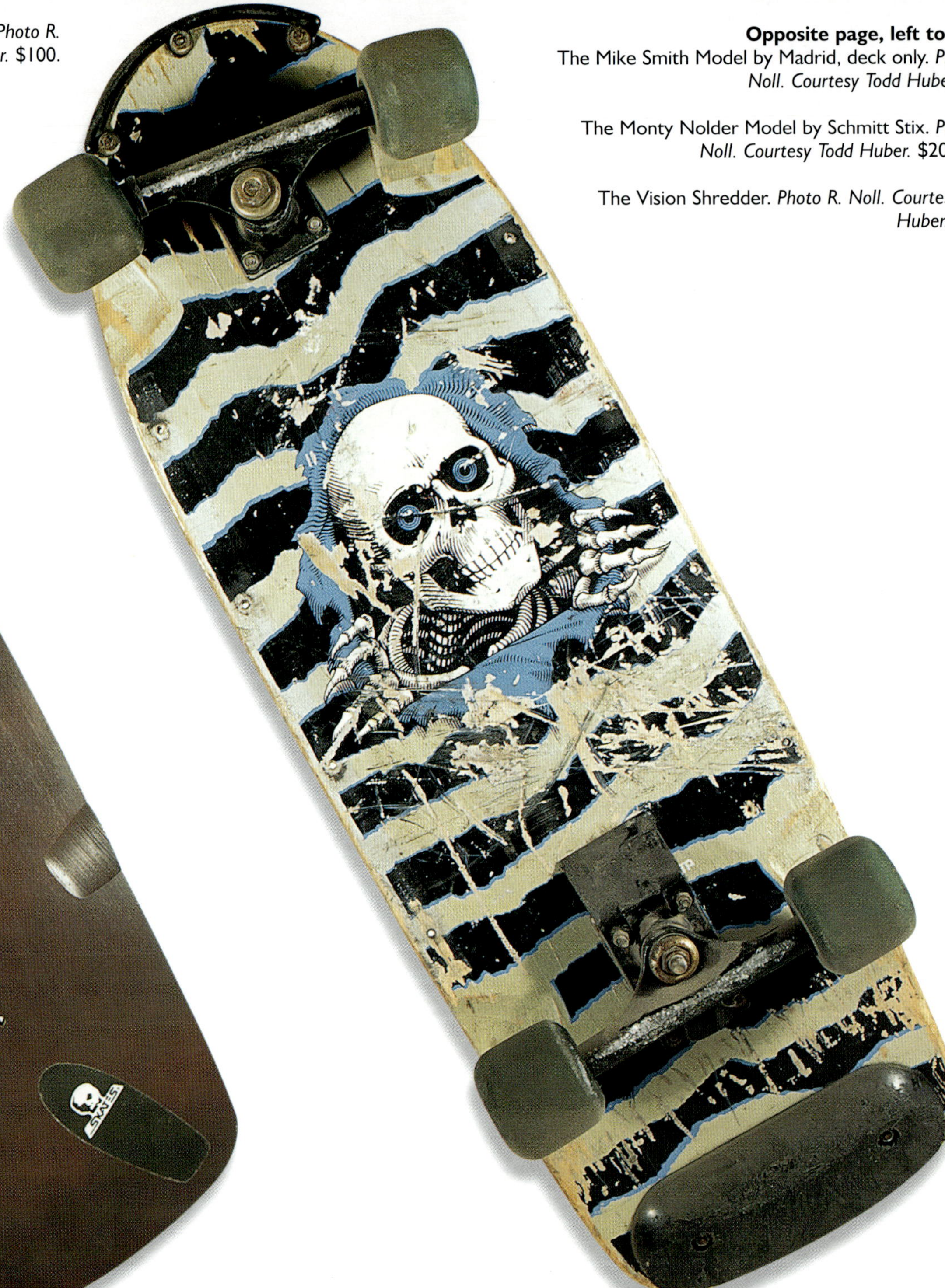

Bones Powell Paralta. *Photo R. Noll. Courtesy Todd Huber.* $100.

Opposite page, left to right:

The Mike Smith Model by Madrid, deck only. *Photo R. Noll. Courtesy Todd Huber.* $75.

The Monty Nolder Model by Schmitt Stix. *Photo R. Noll. Courtesy Todd Huber.* $200-300.

The Vision Shredder. *Photo R. Noll. Courtesy Todd Huber.* $150.

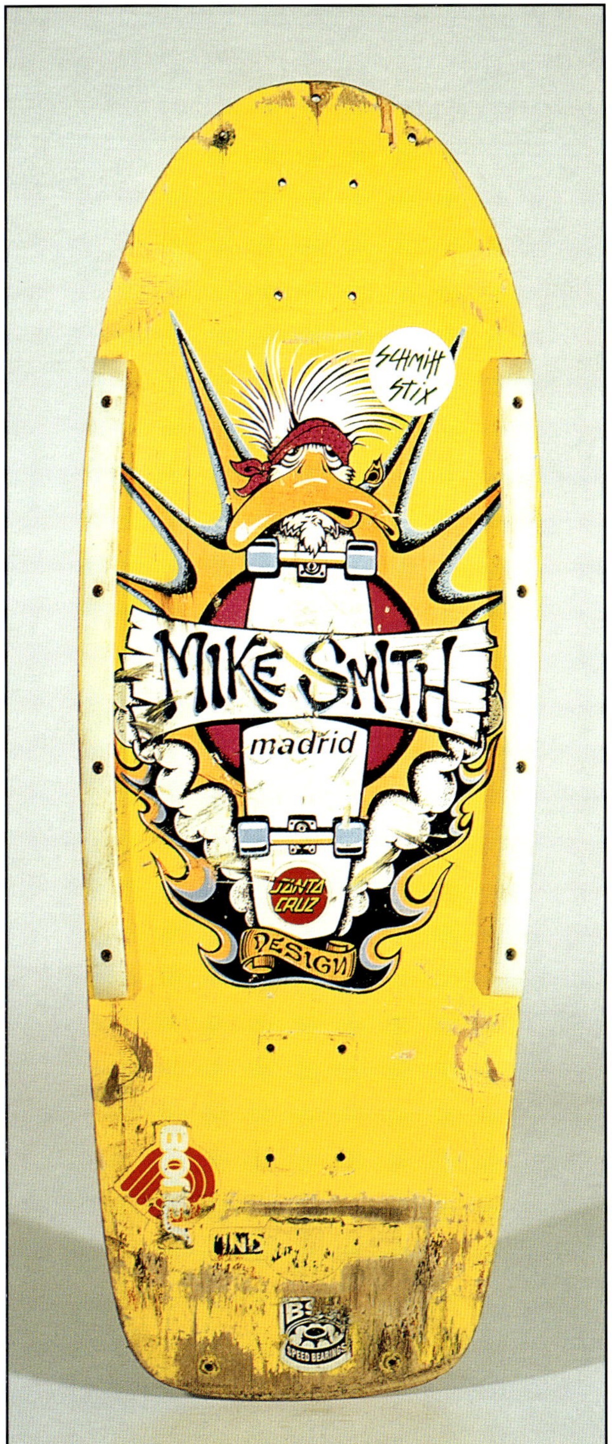
SCHMITT STIX
MIKE SMITH
madrid
SANTA CRUZ
DESIGN

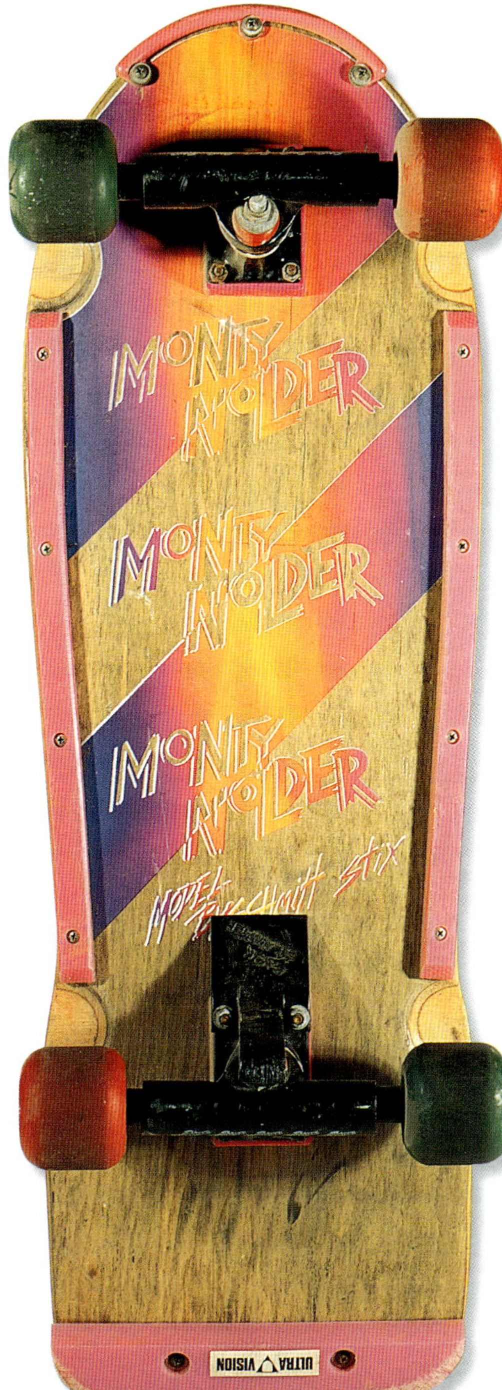
MONTY NOLDER
MONTY NOLDER
MONTY NOLDER
ULTRA VISION

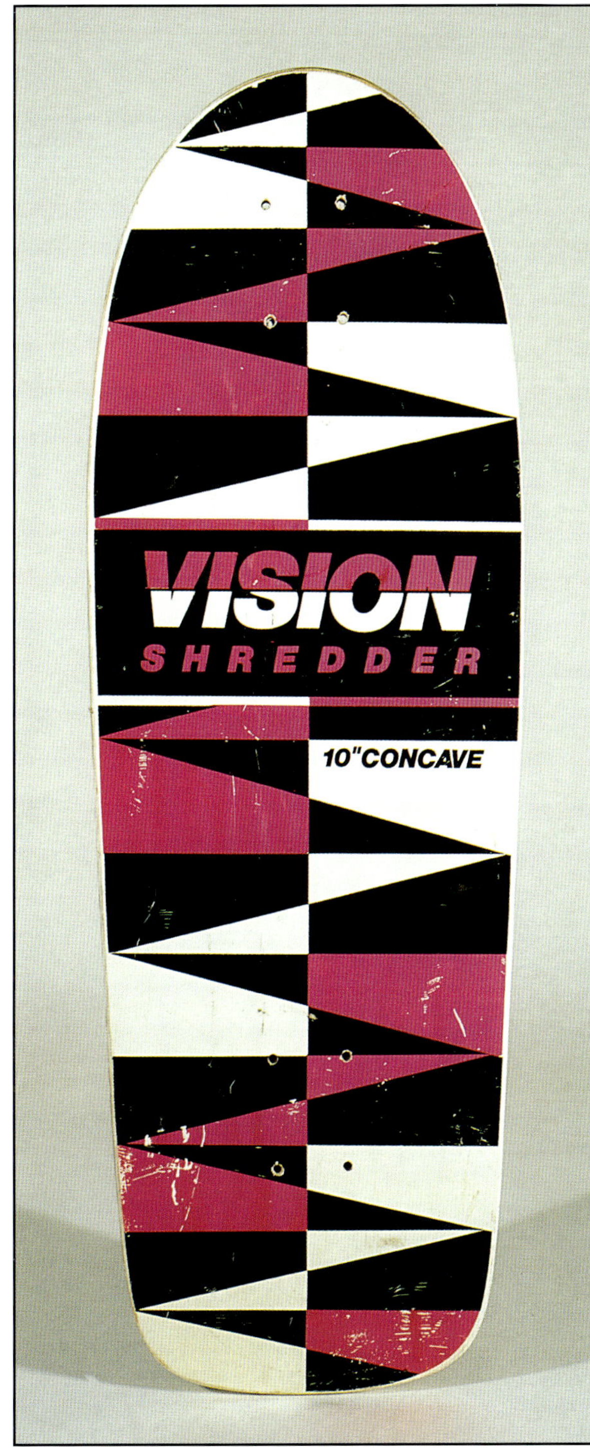
VISION
SHREDDER
10"CONCAVE

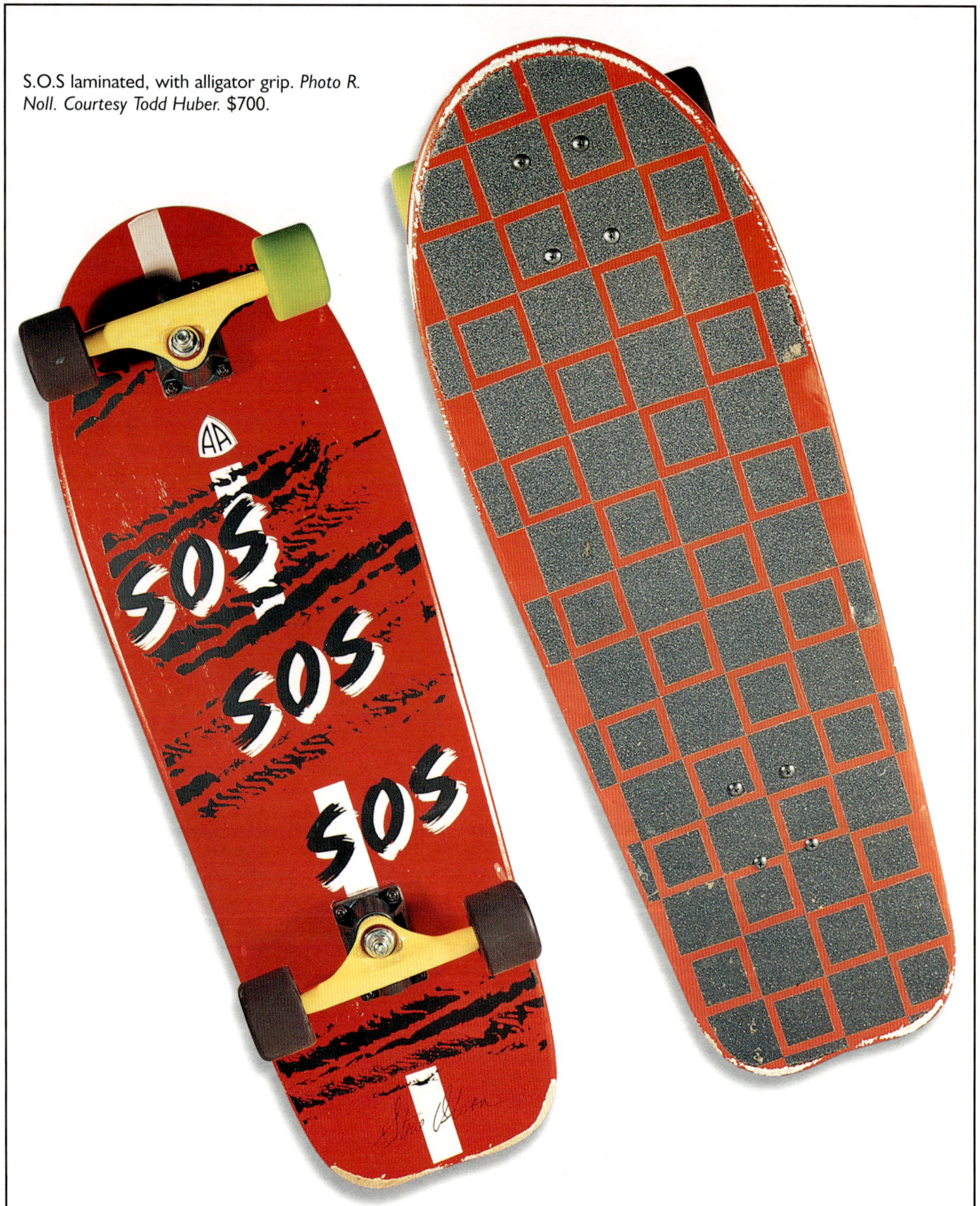

S.O.S laminated, with alligator grip. *Photo R. Noll. Courtesy Todd Huber.* $700.

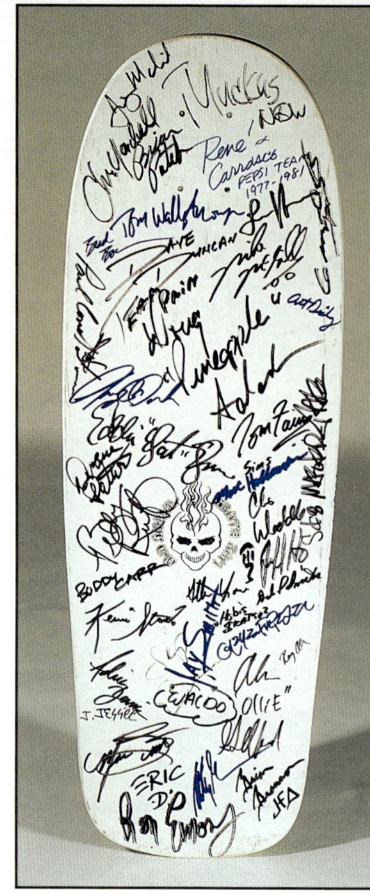

1980s board signed by a myriad of skate moguls. *Photo R. Noll. Courtesy Todd Huber.* $1000.

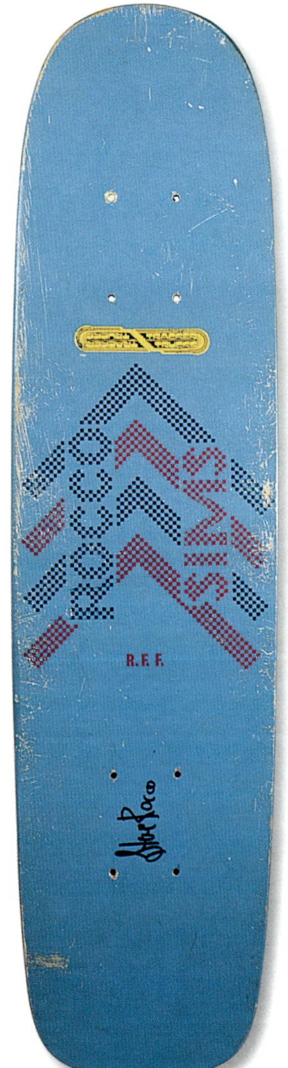

A Rocco Sims freestyle board. *Photo R. Noll. Courtesy Todd Huber.* $200.

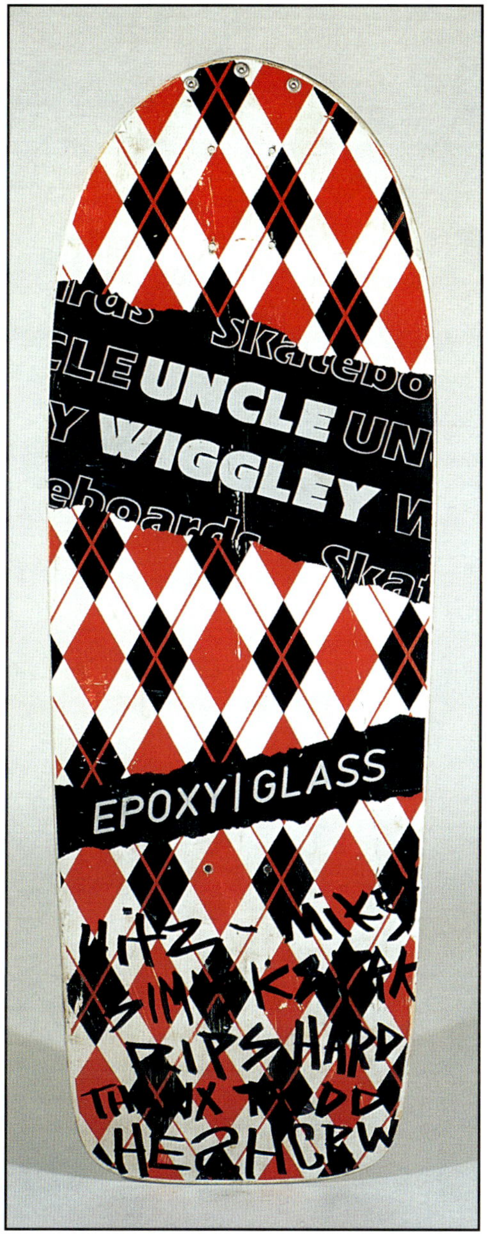

Uncle Wiggley with an epoxy glass kicktail, signed by Sam Hitz. *Photo R. Noll. Courtesy Todd Huber.* $150.

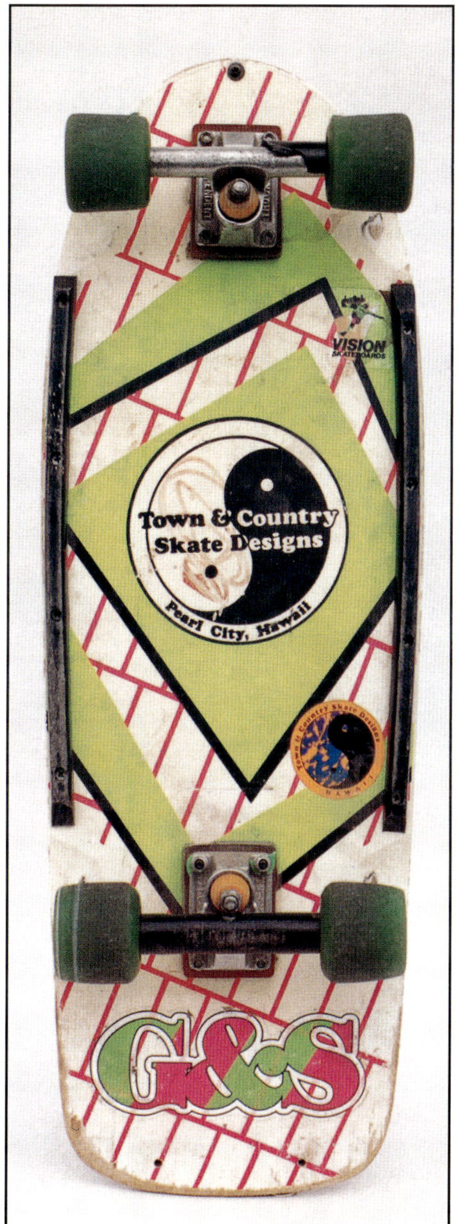

G & S's Town & Country Skate Designs, Pearl City, Hawaii. *Photo R. Noll. Courtesy Gene Cooper*. $200.

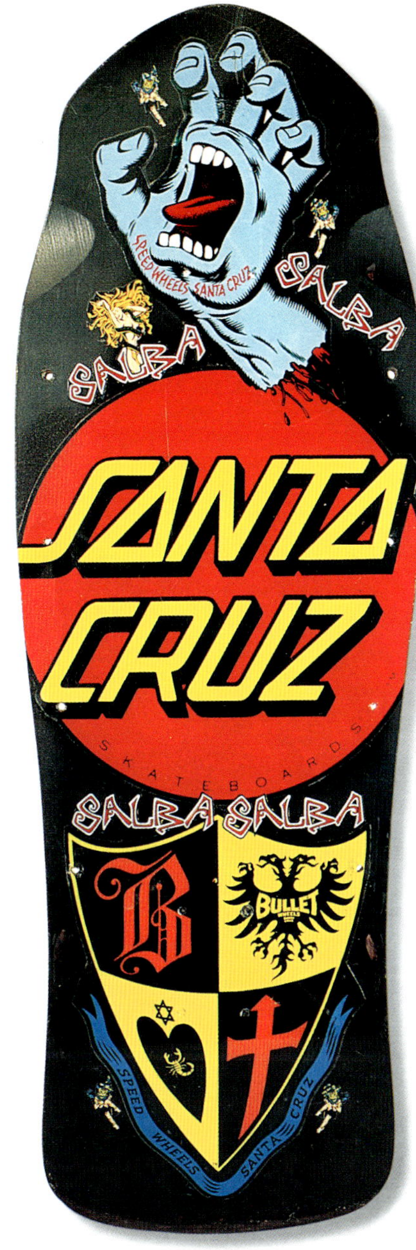

Santa Cruz deck, Salba. *Photo R. Noll. Courtesy Todd Huber.* $150-200.

The El Gato by Veriflex. *Photo R. Noll. Courtesy Todd Huber.* $200.

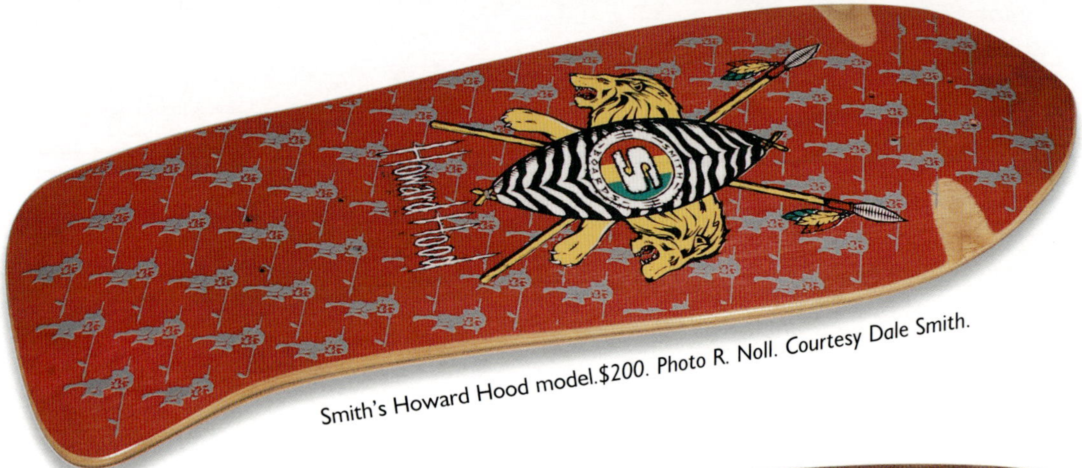

Smith's Howard Hood model.$200. *Photo R. Noll. Courtesy Dale Smith.*

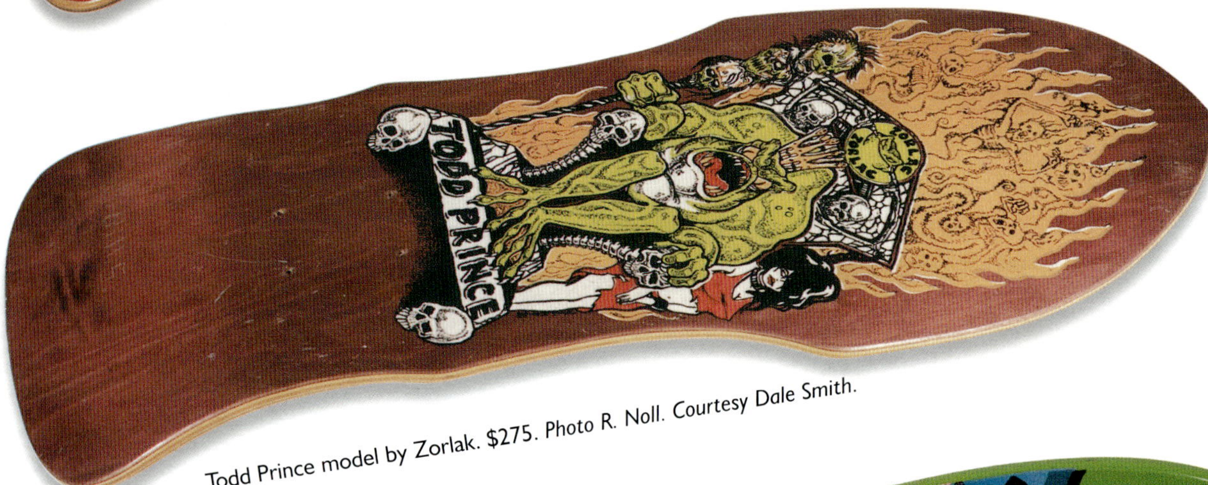

Todd Prince model by Zorlak. $275. *Photo R. Noll. Courtesy Dale Smith.*

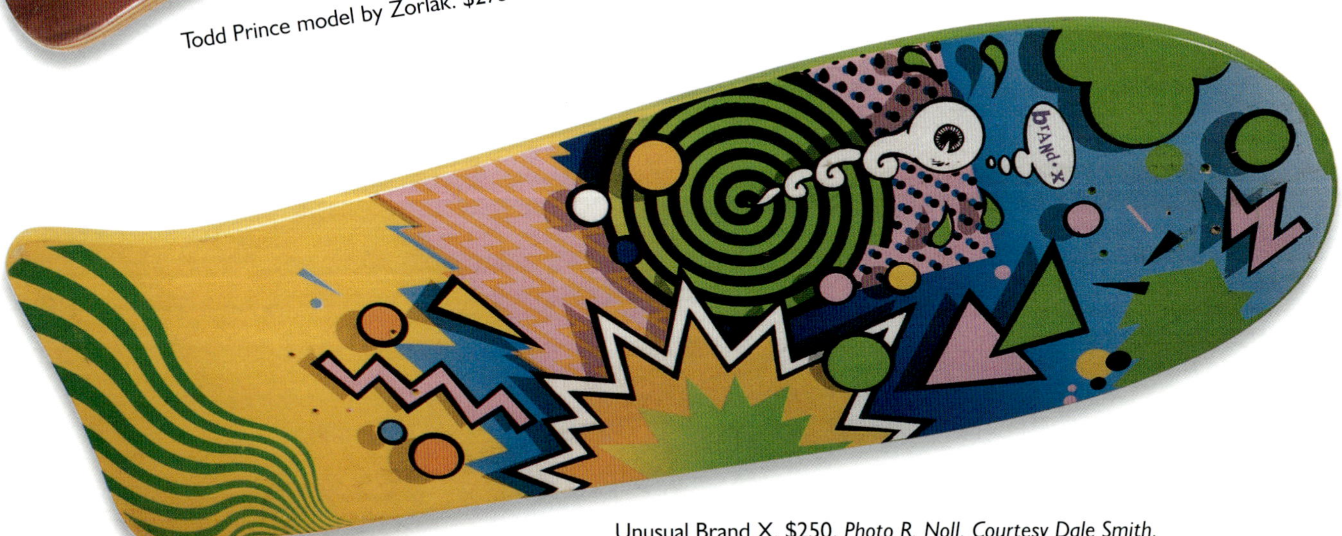

Unusual Brand X. $250. *Photo R. Noll. Courtesy Dale Smith.*

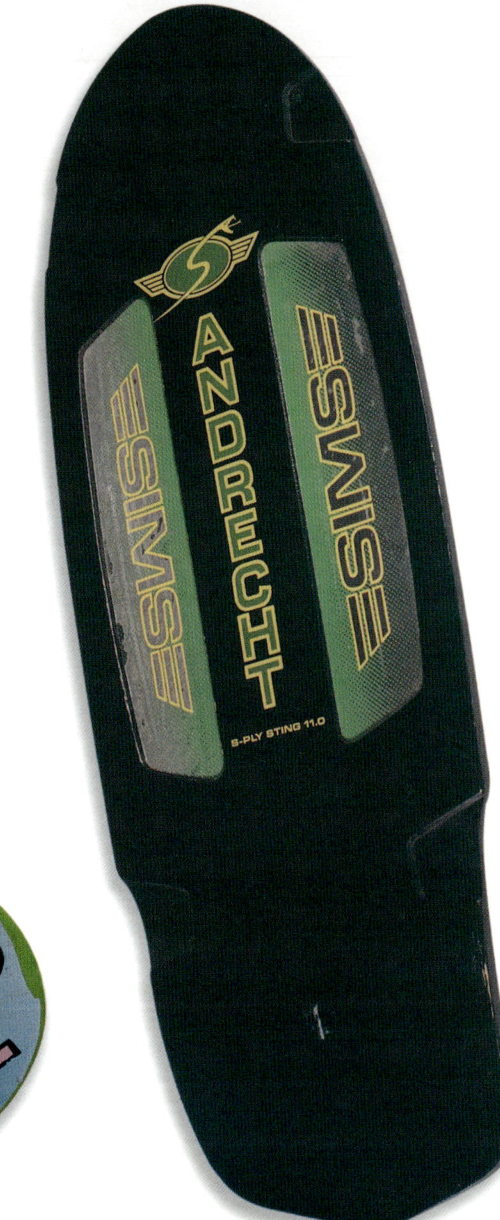

Sims' Andrecht winger. $200-250.
Photo R. Noll. Courtesy Dale Smith.

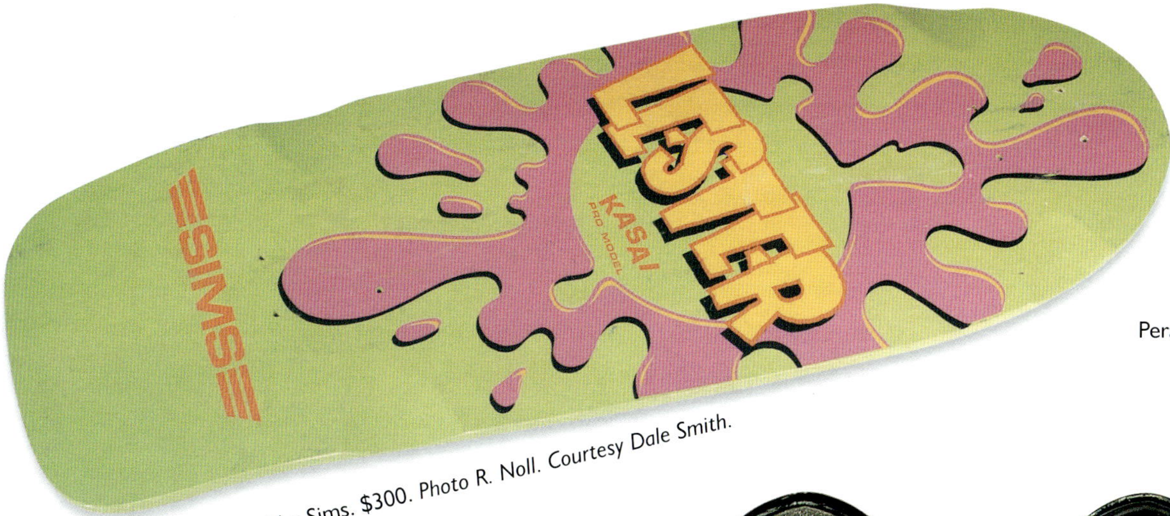

Lester Kasai model by Sims. $300. *Photo R. Noll. Courtesy Dale Smith.*

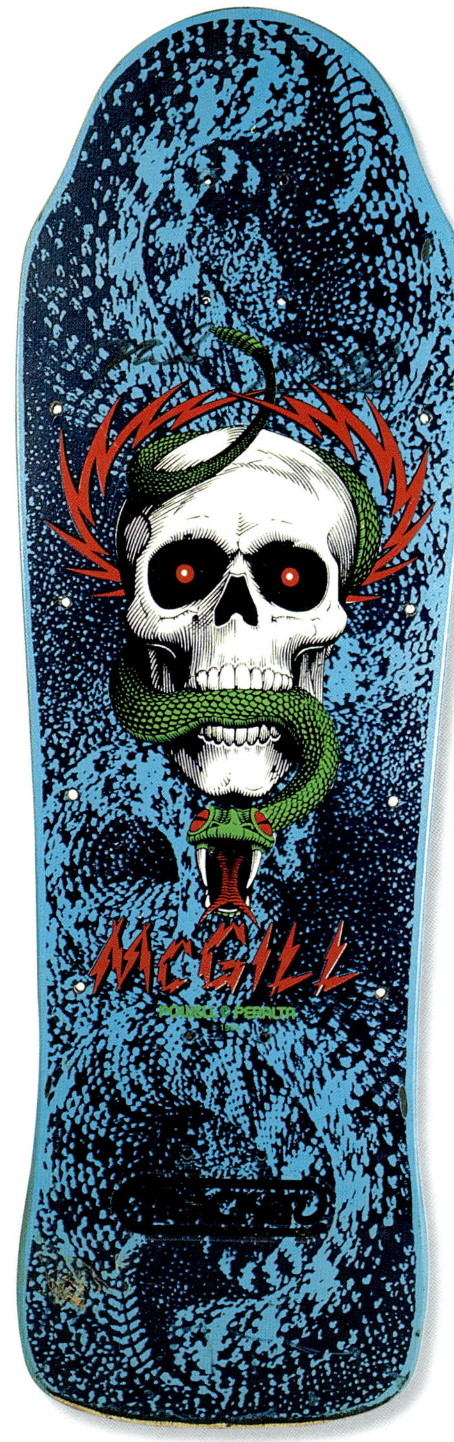

McGill model by Powel Peralta. *Photo R. Noll. Courtesy Todd Huber.* $200-250.

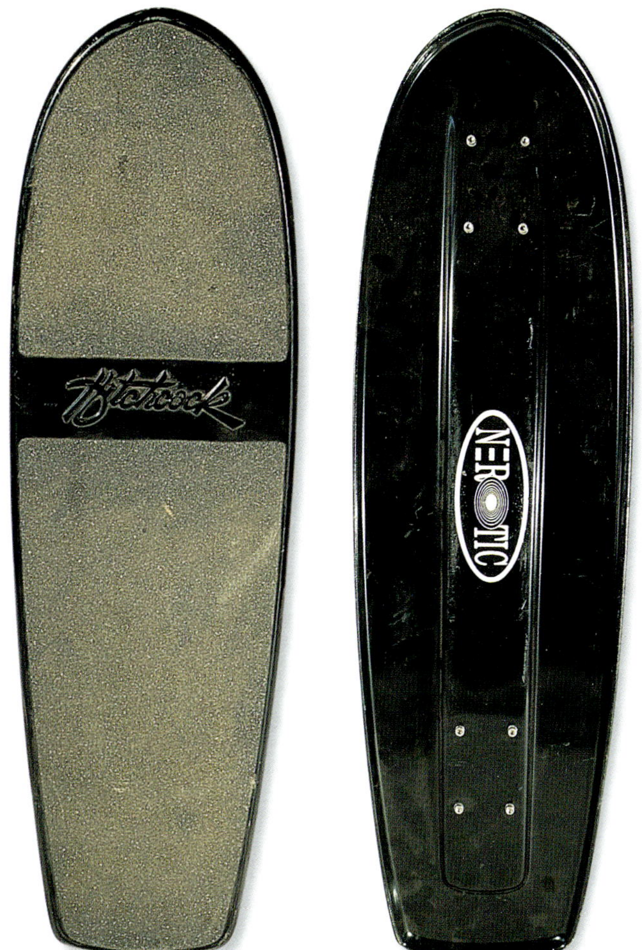

A unique Nerotic fiberglass molded skateboard from Hitchcock. *Photo R. Noll. Courtesy Todd Huber.* $300.

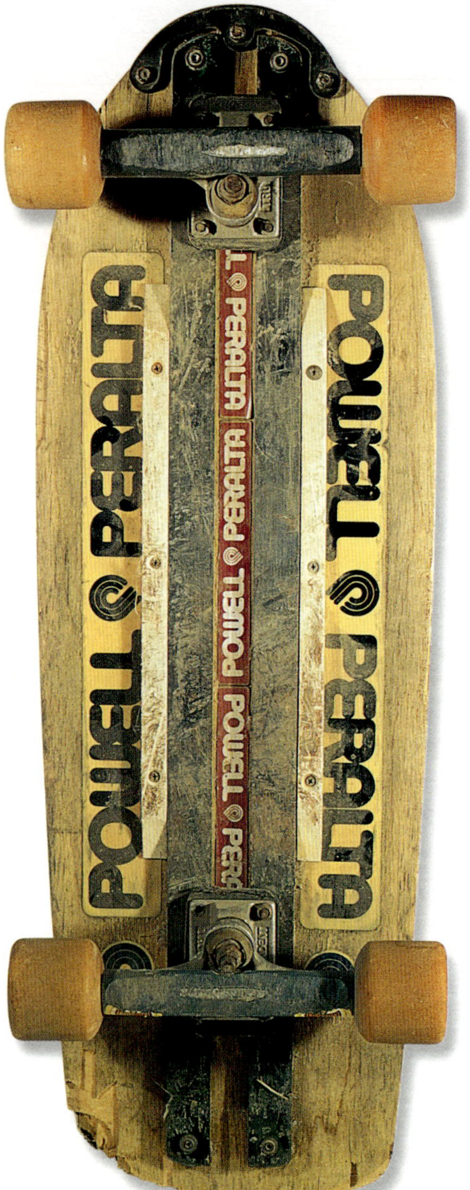

An early Powell Peralta. *Photo R. Noll. Courtesy Todd Huber.* $200.

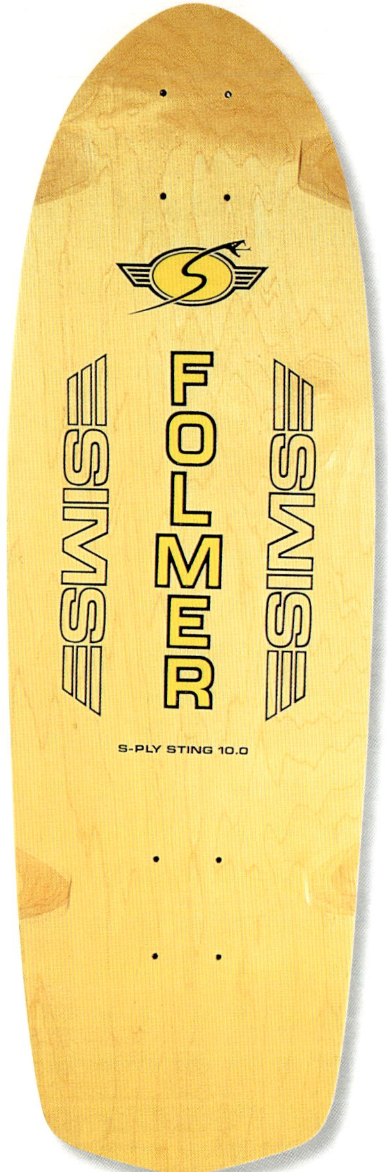

Sims' Folmer model, deck only. *Photo R. Noll. Courtesy Todd Huber.* $400.

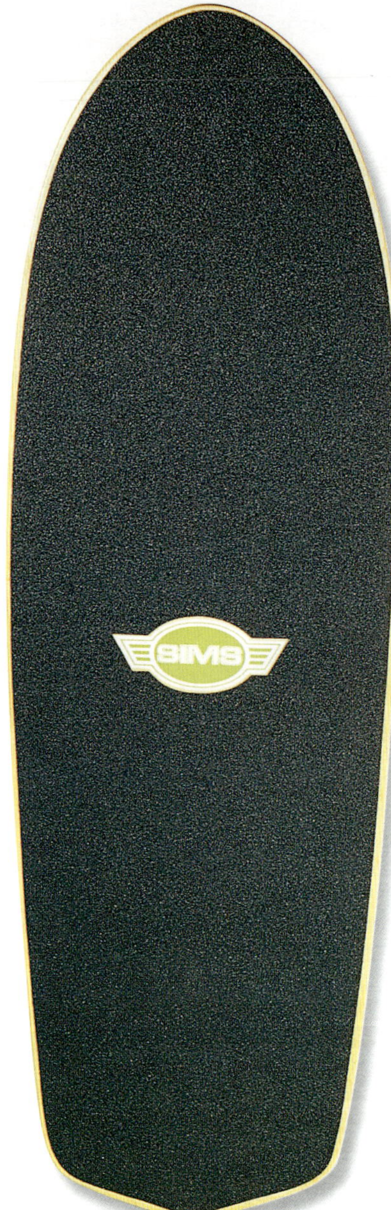

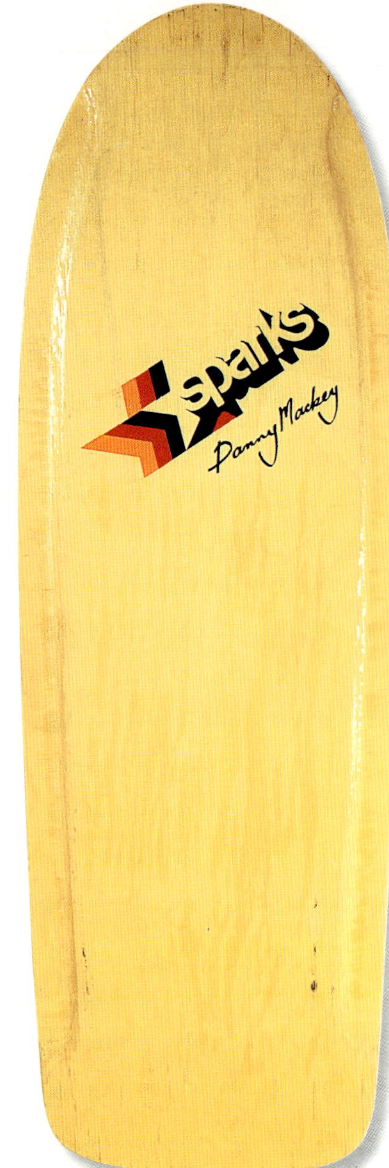

Sparks by Danny Mackey, molded wood. *Photo R. Noll. Courtesy Todd Huber.* $200-300.

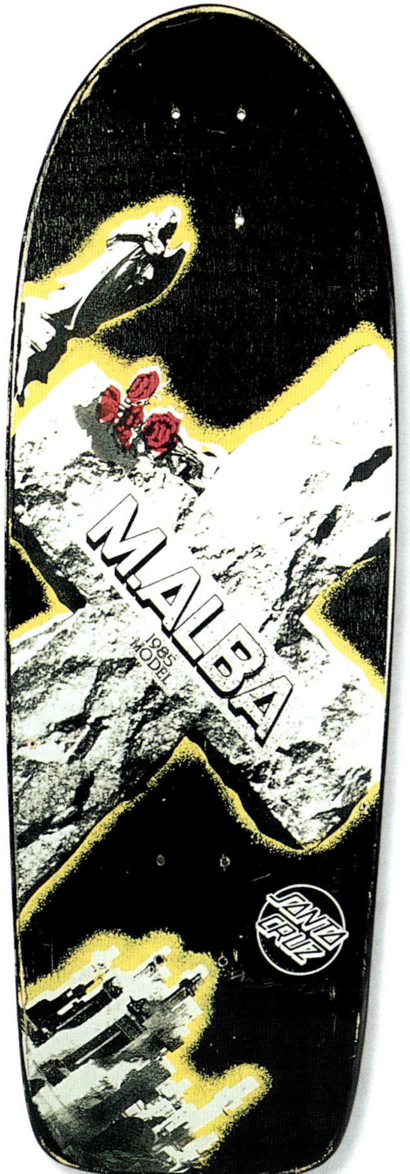

The Mickey Alba model by Santa Cruz. *Photo R. Noll. Courtesy Todd Huber.*

The Bruce Walker Nightmare, 1986, singed by Bruce. *Photo R. Noll. Courtesy Todd Huber.* $75-100.

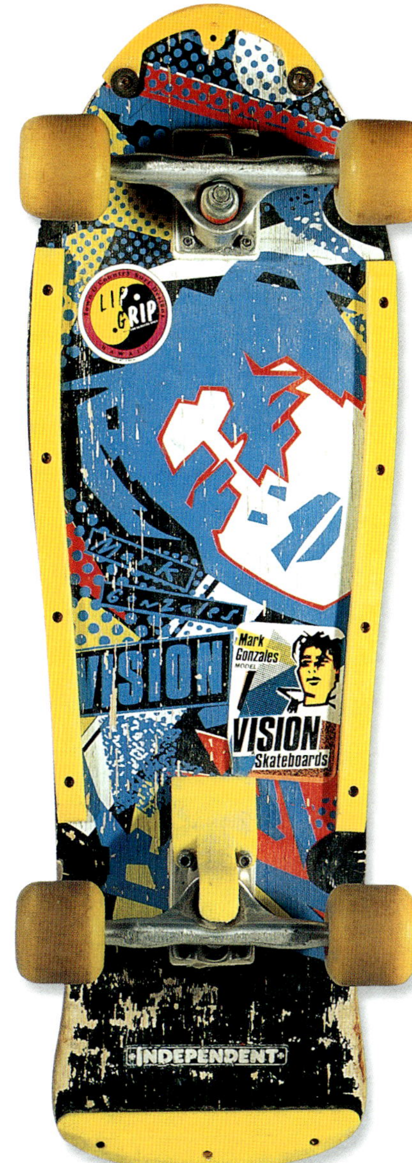

Vision's Mark Gonzales mode, fully equipped. *Photo R. Noll. Courtesy Todd Huber.* $150-200.

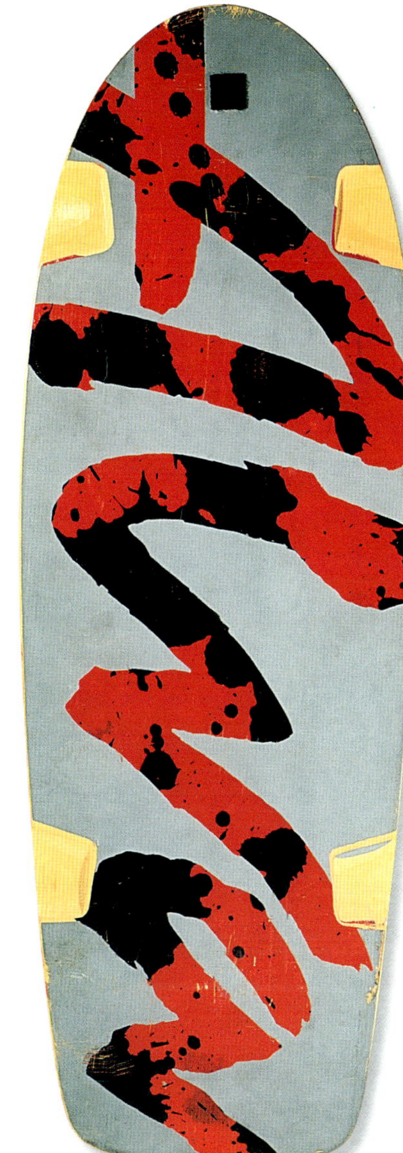

A rare Tony Alva board. *Photo R. Noll. Courtesy Todd Huber.* $3000.

Santa Cruz Deck Rat graphics. *Photo R. Noll. Courtesy Todd Huber.* $200-300.

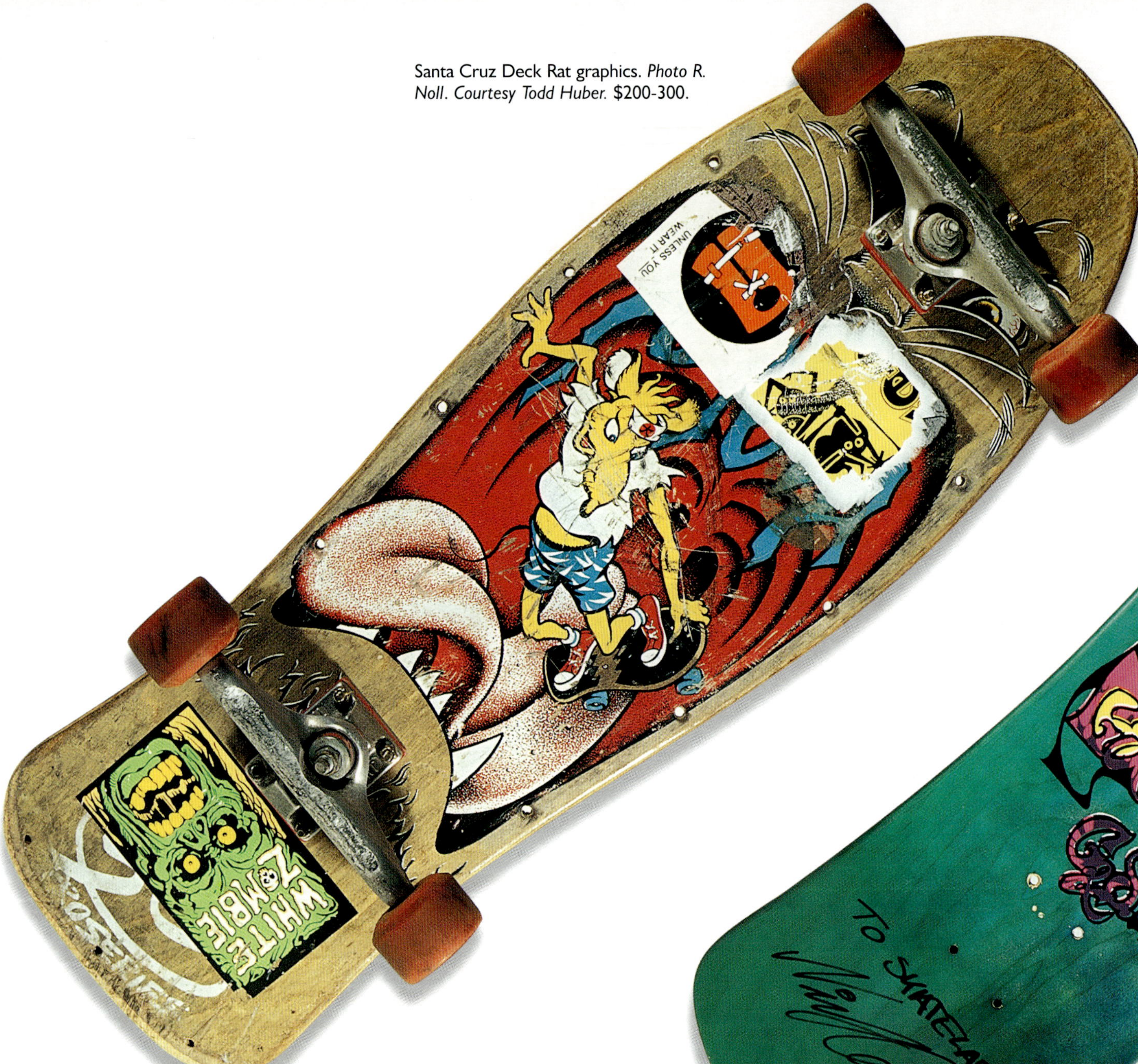

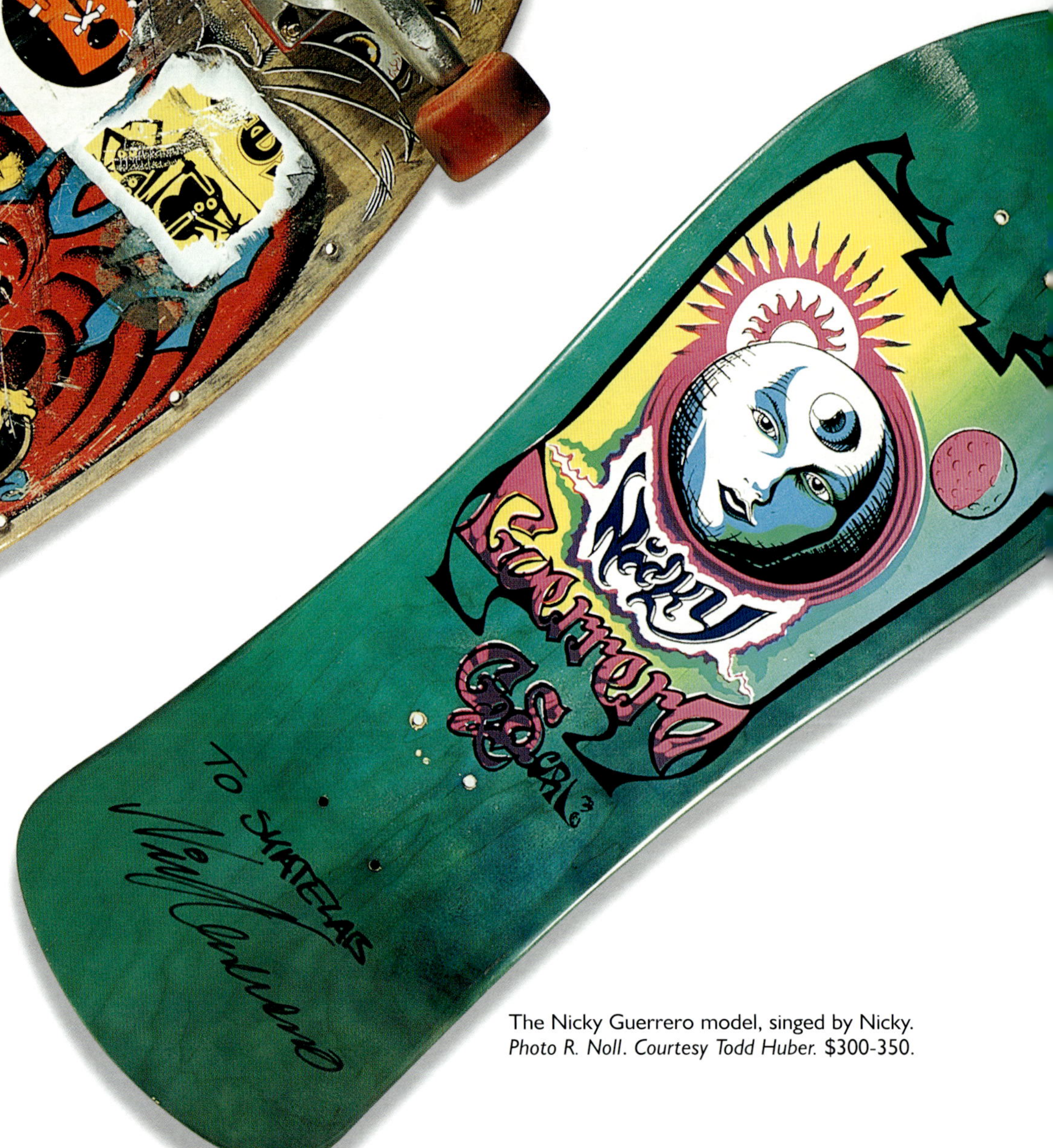

The Nicky Guerrero model, singed by Nicky. *Photo R. Noll. Courtesy Todd Huber.* $300-350.

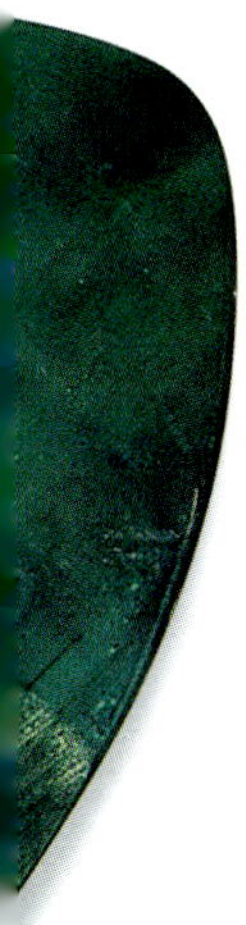

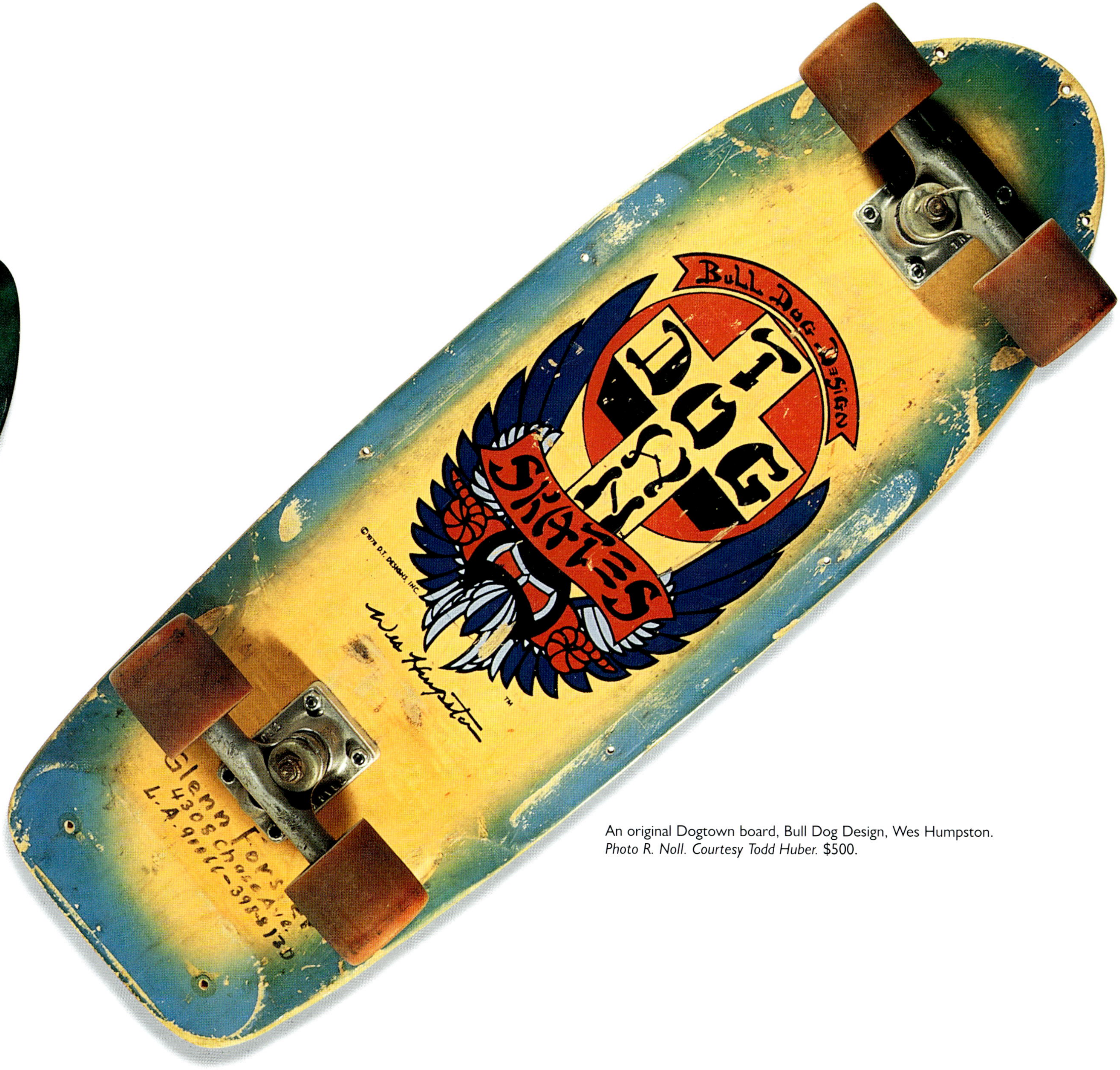

An original Dogtown board, Bull Dog Design, Wes Humpston.
Photo R. Noll. Courtesy Todd Huber. $500.

1990s Skateboards & Beyond

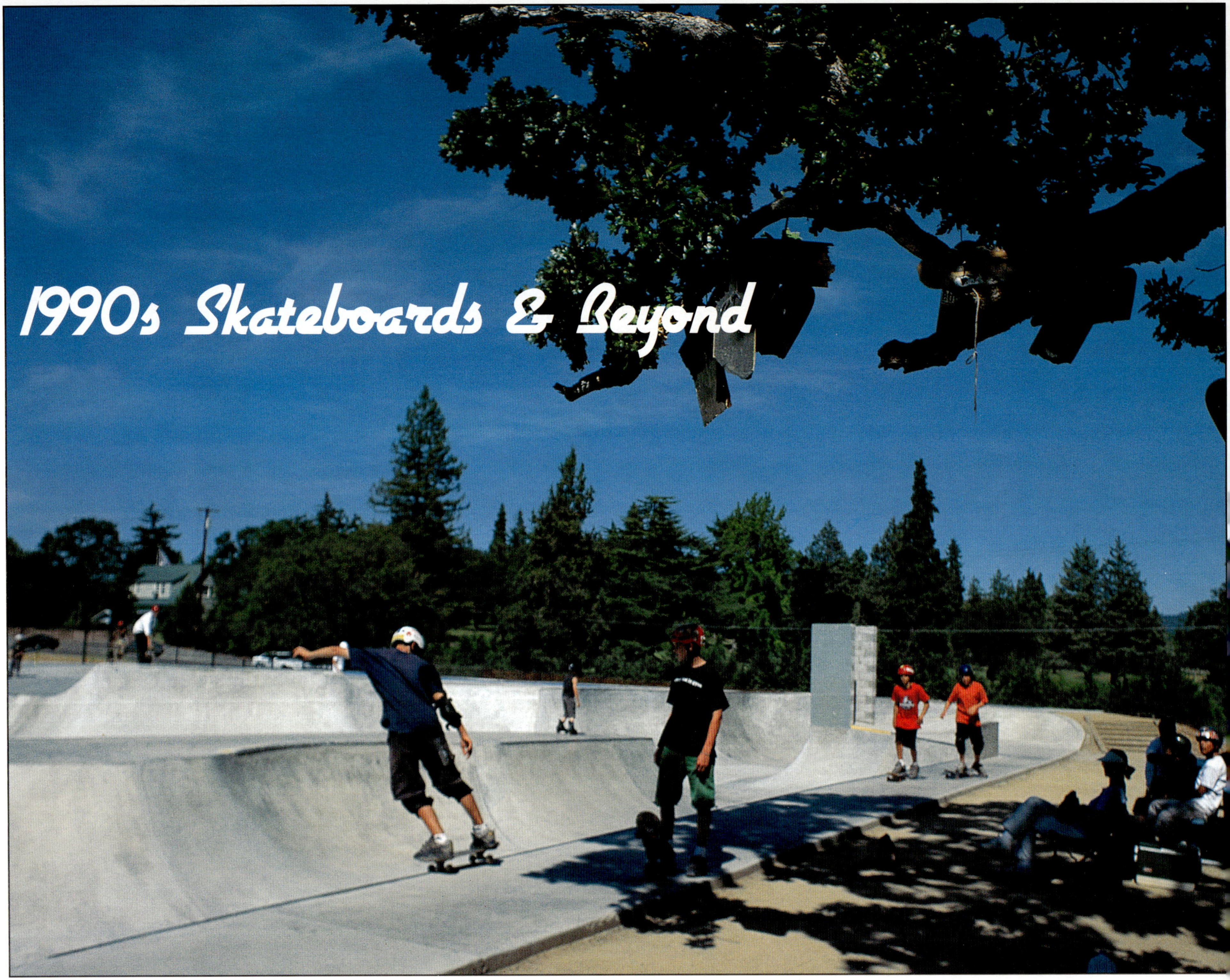

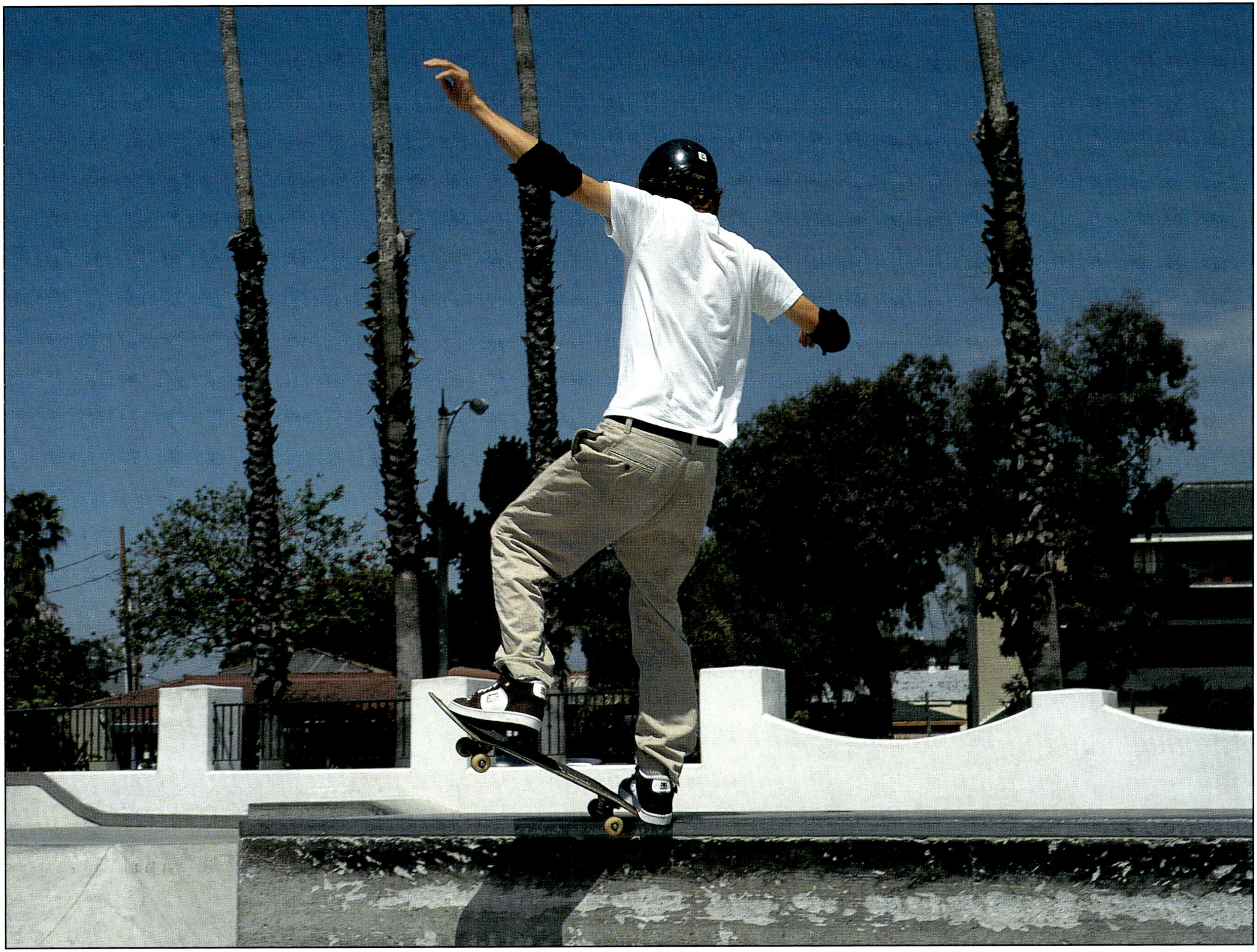

Back to that old Santa Barbara grind. *Photo R. Noll*

Opposite page: The Medford tree where broken and discarded boards end up. *Photo R. Noll*

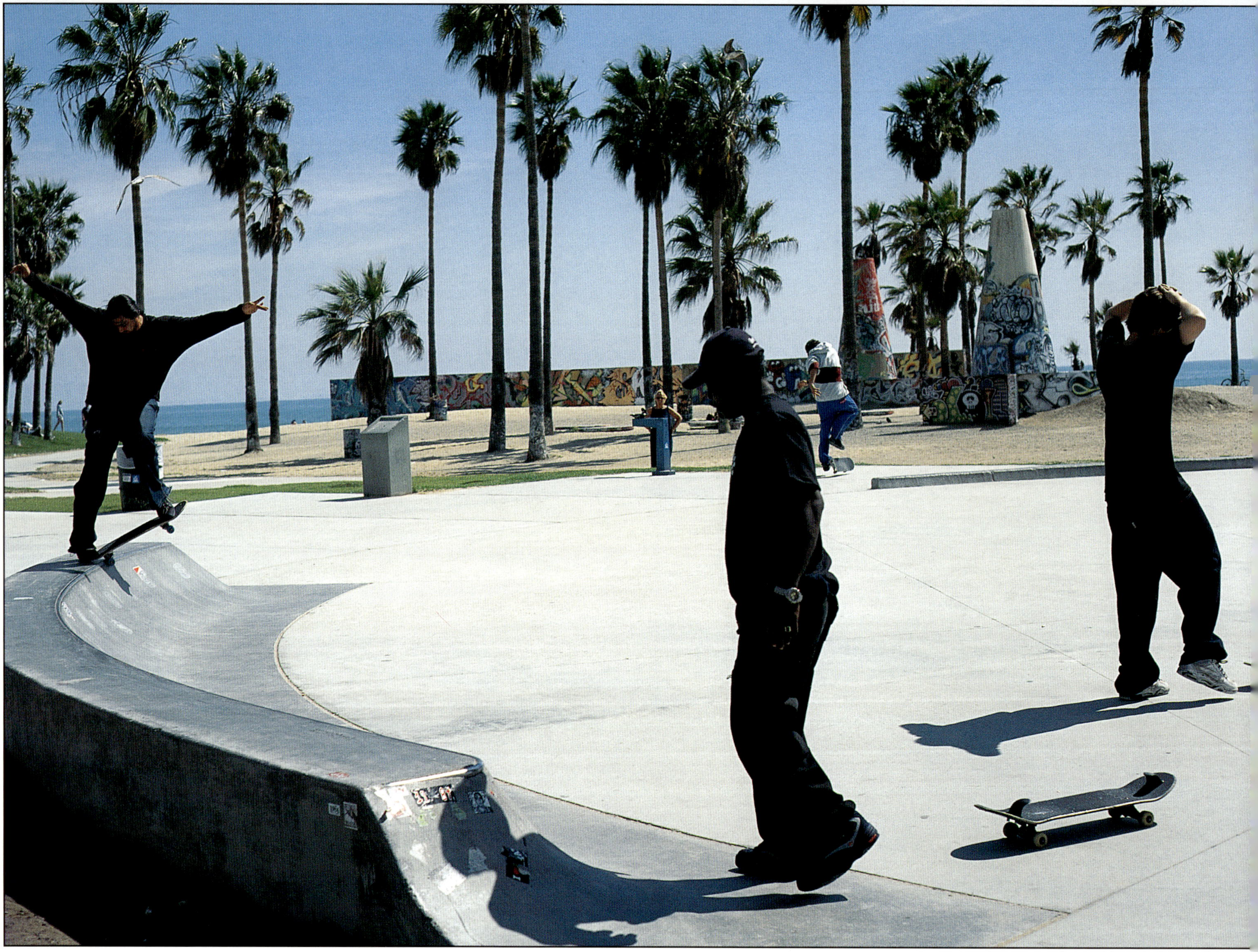

Venice, California. *Photo R. Noll.*

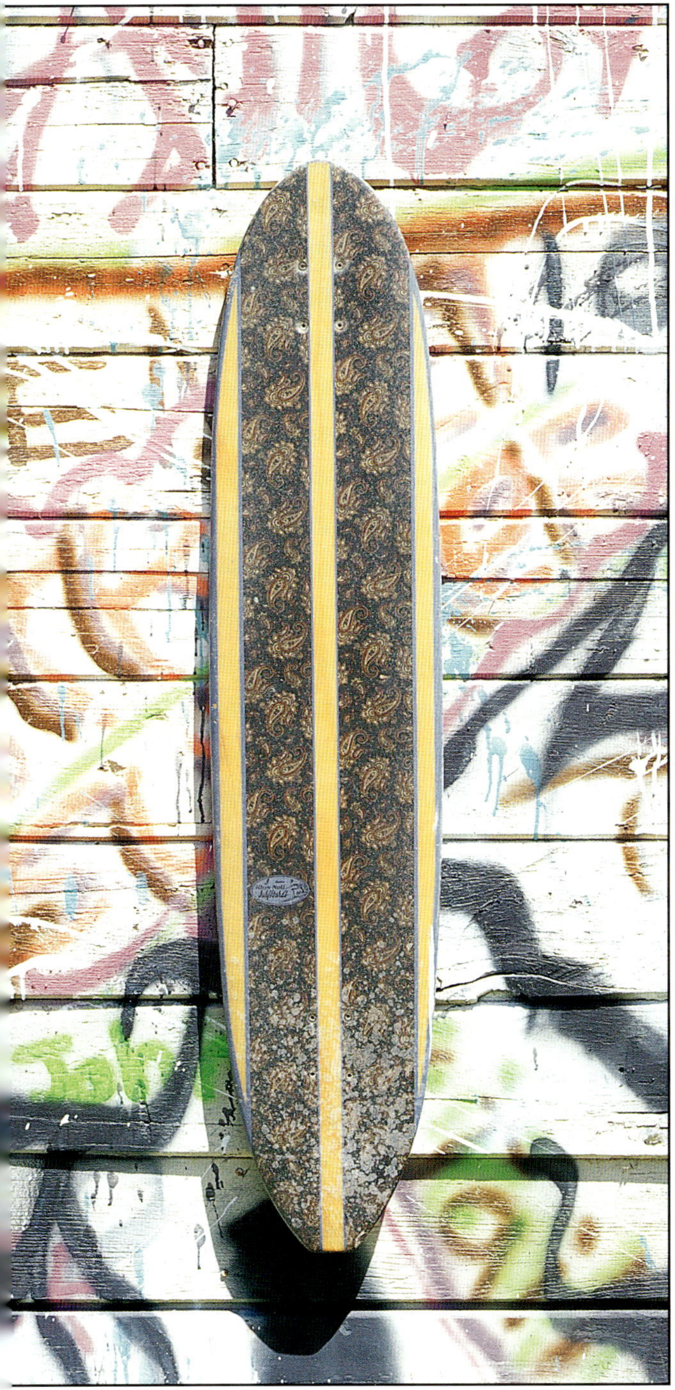

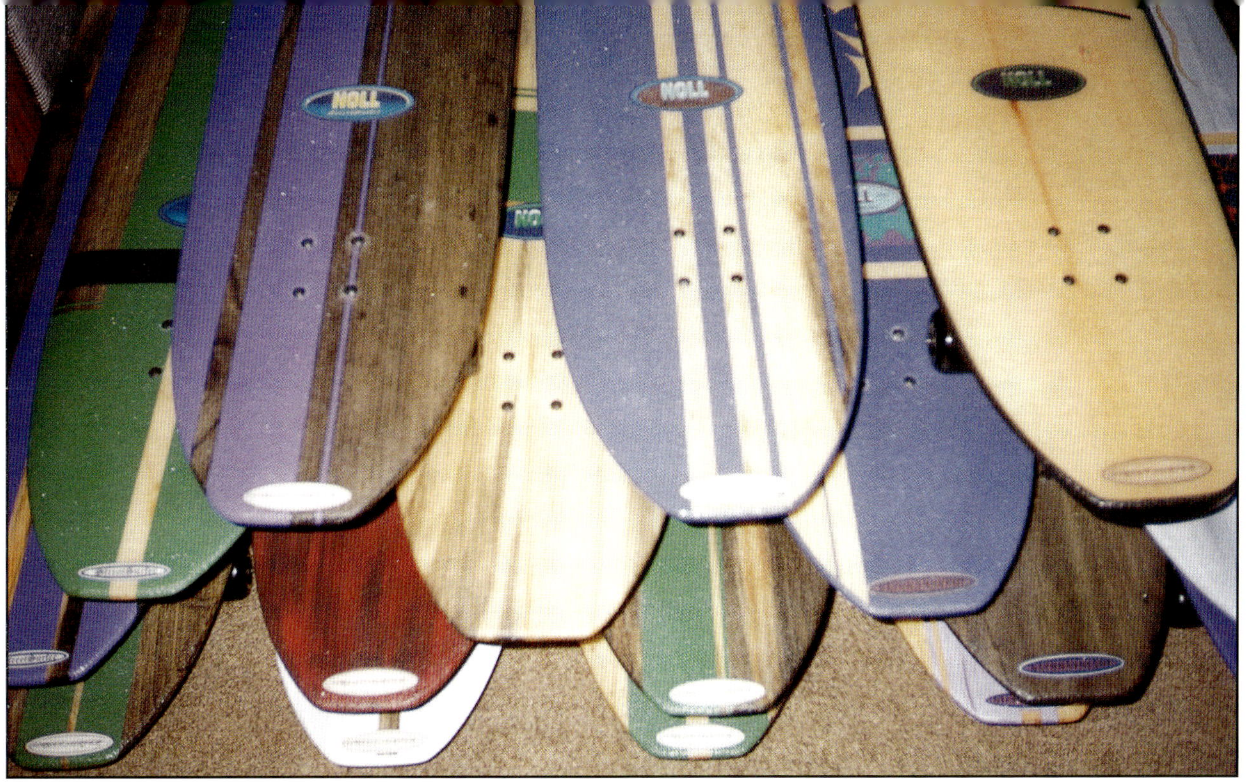

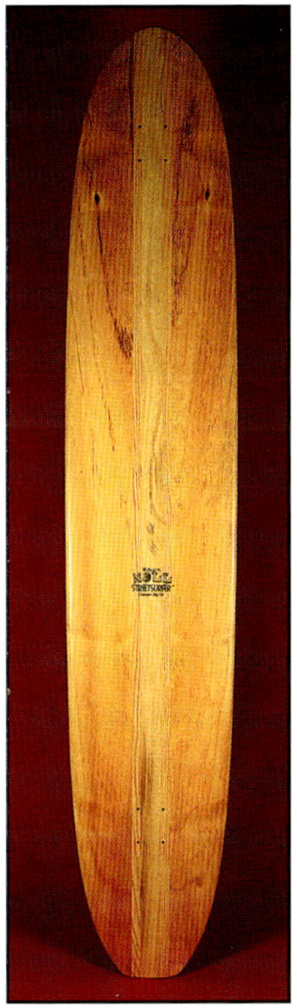

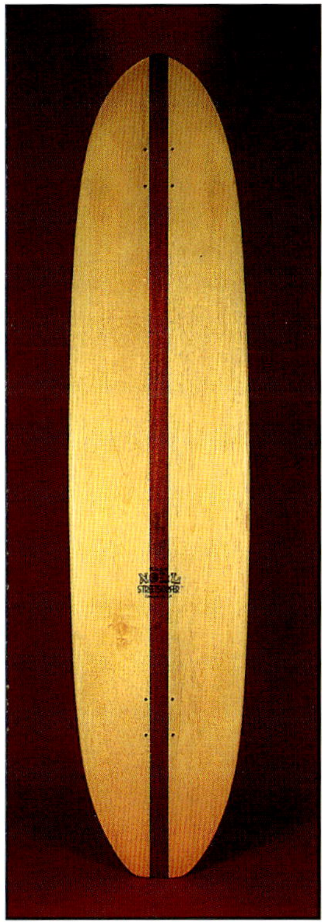

Above: Killer old stack of original Streetsurfers, 1996. *Photo R. Noll. Courtesy Streetsurfer.*

Far left: This is the first generation of longboards that came out of the Streetsurfer Company, 1994. The author's personal board. *Photo R. Noll. Courtesy Streetsurfer.* $700-800.

These two boards are the second generation of Streetsurfers. *Photo R. Noll. Courtesy Streetsurfer.* $200-400 each for the decks only.

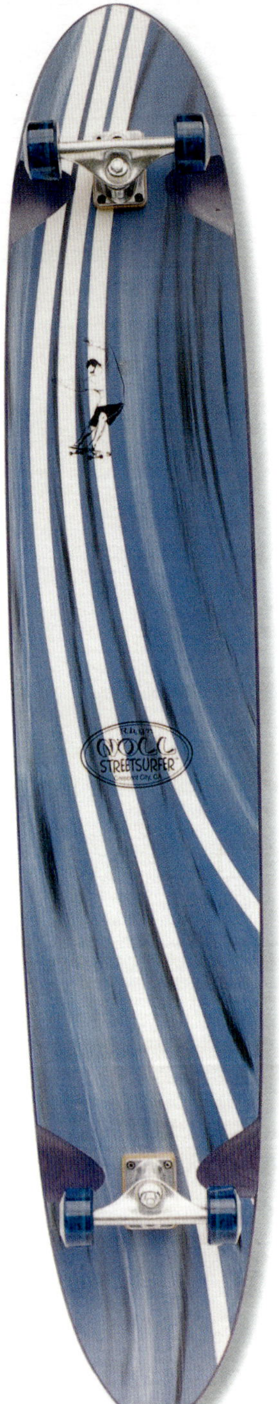

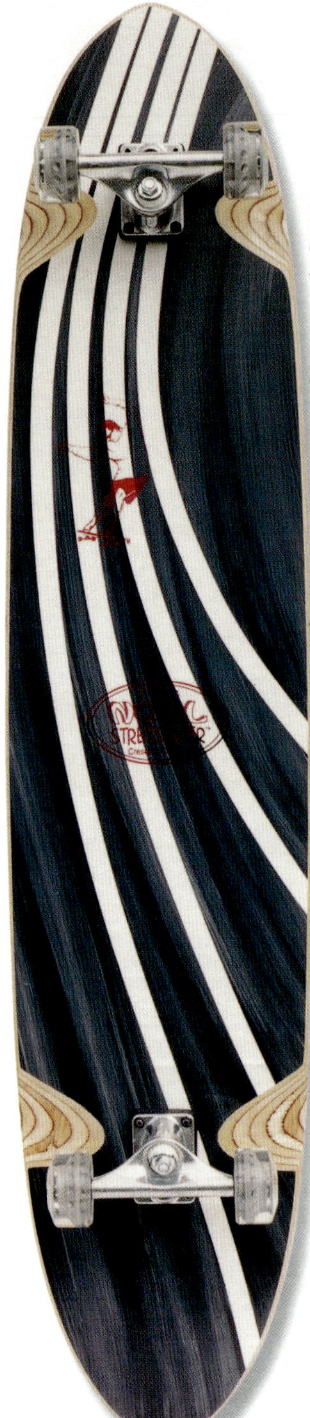

Left: A Streetsurfer 5-footer. *Photo R. Noll. Courtesy Streetsurfer.* $200.

Right: A 4-foot Streetsurfer pro model. *Photo R. Noll. Courtesy Streetsurfer.* $200.

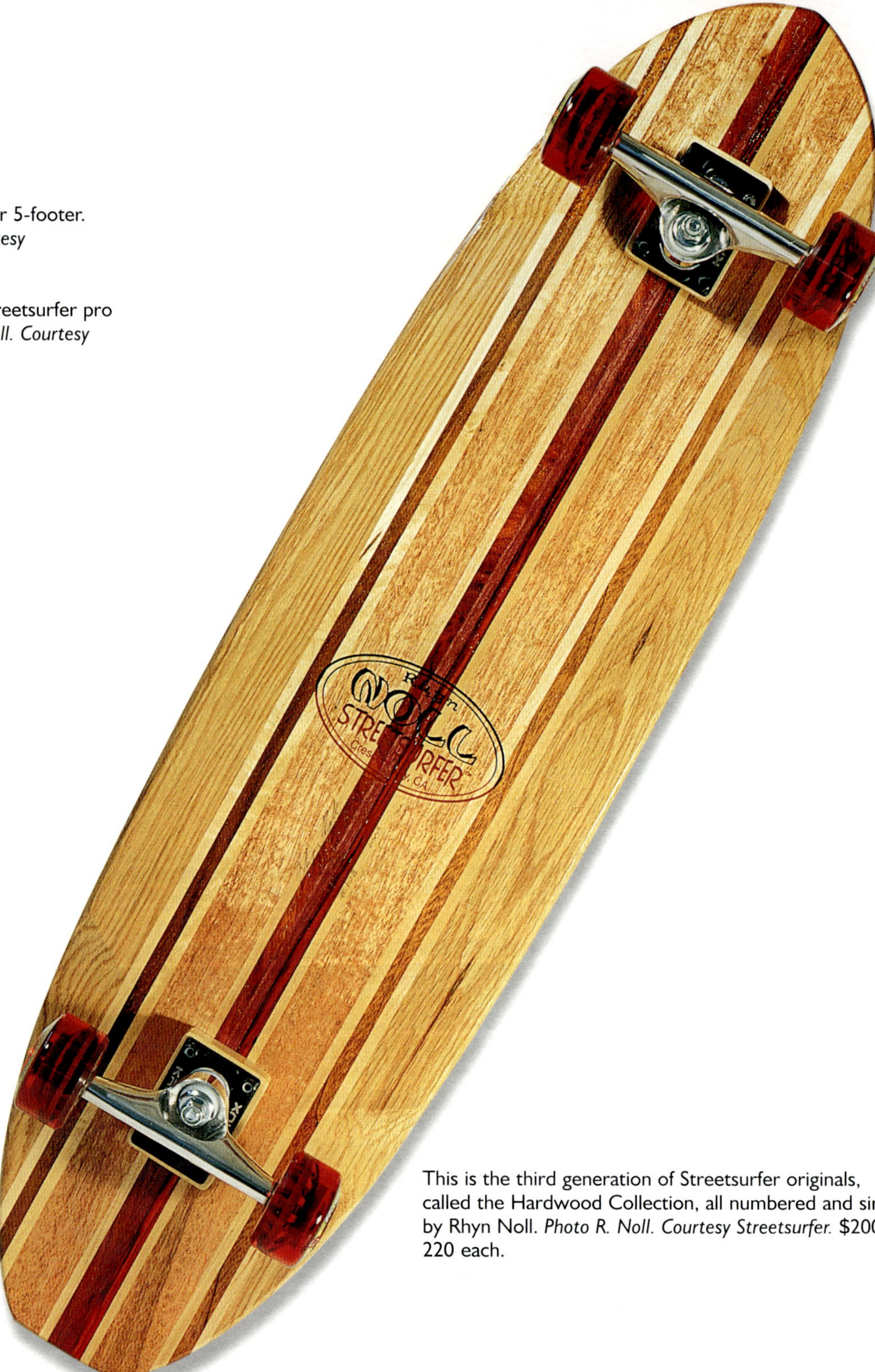

This is the third generation of Streetsurfer originals, called the Hardwood Collection, all numbered and singed by Rhyn Noll. *Photo R. Noll. Courtesy Streetsurfer.* $200-220 each.

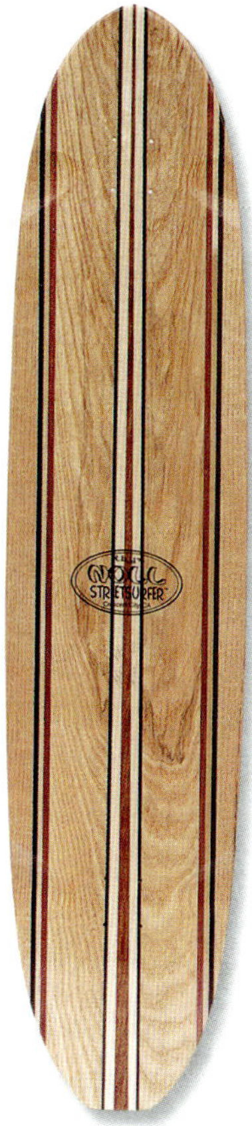

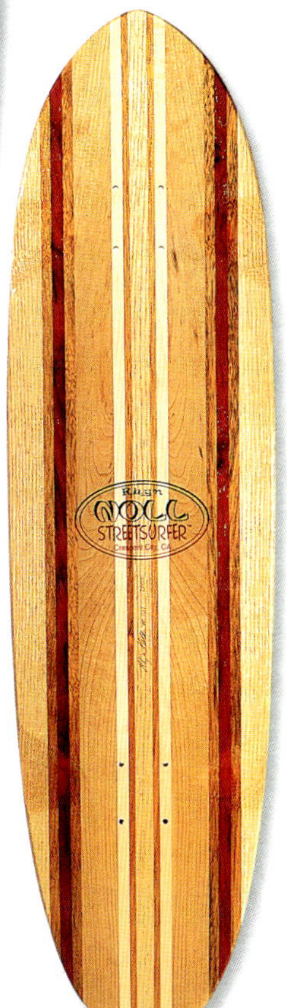

4-foot, hardwood Streetsurfers. *Photo R. Noll. Courtesy Streetsurfer.* $210 each.

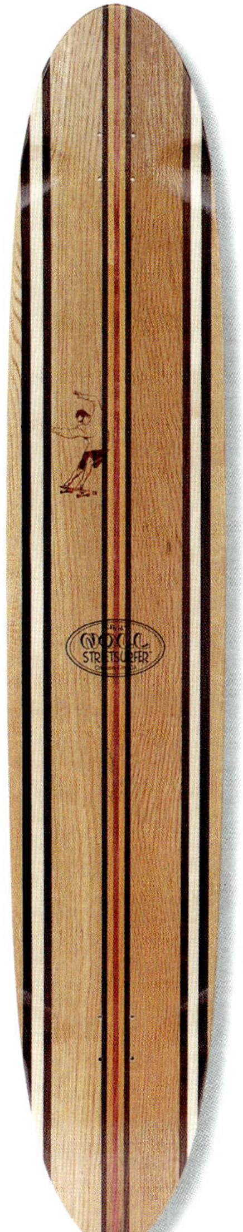

5-foot hardwood Streetsurfer. *Photo R. Noll. Courtesy Streetsurfer.* $220.

Noll's Jail House model. *Photo R. Noll. Courtesy Jail House.* $30-40.

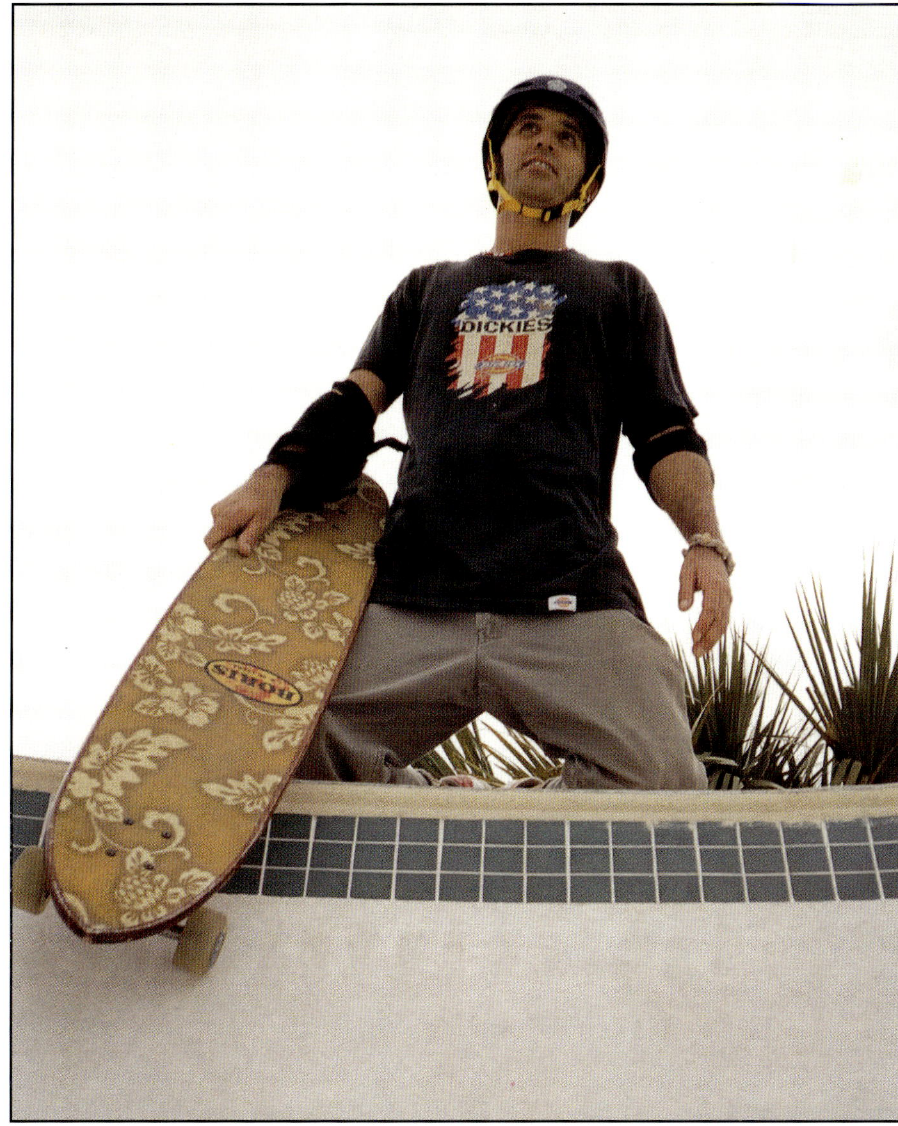

Boris, an east coaster, hanging out poolside. *Photo R. Noll. Courtesy Boris.*

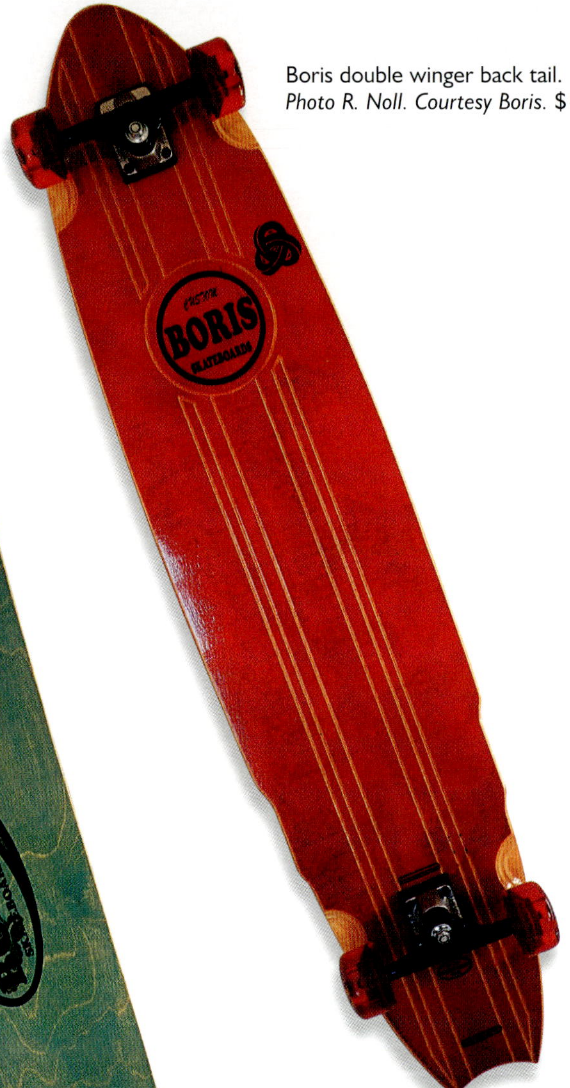

Boris double winger back tail. *Photo R. Noll. Courtesy Boris.* $185.

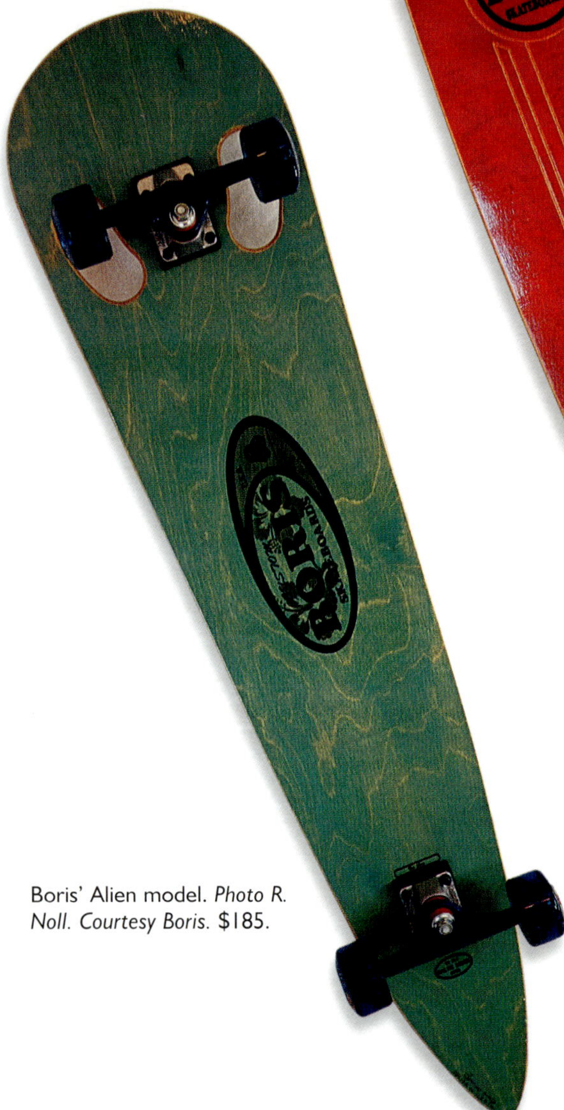

Boris' Alien model. *Photo R. Noll. Courtesy Boris.* $185.

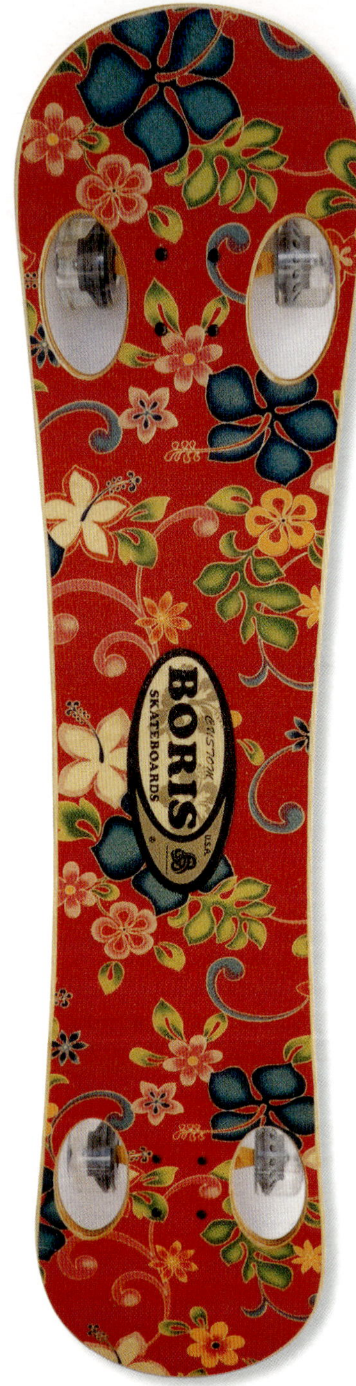

Boris twin. *Photo R. Noll. Courtesy Boris.* $185.

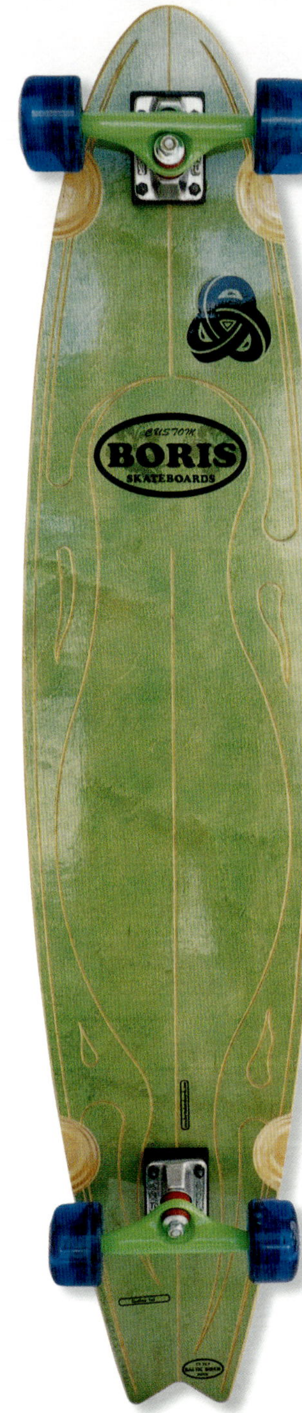

Boris swallowtail. *Photo R. Noll. Courtesy Boris.* $185.

The Snowboard Connection

Every sport has its own evolution over time. Attitudes adapt themselves to the sport and become what you know today. For instance, skateboarding comes from surfing, skateboard ramps are derived from swimming pools, and snow boarding comes from skateboarding. What will be next?

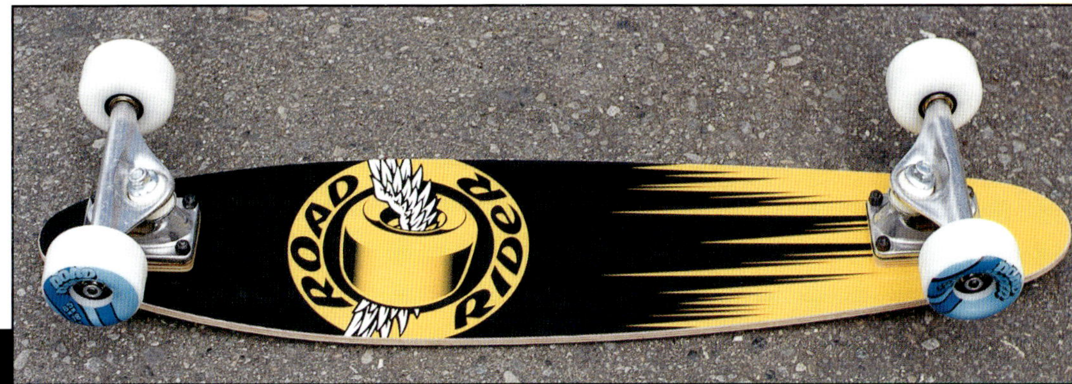

When I visited Rich Novak, he turned me on to this really cool slalom board they're making now, with Road Rider wheels. *Photo R. Noll. Courtesy Rich Novak NHS.*

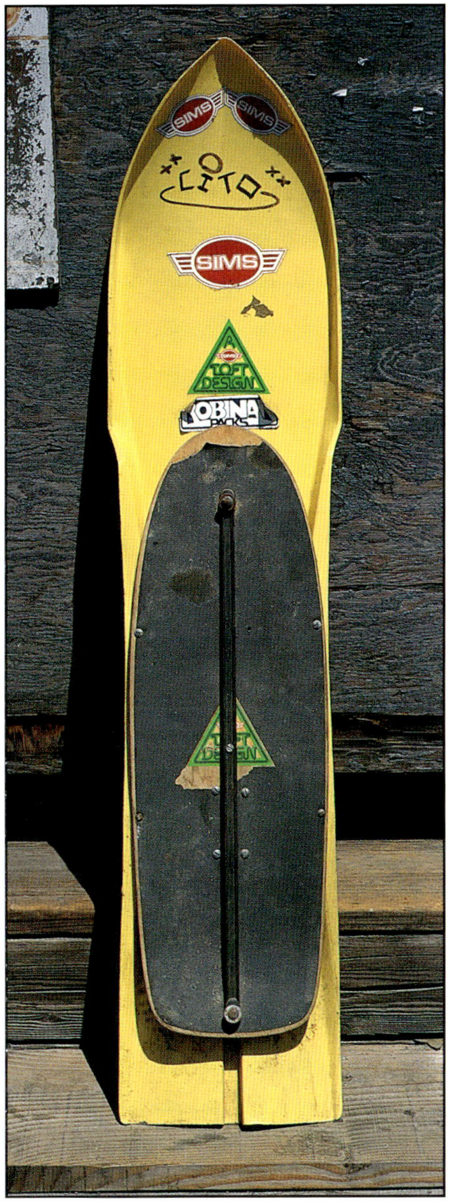

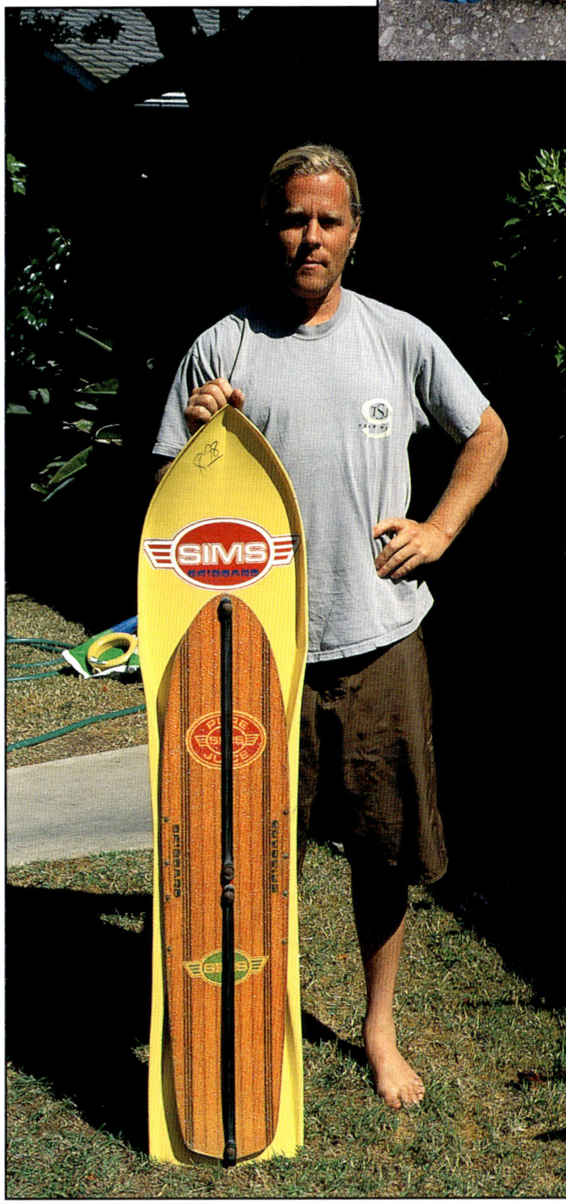

Left: An early Sims snowboard with skate deck and bungee. *Photo R. Noll. Courtesy Jim O'Mahoney.* $700.

Right: A Sims snowboard in mint condition. *Photo R. Noll. Courtesy Scott Starr.* $1300-1500.

Hobie Keepers

In June of 1964, director Bruce Brown premiered his surf movie, *The Endless Summer* and Hobie Alter debuted his first skateboard, The Hobie Super Surfer, one of the best selling skateboards of the sixties. The first Hobie Super Surfer had a beautiful mahogany laminated wood deck with a maple stringer and clay wheels that gripped for carving turns. The design was advanced from the typical boards of its era that used plywood decks, steel wheels, and trucks made for roller skates.

Today, still on the cutting edge of design and development, Hobie has reintroduced the Super Surfer with the latest technology. The beautifully hand crafted decks are mounted with Baku® die cast aluminum heat-treated trucks specifically designed for high performance longboarding. The custom 63.5mm Super Surfer wheels are made with a special blend of urethane with an 82-durameter rating that gives the board unbelievable grip and a smooth ride. The custom wheels combined with ABEC 5 bearings allows for longer glides on the flats. The new Hobie Super Surfer 36" and 47" are ideal for making tight radius turns, hot dogging, or just cruising along the beach front. Enjoy the glide.

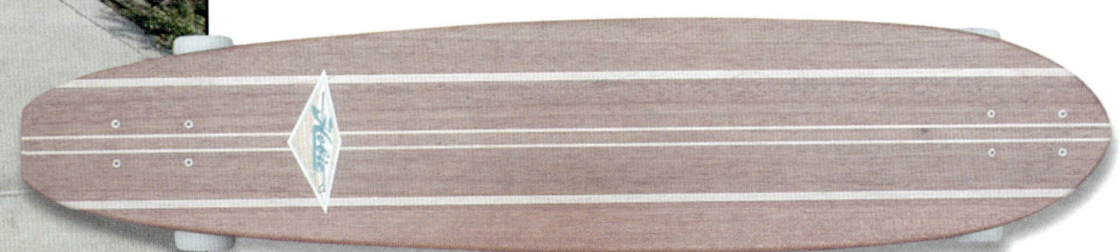

The current Hobie Super Surfer. The 39" deck is custom made with maple and mahogany stringers on top with a laminated Baltic birch bottom. The 47" deck is custom made with laminated Baltic birch core between mahogany and maple stringers top and bottom, reminiscent of the original Super Surfer wood pattern. *Courtesy Hobie.* 39" deck, $175. 47" deck $199.

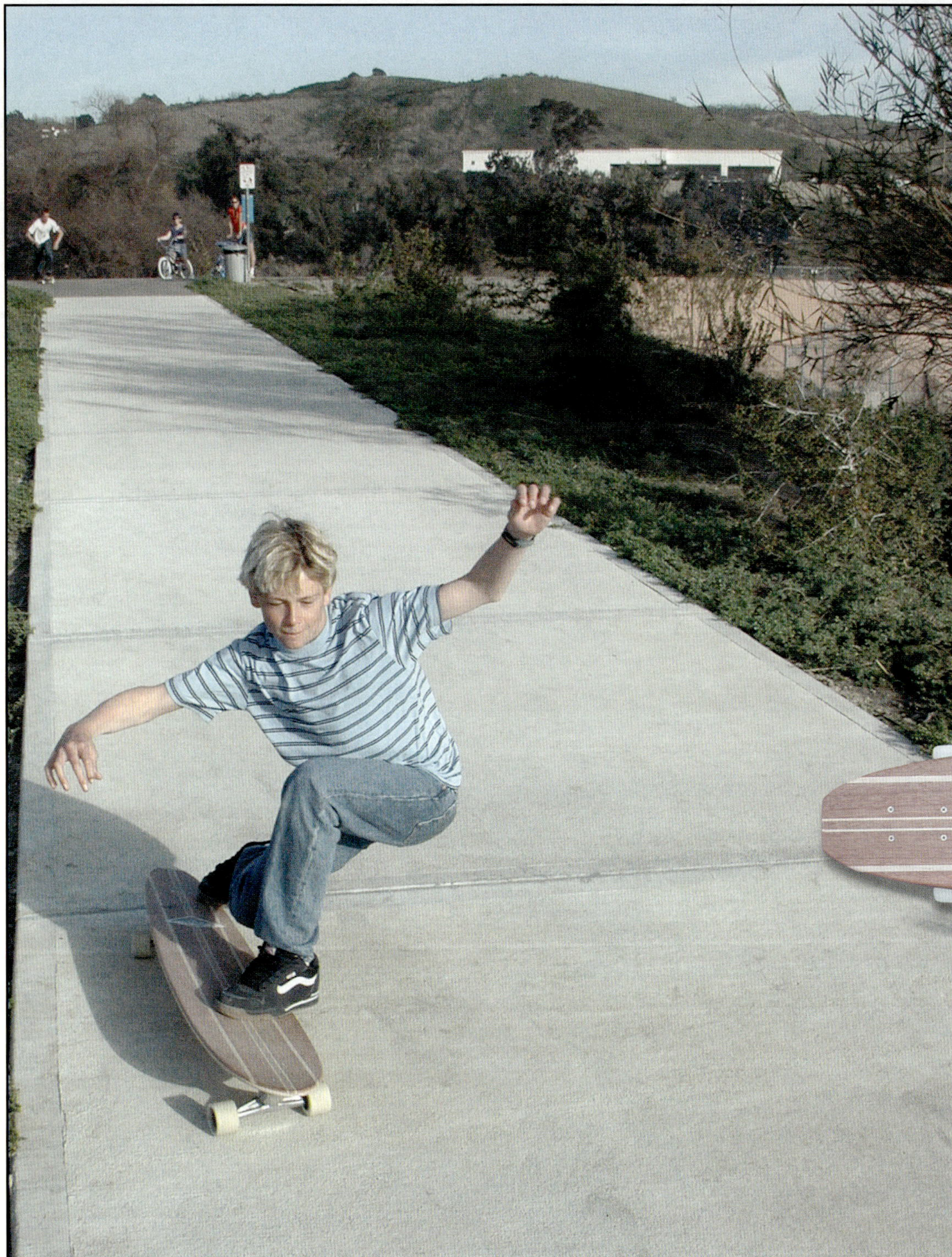

A Hobie keeper. *Courtesy Hobie.*

The Latest Designs

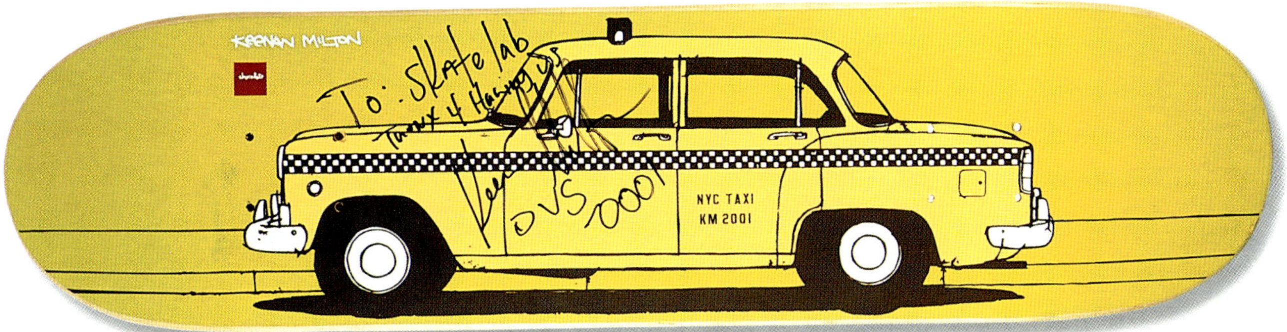

The Keenan Milton model signed by Keenan. Todd Huber says signed boards from pros or otherwise adds $100 to the original price. *Photo R. Noll. Courtesy Todd Huber.* $200.

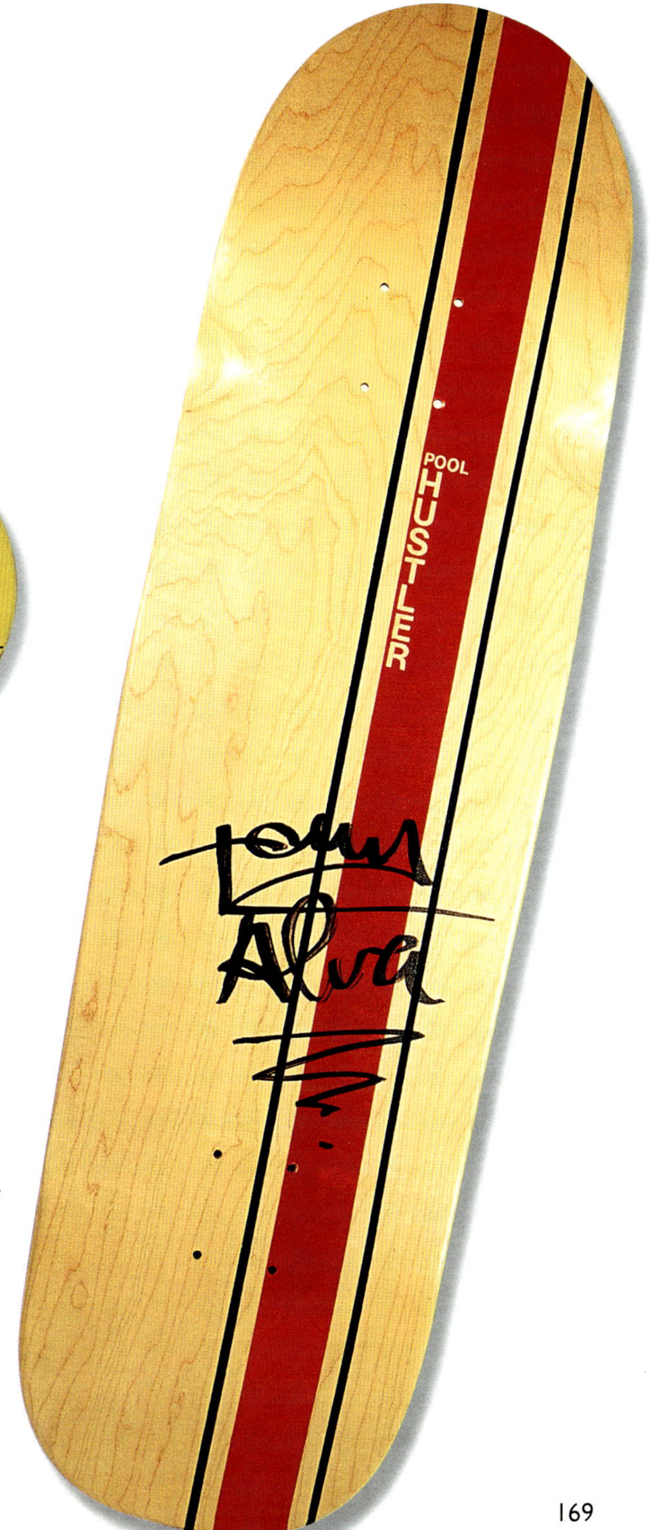

The Pool Hustler, signed by Tony Alva. *Courtesy Todd Huber.* $100-150.

Here we show off a few of today's vert/street boards. As in yesteryear, graphics are pivotal. *Photos R. Noll. Courtesy Todd Huber.* $30-50 each

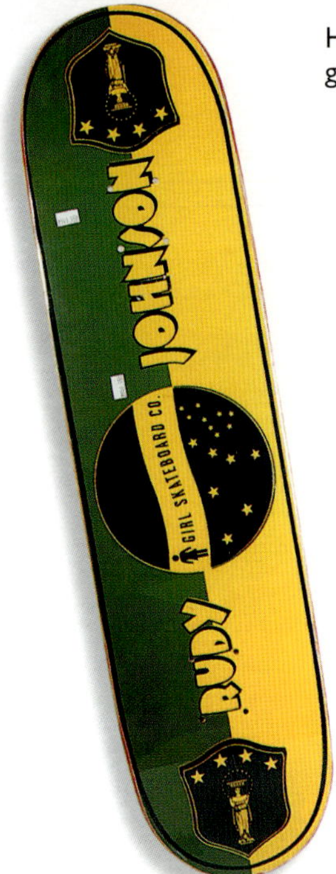

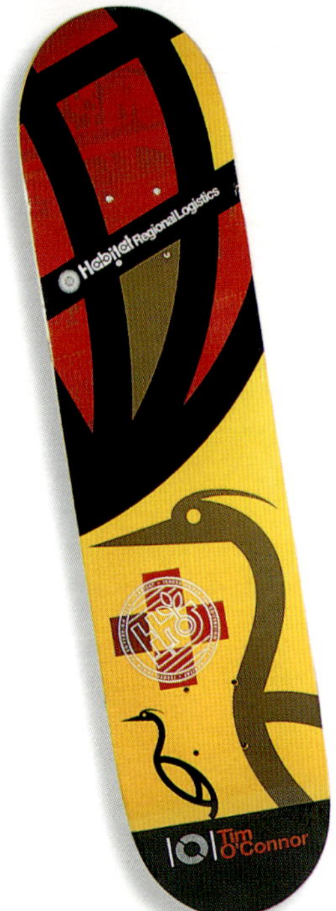

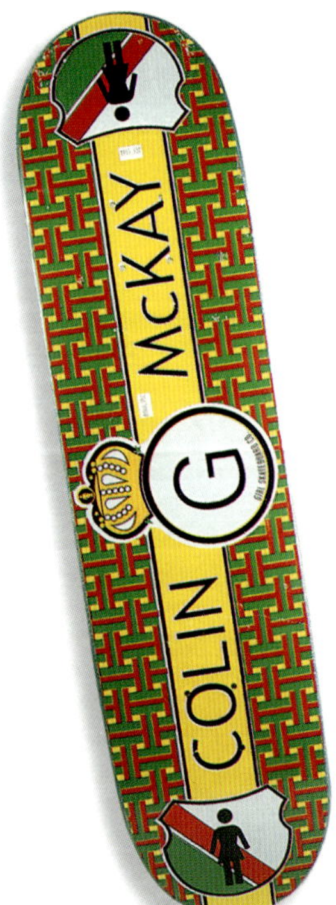

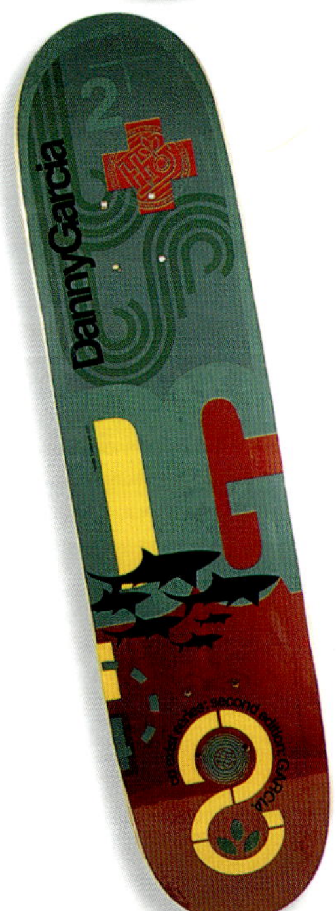

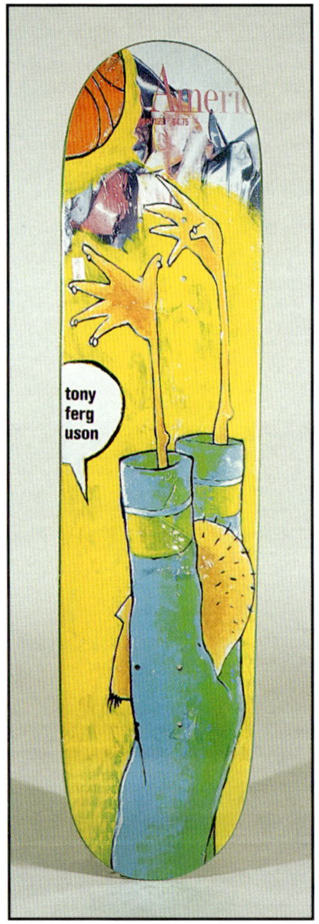

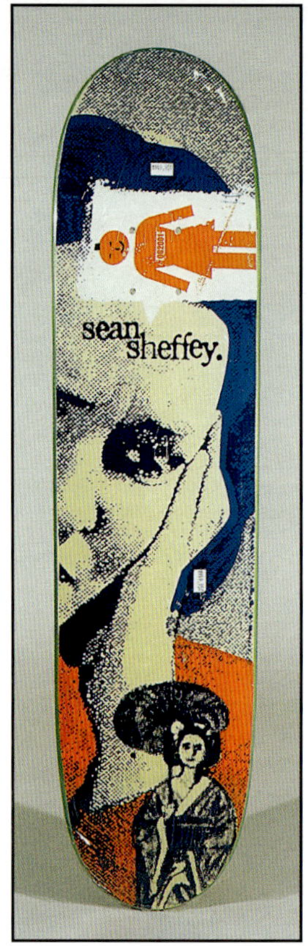

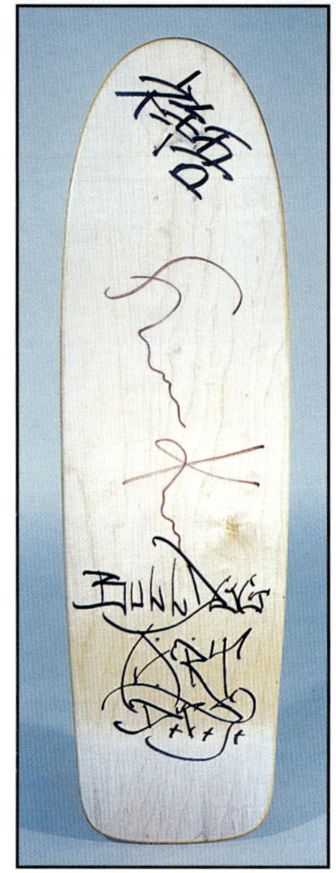

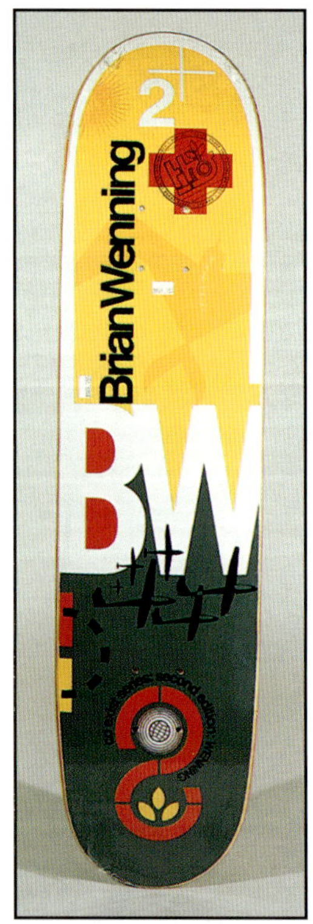

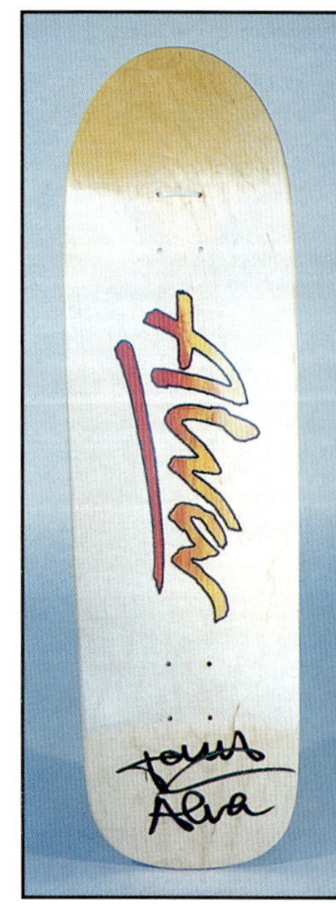

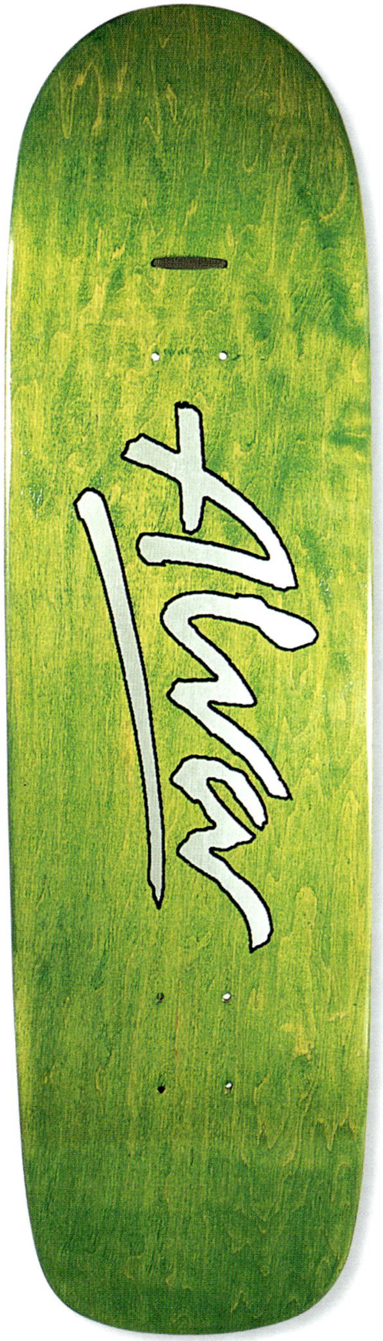

Courtesy Todd Huber.

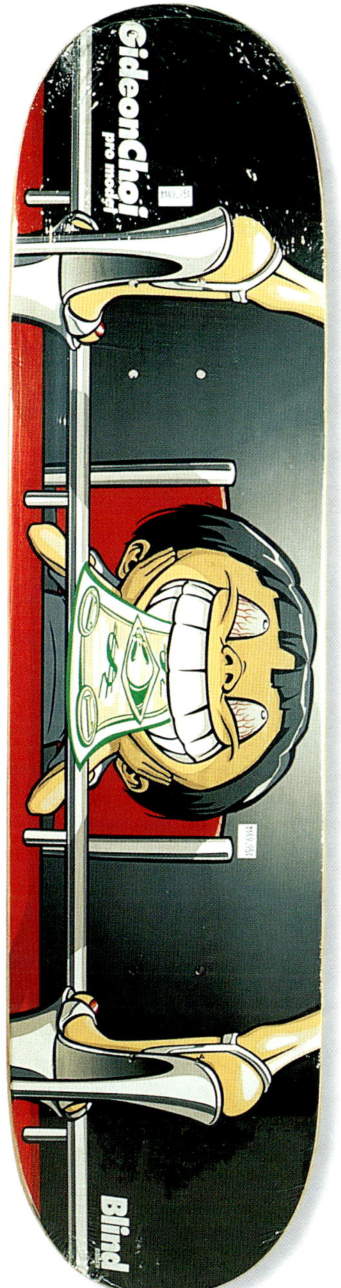

Courtesy Todd Huber.

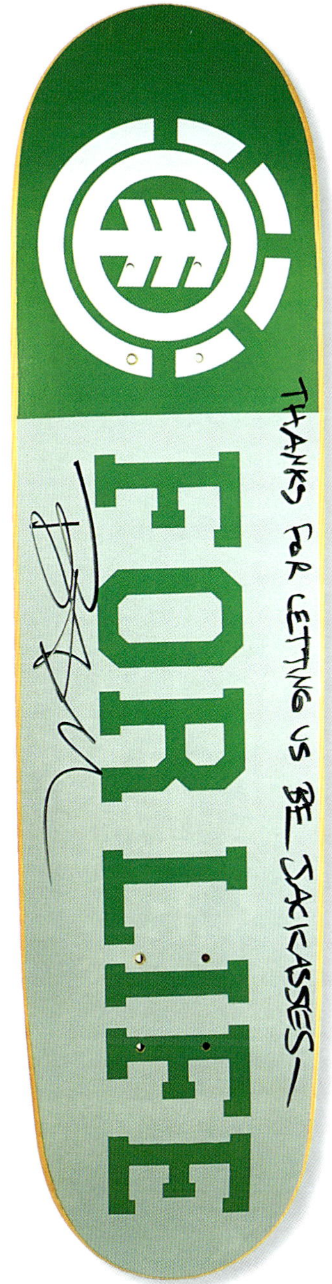

Signed by Bam Magara. *Courtesy Todd Huber.*

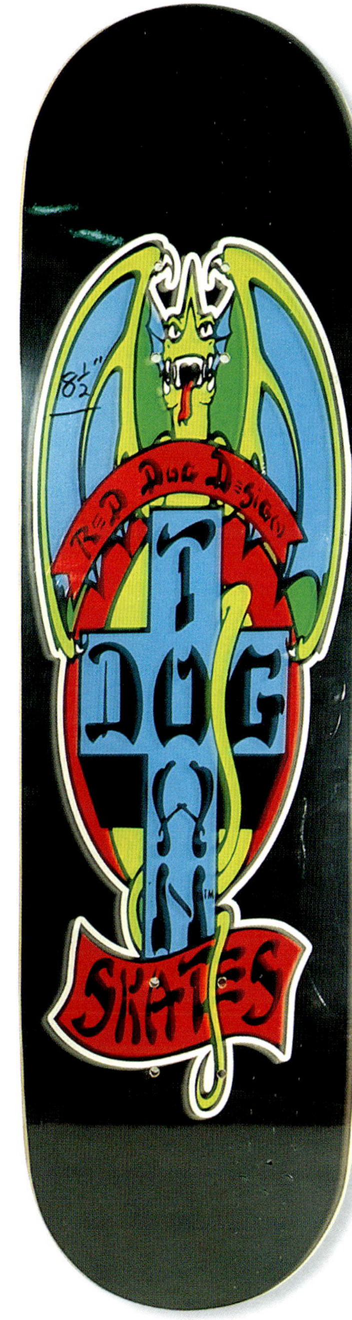

Modern Dogtown. *Courtesy Todd Huber.* $50.

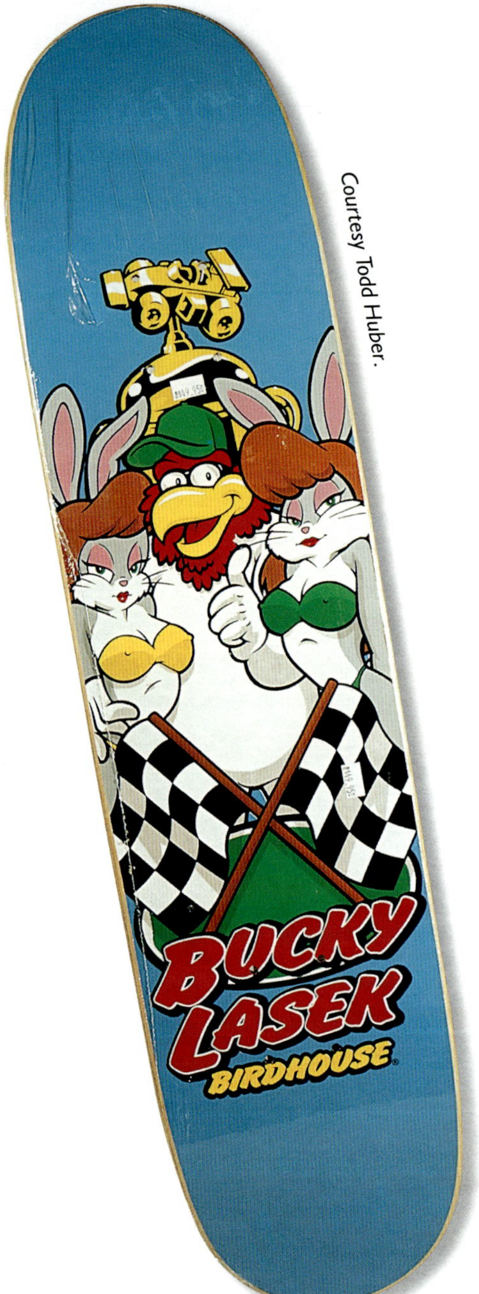

Courtesy Todd Huber.

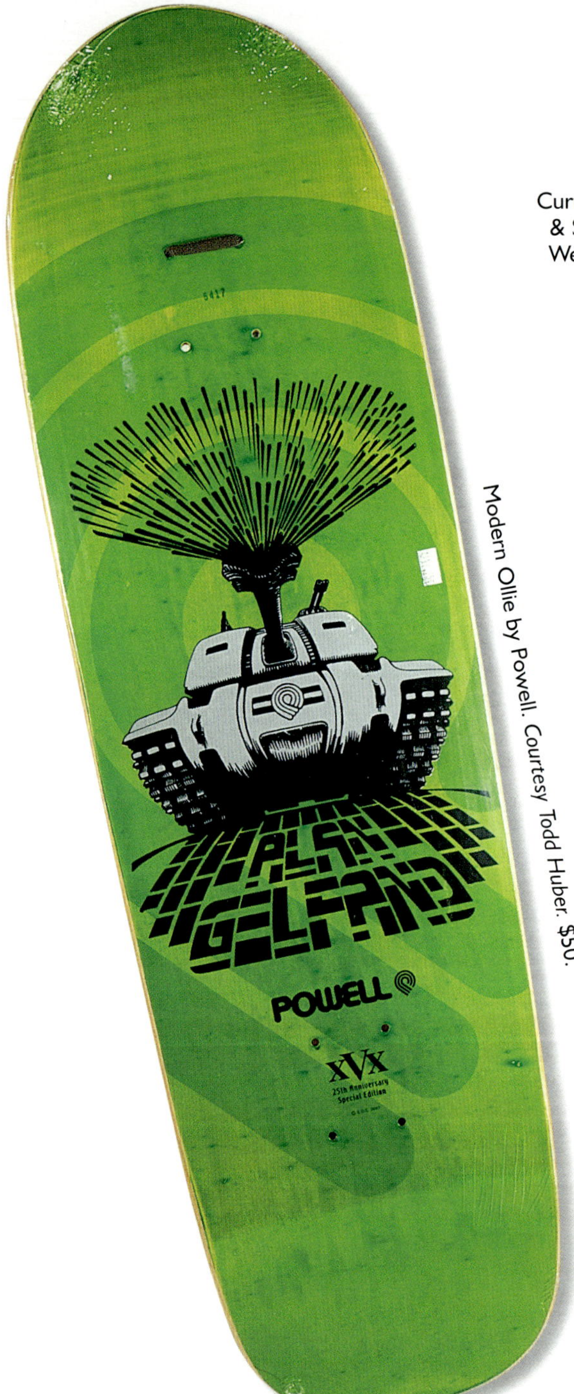

Modern Ollie by Powell. Courtesy Todd Huber. $50.

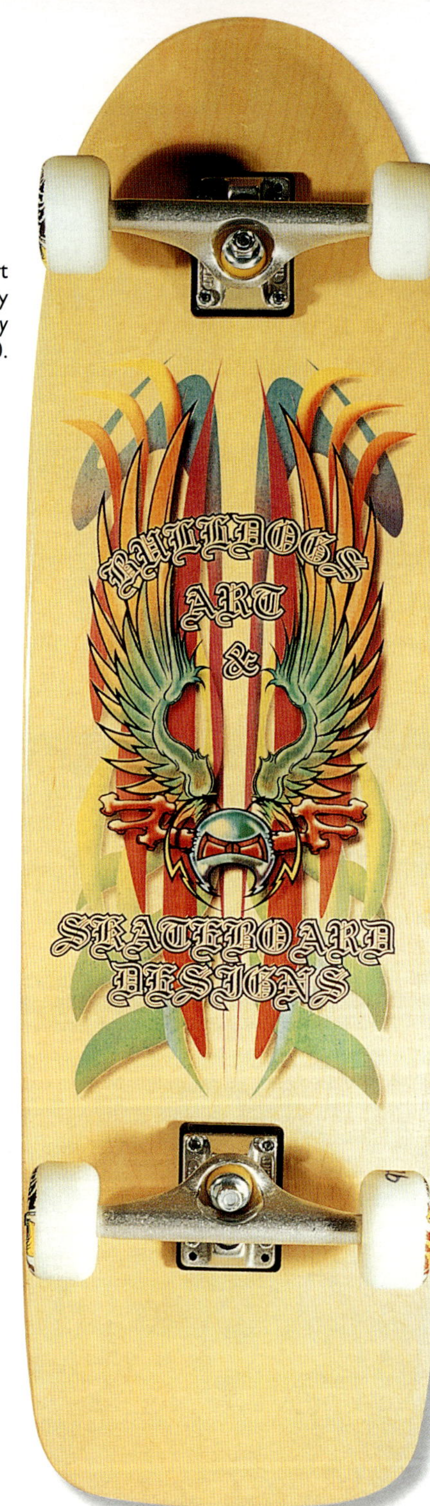

Current series Bulldog Art & Skateboard Designs by Wes Humpston. *Courtesy Jim at Rip City.* $150.

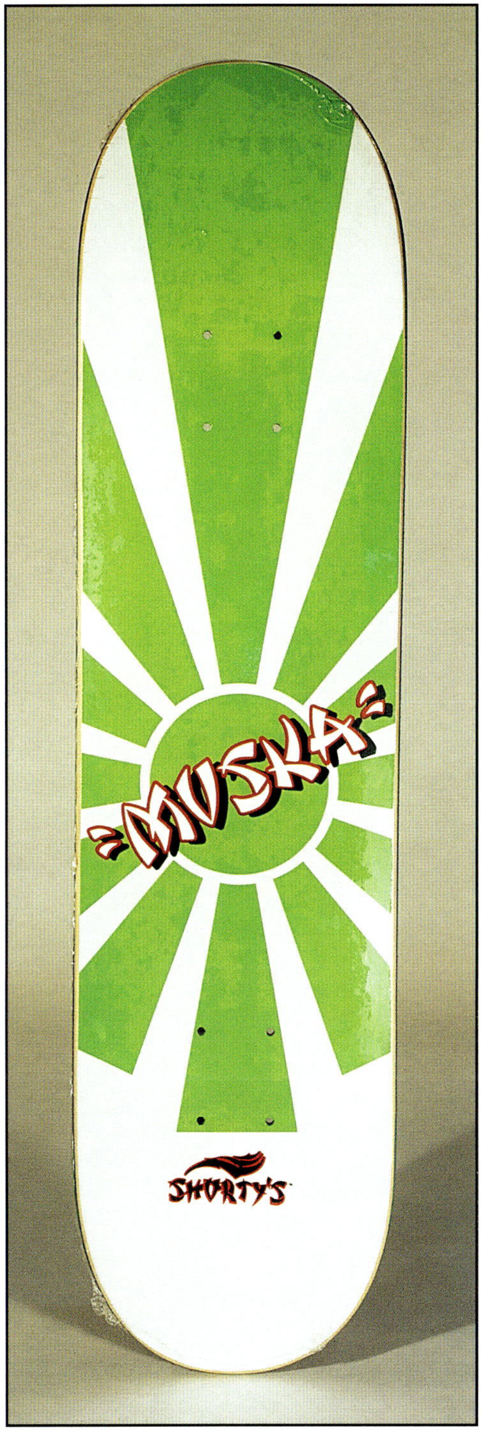

Muska by Shorty's. *Courtesy Todd Huber.* $50.

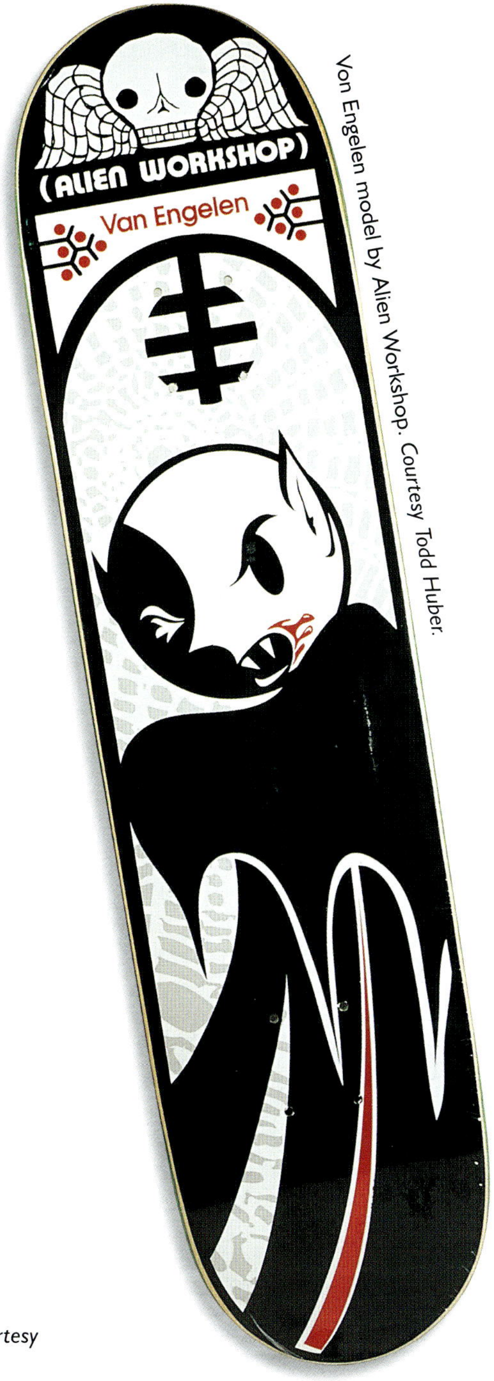

Von Engelen model by Alien Workshop. Courtesy Todd Huber.

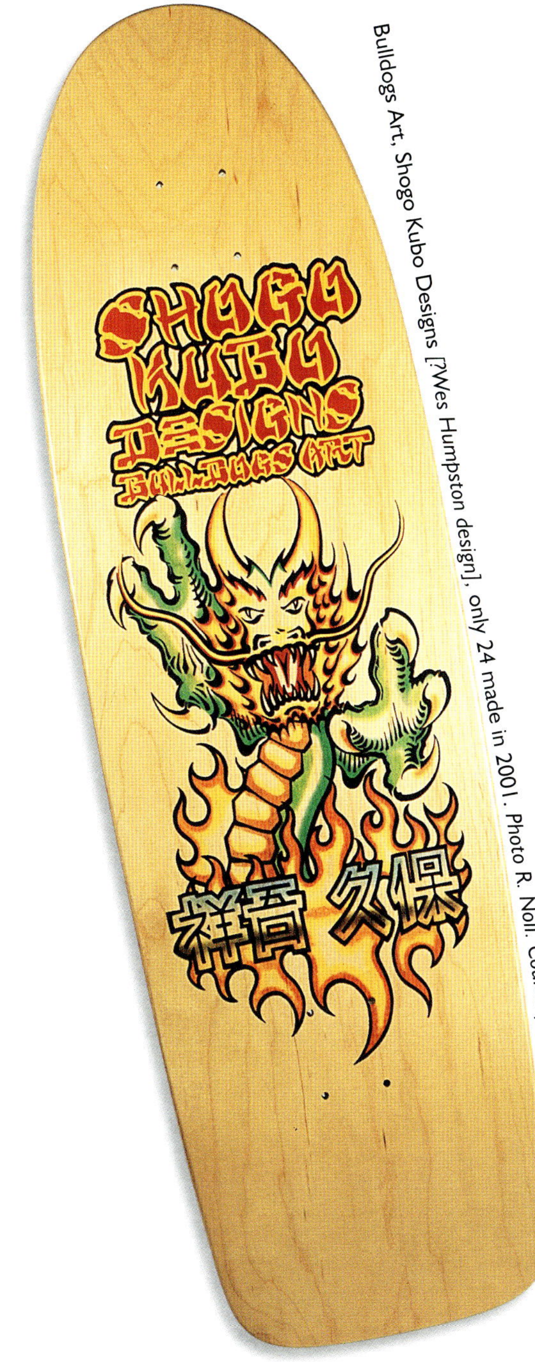

Bulldogs Art, Shogo Kubo Designs [?Wes Humpston design], only 24 made in 2001. Photo R. Noll. Courtesy Todd Huber. $300.

These boards all are of the new school. *Courtesy Todd Huber.* $30-50.

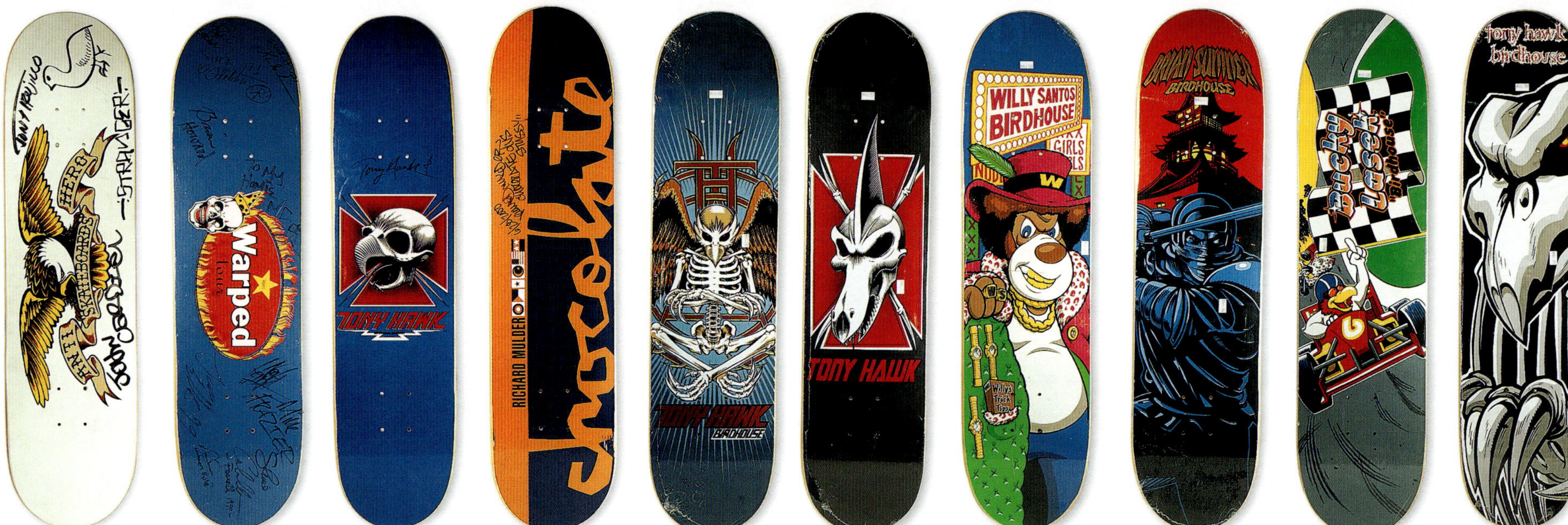

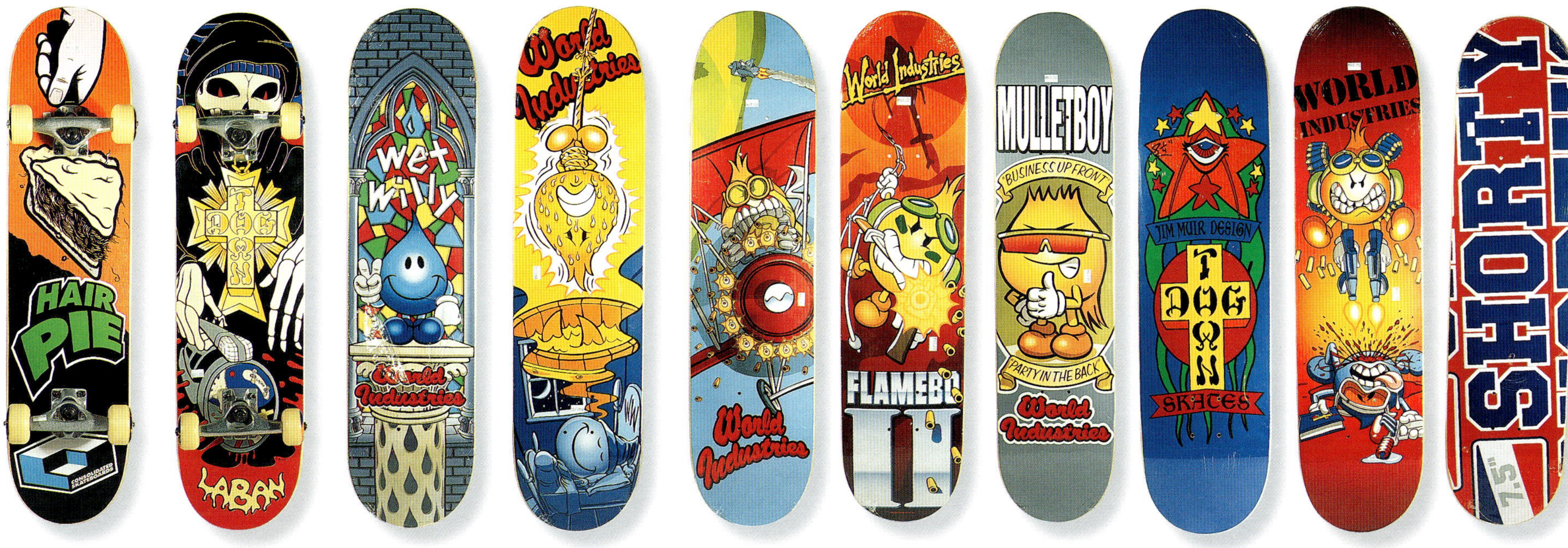
HAIR PIE
LABAN
wet willy
World Industries
World Industries
World Industries
World Industries
MULLETBOY
"BUSINESS UP FRONT"
PARTY IN THE BACK
World Industries
JIM MUIR DESIGN
DOG TOWN
SKATES
WORLD INDUSTRIES
SHORTY
7.5"

Almost the whole Hook-ups collection. Courtesy Todd Huber. $30-50 each.

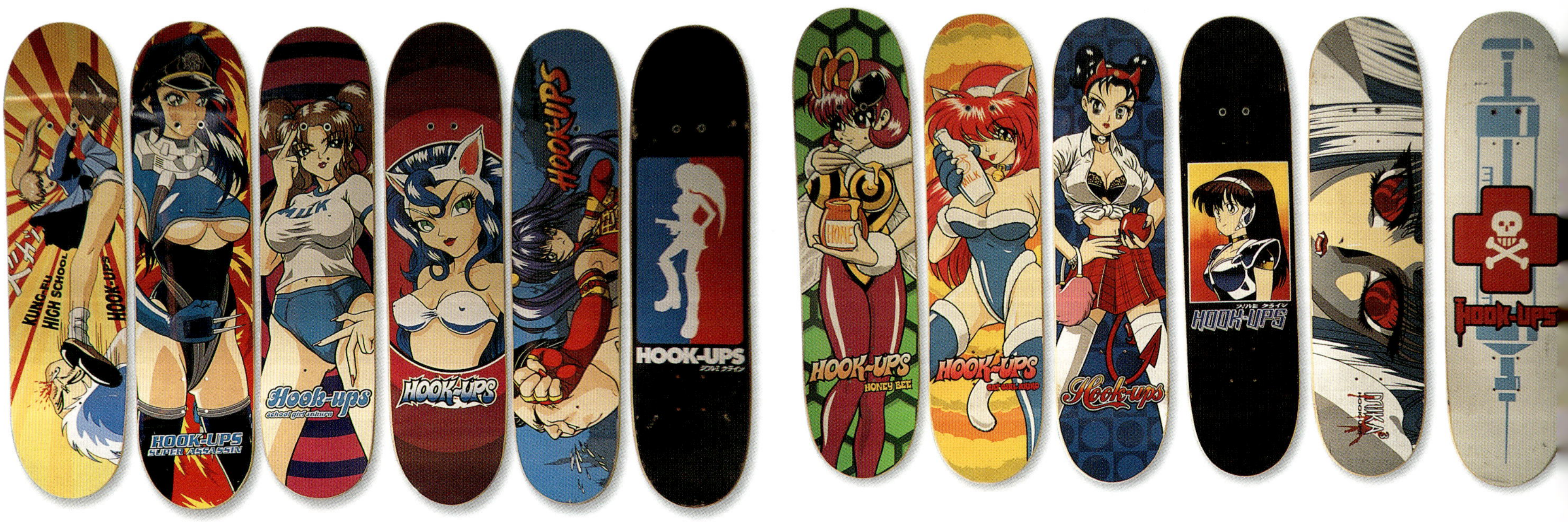

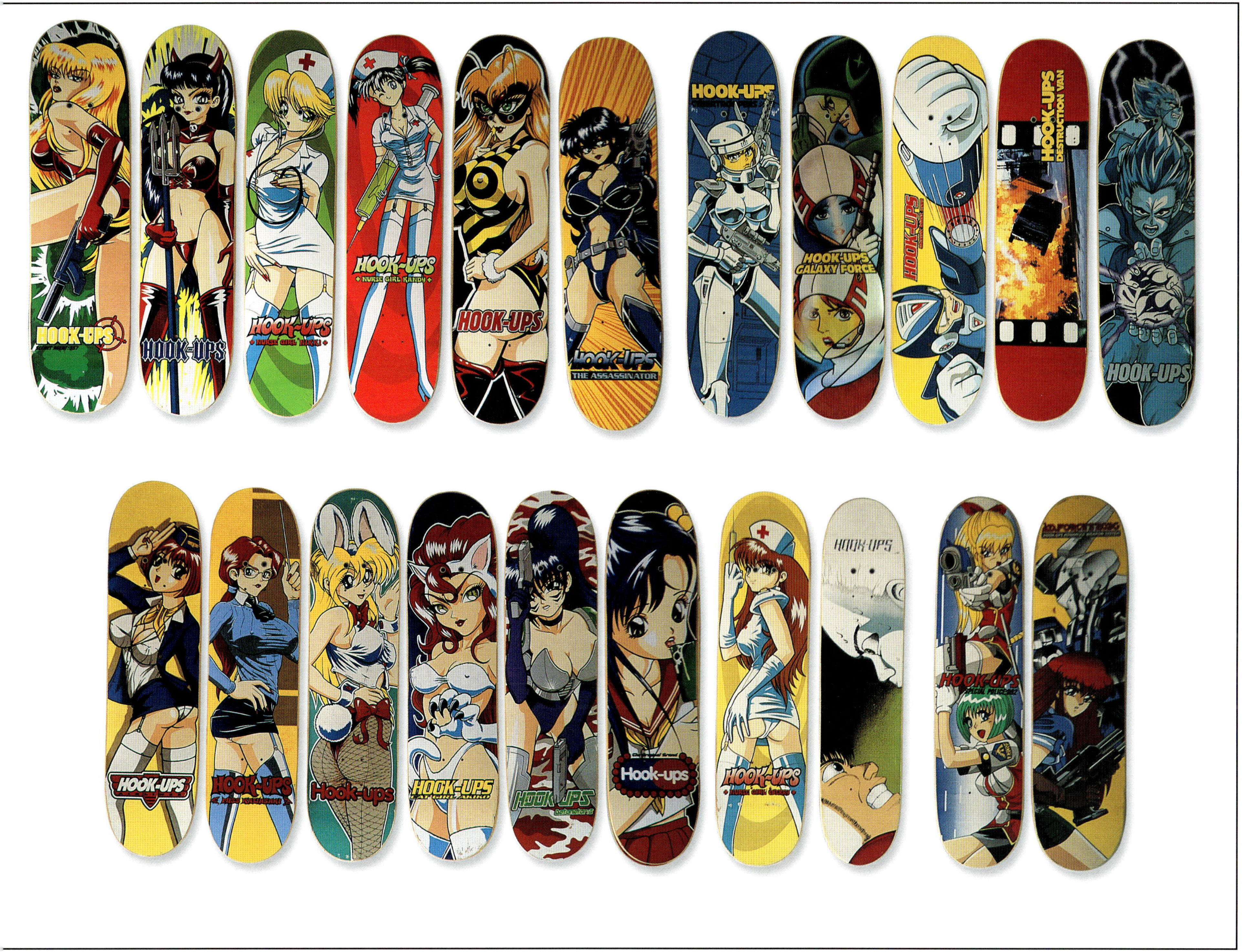
HOOK-UPS
HOOK-UPS
HOOK-UPS
HOOK-UPS
NURSE GIRL KANDY
HOOK-UPS
HOOK-UPS
THE ASSASSINATOR
HOOK-UPS
HOOK-UPS
GALAXY FORCE
HOOK-UPS
HOOK-UPS
DESTRUCTION VAN
HOOK-UPS
HOOK-UPS
HOOK-UPS
Hook-ups
HOOK-UPS
HOOK UPS
Hook-ups
HOOK-UPS
HOOK-UPS
HOOK-UPS

Skateboard Ads & Art

Great art permeates all of us, even the skaters. Jim Phillips has helped me understand the roll artists have played in the history of skateboarding. Skate ads and art from the 1980s typify the era.

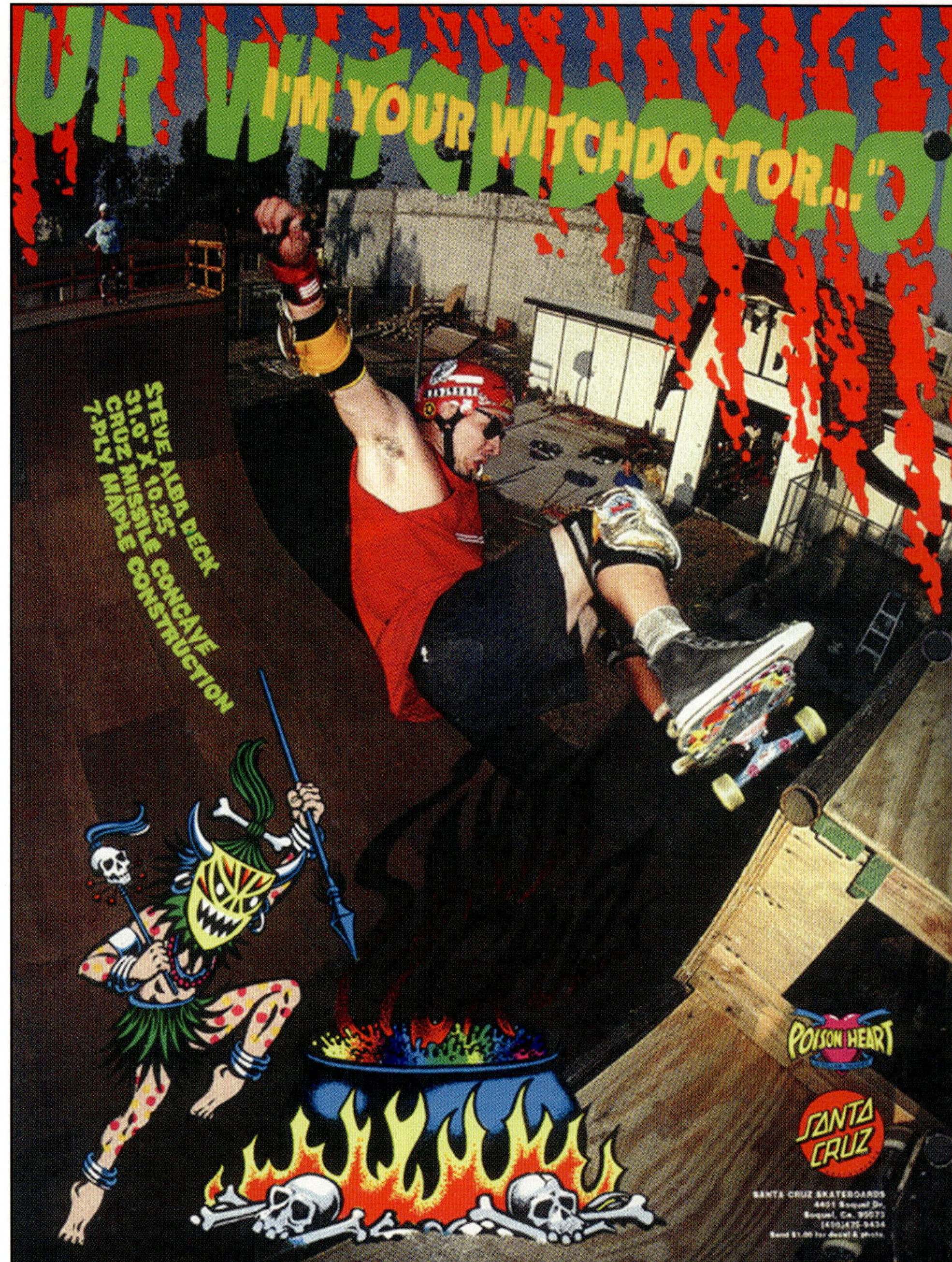

Steve Alba interning as your witchdoctor.
Courtesy Jim Phillips.

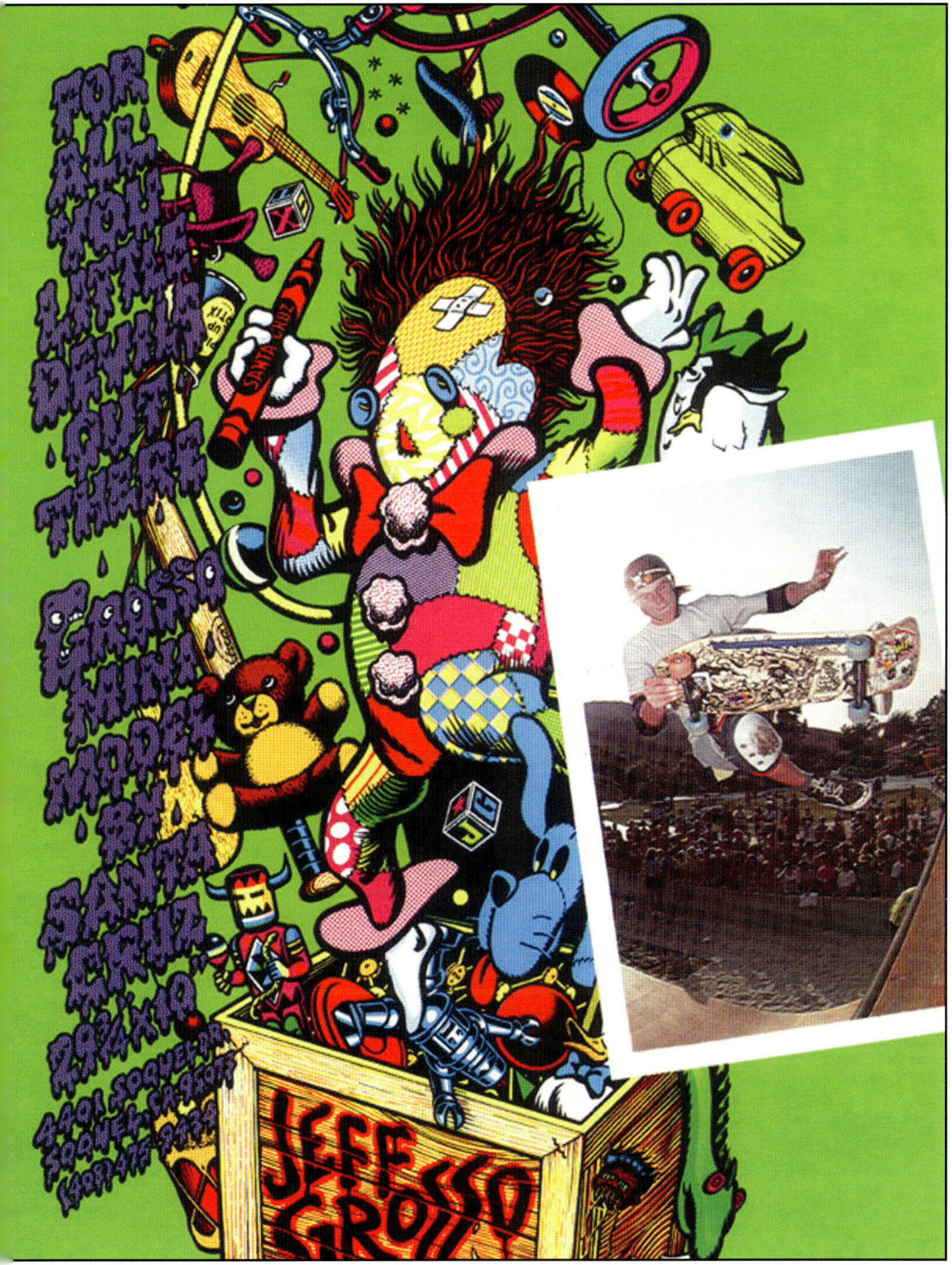

Grosso beguiling us with his menagerie of toys. *Courtesy Jim Phillips.*

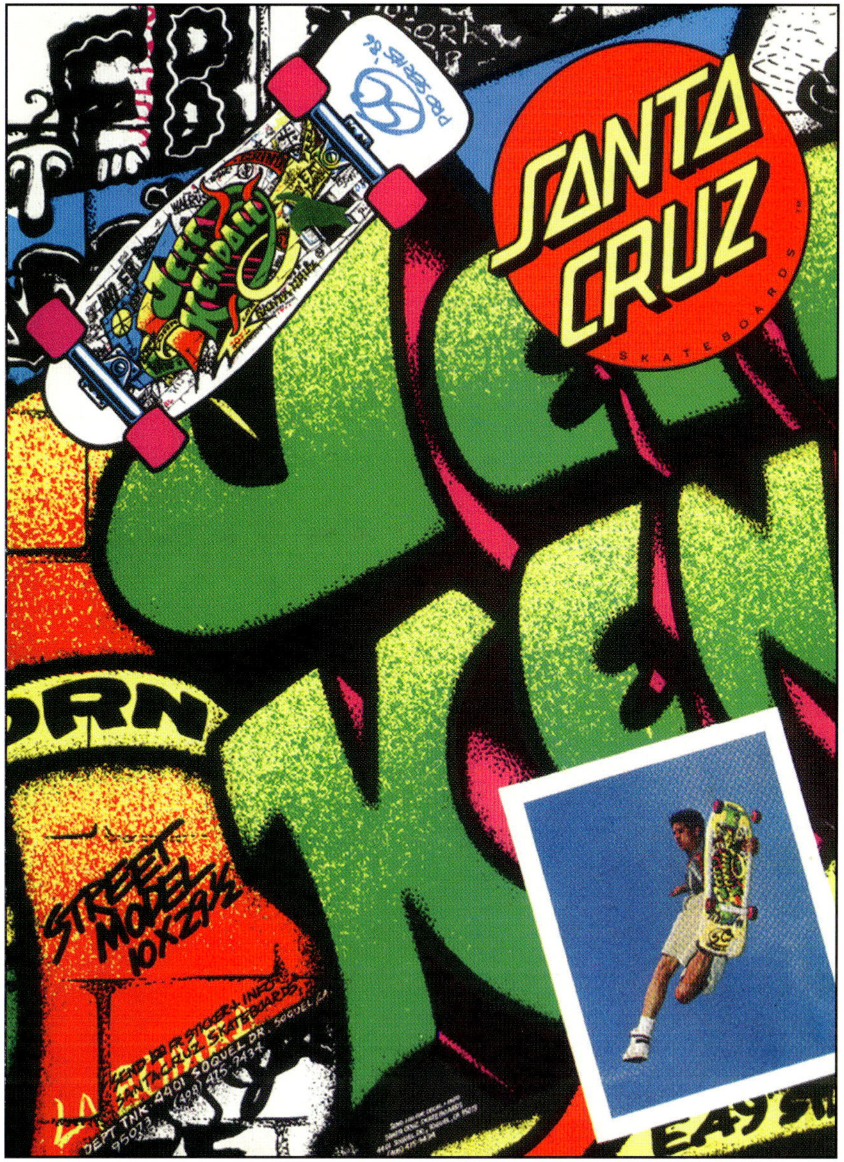

Jeff Kendall. *Courtesy Jim Phillips.*

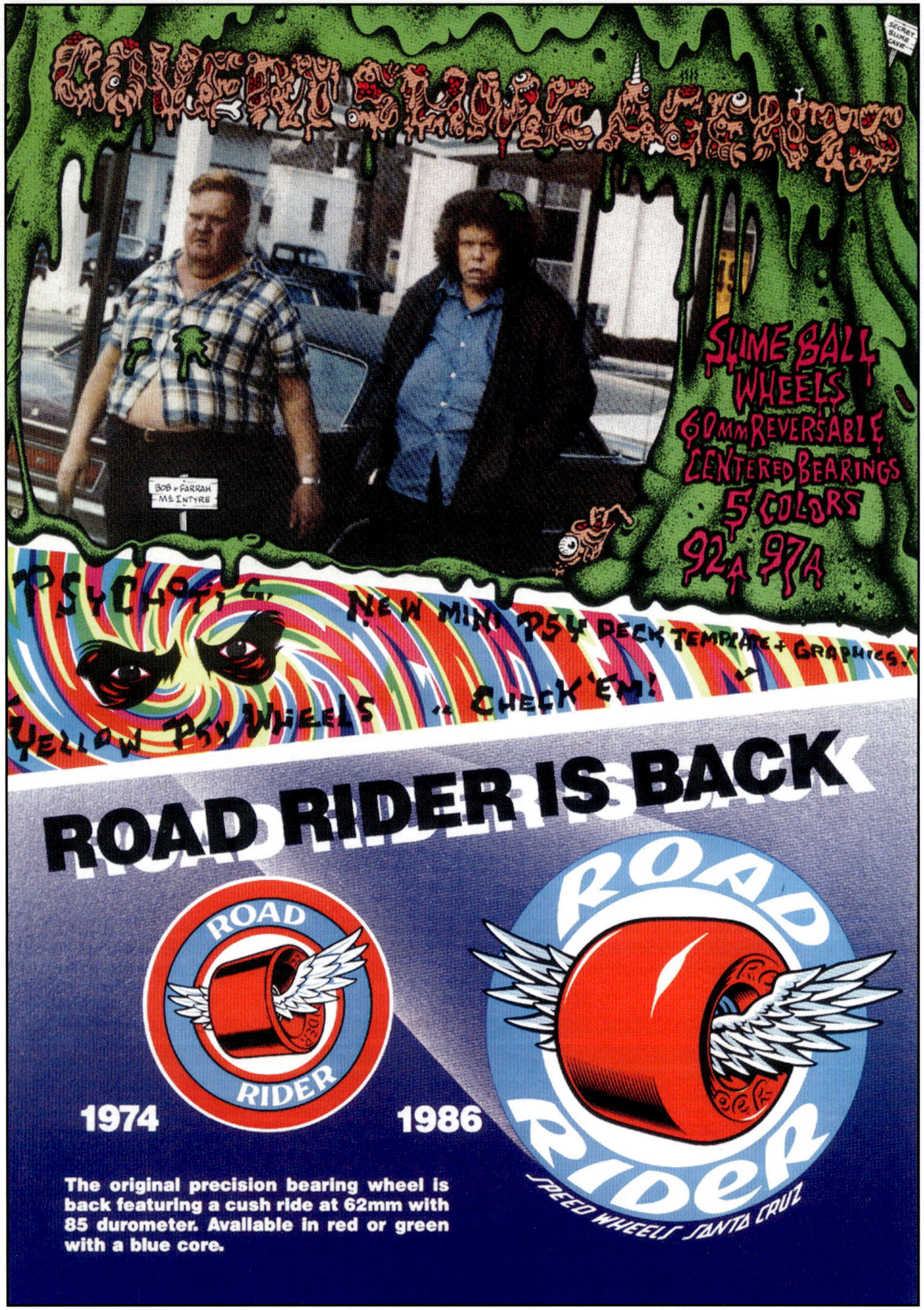

Slime ball add ride beside a road rider ad. You can almost witness the changing of the guard. *Courtesy Jim Phillips.*

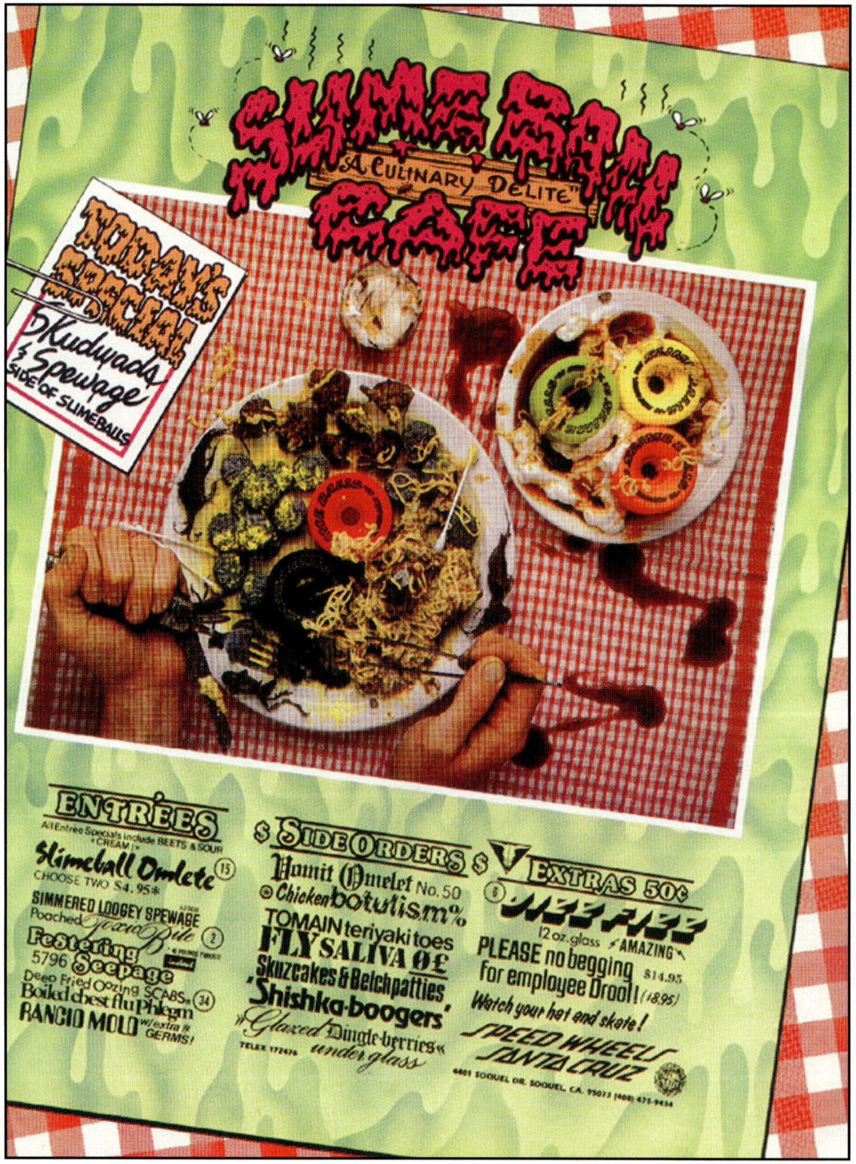

Slime ball cafe. Delectable treats, yum. *Courtesy Jim Phillips.*

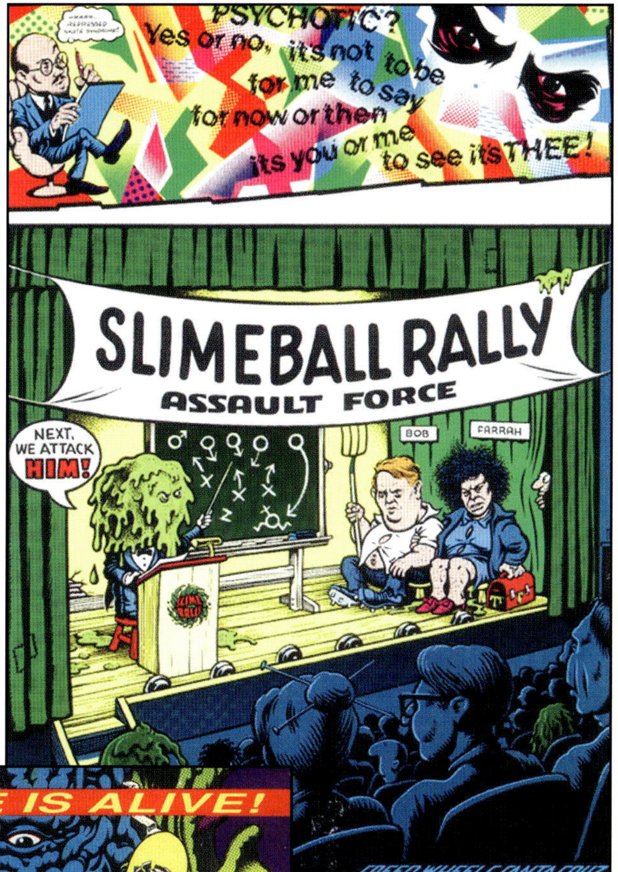

It's disgusting. It's beautiful. It's a slime ball ad. *Photo R. Noll. Courtesy Jim Phillips.*

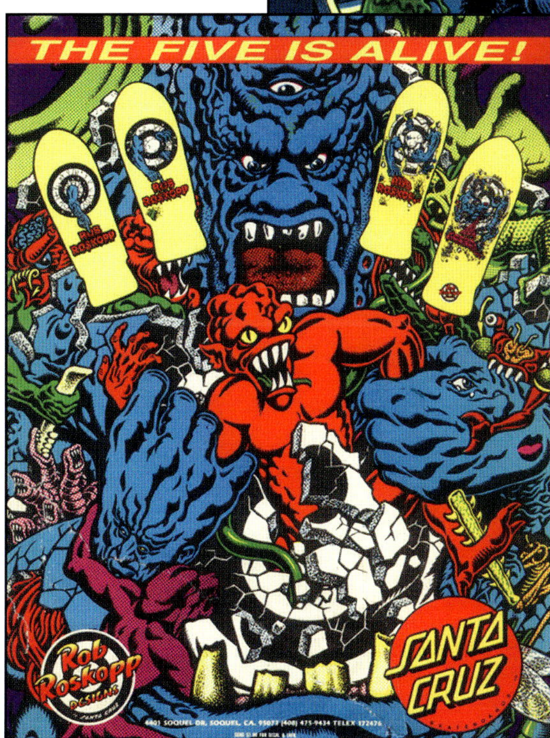

Hard core attitudes ring out in this era, Rob Roskoskopp. *Courtesy Jim Phillips.*

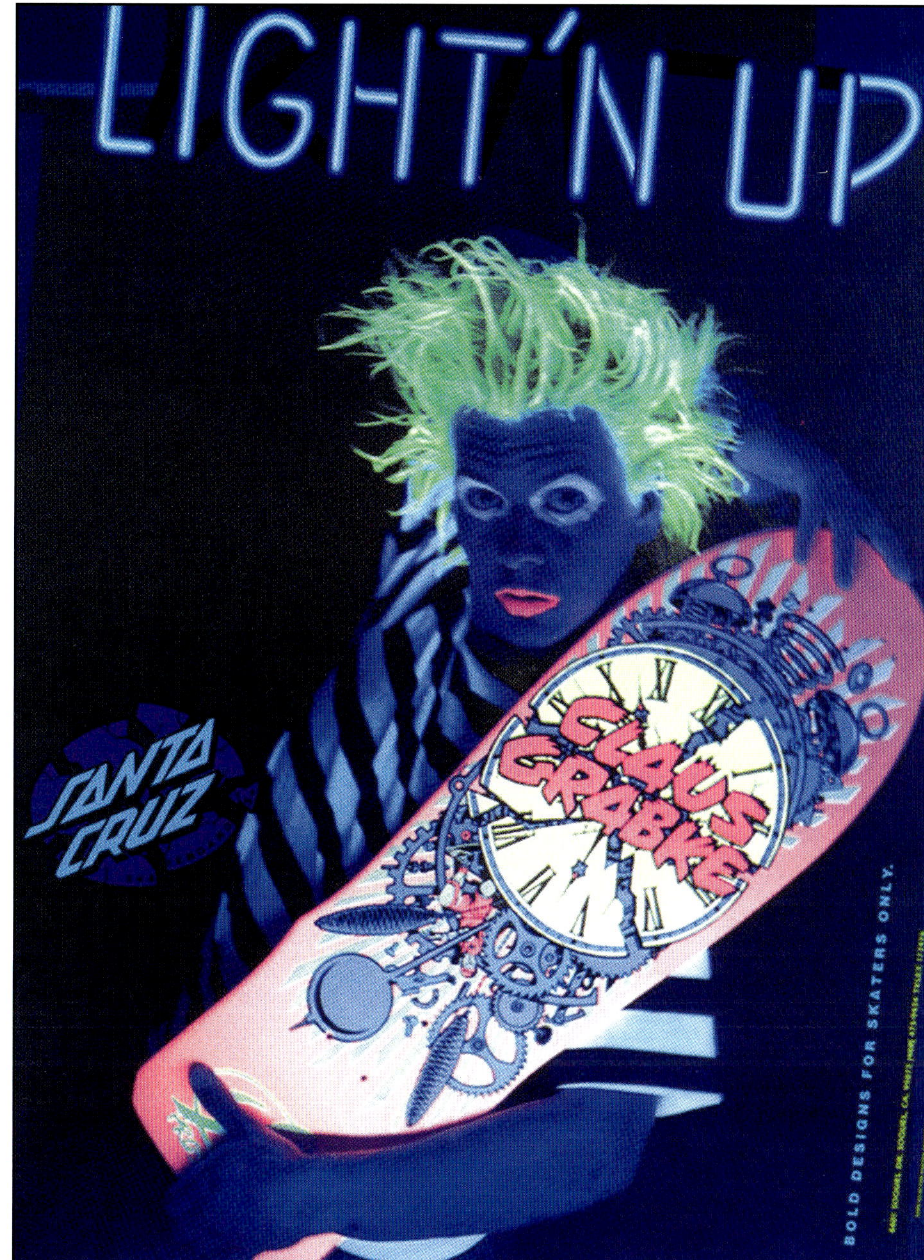

A neon was literally lighting up the '80s grabke. *Courtesy Jim Phillips.*

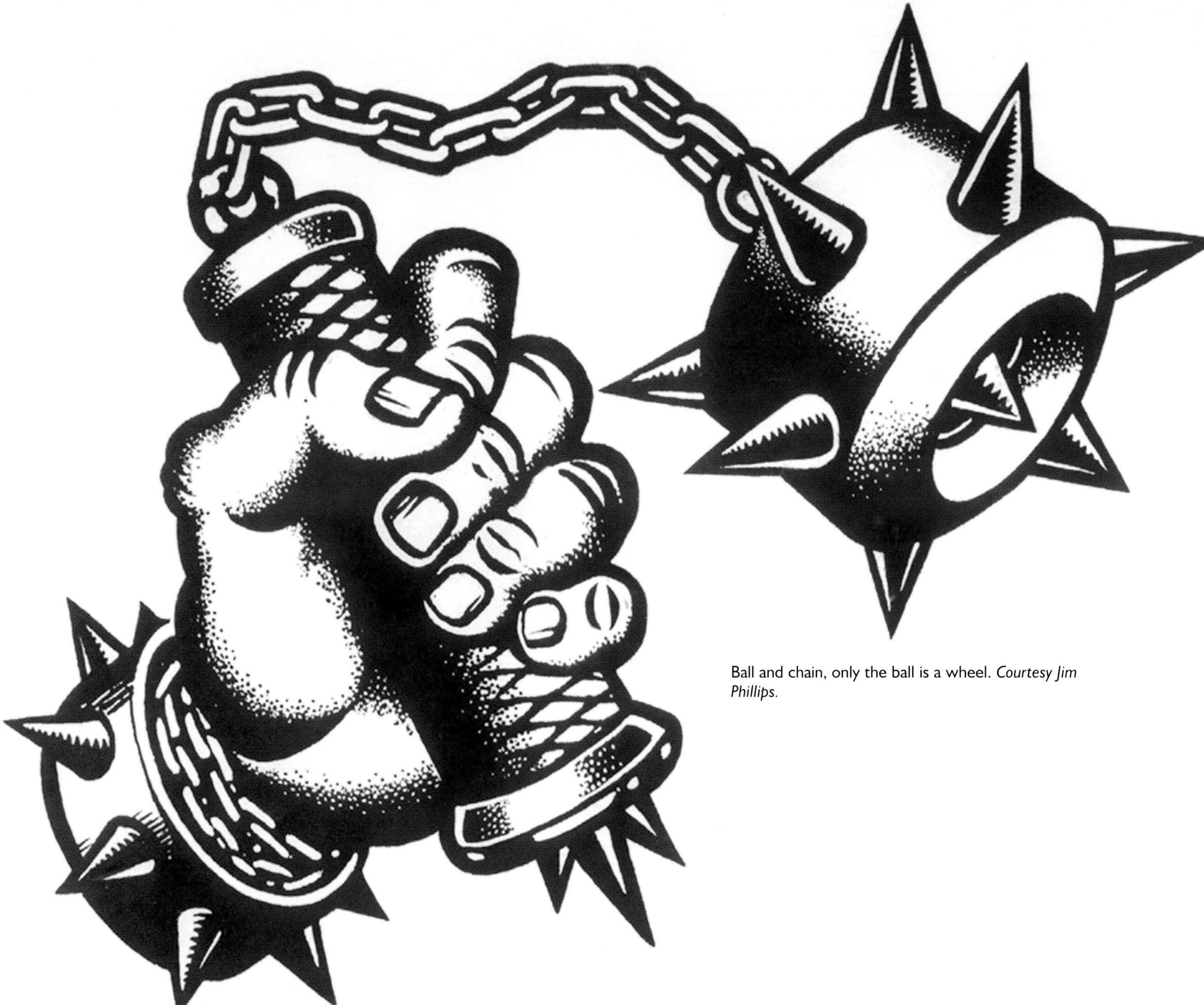

Ball and chain, only the ball is a wheel. *Courtesy Jim Phillips.*

Grimacing cellblock ad. *Courtesy Jim Phillips.*

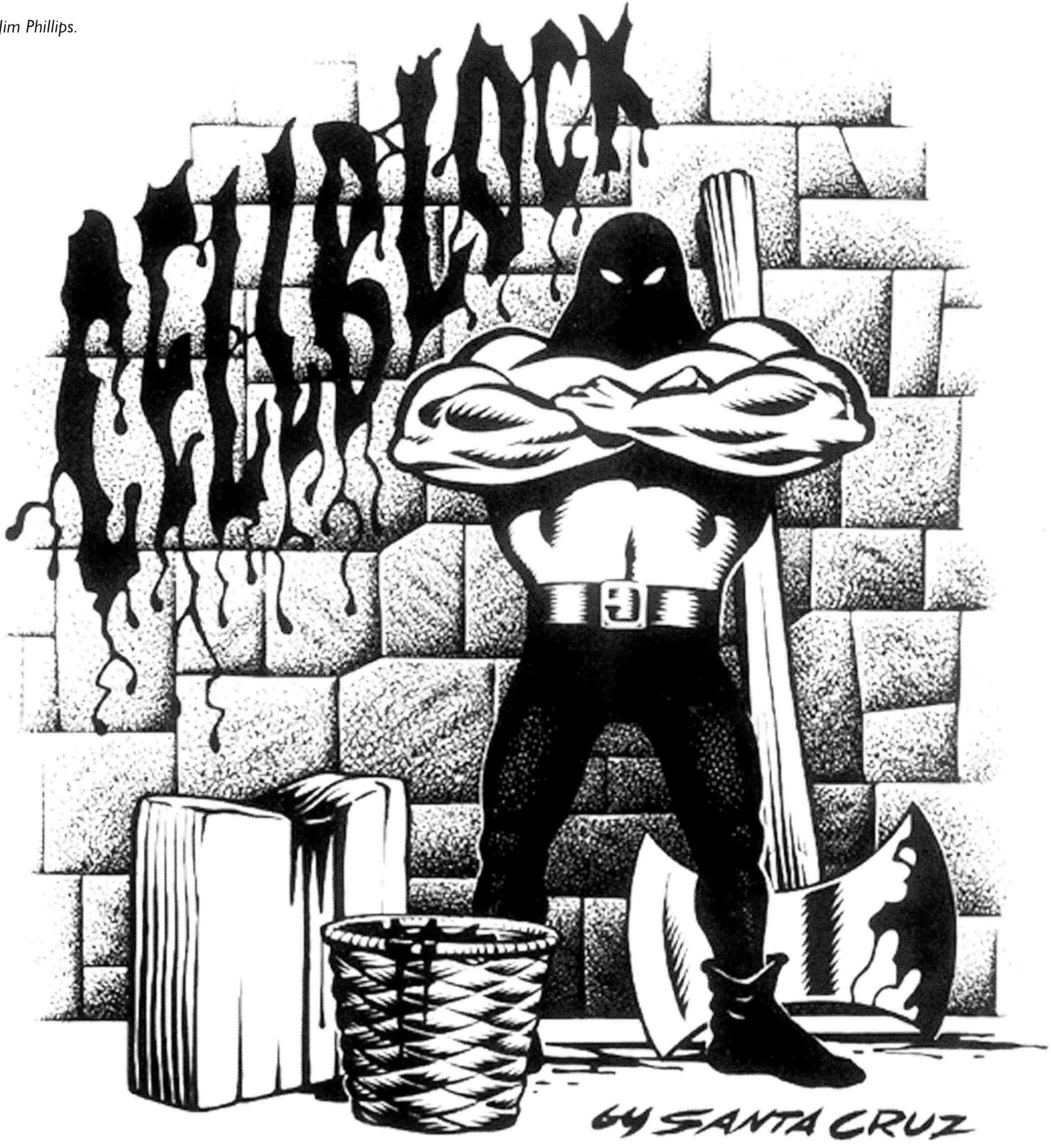

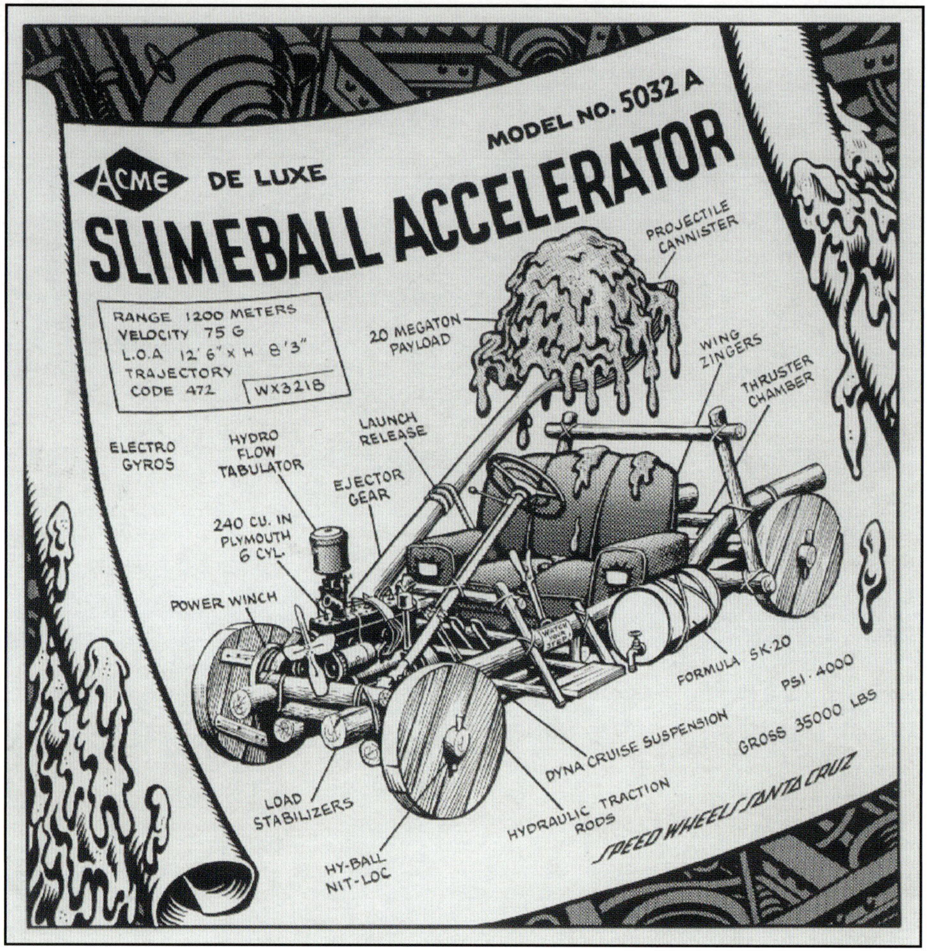

A truly classic Flinstonemobile ad for slimeball wheels. *Courtesy Jim Phillips.*

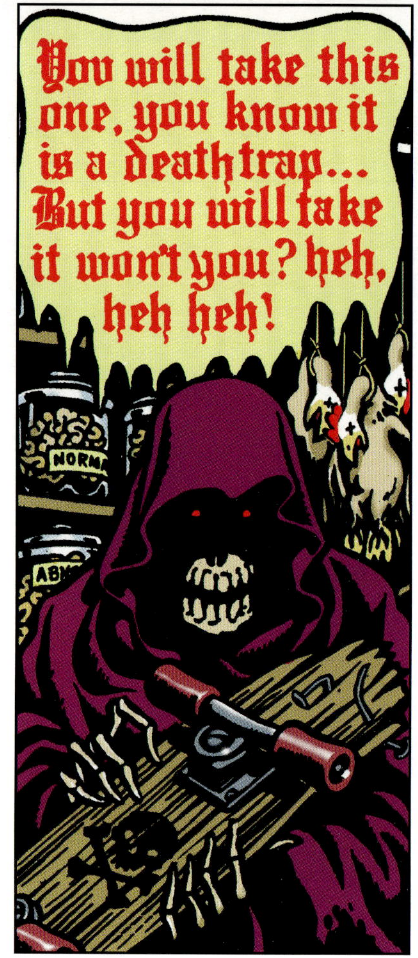

The Grim Reaper. *Courtesy Jim Phillips.*

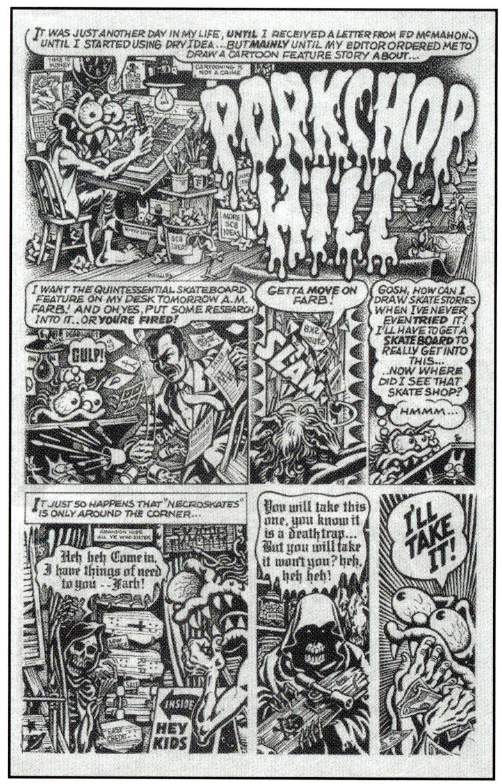

The things. Intro to skate boarding—let's hope your's is better. *Courtesy Jim Phillips.*

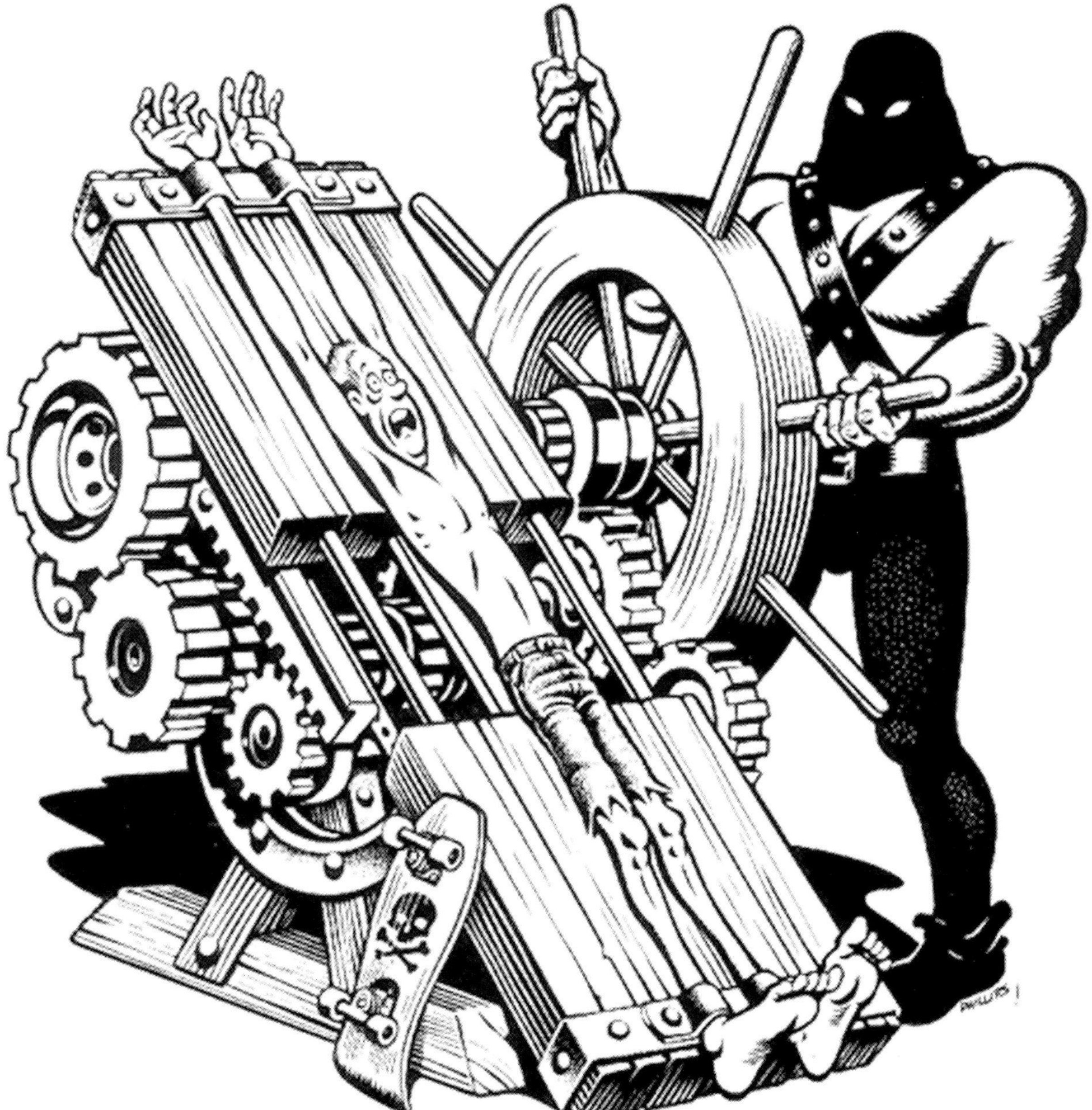

Slime ball ad— cryp, skate art. *Courtesy Jim Phillips.*

Change is always unsettling, but with time you can settle into change. By the time an individual has witnessed an event, it has already become history, and every day that unfolds is history happening. Skateboarding is the fantastic journey through time and will continue into the future. Skateboarding is already 40 years old.

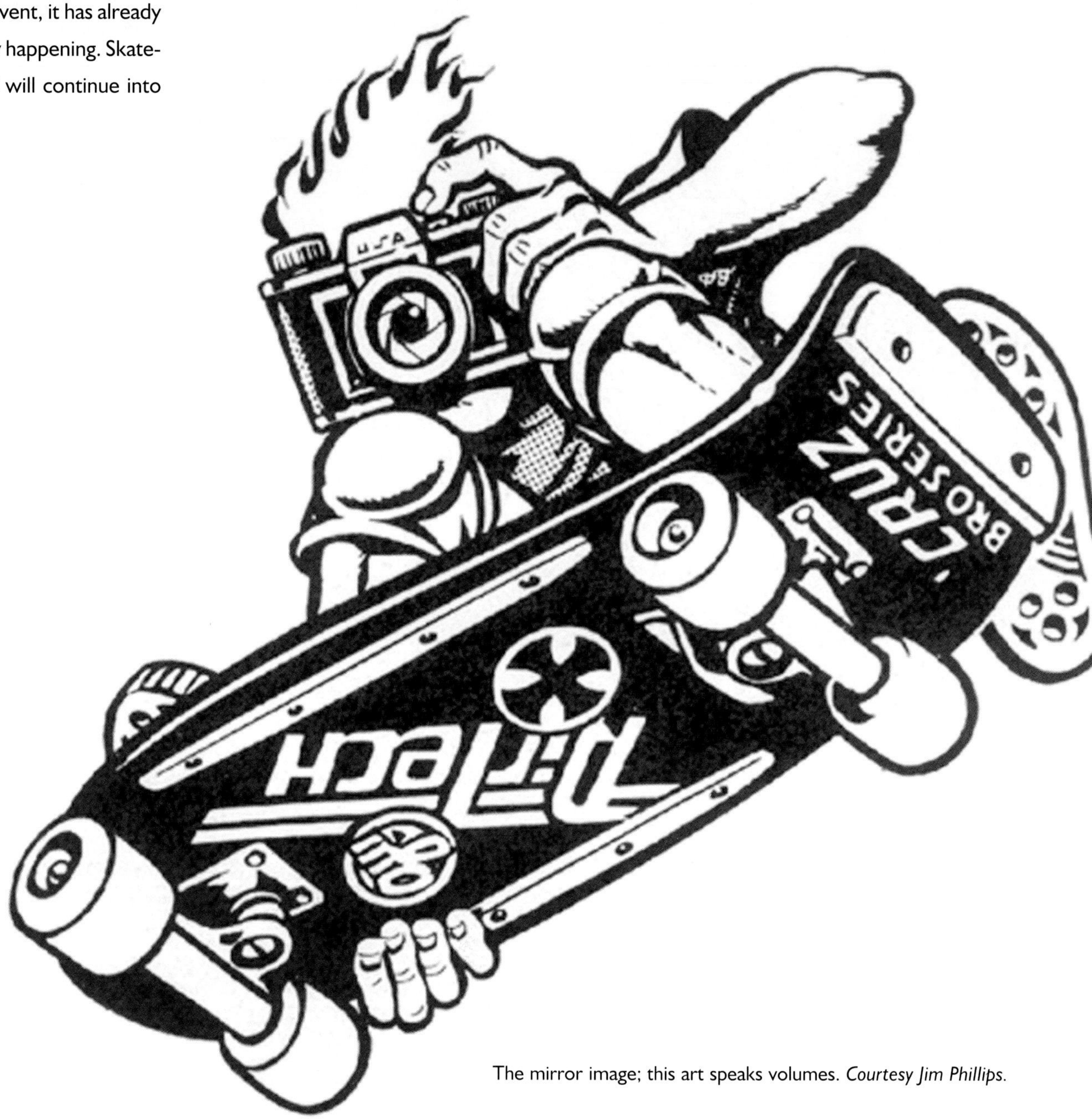

The mirror image; this art speaks volumes. *Courtesy Jim Phillips.*

Glossary of Skateboard Terms

180: One Hundred and eighty degrees. Measure of rotation. Used to describe skateboarding tricks

360: Three hundred and sixty degrees. Measure of rotation. Used to describe skateboarding tricks.

5-0: Grinding with the axle of the rear truck on the edge of the object.

5O-5O: Grinding with the axles of both truckson the edge of the object.

900: Two and a half revolutions or rotations. Achieved by Tony Hawk in 1999.

A: A measurement for the hardness of skateboard wheels.

ACID DROP: Skating off the end of an object while ollieing or touching the board with your hands.

AIR: When skateboard and skater leave the ground/ramp without ollieing.

ALLEY-OOP: A move in which you turn one way while rotating another.

ARMOR: Your pads.

ANTI-ROCKER: A wheel setup with small wheels in the middle of the skates and larger wheels on the outside. Supposed to allow easier grinds due to the bigger area between wheels.

AXLE: The metal rod running through the hanger, with the wheels screwed on either end.

BACKSIDE: Originated from surfing, the direction you turn if you are traveling up a wave and turn so your back faces the wave. Used to describe your direction of rotation in skating. The opposite of frontside.

BACKSLIDE: A Grind using only the back foot, balancing carefully on the boot and frame.

BACON IN THE PAN: When you wipe out major on a ramp. You slide around and shrivel up like frying bacon.

BANANA: Another term for switch.

BAR: Name for grinding bar or rail.

BANK: An elevated surface, A common urban form of ramp.

BASEPLATE: The flat part of the truck that fixes to the board via four drilled holes for truck bolts. Also has an area to attach a pivot cup and kingpin.

BEARING: The part of the board that bears the friction of movement. There should be two contained within each wheel.

BERANI: A front flip with a 180 in it.

BIGSPIN: A 360-degree shoveit with a 180-degree turn in a backside direction.

BIO: Sideways spin.

BLINDSIDE: A trick where you turn away from the grinding object to grind it.

BLUNT: Going up over an object and landing with the tail along the edge of the object and the rear two wheels on top of the object. The board should then be pointing in a near vertical position.

BOARD: Main platform area of a skateboard.

BOARDWALK: A topside soul with back foot rolling on its toe.

BONED: Pushing the board out in front and pointing downwards in mid-air.

BONELESS: Take the front foot off the board and grab the board with your hand. With you back foot still on the board, jump up. Then place your front foot back on the board and remove your hand before landing.

CAB: Fakie 360

CABALERNO: A backflip with a 180 in it.

CAMEL: Toe-Tap

CASPER: With the board upside down, place the front foot underneath the board and back foot on the tail, pointing the board into the sky.

CAVEMAN RAIL: A rail that is really high and hard to get on.

COMP: Short for competition.

CONCAVE: The contour given to decks. The concave will dip down from the left to right and should be asymmetrical. Provides strength to the board and aids the skater when performing tricks.

COPER: Protective covering for the truck that attaches to the hanger. Protects the truck against grinding.

COPING: Metal piping running along the top edge of park bowls and ramps. Provides a longer life to the ramp and increases the range of skateboarding tricks.

CURB: Concrete up-cropping at the edge of roadways. What coping is to ramps, curbs are to streets.

CURB GRIND: A grind that is done on a curb.

CUSHION: Donut-shaped rubber components found on trucks, slotted onto the kingpin. Provide steering and act as shock absorbers. Can be bought in a range of colors and hardness. Two are needed per truck; the one that's slightly cone shaped fits furthest up the kingpin.

DARKSIDE GRIND: A grind that flips the board upside down; the rider stands on the underside of the board.

DECK: Main platform area of a skateboard.

DELAM: Damage done to a deck through skating as a layer is chipped from the plywood deck. The thin layer removed is called a "delam."

DISASTER: Placing the rear wheels on top of an object with the rail of the board on the edge. The front two wheels are therefore hanging off the object.

DOUBLE ORE-IDA: Vert trick in which you alley-oop 720.

DOWNHILL: Skating as fast as possible down the steepest of hills.

DROP BEARINGS: Loose ball bearings used in the'70s.

DROP-IN: When you enter a ramp from the top.

ELBOW: One mini-half pipe placed at an angle next to another one, allowing you to transfer between them.

EGG PLANT: Hand plant where you plant only the outside hand.

EMB: Embarcadero, San Francisco, America. Once the greatest urban Mecca for skateboarding.

EXPRESS AIR: Grabbing the inside of the skate with the same side hand.

FAKIE: Traveling backwards. Driving a car in reverse is, in effect, "going fakie."

FARSIDE: A grind where you go over the bar and land on the "far side" to start grinding.

FAST SLIDE: A grind using only the front foot.

FAT: Adjective meaning high or far. Used to express a skateboarding trick that is per formed over a long distance or a great height. Also spelled "Phat."

FEEBLE GRIND: Grinding with the rear truck while the front truck goes over the top of the edge of the object, putting the board at a slight angle to the direction of movement.

FLATLANDER: A skater who skates only street and no vert.

FLIP: Developed from freestyle skating. It involves the board turning upside down in a variety of combinations. A flip is generally considered to be a complete flip over to land back on the wheels.

FOCUS: Snapping the deck into two pieces. It was once "fashionable" to do this when you became frustrated, said to be conjured up by a part of the industry who wanted to sell more boards by making people think it was cool to focus the board they were riding.

FREESTYLE: An area of skating that has now become part of street and vert skating. Used to be performed on low-riding, skinny boards. Tricks consisted of numerous balancing tricks, flips, and shove-its.

FRONTSIDE: Originated from surfing, the direction in which you turn if you are traveling up a wave and turn so you face the wave. Used to describe direction of rotation in skating. The opposite of "backside".

FUN BOX: A platform object with banked sides plus a handrail, if you're lucky.

GOOFY: You skate goofy if you skate with your right foot forward. The opposite of regular.

GRAB: Using your hand to "grab" onto your board.

GRAPHICS: The artwork on the bottom of a deck. It helps in telling one deck from another.

GRIND: Moving along the edge or on top of an object with the axles of both trucks.

GRIP TAPE: A sticky-back sandpaper material. Usually black but can be bought in a range of colors, even clear. It is used to cover the top of the deck, to create friction that aids the skater.

HALF CAB: Going from skating backwards to skating forwards.

HALF PIPE: A ramp, usually made out of wood, that looks like half of a pipe.

HANDPLANT: A form of handstand where the board is held in the air either by a hand or feet.

HANDRAIL: Common urban feature, designed for holding on to while traveling up and down stairs, though used by skaters for a whole range of tricks.

HANGER: Part of the truck that gets the most abuse. When you grind, you are grinding along the top of the hanger. Contained inside the hanger is the axle.

HEELFLIP: Flipping the board with your heel. Your front foot should move up and across the board, flipping it in the opposite direction of a kickflip.

HELMET: Protective equipment for your head. Nearly always used in vert skateboarding.

IMPOSSIBLE: Freestyle trick invented by Rodney Mullen. Consists of spinning the board around either foot.

INVERT: Going upside down on the ramp and doing a handstand.

INDY GRAB: Grabbing the board in front of you with the rear hand.

JAM: Getting a load of skaters together for a skateboard session.

K-GRIND: Stands for "Crooked Grind". Grinding along on the leading truck without having the board over the object.

KICK FLIP: Flipping the board by kicking it.

KICK TURN: Rotating on the rear wheels of the board with the front wheels raised from the surface.

KINGPIN: The bolt that holds the hanger, cushions and baseplate together of the truck.

KINK: Used to describe handrails. A kink is the changing of the handrail's angle. A handrail that runs down a set of steps then goes horizontal is a two-kink rail.

LAUNCH RAMP: A portable street ramp made for skaters to launch from.

LIP: The top edge of a ramp.

LIPSLIDE: Sliding along on the rails of the board with the rear wheels going over the object.

MANUAL: What people commonly call a wheelie-traveling along while balanced on the two rear wheels.

McTWIST: 540-degree backside air with a mute grab. Invented by Mike McGill.

MELLONCOLLIE: While in mid-air in an ollie, grabbing the board behind you with the leading hand.

MINI-RAMP: A ramp (two transitioned banks facing each other with flat bottom and platforms) that does not have any vert, usually around 6-feet high.

MM: Millimeters. The standard measurement for the diameter of skateboard wheels.

NOCOMLY: Old-school street skating trick. There are many variations but it basically means to travel along with the rear foot on the tail, then place the front foot on the ground and pop the board into the air.

NOLLIE: Follows the same Concepts. as an ollie. While traveling along, place the front foot on the nose and pop up into the air using the nose (rather than the tail in an ollie). The exact same as a switch-stance fakie ollie.

NOSE: The part of the deck in front of the front truck. Opposite end to the tail.

NOSEGRAB: Grabbing the front of the board (nose) with the leading hand.

NOSESLIDE: Sliding along an object using the underside of the nose.

OLLIE: Invented by Ollie Gelfand and brought to the streets by Rodney Mullen. Taking air without using your hands. The basis for most skateboarding tricks.

PADS: Protective equipment for the knees and elbows. These are mainly used by vert skaters.

PARK BOWL: A simulated pool or bowl-shaped area in a skatepark.

PIVOT CUP: A plastic cup that fits into the base plate and stops the metal hanger from coming into contact with the metal base plate.

PLATFORM: An elevated flat surface.

PLY: Short for plywood. The most commonly used material for the deck.

POP SHOVEIT: A shoveit mixed with an ollie. Enables shoveits to be performed higher.

PRO: A professional. Someone who gets paid by a company to skateboard. Often has his/her own signature model deck of which he/she has a percentage of the sales.

QUARTER PIPE: One side of a mini-ramp or vert-ramp, but not as wide. Used for gaining speed on a street course or practicing ramp tricks.

RAILS: On the underside of the board, the edges of the deck running along each side of the trucks. They used to be plastic strips attached to the bottom of the board.

RAIL SLIDE: Sliding along an object on the part of your board that is the bottom between the trucks.

REGULAR: Skating with your left foot forward. The opposite of "goofy."

REVERT: Finishing a trick coming out forwards, then quickly sliding round 180 to come out backwards.

RIP GRIP: Thin, sticky, back-sponge material stuck to the bottom of boards to give your fingers some grip when grabbing.

RISER: Usually made from plastic or rubber. Fits between the deck and base plate of the truck. Helps absorb shock and lift board.

ROCK-AND-ROLL: Ramp trick. Go up to the lip and push the front truck over it. Stall, then turn 180 back down the ramp.

ROLL-IN: To skate along the platform of a ramp, over the lip and down onto the transitions. The part of a ramp that curves onto the platform is also called a roll-in, because of the purpose it serves.

RUBBER: Another name for bushings.

SADPLANT: A variation of a handplant, where your grab the inside rail and straighten your front leg.

SAUSAGE GRIND: Grab your tail while doing a smith grind on your front truck.

SESSION: The act of skateboarding.

SHOVEIT: Turning the board without turning your body, so the board spins round under your feet.

SKETCHY: A term used in dangerous situations, usually meaning insane.

SLALOM: Zig-zag motion that skiers do, except on hard ground usually with a dedicated skateboard.

SLAM: Another word for failing off your board and hurting yourself.

SLAPPY: Doing grinds along such things as curbs without ollieing onto it.

SLICK: Special plastic layer fixed to the bottom of a deck, supposed to aid sliding.

SMITHGRIND: Grinding with the rear truck while the front truck runs along the side

of the object, not over the top. The center of the board my also be touching the edge of the object.

SNAKE: If you're skating an object in which only a limited number of people can skate, a snake is the person that seems to have more goes than anyone by jumping the naturally occurring "queue."

SNAKE RUN: Twisting path with banked sides.

SPACER: A small hollow cylindrical object, usually made from metal, placed between two bearings inside a wheel.

SPINE: If two ramps are back-to-back and do not have a platform at the point of connection, the upside down "V" shape is called the spine.

STALE FISH GRAB: Grabbing the board behind you with the rear hand.

STANCE: Either regular of goofy. The way in which you stand on your board.

STOKED: The feeling of doing something well.

STREET-SURFING: A traditional old-school approach to skateboarding that emulates surfing style.

SWITCH STANCE: The art of skating the stance that you did not learn to skate with. If you do tricks skating goofy, to skate switch stance you must perform tricks with a regular stance, and vice-versa.

TAIL: The part of the deck behind the rear truck.

TAIL GRAB: Grabbing the rear of the board with the rear hand.

TAIL SAVER: A piece of plastic that attaches to the underside of the tail, designed to prevent wear and tear on the tail.

TAIL SLIDE: Sliding with the tail of the board upon the object and the rest of the board hanging off the object, without having gone over it.

TECHNICAL: The name given to complex skating.

THRASHED: The wear and tear of an object due to skateboarding.

TOSS: Such as "product toss" or "sticker toss". An event usually found at sponsored competitions where products are thrown to the crowd.

TRANSITION: Part of a bank/ramp that inclines in an upward direction.

TRUCK: Fixes to the board, and the wheels fit to the truck. A complete truck is made up of a base plate, hanger, axle, kingpin, cushions, two special washers and two bolts for the axles.

TRUCK BOLTS: Keep the truck attached to the board.

TWEAK: To point the board in a different direction than normal.

VERT: Part of an inclined surface that is vertical in gradient.

WALLIE: Skating onto, up, and over a street object.

WALL RIDE: The act of skating up a vertical wall.

WAX: Used to make objects increasingly slippery for skateboard tricks.

WHEEL SLIDE: The technique of slowing down without putting your feet down. It is what people may commonly call a skid.

WOOD: The material used for decks.

WRISTGUARD: Protective equipment for the wrist. A type of glove containing a plastic/metal splint running along the underside of the wrist onto the palm of the hand.

Resources

Juice magazine. 52 Market, Suite D, Venice, California 90291

Skate Boarder magazine. Surfer publications, Inc. Dana Point, California 92629

Skate Boarder Quarterly. Surfer Publications, Inc. Dana Point, California 92629

Transworld Skaterboarding Business. Times Mirror Magazines. 353 Airport Road, Ocean side, California 92054

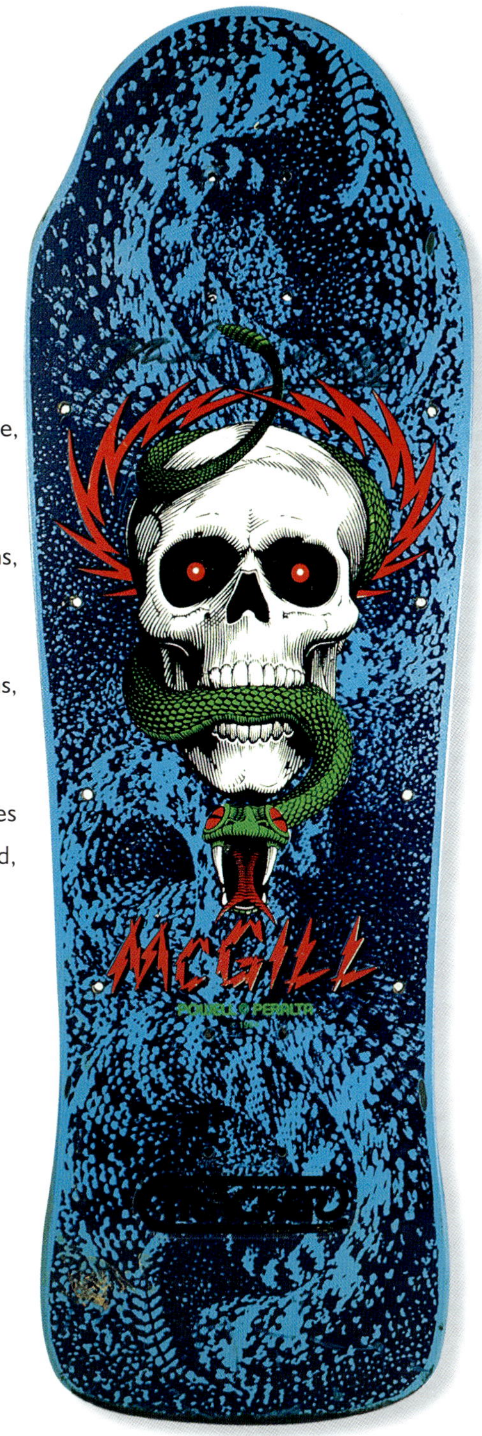

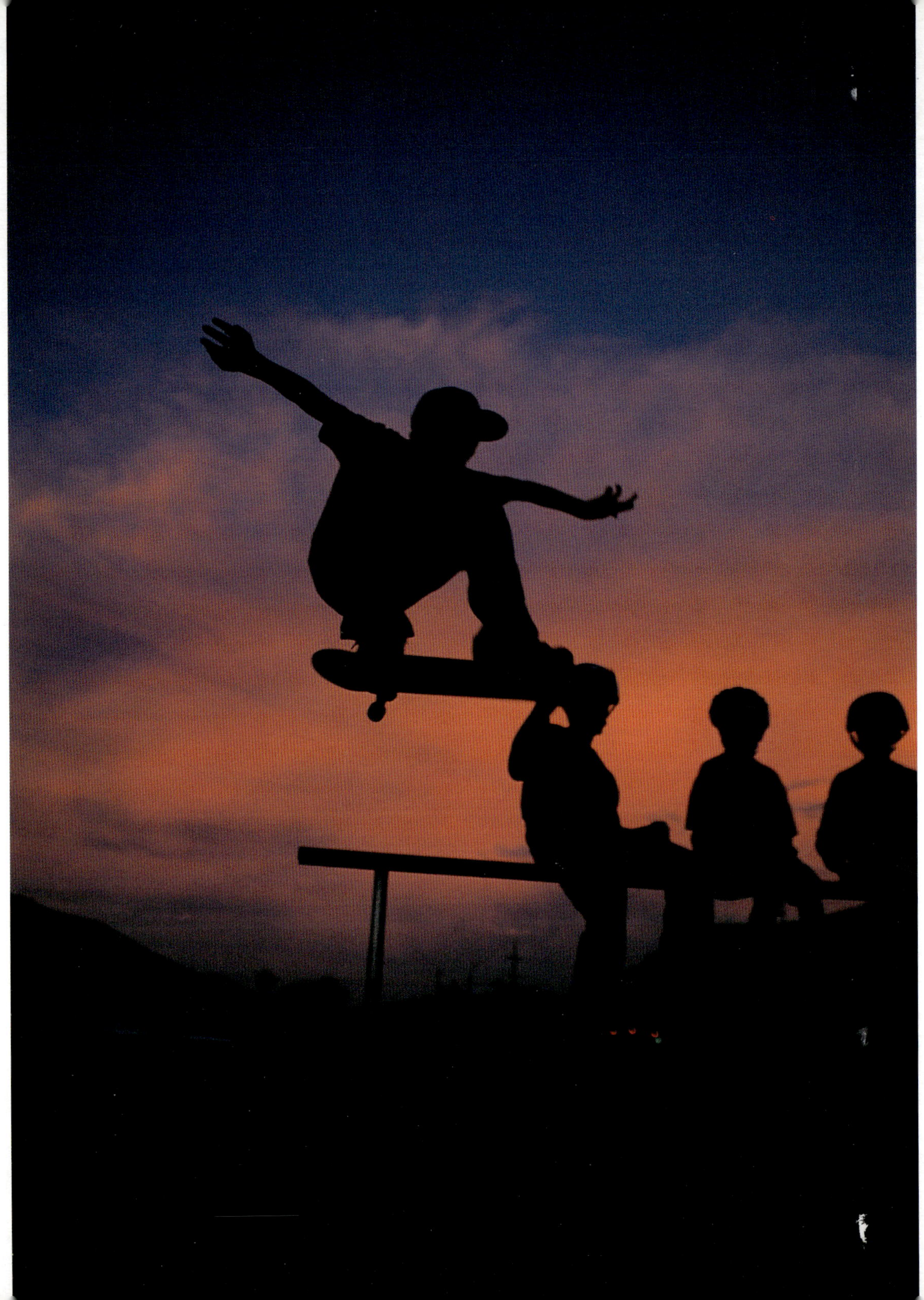